NELSON'S ENCYCLOPEDIA FOR YOUNG READERS

NELSON'S ENCYCLOPEDIA FOR YOUNG READERS

EDITED BY

LAURENCE URDANG

CLIFTON FADIMAN

MILLICENT SELSAM

R. J. UNSTEAD

WILLIAM WORTHY

VOLUME I
ABACUS -- MacARTHUR

THOMAS NELSON PUBLISHERS

NASHVILLE

Editor in Chief
Laurence Urdang

Managing Editor
George C. Kohn

Consulting Editors
Clifton Fadiman
Millicent Selsam
R. J. Unstead
William Worthy

Editors
Hope Gilbert
Walter C. Kidney
Lynne C. Meyer

Assistant Editors
Anthony J. Castagno
Janet Miller

ISBN 0–8407–5184–2

Library of Congress Catalog Card No. 80–14522

TO THE READER

This *Encyclopedia* will answer many of your questions about the world in which you live. It will guide you from very early times through the present day and point you toward tomorrow. It will take you to every major country of the globe and let you explore the depths of outer space. It will tell you how machines work, why nature behaves as it does, and when the important events of history occurred. You will find it fascinating.

The *Encyclopedia* is laid out in alphabetical order. If you don't find an article about a certain subject, check the index at the end of the last volume. The index may show that you can find the information under a different heading. Or perhaps you wish to find more information about a particular subject. Again, try the index; it may direct you to other articles that will give you the details.

Some words are printed in small capitals, like this: ABBEY. This means that the *Encyclopedia* has an entire entry on that subject, in case you want to know more about it.

We hope you enjoy using *Nelson's Encyclopedia for Young Readers*. The editors have prepared it with your special interests in mind. It will introduce you to many exciting ideas and will challenge you to learn more.

THE PUBLISHERS

ABACUS

Man has used counting machines throughout history. One of the earliest, still in use today in Asia, is the abacus. It is a simple device, as the illustration shows, having frames with sliding beads on strings or wires. The beads in the top row stand for units. Those in the second row stand for tens, in the third row for hundreds, and so on.

A very primitive abacus was simply a board with lines on it. Counters were then moved along the lines. Thus, if a person needed an abacus, he might draw one in the sand and move pebbles or other movable counters along the rows drawn. The ancient Egyptians, Greeks, Romans, and Chinese all used types of abacuses. The abacus made it much easier to add and subtract numbers written in Roman numerals, such as CXLVII (147) and MCXX (1120).

Besides adding and subtracting, the abacus can also be used for multiplying and dividing. Some Asians have shown they can solve problems in ARITHMETIC faster than a modern computer can.

ABBEY

An abbey is a large MONASTERY (for men) or convent (for women). The leader of an abbey is called an abbot or abbess. The most famous abbeys existed in England in the MIDDLE AGES. They were very large and wealthy, but Henry VIII had them closed in the 1530s. Many became ruins that can still be seen. Others were made into private houses, some of which still have "Abbey" in their names. Often

1

the abbey church was saved for public use. WESTMINSTER ABBEY is such a church.

In the Middle Ages, there were abbeys all over Europe. Today, there are still many in Europe and some in America. SEE ALSO: MONASTERY.

ABORIGINES

The first people to inhabit any region are called aborigines. The name generally refers, however, to the earliest known people in AUSTRALIA. These primitive Australians were discovered by the white European settlers in the late 1700s. The original aborigines are thought to have come to Australia from southeast Asia.

Aborigines have short, broad faces and are usually not tall. Their noses are wide, their hair black and crinkled. Today, most live among the white people, but some maintain their old ways of life.

In the past they were nomads, wandering from place to place, hunting and fishing for food. They ate lizards, turtles, ants, grubs, kangaroos, and wallabies. Their weapons were the *boomerang*, the *waddy* (a war club), and the *womera* (a three-pronged throwing-spear).

Aborigines believed in magic, made cave-paintings, and adhered to complicated laws that bound families closely together. They revered nature and its wild creatures.

Today there are only about 40,000 full-blooded aborigines and 80,000 part-aborigines in Australia. The government has sought to help and educate them, but some prefer to keep their old ways and to live on reservations in the Northern Territory, Queensland, and Western Australia. The Australian aborigines speak about 200 different languages.

ABRAHAM

Abraham, or Abram, is the forefather of the HEBREWS and the first leader of JUDAISM. He was born around 2000 B.C. in the city of UR in SUMERIA.

In the BIBLE (Gen. 11-25), God promised Abraham the land of Canaan (now called Israel) for his people. Obeying God, he moved with his wife, Sarah, and his servants and cattle to the "land of milk and honey," where he lived as a nomad.

Later, God demanded that Abraham sacrifice his son Isaac as a test of faith. Abraham prepared to kill Isaac at God's command, but because of his father's unquestioning obedience, Isaac was spared.

Abraham is said to have died at the age of 175.

ACCORDION

This is a kind of small reed ORGAN, slung from the neck. With his right hand the player operates a keyboard to play the melody. His left hand is strapped to a board with buttons that are pressed to produce chords. The left hand also works a bellows between the boards that forces air over the reeds whose vibrations produce the sound. The accordion's rather harsh, cheerful sound is often heard at dances in Spain, South America, Scotland, and elsewhere.

ACHILLES

Achilles was the chief hero of the Trojan War, described in the *Iliad*, which probably was written by HOMER. He was a great warrior, but had a fierce temper.

According to legend, his mother, Thetis, was a sea goddess, and knew that Achilles was fated to die at TROY. Therefore, she dipped him when he was a boy into the River Styx to make him immortal. She held him by his heel, however, and that remained the one vulnerable part of his body.

With his warriors in 50 ships, Achilles went to Troy and fought alongside the other Greek princes, such as Agamemnon and Odysseus. Achilles became enraged at the death of Patroclus, his best friend, and killed Hector, a great Trojan warrior. Refusing to give him an honorable burial, Achilles dragged Hector's body in the dust behind his chariot as he drove it around the walls of Troy.

Later, when the Greeks were about to seize the city, Achilles was wounded in his heel by an arrow shot by the Trojan prince, Paris. As foretold to Thetis, he soon died from it: the proverbial "heel of Achilles." SEE ALSO: HECTOR, HOMER, TROY.

ACROBATS

To the Greeks, "one who walks on tiptoes" and "one who climbs high" were acrobats. In ancient Egypt, China, or Greece, performers were admired who could move quickly and keep their balance high above the ground. In ancient Crete, acrobats sprang skillfully from the horns of a charging bull onto its back, then somersaulted to the ground.

Tight-rope walkers were greatly admired by the Romans. During fairs in the Middle Ages, people loved to see the "tumblers" walking on their hands and performing somersaults and back-flips like the gymnasts of today.

Generally, circus acrobats are specialists in one particular act. *High-wire walkers* balance with a pole high above the ground. Acrobatic clowns use the *slack wire. Trapeze artists*, or *aerialists*, swing and somersault high up on a trapeze, a bar at the ends of two suspended ropes. Often they dive to catch the hands of another acrobat who is hanging upside down on another trapeze.

ACROPOLIS

"Acropolis" is Greek for "high city," the raised part of town that was fortified in case of war.

The most famous acropolis is that of ATHENS. The ruins there today are of temples built in the 5th century B.C. and later. The Persians had destroyed the old temples in 480 B.C., and PERICLES, the political leader of Athens, had them rebuilt in a magnificent new form.

The Propylaea was the gate structure, through which visitors and processions passed. It included a small museum of art.

The Parthenon, regarded as one of the most beautiful buildings in history, was the temple of Athena, goddess of Athens. It was made of marble, brilliantly painted, with 46 Doric columns outside. Inside was a statue of Athena faced with ivory and gold. Later the Parthenon became a church, and eventually was ruined by an explosion. Some of its statuary, by the great sculptor Phidias, was taken to the British Museum in London.

The Erechtheion is another temple, beautiful in its individual parts but strange in appearance. It was built on a place sacred for several reasons, and had to house a number of ceremonies.

There were also a number of smaller structures. The temple of Nike (Victory) next to the Propylaea has been rebuilt to its original appearance. Between the Parthenon and the Erechtheion was a bronze statue of Athena, 70 feet (21 m) high. The gold tip of its spear could be seen by sailors at sea.

Acropolis

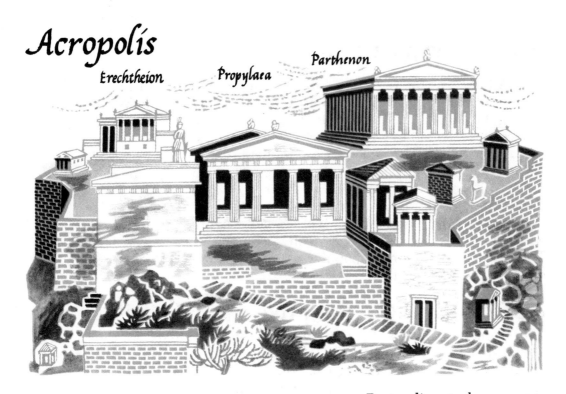

Erechtheion   Propylaea   Parthenon

ACTORS and ACTING

Pretending to be someone else and to have adventures is a favorite game with children the world over. Adults do this, too. The lives of great people and the experiences of ordinary people have been represented in speech, song, and dance through the ages.

Professional actors are dedicated to their work. It takes years of learning to speak and move properly before they are ready for important roles. And each role they play has to be studied carefully as well, so that the actor or actress can make the person they are playing seem real. Many prefer acting on the stage to acting in the movies because of a need to get a response from an audience they can see. Acting can be difficult, but some persons would not be happy doing anything else.

John ADAMS (1735–1826)

John Adams was the first Vice President and second President of the United States. He helped draft and defend the DECLARATION OF INDEPENDENCE. During the AMERICAN REVOLUTION, Adams went to France and Holland to seek support for the colonies.

Adams served as U.S. Vice President under George Washington, becoming President himself in 1797. In Europe, war was then developing between France and Britain, both of which claimed the right to seize American ships. Adams worked out a treaty with France and avoided American involvement. The treaty made Adams unpopular, and he was not reelected President in 1800.

John Quincy ADAMS (1767–1848)

John Quincy Adams was the sixth President of the United States. As a boy, he accompanied his father, JOHN ADAMS, on diplomatic missions to Europe. He helped to arrange the peace treaty that ended the WAR OF 1812. Adams was then appointed minister to Britain. Soon President Monroe recalled him and made him Secretary of State. In that position, Adams played a major part in obtaining Florida and in writing the famous MONROE DOCTRINE.

In 1824, Adams was elected President after a close and bitter contest against ANDREW JACKSON. He was defeated by Jackson in 1828. Later, he served as a congressman from Massachusetts for 17 years. He attacked slavery and opposed the MEXICAN WAR.

Samuel ADAMS (1722–1803)

Samuel Adams, older cousin of JOHN ADAMS, was a brewer in Massachusetts. He was a member of the Massachusetts legislature and spoke out against England's taxation of the American colonies. Adams stirred up public anger and organized a group of rebels, the Sons of Liberty. With the help of men like John Hancock and PATRICK HENRY, Adams encouraged Americans to revolt against British rule. The BOSTON TEA PARTY was planned and led by Sam Adams in 1773.

He voted for and signed the DECLARATION OF INDEPENDENCE.

ADRIATIC SEA

The Adriatic Sea is an arm of the Mediterranean between Italy and Yugoslavia. It was an important trade route during the Middle Ages. Many ships laden with rich cargoes from the East sailed up the Adriatic to the port of VENICE. The merchants there sold these riches—silks, spices, jewels—to other Europeans. The wealth of Asia and Europe could be seen on the piers and wharves of Venice during the 14th and 15th centuries. This city became rich and mighty and was called the "Queen of the Adriatic." SEE ALSO: VENICE.

ADVERTISING

Anyone with something to sell has to let the public know that it is for sale. The process of telling the public is called advertising. A few dollars will buy a small advertisement in a newspaper. On the other hand, some advertisers, such as large companies, spend millions of dollars at a time, letting a whole nation know about a product.

Advertising can be done in newspapers and magazines, on television and radio programs, on billboards, in telephone directories, and in many other ways. The advertiser's message can be handed to passers-by in the street, or even written on the sky in smoke.

Some people object to advertising. It can injure the look of a landscape or a city street. It sometimes makes false claims. Yet advertising of some sort is necessary for business. SEE ALSO: COMMERCE.

7

AEGEAN SEA

The Aegean Sea, between Greece and Turkey (previously called Asia Minor), is part of the Mediterranean Sea. The large island of CRETE lies at the south end. Most of the islands in the Aegean are owned by Greece and are "dead" volcanoes, with their tops above the surface of the water.

The sea was famous in Greek legend and history. Four thousand years ago, prosperous cities arose among its islands and along its coasts. One such city, Troy, controlled the passage of ships and trade between the Aegean and the Black Sea ports.

Cnossus in Crete was the capital of the great Minoan civilization that flourished about 2000 B.C. The Minoans built huge palaces and traded throughout the Aegean and with Egypt. The buried cities on the island of Crete, especially Cnossus, were excavated by Sir Arthur Evans from 1898 to 1935. Since then, other archeologists have carried on his work.

The ancient vase, shown on this page, was found on Crete and is more than 3500 years old.

AFRICA

Africa is a giant continent, more than three times the size of the United States; only Asia is larger. Africa is linked to Asia by a narrow bridge of land in the northeast. Here the SUEZ CANAL has been cut, connecting the Mediterranean with the Red Sea. The Gulf of Aden and the Indian Ocean lie to the east of Africa, and the Atlantic Ocean is to the west.

Not until the Portuguese navigator VASCO DA GAMA sailed around the Cape of Good Hope in 1497 were the size and shape of Africa fully realized. Dense jungles and vast deserts hindered much early exploration of the interior. In the last hundred years, men like DAVID LIVINGSTONE and SIR HENRY STANLEY have penetrated and explored the land. Most trade with the interior had previously been done with the aid of the ARABS.

All of the former European colonies have gained their independence and are now self-governing African nations.

Much of Africa lies in the hot TROPICS. The many highlands, however, create a cool, comfortable climate in many places. Near the equator it is hot and wet, with thick rain forests. Many grasslands, known as *savannas*, extend northward to the SAHARA Desert and southward to the

Kalahari Desert. Along the Cape of South Africa and the Mediterranean coast, the summers are dry and pleasant, and the winters are rather rainy.

Africa's longest range is the Atlas Mountains in the northwest. In the east-central highlands near the equator are Mount Kilimanjaro, Africa's highest mountain, and Mount Kenya. Here also are the largest lakes, including Lake Tanganyika, the longest freshwater lake in the world. These eastern lakes feed three great rivers, the NILE, the Congo, and the ZAMBEZI, on which the mighty VICTORIA FALLS are situated. Another important river, the Niger, drains the heavy equatorial rains of west-central Africa.

The steaming jungle heat and rain near the equator make the area a vast greenhouse. The forests here are thick with fruit trees, oil palms, and large hardwood trees such as ebony and mahogany. In the tangled vines and trees live monkeys, chimpanzees, gorillas, colorful birds, and a variety of snakes and insects.

The savanna has coarse "elephant grass," which grows tall enough to hide lions, zebras, giraffes, elephants, and hippopotamuses. Heavy rainfall occurs for 4 to 5 months on the savannas. There may be drought the rest of the year. Animals often have to wander hundreds of miles to find water.

The largest group of African people are the NEGROES, who live mainly south of the Sahara Desert. Arabs and Berbers live in Egypt and north of the Sahara. White people of British, Dutch, or French descent have settled in the southern parts and along the Mediterranean. A million or so Asians, mainly Hindus from India, live in eastern Africa.

The continent has vast natural resources. The earliest traders were interested in gold, ivory, and spices. Today, lumber, minerals, coffee, cotton, cocoa, and ground-nuts ("monkey-nuts") are produced for export around the world. Dates from the palms that grow in Morocco, Tunisia, and Egypt are well known. Egyptian cotton has a special quality all its own. Half of the world's gold is mined in South Africa, and over half of all industrial diamonds come from Zaire. Niger and Mozambique are now mining uranium to be used in nuclear power plants.

The MOSQUITO is a menace to man in Africa because its bite can cause an illness called MALARIA. Another enemy of man there is the blood-sucking tsetse fly. It carries germs that cause sleeping sickness and other diseases, which kill thousands of Africans and cattle each year. These insects are common in tropical areas, and scientists are now discovering ways to control or exterminate them, making Africa a healthier place to live. SEE ALSO: ARABS, NEGROES, SAHARA, TROPICS.

Rainfall   Vegetation

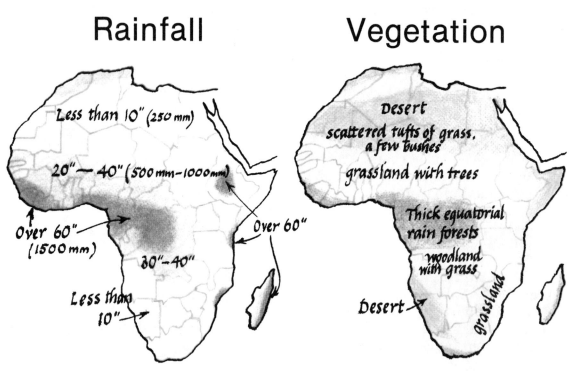

Africa — Countries

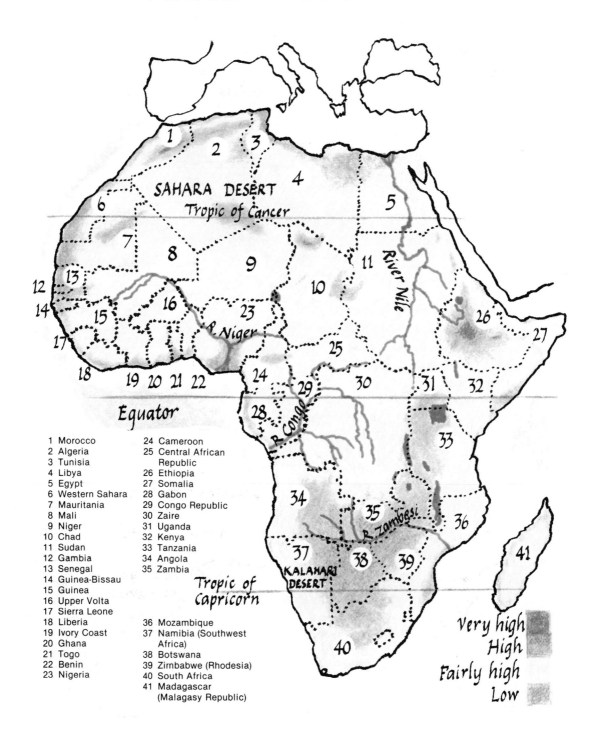

1 Morocco
2 Algeria
3 Tunisia
4 Libya
5 Egypt
6 Western Sahara
7 Mauritania
8 Mali
9 Niger
10 Chad
11 Sudan
12 Gambia
13 Senegal
14 Guinea-Bissau
15 Guinea
16 Upper Volta
17 Sierra Leone
18 Liberia
19 Ivory Coast
20 Ghana
21 Togo
22 Benin
23 Nigeria

24 Cameroon
25 Central African
   Republic
26 Ethiopia
27 Somalia
28 Gabon
29 Congo Republic
30 Zaire
31 Uganda
32 Kenya
33 Tanzania
34 Angola
35 Zambia

36 Mozambique
37 Namibia (Southwest
   Africa)
38 Botswana
39 Zirnbabwe (Rhodesia)
40 South Africa
41 Madagascar
   (Malagasy Republic)

Very high
High
Fairly high
Low

11

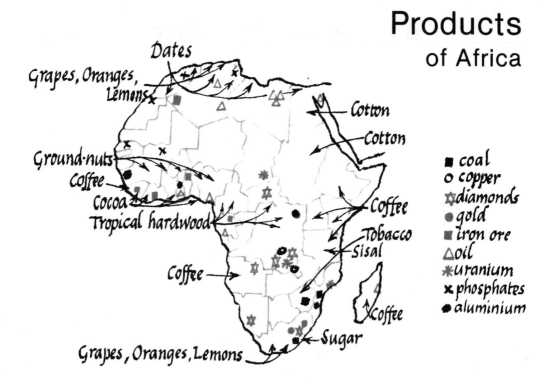

Products
of Africa

Dates

Grapes, Oranges, Lemons

Ground-nuts

Coffee

Cocoa

Tropical hardwood

Coffee

Grapes, Oranges, Lemons

Cotton

Cotton

Coffee

Tobacco

Sisal

Coffee

Sugar

■ coal
o copper
✡ diamonds
● gold
■ iron ore
△ oil
✱ uranium
✗ phosphates
◆ aluminium

AGRICULTURE

Agriculture, or FARMING, is the cultivation of land for food. In a broader sense, it is the science of producing crops and livestock, using the natural resources of the Earth. It is one of the oldest and most important occupations in the world.

Primitive men learned how to grind the seeds of wild grasses into flour. Then they discovered that these seeds could be planted and harvested near their homes. This encouraged the establishment of farm communities, and soon men were growing fields of wheat, rice, barley, and millet, a kind of cereal grass.

For thousands of years, farming tools were very simple. The earliest PLOWS were just small, crooked pieces of wood, often pulled by the men themselves. Later, stronger and larger plows were built that were pulled by oxen. The digging stick, the hoe, and the scythe were other early tools. Through the centuries, man made better and stronger tools; he made ingenious irrigation systems in order to control the water supply in dry regions.

In the last 200 years, agriculture became mechanized with the invention of large farm machinery, like the reaper, the cultivator, the thresher, and the combine. Powerful tractors have helped develop large-scale agriculture. A group of plows, today, can make as many as twenty furrows at a time. The modern combine harvester can cut and thresh grain in a large field in a few hours. It does what it used to take several men many days to do.

A great deal is continually being learned about enriching the soil with the use of fertilizer, selecting and rotating of crops, and improving through careful breeding the quality of livestock and poultry. SEE ALSO: PLOW.

AIR

The Earth

Air is a mixture of gases that surrounds the Earth and forms its atmosphere. About one-fifth of the air is OXYGEN, which animals need in order to live. Almost four-fifths of the air is NITROGEN, which is very important in making fertilizers.

There are also very small amounts of other gases in the air, such as argon, neon, helium, ozone, carbon dioxide, and water vapor. Each of these gases is useful in some way. Argon is used in electric light bulbs; neon in electric lighting and advertising signs; helium in balloons and airships. Ozone, found mainly in the region 6 to 30 miles (9.6–48.3 km) above the Earth's surface, absorbs dangerous radiation from the sun. Carbon dioxide is used by plants to help make their food. Water vapor is the source of all kinds of precipitation (rain, snow, hail).

Pure air is colorless, odorless, and tasteless. It is all around us, and yet we can not see it. We can, however, feel air when it is moving—when there is a breeze or a wind. No plant or animal could exist on Earth without air.

At sea level, nearly 15 pounds of air presses on every square inch (about 1 kg per cm²). Therefore, many tons of air press on our bodies, which are not flattened by this pressure because the air and blood inside our bodies press outward with an equal force.

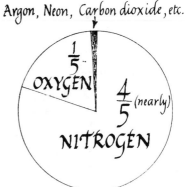

Argon, Neon, Carbon dioxide, etc.

$\frac{1}{5}$ OXYGEN

$\frac{4}{5}$ (nearly) NITROGEN

The layer of air surrounding the Earth is several hundred miles thick. As the air particles move farther away from the Earth's surface, they become farther apart from each other. Thus we say the air gets thinner. The air that is 50 miles (80.5 km) up is so thin that it can scarcely be detected. On the top of Mount Everest, about 5 miles (8 km) up, the air is so thin that breathing is very difficult.

Man has harnessed and used the power of moving air. Windmills for grinding and pumping are driven by the wind. Sailboats are moved also by wind. SEE ALSO: BAROMETER, WIND.

AIRPLANE

To fly was long an ambition of man. The ancient Greek legend of Daedalus and Icarus, who escaped from prison on man-made wings, is an example. Now and then, men really tried to fly on such wings, but had not the strength to do so. The great artist and inventor LEONARDO DA VINCI drew such a flying machine.

Most early attempts involved wings that flapped like those of birds, but the first successes were with the KITE, kept aloft by the motion of the air, the BALLOON, which was lighter than the air, and the GLIDER, whose wings were fixed and which was launched by a force outside itself.

The airplane is a flying machine that is heavier than the air, that has fixed wings, and that moves itself. Model airplanes were tried out in the 1890s, and a steam-powered model flew about a half mile (0.8 km) in 1896. But the steam engine was too heavy to be practical; the gasoline engine was the answer to the weight problem.

On December 17, 1903, Wilbur and Orville Wright first succeeded in flying at Kitty Hawk, North Carolina. Their kite-like airplane, powered by a gasoline engine, flew 120 feet (37 m) in 12 seconds. By 1905, they could fly 25 miles (40 km) at a time. In 1909, the Frenchman Louis Blériot flew from France to England.

The First World War, like most wars, encouraged invention, and the airplane began to assume something close to its modern form around 1915. After the war, aviators began to make new speed and mileage records. Two English aviators made the first crossing of the Atlantic in 1919, and in 1927 the American Charles Lindbergh flew non-stop from New York to Paris.

Until the 1960s, most airplanes were moved by propellers, but jet propulsion—another military invention—has come more and more into recent use. The airliner shown here has four jet engines, placed at the tail. This plane carries more than 160 persons, including crew.

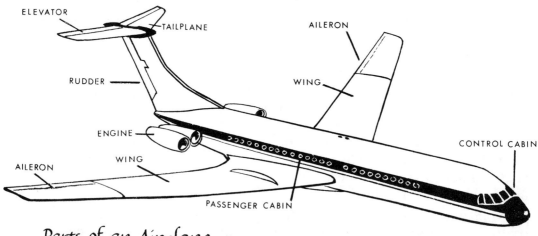

Parts of an Airplane

The airliner illustrated below is the Concorde, able to fly 10 miles (16 km) up and to cross the Atlantic in 3 hours. It can go about 1500 miles (2300 km) an hour, about twice the speed of sound. Its usefulness is limited by the problems it can make for the environment. Military planes have flown even faster, though —over 4000 miles (6400 km) an hour.

The Concorde

A large airliner needs a very long runway for its takeoffs and landings, but aircraft now exist that require almost no runway at all. The HELICOPTER can go straight up, and the VTOL (Vertical Takeoff and Landing) planes, whose wings pivot, can do almost the same. The wings and the engines point upward when the VTOL takes off or lands, then point forward when the plane is in the air.

Airplanes have come in many forms during their brief history. Most planes today have only one wing (monoplanes), but fifty years ago most planes had two. There was even one plane (which never flew successfully) that had nine wings! Modern planes usually have no more then four engines, but some planes in the past had eight or more; these engines were not very powerful.

Modern planes come too in many forms, from the two-seater propeller-driven ones to be found at any small airport to the jet-propelled Boeing 747, which can carry over 500 passengers. The U.S. Air Force Galaxy is even larger. It is a freight plane that can carry 265,000 pounds (120,000 kg) of cargo.

Seaplanes can land and take off on water. They have watertight bodies that float in the water like a ship. Some seaplanes, called *amphibians*, have wheels attached to their hulls. These wheels can be let down so that these seaplanes can operate on land if necessary. *Floatplanes* are seaplanes with large floats instead of wheels.

Helicopter

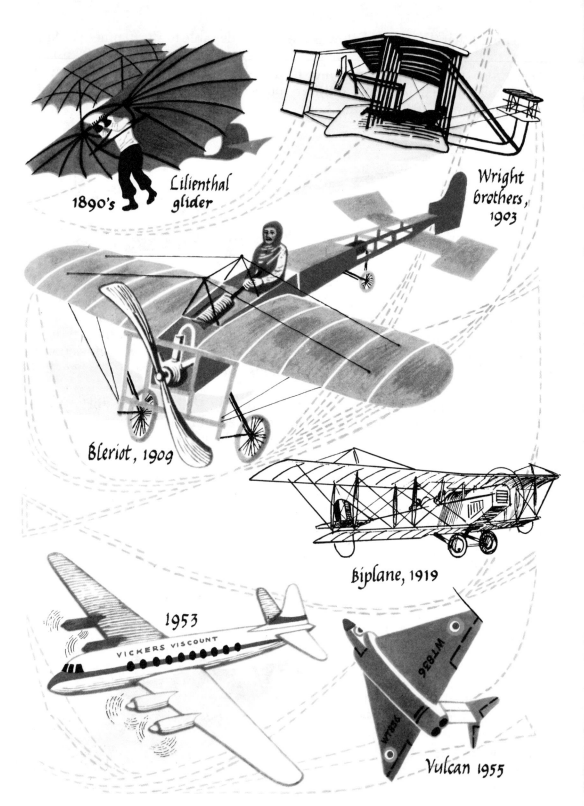

1890's Lilienthal glider

Wright brothers, 1903

Bleriot, 1909

Biplane, 1919

1953 VICKERS VISCOUNT

Vulcan 1955

HOW AN AIRPLANE FLIES

A large modern airplane is so large that it requires more than one person to run it. A big airliner needs pilots, a navigator, and a radio operator. Controls are very complicated. Still, large and small airplanes operate in much the same way. Here is a small plane, flown by one person.

Once the plane is moving, the pilot can raise it by pulling back on a lever (called a *stick*) that rises from the floor. This raises the *elevators*, parts of the wing-like *tail plane*. The elevators act like rudders to turn the plane upward. If the pilot wants to go down, he pushes the stick forward, and the elevators go down.

To turn, the pilot moves his stick to one side or the other. Parts of the wing called *ailerons* rise and fall so as to bank (tilt) the plane. At the same time, the pilot moves a bar on the floor (or else pedals) that control the rudder. The plane banks to get more of a hold on the air than the rudder could do alone. If the pilot used only the rudder, the plane would slide sideways so that he could not control his turn.

The controls and instruments of the cockpit are simple in such a small plane, and many persons have learned to fly them. Even so, there are engine controls, an *altimeter* to measure height above ground, a COMPASS to show direction, a radio for talking with AIRPORTS, and gauges that show the amount of fuel left, pressure of lubricating oil, the temperature of the engine, and so on. In a large airplane, this system of controls and gauges is very complicated. The plane crew often includes a flight engineer, whose job is to watch everything and take care of whatever changes are needed, leaving the pilots to steer the plane. SEE ALSO: AIRPORT, BALLOON, GLIDER, HELICOPTER.

rudder

elevator

aileron

With his hands the pilot moves the 'stick' which controls the elevators and ailerons. With his feet he moves the 'bar which controls the rudder.

AIRPORT

An airport is a place where aircraft take off and land. Aircraft are also kept, supplied, and repaired there.

A small airport may have only one runway with a building that houses the control tower (from which planes are directed by radio). A large passenger airport is much bigger and much more complicated. The control tower is a very tall structure, from which the controller and his crew watch and guide every plane that approaches or leaves the airport, or that moves on the runways. There is a place for observing and reporting the weather. There are hangars for storing and repairing planes. There have to be rooms and hallways for passengers, freight, supplies, plane crews, and airport employees. There are usually restaurants and shops. The baggage of people coming from another country has to be inspected in a special place.

Outside there are not only airplanes and helicopters but fuel trucks, baggage trucks, and other vehicles. Fire trucks and ambulances are ready for accidents.

Airports are usually as far from city areas as they can be, both to prevent accidents and to keep airplane noise from annoying many people. Flat land in areas without smoke or fog is best. If pilots cannot see for miles, airplanes may be stopped from coming in or out.

ALABAMA

Alabama lies in the southern part of the United States. Except for the Appalachian foothills in the northeast, the state consists of rolling and flat coastal plains, drained by the Alabama and Tombigbee Rivers and their tributaries. Central Alabama is called the Black Belt, for its rich, dark soil is excellent for growing cotton, corn, soybeans, and peanuts and for raising poultry and livestock.

Hydroelectric and nuclear power plants have turned Alabama into an important manufacturing state, which also has valuable deposits of coal, iron ore, stone, and petroleum. Iron, steel, and metal products are made in Birmingham, the largest city. Other important industries include chemicals, fertilizers, textiles, lumbering, and fishing.

The Spanish explorers in the 1500s found a number of Indian tribes in Alabama, including the Chickasaws, Cherokees, and Creeks. In 1702, the French built the first permanent settlement near present-day Mobile. Later, the British took control of Alabama, but Spanish Florida claimed the area around Mobile Bay until the U.S. seized it in 1813. In 1861, the southern states were organized as the Confederacy in Montgomery, the capital. The state suffered greatly during and after the Civil War. Today, it has overcome many of its racial and civil rights problems. Alabama has a population of about 3.75 million.

ALAMO

The Alamo, a building in San Antonio, TEXAS, is known as the "Cradle of Texas Liberty." Erected in 1718, it was first a Spanish mission and then a chapel run by the Franciscans, who were trying to Christianize and educate the Indians. The chapel was later converted into a fort and nicknamed the "Alamo," meaning "cottonwood" in Spanish, because of a grove of cottonwoods nearby.

In 1835, American settlers in Texas established their own government. Mexico, which controlled the area, sent 4000 troops under General Santa Anna to retake San Antonio and to crush any opposition. Less than 200 Texas volunteers under the command of Colonel William B. Travis retreated into the Alamo and refused to surrender. During a 12-day siege, every fighting man in the Alamo was killed by the Mexicans. DAVY CROCKETT and Jim Bowie, two American frontiersmen, were among the brave defenders. This heroic stand aroused the Texans, who rallied to the cry, "Remember the Alamo." Led by General Sam Houston, they defeated Santa Anna's Mexicans at San Jacinto and secured independence for Texas.

ALASKA

Alaska is the largest state in the United States, occupying the northwest part of North America. It has mountain ranges, volcanoes, glaciers, and fiords, as well as many islands along its southern coast. The Alaskan climate varies from moderate and rainy in the southeast, where Juneau, the capital, is situated, to extremely icy and cold on the Arctic (or North) Slope. About one-sixth of Alaska's population of about 500,000 are Eskimos and Indians.

Vitus Bering, a Danish explorer, visited Alaska in 1741, and the Russians established the state's first white settlement on Kodiak Island in 1784. The

Russians, facing severe competition from Canadians and Americans as fur traders, sold Alaska for $7.2 million to the U.S. in 1867. For many years, Alaska was called "Seward's Folly," because U.S. Secretary of State William H. Seward had bought it and because it was considered a frozen wasteland without any value. In 1896, gold was discovered and the famous gold rush was on.

Alaska is potentially one of the richest states, particularly with regard to the vast oil fields in Prudhoe Bay off the state's North Slope. The trans-Alaskan pipeline carries oil from there to the southern port of Valdez. Other valuable industries are commercial fishing, lumbering, and tourism.

ALBANIA

Albania is a small, mountainous country bordering the Adriatic Sea. Yugoslavia lies to the north and east, and Greece to the south of it. Its 2.5 million population consists mainly of farmers who raise tobacco, fruits, vegetables, and livestock. Some work as fishermen and coal miners.

The climate is moderate in the mountains. Many mountain villages can only be reached by pack animals. But Albania's capital, Tirana, rests in a fertile plain that is quite easy to reach. Albania has been a Communist country since 1946. It broke off relations with the Soviet Union in 1961 and became an ally of Communist China.

ALBERTA

Alberta is one of the largest provinces of CANADA. The towering Rocky Mountains rise on its western border with British Columbia. Most of Alberta consists of rolling prairies and wooded country, broken by many small lakes, streams, and rivers. Irrigation has made the very dry southern and eastern regions productive for agricultural purposes. Wheat, sugar beets, and vegetables are grown, and much livestock is raised. Alberta has a large mining industry, producing much oil, natural gas, and coal for use at home and abroad. The province's main cities are Edmonton, the capital, Calgary, Lethbridge, and Medicine Hat. There are nearly two million people in Alberta.

In the late 18th century, the British Hudson's Bay Company and the French Northwest Company established fur trading posts in the area. In 1821, the companies merged as the Hudson's Bay Company, which controlled and governed the area until 1869. The territory then became part of Canada, and in 1882 was named Alberta after a daughter of Queen Victoria.

Louisa May ALCOTT (1832–1888)

Louisa May Alcott, American author, was born in Germantown, Pennsylvania, but lived most of her life in and near Concord, Massachusetts. She was taught by her father, a writer and teacher, who encouraged Louisa's early interest in writing. Determined to help support her poor family, Louisa worked as a domestic servant, governess, and seamstress before she made money as a writer.

By 1860, her short stories and poems had been published in the *Atlantic Monthly*. As a nurse during the CIVIL WAR, Louisa wrote letters to her family about her experiences in the hospital. These letters, revised and published as *Hospital Sketches* in 1863, attracted wide attention.

While editor of a children's magazine, her autobiographical book, *Little Women*, was published in two volumes in 1868 and 1869. It was an immediate success, and became one of the most popular books for children ever written. Louisa now had enough money to continue writing. Her other books, including *Little Men*, were popular and brought financial security to the Alcott family.

ALEXANDER the GREAT (356–323 B.C.)

Alexander was a mighty king who became one of the greatest military leaders in history.

He was born in Pella, in northern Greece. Aristotle, the famous Greek philosopher, taught him geography, politics, literature, medicine, and science. His father, Philip II, taught him how to plan and win battles.

When Philip died, Alexander became king of Macedonia, at only 20 years of age. He led his armies on a series of long marches until he had conquered most of the then-known world.

He took control of Greece, driving the Persians out. He went on to take all of civilized Europe, Egypt, and PERSIA. He was made king of Egypt and Asia.

With his soldiers he traveled more than 11,000 miles (17,710 km) and spread the language, customs, and ideas of Greece wherever he went. He also brought back to Greece a great deal about the countries he conquered. He reported on the customs, beliefs, and learning of distant people, as well as details about the land, plants, and animals he found during his conquests.

In India his men refused to go any further. Worn out, Alexander turned back but caught fever and died, at 33 years old, in Babylon. He was buried in Alexandria, Egypt, a splendid city and maybe the greatest monument to his name.

ALFRED the GREAT (A.D. 849–899)

In A.D. 871, Alfred became king of Wessex, the southernmost kingdom in England at that time. He was only 23 years old.

Six years later a mighty Danish army invaded Wessex. Alfred was defeated in battle. He escaped to lead his army to victory the next year. To protect Wessex, he then built a fleet of ships and towers along the coast, should the Danes break the peace. Several years later, the Danes tried to take control, and Alfred finally drove them from southern England in A.D. 897.

He is also remembered for his wise rule and his interest in education. Teachers from Wales and Europe were invited to his kingdom to teach his people, the West Saxons. He helped to translate some books from Latin into Anglo-Saxon (Old English), something that had not been done before. He urged that a history of the times be written; it is now known as the "Anglo-Saxon Chronicle." SEE ALSO: ENGLAND.

A beautiful jewel made for Alfred

Ethan ALLEN (1738–1789)

Born in Connecticut, Ethan Allen, as a young frontiersman and veteran of the French and Indian War, settled in what is now Vermont. At the outbreak of the AMERICAN REVOLUTION, he organized and led the famous "Green Mountain Boys." With only 83 men, his force captured the British forts at Ticonderoga and Crown Point (New York) on May 10, 1775.

The following September, he volunteered to conduct a secret mission to take MONTREAL. He was captured and remained a prisoner until he was exchanged two and a half years later for an English officer. After being released, he was appointed general of the state militia but did not serve in the American Revolution. Instead, he turned his attention to politics, his special interest being Vermont's statehood. Failing to achieve statehood for Vermont, he tried to get Vermont annexed (joined) to Canada. He also wrote about his captivity and about politics.

ALLIGATORS

Alligators are large reptiles belonging to the CROCODILE family. An alligator's snout is rounded and shorter than a crocodile's. When an alligator's mouth is shut, its teeth do not show, whereas two huge teeth stick out of a closed crocodile's mouth.

Alligators are found in the swamps and rivers from North Carolina to Florida and in the Gulf states. A Chinese species, smaller than the American, is found along the Yangtze River in China. Alligators eat fish and other water life, but are not known to attack man unless in self-defense. They lay from 20 to 50 eggs in the mud or sand, and the hot sun helps to hatch them. The demand for alligator leather greatly reduced a number of wild alligator species. For this reason, the use of alligator skins for belts, handbags, and other products is no longer allowed in the U.S. SEE ALSO: CROCODILE

ALLOYS

Alloys are metallic substances. They are formed when two or more METALS or a metal and a non-metal, such as carbon, are mixed together. BRONZE was the first metal alloy used by man. It is a mixture of copper and tin, and is much stronger than either of these pure metals used separately. Brass is an alloy of copper and zinc. STEEL and pewter are also alloys.

Metal alloys produce products that are hard, strong, and light, and that resist corrosion and rust. Depending on the mixture, they also make products of high or low melting point and products that conduct electricity in different ways.

Alloys are widely used in making space satellites, coins, cooking and eating utensils, jewelry, fire alarms, dental fillings, fuses, and thousands of other useful modern conveniences. SEE ALSO: METALS.

ALMANAC

An almanac is a book full of useful information. It tells you the important things that happened last year, both in the United States and everywhere in the world. It describes the states of the nation and the countries of the world. It tells you about religious groups, about the world of sports, about the arts, and many other things that interest people in the United States. It changes every year to keep the information as up-to-date as possible. If you want to know about something, try the almanac. SEE ALSO: DICTIONARY, ENCYCLOPEDIA.

ALPHABET

An alphabet is any system of characters or signs with which language is written. In it there is a definite relation between symbol and sound.

In ancient EGYPT, the people used simple pictures called HIEROGLYPHICS for writing. Thus, every thing and idea had to have its own picture.

Slowly this pictorial language was made simpler, until some pictures were used as *letters* for the first time. The Assyrians, Babylonians, and Persians used CUNEIFORM, a system of wedge-shaped syllables. Little by little, separate syllables of words were symbolized by simple shapes or marks.

The PHOENICIANS, who lived at the east end of the Mediterranean, were the first to use only letters for writing. Phoenician letters stood for separate sounds of the language. "Aleph" and "beth" were the first two letters in their alphabet, meaning ox and house, respectively.

The Greeks used the Phoenician letters but made numerous changes. They developed *vowel* sounds, for the Phoenicians had no vowels. "Aleph" became *alpha* and "beth" became *beta*. Together, these two letters make *alphabet*.

Hieroglyphics (Egypt)

Cuneiform

The Romans later copied the Greek alphabet. Our own ABCs are Roman letters, as can be seen in the illustration on the page. In column 1 are Phoenician letters, in 2 ancient Greek letters, in 3 the later Greek letters, and in 4 the Roman (Latin) letters. Column 5 gives our own alphabet. Examples of hieroglyphic and cuneiform writing are also shown. SEE ALSO: CUNEIFORM, HIEROGLYPHICS.

ALPS

The Alps are a great mountain chain in south central EUROPE, stretching from France through Switzerland to Italy and Austria. The Swiss gave the mountains their name. (An *alp* once referred to the high, green pasture on the mountain side.)

The highest mountain is Mont Blanc ("White Mountain"), rising 15,781 feet (4892 m), located on the French-Italian border. The majestic Matterhorn on the Swiss-Italian border, near Zermatt, is only 1000 feet (310 m) lower.

Today most of the people in the Alps live in villages in the meadows between the mountains. Some herd cows, sheep, and goats. Others are farmers, making butter and their famous cheeses. Also there are craftsmen who make clocks, toys, and wood carvings.

People flock to the Alps to ski during the winter. They come also to enjoy the lovely scenery in the summer. SEE ALSO: EUROPE.

ALUMINUM

The Earth's crust contains more aluminum than any other metal. No one had ever seen aluminum until a little more than a century ago. Although it is plentiful, it is never found in its pure state, but is joined chemically with other materials. All clay, many rocks, and the common mineral, bauxite, contain aluminum. In 1886, a cheap process was discovered for obtaining pure aluminum. A very powerful electric current was passed through a hot solution of bauxite. This process is essentially the method by which aluminum is produced today.

Aluminum is a useful metal because it is very strong and light in weight. It does not rust and can be rolled or stretched into sheets, rods, and wire, or hammered into a thin foil for wrapping and storing foods, chewing gum, and cigarettes.

It is widely used for cooking utensils, airplanes, toys, railroad cars, electric cables, automobiles, and even metallic yarns, from which beautiful fabrics are woven. By a specific process, aluminum items can be made different colors.

AMAZON

The Amazon River begins high in the Andes Mountains in SOUTH AMERICA. It then flows eastward through dense jungle across northern Brazil for about 3700 miles (5957 km) before emptying into the Atlantic. With its tributaries (smaller rivers) from Peru, Venezuela, Colombia, Ecuador, and Bolivia, the Amazon carries more water than any other river system in the world. The mouth of the river is more than 60 miles (97 km) wide, and the main stream is navigable for large ocean-going vessels as far as Iquitos, some 2300 miles (3703 km) from the ocean. For much of its course, the Amazon meanders in a maze of channels through countless islands. Its banks shift with constant erosion. SEE ALSO: SOUTH AMERICA.

AMBER

In primitive times, cone-bearing trees with their sticky gum, or RESIN, fell into swamps and were covered with mud. Slowly, as centuries passed, the sticky resin hardened and changed to a clear, brownish yellow material we call amber. Amber is fossilized resin.

In some amber, insects were trapped and preserved. Scientists can see in perfect detail those insects that existed many years ago.

The ancient Greeks noted how amber (called *elektron* in Greek) attracted bits of straw when rubbed with fur. Men realized later that this action produced static electricity.

Amber makes beautiful beads and combs. Also, amber dissolved in linseed or tung oil produces a commercial varnish.

AMERICA

"America" is frequently used to refer to just the United States of America. However, America refers broadly to the lands of the Western Hemisphere—NORTH AMERICA (which includes CENTRAL AMERICA) and SOUTH AMERICA. These two continents are joined by a narrow strip of land through which the Panama Canal runs.

North and South America are somewhat triangular in shape, with the Pacific to the west and the Atlantic to the east. North America is mostly in a temperate climate, whereas South America lies mostly in the tropics. Some scientists have said the climate is one reason that the United States has developed more rapidly than most South American countries.

North America was explored in the 1490s by CHRISTOPHER COLUMBUS, and South America about 1500 by Amerigo Vespucci, after whom "America" was named. Since then many people from England, France, Germany, and the Scandinavian countries have settled in North America, and many from Spain and Portugal have gone to South America.

The United States is the richest and most powerful of all the countries of "the Americas." Canada has much untapped mineral wealth, large tracts of forest land, and enormous expanses for wheat-growing. The mineral resources of Venezuela (oil), Peru and Chile (iron ore and copper), and Bolivia (tin and silver) have made these nations rich. Argentina is known for its beef, and Brazil exports coffee, soybeans, and cotton.

The mountains of North and South America are the highest in the west. The Rocky Mountains extend from Alaska to Mexico; the Andes Mountains stretch almost the entire length of South America. Also, several great rivers drain large areas of both continents: the Mississippi-Missouri and Rio Grande in North America, and the Amazon and Paraná-La Plata in South America. SEE ALSO: NORTH AMERICA, SOUTH AMERICA, U.S.A.

AMERICAN REVOLUTION
After the British won the FRENCH AND INDIAN WAR in 1763, they had a large empire in North America. They needed more money to pay for the war and for the increased troops stationed in the New World. The British Parliament, supported by King GEORGE III, tried then to make the American colonies share these costs.

In 1764, a tax was put on molasses and sugar, angering New England merchants and makers of rum. The next year, the Stamp Act forced Americans to buy stamps for wills, deeds, and other documents. Newspapers, magazines, and almanacs sold in America also had to have stamps. Everywhere leaders like Samuel Adams and Patrick Henry denounced the act and protested that Parliament was violating the rights of Americans. The angry colonists said that they should not be taxed without representation in Parliament in London—that is, without someone speaking and voting for them when tax laws were made. The Quartering Act also upset the colonists, who were forced to quarter (house and feed) British soldiers.

In 1770, violence occurred in Boston. British redcoats (soldiers) fired into a noisy crowd of Americans who were angry over the taxes. Five Americans were killed at what became known as the Boston Massacre. Then, in 1773, Boston colonists disguised as Indians boarded three British ships and dumped all the tea into the harbor. They were angry about the British tea tax— another tax that Americans had not voted on. The BOSTON TEA PARTY led to further British restrictions on the colonists. In 1774, the First Continental Congress met in Philadelphia and decided not to import any British goods. The King of England was sent several petitions of American grievances (complaints).

In order to seize guns and ammunition belonging to American patriots, the British began a secret march to Concord in April, 1775. Two Americans, PAUL REVERE and William Dawes, rode through the night to warn the colonists. At Lexington, the British encountered and fought a band of Minutemen (American shopkeepers and farmers who were "ready at a minute's notice"). The British then continued on to Concord, where they burned some buildings. On their return march, angry Minutemen fired upon the British, killing and wounding about 200.

Soon the main British fort north of the Hudson River, Fort Ticonderoga, was captured by the Green Mountain Boys of Vermont. Realizing that the colonies were now at war with Britain, American delegates at the Second Continental Congress in Philadelphia appointed GEORGE WASHINGTON commander of the Continental Army. On June 17, 1775, Americans were beaten at the Battle of Bunker Hill, the first major battle of the American Revolution. Now the war began in earnest against the British. But some Americans—called Loyalists—remained loyal to Britain, while the Patriots fought for independence.

THOMAS JEFFERSON wrote the first draft of the DECLARATION OF INDEPENDENCE. On July 4, 1776, representatives of the THIRTEEN COLONIES signed this document, announcing the separation of the colonies from Britain and the formation of the United States.

At first, Washington's small army was beaten and forced to retreat into

Pennsylvania. During the winter of 1776-77, Washington crossed the icy Delaware River and defeated the Hessians (German soldiers paid to fight for the British) at Trenton and Princeton, New Jersey. The British then tried to split the colonies in half by moving an army south from Canada. The British General Howe, instead of advancing north to meet this army, marched his men into Pennsylvania and defeated Washington at Brandywine. Howe then took Philadelphia, the colonial capital. Meanwhile, in the north, the British army under General Burgoyne surrendered to the Americans under General Gates at the Battle of Saratoga in New York. This American victory was the turning point of the war. Soon the French gave soldiers, ships, and money to aid the American cause.

In the cruel winter of 1777-78, Washington's loyal army almost starved and froze to death at Valley Forge, in Pennsylvania. LAFAYETTE, a young Frenchman, and Steuben, a German officer, helped organize and train the suffering American soldiers, so that in the spring Washington had a good, disciplined army.

On the western frontier, Americans under George Rogers Clark captured several British forts. In the South, forces under Nathanael Greene, Daniel Morgan, and Francis Marion won important battles against the British. John Paul Jones became an American hero at sea. With his ship, the *Bonhomme Richard* (in honor of BENJAMIN FRANKLIN), Jones captured the British warship *Serapis* in 1779.

Battle Sites of the American Revolution

The Americans, however, suffered many defeats and were always plagued by lack of food, supplies, and money. Finally at Yorktown in 1781, Washington's army surrounded the British under Lord Cornwallis. The French navy blocked any escape by sea. Cornwallis surrendered, thus ending the American Revolution. In 1783, the Treaty of Paris was signed, granting independence to the new United States of America. SEE ALSO: BOSTON TEA PARTY, DECLARATION OF INDEPENDENCE, U.S.A.

The AMISH

In the 17th century, many German-speaking people belonged to a Protestant sect called the Mennonites. One group that separated from the others was called Amish because they were led by Jakob Ammann. They started to come to eastern Pennsylvania around 1720. Today they are also in western Pennsylvania, parts of the Midwest, and Ontario.

Some Amish people have no churches, but meet in homes. Their services are in the Pennsylvania Dutch language, which is really a kind of German. They wear plain, simple clothes fastened with hooks instead of buttons. The clothes are mostly black. The Amish live very simply. Most are farmers, but will not use machinery. The horse is still important on an Amish farm. They are very good farmers even though they have no tractors. They are afraid of the bad habits of the non-Amish, and sometimes refuse to send their children to public schools.

AMOEBA

The amoeba (also spelled ameba) is a one-celled animal. It is one of the tiniest and simplest animals. It can be seen only with the help of a microscope. It is found in damp ground and stagnant water in most parts of the world. Sometimes it is found inside the bodies of animals, where it can cause illness and death.

The amoeba's body looks like a bit of colorless jelly. Nevertheless, it can do many things that the bodies of larger animals can do. It is a most interesting animal to watch.

The part of the cell that controls all the activities is the *nucleus*—a kind of primitive brain. The amoeba takes in food, digests it, and eliminates waste. It moves about slowly by forming foot-like sacs or projections called *pseudopods* (or "false feet") into which the *protoplasm* (the liquid material inside the cell wall) flows. Thus, the amoeba's shape constantly changes and no two amoebas look exactly alike. Amoebas breathe. They also reproduce themselves by simply dividing in half.

AMPHIBIANS

Amphibian comes from a Greek word meaning "living a double life." Amphibians are cold-blooded, vertebrate animals that spend their early life in water and their adult life on land, though near water. They are an intermediate animal between the fish and the reptile. Common amphibians today include FROGS, TOADS, NEWTS, and salamanders.

They undergo a change from an aquatic (living in water) form to a terrestrial (living on land) form. First, amphibians lay their jelly-like eggs in water. From the eggs hatch larvae or tadpoles, which have GILLS. They propel themselves through the water with their tails. These aquatic animals gradually grow legs, and their gills wither away, being replaced by lungs. They are then ready to live completely or partly on land.

Some amphibians of primitive times were about 8 feet (2.4 m) long. All of these large amphibians have died out. The amphibians that are now on Earth are small in size and rather harmless. They have no scales, fur, or feathers, and their skins are bare and moist. They inhabit damp places. In the larval stage, they eat plants and small dead animals; as adults, they eat insects, too.

AMSTERDAM

Amsterdam is the capital of The Netherlands (HOLLAND) and often called "the Venice of the North." It is cut by more than 50 canals and crossed by some 400 bridges. Millions of strong wooden and concrete pilings support the old and modern buildings. Boats and barges can come right into this beautiful city, and people still live in many of the tall and narrow houses that were built in the 14th century.

Amsterdam is a major European port, a center for the diamond-cutting industry, and the headquarters of many international banks. In the 17th century, REMBRANDT VAN RIJN, the famous Dutch painter, lived here. Many of his paintings hang in the city's Rijks museum. SEE ALSO: HOLLAND.

Roald AMUNDSEN (1872–1928)

Roald Amundsen, a Norwegian explorer, was the first man to reach the SOUTH POLE.

In 1910, he headed for the NORTH POLE, but soon heard that PEARY had already reached it. He then changed plans and sailed to the Antarctic. With a dog team, skis, and four companions, he climbed glaciers and fought blizzards and finally reached the South Pole in December, 1911. A month later an English explorer, SCOTT, found the Norwegian flag there.

In 1926, Amundsen, with two others, flew across the North Pole for the first time. Their dirigible (airship) *Norge*, built and piloted by an Italian, Umberto Nobile, succeeded after two attempts by airplane had failed.

Two years later he died when his plane crashed on a rescue mission. SEE ALSO: NORTH POLE; PEARY, ROBERT; SCOTT, ROBERT; SOUTH POLE.

Hans Christian ANDERSEN (1805–1875)

Hans Christian Andersen was born at the village of Odense in Denmark. He grew up to be one of the world's greatest storytellers, writing poems, novels, and fairy tales.

His father, who died when Hans was 11, was a poor shoemaker, and his mother washed clothes to make money. His time was often spent making up stories and playing with his puppets.

At 14, he left Odense to seek his fortune as an actor in Copenhagen. His acting was not successful, but his writing drew the attention of the King of Denmark, who educated him at public expense. His first poems and a novel brought him some money, and friends encouraged him to continue. His first book of fairy tales was printed in 1835.

Soon he became famous. Among his 168 stories are the well-known "The Emperor's New Clothes," "The Little Mermaid," and "The Red Shoes." A statue of the Little Mermaid on a rock in the harbor of Copenhagen and a statue of Andersen in Central Park in New York City honor this author.

ANESTHETICS

Anesthetics are DRUGS which take away pain. They also relax muscles. They may be used to produce unconsciousness in surgical operations.

There are two kinds of anesthetics: *general* and *local*. General anesthetics are used when a complete loss of consciousness is desired, especially in operations on deep-lying organs. General anesthetics can be inhaled or injected. They include ether, chloroform, and sodium pentothal. Local anesthetics are used in amputations, childbirth, dental surgery, and even brain operations when talking with the patient is necessary for the doctor. Local anesthetics are usually injected. Some local anesthetics are applied by a spray, which numbs the area with cold. Novocaine is an example of a local anesthetic.

Until the 1840s, patients were often given brandy or whiskey or even knocked unconscious before an operation. Some patients were simply tied down and operated on.

In 1846, the world's first modern operation was performed. William Morton, a Boston dentist, used ether to put a patient quietly to sleep before surgery. Anesthetics have been called America's greatest gift to mankind.

ANGLO-SAXONS

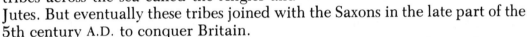

Until about A.D. 400, the Roman armies protected Britain from invaders. Many Germanic-speaking tribes tried to take control of Britain, attacking the coastal settlements in their long, open boats.

When the Romans left to guard their other territories, a people called SAXONS, or "men of the long knives," made successful raids along the coast and up the rivers. The British sought help from other foreign tribes across the sea called the Angles and Jutes. But eventually these tribes joined with the Saxons in the late part of the 5th century A.D. to conquer Britain.

Their first settlements were on the south and east coasts, but within two centuries they spread across the country, leaving only Cornwall, Wales, Cumberland, and much of Scotland untouched.

These Anglo-Saxons, as they are called, were good sailors, warriors, and farmers. They usually lived in little villages in forest clearings. Their huts of wood and clay had thatched roofs and earthen floors. The houses of the chiefs were somewhat larger and rather like the barns in the Middle Ages. The chief lived with his men in the "hall," whose walls were hung with shields and weapons and where they had

great banquets. Bards and minstrels told heroic stories here, often accompanied by music. They recited exciting tales of fights with dragons and monsters, such as the story of BEOWULF.

A tall fence enclosed this hall and the other buildings of the settlement. Outside the fence there were several large fields, where crops were grown. Usually only one or two of the fields were worked each year, the others lying fallow. Every freeman cultivated several strips of field, while his cattle and pigs roamed the forest and pastures for their food. Each house had a weaving loom, on which beautiful fabrics were sometimes made.

ANIMALS

Unlike most PLANTS, animals are living beings that have the ability to move about in search of food. Whereas plants make their food from inorganic substances, animals must secure their food from substances that are already organic—that is, from either plants or other animals which eat plants.

Moreover, animals move in specialized ways, have nervous systems and sense organs, and breathe in oxygen and breathe out carbon dioxide. They also digest their food, give off waste, and reproduce their own kind.

Animals have been divided by zoologists, scientists who study animals, into two main groups. There are animals with backbones called *vertebrates* and animals without backbones called *invertebrates*.

Vertebrates include MAMMALS, BIRDS, REPTILES, AMPHIBIANS, and FISH. Most people use the word "animal" when they are talking about mammals (those that have hair or fur and nurse their young), such as the dog, cat, cow, horse, rabbit, or monkey. Mammals are considered the most complex animals.

Invertebrate animals have a simpler structure. In size, they range from the microscopic one-celled *protozoa* to the giant squid, which may grow to 50 feet (15.5 m) in length. Most invertebrate animals live in water because the pull of GRAVITY makes it difficult for them to move about on land.

The largest animal on Earth is the blue whale, which often grows more than 100 feet (31 m) long and weighs more than 100 tons (91 metric tons). The elephant is the largest land animal, and the ostrich is the largest bird. SEE ALSO: MAMMALS, VERTEBRATE.

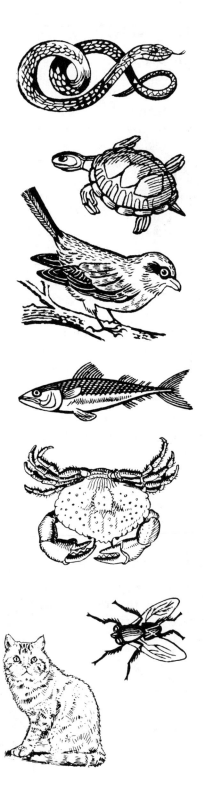

ANTENNAE

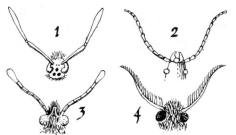

Antennae, often called "feelers," grow in pairs from the head of almost all arthropods, such as insects, centipedes, lobsters, and shrimps. Spiders do not have antennae. The single pair of antennae of all insects looks like long, jointed, flexible rods.
An insect's sense of touch is located in very tiny hairs that grow on the antennae. Also, an insect's sense of smell, which is its keenest sense, is located in minute holes on its antennae. By means of these two senses, insects find food and friends and avoid enemies. The antennae of four different insects are illustrated here: (1) wasp, (2) beetle, (3) butterfly, and (4) moth.

ANTISEPTICS

An antiseptic is a medical or chemical agent that either kills germs or prevents their growth so that your body can get rid of them. When you put Mercurochrome or iodine on a minor cut or wound, you are using an antiseptic. Other common antiseptics include boric acid, alcohol, Merthiolate, mouthwash, and soap and hot water. Chlorine is often used to kill germs in swimming pools and in public water supplies. Special sulfur drugs are sometimes used in surgical wounds as antiseptics.

Until the mid-1800s, about half of the people who were operated on died of infected surgical wounds. After the discovery by LOUIS PASTEUR that germs are the cause of infection, an English doctor named JOSEPH LISTER became the first to use an antiseptic in surgery. He also realized the importance of cleanliness in the operating room. To kill germs, Lister boiled his instruments in hot water and rubbed carbolic acid on wounds and on surfaces in the operating room. Today, sterilization based on his ideas is the chief way of avoiding infection.

ANTS

Ants are one of the most common insects in the world. There are thousands of kinds. Like bees, ants are called social insects. They live in groups or colonies and divide up the work that needs to be done.

Their underground nest is often marked by an anthill. Sand from under the surface is carried by the unfertile females or workers to make the various rooms and tunnels. Some varieties of ants in Africa and Australia build anthills that are several feet high.

An ant colony contains winged males, future queens winged until after mating, and wingless, unfertile female workers. The queen's only function is to lay eggs. The males die after mating; queens and workers may live several years. The work of the colony is done by the unfertile females. The worker ants have many duties. Some workers attend the young by feeding and cleaning them. Some take care of the queen, and some guard the nest.

The workers of some species have highly developed farming habits. A species found in Texas cultivates a certain type of grass and harvests and stores the seeds for food. Some worker harvester ants have specially enlarged strong jaws that are used for cracking open kernels of grain for the colony to eat. Other ants found in the southeast United States grow a fungus which they plant, weed, and eat.

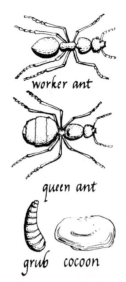

worker ant

queen ant

grub   cocoon

Many ants drink a sweet juice called "honeydew." Honeydew is given off in tiny drops from the bodies of plant lice when stroked by the worker ant. These aphids are called the "cows" of the ant world. Other workers are simply the living vessels for containing honeydew. Their bodies become so swollen with this fluid that walking is impossible for them. Their job is to release droplets of honeydew to the colony as needed. The workers of many colonies will actually capture the grubs of other ant colonies to raise as slaves.

Ants may save themselves work by dropping their loads to other ants below. Several ants will work together to carry a heavy load or dig up a buried, injured fellow worker.

The fierce army ants of tropical Africa and Latin America march from place to place in columns that are sometimes 4 yards (3.6 m) long. They build bridges out of their own bodies. They attack plant and animal life in their path. Even elephants stampede to get out of their way.

APES

Apes are animals closely related to the MONKEY, but are much larger. The four main kinds of apes are GORILLAS, chimpanzees, orangutans, and gibbons. They are native to Africa, Borneo, and the warmer parts of Asia.

An ape walks on all fours, and has longer arms and shorter legs than a man. An ape also has a thumb on each foot.

The ape's brain is only half as large as a man's; it is one of the most intelligent of all animals. The ape can learn to do many simple tricks, and can even use tools. Many chimpanzees have been trained to act as simple astronauts. "Ham" was the first chimpanzee sent into space by the United States.

Gorillas are the biggest and strongest apes. They can grow to be 6 feet (1.86 m) tall and weigh 500 pounds (225 kg). Gibbons are the smallest of the apes. They weigh between 12 to 20 pounds (5.4–9.0 kg) and are 17 to 39 inches (43–99 cm) tall.

Apes often suffer from the same diseases as man does, so they have been helpful in scientific research.

APOLLO

Apollo, the son of ZEUS, was one of the most important gods in Greek mythology. He was regarded as the god of the sun and of song. He entertained the Olympic gods and goddesses with beautiful songs, accompanied by music from his seven-stringed lyre.

In the legends of Homer, Apollo was chiefly the revealer of the future, the god of prophecy, and his oracle at Delphi was believed to foretell the future.

In addition, people believed that Apollo took care of the flocks and herds and taught men the art of healing. His worship was widespread in Greece, where many temples and statues were built in his honor. The most remarkable statue that exists today of Apollo stands in the Vatican at Rome, and is called *Apollo Belvedere*.

APOSTLES

JESUS selected twelve men from among his disciples to preach the Gospel. These chosen disciples, or apostles, were to spread abroad what Jesus had taught them.

The original twelve apostles were Simon PETER and his brother Andrew; James and his brother JOHN,

sons of Zebedee; Philip; Bartholomew; Thomas; MATTHEW; James, the Younger; Thaddaeus; Simon, the Canaanite; and JUDAS ISCARIOT, who later betrayed Jesus and then killed himself. Matthias was then chosen to replace Judas. PAUL is known as an apostle because Jesus appeared to him in a vision and ordered him to preach the Gospel.

Peter, Andrew, James, and John were fishermen; Matthew was a tax-collector. We know little about the others. The twelve stayed with their Master every day, receiving his special teaching and training.

After Christ's crucifixion, the apostles suffered hard times in their work. All of them were arrested, imprisoned, or put to death for their preaching. Paul traveled widely throughout the Mediterranean area. His epistles, or letters, in the New Testament contain much about Jesus' life, death, and resurrection. SEE ALSO: BIBLE, JESUS.

APPLES

Apples belong to the rose family and are probably the world's best known fruit. They may be red, green, or yellow when ripe, but they all develop from the aromatic pink and white flowers that cover apple trees in the spring. The apple blossom is the state flower of Arkansas and Michigan.

As long ago as 2000 B.C., lake-dwellers used apples as food. Apples were a favorite fruit of the early Greeks and Romans, who later brought them to England. Traders, explorers, and missionaries in America carried apple seeds westward with them. One of them, John Chapman, planted and distributed so many apple seeds that people nicknamed him JOHNNY APPLESEED.

Apples grow best in a temperate climate. Many are grown in Europe, especially in France. In the United States, more apples are grown in New York and Washington than in any other state.

Apples can be eaten fresh, baked, or dried, and are often preserved by canning. Apple juice is used in making jellies, cider, and vinegar.

Johnny APPLESEED (1774–1845)

Johnny Appleseed's real name was John Chapman. Born in Leominster, Massachusetts, he was a nurseryman (someone who runs a place where plants and trees are raised for transplanting or for sale). He sold and gave many apple seeds and seedlings (small trees) to people heading west.

About 1800, John started collecting apple seeds from a cider mill in Pennsylvania. Soon he traveled westward, planting seeds as he wandered through Ohio, Indiana, and beyond. He helped settlers establish apple orchards and then moved on.

On the American frontier, a legend grew concerning this familiar man with the apple seeds. "Johnny Appleseed," as he was called, was cheerful and generous and loved by all—pioneers, Indians, and animals. The Indians believed he was protected by the Great Spirit, and the settlers always welcomed him and his Bible. He brought God's blessing.

APRICOT

The apricot is a fruit belonging to the PLUM and PEACH family. It is native to eastern Asia, where the climate is temperate. Moreover, we believe that the apricot was grown 5000 years ago in China and was brought to Europe by Alexander the Great. It was carried to England from Italy more than 400 years ago.

The apricot tree is small, with fragrant leaves on long stalks. The fruit resembles the peach in shape and color. It flowers very early in spring so that late frosts can easily damage it. More than twenty kinds are grown, including the Newcastle, Royal, and Moorpark.

Half of the world's apricots are grown in the western U.S., especially California. It is also a profitable crop in France, Spain, Italy, Australia, Iran, Syria, Yugoslavia, Canada, and South Africa.

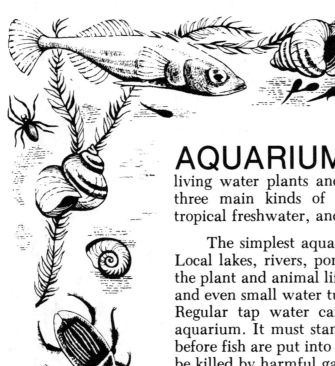

AQUARIUM

An aquarium is usually a glass tank containing living water plants and animals for viewing. The three main kinds of aquariums are freshwater, tropical freshwater, and marine or saltwater.

The simplest aquarium is the freshwater type. Local lakes, rivers, ponds, and streams can supply the plant and animal life. Carp, catfish, small bass, and even small water turtles can be captured for it. Regular tap water can be used in a freshwater aquarium. It must stand for a few days, however, before fish are put into it. Otherwise, the fish might be killed by harmful gases dissolved in the water.

Setting up an aquarium is easy but care must be taken. First, the bottom of the tank is lined with 2 inches (5 cm) of washed sand. Boiled water is added next. (*Hint:* a clean piece of newspaper laid on top of the sand will keep it from becoming stirred up.) Next, carefully press in some water plants. Water plants are an important addition to the tank because they provide oxygen for the fish to breathe.

A few water snails are most useful. They eat rotting leaves off the plants and keep the glass sides free of green scum. Snails reproduce very rapidly and can throw off the balance of living things in the tank. So, be sure to remove the clear ball-shaped snail eggs at once.

Water fleas provide food for the freshwater fish. Young fish in pairs are healthier and will reproduce. They can be bred quickly in a small jar if fed with a piece of ripe banana skin. Carp and catfish will eat almost anything, dead or alive. Never give fish more than they can eat in a short period of time.

The stickleback, the tadpoles of frogs and crested newts, the water spider, the black water beetle, and pond snails pictured on the preceding page are all freshwater animals. However, this particular combination could not exist in the same aquarium, because sticklebacks eat tadpoles, and the black water beetle would attack the stickleback.

AQUEDUCT

An aqueduct is a pipe or channel for carrying water. Usually we think of it as a kind of bridge, out in the open, but most aqueducts are underground pipes for most of the way. Some are very long. An aqueduct that supplies San Francisco is 156 miles (256 km) long.

A modern aqueduct uses pumps to raise the water from the low places to the high ones. The ancient Romans did not do this. They moved water only downhill. To get over valleys, they built magnificent bridge-like structures.

Many of these have survived around the city of Rome and in other parts of the old Roman Empire. The aqueduct shown here is 2000 years old. It crosses a river in the south of France, and is 150 feet (47 m) above the water. It is made of solid stone.

Some aqueduct bridges are also traffic bridges. In Washington, one bridge is carried on iron water pipes formed like arches. Sometimes ordinary bridges carry aqueducts. If you look under a steel bridge, you may see the large water pipe.

ARABIA

Arabia is the old name for all the land in southwestern Asia lying between the Red Sea and the Persian Gulf. It is about one third the size of the United States, but with one tenth the population. Arabia is mainly a great plateau sloping from west to east. Much of the coast is raised above the interior, where there are large deserts with little or no rainfall. Vegetation is, therefore, quite scarce, but there is enough rain in the southern countries—Oman, South Yemen, and Yemen—for the farming of dates, fruits, and grains.

In the past, Arabia was important as a trading link between East and West. The Arabs invented the number system we use (Arabic numerals), and there were, in ancient times, many famous Arabian doctors of medicine. Today, Saudi Arabia, Kuwait, Qatar, Bahrein, and the United Arab Emirates are rich countries because of their large, underground oil deposits. The oil is pumped up and piped to the super-tankers waiting at coastal ports. Much oil goes to the U.S. to be turned into fuel oil and gasoline.

MUHAMMAD, founder of ISLAM, was born in MECCA. He unified Arabia by converting millions of Arabs, rich and poor, to his new religion. Later his teachings spread into India, Africa, and Spain. When they pray, which is several times a day, Muhammad's followers must bow toward Mecca, the holy city. Another holy town, Medina, is where Muhammad was buried in A.D. 632. SEE ALSO: ARABS, ISLAM, MUHAMMAD.

ARABS

In the broadest sense, Arabs are persons whose primary language is Arabic. But some still confine the term "Arab" to the MUSLIMS (followers of ISLAM) living in ARABIA. However, millions of Arabs are found in Syria, Lebanon, Jordan, Iraq, Egypt, Morocco, Tunisia, and Libya.

In the 6th and 7th centuries, the early Muslims from Arabia conquered the lands between the Atlantic on the west, across North Africa and the Middle East, to central Asia on the east. They spread the Arabic language and Islam, building a vast Arab empire. In the 9th to 11th centuries, learning

flourished in the Islamic lands. The Arabs preserved much literature and scientific and medical knowledge which were lost during the DARK AGES in Europe.

Arabs today can be divided into three groups: the nomadic Bedouins, who lead a wandering life in the desert; the small farmers, who grow a few crops on a little land; and the villagers or townspeople, who are craftsmen or merchants.

Bedouins roam the deserts searching for the thistles and thorny bushes on which their camel herds feed. The Bedouin is dependent on the camel whose hair is used to make clothes and tents. In addition, camel's milk is drunk and is made into cheese, and camel's meat is eaten by some Bedouins.

The tough Bedouins live in tents in the desert or in oases. These tents may be more than 30 feet (9.3 m) long and 15 feet (4.7 m) wide, especially the chiefs' tents. The women live and cook in one part. A larger part is used for meals and the entertaining of friends and strangers by the men. Bedouins are hospitable people, always preparing food and drink for a guest, whether a stranger or a friend. Even the poor will give a guest their usual meal—a handful of dates and some bread.

Many Arabs wear traditional clothing, often consisting of a long white robe with a leather belt and a camel's hair coat. This clothing protects them from the heat and cold, for winter temperatures can drop below freezing in the desert. A black braid or rope holds the cotton or silk headdress in place.

The Arab farmers are usually poor and must work hard to make a living. Their small farms produce vegetables, dates, and crops of wheat and barley. Some sheep, goats, donkeys, and even camels may also be owned by the farmers. In Egypt, there are some rich farms that grow good cotton and sugarcane. Olive groves and vineyards are cultivated by the Arabs in North Africa.

In many Arab villages and towns life today is very much as it has been for centuries. Streets are often crowded with people and animals. Small, colorful shops offer the services of shoemakers, tailors, blacksmiths, and silversmiths. The newer parts of Arab towns reflect the modern world and its associated wealth brought by the sale of Arab oil. There are factories, highways, schools, and hospitals.

Many larger and older towns in North Africa show the old and the new side by side. Elegant, fine, European stores on wide avenues are near shabby, small shops on narrow streets, crowded with noisy people. Arab women often scurry by in long robes and with veiled faces. Most of the Arabs live in the older parts of town.

Arabians live in large family groups. Girls usually marry before they are 16. They go to live with their husband's mother and father. The Arabian family

usually consists of father, mother, unmarried daughters and sons, and married sons with their wives and children. Arabian women have fewer rights than men. In the home and on the street, women wear veils to hide their faces from strange men—a traditional Arabian practice. In recent years, women have been given more freedom. SEE ALSO: ARABIA, ISLAM, MUSLIMS.

ARCH

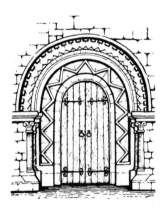

If you drive a wedge between two objects hard enough, you separate them. If you do not drive it hard enough, they will hold the wedge up between them. An arch is like a wedge held in place by the things it is trying to separate. You can rest heavy objects on top of such a wedge. Men have been using the arch to support walls, bridges, and roofs over empty space.

Most arches are curved, using wedges of stone or brick. A frame is built under them until the last wedge, sometimes called a *keystone*, is in place. Then the arch will support itself. Some arches are made of long, curved pieces of steel or wood.

ARCHBISHOP

An archbishop is the chief BISHOP, who oversees the activities of other bishops in an area known as an archdiocese or province.

In the early Christian church the title was merely honorary. Later, the archbishop gained more authority, especially in the Roman Catholic Church. Today there are 30 Roman Catholic archbishops in the United States, each directing his own archdiocese. In England, the Church of England (Anglican Church) has two provinces, Canterbury and York, each with its archbishop. The Archbishop of Canterbury always places the crown on the new king or queen of England during CORONATION.

ARCHEOLOGY

Archeology is the scientific study of ancient civilizations and their ways of life.

We can learn about the lifestyle of ancient man by studying the belongings he left behind. These objects are found by archeologists who dig very carefully among ancient ruins. Among the common objects found are broken pots, dishes, weapons, tools, baskets, jewelry, statues, and money. Animal bones show us which animals were domesticated, hunted, and eaten by ancient man.

One of the most exciting archeological discoveries was the Roman city of Pompeii. Pompeii was covered by a deep layer of ashes and mud when Mount Vesuvius erupted in A.D. 79. Two thousand people were suddenly buried alive. Its ruins give us a fairly complete picture of an earlier, but highly developed, civilization.

Relics of the past have been discovered all over the world—in ancient excavated cities, in burial grounds, in sunken ships, and in the Egyptian pyramids. For instance, in caves near the northwestern shore of the Dead Sea, ancient writings were discovered in the late 1940s and 1950s. These Dead Sea Scrolls include all of the books of the Old Testament except Esther and are the oldest known writings of any books of the Bible.

In 1964, archeological excavations began at Ebla, site of a wealthy and powerful city-state that flourished in the 2000s B.C. Eleven years later, 15,000 clay tablets were uncovered that showed Ebla's economic and political history, as well as its laws and religious thought, which appears to have a strong Biblical basis.

ARCHITECTURE

The art of designing useful and beautiful buildings is called *architecture*. An *architect* is a practical person, who knows how to plan good, useful buildings. He is also an artist, who knows how to give pleasure to persons who see the buildings. He uses shapes, colors, and patterns to turn a house, a church, or a school into a work of art.

ARCTIC and ANTARCTIC

The arctic is the northernmost area around the NORTH POLE, and the antarctic is the area surrounding the SOUTH POLE. Throughout the year both regions are covered with thick ice. However, the arctic ice-cap is much smaller than the antarctic one because the North Pole is in the center of the Arctic Ocean. Warm ocean currents flow toward it, and warm winds in summer blow from the land. During an arctic summer, at least one month has a temperature above freezing.

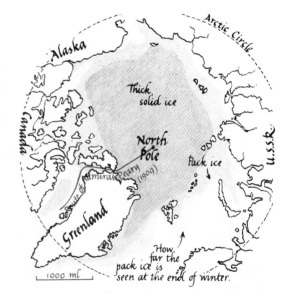

46

The antarctic region consists mainly of the continent of Antarctica. The South Pole is near the middle of this great land mass of snow and ice. There are no warm winds or currents here, and the ice does not melt as it does in the arctic. Antarctica is the coldest place on Earth.

The ice over the antarctic land mass is thousands of feet thick, sometimes three miles (4.8 km) deep. Nothing can grow there except some simple mosses and algae. Along the coasts of Antarctica live many penguins and some birds, as well as many seals, whales, and fish that find food in the waters.

There is, however, much more vegetation and animal life in the arctic area. Grasses and flowers grow abundantly in some parts, and polar bears, caribous, seals, reindeer, wolves, and foxes live on this vegetation. Often ducks and terns are seen on the summer lakes and on the rocky coasts. Tribes of ESKIMOS have used this animal life to support themselves in the arctic.

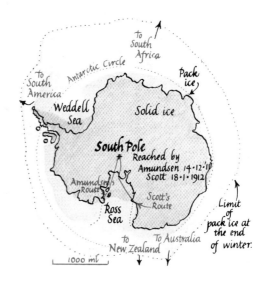

The Norsemen were the first to explore the arctic. From the 16th to 19th century, English and Dutch traders searched for sea routes to the far east through the area. An American named PEARY was the first to reach the North Pole. The antarctic was an important whaling area, and not until the late 19th century were there any serious expeditions. AMUNDSEN, a Norwegian, became the first to reach the South Pole. Much still remains to be discovered there. Today, several countries have sent scientists to work together in laboratories and observatories throughout the year. Various regions in Antarctica have been found to contain deposits of coal, iron, mica, and graphite. Also, scientific interest here has centered on understanding more about past ice ages and present climates in the world. SEE ALSO: NORTH POLE, SOUTH POLE.

ARGENTINA

Argentina is the second largest country in SOUTH AMERICA. The high Andes Mountains run along its western border with Chile. Mount Aconcagua in the Andes is the highest peak in the Western Hemisphere, rising 22,834 feet (7079 m). Argentina's north consists of subtropical lowlands called the Gran Chaco. In the central region are the Pampas, a vast, treeless, fertile plain that is excellent for raising wheat and cattle. Patagonia, in southern Argentina, is the large, windswept, dry plateau, sloping toward the Atlantic in the east. Oil, natural gas, and coal are found in large amounts, and sheep raising is a major occupation.

47

Argentina's capital and largest city is BUENOS AIRES, and the country has more than 26 million inhabitants, most of whom speak Spanish.

In 1516, Spanish explorers, led by Juan Díaz de Solís, landed on the shores of the estuary (inlet of the sea) now called Río de la Plata. FERDINAND MAGELLAN entered this estuary four years later during his voyage around South America. Sebastian Cabot, son of JOHN CABOT, is said to have given the name "Argentina" to the area during his explorations from 1526 to 1530. Juan de Garay traveled overland from Paraguay in 1580, making what is now Buenos Aires a permanent Spanish settlement. Spain then ruled Argentina until it won its independence in 1816. The country's national hero, General José de San Martín, led the people in their fight against the Spanish. Argentina has since been ruled by democratic presidents and military dictators. SEE ALSO: BUENOS AIRES.

ARISTOTLE (384–322 B.C.)

Aristotle was one of the greatest thinkers of all time. For 20 years he studied under another great philosopher, PLATO, who ran a school in ATHENS.

Aristotle became a teacher and wrote about logic, politics, ethics, and literature. He was called upon by the king of Macedonia in 342 B.C. to teach his son, who later became famous as ALEXANDER THE GREAT. Aristotle received money from Alexander to set up his own school, the *Lyceum*, in Athens. Aristotle walked and talked with his students in the Lyceum gardens. He also founded the first important library in Athens and a laboratory for the study of animal life. Aristotle sent students with Alexander the Great on his military expeditions to collect animals for his laboratory. After Alexander's death, Aristotle left Athens to escape anti-Macedonian persecution and lived for the rest of his life on the island of Euboea, his mother's home.

Aristotle tried to collect and explain simply every bit of knowledge known to the Greeks. Only a few of his works have survived, but he remains important because of his ideas about life. SEE ALSO: PLATO.

ARITHMETIC

Arithmetic comes from a Greek word meaning "number." Arithmetic began as counting. Arithmetic symbols are even older than writing. The symbols were used by early man to count the number of baskets of grain paid in taxes. Even today, a child learns to count and use numbers before he can write.

In early times, when a shepherd wanted to count his sheep, he probably used his fingers. The word *digit* comes from the Latin word for "finger." For larger numbers beyond 10, notches would be made on a stick, each mark standing for one. This system was very cumbersome for writing very large numbers.

The Egyptians later used a sign for ten, another for hundreds, and so on. This was a big improvement in arithmetic. The PHOENICIANS invented a very clever system of numbers similar to our own. Their system was, however, based on 60 rather than 10. They also used different symbols. We have inherited from the Phoenicians the division of one hour into 60 minutes, and one minute into 60 seconds.

The Greeks and Romans used Roman numerals (such as, CLXVIII), which were awkward to use in computing. They resorted to using the ancient ABACUS, a simple device still in use in Asia. It consists of a wooden frame with beads for counters that move along wires.

The numerals we use today (0, 1, 2, 3, 4, 5, 6, 7, 8, 9) were invented by the Arabs about A.D. 750. Originally, the zero was used by other cultures not as a number but only as a position marker. As a position marker, it was simply used to show the difference between 123, 1203, 1230, and 1023, for example. The idea of the zero as a number did not come into being until hundreds of years after symbols for the other numbers were invented.

Amazingly enough, the arithmetic methods of quickly solving problems with Arabic numerals were not discovered until the 1700s. SEE ALSO: ABACUS.

ARIZONA

Arizona lies in the southwestern part of the United States. It has hot deserts, wooded highlands, and high mountains. The state is famous for the magnificent GRAND CANYON of the Colorado River, situated in the northwestern region. Other beautiful sights of nature are in the Painted Desert, the Petrified Forest, Canyon Diablo, and Meteor Crater. The warm, dry, healthful climate of Arizona's southern region, which includes the state's two largest cities, Phoenix (the capital) and Tucson, has attracted tourists in summer and winter. Many retired persons have also made their home there.

Indian tribes lived in Arizona for several centuries before the Europeans came. They were probably ancestors of the Pueblos, Navahos, Apaches, and Hopis, who live on reservations in Arizona today. The first Europeans were Spanish explorers in the 1500s. Later Spanish missionaries taught the Indians of Arizona, which was part of Mexico until the U.S. took control at the end of

the Mexican War in 1848. When American pioneers moved into Arizona, terrible wars were fought between the white men and the Apaches, whose leaders included the great warriors Cochise and Geronimo.

Arizona is rich in copper, silver, gold, and other minerals. It has good timberland and irrigated farmland, on which cotton, lettuce, and fruit are grown. Manufacturing is the state's chief source of income. Arizona's population is more than 2.25 million.

ARK

The word "Ark" in the Bible stands for two different things: (1) the famous boat that NOAH built at God's command to save his family and the animals of the Earth from the Flood; (2) the sacred wooden "chest" that the HEBREWS carried everywhere with them, to remind them that God was always with them.

The ark Noah built was a huge ship made of wood, and sealed with tar to keep the water out. Noah and his sons took animals of every kind into the ark to protect them from the Flood, which God sent to destroy all other life on the Earth (Gen. 6–7).

The second ark was called "Ark of the Covenant." It was a chest made of cedar wood and overlaid with gold inside and out. It contained the stone tablets on which God had written the Ten Commandments, the wooden rod that Aaron used to demonstrate God's miracles to Pharoah, and a pot of

manna, the bread that God gave the Hebrews as they wandered in the wilderness. It was always veiled, and only the high priest was allowed to see it uncovered.

Hebrew warriors believed the chest brought victory, and so they carried it into war. For a while it rested in Solomon's Temple at Jerusalem. No one knows what happened to it after the Temple was destroyed by NEBUCHADNEZZAR in 587 B.C. SEE ALSO: NOAH.

A picture of the Ark, from an old book

50

ARKANSAS

Arkansas is in the south central part of the United States. The broad Mississippi River flows lazily along the eastern edge of the state, and the Arkansas River passes through the middle, separating the Ozark Plateau from the Ouachita Mountains. The farmland of the river valleys is excellent for growing cotton, rice, and soybeans and for raising livestock and poultry.

Much of the state is wooded, forming the basis of a large lumber and paper-making industry. There is plenty of oil, natural gas, and bauxite. Arkansas has an abundant water supply, convertible to hydroelectric power for use in homes and factories. Today, more than half of the population of 2.25 million live and work in towns and cities, such as in Little Rock, the capital, or Hot Springs, where visitors bathe in the thermal waters. Tourists come to Arkansas to fish and hunt in its lakes, parks, and forests. Some even hunt for diamonds in the only diamond mine in the U.S., situated near Murfreesboro.

The first Europeans in the area were the Spanish, led by Hernando de Soto in 1541. The Frenchmen, Marquette and Joliet, explored in 1673 the land near the mouth of the Arkansas River, and La Salle claimed the region for France in 1682. The United States received all of what is now Arkansas as part of the Louisiana Purchase in 1803.

ARMADA

King Philip II of Spain had long been trying to overthrow Queen ELIZABETH I of England. The Spanish had grown more and more angry because the English had not only robbed their trading ships and helped the Netherlanders rebel against Spanish rule, but Elizabeth had knighted SIR FRANCIS DRAKE for his attacks on Spanish galleons and colonies in the New World. Finally, when Elizabeth ordered the execution of MARY QUEEN OF SCOTS in 1587, Philip decided to invade England and seize the throne. Philip also hoped to end the English attacks and to make England a Catholic country once again.

Philip assembled a great *Armada* (which means "fleet" in Spanish) and planned to land his army in England. But, before the Armada could sail, Drake made a surprise attack on Cadiz harbor and destroyed many warships. The Spanish Armada was delayed until the next year, 1588.

In July, near Plymouth, England, the Armada found the main English fleet under the command of Lord Howard. The smaller and swifter English ships attacked the huge, slow-moving Spanish galleons for eight days. The Armada remained intact but much damage was done to it. The Spanish commander, Duke of Medina Sidonia, then anchored his fleet off Calais on the Strait of Dover. Spanish troops and fresh supplies were to be put on board. That night, Drake set fire to eight English ships and sent them drifting toward the anchored Armada. The Spaniards in panic cut their cables and drifted out to sea, breaking up their formation once and for all.

The next day the English drove headlong into the Armada, battering many ships. Some ships drifted aground; others fled northward around Scotland, but many were wrecked in storms off the Irish coast. Many Spaniards died of lack of food and disease on the return home. Only 53 of the original 130 warships finally returned to Spain. The English lost no ships and not more than 100 men in the battle.

The defeat of the Spanish Armada was a great blow to the prestige of Spain, the strongest country in the world at that time. Spain remained strong after the battle, but England now challenged the Spanish with more confidence than ever before. SEE ALSO: DRAKE, SIR FRANCIS.

ARMOR

The use of armor in combat has been common in many places and times. People have protected themselves with many materials. Steel, bronze, plastic, leather, heavy cloth, bone, ropes, bark, and even ivory have been made into armor.

The earliest armor was probably made of animal hide. Armor from rhinoceros skin was made in China 3000 years ago, and ordinary soldiers were still using leather armor in England 350 years ago.

Bronze armor is also very old. Some found in Greece was made in 1450 B.C. Ancient Greek armor of 2500 years ago included a bronze helmet, a breast protector (*cuirass*) and shin protectors (*greaves*) all of bronze. Roman armor had an iron or steel helmet and a cuirass of leather with steel plates attached. Bronze cuirasses were used by Roman officers.

In the Middle Ages, armor developed rapidly. The medieval soldier, the knight especially, had to protect himself against the thrust of lances held by men on horseback, and against the thrusting and slashing of heavy swords. At first, knights protected their bodies with *mail*. Mail is armor that bends. It is made of rings of iron linked together in all directions, or of pieces of metal riveted to cloth. Under the mail was heavy, padded cloth. The helmets that protected their heads were first pointed and open at the face, but were later made like cans, with slits for sight and breathing.

Mail did not give enough protection, and in the 14th century *armorers* began to make real suits of armor out of steel plates. Only a man of wealth could afford a suit of *plate armor*. By the middle of the 15th century, the knight was dressed in a beautiful suit of steel, strong, light, and cunningly made to allow him free movement. Horses were also armored. Horse armor was covered with a *caparison*, a cloth decorated with the knight's personal insignia (coat of arms).

Armor went almost out of use in the 18th century, but the dangers of World War I caused soldiers to wear helmets again. Machines of war wear armor too: tanks are a modern example. SEE ALSO: CRUSADES, HERALDRY.

ARMY

Throughout history, men have been organized and armed for the primary purpose of warfare on land. The importance of a king or a state has often depended upon the army, whether it be made up of infantry, cavalry, artillery, or men in tanks or other vehicles.

The earliest known armies are believed to have been organized in Mesopotamia and Egypt in the 4th millennium B.C. The Greeks made military service obligatory for all male citizens. At first the Roman armies were composed of citizens but later consisted mainly of barbarian mercenaries (soldiers fighting solely for pay). In the Middle Ages, the army consisted of armed knights and yeomanry (men who owned land). These men owed a set number of days of military service to their lord or king. Mercenaries and, later, professional soldiers made up most of the armies from the 14th to the 18th century.

In recent wars, professional or career soldiers have formed only part of the regular army. Many countries have relied on conscription (compulsory enrollment or "the draft") to get manpower in time of emergency. The U.S. today maintains its peacetime army by voluntary enlistment.

ARTERIES and VEINS

Arteries and veins are BLOOD vessels. The arteries carry blood away from the HEART. Rich in oxygen picked up from the lungs, this blood is bright red in color. Arterial blood moves with great force as it is pumped to the various parts of the body. We know immediately that an artery is cut if the blood is bright red and comes out in little spurts.

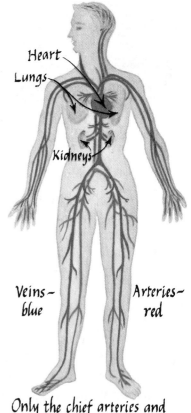

The arteries closest to the heart are quite big. The main artery leading from the heart is called the *aorta*. It divides like the branches of a tree. The tiniest branches which go to the body cells are called *capillaries*. Capillaries are no wider than a hair, and the blood cells must pass along them in single file. When the blood reaches the capillaries serving the individual body cells, oxygen is exchanged for carbon dioxide. Carbon dioxide is a waste product of the body cells.

The veins are the vessels which carry the blood rich in carbon dioxide slowly back to the heart. This blood then goes on to the lungs where the carbon dioxide is breathed out. When a vein is cut, the blood is purplish in color and does not spurt out.

Only the chief arteries and veins are shown

ARTHROPODS

The animal kingdom is divided into 30 major groups or *phyla*. The arthropod phylum contains about four-fifths of all known species of animals.

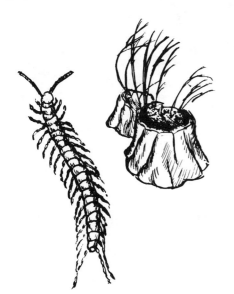

Arthropods do not have backbones. Their hard outer shell is their skeleton. As they grow in size, they must molt the shell and replace it with a larger one. They have jointed legs, and their bodies are divided into two or more sections. In Greek, arthropod means "jointed feet."

Arthropods have a very simple circulatory system, and their blood is either colorless or pale yellow. They do not have lungs. Those that live on land get oxygen as gases simply dissolve into their systems; those living in water have either internal or external gills.

Arthropods include horseshoe crabs, CRUSTACEANS, millipedes, centipedes, SPIDERS, and INSECTS.

King ARTHUR

Many old stories have grown up around King Arthur. His real name may have been Artos. He was probably a strong war leader who lived in England in the 5th or 6th century A.D. Some say he was a leader of the Celts, the people who lived in England before the Saxons invaded around A.D. 500. The British have handed down many wonderful tales of Arthur's bravery and deeds.

Sir Thomas Malory wrote a book in the 15th century about Arthur, called *Morte d'Arthur*—the "Death of Arthur." Malory's dramatic narrative helped to make famous this legendary king, who lived with his beautiful queen Guinevere at Camelot.

Malory's book contains eight tales: King Uther and the Coming of Arthur, King Arthur's War with Rome, Lancelot, Gareth, Tristram, Sangreal (Holy Grail), Knight of the Cart (Lancelot again), and the Death of Arthur. They show the ideals of courage and courtesy during the Middle Ages.

The first story tells how Arthur became king. As a child, Arthur had been cared for by Sir Ector, a loyal knight unaware that Arthur was the illegitimate son of King Uther Pendragon. When Uther died, the nobles fought among themselves to be king. Merlin the Magician arranged that they notice a large stone with a long, beautiful sword stuck in it. On the stone was written, "Whoever can draw out this sword is the rightful King of Britain."

The nobles could not remove the sword. Several months later, a great tournament was planned, and Sir Ector came with his son, Sir Kay, and Arthur, who was still a very young man. Sir Kay had forgotten his own sword, and Arthur was sent to get it. Remembering the sword in the stone, Arthur removed it easily and brought it to Sir Kay. Arthur was quickly recognized as the rightful king. He named the sword Excalibur.

The last story tells how Arthur was fatally wounded in battle by one of his knights, Sir Modred, who wanted to be king. Arthur was then taken to the lakeside by Sir Bedivere, where he was carried in a barge to the Isle of Avalon.

The exciting adventures of his Knights of the ROUND TABLE have been written about by many of the world's best poets and musicians.

ASBESTOS

Asbestos is a Greek word meaning "will not burn." It is a mineral used in making fireproof articles such as firemen's gloves and suits, as shown in the picture. It is also used for theater curtains, roofing shingles, coverings for electric cables and flue pipes, and brake linings.

Asbestos is usually found in layers in other rock. It can be mined in open quarries or underground. The ore is crushed, dried, and screened to remove the fine fibers of asbestos, which is then graded and sold to manufacturers of asbestos products.

In the Middle Ages, the famous emperor CHAR-LEMAGNE had an asbestos tablecloth. To clean it of spilled grease and food, he simply tossed it into the fire. The tablecloth would remain undamaged.

Today, Canada is the world's largest supplier of asbestos. SEE ALSO: FIRE FIGHTING.

ASIA

Asia is the largest continent, larger than North and South America together. It stretches about 6900 miles (11,109 km) from east to west, from Turkey across SIBERIA. From north to south, Asia extends about 5300 miles (8533 km), going from far above the Arctic Circle to the equator. The Arabian peninsula and the Middle East are on the southwestern side of Asia. The many Asian countries are shown on the map.

The highest and lowest land in the world is in Asia. The highest peaks are found in two mountain ranges, the Karakorams and the HIMALAYAS. These ranges, situated mainly in India, Tibet, and Nepal, cut off the Indian subcontinent from China. The tallest mountain in the world is Mount EVEREST in the Himalayas, at 29,028 feet (8999 m). On the border of Jordan and Israel is the DEAD SEA, the lowest valley on land, about 1300 feet (403 m) below sea level.

In the high Asian ranges rise many of the great rivers of the world. The Indus, the Brahmaputra, and the GANGES flow south to the Indian Ocean. The Yangtze-Kiang and the Hwangho, or Yellow, Rivers flow east through China. Millions of people live and farm along the vast fertile plains of these rivers.

Large areas of Asia are either too cold or too hot and dry for people to live. Some places, like Cherrapunji, India, have more than 400 inches (1016 cm) of rainfall each year. However, in the Gobi Desert in Mongolia and China there is less than two inches (5 cm) of rainfall each year. Temperatures can go to 120°F (49°C) in parts of India, and can drop to −100°F below zero (−73°C) in northern Siberia. In spite of this, much of the weather is pleasant

Very high
High
Fairly high
Low

Leningrad
Moscow
RUSSIA
EUROPE
SIBERIA
R. Ob
R. Yenisei
R. Lena
U.S.S.R.
R. Amur
TURKEY
Caspian Sea
MONGOLIA
Tokyo
JAPAN
SYRIA
Teheran
KOREA
IRAQ
IRAN
AFGHANISTAN
Peking
Shanghai
ARABIA
PAKISTAN
TIBET
CHINA
R. Hwangho
Kiang
PACIFIC OCEAN
R. Indus
Everest
NEPAL
R. Ganges
R. Yangtse Kiang
TAIWAN
Calcutta
Hong Kong
Bombay
INDIA
BURMA LAOS
PHILIPPINES
INDIAN
OCEAN
SRI LANKA
THAI-LAND
VIETNAM
CAMBODIA
MALAYSIA
Singapore
BORNEO
SUMATRA
INDONESIA
JAVA

Less than 10"
10"–20"
10" – 20"
20"–40"
20"
10"
5"
5"–10"
10"
Less than 5"
20"
Less than 5"
5"
10"
40"
40"
over 100"
80"
60"
60"
80"
80"
Over 100"
Over 100"
Rainfall (annual)

Cold deserts
Cool Forests
Pine Forests
Grasslands
Grass lands
Dry scrubland & desert
Warm Forests
Hot grasslands
Hot Forests (jungle)
Hot grass-land

58

for living. Almost half of the world's people live in Asia; about 1500 million live in India and China today.

The U.S.S.R. stretches across the entire northern half of Asia. The Ural Mountains divide Europe from Asia. Extending from the Urals to the Pacific, a vast, isolated area is found, called Siberia. Little is known about this region, except that plenty of iron ore, coal, oil, lead, copper, nickel, bauxite, gold, and other minerals are mined here, as well as in the Urals.

In northern Siberia the vegetation is sparse, with only mosses and lichens. To the south, there are huge timber forests. Further south are vast plains called *steppes*, where wheat and other grains are grown. India is hot and often rainy, especially during the monsoon season. Here, millions of tons of rice are grown each year in the flooded fields. Huge plantations in southeast Asia supply crops of rubber, coffee, tea, sugar, and spices. But there are so many people that the food is not enough, and millions sometimes go hungry. In the extremely hot and wet tropical forests and jungles of Burma and Malaysia grow teak, sandalwood, and other exotic woods.

Some of the oldest known civilizations in the world existed in Asia. One such existed in the Indus River valley in Pakistan. More than 5000 years ago great cities were built near the EUPHRATES River in Iraq. Also, at about the same time, people in China had wheeled carts, boats, and musical instruments and had invented paper and printing and gunpowder. Mongol hordes from the north attempted to destroy the wonderful Chinese civilizations during the 13th and 14th centuries. The Arabs also had an advanced culture between the end of the Roman Empire and the Middle Ages.

From the 16th to the 19th century, many European nations seized rich parts of Asia for colonies. However, after World War II, most countries won independence, such as India, Burma, Indonesia, and Malaysia. SEE ALSO: ARABIA, CHINA, INDIA, SIBERIA, U.S.S.R.

ASIA MINOR

Asia Minor is the old name for that part of western Asia we now call TURKEY. It is bounded by the BLACK SEA on the north, the AEGEAN SEA on the west, and the MEDITERRANEAN on the south. The narrow straits of the Bosporus and Dardanelles separate Asia Minor from Europe. Many towns on the west coast were famous in Greek history, such as Smyrna (modern Izmir), Ephesus, and TROY, where some of the greatest battles of the world were fought. ALEXANDER THE GREAT won some of his earliest battles in Asia Minor, and PAUL first preached in the villages along its Mediterranean shore. Asia Minor became an important part of the Byzantine Empire (Eastern Roman Empire). The Turks invaded Asia Minor and in 1453 conquered the Byzantine Empire. The Turkish, or Ottoman, Empire lasted until World War I, when the republic of Turkey was founded. SEE ALSO: TURKEY.

ASTROLOGY

Astrology is supposed to be a way of predicting future events based on the positions of the heavenly bodies. Astrology is not a science. Because ancient peoples did not understand the real causes for many happenings, they turned to MAGIC and stargazing to explain life about them.

Ancient kings all had court astrologers to advise them on the most favorable time for war, and for the end of plagues, famines, and other natural disasters. Astrologers gave advice on when to travel and on when (and whom) to marry. They also told the best time to plant crops and harvest them. No important person would make a major decision without first consulting an astrologer, because people commonly believed that the stars had magic power.

Astrologers divided the sky into twelve parts, each having its own special sign. These are known as the Signs of the Zodiac and are pictured here.

Some people today still believe in astrology.

Aries Taurus Libra Scorpio Gemini Cancer Sagittarius Capricorn Leo Virgo Pisces Aquarius

ASTRONAUTS

The word *astronaut* comes from Greek and means "sailor of the stars." The Russians use the *cosmonaut*, meaning "sailor of the universe."

The Space Age began in 1957 when the Soviet Union launched Sputnik I, the first man-made satellite to orbit the Earth. The first successful manned space flight was on April 12, 1961, when Yuri Gagarin, a Russian cosmonaut, completed one orbit of the Earth in 89.34 minutes. On May 5, 1961, Alan B. Shepard, Jr. became the first American astronaut in space. In 1969, American astronauts Neil Armstrong and Edwin Aldrin were the first men to walk on the moon.

In order to "sail" a spacecraft, many tests must be passed. Most astronauts are former jet pilots; some are scientists. All must be in excellent health and in top physical shape. The astronauts of the United States are trained by the National Aeronautics and Space Administration (NASA) in Houston, Texas. Future astronauts spend a year learning how to fly. They study mechanics, communication, navigation, astronomy, and geology. Also, a knowledge of photography, survival, and first aid is important for a successful flight and landing.

Each astronaut during his training becomes part of a crew. He trains for one special job to do as a member of a team. The crew spends thousands of hours "flying" special training machines called simulators. Thus, astronauts are able to experience weightlessness and space emergencies, and practice mechanical techniques without ever leaving the space training center. Astronauts as scientists will become more important in the future because their scientific knowledge and training will be used more on space flights.

ASTRONOMY

Astronomy is the study of all the objects in the sky beyond the Earth's atmosphere. Astronomy is the oldest science. Early astronomers invented the first calendar based on the various monthly phases of the moon. These calendars were not as accurate as those of today, but they were helpful to sailors and farmers.

Almost 5000 years ago, the ancient Chinese built large observatories. They were able to predict ECLIPSES, but they thought they were caused by a dragon trying to swallow the sun. Early astronomers gradually realized that they needed to explain what they saw happening in the sky.

Two thousand years ago, the Greek astronomers tried to understand and explain events in the heavens. At that time, Aristarchus taught that the Earth and the other planets move about the sun. Not many people believed him. Most people believed PLATO and ARISTOTLE, the famous Greek philosophers of the time. They claimed that the Earth was the center of the universe.

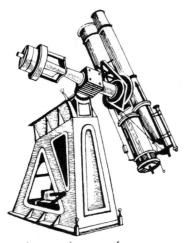

A modern telescope

Astronomy did not become completely separated from myths and folklore until the invention of the telescope in the late 1500s.

GALILEO was the first astronomer to use a telescope. The telescope aided this Italian scientist to prove to those who doubted that the Earth really does go around the sun. His telescope, pictured on the preceding page, was not very powerful compared to those used today. The period from about 1550 to 1750 was rich in important astronomical discoveries. Besides Galileo, some of the other famous astronomers of that period were COPERNICUS and SIR ISAAC NEWTON.

Without a telescope, one can see about 3000 stars on a clear night. With a modern telescope, over 1 billion stars may be seen. Radio telescopes have detected stars too far away to be seen. They detect radio waves rather than light.

Today astronomers are able to measure and weigh stars billions of miles away. They have been able to calculate their composition and speed by studying their light. Astronomers have figured out that the nearest star is almost 25 million million miles away (40 million million km).

ATHENS

Athens, the capital of GREECE, is an ancient city with an important history. The foundations of Western culture come from the art, literature, philosophy, and law of the Athenians of the 5th century B.C. Piraeus is still the port city of Athens.

Modern Athens is built around a central rocky hill called the ACROPOLIS. The Acropolis, which means "city at the top," was a fort when Athens was founded. Later the people built temples there. Many believe that one of the temples, the *Parthenon*, is the finest structure designed by man. Around the Acropolis are grouped the Areopagus, where the ancient council of elders met, and the Pnyx, where free citizens met to discuss important matters.

Pericles.
490 –
429 B.C.

According to legend, Athens was founded in 1550 B.C. by Cecrops, a mythical hero. It was later named in honor of Athena the goddess of wisdom. Between 500 and 400 B.C., the city-state attained its greatest glory. The Per-

Athens during ancient times

sians were no longer a threat, a peace having been made in 449 B.C. after more then fifty years of war between the Greek city-states and the Persian Empire.

The population of Athens at that time consisted of a few nobles, many free men, and a large number of slaves. These slaves worked as tradesmen, craftsmen (masons, carpenters), and teachers. Athens became rich and famous through trade, and other city-states grew jealous.

One of them, Sparta, attacked Athens and defeated her after 30 years (the Peloponnesian War). Although Athens later managed to regain great prosperity, she never again achieved the leadership she once had in the culture of the eastern Mediterranean.

Despite the wars, the glory of Greece reached its peak in Athens. Within a space of about 150 years, Athens had produced such men as Pericles, Aeschylus, Sophocles, Euripides, Aristophanes, SOCRATES, Thucydides, Phidias, PLATO, and ARISTOTLE—men whose equals are hardly found in the history of the rest of the world. SEE ALSO: ACROPOLIS, GREECE, SPARTA.

ATLANTIC

The Atlantic Ocean is the second largest ocean in the world, stretching from the arctic to the antarctic, some 9000 miles (14,500 km). Europe, North America, South America, Africa, and Antarctica border on the Atlantic. It varies in width from about 4500 miles (7245 km) between Europe and the U.S., to about 1700 miles (2737 km) between Brazil and Liberia.

The Atlantic has a large submarine plateau in mid-ocean, extending from the southern part of Africa north to Iceland. Thus, the Atlantic basin is divided into eastern and western valleys. The western valley is the deeper, averaging 18,000 feet (5580 m); the eastern averages about 13,000 feet (4030 m) in depth. The greatest Atlantic depth yet discovered is north of Puerto Rico, where it is 30,000 feet (9300 m) deep.

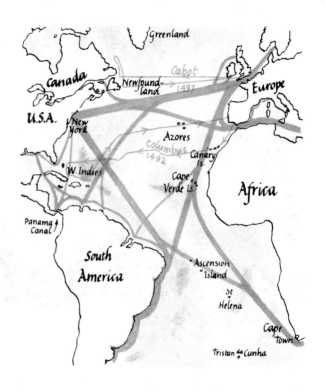

The water from Newfoundland to Ireland is sometimes less than a mile deep. In this part of the Atlantic most of the communications cables are laid that connect the United States and Europe.

The Vikings were probably the first to cross the Atlantic about a thousand years ago. The Portuguese under the leadership of Henry the Navigator opened trade routes in the South Atlantic during the 15th century. COLUMBUS and CABOT led the way for European settlements in the New World. It took Columbus about five weeks to cross the Atlantic, but today a supersonic jet takes about three hours.

The Atlantic abounds with many kinds of fish. The Georges Bank east of Massachusetts and the Grand Banks south of Newfoundland are rich fishing grounds for cod and lobster. Whales are also seen in the North and South Atlantic. Much of the ocean floor is covered by a grayish mud, formed of the hard parts of billions and billions of animal organisms. Below this ooze is found red clay of meteoric or volcanic origin.

Near the West Indies, in an area known as the Sargasso Sea grow thick clusters of gulfweeds or Sargassum seaweed. Baby eels drift and swim from here across the Atlantic to European rivers. The eels are only a few inches long when they make this three to four thousand mile (4830–6440 km) migration. Later, the mature eels cross the Atlantic again to their spawning grounds in the Sargasso Sea.

The island of "Atlantis" is said to have been destroyed by an earthquake or to have sunk beneath the ocean because its people were very wicked. The ocean was named after this legendary country.

ATOMIC BOMB

The atomic bomb works in either of two ways: by splitting the nuclei of the atoms of certain heavy chemical elements, or by fusing hydrogen atoms together. Either one of these actions releases tremendous energy that destroys practically everything over a wide area.

Early in World War II, the Germans tried to make an atomic bomb, but daring commando raids damaged a factory they needed for materials and a scientist working on the bomb was smuggled away to England. The United States dropped the first atomic bomb on August 6, 1945, on the Japanese city of Hiroshima. Japan had to surrender. The U.S.S.R. had an atomic bomb a few years later. People began to worry about the terrible wars that "the Bomb" would make possible. So far, thanks to common sense, we have avoided them. In such a war, everybody would lose. SEE ALSO: ATOMS, NUCLEAR ENERGY.

ATOMS

The building blocks of all the millions of substances in the world are ELEMENTS. There are over 100 elements known. Hydrogen, oxygen, copper, gold, silver, iron, and uranium are elements.

The smallest piece of an element that can exist is called an atom. Atoms are too small to be seen with a microscope. There are more atoms in the ink in the period at the end of this sentence than there are people in the world. We know about atoms from the way they behave.

Atoms themselves are made up of smaller particles. The center of an atom is called the nucleus. It is made up of one or more particles called *protons*. Each proton has a positive electrical charge. All atoms, except the simplest form of hydrogen, also have electrically neutral particles called *neutrons* in the nucleus. Neutrons have about the same mass as protons. In one or more orbits about the nucleus are electrically negative particles called *electrons*. They equal the number of protons. They are so extremely small that they do not affect the atomic weight.

An atom is mostly space. If the simplest atom, hydrogen, with only one orbit were magnified so that it was the length of a football field (100 yards or 91 m), the nucleus would sit on the 50 yard (45.5 m) line and be the size of a pea.

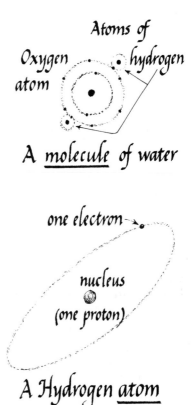

Atoms of
Oxygen hydrogen
atom

A *molecule* of water

one electron

nucleus
(one proton)

A Hydrogen *atom*

65

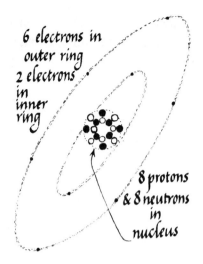

6 electrons in outer ring
2 electrons in inner ring

8 protons & 8 neutrons in nucleus

An Oxygen _atom_

Although electrons are insignificant in weight, they are still very important. An element which does not have enough electrons in its outer ring to be complete either gives off or takes on electrons. In so doing, one element can join with another element. This joining together of two or more atoms is called a *chemical reaction*. When 2 atoms of hydrogen join with 1 atom of oxygen, a molecule of water (H_2O) is formed. A molecule of water is the smallest piece of water that can exist.

It has been found that no element has more than two electrons in the first orbit, nor more than eight in any of the other orbits. The orbits are at angles to one another.

The mid-twentieth century ushered in the Atomic Age. Scientists discovered how to create atomic energy. One way to create this energy is by splitting the nucleus of an atom. The atomic bomb's enormous and dangerous energy is produced in this way when it explodes. Another way of creating this energy is by fusing hydrogen atoms together. The destructive power of the hydrogen bomb is produced in this way. Man is learning to harness the atom's energy for peacetime uses. Already nuclear power plants split uranium atoms to generate electricity for factories and homes. SEE ALSO: ATOMIC BOMB.

John James AUDUBON (1785-1851)

John James Audubon is world famous for his detailed paintings of American birds.

The facts concerning Audubon's early life are shrouded in mystery. At the age of four, he was brought home to France from the West Indies by a kindly French naval captain, Jean Audubon. In 1794, the boy was legally adopted by the captain and his childless wife. Audubon was taught the gentlemanly arts of hunting, fencing, and playing the violin. He was uninterested in school, preferring to roam the woods and sketch the birds and animals he saw.

His father hoped he would join the French navy, but instead Audubon left for

America at the age of 18. The young, charming Audubon soon had many friends. However, one business venture after another failed. He tried many jobs—teaching French, dancing, and swimming, running a mill, tending a store, and painting portraits, landscapes, and signs.

In 1808, he married Lucy Bakewell. Despite his repeated failures and imprisonment for bankruptcy, his faithful wife encouraged him to paint. She became a governess to allow him the freedom to roam America in search of new bird species to record on canvas. The more than 1000 pictures he painted are now very valuable.

In 1886, the Audubon Society, made up of people concerned about bird CONSERVATION, was named in his honor.

AUSTRALIA

Australia is the smallest continent or the largest island in the world, according to definition. It stretches from east to west about 2400 miles (3864 km), and from north to south nearly 2000 miles (3220 km).

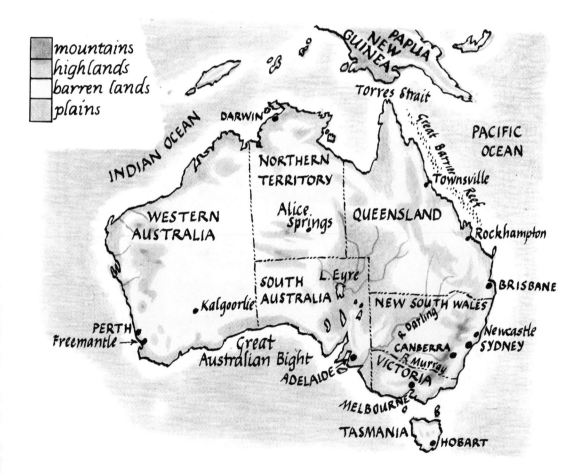

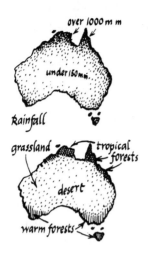

over 1000 mm

under 150 mm.

Rainfall

grassland — tropical forests

desert

warm forests

Australia has low mountains, wide beautiful beaches, and a very dry, nearly desolate interior called *the outback*. Most of the good farmland and good ports are in the east and southeast. Here the climate is comfortable and the population is largest. The northern part of Australia has areas of desert and tropical jungle. The south-central area has a few large lakes. From these lakes to the west, the desert goes nearly to the ocean.

The Great Barrier Reef lies 60 miles (97 km) off Australia's northern coast. It is the largest coral formation in the world, extending more than 1200 miles (1932 km). Of the 600 islands along the reef, Heron Island is maybe the most interesting, with giant green turtles coming there to lay their eggs in the hot sand.

When Europeans started exploring the continent in the 17th century, they found different groups of primitive natives, including the ABORIGINES, who offered little resistance to the foreigners. Abel Tasman, a Dutch sailor, landed in 1642 on an island south of Australia, later named Tasmania in his honor. In 1688, William Dampier, an English adventurer, visited the mainland and published an account of it. Later, in 1770, Capt. JAMES COOK reached Botany Bay, near Sydney, and claimed the east coast region for Britain. The first British settlement in 1788 was a prison colony near Sydney.

During the first half of the 19th century, Australia was a dumping ground for criminals and other undesirables from Britain. However, in 1851, a gold strike in Victoria brought traders and families. This and other strikes brought people from all parts of the world. By 1860, Victoria's population had tripled. Australia developed rapidly, and today there are more than 14 million people living in the "Land Down Under."

68

Koala Bear

The plants and animals of Australia are quite different from those found elsewhere in the world. About 400 unusual kinds of animals live in Australia. The kangaroo, for example, lives only on this continent and the island of Tasmania. Other animals found living here include the small, cuddly koala bear, the duck-billed platypus, and the spiny anteater. The wild Australian dog called the *dingo* was apparently brought by the aborigines when they migrated from Asia to Australia. The Europeans brought domestic animals to the continent, such as cats, pigs, horses, and sheep.

Sheep raising is one of Australia's richest occupations. Some of the sheep farms cover thousands and thousands of acres. Today, one-third of all the world's wool comes from Australia. Where the grasslands are better, large herds of cattle are raised. Also, in the south there is plenty of rain and sun to grow wheat. In the most southern regions, apples, pears, oranges, lemons, and grapes grow.

Gold, diamonds, sapphires, opals, and other jewels are found in Australia. Ample quantities of lead, copper, iron, uranium, and coal are mined, too. In the waters off the coasts, divers find valuable pearls. The country produces the largest quantity of pearly shells in the world. They are made into buttons and decorations.

Australia is divided into six states: New South Wales, Victoria, Queensland, South Australia, Western Australia, and Tasmania. It also has one internal territory—Northern Territory—and one capital territory. The main ports are Melbourne, Sydney, Adelaide, Fremantle, and Brisbane.

Australia today is really two places. The small and large cities contain three-fourths of the people and most of the modern industries. However, in the outback, thousands of aborigines still live as their ancestors did in the STONE AGE. The contrast between these two is evident in the great engineering projects, like the Snowy Mountain Hydro-electric Scheme that brings power and irrigation to many new areas, and the reservations set up by the Australian government to protect the aborigine culture.

A long modern bridge spans the harbor at Sydney (see picture).

AUSTRIA

Austria is a small country in central Europe, about the size of Indiana. Until 1919, however, Austria ruled the powerful Austro-Hungarian Empire, a monarchy of diverse kingdoms and peoples.

It is bounded by Switzerland and Liechtenstein in the west, by Yugoslavia and Italy in the south, Germany and Czechoslovakia in the north, and Hungary in the east. The ALPS stretch through Austria from west to northeast, where the DANUBE River flows. The capital, VIENNA, rests by the side of the river and is the crossroads

between central and eastern Europe. Vienna, where one fourth of all Austrians live, Innsbruck, and Salzburg are all known for their music festivals. BEETHOVEN, MOZART, Schubert, Strauss, and Haydn lived and wrote their music in Vienna.

Many of Austria's 7.5 million people are engaged in farming and forestry; others work in manufacturing—textiles, chemicals, and machinery. Some run popular winter ski resorts in the Tyrol, an alpine province in western Austria.

Its plains are full of wheat and sugar-beets; its vineyards are producing some of the world's best white wines. Huge power-plants make enough electricity for Austria and for parts of Italy and Switzerland. Some of its important minerals are copper, zinc, iron-ore, and aluminum. SEE ALSO: VIENNA.

AUTOMOBILE

The idea of a self-propelled road vehicle goes back to the 15th century at least. Early inventors suggested sails, windmills, springs, steam, compressed air, and gunpowder explosions. The first real automobile was that of Nicolas-Joseph Cugnot, in 1769: a steam-powered wagon. Steam stagecoaches were used in England in the 1830s, but attention soon shifted to the new railroads.

Benz, about 1900

In 1885, Carl Benz of Germany ran the first car with a gasoline engine. The first such car in the United States was probably built in 1890, and by 1898 there were over 50 American automobile makers. Automobiles became really popular shortly after 1900. The Ford Motor Company went into production in 1903. HENRY FORD, a brilliant man, not only made cars much more cheaply than ever before, but found ways of manufacturing them that were very useful to every type of industry. His invention of the *assembly line* allowed each worker to do just one thing, over and over, as the cars being built came past him. (Some workers hated such a boring job, though.)

For a while, steam-powered automobiles were made, but INTERNAL-COMBUSTION ENGINES, exploding gasoline or oil, were soon the only ones used for cars and trucks. Recent worry about pollution has caused people to be interested again in the steam engine and the electric car.

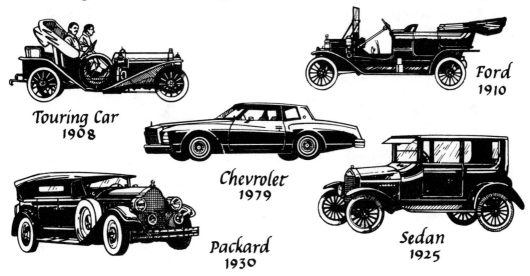

Touring Car
1908

Ford
1910

Chevrolet
1979

Packard
1930

Sedan
1925

Streamlining is one of the many ways in which cars have been improved over the years. Instead of wasting energy pushing air away, a streamlined car parts the air as gently as possible.

Chrysler Airflow
1935

HOW AN AUTOMOBILE WORKS

The modern car is almost always run by a gasoline engine, while heavier vehicles like trucks and buses are usually run by diesel (oil) engines.

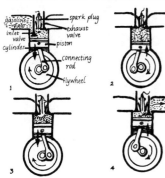

In the gasoline engine, an explosive mixture of gasoline and air comes from a *carburetor*, is lighted by a *spark plug*, and in exploding pushes down a *piston* in one of the engine's *cylinders*. By means of a rod, the piston sends a crank on the engine's *crankshaft* part of the way around. Meanwhile, other pistons are pushing on other cranks of the crankshaft. The piston we see here is sent up again by the turning of its own crank, and is then ready for the next explosion. Thousands of these explosions take place in the engine every minute. Thanks to the *muffler* through which the burned gases pass to the outer air, we hardly hear them.

The crankshaft is connected to a *transmission,* a set of gears that allow the driver to choose between high speed and low power or low speed and high power, or to reverse the car. The transmission then turns the *drive shaft,* which turns the *differential gear.* This last actually turns the wheels of the car. Most cars have two-wheel drive: the rear wheels usually move the car, while the front ones are only for steering. There are cars with four-wheel drive, however.

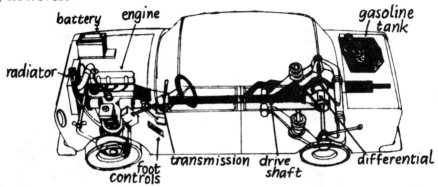

Under the *hood,* usually in front, are other important things besides the engine. The radiator is at the front of the hood; its purpose is to cool the engine, which gets very hot. There is also a *generator* that makes electricity for the spark plugs and for the battery that stores electricity for the *starter,* the lights, horn, and other devices.

Inside the driver controls his car with an *ignition,* which shuts the electricity on and off, and pedals for the *starter,* an *accelerator* for controlling speed, and perhaps a *clutch.* There is also a *gearshift* for controlling the transmission, and brake controls. SEE ALSO: INTERNAL-COMBUSTION ENGINE.

AVALANCHE

In the mountains masses of ice and snow, earth, or rock tumble down, causing what are called avalanches. The weight of ice and snow on the mountainsides can be so heavy that avalanches begin during winter. In spring, melting snows can cause the earth to come loose and be washed with the snow down the mountain. As these avalanches gather speed, they make a thunderous noise and winds strong enough to destroy buildings and forest trees.

In the ALPS in Europe, ice avalanches from upper glaciers commonly cause loss of property and lives. In the ROCKY MOUNTAINS, avalanches are often referred to as snowslides. The term is also applied to landslides, which occur when huge amounts of earth slide down a mountainside. Sudden shocks from an explosion or EARTHQUAKE can sometimes create an avalanche.

BABYLON

Babylon was one of the oldest and most important cities ever built. It was on the EUPHRATES River, about 700 miles (1127 km) northwest of Ur. Babylon is mentioned in written records of the 3rd millennium B.C.

When Hammurabi became king of Babylon around 1720 B.C., he built a huge empire (Babylonia), conquering the other tribes and cities around him. His code of laws is one of the greatest of all times; it is written in CUNEIFORM on columns and

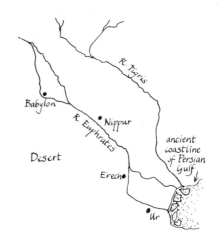

clay tablets. Around 690 B.C., Babylon was destroyed by the Assyrians under Sennacherib. Many beautiful houses and temples were ruined.

Babylon's real splendor began after the city was rebuilt under another king, NEBUCHADNEZZAR. In the 6th century B.C., he conquered other tribes and seized several Phoenician towns. He also captured Jerusalem and transported many Hebrews to Babylon to be used as slaves (2 Kings 24:10-13).

Nebuchadnezzar made Babylon one of the most colorful and luxurious cities in the world. To protect it, he built thick walls and high towers with glazed brick. Inside the city were the famous *Hanging Gardens*, one of the SEVEN WONDERS OF THE WORLD, which he built to please his wife. There were also many *ziggurats*, pyramid-shaped towers, decorated with glazed and colored

tiles. Exotic plants and trees grew all over the city. The people lived well, enjoying many rich foods and comforts of the ancient days. In his later years, Nebuchadnezzar went mad until he finally accepted the God of the Jews (Dan. 4:32–37).

In 538 B.C., Babylon was captured by Cyrus the Great and used as one of the capitals of the mighty Persian Empire. Later, Alexander the Great conquered it. Babylon never again regained its past glories. SEE ALSO: NEBUCHADNEZZAR.

Johann Sebastian BACH (1685–1750)

The Bachs were a family of musicians, but Johann Sebastian Bach is considered to be the greatest of them, and in fact one of the greatest composers in history.

He was born in Eisenach, Germany, in 1685, and died in Leipzig, Germany, in 1750. His father died when he was 10, and at 15, he began to support himself, first as a choirboy, then as a violinist, an organist, and finally as a choir director at St. Thomas' Church and School in Leipzig. He stayed at St. Thomas' for 30 years.

His music is of three kinds: organ music, religious choral music, and music for harpsichords and other instruments to be played in the courts of the German princes. He is regarded as one of the great masters of *counterpoint*, that is of mingling and contrasting the "voices" of different singers or instruments in a beautiful way. He wrote an enormous amount of music, enough to fill 50 volumes.

Little of his music was printed in his lifetime, and soon after his death he was forgotten. Early in the 19th century, though, a few musicians—one of them was the great composer Felix Mendelssohn—rediscovered Bach and began to publish his work. Since then his popularity has grown steadily.

BACON

Bacon is obtained from the sides and back of the pig and then cured. Two hundred years ago bacon was chiefly a food eaten by the poor, but today it is readily eaten by almost everyone.

Meat is cut from the pig in large pieces, generally from that part where

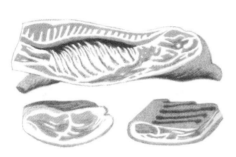

the fat is mixed with lean meat. Salt is pressed into the dry, raw meat. Afterward it is smoked, usually by hanging the dry, salted meat in the smoke of pine or oak fires. This produces the right flavor for eating.

In the United States, packing houses prepare large amounts of bacon to be sold in the supermarkets or to be exported to other countries.

Francis BACON (1561–1626)

Francis Bacon was an important English philosopher, writer, and statesman. He served at first in the court of Queen ELIZABETH I and later became Lord Chancellor under King JAMES I.

However, in 1621, he was accused by his enemies of accepting bribes and of misusing his office. After pleading guilty, he was fined and imprisoned for a short time. His career as a public official was ended.

He then spent the rest of his life writing at his country estate in Hertfordshire. His philosophical ideas became the basis of all modern natural science for the next 300 years. His "Essays" and his book *The Advancement of Learning* are noted for observations about life and are still read today.

Perhaps his scientific principle of first speculating about something and then testing to prove it helped cause his own death. On an icy winter's journey he left his carriage to stuff a dead chicken with snow: he believed the cold would preserve the meat. He died from a chill soon afterward.

Roger BACON (1214?–1294?)

Roger Bacon was an early English philosopher and scientist. A Franciscan monk, he was a well-known teacher at Oxford University in England.

Bacon was far advanced for his time in natural science. He believed in first making an accurate observation of an event and then making controlled experiments. This was the only basis of certainty for him; but he also believed that faith and wisdom were connected somehow in the search for truth.

He was one of the first to believe the Earth was round. He predicted many modern inventions, such as cars, submarines, and aircraft. Also, he is credited with the invention of gunpowder in Europe.

In the MIDDLE AGES, his writings about science were attacked by many as magic and as being against the teachings of the Church. He was kept in prison for 14 years, and was finally freed shortly before his death. Three of his most important books were written secretly for the Pope in one year (1267–68) —*Opus Majus*, *Opus Minor*, and *Opus Tertium*. SEE ALSO: MIDDLE AGES.

BACTERIA

Bacteria are very tiny one-celled organisms or plants. Unlike animals, they have firm cell walls. Only a colony of thousands of bacteria growing together can be seen by man's naked eye. Bacteria were first observed by Anton van Leeuwenhoek, a Dutch scientist, in the late 17th century. He saw them in a drop of water while he was looking through his microscope, and he named them his "very little animalcules."

In 1865, LOUIS PASTEUR, a French scientist, discovered how bacteria multiply and cause disease. He also found out how to prevent many diseases by vaccination. Bacteria began to be studied thoroughly after the 1870s. At that time, Robert Koch, a German doctor, discovered a way of staining bacteria with dyes and then growing them for identification on special jellies.

Bacteria are everywhere—in the air, in the soil, and in our bodies. Most are harmless, and many are helpful and necessary for life. Helpful bacteria cause decay, thus making more room on Earth for living things. Bacteria are

pneumococcus
(cause of pneumonia)

bacillus diphtheriæ
(cause of diphtheria)

bacillus typhosus
(cause of typhoid fever)

pea plant

roots with lumps containing bacteria

one of the 'lumps' cut in two and magnified

bacteria

necessary in our digestive tracts because they help break down food to be absorbed by the bloodstream. Bacteria help to make vinegar, cheese, wine, and yogurt. They aid in tanning leather and curing tobacco. They help some plants, such as the pea family, to enrich the soil with more nitrogen by drawing nitrogen out of the air.

Other bacteria are harmful. We call them GERMS. Germs can cause such things as tooth decay, food poisoning, rancid butter, tetanus, and tuberculosis.

Bacteria come in three basic shapes. Rod-shaped bacteria are called *bacilli*; some have hairs which help them move. Some are spherical and are called *cocci*. Others are spiral-shaped and are called *spirilla*.

To multiply, bacteria simply divide in half when they reach a certain size. In theory, one bacterium could produce about 3 billion offspring— almost the population of the Earth—in less than a day. Fortunately, many die, but their ability to increase rapidly explains why diseases can spread so quickly.

BADGER

The badger is a burrowing mammal of the weasel family, related to the SKUNK. It has a broad, stocky body covered with grizzled hair. Unlike most mammals, the badger's coat is light (gray) above and dark (black) below. Its name *badger* comes from the white markings or "badge" on its face. The badger is found throughout Europe and Asia, while a completely different species lives in North America.

Badgers are nocturnal (active at night) in habit. Their sense of sight is not good, but they have very keen senses of smell and hearing. With their long pointed snouts and strong sharp claws, they sniff out and dig up the burrows of mice and rabbits, their chief source of food. They also eat roots, grubs, frogs, and eggs. Their food is crushed rather than chewed by their strong flat teeth.

Foxes, coyotes, and hawks have been known to follow badgers in order to seize the small animals that badgers have uncovered.

BAGPIPE

The bagpipe is found in many countries, although people think of it as belonging only to Scotland.

The bag, into which the player blows, is squeezed to keep air flowing into the pipes at the right rate. Each pipe has a reed that makes the peculiar sound of the instrument. In a Scottish bagpipe, the player covers and uncovers finger holes on the *chanter* to play the melody. Other pipes, called *drones*, play the same notes all the time.

The bagpipe is used as a solo instrument and in military bands. The ancient Romans used a type of bagpipe.

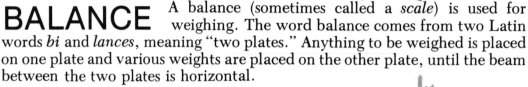

Drones

Chanter

BALANCE

A balance (sometimes called a *scale*) is used for weighing. The word balance comes from two Latin words *bi* and *lances*, meaning "two plates." Anything to be weighed is placed on one plate and various weights are placed on the other plate, until the beam between the two plates is horizontal.

The upper picture is copied from one painted in an Egyptian tomb 3500 years ago. The weights are in the form of animals' heads and the material being weighed is gold. The oldest known weights were made of stone. Some were found in an Egyptian tomb 7000 years old.

The other balance that is pictured is a modern one. It works basically the same way as the ancient one. It is capable of weighing accurately to one thousandth of an ounce (.028 g). The glass case protects it from dust, moisture, rust, and drafts, all of which would make it weigh inaccurately. The weights are handled with tweezers as the perspiration and body oils on one's hands would affect the accuracy of the weights. The balance used by some scientists is so sensitive that it can measure the weight of a speck of dust.

The *spring balance* (not really a balance) is used by some markets to weigh meat and groceries.

Vasco Núñez de BALBOA (1475?–1519)

Vasco Núñez de Balboa was the first European to see the Pacific Ocean, in 1513. Latin Americans of Spanish and Indian ancestry consider him a great hero. His discoveries opened the way for Spanish exploration and conquest along South America's west coast

Balboa was a Spanish explorer who sailed in 1500 to the Caribbean area. After an unsuccessful attempt to establish a colony near Cartagena, in northern Colombia, Balboa started a colony at Darien (now in Panama) in 1511. Instead of killing the Indians, as most Spanish conquistadors (conquerors) did, Balboa made friends with them. Soon he learned about a great sea not far away. With about 1000 Indians, he and his men fought through thick jungle and swamps to the top of a hill. From there Balboa discovered the Pacific Ocean. When he got to the ocean, Balboa claimed it and all the land that the ocean touched for Spain.

Balboa did not live to realize the size of the "Southern Sea," his name for the Pacific. His enemies at the court of Spain seized him a few years later and tried him on false charges of treason. He was found guilty and was beheaded.

BALKANS

The Balkans is the name given to the countries that make up the southeastern section of Europe. The Balkan Peninsula lies between the Black Sea in the east, the Aegean in the southeast, the Mediterranean in the south, and the Adriatic in the west. The Danube River is usually considered the northern limit of the Balkans.

The area consists of ALBANIA, BULGARIA, continental GREECE, and parts of YUGOSLAVIA, TURKEY, and RUMANIA. Its climate is mostly moderate, with cold winters and hot summers. Many different people with their own languages, customs, and religions live in the Balkans. Wars and revolutions have occurred among these people throughout recorded history.

Sometimes, the Balkans refer to the northern mountain range running east to west through Bulgaria.

BALL

The ball has been used for play throughout history. There are numerous games in which a ball is thrown, kicked, rolled, or struck with a stick.

Boys and girls many years ago probably played with round stones that their fathers threw at birds and animals. A kind of ball game is pictured on early Egyptian monuments, and balls are mentioned in ancient Hebrew books.

The ball was used by the Greeks and Romans in their play. Ball games were a way to keep their bodies fit, and they threw a small ball called the *harpastum* in a game like football. The Romans had a large leather ball with an air-filled bladder, called a *follis*.

In the 16th century, different ball games became very popular, such as early forms of rugby-football, cricket, tennis, and golf. The Indians in North America were tossing a ball around in a game called lacrosse long before Columbus sailed the Atlantic.

Over the years the shape and size of balls in sports have changed to make play more interesting. For instance, the American football changed from the egg-shaped rugby ball in order to make the ball easier to throw and to liven up the game. About 1920, the baseball was improved, which made hitting a more important part of the game. Today, most balls are produced from man-made, not natural materials.

BALLAD

A ballad is usually a song that tells a story. The MINSTRELS used to sing them as they went from house to house. For centuries, during the Middle Ages, ballads were not written down, and each minstrel sang them in whatever way he pleased. As a result, the words became changed, and even today we know of several versions of the same song. The common people sang the ballads they heard, and may have made up their own. The same songs were sung for hundreds of years, and scholars like SIR WALTER SCOTT finally wrote them down. Some ballads came to America, and are still sung over here, especially among some Southern and Western mountaineers.

After printing was invented and after more people began to learn to read, ballads were sold in the marketplaces. Peddlers would sing the ballads, then sell sheets with the words and music printed on them. Often they sang about recent events, such as murders and executions. But they also sang about politics, and the ruling officials often tried to have ballad-selling stopped.

A hundred and fifty years ago, composers began to write love songs with many stanzas, that is repetitions of the tune to different sets of words. These were also called ballads, though they usually told no stories. Such songs are still composed, and are still often called ballads.

BALLET

Ballet (pronounced bal'ā) is the art of dancing in the theater. It is usually done by professional dancers, and often acts out a story. It is like a play that is danced, not spoken. Ballet dancers' *technique* (way of performing) is different from that of other dancers. Many ballet movements are unnatural for the body. However, ballet dancers make these movements easily and gracefully.

Several hundred years ago, royal courts enjoyed *masques*, plays performed with poetry, songs, and dances. It was from the masque that ballet came. One of the earliest ballets we know was given at a royal wedding in Paris in 1581.

The earliest ballets were given on a floor surrounded by the audience. But soon ballets were being given on the stages of regular theaters, with elaborate scenery.

Louis XIV of France (1638–1715) loved ballet. He himself danced in those that were given at his court. He decided that France should lead the world in this art, and began a Royal Academy of Dancing in 1661. It is still going on today under another name.

Most people who study ballet do not want to become professional dancers. They go through the exercises because they make people strong, quick, and graceful. Those who want to become dancers often begin at the age of 10 and study for at least six years. They begin with easy exercises and go on to hard ones. Every movement has to be learned perfectly. In "classical" ballet, the sort most often seen, the movements all have French names. For example, there are the *plié* (bend), *glissade* (glide), *fouetté* (quick turn), *sauté* (jump), *pirouette* (spin on one toe), and the *pas de deux* (dance for two).

Once the steps and movements are mastered, the ballet student can combine them in various ways.

Even though we speak of classical ballet, it took centuries for all the steps to come into use. Dancing "on points" (that is, on tiptoe) seems so typical of ballet that we cannot imagine ballet without it. But it was probably introduced around 1820.

A ballet is made up of:

A *libretto*, or story. Most ballets act out a story, like TCHAIKOVSKY'S *Sleeping Beauty*. Some do not, though. *Les Sylphides* is pure, graceful dancing, watched for its own sake.

The *choreography*, which tells the dancers what moves to make and when. Since the dancers move in time to the music, the choreographer, who works out the choreography, and the composer of the music must work together. Sometimes the choreographer has the first idea, and the composer writes his music to suit the dancers' steps.

The *music*. Usually music is composed especially for a ballet. An example is Tchaikovsky's *Nutcracker*. But sometimes the choreographer finds music already written to use. *Les Sylphides*, for instance, is set to music that FREDERIC CHOPIN wrote for the piano. The piano music of Rossini has been used several times. On the other hand, ballet music is often given in "concert" version, without dancing.

The *scenery and costumes*. The scenery provides a beautiful background for the dance. The costumes must also be beautiful and are often quite fancy, but they must always be easy to move in.

A ballet is something to be enjoyed in several ways, as you can see. Some are long and have several acts, like a play. *The Sleeping Beauty* is such a ballet. Others last only twenty minutes or so, and several such ballets may be given the same evening.

BALLOONS

A balloon is a light, flexible bag that can be filled with air or some other gas. A toy balloon may be quite small and made of rubber, so that it will expand easily. But balloons may also be quite large—in fact, several hundred feet long—depending upon their use.

A passenger balloon rises in the air because it is lighter than air. The bag is filled with hot air (which is very light) or with light gases such as helium or hydrogen. Many balloons are huge because they must contain large amounts of gas.

Two French brothers named Montgolfier were the first to use balloons. They sent up hot-air balloons in 1783. One lifted a rooster, a duck, and a sheep. The same year Pilâtre de Rozier and the Marquis d'Arlandes became the first men to fly. A little later, a professor named Charles traveled 27 miles (43 km) with a friend in a hydrogen balloon.

These were *free* balloons: they had no motors or steering mechanisms, and only the winds moved them. *Dirigible* balloons, which could be steered where the balloonist pleased, came much later. Early in the 1900s, the ZEPPELINS, named after the German count who invented them, first appeared. These were huge, rigidly framed dirigibles. During World War I, they were used to bomb England. Germany tried to use dirigibles for passenger service, as did England, but they were too clumsy and

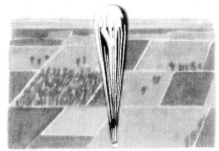

dangerous. The dirigible *Hindenburg* exploded near New York in 1937 when its hydrogen caught fire.

Besides dirigibles there are *blimps*. Instead of having rigid frames as the dirigible does, they are inflated, like free balloons. Blimps and free balloons are still much used. Balloons are used for sport, weather research, and many other things. They have gone up as far as 30 miles (48 km). SEE ALSO: ZEPPELIN.

BALLOT

A ballot is a sheet of paper on which someone marks or writes his choice during an election. It might be used to pick a team captain, a school president, or a U.S. President. It can also be used to decide an issue, such as whether to spend money on new roads or not.

The ballot was used in Athens in the 5th century B.C. by the popular courts. It fell into disuse in the Middle Ages, and reappeared in the 16th and 17th centuries. The British colonies in America were the first to use the secret ballot in their elections.

Widespread voting abuses led to the use of the Australian ballot, which became very popular in the U.S. after 1888. The Australian system has all candidates' names printed on a ballot and placed at voting booths at public expense. In secret, the voter marks his own ballot.

The voting machine is now widely used in local and national elections throughout the United States. The voter enters a booth, and as he closes the curtain behind him, the machine unlocks for voting. By pulling down levers, the voter indicates his choices. When he opens the curtain to leave, he automatically registers his vote and wipes clean the face of the machine. Using machines, the ballots can be easily and quickly tabulated for the total vote. It is believed that the accuracy, secrecy, and honesty of the ballot are helped by modern voting machines, as long as they are not tampered with. SEE ALSO: DEMOCRACY.

BALTIC SEA

Denmark guards the entrance to the Baltic Sea, an arm of the Atlantic that makes an indentation in the coastline of northern Europe. The Baltic is connected with the North Sea by a narrow channel between Denmark and Sweden. It also touches the countries of Germany, Poland, Finland, and the Soviet republics of Lithuania, Latvia, and Estonia, as well as the U.S.S.R.

Most of the Baltic is shallow, and northern parts of it freeze over in the winter. Many rivers run into the Baltic, such as the Oder, Vistula, Neva, Niemen, and Dvina. Because of its narrow outlets, shallowness, and the rivers feeding it, the Baltic has a low salt content.

Today it is important as a fishing ground for salmon, trout, and herring. Ships are continually carrying goods among the Baltic ports of Leningrad (U.S.S.R.), Helsinki (Finland), Danzig (Poland), Riga (Latvia), Stockholm (Sweden), and Copenhagen (Denmark).

In winter, icebreakers are commonly used to keep the northernmost ports open. Ports on the Gulf of Finland, the northern arm of the Baltic, are often closed entirely for four months due to ice.

The 61-mile-long (98 km) Kiel Canal is a shortcut between the Baltic and the North Sea. Other canals connect the Baltic with the Volga River (U.S.S.R.) and with the Arctic Ocean. SEE ALSO: NORTH SEA.

BANANAS

Bananas are a tropical fruit that grows on a palmlike plant. The banana plant is about the size of a small tree, but it is really a huge woodless plant. It has very large, bright green leaves, sometimes 10 feet (3.1 m) or more long. These leaves form a kind of crown at the top of the stem of the banana plant.

On the banana plantations, young shoots are cut from the base of mature banana plants and then planted about 12 feet (3.7 m) apart. The plants grow very rapidly in hot, moist climates, reaching more than 20 feet (6.2 m) tall in less than a year. When a banana plant blooms, a long stem

pushes up through the hollow stem and a cluster of yellowish flowers forms. From these clusters, bunches of bananas develop. Since the plant's stem bends downward, the individual bananas bend upward on the bunch hanging from the "tree."

One bunch of bananas consists of about 100 bananas and weighs about 70 pounds (31.5 kg). Only one bunch of bananas is produced during the lifetime of a banana plant. The green, unripe bunch will spoil quickly after it is cut down. Fast ships with special storing and cooling rooms to prevent early ripening are essential if the bananas are to be marketed successfully. The bananas sold in the United States come mainly from Central America, Mexico, and the West Indies.

In the tropics, the leaves from the banana plant are sometimes braided to make rugs and bags. The plant's fibers are used to make rope, cloth, and even paper. The bananas themselves are usually eaten raw, but they can be baked or fried to make delicious dishes.

BAND
A band is a group of musicians who play certain instruments and not others. A military band plays brass instruments, such as trumpets and trombones, WOODWINDS such as clarinets, and percussion instruments such as drums and glockenspiels. All these can easily be carried while marching. A dance band uses many of the same instruments, but probably also uses a piano. Stringed instruments like violins, are never found in a military band, but sometimes are used in a dance band. When there are many strings, a group of musicians is called an ORCHESTRA.

The compositions and leadership of JOHN PHILIP SOUSA did much to promote interest in band music. SEE ALSO: ORCHESTRA; SOUSA, JOHN PHILIP.

Band Instruments

Tuba

Cornet

trombone

Horn

Bass Drum

BANK A bank looks after money. People can borrow money from banks to buy homes, cars, and other things. Banks lend money to cities and towns to build roads and schools. Banks lend money to manufacturers of airplanes, cars, drugs, clothing, and machinery to help them make their products, buy supplies, or build new factories.

The money that we or a business borrow from a bank must be paid back with *interest*. That means we must pay the bank a little more than we borrow. However, if we deposit, or put, our money into the bank to be saved (a *savings account*), then the bank pays us interest. Businesses then borrow the

The **Bank of England**

bank's (really our) money. We also borrow on *credit*, meaning the bank believes we earn enough to be able to pay back the loan plus the interest charge. Banks make a profit by making loans because the interest charges for lending money are higher than the interest they pay to depositors.

A depositor may write *checks*, a written order to take money out of his or her bank account to pay bills. The check directs the bank to pay a certain amount of money to the person or company to whom it is written. We do not have to carry large amounts of cash when we have *checking accounts*.

Banks also give advice to people about how to use money. A bank may take care of money "in trust," looking after the way our money is saved, invested, or spent during our life or after we die.

The money in the bank is stored in strong vaults that have heavy, steel walls and doors with complex locks. People can rent boxes inside the vault to provide safe-keeping for jewelry, papers, and other valuables.

BARGES

Barges are large boats, usually flat-bottomed, used for transporting goods. Some have their own engines, but many are towed, especially on inland canals, by tugboats.

On the GREAT LAKES and along the coast of the U.S., huge steel barges carry bulk cargoes like coal or oil. Barges regularly travel many great rivers, such as the MISSISSIPPI, the RHINE, and the Volga, moving freight that would be more expensive to carry across land.

Since ancient days barges have been used. At first, men, horses, and mules pulled them, until steamboats were invented in the 19th century. Today, the sight of three or four barges linked together is a familiar one on many large waterways.

BARNACLES

Barnacles are CRUSTACEANS, yet they do not look like a crab or a lobster. Barnacles live in salt water. There are two main types of barnacles.

Acorn Barnacles

Those that attach themselves to rocks, piers, floating logs, sea shells, and other sea animals are called *acorn* barnacles. They look like miniature volcanoes. More than 2000 have been known to grow in a space the size of this page. *Goose* barnacles attach themselves to the undersides of ships by means of a long stalk. They are a nuisance because they prevent a ship from gliding smoothly through the water. Today, large ocean steamships have to have their hulls thoroughly scraped at intervals in order to get rid of barnacles.

Baby barnacles swim freely about without any shell. In this larval state (see illustration on page 88), they have one eye and swim with the help of feathery feelers (1). Next, they grow a transparent double shell, which is hinged on one side (2).

Acorn barnacles develop suckers and grow a conical shell (3). The goose barnacle grows a stalk out of its head for attaching itself to ships (4).

Barnacles remain fixed in one spot for life. They stay inside their shells except when they stick out their feathery feet to draw in tiny plants and animals for food. When not covered by water, even the feet are drawn into the shell.

BAROMETER

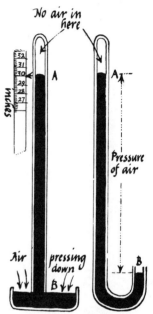

A barometer is an instrument for measuring changes in the pressure of the atmosphere. As air gets colder, it becomes heavy or dense as particles of air move closer together; therefore, air pressure increases. As air gets warmer, air particles rise and move farther apart; therefore, the air pressure drops.

The barometer is the basis for accurate weather forecasting. It is also an important instrument for pilots as it tells how high a plane is above sea level. Mountain climbers find barometers useful in the same way.

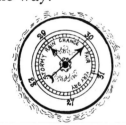

The face of an aneroid barometer

A simplified diagram to show how the aneroid barometer works

In 1643, Torricelli, a student of GALILEO, built the first barometer. It looked much like the one in the top right-hand picture. His simple barometer measured how much *mercury* the air pressure can hold up. Cold air presses down on the mercury in the open dish and causes the column of mercury to rise in the tube. Since warm air exerts less pressure on the mercury in the dish, it causes the column of mercury to drop.

A water barometer could be used but the tube would have to be 34 feet (10.5 m) high. Since mercury is 13.6 times heavier than water, a column 30 inches (0.8 m) high is sufficient. Mercury also has the advantage of not evaporating at ordinary temperatures. Today, mercury barometers are often curved like the one pictured in the top right-hand picture.

The more modern aneroid ("without air") barometer looks more like a round wall clock. Behind the dial is a metal box with some of the air removed. As the air pressure changes, the center of the box is pushed up or down by the air. This change activates a number of complicated levers attached to a central stump. When the stump moves up or down, it causes a pointer to move over a scale to produce a reading.

BARROWS

A barrow is a mound of earth that ancient people heaped over the dead. The *long barrows* of England are divided inside into hallways and chambers used for the burials. The largest is more than 300 feet (about 100 m) long.

Round barrows were built later in western England. Only one person was buried in each. People called the Beaker Folk (because of the drinking cups buried with them) built these.

Some VIKING chiefs were buried in barrows. They were placed in their boats with their weapons and treasure, and covered with earth.

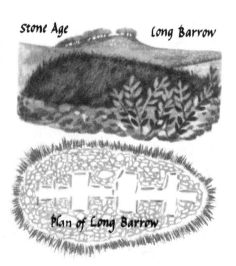

Stone Age   *Long Barrow*

Plan of Long Barrow

Clara BARTON (1821–1912)

Born on Christmas day, Clarissa Harlowe Barton led a life dedicated to giving to others. A former schoolteacher, she founded the American RED CROSS and became known as "the angel of the battlefield."

At the outbreak of the CIVIL WAR, Clara organized an agency for distributing supplies to the wounded Union soldiers. She was a fearless nurse. Under fire during battles, she carried food and bandages to wounded soldiers. In 1865, President Lincoln asked her to organize the search for records of missing soldiers. In 1869, while vacationing in Europe, Clara found herself in the midst of the outbreak of the Franco-Prussian War and gave aid to the war victims.

In Europe, she became involved with the International Red Cross and in 1881 organized the American National Red Cross. In 1882, she succeeded in getting the United States to sign the Geneva agreement dealing with the treatment of victims and prisoners of war. She was also responsible for getting the Red Cross to deal with peacetime emergencies, such as famines, floods, cyclones, earthquakes, and epidemics. She remained president of the society until 1904 and personally aided in disasters whenever needed.

BASEBALL

Baseball is a game between 2 teams of 9 players each. It is played with a hard ball, a wooden bat, and padded gloves. Four bases are laid out on a large field having an infield or diamond (a 90-foot [27.4 m] square with a base at each corner) at one end. The teams alternate as batters and fielders, exchanging places when three of the batting side are "put out."

A batter tries to hit the ball thrown by the opposing team's pitcher, trying to put the ball out of reach of the fielders. After hitting the ball, a batter runs from base to base counterclockwise around the diamond. A complete circuit of the bases counts as one run. To win, a team must score more runs in 9 innings than its opponent. An inning is finished when each team has succeeded in "putting out" three of the other team's batters. A batter is "out" if he strikes out, if he hits a ball in the air that is caught before it touches the ground, if the struck ball gets to the first baseman's hands before he can run to that base, or if he is tagged with the ball while off base.

BASKETBALL

Basketball is a game played usually indoors on a rectangular court, 94 feet (29 m) long and 50 feet (15.5 m) wide. There are 2 opposing teams of 5 players each. At each end of the court is a basket mounted 10 feet (3.1 m) above the floor on a backboard. Players may dribble the ball or pass it to a teammate, but they may not walk or run with the ball.

The object is to score by tossing the ball through the basket guarded by the other team. Two points are usually scored for a field goal (when the ball goes through the basket during play). Illegal body contact between opposing players is a foul, penalized by awarding free throws (an unhindered shot at the basket from a line 15 feet [4.6 m] away) to the player who was fouled (hit, shoved, held, or tackled). Each basket made by a free throw counts one point. Players who commit more than the permitted number of fouls must leave the game.

A referee and an umpire conduct the play of the game, which is divided into 4 quarters or 2 halves.

BATS

Bats are the only MAMMALS that fly. Unlike birds, they have fur and nurse their young.

Some bats have a small mouse-sized body with a wing span of only a few inches or centimeters; the largest, found in the tropics, has a body about a foot (30.5 cm) long with a wing span of about 3 feet (92 cm).

Although there are over 1200 different kinds of bats found all over the world (except in the freezing polar regions), people hardly ever see them. Bats are nocturnal— that is, they are active at night and sleep during the day. They sleep hanging upside down in such places as caves, hollow trees, attics, and steeples.

Bats are very strange-looking. Their mouse-like bodies have short, weak legs and short arms with large "hands" and long, thin, bony fingers. The fingers are even longer than the body. A thin sheet of skin is stretched over the fingers and attached to the ankles and the feet. They sleep in high places so that they can launch into flight easier.

Most bats are helpful as insect-eaters. Some bats are fruit-eaters and can damage an orchard. Many dine on fish, meat, or nectar from flowers. The vampire bat of South America is the only one known to harm people or animals. It nips very gently the skin of a sleeping victim and sucks its blood. The nip does not waken the victim, but it is possible to contract (catch) rabies from such a bite.

Bats are expert flyers. They are able to fly rapidly through a room criss-crossed with wires without bumping into them. Bats have a built-in sonar system. As they fly, they send out high-pitched squeaks, which humans usually cannot hear. The obstacles in the bat's path echo back these sound waves. The big sensitive ears of the bat catch these echoes. The bat then changes direction.

BATHYSCAPHE

Until this century, men had not been able to venture far beneath the surface of the sea. The tremendous water pressure, the need for oxygen, and the total darkness at depths below 300 feet (93 m) presented tremendous problems.

In 1947, Auguste Piccard, a Swiss physicist, invented the first bathyscaphe. A bathyscaphe is a small submarine with a spherical observation chamber under its hull for viewing the ocean at great depths. In 1960, Piccard set the world deep sea diving record. His bathyscaphe descended 35,820 feet (11,104.2 m) off the coast of Guam.

The picture on this page also shows an earlier diving chamber called a *bathysphere* (lower left). It was invented by Dr. Charles Beebe, an American, who succeeded in making the world's first dive of more than 3000 feet (930 m), in 1934.

BATTERIES

A battery is a device for providing ELECTRICITY by a chemical process. There are two main types of batteries: (1) *dry cell* used in flashlights, toys, and flash cameras, and (2) *wet cell* (or *storage*) used in car batteries. Dry cell batteries provide electricity for a while and then have to be thrown out. Wet cell batteries last for years.

Two or more cells work together in a battery. All batteries have positive and negative terminals through which electricity flows when they are connected. Electricity can be made to flow through the fine wire inside a light bulb, which produces light when it becomes white hot, or electricity can drive a motor.

The inside of a dry cell battery—like the common flashlight battery—is shown in the top picture. The cell dies when one of the chemicals packed inside is used up.

In a car battery, as shown in the bottom picture, the chemicals do not get used up and the chemical reaction can be made to reverse itself. When the cell runs down, it can be connected to an outside current and recharged. This process puts the electrons back where they were at the start of the reaction. The battery can be again used for producing a current of electricity.

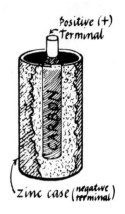

Positive (+) Terminal

Zinc case (negative terminal)

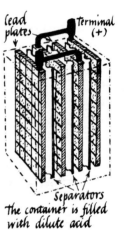

lead plates

Terminal (+)

Separators
The container is filled with dilute acid

BEARS

Bears are classed as *carnivorous* (meat-eating) MAMMALS, but their diet also includes leaves, roots, acorns, fish, rodents, snakes, and honey.

The Alaskan brown bear is the heaviest carnivorous land animal. Males weigh up to 1600 pounds (720 kg).

The polar bear is the tallest bear. Polar bears may grow to be 11 feet (3.4 m) tall. They may live an entire lifetime on an ice floe and in the water around it. They eat mainly fish, seal, and walrus.

The large grizzly bear has the reputation of being one of the most

ferocious wild animals. This bear has been nearly exterminated (done away with), except where it is protected in national parks.

Many bears hibernate (sleep) during cold weather. When warm weather returns and they awake, the expressions "hungry as a bear" and "cross as a bear" fit them well!

BEAVERS

Like the rat, the beaver is a rodent or gnawing mammal. In fact, it is the largest rodent in North America and is about 3 feet (91 cm) long. Its wooly undercoat is covered by thick coarse brown fur which is waterproof. Its webbed back feet and peculiar broad flat scaly tail make the beaver a good swimmer. The front feet have sharp claws for carrying and digging.

Beavers are well-known for their amazing energy and engineering skill. They build dams across ponds and "houses" or lodges near the dams. Their dams and lodges are built of wood, mud, and clay. The entrances are underwater. They also construct canals for floating the lumber to the building site. The lodges are the storage places for their food—berries, roots (particularly water lily roots), leaves, and bark from willow, poplar, and birch trees.

BEES

Early cave drawings show that primitive man gathered honey from bees. Honey was man's first source of sugar.

Queen

Drone   Worker

There are many thousands of species of bees. Some live alone, but most live together in large groups. The wild bumblebee lives with two or three hundred others, while the honeybee may live in a colony of 70,000 or more. Honeybees are social animals that work together diligently for the good of the group.

There are three types of honeybee: the queen bee, the drones, and the workers. The queen's only task is to lay eggs. The few stingless drones have the job of mating with the queen. The thousands of workers are unfertile females. They are the ones seen

Hind leg of worker bee with pollen sac

gathering the nectar and pollen from the flowers. They make honey and beeswax. Some build the hive; some guard it and will sting any enemy that comes near. Some take care of the young; some care for the queen and the drones. Some keep the hive ventilated by fanning the air with their wings. Others clean the hive. Workers live only about six weeks. However, the queen can lay more than a thousand eggs a day to replace them.

Inside the hive is a *honeycomb*. It is formed from wax secreted by glands on the abdomens of the workers. The honeycomb is made up of thousands of six-sided chambers or *cells*. Eggs are laid in some cells; honey, in others.

Like many other insects, the honeybee goes through many great changes between the egg and adult stages of its life. The actual bee egg is no bigger than the period at the end of this sentence. In three days the

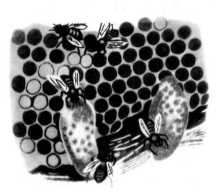

eggs hatch. The wormlike grubs (or *larvae*) are fed first liquid food and then "beebread" a few days later. Beebread is a mixture of pollen, honey, and water. The larvae grow quickly. Soon the cells are sealed off and each grub becomes a *pupa* inside the waxy cocoon. After twelve days, the adult gnaws its way out of the cell and joins the work force.

The workers, though sterile and incapable of mating, can under certain circumstances lay eggs. These eggs, however, produce only drones.

At the height of the summer, some extra large cells are constructed and eggs are laid in them. The grubs that hatch out are fed only a special rich food, called "royal jelly." This food is produced in special glands in the workers' heads. These grubs eventually turn into queen bees.

Before these queens hatch, the old queen and several thousand of the other bees fly off in search of a new home. The bees cluster around the queen when she settles on a suitable place for a new hive. This is called *swarming*. Beekeepers often capture swarms and put them into an empty hive. The bees quickly start building a new hive. A new colony is soon busy at work.

When the first queen emerges from her cell back at the old hive, she takes her mating flight. She returns to the hive, kills all the other emerging queens, and begins laying eggs.

In winter, bees live on their stored honey or sugar water that may be provided for them.

BEET

The beet is a plant grown for food and as a source of sugar. Four types of beet are cultivated: the red, or garden, beet; the white sugar beet; the mangel-wurzel or mangold; and the Swiss chard.

Red beet

Sugar beet

The red beet's root is a tasty vegetable that can be eaten fresh, canned, or pickled. Its young leaves can also be eaten as a green vegetable. The white sugar beet is raised for the production of sucrose or "cane" SUGAR. Its roots yield much sugar. At present, about one-third of the world's sugar is from beets. In the U.S., California is the principal beet-sugar producing state.

The mangel-wurzel, meaning "beet root" in German, is grown for feed for livestock in Europe and Canada and, to a lesser extent, in the U.S. Swiss chard is grown for its edible, spinach-like leaves.

Beets grow best in deep, crumbly soil and in temperate to cool regions. Chemical fertilizers and manures help produce an abundant beet crop.

Ludwig van BEETHOVEN (1770–1827)

Beethoven is regarded as one of the greatest of all composers. He was born in Bonn, Germany, in 1770. His father, a singer, made him learn the violin and piano at the age of four. At 17 he was in Vienna, where he was taught by MOZART. Later he settled in Vienna, where he was famous as a pianist. A few noblemen helped him to live while he played and composed his music.

In 1798, when he was only 20, he found that he was going deaf. He was entirely deaf by 1810, but went on composing. He never heard some of his best work. He was upset by his deafness, and could be hard to get along with as a result. In 1827, his real greatness not yet understood, he died.

BEETLES

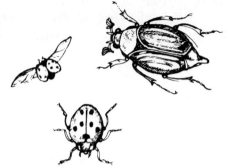

Beetles are the most common type of INSECT. They are characterized by their hard wing cases. Their flying wings are folded underneath these protective cases.

The beetle in the upper picture is a European cockchafer, which, like the BOLL WEEVIL and JAPANESE BEETLE, damages trees and crops. The lady-bug in the lower picture is beneficial to the farmer in controlling harmful garden pests.

Some beetles, like the cucumber beetle, give plants virus diseases. Some species produce a chemical which causes human skin to blister. A few are hosts to parasites which occasionally infect man.

European ground beetles have been introduced into the U.S. to control the gypsy moths.

BELGIUM

Belgium is a small country in northwest Europe, between France and Holland. It is a little larger than Maryland, with a population of about 10 million. BRUSSELS is its capital and largest city.

The land is mostly low and flat, although the heavily forested Ardennes Hills in the southeast rise to about 2000 feet (620 m). Cattle raising, wheat growing, and truck farming are important in Belgian agriculture. In the richer soil near Holland, fruits and vegetables are grown.

The Belgians are divided into several language groups. A Dutch dialect called *Flemish* is spoken in the north, and a kind of French called *Walloon* is used in the southern half. French is spoken mostly in the south, and German is used in the western provinces of Belgium. During the 1960s, tensions increased between the Flemish and the Walloons. New political parties concerned with the language problem gained strength. By 1971, Belgium's Parliament had revised the constitution, establishing three main cultural groups: Dutch speakers, French speakers, and German speakers. The constitution also divided the country into three economic regions: Flanders, Wallonia, and Brussels.

The main industries are steel and metal manufacturing, textiles (cotton, wool, and linen), chemicals, lace, and diamond cutting. Belgium's chief port is Antwerp, which handles much trade to and from other European countries and the U.S. SEE ALSO: BRUSSELS.

98

BELGRADE

Belgrade is the capital and largest city of YUGO-SLAVIA, with a population of more than 1 million. It stands on and around a hill (479 feet or 149 m) at the juncture of the DANUBE and Sava Rivers.

Because of its strategic position, Belgrade was called the key to the BALKANS and was always a busy river port. In history it has been held successively by the Celts, Romans, Huns, Goths, the Byzantines, Turks, and the Serbians. In World War I, it was occupied by Austrian troops, and for most of World War II, it was held by German forces.

Belgrade has many handsome parks, palaces, museums, and churches. Fine old buildings built of white stone surround the city's fortress of Kalemegdan. Belgrade means "white fortress" in Serbo-Croatian, the principal Slavic language of Yugoslavia. SEE ALSO: YUGOSLAVIA.

Alexander Graham BELL (1847–1922)

Alexander Graham Bell was born in Edinburgh, Scotland. In 1870, he emigrated to Canada and a year later to the United States. He began teaching deaf-mutes and publicizing a system of instruction for them that had first been developed by his father. In Boston he founded a school for deaf-mutes that later became a part of Boston University, where he was appointed professor of vocal physiology.

While at Boston he invented the telephone, which was a crude device with two simple microphones. He found a way of sending sound through wires by changing it into electrical impulses. On March 10, 1876, the first words were transmitted over the telephone. Bell spoke from an attic to his assistant in the cellar: "Mr. Watson, come here; I want you."

His invention was exhibited at the 1876 Philadelphia Centennial Exposition and led to the organization of the Bell Telephone Company a year later.

Bell lived a creative life for more than 45 years after the invention of the telephone. He invented a device, called a photoplane, to transmit sound over short distances with a beam of light. He helped discover a method for making phonograph records on wax discs. Bell was also interested in sheep breeding and did research with his flocks, especially at his home on Cape Breton, Nova Scotia. SEE ALSO: TELEPHONE.

BELLS

Bells have been used for centuries in many parts of the world. They have been made, too, of many materials—including wood—and in many shapes. The kind of bell we know best curves downward from a flat top, then flares out at the bottom. Such a bell is usually made of bell metal, an ALLOY of copper and tin (in other words, a kind of bronze). The usual proportions are 13 parts of copper to four of tin. Bells are so familiar that we can easily picture anything described as bell-shaped.

Bells are usually cast at *foundries*. A mold is made whose outside is shaped like the inside of the bell. Then another mold is put over it. The inside of this mold is shaped like the outside of the bell. The molten bell metal is poured between the two molds and allowed to harden before they are removed. Then the bell must be *tuned*. Bits of metal are shaved off inside until the bell sounds the right note. Some of the best bells are made in England and Holland. One London foundry has been making bells since 1570.

Bells come in many sizes. The largest ever made is in Moscow. It weighs 180 tons (164 metric tons). Like our own LIBERTY BELL, it is now broken and cannot be used.

Other kinds of bells that we see often are hammered out rather than cast: electric bells, like half a ball, cowbells, which are rectangular, and ball-like sleighbells.

BEOWULF

Beowulf is the oldest English epic poem. It is the most important literary work of the ANGLO-SAXONS, dating from the 8th or 9th century. The original manuscript is now in the British Museum; it is written in *Old English*, which is very different from modern English, and some of its pages are unclear, having been charred by fire, or lost. This manuscript is very valuable, for

Beowulf is the only complete Old English poem which has been found.

The story takes place in Sweden and Denmark. The monster Grendel comes each night from his lair among the marshes into the hall of Hrothgar, King of the Danes, where he seizes warriors and carries them off to be devoured. Beowulf, a Swedish prince, crosses the sea with his men to kill the monster. In a mighty struggle, Beowulf wrenches Grendel's arm from its socket. Grendel flees to his lair to die. Hrothgar is happy to be rid of Grendel at last. He celebrates with a great feast, welcoming Beowulf and his brave warriors.

The next night Grendel's mother, mad with grief, comes to the hall to avenge the death of her son. She carries off one of Hrothgar's men. Again Beowulf is sent for and descends to her cave under the marshes. While the other warriors watch at the water's edge, Beowulf slays her with a magic sword.

Loaded with gifts from the grateful Danes, Beowulf returns to his own country, where he becomes king for 50 years. Then a fire-dragon ravages the land because a cup has been stolen from its huge treasure hoard. Beowulf, though very old, kills it in a dreadful fight, during which all his followers desert him except one, Wiglaf. Beowulf is fatally wounded, however, and dies.

Many parts of this epic poem have nothing to do with Beowulf. Some episodes describe Scandinavian tradition. Scholars believe the story of Beowulf was sung by minstrels long before it was written down. SEE ALSO: ANGLO-SAXONS.

BERLIN

Berlin is divided, like Germany itself, into two parts or zones. The city of East Berlin is the capital of East Germany and is controlled by the communists. West Berlin is non-communist, linked to West Germany, but governed under the supervision of the Americans, Soviets, British, and French. The communists have built a wall between the two parts of the city.

Berlin was a small town in the Middle Ages and grew slowly in size until the beginning of the 18th century, when it became the capital of Prussia, the former German state. Berlin's location, on the banks of the Spree and on a flat, sandy plain, made it the center of a great canal system. By these canals, roads, and later railroads, Berlin gathered trade and became an industrial power. During World War II its huge factories were destroyed; after Germany's surrender, the city was split into sectors.

Much of West Berlin has been rebuilt. Today, iron and steel are its main industries, and there are factories making electrical instruments, furniture, paper, and processed food. SEE ALSO: GERMANY.

BETHLEHEM

Jesus was born in Bethlehem, a small town in Palestine, six miles (9.6 km) south of JERUSALEM. It is on a hill in green, fertile land and looks toward the Dead Sea. The Old Testament of the BIBLE tells how Bethlehem was also the birthplace of Benjamin and DAVID, the second King of Israel.

People today visit Bethlehem's Church of the Nativity, built by Constantine I in the 4th century A.D. In a cave under the church may be the spot where Jesus was born in a manger.

102

BIBLE

The Bible is the sacred book of Jews and Christians, put together over a period of more than a thousand years.

It has two main sections: the *Old Testament*, which describes the ancient Jewish people and their religion, and the *New Testament*, which tells of the life of Jesus and the missionary work of his disciples.

The Old Testament was first written in Hebrew, the language of the Jews. The first five books are called the Pentateuch. They tell of the creation of the world, the early history of the Jews, and the commandments and laws given by God.

The writings of the PROPHETS—Isaiah, Ezekiel, Jeremiah, and others—brought God's word to the Jews in later years. The prophets warned the Jews when they misbehaved.

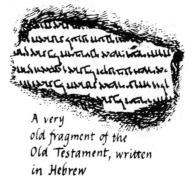

A very old fragment of the Old Testament, written in Hebrew

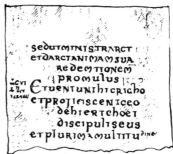

Part of the New Testament, written in Latin

Bible on a medieval lectern

Other books of the Old Testament are the so-called Writings. They include the PSALMS (hymns and poems), the Proverbs, and the book that tells the sufferings of Job.

The New Testament begins with the four *Gospels*, which record the life and sayings of Jesus. These were written by MATTHEW, MARK, LUKE, and JOHN. Greek is the language in which the Gospels were written. John wrote his Gospel last.

Luke also wrote the Acts of the Apostles, which tells how the Christian church began and how its message spread to Asia Minor, Greece, and Rome.

After these books we find the *Epistles* (letters) that PAUL and others wrote to the new churches advising them on the Christian way of life.

The Bible has been translated (put into other languages) many times. In the third century before Christ, 70 Hebrew scholars translated the Old Testament into Greek because many Jewish people spoke Greek rather than Hebrew.

In the 4th century A.D., Jerome translated the whole Bible into Latin. It took him 25 years, but it was so well done that the Roman Catholic Church still uses this translation. It is called the *Vulgate*. Catholics also use several English translations of the Bible.

Parts of the Bible were translated into English in the early Middle Ages. Much later, JOHN WYCLIFFE and William Tyndale made English translations. But the church did not want English translations in Tyndale's time (the early 16th century), and he was burned at the stake.

The Authorized Version of the Bible was put together by a group of English scholars in the reign of King James I, early in the 17th century. Other English translations have been made since, some very recently. The Bible has been translated into most of the languages of the world, including those of American Indians and African natives.

Artists have decorated and illustrated Bibles in thousands of beautiful ways, for it is a very important book. In the early days, when each single book had to be written by hand, several artists might work on different parts of a Bible. This was extremely expensive. But even printed Bibles are often works of art, printed on fine paper and illustrated. SEE ALSO: CHRISTIANITY.

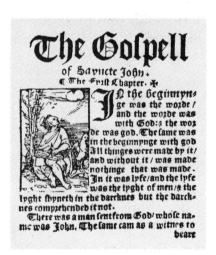

BICYCLE

The first bicycle was invented in Paris around 1818. The English called it a hobbyhorse. The rider kicked against the ground to move it, for it had no pedals. It was tiring to use.

In 1839, a Scot named Kirkpatrick Macmillan invented a way of driving the rear wheel with pedals and levers, but the idea did not get much attention.

In 1865, a Frenchman put pedals on the axle of the front wheel. This introduced a kind of bicycle used until about 1885. Such bicycles were different from modern ones. They had a very large front wheel and a very small rear one, or a very large rear wheel and a very small front one. The rider sat up high, so that these bicycles were tricky to use. The rider had to have a very good sense of balance.

In 1874, H. J. Lawson put the pedals between the wheels. These turned a gear wheel, which drove an endless chain, which turned the rear wheel. He also made the front and rear wheels more nearly the same size, as the "Bicyclette" of 1879 shows. Around 1885, J. K. Starley began to make the "safety" bicycle, which had a chain drive and wheels of the same size. This is almost the same as the bicycle used today. In 1888, the Dunlop pneumatic tire (filled with air) replaced the solid rubber tires used before. Other improvements about this time included the coaster brake and adjustable handle bars. The bicycle became a popular means of transportation in the 1890s. After some changes were made in gears and brakes, the modern bicycle was created.

The bicycle has been very important in modern life. It has given pleasure, cheap transportation, and a chance to see the world. Even armies and policemen find it useful.

10 – Speed

'Bicyclette'

BILL OF RIGHTS

The first ten Amendments to the U.S. CONSTITUTION are often referred to as the Bill of Rights. These rights protect each citizen against his or her government.

The First Amendment guarantees freedom of speech, of religion, and of the press. It also insures the right of assembly and the right to ask the government for justice. The Second Amendment guarantees the right to possess weapons. The Third states that citizens cannot be forced to provide room and board for soldiers in their homes. The Fourth says that citizens and their property cannot be searched or taken away without a warrant (legal permission). The Fifth says that a citizen cannot be tried twice for the same crime and cannot be made to testify (speak out) against himself. The Sixth and Seventh guarantee the right of a trial by jury in both criminal and common law cases. The Eighth prohibits cruel and unusual punishment. The Ninth says that rights not mentioned in the Constitution belong to the people. The Tenth says that powers not given to the federal government are reserved for the States or the people.

BIOLOGY

Biology is the scientific study of all living things. Biology is divided into two main parts: BOTANY, the science of plants, and ZOOLOGY, the science of animals. Biologists discover and help us to understand more about the origin, development, reproduction and structure of all forms of life. They study the causes of and cures for plant and animal diseases, and the importance of the balance of plant and animal life in nature.

BIRDS

Birds are the only animals that have FEATHERS. Like mammals, they are warm-blooded and usually have a body temperature higher than man's. All birds lay eggs.

The *archeopteryx* (illustrated here) was the earliest known bird and looked very much like a lizard. It lived during the age of dinosaurs and was only about the size of a crow. It had a long "mouth" with sharp teeth, and its wings and feet had sharp claws.

Birds have large, strong breastbones that make it possible to move their wings in flight. Their bones are hollow and lightweight. However, some birds like the ostrich are too big to fly.

Hawfinch

Duck

Missel Thrush

Eagle

Birds have very keen hearing and sight. Robins can be seen tilting their heads as they listen for the movement of worms under the soil. Some kinds of owls have night vision that is 50 to 100 times greater than human night vision. The golden eagle can detect a rabbit 18 inches (45.7 cm) in length at distances up to two miles (3.2 km).

There are about 9000 species of birds in the world. Some birds live on land and feed on fruit, grain, insects, snails, snakes, frogs, or mice. Some live near water and eat water plants, fish, or mollusks, such as clams.

A bird's beak and claws determine its food and lifestyle. Birds of prey, like the eagle, have fearsome claws and strong, sharp beaks for clasping and tearing apart their prey. Eagles have even been known to carry off young lambs. Water fowl, like ducks, have webbed feet for swimming and bills to help them search for food under the water.

The seed-eaters have short, strong beaks for cracking shells; the insect and worm-eating birds have longer, sharper beaks.

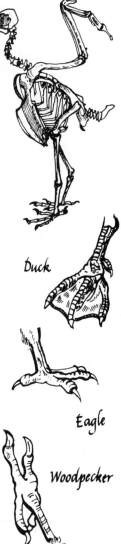

Duck

Eagle

Woodpecker

Parrot

Pelican

Ostrich

Birds have two types of feathers: large flight feathers on their wings and tails, and downy feathers to keep them warm and dry. Periodically, all birds molt or change their feathers, sometimes to different colors. Male birds often have much brighter plumage before mating time.

The nests and eggs of a bird species are always the same type and are easily identified. Some nests, such as those of the penguin and plover, are simply hollows in the ground or among stones. These nests are used only for one season. Other birds build very elaborate nests. The wren makes an egg-shaped nest with the entrance near the top. Leaves and moss are pressed carefully on the outside; downy feathers line the inside.

The number of eggs laid by different bird species varies greatly. Large numbers of eggs are laid by birds that have many enemies. Nests easy to reach often have eggs with camouflaged coloring. Eggs are laid one a day until the number is complete. After being sat on by the female (and sometimes the male), they hatch in about 2 or 3 weeks.

A baby bird can eat nearly its own weight in food each day. The parents may make 30 or 40 trips for food in an hour. This feeding of the young continues for 10 days or more until they are ready to fly.

Many species of birds lay their eggs in one country and fly enormous distances to live the rest of the year in another country. Many birds fly to warm climates when cold weather comes, and return when it is warm again. The map shows some migration patterns. SEE ALSO: MIGRATION.

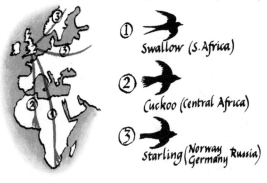

① Swallow (S. Africa)

② Cuckoo (Central Africa)

③ Starling (Norway, Germany, Russia)

BISHOP

A bishop is a clergyman who is in charge of a number of *parishes* (local Christian congregations). Each parish is cared for by a priest or minister. The group of parishes under a bishop is called a *diocese*, and the bishop's own church is a *cathedral*. Some bishops are supervised by *archbishops*. The Roman Catholic, Protestant Episcopal, Orthodox, and Methodist Episcopal churches all have bishops.

BLACKBEARD (died 1718)

Blackbeard was one of the most famous English PIRATES that ever lived. His real name was Edward Teach, but he became known as "Blackbeard" because of his long, black beard that made his face look fierce. From 1716 to 1718, Blackbeard in his 40-gun ship, *Queen Anne's Revenge*, preyed with cruelty on many defenseless merchant ships. His headquarters were either in the Bahamas or the Carolinas. Robbing and killing in the WEST INDIES and along the coasts of the American colonies, Blackbeard became a dreaded pirate until an English warship forced his ship aground off the coast of North Carolina. Blackbeard then fought the English captain with pistol and sword, but was slain. Many romantic stories and legends have grown up around Blackbeard.

BLACK DEATH

In the Middle Ages, an epidemic disease called the "Black Death" spread throughout Europe, killing almost three-quarters of the population in less than 20 years. Famine and sickness were quite common then, and plagues swept quickly in hot weather through walled towns where dirt and overcrowding were familiar sights.

The Black Death that plagued Europe in the mid-1300s began in Constantinople or Sicily, probably coming from China. It was transmitted to human beings by fleas from diseased rats.

The ship that brought the rat that carried the flea which brought the plague to Europe

During 1348, a ship arrived at Weymouth, England, and within months people were dying of the disease. By the next year London, Wales, and Scotland were fighting to contain the plague.

The Black Death was characterized by a very high fever, chills, delirium, and dark swellings under a victim's skin, thus giving the name "Black Death" to the disease. A person could die in 3 to 4 days. Doctors were helpless, and people fled wildly from the cities, leaving their jobs and even their children. The contagious dead were left unburied and fields were left unharvested. In England alone a third of the population died in three years. The plague ravaged Europe, destroying entire villages.

The leaders of Venice quarantined foreign travelers and ships in order to contain the plague. "Quarantine" derives from the Italian word for forty, the

number of days a quarantine lasted. That is the term of isolation imposed upon ships or persons suspected of carrying the contagious Black Death.

Afterward there were few workers to do what the feudal lords demanded in the manors and the fields. Higher wages were also demanded by the peasants. In England Wat Tyler led the Peasants' Revolt in 1381 against high taxes and bad treatment by the lords.

Plague is still prevalent in parts of Asia, and the World Health Organization has begun sanitation programs for rodent control in areas of known infection.

BLACK SEA

The Black Sea is a large inland sea between Europe and Asia, connected with the Aegean Sea by the Bosporus, the Sea of Marmara, and the Dardanelles. The Bosporus is an 18-mile (29 km) strait, and the Dardanelles is a narrow 40-mile (64 km) strait. The Black Sea was probably called "black" because of the thick fogs that make the waters appear black during winter.

Because of its narrow outlet, the sea is almost tideless, but bad storms have swept it since ancient times. The DANUBE and three Soviet rivers—the Dnieper, the Dniester, and the Don—flow into the Black Sea, making it less salty than most seas.

Fishing boats unload herring, mackerel, pike, and sturgeon at Istanbul, Odessa, and other ports. Fruit, tea, and cotton can be raised on the hot, humid, northern shore, a favorite winter vacation place for the Russians.

Odessa

R. Danube

Black Sea

Bosphorus

Istanbul

Sea of Marmara

Dardanelles

200 miles

BLAST FURNACE

To get IRON from ORE, a blast furnace is used. This is a tower more than 100 feet (30 m) high, made of steel and lined with bricks that can resist high temperatures.

Small cars bring ore, limestone (which helps melting), and coke (a refined coal used for fuel) to the top of the furnace. These materials fall through a pair of cone-shaped doors so arranged that little of the heat inside escapes. The mixture burns fiercely, fed with air under pressure (the *blast*) from below. Temperatures rise above 2800°F (1500°C) as the molten iron trickles downward.

The iron settles into the *hearth* of the furnace, a well below the place where the blast comes in. As the iron gathers, a mixture of unwanted materials called *slag* begins to float on top. When there is enough iron in the hearth, the slag is allowed to pour out of the furnace into ladles, tubs on wheels that are used to carry it away. (Slag is made into building materials.) When the slag is gone, the iron flows through a hole in the bottom of the hearth. It is either allowed to harden in molds on the floor beside the furnace or is carried away in other ladles. The castings on the floor are called pigs, and iron from a blast furnace is called *pig iron*. This can be used as it is to make cast-iron objects, or it can be converted into steel.

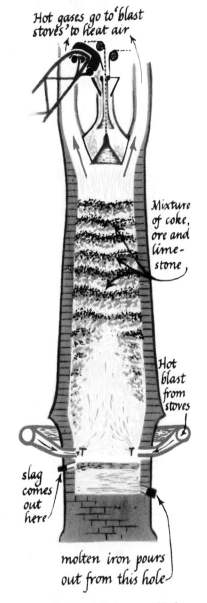

Hot gases go to 'blast stoves' to heat air

Mixture of coke, ore and lime-stone,

Hot blast from stoves

slag comes out here

molten iron pours out from this hole

The heat produced by the furnace does more work. It is drawn off the top of the furnace through large pipes, which send it through *stoves*. The stoves pick up and store much of the heat. The air used for the blast should be as hot as possible when it reaches the furnace. This air is sent through the hot stoves on its way to the furnace and also becomes hot.

A large furnace may be "in blast" (at work) for two years at a time. By that time the fire-resistant brick lining is worn out and has to be rebuilt. The furnace is shut down until this is done.

111

BLOOD

Blood is the fluid that flows through ARTERIES AND VEINS. A microscope reveals that it is a pale yellow liquid (*plasma*) in which float a huge number of small red and white cells (*corpuscles*).

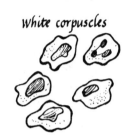

Red corpuscles
(magnified 4000 times)

white corpuscles

The round, disc-shaped red corpuscles are so small that a pile of 3000 would only be one inch (2.54 cm) in height! These corpuscles contain *hemoglobin*, an iron compound which carries oxygen from the lungs to the body cells. The arterial blood is bright red because the hemoglobin carries the oxygen breathed in; the venous blood is bluish-purple because it carries carbon dioxide from the body cells to the lungs to be breathed out.

Red corpuscles wear out in a few weeks. The bone marrow replaces worn-out red cells with millions of new ones every minute.

A healthy person's blood contains about 500 times more red cells than white cells. White cells are somewhat larger than the red cells. The most common types are shown in the picture. White corpuscles act somewhat like AMOEBAS. Their job is to fight infection by surrounding and absorbing germs and foreign particles.

The watery plasma contains chemicals for keeping the body active and healthy. The digested food from the linings of the intestines is carried by the plasma to wherever it is needed.

Red corpuscles are made in the bone marrow

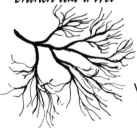

The veins & arteries branch like a tree

Many people donate some of their blood to "blood banks." Whole blood and plasma are refrigerated and available for surgical and accident cases. There are different types of blood, such as "A," "B," "AB," and "O," and great care must be taken in giving a person the right type.

There are about 9 pints (4.3 liters) of blood circulating in the body of a man, and it takes about 30 seconds to be pumped once through his system. The blood keeps our body temperature at about 98.6° F (53.7° C), but during illness it can rise to 102° F (56.7° C) or more.

BOATS

When we call something a boat, we usually mean that it is a small vessel. (A vessel is something that floats by keeping water out of its inside.) Anything larger is a SHIP. But some very large vessels on rivers, canals, and lakes are also called boats.

The first boat was probably a large log, burned hollow inside. This was clumsy to handle, and most boats have been made of light framework. This frame is covered with bark, animal skins, wooden planks, thin steel or aluminum, or other materials. Most boats today are driven by motors, SAILS, oars, or paddles.

Motorboats have either outboard (hanging outside the boat) or inboard motors. When they run fast, they skim on top of the water instead of floating.

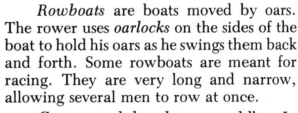

Rowboats are boats moved by oars. The rower uses *oarlocks* on the sides of the boat to hold his oars as he swings them back and forth. Some rowboats are meant for racing. They are very long and narrow, allowing several men to row at once.

Canoes and *kayaks* use paddles. In rowing, you face backward and pull forward on the oar. In paddling, you face forward and move the lower end of the paddle backward.

Sailboats are very popular, but can be very expensive. The most popular type is called the *sloop*. It has one mast and two triangular sails, and two people can handle it easily. There is also the catboat, which has one sail on a mast all the way up at the bow. There are two-masted boats that are almost ships in size. Depending on the sizes and positions of the masts, these are called schooners, ketches, or yawls. Boats sometimes can house people for several days. When they have living space, they are called *yachts*. Although yachting costs a great deal, many people are able and willing to spend the money it takes.

Boating should be done as safely as possible, since accidents can happen. SEE ALSO: RIVERBOAT, SAILS, SHIPS.

113

Simón BOLÍVAR (1783–1830)

Simón Bolívar was one of South America's greatest generals and statesmen. Known as "The Liberator," he became the leader of the war for independence from Spain.

Born in Caracas, VENEZUELA, Bolívar came from a wealthy family that encouraged him to study and travel abroad. As a young man, he saw how revolutions in other countries had brought freedom for the people.

In 1807, he joined South America's fight for freedom from Spanish rule. At first, he and his soldiers suffered military defeats. But, with more money and weapons, his army defeated the Spanish at the Battle of Boyaca, in New Granada (now Colombia), in 1819. He became the president of New Granada and drew up a constitution. In renewed fighting, Bolívar successively defeated the Spanish in Venezuela (1821), Ecuador (1822), PERU (1824), and Upper Peru (1825). This last area named itself BOLIVIA after its liberator, Bolívar.

In the following years, Bolívar's attempts for a united South America failed. When he died, warfare had begun between the new countries.

BOLIVIA

Bolivia is a landlocked country in SOUTH AMERICA. The western half consists of high, bleak mountains—part of the Andes—and high plateaus. Near the *altiplano* ("high plain") rest most of Bolivia's cities, including La Paz, the administrative capital, and Sucre, the legal capital. Here also is Lake Titicaca, the world's highest lake, 12,506 feet (3877 m) above sea level. Eastern Bolivia is made up of fertile valleys and lowlands and dense rain forests.

Coffee, cacao, sugar, potatoes, corn, and fruits are grown in Bolivia. However, mining earns the most money for the country. In the Andes Mountains are found large deposits of tin, tungsten, copper, silver, gold, lead, oil, and other minerals.

More than half of Bolivia's population—about 6 million people—are Quechua and Aymara Indians, who have their own customs and language. The rest are of European, mainly Spanish, or of mixed Indian and white origin (Cholos).

Bolivia's altiplano was conquered by the INCAS in the 13th century. The Spanish took control of the region in the 1530s and made the Indians work as slaves in the rich silver mines. For almost 300 years, Spain ruled Upper Peru, as the region was then called. Through revolution and war, it gained independence in 1825, naming itself Bolivia after General SIMÓN BOLÍVAR, South America's famed "Liberator." Bolivia has been generally ruled by military groups, who have had to contend with peasant uprisings, guerrilla civil war, and labor strikes.

BOLL WEEVIL

The boll weevil is a BEETLE. It is the most serious pest of COTTON in the United States. The grayish adult is about .25 inch (0.64 cm) in length, half of which is its snout.

The insect, which only feeds upon cotton, was first known in Central America. By the early 1890s, it had entered the United States at Brownsville, Texas. The boll weevil moved outward from this point at a rate of about 70 miles (113 km) a year. Since 1922, it has been found in every part of the cotton growing areas east of the Rockies.

The adult punctures the buds and bolls (pods) of the cotton plant and lays its eggs in them. The pale yellow grubs (LARVAE) that hatch out, feed upon the buds and bolls. The entire life cycle is about three weeks. The larvae do the most damage, but the adults live several weeks and continue to produce four or more generations.

In autumn, the adults hibernate until spring; fortunately about 95 percent die during the winter.

BONES

The SKELETON of the body in vertebrate animals is made up of bones. In the human body there are more than 200 bones. They assume a variety of shapes and sizes, as you can see in the illustration. The skull and rib bones cover parts of the body that can be easily hurt. The backbone and the main bones in our legs and arms furnish the framework to which our muscles are attached.

Bones are not really solid. They are hard on the outside, but they have millions of tiny holes through which BLOOD flows to feed nourishment to the bone cells. Inside the bones is a spongy, web-like mass that contains the blood vessels and nerves. In certain bones, there is also the *marrow*, soft tissue where the red corpuscles of our blood are made.

The circulation of blood within our bones makes possible their growth when we are young; it also enables bones to mend when they are broken. Besides fracture, bones are subject to various infections and diseases.

BOOKS

The earliest books we know are clay tablets. The Sumerians and the Babylonians scratched words into the clay of these tablets as long as 5000 years ago. The ancient Egyptians, around the same time, found a handier way of making books. They crushed the stems of the *papyrus* reed to make a sort of paper, and wrote on long rolls of this. The Book of the Dead, buried in an Egyptian tomb in 2600 B.C., is a papyrus roll over 70 feet (22 m) long and 15 inches (38 cm) wide. The ancient Romans also used *scrolls* (rolls) of papyrus. But later they began to use *parchment*. This was a thin, stiff, strong material made from the skins of sheep and goats.

In the Middle Ages, the use of papyrus died out, and only parchment was used. Medieval books were written out by hand, and were often decorated with beautiful paintings that were covered with gold in places. Parchment was a good material to use for such books. Most monasteries had a scriptorium, where books were written. And every city had *copyists*, whose job was to copy books for customers, and *miniaturists*, the artists who decorated them.

A folded 'codex'

Books in the Middle Ages were in the form we use today, which is called a *codex*. The sheets of papyrus were sewn together at one edge to make pages, and a sturdy cover was glued on over the sewn edge.

Hand-written books were very expensive. The time needed to make them was long, and the artists were well paid. Some of the paints were costly too. The printed book was the answer to the problems of cost and speed. Books were first printed in Germany around 1460. Instead of being on parchment, they were on a new material, paper, which was made of tiny fibers of cloth. Paper soaked up the printer's ink. Printing allowed many books to be made in a very short time. And the book itself was more likely not to have mistakes, since the words could be checked over before any books were printed. Printing presses soon appeared all over Europe.

A medieval library

A line of printing type

At first people had miniaturists decorate some parts of the printed books, but soon they got used to the black-and-white illustrations and decorations the printer supplied.

A modern book is made up of groups of pages. A number of pages, 16 perhaps, are printed on both sides of a large sheet of paper. Then the sheet is folded and cut to make one section of the book. All the sections are sewn together, and a cover is glued on, just as it was in the Middle Ages. SEE ALSO: PRINTING.

Daniel BOONE (1734–1820)

Daniel Boone was a famous American explorer and frontiersman. He grew up in Berks County, Pennsylvania, where he was taught by friendly Indians how to survive alone in the deep woods. As a boy, he moved with his family to North Carolina and became a wandering hunter and trapper.

In the 1760's, Boone explored the Kentucky region. His first attempt to establish a settlement there in 1773 failed because of Indian attacks. Two years later, Boone was hired by the Transylvania Company to blaze a trail through the Cumberland Gap, a pass through the Appalachian Mountains. It became the famous Wilderness Trail, going from eastern Virginia to Kentucky and beyond. Boone built a stockade and fort, known as Boonesboro (or Boonesborough), on the Kentucky River. Indians constantly attacked the settlement. For about five months, Boone was held captive by the Shawnees. He escaped in time to warn Boonesboro of an attack, which failed.

In his later years, Boone lived in West Virginia and Missouri, becoming a lawmaker and continuing to hunt and trap.

BOSTON

Boston, the capital of MASSACHUSETTS, is the largest city in New England. Situated at the head of Massachusetts Bay, it is a major seaport of the U.S. and an important market for fish and wool. It is also a large banking and industrial center. About 650,000 people live in the city.

In 1630, a colony was established there by the PURITANS under John Winthrop. Later, Boston became a center of opposition to British rule. The BOSTON TEA PARTY and many battles during the American Revolution occurred in and around Boston. In the 1800s, the city grew prosperous from shipping and from textile mills and shoe factories. Education and culture became very important to Bostonians.

The city today has broad avenues and tall skyscrapers, as well as old crooked streets and red-brick buildings. Among its historic attractions are Old North Church, where lanterns were set for PAUL REVERE, and *Old Ironsides*, the most famous ship in the U.S. Navy. Boston has lovely parks, art museums, and many universities. Harvard, in nearby Cambridge, was founded in 1636, and is the oldest institution of higher learning in the U.S. SEE ALSO: MASSACHUSETTS.

BOSTON TEA PARTY

In the 1770's, the American colonies were angry about the taxes that Britain forced them to pay on imported goods. They agreed not to accept British goods. However, Britain declared its right to tax the colonies and sent cargoes of extra tea to American ports.

The colonists did not accept the taxed tea at Charleston, Philadelphia, and New York. At Boston, British tea ships remained unloaded in the harbor, while the governor tried to make the Bostonians pay the tax.

A small group of colonists, led by SAMUEL ADAMS, PAUL REVERE, and others, dressed themselves up as Indians, with war paint, feathers, and tomahawks. Late at night on December 16, 1773, they boarded the ships and threw 342 cases of tea into Boston harbor. Then they quietly left the ships.

When the British discovered what had happened, they took revenge by closing the port of Boston. Also, Massachusetts lost its charter. Colonists had to let British soldiers live in their homes. SEE ALSO: AMERICAN REVOLUTION.

BOTANY

Botany is the scientific study of plants. Botany and zoology together form the science of biology. Botanists identify, name, and assign plants to various classifications according to their similarities and differences. They study the structure of the roots, stems, trunks, leaves, flowers, fruits, and seeds of all plants. The vital processes of plants are also studied, including the intake of carbon dioxide from the air, the intake of water and food from the soil, and photosynthesis.

Botany is concerned with the stages of plant growth and plant reproduction. There is also the study of plant diseases, trying to develop ways of treating and preventing them. Finally, botany examines the fossil remains of extinct plants to determine how plants have changed through the ages.

BOW AND ARROW

The bow and arrow is a simple type of weapon that has been used for many centuries, mainly for hunting. The bow propels the arrow (a sharp pointed stick) to the target. Because the arrow moves at a fast speed, it can puncture the skin of most animals. Also, because the bow and arrow work quietly, they do not frighten other animals away.

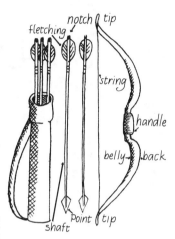

When a tough young sapling is bent, it stays bent only as long as it is held. After it is let go, it whips back into a straight form. Certain kinds of wood and other materials have so much of this springiness that they are good for making bows. The bow is held in a slightly bent position by its string. When the notch in the arrow's tail is fitted over the string the archer bends the bow still further, then releases it. This is enough to send the arrow many yards.

One special type is the *crossbow*, a very small, strong bow that has to be bent with a small machine.

Bows and arrows have been used all over the world. Even the invention of guns has not put an end to them. Archers still compete in target shooting, or hunt for sport. Even some industrial plants use archers. They have gases that must be burned at the tops of tall pipes, and archers may be called to light them with flaming arrows.

BOXING

Boxing is the sport of fighting with the fists. Its origin goes back to the Greeks and Romans, who bound the fists with leather, weighted gloves. Boxing died out until it was revived in England in the late 1600s. For a while, bare fists were used by the fighters (boxers), and a contest lasted until one fighter was knocked out or could not continue. Finally, in 1865, an Englishman introduced a set of boxing rules, which became the basic rules of modern boxing.

Today, the two opponents who fight (box) each other wear gloves weighing upward from 5 oz. (142 g) each. They fight in a roped-off ring that is usually 20 feet (6.2 m) square. Most boxing matches are divided into 3-minute rounds (there may be as many as 15 rounds) with 1-minute breaks between rounds. Unless one boxer is knocked out or unable to get up after 10 seconds, a match is decided on points from punches delivered and skillful action in avoiding them. A referee calls fouls when a boxer hits below the belt, kicks, wrestles, or gouges. So that matches will be even, boxers are divided into different weight classes.

BOY SCOUTS

The Boy Scouts is a boys' organization that was founded by a British army officer, Sir Robert Baden-Powell, in 1908. He organized a boys' camp and published a handbook of activities, called *Scouting for Boys*. In 1910, Daniel Beard and William Boyce founded the Boy Scouts of America.

A boy's age determines the scouting group that he can join. He becomes a Cub Scout when he is 8 to 10. By performing 12 achievements, Cub Scouts go up in rank from Bobcat to Wolf, Bear, and Webelos. Boy Scouts are 11 to 17 years old. They begin as Tenderfoot Scouts and then are Second Class, First Class, Star, Life, and finally Eagle Scouts. They move up in rank by earning merit badges in such activities as

first aid, life saving, swimming, and wildlife management. At 15, a Boy Scout may join an Explorer post, or ship, and win other awards.

The famous motto of the Boy Scouts of America is "Be Prepared!" Scouts pledge to obey the Scout Law, which includes the phrase, "To help other people at all times."

There are Scout associations in more than 100 countries around the world. The World Scout Bureau, located in Geneva, Switzerland, coordinates the activities of the Scout associations. International gatherings of Boy Scouts, called jamborees, are held every four years. The U.S. also holds a national jamboree every four years.

BRAILLE

A way of allowing the blind to read was invented in 1829 by Louis Braille, a Frenchman who was blind himself. The idea was not new, but it is Braille's system that is now used.

The alphabet is shown here. Each letter is made up of from one to six dots, which are embossed (pushed up) from a thick piece of paper. The fingers of the blind can tell the pattern of dots, and thus tell which letter it is. Some patterns stand for very ordinary words or parts of words. The letters are about as large as they are shown here, and their pages are thick, so that a book in braille is large and clumsy.

The making of books and other writings in braille is called *encoding*.

BRAIN

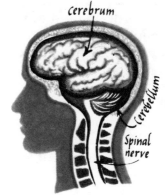

The brain, which is protected by the hard bones of the skull, is a soft mass of gray and white CELLS. There are more than 10 billion cells in the brain, connected with one another in ways that scientists do not yet fully understand. All parts of the body are connected to the brain by NERVE fibers in the spinal cord.

All parts of the body have many nerve endings. If you burn your finger, the nerve endings are affected. Then the nerve sends a high-speed signal to the brain. The brain causes the muscles in your hand and arm to move so that your finger is yanked away from the source of pain.

The brain is divided down the middle of the skull into two halves, or *hemispheres*. The left side of the brain controls

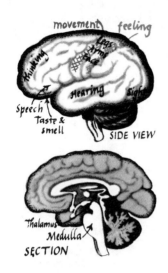

movement feeling

Thinking

Hearing Sight

Speech
Taste & smell

SIDE VIEW

Thalamus
Medulla
SECTION

the right side of the body, and the right side of the brain controls the left side of the body. Different parts of the brain control different bodily functions. Some of the body's functions, like the beating of the heart and breathing, are *involuntary*. The brain directs such functions without our having to think about them.

In some ways the brain is like a computer. But if we were to build a computer with circuits that copied the circuits of the brain, that computer would occupy several buildings, each about 110 stories high.

The brain of a 3-month-old baby weighs a little less than 1 pound (0.45 kg). The adult brain weighs about 3 pounds (1.4 kg).

All animals that have backbones (*vertebrates*) have brains. Some have huge brains, like the whale and the elephant. Many have tiny brains, like the HUMMINGBIRD. The size of the brain is less important than its weight compared to the weight of the whole body. When the brain is measured in this way, man has the largest brain.

BRASS

Brass is an ALLOY of essentially copper and zinc. Since prehistoric times, it has been important because of its hardness and workability. In the Middle Ages and later, brass was used for cannons. Today, it is beaten and hammered into many shapes, rolled into thin sheets or tubes, and drawn out into wires. Brass is widely used in the manufacture of bolts and screws, faucet handles, window and door fittings, and other items in the building industry.

BRAZIL

Brazil is the largest country in SOUTH AMERICA and the fifth largest in the world. The great AMAZON·RIVER and its tributaries drain most of northern Brazil. There is dry scrubland in the northeast. Southern Brazil consists of fertile plains and highlands. This area has many cattle ranches and coffee plantations (Brazil is the world's greatest coffee grower). Cotton, soybeans, sugar, cocoa beans, and many fruits are also grown in the country.

Brazil's enormous mineral wealth, which is gradually being exploited, includes coal, iron ore, manganese, chromium, nickel, oil, lead, asbestos, gold, quartz crystal, and various gem stones. Rubber, timber, and other forest products come from Brazil, too.

Most of the country has a hot, wet climate all year long, but along the

coast and in the south the weather is often cool and dry. Most of Brazil's major cities lie along the Atlantic seacoast, including beautiful RIO DE JANEIRO and industrial São Paulo, the two largest cities. The capital is Brasilia, a modern city built out of the dense jungle near the center of the country. Brazil's population is more than 112 million people, most of whom are descended from early Portuguese colonists and slaves. Portuguese is the main language.

In 1500, a Portuguese navigator, Pedro Alvares Cabral, landed on the coast and claimed the region for PORTUGAL. Soon Portuguese settlers brought Negro slaves from Africa to work in the sugar cane fields. In the early 1800s, Brazil became the center of Portugal's government, but in 1822 the colony declared its independence. The country has since been ruled as a monarchy, democracy, and dictatorship.

BREAD

Bread was the world's first man-made food, but bread in ancient times was probably very different from the bread of today. The first breads were probably made of a coarse flour ground from nuts or the seeds of wild grasses. The flour was then mixed with water to make flat cakes of dough, which were then placed among the embers or near the edge of the fire. The ancient Egyptians discovered how to make bread more digestible and better tasting by *leavening* it.

The leavening we use today is yeast. It is the yeast that produces the tiny air spaces we find inside a loaf of bread. Yeast mixed with warm water and sugar gives off bubbles of carbon dioxide which cause the bread to "rise."

The type of flour used determines the flavor and appearance of bread. White flour is made by grinding the inside of the wheat grain, after removing the seed coat; brown flour is made by grinding the whole grain. Other flours are made from corn or rice, particularly in hot countries, and from oats and rye in colder countries.

Some modern yeast breads are coffee cakes, yeast rolls, and sweet breads. Some breads are made with baking powder, baking soda, or both instead of with yeast. These breads do not have to rise before being put into the oven. They are called *quick breads*, and include biscuits, muffins, and fruit breads.

Today huge bakeries have special machinery to make bread so that it never gets touched by human hands. Machines mix the dough, add preservatives, vitamins, and minerals to enrich the bread, and then cut it into pieces of the correct weight. Machines then place the pieces in pans which are conveyed through heated tunnels to allow the dough to rise, and then on into precisely heated ovens. Another machine wraps the loaves when they are cool.

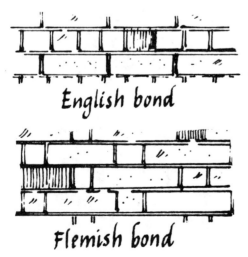

English bond

Flemish bond

BRICKS

Many centuries ago, people in western Asia discovered that rectangular pieces of hard, dried mud could be used for building. The earliest bricks were simply dried under the hot sun, but these crumbled under rain. People soon discovered that burning the bricks made them harder, stronger, and waterproof.

The art of brickmaking soon spread westward to ancient Egypt and eastward to India and China.

Until the 19th century, bricks were made by hand. Clay was rammed into a little box that was used as a mold and allowed to dry. Then it was piled up with other bricks, and a fire was built inside the pile. The bricks closest to the fire were the best burned, and were used where hard bricks were needed. The softer bricks were used where they were not exposed to the weather. About 150 years ago, people began to invent machines for molding bricks automatically. They also invented *kilns* (ovens), where bricks could be baked more evenly than before.

Most bricks are made of ordinary clay, and people have even used the clay dug up in making a house cellar to make the bricks for the walls. Some bricks need special materials, such as the bricks inside BLAST FURNACES. These must be able to resist great heat.

Egyptians making mud bricks

Loading bricks into kiln

Bricks have had many different forms and sizes. The ancient Roman brick was low and square, like a big, thick floor tile. Medieval bricks looked much like modern ones, but were often smaller. An ordinary modern brick is a little over 8 inches (20 cm) long, about 4 inches (10 cm) deep, and about 2 inches (5 cm) thick.

Bricks are laid in a mortar of some kind, usually made with cement or lime. They are laid in *bonds*, patterns that make the wall strong in all directions or that have a decorative effect. Each level row of bricks is called a *course*. A brick with its side exposed in the wall is a *stretcher*; a brick with its end exposed is a *header*.

125

Primitive Stone Bridge

Primitive Suspension Bridge

Arched Bridge

Modern Suspension Bridge

Cantilever Bridge

BRIDGES

The first bridges were probably trees that fell across deep places that people wanted to cross. Many modern bridges are really no different. A level object acts as a beam to support traffic crossing from side to side. Old bridges use beams of wood or even stone. Modern bridges are likely to be built with *girders*. These are beams of steel or of concrete made stronger with lengths of steel buried in them (reinforced concrete). Many bridges use *trusses*. A truss is really a kind of beam, but it is made of lengths of steel or wood arranged in triangular patterns. A triangle will not bend anywhere, and is thus strong. If a bridge needs more than one beam to get across the deep place, tall constructions called *piers* are built to help hold the beam in the middle. A road bridge with many piers is called a *viaduct*.

Bridges can be built without beams or trusses. The Romans and many other peoples supported bridges with ARCHES. Arched bridges can be built of stone, brick, steel, or even wood. Old fashioned covered bridges are often built with wooden arches.

Another way of building a bridge is with a *cantilever*. A cantilever is like your arm when you hold it out. It is held up at one end only. Most cantilevers have arms going both ways, as in the illustration at the bottom of the page.

Yet another way of getting across a deep place is with a *suspension bridge*. The Indians of South America have used these for centuries. Ropes hang across a valley, and a walk is built on top of them. Early in the 19th century, European engineers began to make suspension bridges that hung from chains or cables (ropes) of wire. These bridges can be very long. The Verrazano-Narrows Bridge, which crosses the entrance to New York harbor, is 4260 feet (1298 m) long between the towers that hold up the cables. The towers themselves are 690 feet (210 m) high.

BRITISH COLUMBIA

British Columbia is a large, mountainous province in western CANADA. Many islands, such as Vancouver Island and the Queen Charlotte Islands, lie off its deeply indented coast on the Pacific. Along the ocean are the Coast Mountains, in the northwest are the Skeena Mountains, and in the east are the high Rockies. The Fraser River, about 850 miles (1369 km) long, flows through the central and southern areas. British Columbia's capital is Victoria and its largest city is VANCOUVER. About 2.5 million people live in the province.

Vast forests cover much of the land, and lumbering is the major industry. Copper, zinc, molybdenum, natural gas, and oil are found in the province. Many rapidly flowing rivers supply cheap hydroelectric power for the industries. Wood products, paper, aluminum, chemicals, and food items come from British Columbia.

In 1778, Captain JAMES COOK stopped briefly on the coast. Soon fur traders came, and the Hudson's Bay Company ruled the region until 1858, when the British made it a colony. In 1871, it became part of Canada. SEE ALSO: VANCOUVER.

BRITISH ISLES

Two large islands—GREAT BRITAIN and IRELAND—and more than 5000 smaller islands make up the British Isles. The area is about the size of the state of New Mexico.

Highest land
High land

127

Some geologists believe the British Isles were connected to the European mainland when the Earth was first formed. At that time, the coast was roughly along the westernmost edge of Scotland and Ireland. The sea then gradually cut through the low lands, making the Irish Sea, the English Channel, and the NORTH SEA.

Wheat grows mostly in the drier regions of England, and the coal mines are near the industrial areas where much of the population lives. Sheep and cattle are raised in some highland regions. Vegetable gardening and mixed farming are carried on in many places. Herring and white fish are caught abundantly in the surrounding seas.

Various peoples have invaded and settled in the British Isles during the last two thousand years. The Romans conquered the BRITONS and ruled there until about A.D. 400. After the Romans withdrew, the ANGLO–SAXONS settled there, pushing the Britons into the western provinces. Also, the Danes took over and settled in some parts. In 1066, WILLIAM THE CONQUEROR invaded the British Isles with his NORMANS from France.

During the Industrial Revolution in the 19th century, England grew in wealth and importance. She had colonies around the world, protected by her immense sea-power. Her population then increased rapidly, from about 13 million in 1820 to 41 million by 1920. Today the British Isles have about 60 million people. To feed so many people in so small an area much of the food has to be imported, for the home farms are too small.

The British Isles must also import raw materials, like oil, lumber, chemicals, cotton, and hides. To pay for these things, workers in the cities build cars and machinery to be sold abroad. Coal is mined and used to run the plants. Other important exports from the British Isles are textiles, airplanes, and electrical goods. Ships built in the shipyards of England and Scotland carry merchandise all over the world. SEE ALSO: ENGLAND, IRELAND, SCOTLAND, WALES.

Ancient BRITONS

"Ancient Britons" refers to the inhabitants of Britain when the Romans conquered it in 56 B.C. These were the people living there when the ANGLO–SAXONS later invaded the island.

The caves at Torquay, Cheddar, and in Derbyshire reveal that people lived there many centuries before the Romans came. They were hunters who used flint weapons. Historians say that people from the Mediterranean region invaded Britain about

4500 years ago, bringing cattle, sheep, and pigs. They also brought wheat and corn seed, as well as the ability to weave and make pottery. These New Stone Age people were more advanced in farming, knowing the importance of good soil for their crops.

Around 1800 B.C., another group known as the *Beaker Folk* invaded the island; they knew how to make weapons and tools of bronze. Their peculiar name was given them because they made a certain kind of jar, or beaker, which archeologists have found in huge numbers. They were fine workers in gold, too.

Toward the end of the BRONZE AGE, around 1400 B.C., tribes of people known as CELTS came from the continent of Europe and settled in Britain. They knew how to obtain and shape iron. Mirrors, bracelets, swords, helmets, shields, and horse armor all demonstrate great craftsmanship in the working of metal. Many Celtic groups continued to migrate to Britain until the first century B.C.

One Celtic group was called *Brythons*, from which come the names Briton and Britain. The various tribes of Britons, especially in the southern part of the island, developed a primitive civilization with organized communities and iron and gold coins. The Britons made excellent bronze weapons and jewelry.

When the Anglo-Saxons invaded, many Britons fled to a province in northwestern France. The area was later called Brittany, after the Britons, who later were known as Bretons. SEE ALSO: BRITISH ISLES, CELTS.

BRONZE

Bronze is an ALLOY consisting essentially of copper and tin. The ancient Egyptians made bronze, casting and hammering it into utensils, armor, weapons, and statues. The Greeks made beautiful bronze sculpture. Today, the uses of bronze vary with the percentages of copper, tin, and other added elements. Aluminum bronze has great strength and resists corrosion; thus it is used for machine parts. Silicon bronze is used for telegraph wires, and leaded bronze makes heavy duty bearings.

BRONZE AGE

The Bronze Age is the period in history when metals were first used regularly in making weapons and tools. At first, pure copper and an alloy of copper and tin were used. This early period is thus often called the Copper Age. The New Stone Age men in the Middle East, possibly in Iran, found little beads of copper after they had heated certain stones with charcoal. Having discovered this, they probably searched for other colored stones, heated them, and thus found other metals. Soon they learned that if the right amount of copper was melted together with the right amount of tin, the ALLOY was much easier to cast and also produced a harder metal, which we know today as *bronze*.

This early knowledge of making or casting metal was slow to reach other lands. As a result, the Bronze Age started at different times in different places. For instance, it did not reach Britain until about 1800 B.C., long after the civilizations of Mesopotamia had known bronze.

As the centuries went by, new and better ways of casting bronze were invented. Men also made more complicated molds and found that they could hammer out sheets of the metal. By 800 B.C., bronze had been largely replaced by iron, which was more efficient and usually stronger. Archeologists have uncovered many tools of the Bronze Age, such as saws, hammers, knives, swords, axes, spears, anvils, and shields. Even after the coming of the Iron Age, bronze was widely used for coins and objects of art.

On this page are pictures of some articles made by Bronze Age people, including a beaker from the Beaker Folk who were ancestors of the ANCIENT BRITONS. SEE ALSO: BRONZE.

BRUSSELS

Brussels, the capital of BELGIUM, is a thriving industrial, financial, and cultural center. During the Middle Ages, it grew as a trading center, and today it produces lace, gloves, leather, cotton and woolen textiles, and glassware. Belgium's stock exchange is located there, and there are a university, academies of art and science, a music conservatory, and famous museums.

The older parts of the city have winding, narrow streets and fine medieval and Renaissance buildings. The Cathedral of St. Gudule, built between 1220 and 1272, is a fabulous example of Gothic architecture.

More than 1.5 million people live in Brussels today. After Belgium became separated from Holland in 1831, the city built many wide, spacious boulevards and modern buildings. It is the administrative seat of the European Economic Community (E.E.C.). SEE ALSO: BELGIUM

BUD

A bud is a point of growth on a plant. Growing out of the bud can be leaves, flowers, or a new stem with leaves and possibly flowers. A bud has a covering to protect the tightly packed leaves or flowers which are inside.

Those plants which live more than one year (*perennials*) have buds for next year's growth located where the present year's leaves join the main stem. This does not apply to those plants that live for only one growing season (*annuals*).

leaves (a) come from bud (A), and so on.

The illustration shows the buds of a beech tree in autumn, and the leaves which have developed from these buds by early May.

BUDDHA (563?–483? B.C.)

About 150 million people in Asia have a religion called Buddhism. It is named after Buddha, a person who lived from around 563 to around 483 B.C. "Buddha" means "enlightened (full of wisdom) person."

Legend says that Buddha (who was at first named Gautama) was a prince who was kept from knowing the troubles that people have. But one day he saw an old man, a sick man, and a dead man, and decided to try to free human beings of suffering. After studying with holy men for six years, he began to meditate (think about things) by himself. He sat under a large tree, in the position shown in the illustration. Finally, he felt he had discovered the meaning of life. He taught many disciples. Today, there are several kinds of Buddhism in Japan, Sri Lanka, and southeast Asia.

BUENOS AIRES

Buenos Aires is the capital, largest city, and chief port of ARGENTINA in South America. In Spanish, Buenos Aires means "good air." It has broad, treelined streets and many attractive parks, surrounded by modern buildings. Today, almost 9 million people live in or around Buenos Aires.

It stands on the west side of the La Plata River, about 170 miles (274 km) from the Atlantic Ocean. Here the river makes a wide, natural harbor through which pass immense quantities of exports like grain, meat, and wool.

The Spaniards founded the city in 1536. Many fine, old Spanish houses still stand, and close by are modern theaters and museums. Famous Palermo Park has playing fields and botanical and zoological gardens. SEE ALSO: ARGENTINA.

BUFFALO

The buffalo is a cud-chewing mammal. Large and oxlike, it stands 5 feet (1.5 m) or more at the shoulder and weighs up to 1800 pounds (810 kg). For many centuries, tamed buffaloes have been used in India and Egypt to carry loads and to pull plows. Wild buffaloes of North America are really *bison*, which have large heads and high, humped shoulders.

BUFFALO BILL (1846–1917)

Buffalo Bill was a famous American frontiersman, scout, and showman. His real name was William Frederick Cody. However, after he supplied large amounts of buffalo meat to construction gangs on the Union Pacific Railroad, Cody was given his nickname "Buffalo Bill."

He was born in Iowa, but his family moved to Kansas when he was 8. There he worked for a freight company. Later, when he was 14, he became a rider for the PONY EXPRESS.

During the Civil War, Cody served as a U.S. Army scout on the western frontier. Afterward he was hired as a buffalo hunter for railroad workers on the Great Plains. For a while, he appeared on stage as "Buffalo Bill," but returned to scouting in 1876. He fought against the Sioux Indians and supposedly killed Chief Yellow Hand in personal combat.

In 1883, Buffalo Bill went back into show business and organized his famous "Wild West Show." His show toured all over the U.S. and Europe, thrilling audiences with trick riding, sharpshooting, and fake Indian fights. Later, on his land in Wyoming, Buffalo Bill founded the town of Cody.

BUILDING

There are many parts of the world where buildings are still put up as all buildings used to be, with things provided by nature. Sticks, bamboo, grass, mud, and rocks are used just as they are found. The primitive builders who use these things are often very skilled, and make buildings in all sorts of interesting shapes.

In ancient times, men began to give the shapes they wished to natural materials. First they molded mud into bricks. Later, they were decorating the interiors of their houses with paint. These things happened in western Asia. By the time of Abraham, the Egyptians were putting up buildings of cut stone. Builders also learned to carve wood and make decorative colored tiles.

Some early civilizations, like GREECE and EGYPT, used *columns* (posts) and *lintels* (beams) for building, and almost never used the arch. The architects of ROME and the Middle Ages used the ARCH everywhere along with the *vault*, which is really a form of arch but covers square spaces. None of these early cultures had BLAST FURNACES or any of the other equipment we use today, so iron and steel were used very sparingly.

When modern INDUSTRY was introduced in the early 19th century, things changed. Men could build with iron and steel, and railroads could take building materials great distances. Before then, people used the materials their own region supplied. By 1850, all this was changing. In the early 1880s, the first SKYSCRAPERS— buildings held up by iron or steel frames— were being built. Manufacturers were able, by then, to make very large sheets of GLASS. This was very important for the appearance of buildings. *Prefabrication*, the making of large parts of a building in factories, came early. In 1851, the Crystal Palace, an iron-and-glass building 1848 feet (573 m) long, was bolted together in a few weeks from parts made in factories. Prefabricated structures are sometimes made by a process called *modular construction* (the use of a standard measurement for building materials).

BULB

A bulb is a thickened bud having fleshy leaves on a short stem. It contains one or more buds which can develop into new plants. Many common outdoor and house plants, such as tulips, narcissuses, daffodils, and lilies, are grown from bulbs.

The leaves of a plant make starch from the carbon dioxide in the air. This starch is stored underground at the base of the leaves, which slowly thickens to form a bulb. The leaves above ground die and dry up. The picture shows a cross section of a bulb, whose overlapping leaves packed tightly together contain food material that will sustain the plant during the next year's growth.

BULGARIA

Bulgaria, one of the BALKAN countries, is bounded by the Black Sea to the east, Rumania to the north, and Yugoslavia, Greece, and Turkey to the west and south. Agriculture is the chief occupation; the farms produce wheat, corn, fruit, tobacco, and roses. The Communist regime has developed the country's mining and manufacturing, notably of iron and steel, machinery, and chemicals. Its capital is Sofia, famous for its old churches, mosques, and synagogues. Its population is nearly 9 million.

Paul BUNYAN

A folklore hero of American lumberjacks, Paul Bunyan is a fictional character of great strength, speed, vision, humor, and skill. The bigness of all his qualities makes the "tall tales" about Bunyan typically American and in keeping with the seemingly endless land and resources of North America.

The legend of Paul Bunyan was originally told in the 1830s and repeatedly retold by rugged loggers in the lumber camps of Minnesota, Michigan, and Wisconsin. Paul's blue ox, Babe, was "42 ax handles" long and able to swallow whole rivers in a gulp. Paul could hitch her to a crooked logging road and she would pull it straight.

Two other exaggerated, regional, folklore heroes of similar bigness are the cowboy Pecos Bill and John Henry, the hard-working Negro slave.

BUOYS

Buoys are floating objects anchored in one part of a harbor, river, or other place where there are boats. Some are meant for tying up boats, but most are signals. They point out dangerous things like wrecks or mark the edges of the channels where it is safe to sail. In our waters a red buoy marks the right side of a channel as you face the land from the sea, and a black one marks the left side. Some buoys have flashing lights, bells, or whistles. SEE ALSO: LIGHTHOUSES AND LIGHTSHIPS.

BURMA

Burma is about the size of Texas, but has more than 31.5 million people, almost three times the number of Texans. This country, lying on the Bay of Bengal in southeast Asia, is cut off from surrounding lands (China, India, Laos, and Thailand) by high mountain ranges. More than half of Burma is tropical jungle, where teakwood grows. The Irrawaddy River flows through the country,

making a fertile plain for the growing of rice, cotton, rubber, and sugar-cane, the chief exports.

The Burmese follow the Buddhist religion. They lived under the rule of the Mongols from China in the 14th century. The British conquered them and made them part of the British Empire in the 1800s. After World War II, the people became free and established an independent republic. Most Burmese live in small villages, but more than 2 million live in Rangoon, the capital and major seaport.

Robert BURNS (1759–1796)

Robert Burns is Scotland's most beloved poet. He wrote about patriotism, love, and nature in the Scottish dialect. His birthday is often celebrated in Scotland by a special "Burns' Dinner" on January 25th each year.

He was the oldest in a family of seven children, all of whom worked hard on their father's farm. His father encouraged Robert to read and write in his spare time. At 15, he started writing poems himself, though none of them was published until he was 27.

Because he had been unsuccessful in farming and writing, he thought of going to live in Jamaica in the West Indies. To get money for the trip, Burns published his poems himself. They were an immediate success, so much so that he decided not to leave Scotland.

136

He then returned to farming but could not make it pay. To support his family, he became a tax collector but continued to write more and more poetry. The Scots loved his poems that accurately described their rural life. At 37, Burns died after a severe attack of rheumatic fever.

Among the most familiar poems in the English language are Burns' "Auld Lang Syne," "Comin' thro' the Rye," and "The Jolly Beggars." Many of his verses have been put to song.

BUS

People have been able to hire vehicles with drivers since the 17th century. These are what we call cabs or taxis. But in 1829, an Englishman began to run large carriages on special routes that would take any passenger who wanted to board for a small fare. He called his carriages *omnibuses*, from the Latin words meaning "for all." Now we say "buses."

Buses were almost all horse-drawn until early in this century. A few steam stagecoaches ran in England in the 1830s, but not for long. By 1905, there were motor buses in some cities. They soon began to put the trolley companies out of business because of their advantages. Then they started to go from city to city, and began to offer cheaper service than the railroads did. Today there are very many bus lines, which carry passengers, packages, and mail everywhere. SEE ALSO: AUTOMOBILE, TRANSPORTATION.

BUSINESS

A business is any activity in which people pay for something they get. An INDUSTRY makes things or does things for many people, who pay for them. A PROFESSION provides a service for people. Both an industry and a profession are businesses, because money changes hands as part of the activity.

COMMERCE is also part of business. Commerce is the selling of things rather than the making or doing of things. A merchant, who runs a store, is in a commerce (or *trade*), and is thus a businessman. SEE ALSO: COMMERCE, INDUSTRY, PROFESSION.

BUTTER

When milk or cream is agitated or churned (stirred rapidly), tiny globules of fat in the milk or cream unite to form a soft whitish or yellowish substance known as butter. Butter is used in cooking and as a spread on bread.

Butter has been known since about 2000 B.C. In ancient times, it was used less as a food than as an ointment for the bath and as a medicine. The old way of making butter was to put milk in skin pouches, which were then thrown back and forth by hand or by a trotting horse (the pouches were tied to the horse's back). Later, different kinds of hand churns were used. About 1850, the cream separator was invented, which started large-scale butter making. Today, enormous churns that hold hundreds of gallons of cream rotate rapidly, turning the cream with some cold water added into butter.

Afterward, special machines "wash" the butter and remove the excess water. The butter is usually cut into 1 pound (.45 kg) or .25 pound (.11 kg) sticks and wrapped in grease-proof paper to be sold in the supermarkets.

Among the leading producers of butter are New Zealand, Australia, Russia, Denmark, and Canada.

BUTTERFLIES

Butterflies are INSECTS. Like MOTHS, they have three parts to their bodies: the head, thorax (chest), and abdomen. Their legs and wings are connected to the thorax, as you can see in the picture.

Most butterflies have colorful wings. The wings' undersides are, however, much duller in color. This helps them to escape notice when their wings are folded together and they are still.

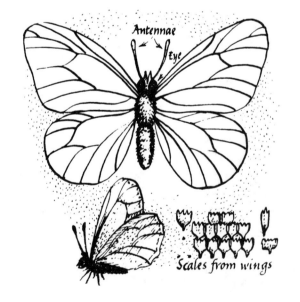

Antennae

Eye

Scales from wings

Peacock

Red
Admiral

Tortoise-
shell

Orange
Tip

Brimstone

Swallow-tail

Small
Copper

Painted
Lady

Wall

Meadow
Brown

Common
Blue

Comma

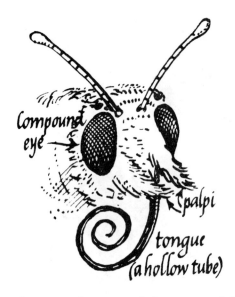

The wings are covered with tiny scales which come off if the insect is handled. These scales, like those greatly magnified in the illustration, contain red, yellow, black, and white pigments, which give the wings their beautiful coloration.

The butterfly has two big eyes, which are *compound* eyes. Each eye is really made up of thousands of tiny eyes. This kind of eye allows the butterfly to see any danger in any direction.

Many butterflies have long, hollow tongues, which they use to suck the nectar (juice) from flowers.

Butterflies lay their eggs on plants which the young caterpillars can eat. These eggs are very small but often beautiful in design. The eggs of the peacock butterfly are shown here. The small caterpillars that hatch out of the eggs grow quite rapidly as they eat. Several times they shed their skins. When they are fully developed, they shed their skins for the final time and turn into *chrysalises*. The chrysalises hang from leaves, twigs, and branches by strands of silk.

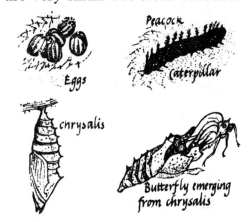

Inside the chrysalis, the body changes into the adult form. Usually in two or three weeks, the chrysalis bursts and a new butterfly emerges. Its crumpled wings gradually unfold as "blood" flows into them. When the wings are fully opened, the butterfly usually flies off and eventually begins the life cycle again from egg to caterpillar to butterfly. SEE ALSO: CATERPILLARS, MOTHS.

Richard E. BYRD (1888–1957)

Richard E. Byrd, the most famous modern American explorer, showed signs at an early age of having an adventuresome spirit. At the age of 12, he left his home in Winchester, Virginia, and circumnavigated the globe—alone.

As a cadet at the U.S. Naval Academy, Byrd was always ready to be the first to accept difficult challenges regardless of physical risk. Because two severe athletic injuries weakened his leg, he was unable to continue his career at sea because he could not stand the strain of long hours on watch. He convinced the Navy to let him fly, and by 1918 he had become a naval aviator. In 1925, he commanded an expedition to Greenland and explored 30,000 square miles (77,700 km²). In 1926, he and his co-pilot, Floyd Bennett, were the first men to fly over the NORTH POLE.

In 1929, he and his crew were the first men to fly over the dogsled trail made by Amundsen to the SOUTH POLE. A grateful Congress promoted him to rear admiral. By his last expedition in 1956, he had mapped approximately 500,000 square miles (1,295,000 km²) of the icy continent, and he had discovered two major mountain ranges there. He spent many months alone in his hut, and had many experiences that nearly cost him his life.

CABBAGE

Cabbage is a leafy garden vegetable. There are many different varieties of cabbage, all developed from the wild, or sea, cabbage. The best known varieties include the common cabbage, Chinese cabbage, cauliflower, broccoli, Brussels sprouts, kale, and kohlrabi.

They all grow well in cool, moist climates. The true cabbages are the white, red, and Savoy type with its curly, loose leaves. Sauerkraut and coleslaw are made from cabbage.

U.S. CABINET

The President of the U.S. has a group of advisers known as his Cabinet. Each adviser is also the head of a government department, such as the State, Justice, or Energy Department. Today the President's Cabinet consists of 12 department heads. They are the Secretary of State, of Defense, of the Treasury, of Commerce, of the Interior, of Agriculture, of Labor, of Health, Education, and Welfare, of Housing and Urban Development, of Transportation, of Energy, and the Attorney General.

The President appoints his Cabinet members with the approval of the U.S. Senate and may remove them when he wants to. They meet in the White House in the Cabinet room, next to the President's office. Sometimes other government officials are given so-called Cabinet level positions but do not head departments. These people help the President deal with new problems. The Director of the Office of Management and Budget and the U.S. Ambassador of the United Nations are two such people with Cabinet rank. SEE ALSO: PRESIDENCY.

CABLES

A cable is a heavy rope. Some cables are made of hemp or nylon, like the hawsers that tie ships to a wharf or that are used for pulling barges. Other cables are ropes of steel wire. Suspension bridges are hung from such ropes. Special cars travel back and forth on a wire hung from the towers of the bridge, carrying the light wires that are bound together to make the bridge cable.

A cable can also be a heavy wire for carrying electricity. Telephone messages, television programs, and electricity for homes and factories pass along cables across the country or under the street. Most cables are *insulated* (wrapped in something that keeps electricity from escaping), but some are not. These are kept away from other objects by insulators, supports that will not carry electricity.

Houses should be wired with armored cable. This has a tough outer layer that keeps animals in the walls or other things from getting through the insulation and letting the electricity out.

Rope cable

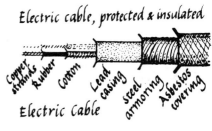
Electric cable, protected & insulated

Copper strands   Rubber   Cotton   Lead casing   Steel armoring   Asbestos covering
Electric Cable

John CABOT (1450–1498)

John Cabot was born in Italy (probably Genoa), as Giovanni Caboto. Cabot migrated to Bristol, England, in the 1480s.

Like Columbus, Cabot believed that the Earth was round, and, with permission from King Henry VII of England, he sailed from Bristol in May, 1497. With a crew of only 18, he set out in the *Mathew*, a ship of 100 tons (91 metric tons). Later that year, he landed on Cape Breton Island, Nova Scotia, and claimed the area for Henry VII, who rewarded Cabot when he returned.

In 1498, he again sailed to America, this time with two ships and 300 men. Seeking a route to Japan, he sailed north along the coast of GREENLAND, until a mutinous crew and icebergs forced him southward. He sailed along hundreds of miles of North American coast, noting in his logbook NEWFOUNDLAND and Cape Cod. Failing to find the oriental trade route and with supplies low, at the latitude of the Chesapeake Bay, Maryland, he turned back to England. Many English claims in North America were based on his exploration.

His son, Sebastian, was an explorer and map-maker in the 1500s. After several voyages to North and South America, he founded a trading company in 1553 and sent an expedition to seek a Northwest Passage to Asia. It reached Russia, and trade began between that country and England.

CACTI

Cacti are plants adapted to living in the hot, dry climate of the desert. Their structure is adapted to an environment where water is scarce. Most have no leaves to give off a lot of water vapor. The thick juicy stems store water and have prickly spines to protect them from thirsty plant-eating desert animals. Their deep roots soak up all available moisture from the ground.

There are 1500 species of cacti; they come in many different sizes and shapes. The giant cactus or saguaro of Arizona (shown at the top of the illustration) is the largest and often grows 40 feet (12.4 km)

143

tall. The Prickly Pear cactus is found in many deserts. Its pear-shaped fruit is very refreshing and can be used to make a jelly tasting much like apple jelly. The Prickly Pear was introduced into Australia, where it spread rapidly, and only recently was brought under control.

Miniature cacti make good house plants. Florists cultivate the Christmas cactus and the orchid cactus for their showy blossoms.

Julius CAESAR (102?–44 B.C.)

Although Julius Caesar was a nobleman from one of the oldest, upper-class families in Rome, he became very popular with the common people. He entered politics as a young man and quickly rose through the ranks, until in 59 B.C., he was elected Consul. With Pompey and Crassus, he ruled Rome and its provinces.

He became the Governor of Gaul, the country known as France today, and commanded a superior Roman army there. Because of Caesar's military genius and his personal interest in his army, he was able to bring all Gaul under Roman control and to acquire strong loyalty from his soldiers. Caesar wrote a very clear account of his wars against the Gauls, entitled *De Bello Gallico* (The Gallic Wars). Boys and girls who are studying Latin often read this book.

Caesar's victories and popular support made Pompey and the senate jealous at Rome. Caesar was ordered by the Roman senate to disband his army or be declared an enemy of the people. With his soldiers, Caesar in 49 B.C. crossed the Rubicon, the stream marking his province, and marched to Rome. For four years he waged war, defeating Pompey's soldiers in Spain, North Africa, and Asia Minor. By 45 B.C., Caesar controlled a huge territory that later became known as the Roman Empire. The Roman government made him dictator.

Caesar now set out to reform living conditions of the people and to rule wisely. He pardoned all his enemies and then passed new farming laws. He built a public library and devised the Julian calendar.

His success and power aroused the jealousy of other great men in Rome, who conspired against him. On March 15 (the Ides of March), 44 B.C., Caesar was stabbed to death in the senate house. Eventually his grandnephew, Octavian, took control of the Roman Empire and ruled as Augustus Caesar.

CAIRO

Cairo, the capital of EGYPT, rests beside the Nile River and is today the largest city in Africa. It is a blend of the ancient and modern cultures. There are donkeys, camels, and carts on narrow, twisting streets, and there are modern cars racing along wide avenues.

In the 7th century, when the Arabs spread over North Africa, Cairo became their capital. It was the Egyptian capital from the late 10th century to 1517, when the Turks took control of Egypt. During the CRUSADES in the 12th century, the famous Muslim leader, Saladin, built a strong fortress there to protect the people. Later, the French and British occupied Cairo during the 19th and 20th centuries.

The Great Pyramids and the SPHINX stand across the Nile to the west, at Gizeh, about 10 miles (16 km) from Cairo. SEE ALSO: EGYPT.

CALENDAR

Until 1752, English-speaking countries used the Julian calendar. This way of reckoning the days of the year was set up by Julius CAESAR in the first century B.C. The astronomer who advised him said that the year was just 365.25 days long, but this was wrong. A year is 365 days, 5 hours, 48 minutes, and 46 seconds long. In the 16th century, the year was off by 10 days. Pope Gregory established the Gregorian calendar in 1582 to correct this. He simply dropped out 10 days. When the English government began to use the Gregorian calendar in 1752, they took out 11 days. September 14th came right after September 2nd. People did not understand that they would live 11 days "longer" at the end and demanded their lost days back.

The names of the months are very old. September through December are taken from the Roman words for 7th, 8th, 9th, and 10th. At some point, July and August, named after Julius and Augustus Caesar, were put in before September. The days of the week have old Saxon and Danish names for gods. The QUAKERS objected to the usual names as un-Christian. They preferred to say Second Month, Fourth Day, etc.

Christians reckon the years from the birth of Christ. Years before this event are years B.C. (before Christ). These years are counted *backward*: 45 B.C. comes before 44. Years after his birth are labeled A.D. (*anno Domini*: year of the Lord). The scholar who calculated the birth of Christ seems to have been wrong because Christ was probably born in 4 B.C. Orthodox Jews count the years from the founding of the world, which was assumed to have been in 3760 B.C. Some Jews who use the Christian system say C.E. (common era) instead of A.D. The Muslims count their years from the Hegira, the flight of Muhammad from Mecca in 622 A.D. The Greeks dated their calendar from the first OLYMPIC GAMES in 776 B.C. And the Romans dated theirs from the supposed founding of ROME in 753 B.C.

CALIFORNIA

From the fir-covered Klamath Mountains in the north to the hot Mojave Desert in the south, California is a land of contrasts. It has Mount Whitney, the highest point in the U.S., outside Alaska, and Death Valley, the lowest point in the Western Hemisphere. California's fertile Central Valley is surrounded by mountain ranges, including the high Sierra Nevada and the Coast Range. Great extremes mark the climate, with many parts having almost no rainfall. Other sections have cold winters and heavy rain, especially in the northern mountains. California is subject to earthquakes caused by the San Andreas fault, and yet the state is the most populous, with about 22 million people.

Manufacturing is the chief industry, and California produces much oil and natural gas. It is the nation's leader in growing citrus fruits and vegetables. Other important activities are real estate, television, movie-making, and tourism.

Sir Francis Drake claimed California for England in 1579, but the first permanent settlement was made by the Spanish in 1769. The region became a

Mexican province in 1822. Soon Americans were settling there, and Mexico finally gave up its claim in 1848. Then gold was discovered at Sutter's Mill, near Coloma, touching off the California Gold Rush of 1849. SAN FRANCISCO grew fast as a boom town, and vigilante groups tried to keep law and order. In 1850, California was admitted to the Union.

Sacramento is the capital, and LOS ANGELES, San Francisco, and San Diego are the principal cities. SEE ALSO: LOS ANGELES, SAN FRANCISCO.

CAMBRIDGE

Cambridge, England, is most famous as the site of Cambridge University. The oldest *college* (division) of the university is Peterhouse, founded in the 13th century. During the following centuries many other colleges were begun, and in the last 100 years three colleges for women were built (Newnham, Girton, and New Hall).

Much of the present town of Cambridge still has a medieval atmosphere and appearance, with old inns, houses, churches, and winding, narrow streets.

CAMEL

There are two species of camel: the single-humped dromedary of Arabia and North Africa and the two-humped Bactrian camel of central Asia. Camels store fat in their humps and excess water in special cells lining their stomachs. A thirsty camel can drink 20 gallons (75.8 liters) of water at one time.

Camels have long necks, small ears, and strong teeth. Their broad, flat, thick-soled cloven hoofs do not sink into the sands of the desert. Without camels, large desert regions could not be inhabited. Used as beasts of burden for thousands of years, they can generally carry loads of about 500 pounds (225 kg).

The wild guanaco and vicuña and the domesticated alpaca and llama of South America are distant relatives of the camel.

CAMERA

Pictures are taken on rolls of film or on glass plates chemically treated to record light and darkness. Here is an ordinary small camera. You hold it in your hand, and look through the *viewfinder* until you see just the picture you want to take. Then you press the lever (L). This allows the *shutter* (S) to open for a fraction of a second. Light then passes through the lens from the object you are photographing in

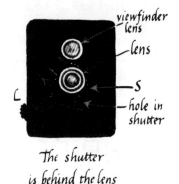

The shutter is behind the lens

such a way that a picture of the object, upside down, is recorded on the film. Modern films record the appearance of the object very quickly, and the time the shutter is open must be just right.

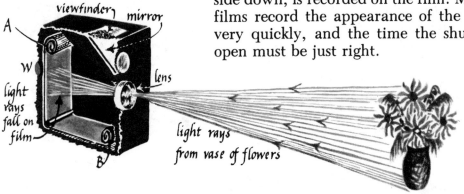

When you have taken your picture, you must wind the film a little way down. It begins on spool A and when all your pictures are taken it will be on spool B. To show you how far to wind, a strip of paper on the back of the film carries numbers. You look for these through the little window W. This window is of a special color so as not to *expose* (cause change in) the film.

CANADA

Canada is one of the independent members of the British Commonwealth of Nations. It is nearly the same size as Europe, and only Russia is larger as a country. However, Canada's population of more than 23 million is less than one-twentieth that of Europe's. The capital is OTTAWA in southeastern Ontario.

Canada occupies all of the North American continent that is north of the United States except for Alaska and the small French islands of St. Pierre and Miquelon. It is a confederation of 10 provinces—Newfoundland, Nova Scotia, Prince Edward Island, New Brunswick, Quebec, Ontario, Manitoba, Saskatchewan, Alberta, and British Columbia—and two territories—the Yukon and the Northwest Territories. Canada and the U.S. are separated by the longest undefended border in the world, marked in part by the GREAT LAKES.

Canada

In the west, the ROCKY MOUNTAINS, ranging from 9000 to 19,000 feet high (2790-5890 m), form a wide belt that stretches from Alaska into the U.S. Eastern Canada is not so elevated, with most highlands not exceeding 4000 feet (1240 m). The interior, extending from the Arctic Ocean to the ST. LAWRENCE SEAWAY, is a great rolling plain that slopes toward Hudson Bay, a shallow but large inland sea.

The INDIANS and ESKIMOS inhabited the land long before the Vikings tried unsuccessfully to settle on Newfoundland about 1000 years ago. In 1497, JOHN CABOT touched the east coast, claiming it for Britain. Jacques Cartier, in 1534, explored the St. Lawrence River and planted the French flag on the Gaspé Peninsula in Quebec. In 1604, Samuel de Champlain founded the first permanent settlement in Canada, on the Bay of Fundy in Nova Scotia. In the 17th and 18th centuries, the

149

French and British continued to explore, make claims, and settle much of southern Canada from the Atlantic to the Pacific. Finally, war broke out between Britain and France over control of Canada. In 1759, the British General Wolfe and the French General Montcalm battled on the Plains of Abraham near Quebec. Both were killed, but the British won, and four years later France gave up its claims in Canada. Today, however, more than six million inhabitants speak French, mostly in the province of Quebec.

In the west, British Columbia borders the Pacific Ocean, having a climate rather like that of the British Isles. It is not too cold or too hot, with plenty of rain for growing fruit. Cedar, pine, and fir trees grow abundantly in its mountains, and LUMBERING is a leading industry. Copper, silver, lead, zinc, and oil are found here, and large amounts of aluminum are produced with the help of huge hydroelectric plants.

To the east, we find the province of Alberta with its enormous oil and coking coal reserves. Further east are the vast prairies of Saskatchewan and Manitoba, where wheat is grown and exported around the world. Here it is hot and dry in summer but bitterly cold in winter.

Plenty of oil has recently been found under the prairies

In Ontario and Quebec (in cities like TORONTO and MONTREAL) are found the largest number of people and the biggest manufacturing plants. Here, also, are rich dairy farms and cattle lands. In the northern woods there are ample trees that provide thousands of tons of pulp used to manufacture paper. To the north of the Great Lakes is a region with much copper, asbestos, zinc, gold, oil, and nickel. A great URANIUM producing district is located in the Northwest Territories. It has a rich fishing industry along the Atlantic coast, and it has more than 1 million square miles (2,590,000 km²) of forests. SEE ALSO: INDIVIDUAL CANADIAN PROVINCES.

CANAL

A canal is really a man-made river. It may be dug to take water to or away from an area of land, or to make a path for ships and boats.

Canals have been very important to some countries. The so-called canals of VENICE are natural, since Venice is built on many islands. The canals of HOLLAND were made for boats and also to drain off the water from the low-lying areas. England, France, and Russia have thousands of miles of canals, built to allow *barges* (freight boats) to carry goods in the days when roads were bad and there were no railroads.

Cape Cod Canal

New York State Barge Canal

Chicago Sanitary and Ship Canal

Gulf Intracoastal Waterway

Intracoastal Waterway

Canals were important in the United States 150 years ago. The famous Erie Canal, opened in 1825, helped make New York City a great seaport. Farmers in the new western states shipped their products from Buffalo to Albany. From there they were shipped down the Hudson River. Goods the farmers needed went back along the canal. In 1834, a canal was built between Philadelphia and Pittsburg, Pennsylvania. It had 37 miles (59 km) of railroad to haul the canal boats ove the Appalachian Mountains. Lake Erie and the Ohio River were connected by a canal in the 1830s. These canals helped the settlement of the West before there were railroads. At one time the United States had 4000 miles (6400 km) of canals. Most of these were abandoned when the railroads offered faster service.

Some canals carry ships from place to place, for instance the Panama Canal, the Suez Canal between the Mediterranean and the Red Seas, and the canals of the St. Lawrence Seaway in Canada.

Canal Locks

Some canals are level from end to end but some climb high ground by means of LOCKS. These are places shut off by waterproof gates. A boat enters the lock, and water is let into the lock from above if it is going uphill, and out of the lock if it is going downhill. The boat rises or falls gently as the water pours. SEE ALSO: LOCKS (ON CANALS).

CANARY

Canaries are small birds of the finch family. They are sometimes kept in cages as pets. In the late 15th century, canaries were brought from the Canary Islands, Madeira, and the Azores to Europe. The wild birds are gray or green in color. However, careful breeding has produced yellow, buff, and sometimes greenish canaries.

They eat mainly grain, seed, and millet. They can be trained to sing. In captivity, canaries breed rapidly and live to be 15 or more years old.

CANARY ISLANDS

These islands lie about 65 miles (105 km) off the northwest coast of Africa. The seven main islands are all mountain peaks of volcanic origin. The two main cities are the ports of Las Palmas, on Grand Canary, and Santa Cruz, on Tenerife, which also has Mt. Teide, more than 12,000 feet (3720 m) high.

Tenerife

The Canaries have belonged to Spain since the 1400s. The people have the same customs, language, and religion as the Spanish, and they make their living by growing bananas, sugar cane, and tobacco, as well as by fishing.

The Romans named the islands "Insulas Canarias" (islands of the dogs), for wild dogs once roamed there. "Canary" comes from *canis*, the Latin word meaning "dog." Later, the birds on the islands were named canaries.

CANDLES

Candles have been used since ancient Roman times. They are a handy sort of light, easy to carry. They burn with a steady flame if kept out of drafts.

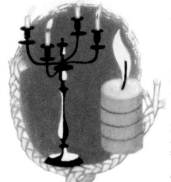

Candles have been used as clocks. If marked with lines in the right places the flame will burn down so as to mark the time. Today, candles are used mostly to give a pleasant light at dinner or at parties. Almost everyone has electricity for regular lighting.

In the past, candles were made of tallow (made from sheep's fat) or beeswax. Such candles were expensive, and few people could afford to light a house brightly with them. Most people used oil lamps or torches, or even relied on firelight. In the early 19th century, candles were made from a substance found in a certain kind of whale. Later, it was found that a product of oil refineries could be made into a cheap wax. The earliest candles were often made by dipping the wick again and again in hot wax. Now, all candles are made in molds. Most modern candles are made of *stearin*, which comes from tallow, and *paraffin*, a mineral wax. Wicks are generally made of woven cord. An interesting thing about the wick: one of its threads is made tighter than the others so that it will curl down at the end and burn more slowly.

CANNIBALS

A cannibal is a person who eats human flesh. The practice of eating flesh has existed since ancient times, but the name "cannibal" originated when COLUMBUS discovered the West Indies, where there was a man-eating tribe called the Caribales, after whom the Caribbean Sea and islands were later named.

Some cannibals eat human flesh for food, as we eat the flesh of animals. Others eat it because they believe the strength and courage of the killed person will become theirs if they eat it. Others eat it during a religious ceremony, at which a human being is killed. Most cannibals eat only certain parts of the body.

Cannibalism was practiced in North America by the Atakapa Indians and by tribes living along the Gulf of Mexico. The Aztec Indians in Mexico ate people after first sacrificing them to their gods. There are still cannibals in some parts of Africa, Australia, and Central America.

CANNON

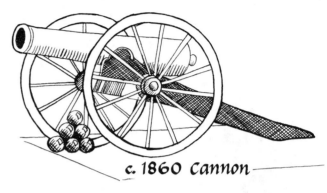

c. 1860 Cannon

Ancient and medieval armies had *catapults*, machines that used springs or weights to hurl stones and arrows. In the 14th century, the cannon first appeared. This was a metal tube that hurled balls with explosions of gunpowder.

The early cannons were made of bronze or iron, and were *muzzle-loading* (loaded at the end toward the enemy). In the 19th century, steel cannons were invented that were *breech-loading* (loaded at the end toward the gunners). This was a big improvement. Instead of the solid balls used for centuries, these guns fired *shells*, pointed missiles filled with explosive. These went further, pierced through armor, and exploded. SEE ALSO: GUN.

CANOE

Canoes are small light boats that are paddled, not rowed. In paddling, the boatman faces forward, holding the paddle upright and pushing back on the water.

The Indians made very light canoes of wooden ribs and birch bark for use on streams and lakes. Today, canoes of this sort are often covered with aluminum or some other factory-made material. The Eskimos use *kayaks*, covered with skin. These are one-man canoes for use in open water. They have two-bladed paddles.

CANTERBURY

Canterbury has been the spiritual center of ENGLAND for a long time. When St. Augustine in A.D. 597 came from Rome to convert the people of Britain to Christianity, he founded an abbey at Canterbury and became the first archbishop.

The first cathedral was burned and rebuilt several times in the 10th and 11th centuries. The first Norman archbishop, Lanfranc, began to erect a much larger cathedral in 1070. This huge church was partially destroyed by fire, but rebuilt and improved during the following centuries.

Visitors to Canterbury can see other fine old buildings and walls built in the Middle Ages. King's School, founded around A.D. 600, and a modern university are located here.

During World War II, much of the cathedral and many other buildings suffered heavy bomb damage. Traces of the old Roman city were then uncovered.

West Gate

CAPE

A cape is a piece of land that sticks out into the sea.

Cape Cod is a famous one in Massachusetts. Other well-known capes in the world include Cape Hatteras in North Carolina, Cape Verde on the extreme western point of Africa, Cape Comorin at the southern end of India, and Cape St. Vincent on the southwestern edge of Portugal.

A very famous cape is Cape Horn at the southernmost tip of South America. Its headland is a rock 1390 feet (431 m) high, first sighted by Sir Francis Drake in 1578. The Cape of Good Hope is located near the southern tip of South Africa. It rises almost 1000 feet (310 m) above the sea, and was discovered in 1488 by Bartholomew Diaz, who first named it the Cape of Storms.

A cape is also a sleeveless outer garment that fits closely at the neck and hangs loosely from the shoulders.

CAPE TOWN

Cape Town is the legislative capital of SOUTH AFRICA, situated on the Atlantic Ocean 30 miles (48 km) north of the Cape of Good Hope. It is also South Africa's oldest city and chief port.

It was founded in 1652 by the Dutch, who used it as a supply station on their trade route to the East. The British captured it in 1806 and made it the capital of the British Cape Colony.

155

As it grew, the city was rebuilt with modern streets and buildings. It is important in commerce and manufacturing. Gold and diamonds are exported from Cape Town, and fruits, wool, skins, and corn have a thriving market there. Its beautiful location on Table Bay, with Table Mountain rising behind it, and its mild climate have brought many tourists, creating a big resort industry. SEE ALSO: SOUTH AFRICA.

CARBON

Carbon is one of the most important ELEMENTS in the world. All living things, plants and animals, are made up of carbon. Because carbon unites chemically with so many other elements, a special branch of chemistry (called *organic* chemistry) was established to deal with the half million COMPOUNDS of carbon.

Most carbon compounds have been made in the last century; more are being discovered each year. Everything we eat, except salt and water, contains carbon. Nylon, plastics, and petroleum are carbon compounds too.

Soot, coke, and charcoal are almost pure forms of carbon. Pure carbon can be black, but *graphite,* which is a form of carbon, is metallic gray in color. Graphite is the "lead" in our lead pencils. Because of its arrangement of atoms, the layers of graphite slide easily over one another; its smooth, slippery quality makes it a good lubricant. Diamonds, formed deep within the earth, are a very hard form of carbon. They are clear and colorless. Because of their extreme hardness, they are used in drills.

When carbon is joined with other elements, its identity is hidden. However, when a material, such as toast, is burned, the black scorching that results is the carbon revealing itself.

Plants make food from the carbon dioxide that is in the air. Animals breathe it out

Some carbon compounds are extremely complex. The hemoglobin that makes our blood red contains 758 atoms of carbon, 1203 of hydrogen, 218 of oxygen, 135 of nitrogen, 3 of sulphur, and just 1 of iron.

An important simple compound of carbon also vital for life is carbon dioxide. For each MOLECULE of carbon dioxide, there are one atom of carbon and two of oxygen. As we grow and move, the substances providing fuel for our bodies are burned. The carbon that remains joins with the oxygen breathed in and is breathed out as carbon dioxide.

Plants use carbon dioxide in the air to manufacture their food.

CARIBBEAN SEA

The Caribbean is an extension of the Atlantic Ocean and borders the east coast of CENTRAL AMERICA, the islands of the WEST INDIES, and the north coast of South America.

This sea was once a favorite hunting ground for PIRATES. Hiding among the many inlets, they waited to attack the ships returning home laden with treasure from the New World.

Now, many ships cross the Caribbean to pass through the busy PANAMA CANAL. Coffee, bananas, and oil are in their cargoes. Cruise ships also travel to this sea, for the area provides a pleasant, warm, winter vacation setting.

However, these waters still bear constant watching by sea captains. Although pirates no longer exist, the Caribbean is the area where dangerous hurricanes blow in from the Atlantic and undersea mountains can cause ships to run aground.

Andrew CARNEGIE (1835–1919)

Born in Scotland, Andrew Carnegie settled with his poor family near Pittsburgh, Pennsylvania, in 1848. As a boy, he worked hard in a cotton factory. Later, he became a telegraph operator and a superintendent on the Pennsylvania Railroad. He saved his money and invested in oil lands and in iron and steel factories. Realizing the future importance of steel, Carnegie began to build and acquire steel companies. In 1899, he combined his businesses to form the Carnegie Steel Company, which made one quarter of the nation's steel using the new Bessemer process. His company controlled iron mines, coke ovens, ore ships, and railroads. Carnegie's genius lay in being an efficient organizer and administrator of business.

In 1901, he retired, selling his business to the United States Steel Corporation for $250 million. Carnegie believed that a rich man should, after providing for his family, use his money to help mankind. He thus gave away about $350 million to found public libraries, museums, and schools and to promote scientific research and international peace.

CARPETS and RUGS

A *carpet* is a large covering of heavy cloth for a floor. A *rug* is a small carpet. The first carpets were brought to Europe about 800 years ago from western Asia. People at that time sometimes hung them on walls, and later they often used them as tablecloths.

Handmade carpets are made in Iran, Turkey, Pakistan, and China. Tufts of wool thread are knotted into stretched threads called *warps*. The tufts rise above the warps to make a fuzzy *pile* in patterns of different colors. Each country has its own group of patterns and colors. To make such a carpet means tying thousands of knots, so they are very expensive.

A corner of a Persian Carpet

Most modern carpets are made by huge machines, able to weave wide areas from wool or synthetic fiber. Such carpeting can be found almost everywhere today.

Lewis CARROLL (1832–1898)

Lewis Carroll was the author of *Alice's Adventures in Wonderland* and *Through the Looking Glass*. His real name was Charles Lutwidge Dodgson.

He graduated from Oxford University and became a mathematics teacher there. He wrote several important books about mathematics, but only when *Alice's Adventures in Wonderland* was published in 1865 under his pseudonym (fictitious name used by a writer to conceal his identity) did he become famous.

This story was first told to a group of friends which included Alice Liddell, the daughter of the dean of Carroll's college. They were the first to hear about "Alice," the little girl who falls down a hole and discovers a strange and wonderful world. Alice meets many strange characters: the Mad Hatter, the March Hare, the White Rabbit, the Mock Turtle, and the Queen of Hearts.

Carroll's books were illustrated by a famous artist, Sir John Tenniel. Today, his drawings are as popular as the stories.

Kit CARSON (1809–1868)

Christopher ("Kit") Carson was an American frontiersman and Western scout. At the age of one year, he moved with his parents from Kentucky to Missouri. Later, he learned to make saddles and other pieces of equipment for horses.

In 1826, Carson joined a group of hunters heading for Santa Fe, New Mexico, and from that time on he devoted himself to hunting, trapping, and traveling, mainly in California and the Rockies.

He served as a hunter and guide for the Fremont expeditions to California in the 1840s. In 1854, he was appointed Indian agent for the Utahs and Apaches at Taos, New Mexico.

During the CIVIL WAR, Carson served in New Mexico, Colorado, the Indian Territory, and Texas, and fought against the Navahos. In 1865, he became a brigadier general.

Founded in 1858, Carson City, Nevada, was named in his honor. It has the distinction of being the smallest state capital in the United States.

Jimmy CARTER (born 1924)

In 1976, James Earl Carter, Jr., was elected the 39th President of the United States. He became the first man from the Deep South to win the PRESIDENCY since the Civil War. (Senator Walter F. Mondale of Minnesota was elected Vice President.)

Carter graduated from the U.S. Naval Academy in 1946 and served in the Navy for the next seven years. He then returned to his hometown, Plains, in Georgia, and built up his family's peanut farming and warehousing business. In 1962, he became a state senator and was reelected two years later. Elected governor of Georgia in 1970, Carter reorganized the state's government.

Barred by Georgia's law from reelection as governor, he spent more than a year campaigning for, and winning, the Democratic nomination for President. In a close presidential election, Carter beat the incumbent President, Gerald R. Ford. He has since concerned himself with problems of energy, welfare, consumer protection, human rights, and armaments, and the establishment of peace in the Middle East.

CARTHAGE

Carthage was one of the most famous cities of the ancient world. It lay near what is now modern Tunis, the capital of Tunisia, in northern Africa.

Where Carthage used to stand

According to legend, the city was founded by Queen Dido, a daughter of a king of Tyre. However, it really was founded by PHOENICIANS from Tyre in the 9th century B.C. Carthage grew to be a wealthy trading city-state that sent out ships to all parts of the Mediterranean. It dominated the area for about 300 years, ruling at various times over parts of Sicily, Sardinia, Spain, and North Africa.

The Carthaginians struggled against the Greeks for control of Sicily. Later, they were completely driven out of Sicily by the Romans, who had grown jealous of Carthage.

Carthage's most important leader was HANNIBAL. In 217 B.C., he crossed the Alps with his army and 50 elephants and invaded northern Italy. Hannibal nearly succeeded in defeating Rome, but he was recalled to Carthage in 203 B.C. to protect the city from an advancing Roman army.

During a later war, Carthage was utterly destroyed by the Romans. JULIUS CAESAR and Augustus, two Romans, later built a fine new city of Carthage, but the barbaric Vandals ruined it and then the Arabs totally destroyed it in A.D. 698. There are today almost no remains of ancient Carthage. Archeologists have discovered a few ancient cemeteries, shrines, and fortifications. Some Roman baths and building still stand. King Louis IX of France, while on a Crusade, died at Carthage in 1270. A chapel in his honor stands on Byrsa Hill, site of the ancient fortress. SEE ALSO: HANNIBAL.

George Washington CARVER (1864?–1943)

George Washington Carver became a great American chemist and agricultural expert. He discovered what the peanut, sweet potato, and soybean were made of. Later he combined the various parts of these plants with other substances to create many new products.

He was the son of a slave woman owned by Moses Carver. At about 12 years old, he left the Carver plantation in Missouri. He wandered about, supporting himself as a farm worker, hotel cook, and laundryman. He managed to get a high school education. After being refused entrance to one university because he was black, Carver entered Iowa State College, where he received two degrees in botany.

In 1896, he became head of the new department of agriculture at Tuskegee Institute, in Alabama. There he taught about soil improvement and plant diseases. He encouraged the cultivation of the peanut, the sweet potato, and the soybean. Later he contributed his life savings to establish a foundation for scientific research at Tuskegee.

CASTING

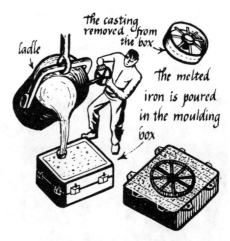

the casting removed from the box

ladle

The melted iron is poured in the moulding box

Casting is the process of pouring liquid material into a special hollow, called a *mold*, and letting the material harden.

It is possible to make casts of plaster or other cool material, but most castings are made of molten metal. The place where such castings are made is called a *foundry*. A *pattern* is made of the thing to be cast. This is an object of the exact same form. Sand or other material is built up around the pattern to make the mold. Then the pattern is removed, and the molten metal is poured in and allowed to harden. Hollow objects, like BELLS, need a *core*, a mold for the inside as well as the outside. This is put inside the outer mold, and the metal is poured between them. There are several ways of casting things, but all of them need a pattern and a mold.

CASTLE

A castle is a nobleman's home that can be defended against attack. Noblemen built them in most parts of Europe, and the Crusaders (see CRUSADES) built them in the Near East.

Early castles, in the 10th or 11th centuries, were built of wood and earth. Often a high mound of earth supported the lord's house. The mound was surrounded by a ditch. Often an outer wall enclosed a yard called a *bailey*.

Much cleverness went into attacking castles, and just as much cleverness went into making them too strong and complicated to capture. By the 12th century, castles were built of stone or brick. Instead of a central mound there was a *keep*, a tall and enormously strong tower where the lord lived. In the keep there was a hall (room for the whole household), a set of rooms for the lord's family, sleeping spaces for the servants and the defenders, and places for the supplies they needed to wait out the *siege* (attack on the castle). Outside the keep were one or more baileys, defended by stone *curtains* (walls) which had towers every here and there, and gatehouses to control the movement of people. The towers and walls had *crenelations* (places

for archers to hide) and *machicolations* (openings below the crenelations for dropping stones, hot liquids, and so on). The gatehouses had *portcullises* (heavy, sliding gates) and *drawbridges* (moving bridges) that could be pulled in or up from the *moats* (ditches full of water) outside the walls. The enemy tried to take the castle by digging under the walls, going onto the walls with ladders and towers, hurling stones from catapults, or waiting until the castle's food supply was gone.

By 1400, the castle was like a complicated fighting machine. Sometimes it could be pleasant inside. The lords had separate houses, and used the keep only during a siege. But the invention of CANNONS put an end to castle building. They could easily knock the walls down.

CAT

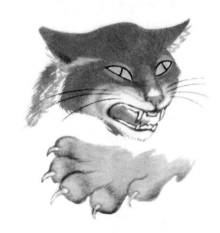

Egyptian tomb paintings show that cats have been tamed since 1500 B.C. The supposition that all domestic cats descended from those in Egypt is not certain but is most likely. Illustrated here are two of the better known house cats: the Siamese and the Persian.

The cat family also includes the LION, the TIGER, the LEOPARD, the cheetah, and the lynx. Like the house

Leopard

Siamese

Persian

Tiger

Lion

cat, they all have strong, sleek bodies for hunting. Their soft padded feet help them to move quietly. All except the cheetah can retract their claws when they are not needed. Their sharp teeth and claws help them tear apart their prey. The rough tongue helps to clean the bones of meat. At night when they hunt, the pupils of their eyes open wide; during the day their pupils are narrow slits. Their whiskers are very sensitive and aid them in hunting at night. They also have a very keen sense of hearing and smell.

The larger members of the cat family are found in the jungles or hot grasslands. The smaller cats are found almost everywhere.

CATERPILLAR

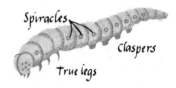

Caterpillars are one stage in the life cycle of BUTTERFLIES and MOTHS. There are four stages in the complete life cycle: egg, larva, pupa, and adult. Caterpillars are the larva stage.

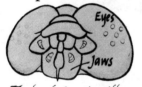

The head of a caterpillar

They chew their way out of the eggs and next begin chewing the plants on which the eggs were laid. The butterfly lays her eggs on plants the caterpillars later use for food.

These drawings illustrate the various body parts of a caterpillar. The large and powerful jaws chew sideways. There are twelve simple, tiny eyes. Three pairs of true legs, each ending in a claw, are located on the front three sections of the body. The other end usually has five pairs of stubby legs called *claspers*.

Each clasper ends with a soft pad edged with tiny hooks with which the caterpillar can grasp very firmly. There are nine pairs of breathing holes, known as *spiracles*, on the sides of the caterpillar's body. Below the mouth is the *spinneret*, a tube which squirts a sticky liquid which hardens into a silken thread. The caterpillar can get quickly from place to place by means of the thread.

As a butterfly eats, it grows quickly and sheds its skin several times. After about a month, it is ready for the pupa stage. The caterpillar seeks a suitable hiding place, attaches itself by a silken thread, and, when the skin splits for the last time, becomes a *chrysalis*. The soft skin of the chrysalis soon hardens into a tough, protective covering.

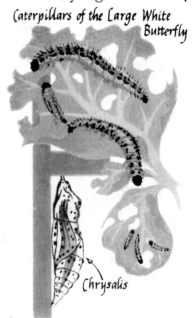

Caterpillars of the Large White Butterfly

Chrysalis

Inside the chrysalis is the pupa or resting stage. Body changes occur inside the pupa until the adult butterfly is ready to emerge in ten or more days. Or the chrysalis can last through the winter.

Caterpillars of moths spin *cocoons* around themselves before changing into a pupa.

Silk is obtained from the cocoon of the silk worm. SEE ALSO: BUTTERFLIES, MOTHS.

CATHEDRAL

A cathedral is the principal church of a BISHOP'S diocese, and so cathedrals are usually larger and more elaborate than local churches. It is called a *cathedral* because it is the place where a bishop worships, and the Latin name for a bishop's chair is *cathedra*. Cathedrals are most common in the Roman Catholic and the Episcopal churches.

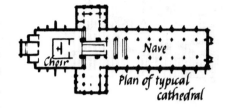
Plan of typical cathedral

Most cathedrals in the Middle Ages were laid out in the form of crosses. Inside, long *arcades* (rows of arches) led toward the main altars. Chapels (small rooms for worship) lined the *nave* (large auditorium for the worshippers) and *choir* (place for clergy). Outside, towers—often three of them—gave the cathedral great height. These towers were made of stone, but *spires* (steep, pointed roofs) often added more height still. The spire of cathedral of Lincoln, England, was over 500 feet (150 m) high, and was once the tallest building in the world.

Chartres Cathedral, France
12th-16th centuries

The cathedrals built in England, France, and Spain from the 13th through the 16th centuries are the most famous of all. They are mostly in the Gothic style, which uses pointed arches and high ceilings. Their system of flying buttresses (arch-like props) was some of the most daring engineering of the past. Sometimes there were collapses.

During the RENAISSANCE, church designers used round arches, classical columns, and round domes.

St. Patrick's Cathedral, New York City 19th century

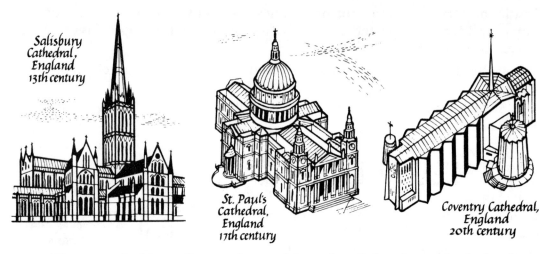

Salisbury
Cathedral,
England
13th century

St. Paul's
Cathedral,
England
17th century

Coventry Cathedral,
England
20th century

There are bishops all over the world, and each has his cathedral. There are cathedrals in the United States too. Saint John the Divine, the Protestant Episcopal cathedral in New York, is so gigantic that nobody knows how to finish it. It is 600 feet (180 m) long inside, and is full of gorgeous art. But the rough stonework shows where the builders have stopped.

CATHOLIC CHURCH
When we speak of the "Catholic Church," most people mean the Roman Catholic Church but actually it is many Latin and Oriental churches which have the same beliefs and the same government under the Bishop of Rome, Italy. He is called the *Pope* (from an Italian word that means "father"). He is elected by *cardinals* for the rest of his life.

The Catholic Church teaches that people are born in original sin, inherited from Adam, which Jesus removes through *grace* (a gift which places one in friendship with God). Catholics believe that a person can find grace through seven special encounters with God, which they call *sacraments*.

The first of these encounters is the sacrament of *baptism*. Water is poured on a new baby while the words of baptism are said. The child thus becomes a member of the Church.

At the age of seven, the Catholic child, for the first time, eats bread and drinks wine that Catholics believe are the body and blood of Jesus Christ. This is called the *Eucharist*, which is taken at formal acts of worship. About the age of twelve, the young Catholic makes a personal commitment to Christ in the sacrament of *confirmation*, in which the Holy Spirit comes in a special way.

In the sacrament of *penance* or reconciliation, a Catholic confesses his or her sins to a minister, the priest. The priest forgives these sins if the person is sorry for them and promises to serve God better.

166

If a Catholic person marries, a priest witnesses the ceremony because Catholics consider *marriage* to be a sacrament too. If a Catholic becomes a minister, he is ordained in a ceremony called *holy orders*, which is another sacrament.

Finally, when a Catholic person is dying, a priest will be called to give the *anointing of the sick*, which is another sacrament. In this ceremony the priest anoints the senses with oil, asking God to forgive any offenses these senses may have given Him.

There are about 145 million Catholics in North America and about 709 million in the whole world.

CAVES

People who explore caves are called *speleologists*, or sometimes *spelunkers*. Most people who explore caves, however, call themselves *cavers*.

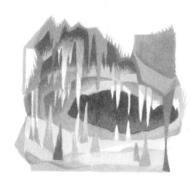

Cavers know that exploring caves can be dangerous, but there is the thrill for them of finding something new or of discovering something old. Many times they come upon unexpected beauty. Dripping water leaves mineral deposits that build forms we call STALACTITES AND STALAGMITES. Stalactites and stalagmites sometimes meet and form giant *columns* that go from the floor to the ceiling of the caves. Other formations, called *flowstone*, look like large curtains and draperies or like frozen waterfalls and cataracts.

Caves are natural openings in the Earth. They can be found in places that have many different types of rock, but they are generally found where limestone abounds. This is because limestone is easily dissolved by ground water containing carbon dioxide. Along shorelines, waves create another kind of cave. *Sea caves* are the result of one kind of *erosion:* the wearing away of rock by the constant movement of water against its surface.

One other kind of cave is the *lava cave*. When an outer crust has formed over molten (melted) lava and the molten lava later flows away, the outer crust, which was its roof, remains. The long cave or tunnel that is left under the crust is a lava cave.

Some caves are very small. Others are very large. Some caves have rivers flowing through them. In Mammoth Cave in Kentucky, visitors can take a short boat ride on its waterway, the Echo River, 360 feet (111.60 m) below the surface of the Earth.

The largest underground chamber discovered so far is at Carlsbad Caverns in New Mexico. This room is 4000 feet (1240 m) long, 625 feet (194 m) wide, and 350 feet (109 m) high.

CELLO

The cello (pronounced chel′ō) is a member of the VIOLIN family. In fact, it used to be called the violoncello. It has four strings, and is much larger than a violin. Its tone is lower than that of a violin. The *cellist* holds it by the neck and between the knees. A single pointed leg holds it up from the floor at the right distance for playing.

An earlier type of cello, in the 16th century, was called a *viola da gamba* (leg viol) because it was held the same way. The first cello was probably made by Andreas Amati of Verona, Italy.

CELLS

Cells are the "building blocks" of all life.

There are some microscopic plants (such as bacteria) and animals (such as the AMOEBA, illustrated here) that consist of only one cell. The body of the amoeba looks like a blob of jelly. It is so tiny that hundreds could fit on the period at the end of this sentence.

An Amoeba

nucleus

the amoeba is about to wrap itself around this speck of food.

Muscle cells

Nerve cells

Taste cells on the surface of the tongue

Most animals and plants, however, are very complex and consist of hundreds of thousands or millions of cells, which differ in shape and function. BLOOD is made up of red and white cells called corpuscles; the red cells carry oxygen to the body and the white cells fight infection. MUSCLE cells are long and thin, but have the power of making themselves shorter and thicker. NERVE cells pass messages through themselves by means of faint electric currents. The gray cells in our BRAINS make it possible for us to think.

Plants also have many different kinds of cells. All green LEAVES have a tough skin made up of small colorless cells packed closely together. Bigger cells lie underneath this layer and contain the green coloring matter, called *chlorophyll*, which enables the plant to produce its food from the carbon dioxide of the air. Thick-walled cells in the stems provide the plant with rigid support. Other cells form long tubes in which water rises to the top of the plant or food travels down from the leaves.

Most cells are microscopic in size, but the yolk or yellow of a hen's egg is one cell.

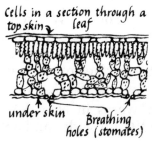

Cells in a section through a leaf

top skin

under skin

Breathing holes (stomates)

CELTS

The Celts were an ancient race that formerly lived in parts of Italy, Spain, and France. In the 3rd and 2nd centuries B.C., they crossed the channel into England, bringing with them iron weapons.

The Celts in England were tall and fair. They were good warriors and skillful workers, making beautiful jewelry, splendid chariots, fine weapons, shields, and armor. They were also good farmers and lived in semi-fortified villages.

The Belgae were one of the last Celtic tribes to arrive in England, settling in the southeast part. The Belgae cleared the forests and cultivated the heavier soil in the valleys, using a strong, wheeled plow.

When the Romans left England, the ANGLO-SAXON invaders drove many Celts into the western and northern parts of the British Isles. The descendants of this race still occupy Wales, Ireland, and Scotland.

CEMENT

Cement is any material that binds two surfaces together. Putty and glue are types of cement.

However, cement usually refers to building cement. Building cement used as *mortar* for bricklaying is a mixture of lime, sand, and water. Cement with more sand, gravel, or crushed stone makes CONCRETE.

The common building cement most used today is *Portland* cement, which was invented by an Englishman, Joseph Aspdin, in 1824. Portland cement is made by heating a mixture of clay and chalk to an extremely high temperature. Then water is added. Gypsum is mixed in to control the hardening time.

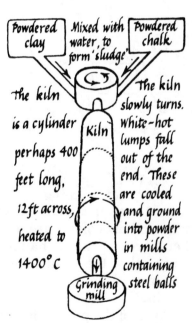

Powdered clay | Mixed with water, to form 'sludge' | Powdered chalk

The kiln is a cylinder perhaps 400 feet long, 12 ft across, heated to 1400°C

Kiln

Grinding mill

The kiln slowly turns. White-hot lumps fall out of the end. These are cooled and ground into powder in mills containing steel balls

Cements made from natural asphalt or coal tar are mixed with small stones to make a tough paving and road material. Plaster of Paris is a gypsum cement used in making casts and in the interiors of buildings. SEE ALSO: CONCRETE.

CENTAURS

Centaurs were creatures in Greek mythology that were half man and half horse. They were savage monsters, known for their drunkenness and lust. They were often followers of Dionysus, the god of wine, and fought brutally with Greek heroes, such as HERCULES. An exception to their violent, savage behavior was Chiron, who had a reputation for goodness and wisdom. Several Greek heroes, like JASON and ACHILLES, were taught by Chiron.

In the myths, the centaurs were driven from Thessaly, a region in eastern Greece, by the Lapiths. They had tried to seize the new bride of the king, as well as other women. Stories about the famous horsemen of Thessaly may have been the source of the mythical centaurs.

CENTRAL AMERICA

Central America is the long, narrow bridge of land between Mexico and South America. Actually, it is too mountainous and forested to make South America easily accessible from North America. The difficult terrain provides natural boundaries for the six independent countries and one British colony. The countries are Guatemala, El Salvador, Honduras, Nicaragua, Costa Rica, and Panama. The colony is Belize.

The land along the Caribbean and the Pacific is low, wet, very hot, and an unpleasant place for most people to live. However, this climate is perfect for BANANA and SUGAR cane plantations, as well as for dense, steamy forests supplying mahogany wood and chicle, a substance used in making chewing gum.

Cacao trees, the seeds of which provide cocoa and chocolate, are also grown here. There are so many banana plantations though, that the Central American countries are often called the "banana republics."

Most of the population, which is either pure or part Indian, lives in the highlands. Here COFFEE and corn are the major crops. The Indians of Central America grew corn

long before white people ever heard of it. Beef cattle are also raised in the highlands. The climate of the highlands provides popular vacation places for tourists. Many travelers enjoy the colorful marketplace and climate of Guatamala City and also the ruins left from the ancient Maya Indians whose great empire flourished long before the time of COLUMBUS.

Unfortunately, civil wars within each of the various countries have often created unstable governments and hindered industrial development.

CERAMICS

The art of baking different kinds of clay in various forms is called ceramics. Dishes, beautiful vases, insulators for telephone poles, tiles for the bathroom floor, and many other things are often ceramic.

The practice of making *earthenware* is very old. Clay is *fired* (baked) to produce it. The natural color of the clay is red, brown, or gray, but a *slip* (watery clay) of another color can be used to hide it, or it can be glazed. A *glaze* can be colorless and let the color beneath show through, or it can have a color of its own. It usually makes the ceramic object shiny.

Stoneware dates from 1400 B.C. To make it, clay is mixed with other materials that turn glass-like in the firing. Much good china and pottery is made from stoneware.

Porcelain is the finest of the ceramic materials. In true, or hard, porcelain, a fine white clay is mixed with a certain kind of rock. The rock turns glass-like in the firing. Unlike stoneware, porcelain allows light to pass through. If thin enough, it rings when tapped. Artificial, or soft, porcelain is made with clay and powdered glass, or with clay and powdered animal bones. There is a kind of true porcelain called *bone china*, for it too has bone ash in it. True porcelain was discovered in China in the 13th century, but Europeans did not know how to make it until early in the 18th century.

Most ceramics are still made of earthenware. For many centuries a round object like a pot was built up with coils of clay pressed together. This is still the way with the Indians of our Southwest. But most people use the *potter's wheel*, which revolves while the potter shapes the clay with his hands. Or, in factories, the clay is shaped in molds much like those used in CASTING. Decoration can be done with slip, dribbled glazes, paints, or things like decals with the designs printed on them. Then the ceramic is fired in an ovenlike kiln.

CEREALS

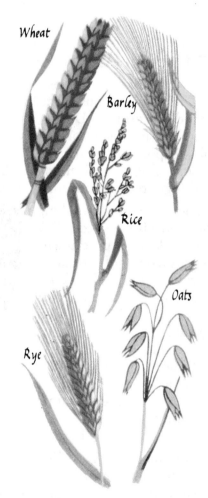

Cereals, or grains, are grasses which have been carefully cultivated for their large, plentiful, starchy seeds.

Cereals were cultivated by early man long before recorded history. Once man became aware he could grow enough food for his daily needs, he ceased to wander in search of food. Towns and civilizations sprang up as a result. The first cereals were grown in the area known as the "Fertile Crescent," which included the valleys of the NILE, Tigris, and EUPHRATES rivers. Grain storehouses have been unearthed that belonged to the ancient Egyptians, Greeks, Romans, PHOENICIANS, Aztecs, Mayas, and INCAS.

The word "cereal" comes from Ceres, the Roman goddess of corn. Wheat is the most widely used cereal for making bread, although rye is more popular in eastern Europe.

WHEAT, barley, oats, and RYE grow chiefly in the world's temperate zones—the United States, Canada, Europe, and the Soviet Union. RICE is grown in warmer, wetter areas—China, India, Burma, and Pakistan. Corn is widely grown in the United States; millet in India.

Cereals are ground into flour and used also for breakfast cereals, cattle food, and starch. Barley is used in making beer.

The valuable vitamins and minerals in the outside covering of the seed coat are often thrown away during the manufacturing of breakfast cereals. Therefore, whole grain food products are much more nutritious.

172

CHALK

Chalk is a soft, white, powdery LIMESTONE. It consists mainly of fossil shells of small creatures that lived in the ocean long, long ago. Thousands of these tiny shells, like those in the picture (greatly enlarged), made thick layers on the ocean's floor.

When great upheavals on the Earth's surface occurred long ago, these chalky layers under the sea were raised up to become hills. In England, the famous white cliffs of Dover on the English Channel are almost pure chalk. There are areas of chalk in Kansas, which is far from the ocean, but which was once covered by a sea that contained ancient sea life.

Chalk is used in making putty, plaster, cement, and rubber goods. Blackboard crayons are also made of chalk.

CHAMELEON

The chameleon is a tree-dwelling lizard with an ability to change color. Light intensity, temperature change, fear, and excitement will cause its skin to change color. There are numerous species of chameleon; most live in Madagascar and in Africa south of the Sahara Desert. The small American chameleon is not related to the chameleon of the Eastern Hemisphere.

Most chameleons grow no longer than 10 inches (25.4 cm); the longest is about 2 feet (61 cm). Their eyes, which move independently, are covered by lids with a tiny peephole in the middle. Their skins are scaly and their tails are often used for grasping around an object. Chameleons have sticky tongues, which they shoot far out to catch insects.

CHANTEY

In the days of sailing ships, the sailors would turn the capstan that raised the anchor or pull on the ropes that raised the sails. Unless they all moved at the same moment, there would not be enough force to do such things. This is where a chantey (or *shanty*) helped. A *chanteyman* led the work crew, singing old verses or making up new ones. On certain sounds everyone pulled or pushed. "What Shall We Do with a Drunken Sailor," "Blow the Man Down," and "A-roving" are three famous chanteys. In the first two the rhythm is especially strong, showing the places at which the sailors moved together.

CHAPEL

A chapel is a small CHURCH. Often it is part of a larger church, where it is used for quiet prayer. A Catholic or Episcopal church usually has one chapel, while CATHEDRALS usually have many. Each has its own services.

A chapel can also be the church of a school, a hospital, or even a prison. It is meant mostly for those who live there.

In England, a chapel is any church not belonging to the state church (Church of England) or the Catholic Church. SEE ALSO: CATHEDRAL, CHURCH.

Charlie CHAPLIN (1889–1977)

Shortly before 1920, American movie audiences began to enjoy the adventures of a little tramp, dressed in a shabby suit and carrying a battered umbrella. He had ridiculous and often frightening experiences, but got out of them somehow.

In real life the tramp was Charles Spencer Chaplin, the son of two English music-hall entertainers, who began to act in American movies in 1913. By 1920, he was famous and becoming rich, for audiences found his acting not only funny but also very lovable. All early movies were silent, but even after sound movies began in the late 1920s, Chaplin went on making ones that were mostly silent. He wanted people to watch him, not listen to him. His early movies were for amusement only, but later he began to be

interested in social problems. In *Modern Times* he made his audience not only laugh but think about the troubles that some people have, and *The Great Dictator* was an attack on HITLER and Mussolini.

Chaplin's public remarks caused him to be accused of being a Communist, and in 1952 he left the United States to live in Switzerland. He continued to act in and direct movies in Europe. In spite of the bad feeling between Chaplin and the United States, his movies are still often shown here, since he is regarded as one of the greatest movie actors.

In 1972, Chaplin received an honorary Oscar at the annual Academy Awards. Queen Elizabeth II of England knighted him in 1975.

CHARCOAL

Charcoal is an impure form of carbon. It is a black substance obtained by burning wood or other organic material in the absence of air. Wood charcoal used to be produced by piling wood into stacks, covering it with sod and damp ashes, and then setting fire to it. Charcoal is now made in huge ovens.

Charcoal produces a greater amount of heat in proportion to its volume than is obtained from a similar volume of wood. As a fuel, it has the added advantage of being smokeless. Charcoal can absorb a great many gases. Thus, it is used in gas masks to remove toxic vapors. It is also used in decolorizing sugar and in purifying air, water, and natural gas. Explosives and briquettes for barbeques are made from charcoal. SEE ALSO: CARBON.

CHARLEMAGNE (A.D. 742–814)

Charlemagne, whose name in Old French means "Charles the Great," was one of the greatest military leaders of the MIDDLE AGES. In A.D. 771, he was proclaimed the sole king of the Franks, a Germanic people who lived in France and parts of Germany and the Netherlands.

As a Christian king, he set about conquering and converting the rest of Europe, which was then made up of many kingdoms. He took control of the Lombards, a tribe in northern Italy that had previously been threatening the Pope at Rome. He invaded Spain and was repulsed by the Moors, but he managed to seize a northeast region in the country. The Saxons in northwestern Germany were conquered by him. Through his conquests, he established Christianity in a large part of Europe.

Charlemagne went to Rome, where the Pope on Christmas Day, A.D. 800, proclaimed him Emperor of the Holy Roman Empire. He made Aachen (called Aix-la-Chapelle by the French) in western Germany his capital city. His dominion included modern Hungary, Belgium, Germany, Switzerland, France, and portions of Spain and Italy.

He was a wise and energetic ruler, setting up strong, but fair, laws throughout his empire. He built schools and encouraged the spread of learning. But when he died, the empire split up in chaos; his personal control had kept it together.

Geoffrey CHAUCER (1340?–1400)

Geoffrey Chaucer was one of the earliest English poets. He ranks with Shakespeare and Milton among the great poets of the world.

"Whan that Aprille with his shoures soote/The droghte of March hath perced to the roote." ("When that April with its showers sweet/The drought of March has pierced to the root.") These are the first lines of the Prologue to *The Canterbury Tales*, written by Chaucer in Middle English (the modern translation followes the original). During Chaucer's time there was no standard English language, just many different dialects. But his skill in his particular dialect helped make his dialect standard English.

The poem, *The Canterbury Tales*, is about 30 pilgrims on a journey from London to Canterbury. These pilgrims include all sorts of people—a miller, a knight, a nun, a priest, a lawyer, a doctor, a farmer, a sailor, and so on. Each person tells a story to pass the time. Chaucer gives a good picture of the customs and ideas of his day, and also pokes some fun at many of them.

Not a lot is known about Chaucer himself. He was the son of a London wine merchant. As a boy he was a page in a prince's house and later was a soldier and representative for the king. He rose to be a chief customs officer in the port of London, and later he was in charge of the upkeep of many royal buildings. He was the first poet buried in Westminster Abbey in London, in what is now named "The Poet's Corner."

A few of the characters in *The Canterbury Tales* are illustrated here, copied from drawings made several hundred years ago.

CHECKERS

Checkers is an old game, popular since ancient Egypt, Greece, and Rome.

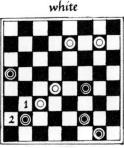

white

black

It is played by two persons with pieces called checkers on a board with 64 alternately colored squares—usually red and black or white and black. Each player has 12 checkers of his own color, and all play occurs on the black squares. Sitting at opposite sides of the board, each player places his pieces on the three lines of black spaces nearest him. The players alternately move their pieces diagonally in a forward direction.

The object of the game is to eliminate from play the opponent's checkers by "jumping" them. A player removes his opponent's piece by jumping one of his own pieces diagonally over it to an empty square immediately beyond it. If a player can keep moving forward, he can take two or more of his opponent's pieces in one jump, provided one empty square lies between each of his pieces. If a player moves his piece into the last line of his opponent's side, the piece is crowned as a king (one of the removed checkers is placed on top of it). A king can move backwards and forwards diagonally. In the picture, the white piece (1) jumps over the black one (2), thus removing it from the board. Then the white piece becomes a king, having reached the far side of the board.

CHEESE

Cheese has been an important food for thousands of years. It is the solid part of milk, consisting mostly of protein and fat. Cheesemakers allow milk to clot or curdle, either by letting bacterial action sour it or by adding special substances to it. It can then be separated into *curds* (the more solid part) and *whey* (the watery part). Cheese is made from curds. Special machines chop the curds into tiny pieces, which are then heated, salted, and pressed into cloth-lined molds. Afterward the molded curds are set in a cool, dry place to "ripen" gradually into the various kinds of cheese we know.

The numerous cheeses (often named for their place of origin) depend for their particular flavors and textures on the kind of milk used, the method of processing the curds, the length of the ripening period, and the added mold or bacteria, if any.

177

Cheeses can be put into two groups: hard cheeses that improve with age under good conditions and soft cheeses that are eaten soon after being made. Very hard cheeses include Parmesan and Romano; hard cheeses include Swiss, Cheddar, Edam, and Gouda. Among the semisoft cheeses are Roquefort, Gorgonzola, and Limburger; soft cheeses include Brie, Camembert, Valencay, and cottage. There are about 500 different kinds of cheese made, ranging in taste from mild cream cheese to strong, smelly Limburger.

CHEMISTRY

Chemistry is the branch of science that studies the kinds of ELEMENTS in the composition of all things. Chemists also explain chemical changes and discover new ways of combining elements to produce new and useful substances. A chemical change results from the exchange of electrons between two or more substances. Digestion, tarnishing, rotting, and corroding are all examples of chemical reactions.

Chemists have discovered, for example, that water is composed of two atoms of hydrogen for every one atom of oxygen. They represent this composition by the formula H_2O. They have also learned that an electric current passed through water will break it down chemically into hydrogen and oxygen gases, and that burning hydrogen in oxygen will reunite them. A long time passed before chemists realized that burning is in fact the joining of the substance being burned with the oxygen of the air. Burning is rapid *oxidation*. Rusting is slow oxidation—that is, the slow joining together of iron with oxygen.

There are many branches of chemistry. *Organic chemistry* is the study of carbon compounds; *inorganic chemistry* is the study of mineral substances; and, *biochemistry* is the study of the chemical processes in plants and animals. Chemists are very important in industrial, agricultural, and medical research.

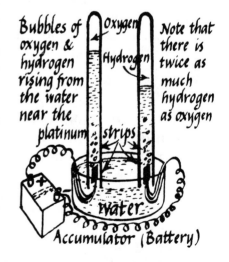

The electric current passing through the water breaks it up into oxygen & hydrogen

Bubbles of oxygen & hydrogen rising from the water near the platinum strips

Oxygen
Hydrogen

Note that there is twice as much hydrogen as oxygen

water

Accumulator (Battery)

An organic substance — an aspirin molecule

● carbon atom

⊘ oxygen atom

○ hydrogen atom

A simple inorganic substance

○ Sodium atom

⊘ Chlorine atom

A molecule of sodium chloride (common salt)

Most of today's knowledge of chemistry was discovered in the last 150 years. The Egyptians, Greeks, and especially the Arabs had a practical understanding of chemistry. The alchemists of the Middle Ages spent their time trying to turn cheap metals, such as lead, into gold. They also sought to discover the "Elixir of Life," a potion to enable them to live forever. Although much magic was mixed into their experimentation and their search proved unsuccessful, they did discover facts about matter and how it acts. Such facts were useful later to scientists.

An alchemist

CHESS

Chess is played by two persons on a board like that used in CHECKERS, having 32 black (or red) and 32 white squares.

Each player has 16 "pieces" or chessmen—one king, one queen, two rooks (or castles), two bishops, two knights, and eight pawns. Some are pictured here. Each chess piece moves in a different way. The rooks move forward or backward, left or right, any number of squares, but never diagonally. The knights have a peculiar L-shaped movement, moving one square forward, and then one square diagonally. The bishops move diagonally any number of squares; the queen moves like a rook and a bishop; the king moves in any direction, but only one square at a time. The pawns advance one square at a time, except a player may move them two squares each the first time he moves them.

Some 12th century chess men

The object of the game is to force an opponent's king to surrender, making his king unable to move to safety or be protected from capture.

Chess is a very old game, probably originating in India in the 6th century A.D. Later it was brought by way of Persia and Arabia to Europe. People all over the world play chess today.

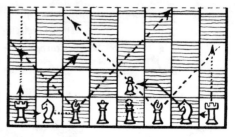

CHICAGO

Chicago is the second largest city in the United States, following NEW YORK CITY. It lies on the southwest shore of Lake Michigan, in the state of ILLINOIS.

A metropolitan area of more than 7 million people, Chicago is the most important Great Lakes' port and the world's largest railroad center. Equally important are its modern expressways and airline terminals, which help carry the huge variety of goods and services that go in and out of the city. Its meat-packing plants and large grain mills and elevators are the most famous in the world. It is a leading producer of steel, telephone equipment, radios, TV sets, diesel engines, and plastics.

In 1673, the explorers MARQUETTE AND JOLIET visited the site of Chicago. A century later a black French merchant, Jean Baptiste Pointe du Sable, founded a trading post there. John Kinzie in 1804 became the first permanent settler in Chicago, at a post called Ft. Dearborn. The Erie Canal and the railroads stimulated growth in the 1800s. In 1871, the city was utterly destroyed by a great fire, but within a few years was rebuilt.

The first skyscraper, ten stories high, was constructed there in 1885. Today three of the world's ten tallest buildings are located there. The famous Merchandise Mart, the Chicago Board of Trade, the Museum of Science and Industry, Art Institute, and the University of Chicago attract many visitors to the city each year. SEE ALSO: ILLINOIS.

CHILE

Chile is a long, narrow country that lies along the southwest coast of SOUTH AMERICA. The towering Andes Mountains extend nearly the entire length of the country. The Atacama Desert in the north is one of the world's driest regions, but it contains rich deposits of copper and sodium nitrate. In central Chile, between the Andes and a low coastal range, is a long, fertile valley where large crops of potatoes, wheat, barley, wine grapes, and fruit are grown. Chile's southern region is rugged and heavily wooded, with deep FIORDS along the coast and many craggy islands offshore. Far to the south is Tierra del Fuego ("Land of Fire"), the largest island. MAGELLAN, who named the island because of its many Indian bonfires, sailed his ship in 1520 through the straits north of Tierra del Fuego. Chile ends at Cape Horn, the southern tip of South America.

Until the Spanish conquered the region in the 16th century, the INCAS ruled the northern part and the Araucanian Indians the southern part. Under the leadership of José de San Martín and Bernardo O'Higgins, Chile gained its independence in 1818, driving out the Spanish rulers. Since then, the country has developed into a modern, industrial republic, despite internal political wars and economic problems. Chile today has more than 10.5 million people, most of whom speak Spanish. Santiago is the capital and largest city.

CHINA

China is located in the eastern part of Asia and is the third largest country in the world, after the U.S.S.R. and Canada. It is the most populous country with more than one billion people.

The Chinese are traditionally hard-working farmers, growing rice, wheat, barley, corn, millet, soybeans, tea, peas, cotton, and fiber crops like hemp and jute. The soil in the Yangtze and Yellow River valleys is very fertile, but floods, hurricanes, and droughts sometimes destroy entire crops.

181

China has rich minerals that are now being used to develop its modern industries. It is the world's third largest coal producer and also mines iron ore, tin, antimony, tungsten, and other minerals. Roads, dams, factories, hydroelectric stations, and airports are turning China into an industrial country. China's trade with the West is growing.

China has the oldest continuing civilization in the world, dating back more than 4000 years. By the time of Christ, the Chinese had lived under a succession of ruling families, called dynasties, that had unified the country. The Great Wall of China was built and rebuilt through the centuries to keep out invaders, who eventually overran much of China in the 1600s. However, during the Middle Ages, science and the arts flourished and were more advanced than in Europe.

The Chinese were the first to develop paper, printing, porcelain, silk, and gunpowder. Around 1300, MARCO POLO and other travelers to China brought back goods and tales of fabulous riches. They marveled at the Chinese skill in painting, poetry, drama, and pottery.

The country was plagued for many years by poverty, revolutions, and wars. After Dr. Sun Yat-sen overthrew the last dynasty and made China a republic in 1912, there was more conflict and competition for power. The communists, led by Mao Tse-tung, who died in 1975, took control of the country in 1950. China, now called the People's Republic of China, has grown to be a powerful, communist state. SEE ALSO: ASIA.

182

Frédéric François CHOPIN (1810–1849)

Chopin was one of the greatest composers of the 19th century. Almost everything he wrote was for the piano. He himself was a great pianist.

He was born near Warsaw, Poland, in 1810. He went to Vienna when he was 20, then went to Paris, composing, teaching, and playing. He became famous. Some of his work was gentle and dreamlike. Some was passionate and vigorous. Much of his work—his mazurkas, for example—is based on Polish music. Poland's attempt to free itself from foreign rule inspired some of his compositions.

At the height of his career, he became sick with tuberculosis. He had an unhappy love affair. A revolution in Paris forced him to move to England. He died in 1849, thirty-nine years old.

CHRISTIANITY

When Jesus died, there were about 100 Christians in the entire world. Now there are more than one billion.

The followers of Jesus believe that He is the Son of God. They believe that Jesus' death on the cross was a sacrifice for mankind, and that his *resurrection* (return to life) made it possible for people who believe in him to enjoy a new life after death.

Jesus was executed in Palestine when it was part of the Roman Empire. After He rose from the dead and ascended to heaven, Paul and other followers of Jesus spread the Christian religion through the Roman Empire. The Roman emperors tried to stop Christianity. For many years the Christians worshipped in *catacombs* (underground tombs). Finally they were allowed to worship in public. In A.D. 324, Emperor

CONSTANTINE made Christianity the state religion of Rome. Thus it spread over the whole Empire.

The Roman Empire divided into two parts in the 5th century A.D., and the Christian Church soon divided into two parts as well. The Western Church, run from Rome, became the CATHOLIC CHURCH. The Eastern Church, run from Constantinople (now Istanbul), became the ORTHODOX CHURCH. Smaller Christian groups have split off from the Catholic and Orthodox churches.

In a catacomb

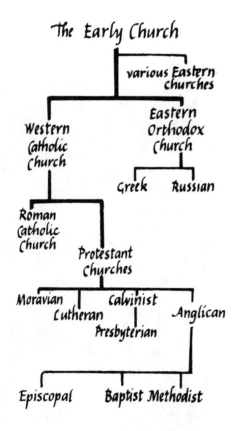

The Early Church

various Eastern churches

Western Catholic Church

Eastern Orthodox Church

Greek   Russian

Roman Catholic Church

Protestant Churches

Moravian   Calvinist
    Lutheran   Anglican
        Presbyterian

Episcopal   Baptist Methodist

The Catholic Church was very powerful in Western Europe during the Middle Ages. People donated money and land to the churches and monasteries. Sometimes local churches became little states, with much land and many people. The POPE himself ruled a large part of Italy.

The Orthodox Church spread from Byzantium into Greece, Russia, and the Near East. In those places, too, it became a great landowner.

In the 15th and 16th centuries, many Christians did not like the things Catholic priests said and did in the name of Christianity. These people were called *Protestants* because they *protested* ("spoke for") the original beliefs of the New Testament. They founded churches of their own, such as the Episcopal, Lutheran, Methodist, Baptist, and Presbyterian churches.
SEE ALSO: BIBLE, CATHOLIC CHURCH, ORTHODOX CHURCH, PROTESTANTISM.

CHRISTMAS

Christmas is the day set aside to celebrate the birth of JESUS. We do not know exactly when Jesus Christ was born, but most Christians celebrate Christmas on December 25th of each year.

The Bible says that an angel told Mary, the mother of Jesus, that she would give birth to the Son of God. At that time she was engaged to marry Joseph of Nazareth, a carpenter. When she was about to give birth, Mary and Joseph had to go to the little town of BETHLEHEM to register for a tax list.

Finding no room in an inn, they slept in a stable, where Jesus was born.

An angel told shepherds that they should go to see Jesus. Wise men, or kings, from a foreign land later brought gifts of gold, frankincense, and myrrh to the Christ child. In the past, Christmas festivities lasted until the Twelfth Night (January 6th), the date when we usually take down our Christmas decorations.

Many customs have grown up around Christmas. Saint Nicholas, a 4th century A.D. bishop in Asia Minor, spent his life doing good deeds. In Holland, Germany, and elsewhere, his feast is celebrated on December 6th, which is a children's holiday for gifts. The English in New York accepted him from the Dutch, moved his day to Christmas, and called him *Santa Claus*. We think of Santa Claus today as a plump, jolly, old fellow who drives a reindeer-drawn sled full of presents.

Christmas has absorbed many other customs: the Yule Log, the boar's head, the goose (in America the turkey), decoration with holly, hawthorn, and mistletoe; the singing of carols, the crèche, the Christmas tree, and the sending of Christmas cards, which first appeared about 1850. SEE ALSO: JESUS.

CHROMIUM

Chromium is a grayish metallic element. It never occurs by itself in nature but always in COMPOUNDS. Chromium is obtained from the mineral chromite, which consists of iron, chromium, and oxygen. This mineral is mainly found in Zimbabwe, Russia, Turkey, the East Indies, South Africa, the Philippines, and Yugoslavia. The U.S. has only small deposits.

Chromium is very hard and does not tarnish in the air. With lead, potassium, and oxygen, it forms various compounds that are used as pigments in paints, in dyeing, and in tanning leather. Chromium, in the form of chromic oxide, gives beautiful tints to certain gemstones, like emeralds, aquamarine, and some sapphires.

Chromium is widely used in plating other metals. It gives STEEL a thin protective coating that is hard, stainless, easily polished. The bright metal trim on automobiles is usually made of chromium. Stainless steel has about 15 per cent chromium.

CHURCH

The word *church* may be used to describe a group of Christians or the building where they worship. The group of all people who follow Jesus Christ is often called "the church." The New Testament of the BIBLE often refers to the church, giving Jesus' promise and instructions for his

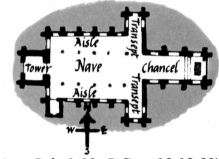

followers (see Col. 1:18, I Cor. 12:13-20). The word *church* may also mean a group of Christians who have certain beliefs. We can speak of the Lutheran church, the Baptist church, the Presbyterian church, and so on—each one is a large group of Christians with unique teachings. Each of these groups is called a *denomination*.

The earliest church buildings were planned like the ancient Roman *basilica*, which was a kind of public hall. A long central space led to an *apse*, a round area at one end. Alongside the central space were narrower spaces for the movement of the crowds.

Most Catholic and many Protestant churches still use this plan. A *nave* (for the congregation) and a *chancel* (for the clergy) make up the central space. Aisles lead to the seats and sometimes to CHAPELS. Some Protestant churches are different. They are more square shape, so that the seats are as close as possible to the preacher's desk or pulpit. Orthodox churches are also square. Instead of being covered by roofs they are covered by domes, like half a ball. SEE ALSO: CHRISTIANITY.

Sir Winston CHURCHILL (1874–1965)

Winston Churchill was a great statesman. He became Prime Minister of ENGLAND during World War II, inspiring the nation by his brilliant speeches and resolute example to fight and endure the hardships of war. Almost everyone has heard his famous words: "I have nothing to offer but blood, toil, tears, and sweat."

Young Churchill went to India in 1896 as a soldier and a reporter. Four years later, he entered Parliament in England. He was Home Secretary in 1910 and held other posts until he became Prime Minister in 1940, when England was already at war with GERMANY. He led his country to victory. Afterward, his party was defeated, but he stayed in Parliament, becoming Prime Minister again from 1951 to 1955. Then he retired.

He was also a painter and an outstanding writer, winning the Nobel Prize for Literature in 1953. His many books include the six-volume *The Second World War* and the four-volume *A History of the English-speaking Peoples*. He died at 90 and was given a state funeral.

CIRCUS

The word "circus" means a "ring" or "circle" in Latin. The first circuses were held in great arenas in Rome. Spectators sat in a round or oval stadium or theater and watched chariot races, athletic contests, gladiator fights, wild beasts, and even naval battles staged on a flooded stadium floor. The *Circus Maximus* was the greatest

Ruins of the Colosseum, Rome

of these arenas, seating over 150,000 people. The Colosseum, a smaller one, can still be viewed today, though it is in ruins. During the Roman Empire, these "circuses" became places of slaughter of animals and men, far different from the circuses we have today.

During the late Middle Ages, jugglers, ACROBATS, tightrope walkers, and musicians roamed from village to village, putting on shows and collecting as much money as the people would give.

Astley's 'Amphitheatre'

The circus that we know today came into being in 1768, when Philip Astley, an Englishman, entertained people while galloping in a circle, standing on his horse's back. Riding and keeping his balance this way, Astley traced

the first circus ring. He gathered other showmen around him and traveled through Europe, establishing 19 permanent circuses during his life. An Englishman, John Ricketts, opened circuses in 1793 in Philadelphia and New York City, the first seen in America. Soon these traveling showmen were using tents, or "big tops," said to have been invented in America about 1826.

Many circuses were formed in the 19th century and all kinds of new acts were developed. Trick riders, wild animal tamers, and children's clowns also became main attractions. About 1880, Phineas T. Barnum joined with another famous circus man, James A. Bailey, to form "The Greatest Show on Earth." The most famous of all circus names is probably Ringling. In 1919, The Ringling Brothers and Barnum & Bailey Circus went on tour as one enormous show. Today it is still the greatest circus of all, though it now performs only in large indoor arenas instead of large, canvas tents. SEE ALSO: ACROBATS.

CITIZENSHIP

Citizenship means that a person is given certain rights, privileges, and duties as a member of a state or nation. As a citizen of a country, a person usually participates in and supports his or her government. Citizens of the United States are allowed to vote and to hold office. Foreigners living in the U.S. are protected by the CONSTITUTION, just as citizens are. However, only citizens have their rights protected by the U.S. government when they travel or live abroad. Good citizenship means voting for officials during elections, making sure those elected will not pass laws and do things that will harm the people and the country. American citizens, through the study of U.S. history and the Constitution, make certain their rights are maintained and the principles of democratic government are always followed. Good citizenship also means obeying the laws and defending the nation in wartime.

Who is a United States citizen? A person is a citizen by birth—that is, he or she was born in the U.S., born to U.S. citizens living in a foreign country, or (under special conditions) born abroad with one U.S. parent. A foreigner can become a U.S. citizen through the process of *naturalization*. A naturalized U.S. citizen must be at least 18 years old, must have lived in the country for at least the last 5 years and in the state where he or she applies for at least the last 6 months, must be able to read, write, and speak English, and must know about U.S. history and the Constitution. The person must also be a legal *alien* (a non-citizen legally in the U.S.) and must have no criminal record.

U.S. citizenship can also be taken away. A person loses it if he or she becomes a naturalized citizen of another country or a member of another country's armed forces without permission of the U.S. government. Voting or holding office in another country, giving up U.S. citizenship before an American official (usually at an embassy), or committing treason are also ways to lose citizenship.

The CIVIL WAR

The U.S. Civil War was fought between 23 Northern states (the Union) and 11 Southern states (the Confederacy) from 1861 to 1865. It was fought over two main issues. One was the extension of SLAVERY into U.S. territories, and the other was states' rights. Many people felt that the federal government was abusing its powers granted by the U.S. CONSTITUTION.

From the 1600s, many Southerners owned black slaves, who worked on the large cotton and tobacco plantations and in the homes. Northerners used slaves for a while, but stopped because slave labor was not practical or economical for them.

In the 1830s, a group of Northerners called the Abolitionists began to work to end all slavery in the U.S. They attacked the South and its way of life. They tried to stop slavery in the new western lands of the U.S. Finally, the South felt its customs and economy were in danger.

After ABRAHAM LINCOLN was elected President in 1860, many in the South thought that he would interfere with slavery in their states. South Carolina, Alabama, Mississippi, Georgia, Florida, Louisiana, and Texas decided to secede (break away) from the United States. On Feb. 4, 1861, they formed the Confederate States of America, also called the Confederacy. Montgomery, Alabama, was chosen the Confederate capital. Jefferson Davis was elected President.

Then, on April 12, 1861, Confederate troops bombarded and seized Fort Sumter, a Union stronghold in Charleston harbor, South Carolina. Lincoln called for volunteers to keep the South in the Union. The Civil War had started. Now four more states —Virginia, North Carolina, Tennessee, and Arkansas— seceded and joined the Confederacy. Richmond, Virginia, became the Confederacy's new capital.

The first Battle of Bull Run occurred on July 21, 1861, near Manassas, Virginia. Confederate troops forced the Union troops to retreat back to Washington. The following year, the North won at the Battle of Shiloh, in Tennessee, but lost many soldiers. At the second Battle of Bull Run in August,

1862, Generals ROBERT E. LEE and "Stonewall" Jackson led their loyal Confederate armies to victory and then invaded the North. The next month, their armies were defeated at Antietam Creek, near Sharpsburg, Maryland, by Union forces under General George McClellan.

After General Lee's army won at Chancellorsville, Virginia, in May, 1863, Lee decided again to invade the North. However, at the BATTLE OF GETTYSBURG in July, Lee's army was stopped and made to fall back. This was the turning point of the war. Confederate losses were so great that the South would never again be able to mount another drive into the North.

Meanwhile, the North blockaded the South's ports. Two armored warships, the *Monitor* and *Merrimack*, engaged in a naval battle at Hampton Roads, Virginia, on March 9, 1862. Neither ship won, but the Confederate *Merrimack* was badly damaged by the *Monitor's* shells. The North's blockade remained intact. In the Gulf of Mexico, the North's fleet under Captain David Farragut captured New Orleans in April, 1862. Two years later, Farragut's ships won the Battle of Mobile Bay and then took the city of Mobile, Alabama. The South was hindered in getting its vital supplies from abroad.

Union troops under General ULYSSES S. GRANT won an important battle in Vicksburg, Mississippi, in July, 1863. Union forces then pushed east into Tennessee, defeating the Confederates at Chattanooga and Knoxville. General William Sherman's Union soldiers marched to Atlanta and then to Savannah, burning and destroying the South's food, supplies, and equipment. Sherman's "March to the Sea" cut the South in two.

In Virginia, General Grant, who had been made commander in chief of the Union army, pursued General Lee, who was forced to fall back to Richmond. Grant's large army defeated Lee's dwindling forces during the Siege of Petersburg and Richmond on April 2, 1865. Lee's army retreated but was caught by Union armies led by General Grant and General Philip Sheridan. Realizing his men were weary and beaten, Lee nobly surrendered at Appomattox Court House on April 9, 1865. Soon the other armies of the South gave up, and the bitter war was over. SEE ALSO: GETTYSBURG, BATTLE OF; GRANT, ULYSSES S.; LEE, ROBERT E.; LINCOLN, ABRAHAM; SLAVERY.

CLAY

After thousands of years of weathering, rocks gradually break up into minute particles. These particles are often carried by streams and deposited in lakes and rivers. As the particles settle, they form layers of very fine-grained mud, called *clay*. Clays vary in color, depending on the kinds of rock from which they have been formed. Natural clays are usually gray or tan, but some are red or pure white.

When wet, clay can be molded into various shapes and figures. When dry, it is very brittle and easily broken. If clay objects are baked at very high temperatures, they become extremely hard. Some coarse types of clay are used in making tiles and bricks; other finer clays are used to make dishes, bowls, and flower pots. Some clays go into the making of CEMENT.

Clay absorbs grease and oil and is therefore used in the preparation of *fuller's*

earth for removing grease from fabrics as well as for making cosmetics.

Man has used clay for thousands of years, and, even today, people of all ages still enjoy working with clay.

CLEOPATRA (69–30 B.C.)

Cleopatra was a beautiful, cunning, and ambitious woman. As queen of ancient Egypt, she tried to gain control of the entire Roman Empire.

When she was 17, her father died, and she and her younger brother shared the throne in Egypt. But she had to flee when her brother's guardians seized the kingdom. With the help of JULIUS CAESAR, she regained the throne. Her brother accidentally drowned in the Nile.

A coin minted in Egypt, with Cleopatra on one side, and Antony on the other

Cleopatra planned to rule Rome with Caesar, who had fallen in love with her. However, in 44 B.C., Caesar was murdered, and Mark Antony became ruler over Egypt. He fell in love with Cleopatra, and together they hoped to rule Egypt and Rome. But Octavian, Antony's enemy, declared war on him and defeated his ships off Actium, in Greece, in 31 B.C.

Later, believing Cleopatra was dead, Antony committed suicide. Cleopatra, faced by a cold, uncharmed Octavian, also killed herself. According to tradition, to avoid becoming a Roman prisoner, she let an asp, a poisonous snake, bite her, causing her death.

CLERGY

Christian and Jewish religious leaders are called clergy. Clergy must first be sure that they really want to be clergymen. Christian clergy feel that God has given them this desire. Then they must be carefully trained by studying the Scriptures, theology—an understanding of God's relation to man—and how to carry out their duties as clergy. If they have studied successfully they are *ordained* and become clergy.

Clergy in the Roman CATHOLIC and ORTHODOX CHURCHES are called *priests*. A priest is a person who can address God directly, can pray for mankind, and can perform the sacrament of the *Eucharist*, by which man comes into contact with God. He has the power to forgive sins in the name of God.

Some Protestant churches call their religious leaders priests, but most call them *pastors* or *ministers*. Protestants believe that every Christian is a priest, able to address God directly. A minister is a priest, like any other Christian, but serves the local group of Christians by teaching, preaching, and praying. In the Catholic and Orthodox churches, the *mass*, at which the ritual of the Eucharist is performed, is of the greatest importance. The Protestant *service*, on the other hand, puts great importance on preaching. The QUAKERS have no clergy; every person may speak at a Quaker meeting.

A *rabbi* is a teacher and spiritual leader in JUDAISM. Any group of ten or more men may hold a religious service and pray to God. The rabbi is the usual leader of such services, though, and it is the rabbi who gives advice on religious matters. SEE ALSO: CATHOLIC CHURCH, JUDAISM, ORTHODOX CHURCH, PROTESTANTISM.

CLIMATE

Climate refers to the kind of weather that a particular region has. Those who study climatic conditions are called *climatologists*. They keep records of temperature, barometric (air) pressure, humidity, rainfall, sunshine, cloudiness, and winds. Though the weather in a region may change daily, it usually falls into a noticeable and typical year-round pattern. Climatologists and meteorologists (those who study atmospheric phenomena as well as climate) have grouped the various kinds of climates around the world as follows:

(a) *Polar*—long cold winters (for example, the North and South Poles);

(b) *Temperate*—moderate temperatures and moderate rainfall (for example, northern coastal regions of the United States);

(c) *Continental*—very hot summers and very cold winters in the interiors of large land masses (for example, Russia, Canada, or the United States);

(d) *Mediterranean*—long dry summers and warm rainy winters (for example, Greece, southern Italy, and southern California);

(e) *Hot Dry*—hot days and cool nights (for example, the desert areas like the Sahara and southern Arizona or New Mexico);

(f) *Hot Wet*—hot and humid throughout the year, with heavy rainfall (for example, tropical regions like central Africa and the southern tip of Florida);

(g) *Monsoon*—warm ocean winds bring heavy rainfall in summer, with a dry period in winter (for example, Southeast Asia).

CLOCKS

Egyptian Clepsydra

17th Century Clock

Sundial

Anything that goes or changes steadily can be used for telling the time. The burning-down of candles, the trickling of water or sand, and the movement of a shadow on a *sundial* have all been used.

These ancient ways of telling the time all had their drawbacks, though. A draft would make the candle burn too fast. Freezing would stop the *clepsydra*, or water clock. On a cloudy day the sundial was useless, and it was useless after sundown. The mechanical clock was the answer. It seems likely that monks in the 14th century invented this. Such a clock turned hands under the power of a falling weight. An *escapement* kept the clockwork moving at the right speed. Spring-driven clocks were first made around 1500. In 1657, the PENDULUM was invented. This made clocks more accurate than before. In 1765, an Englishman, John Harrison, made the first *chronometer*, a very accurate clock. Modern clocks are much more accurate still.

CLOTH

Cloth is any flexible (readily bent) material made out of threads or other fibers. Most fibers are natural animal or plant fibers. These are used in wool, cotton, linen, and silk. But these days many *synthetics* (man-made fibers) are also being used. Rayon, nylon, and Dacron are among them.

felt

weaving

Knitting

There are three ways of making cloth: *Felting*, in which short fibers are wetted, beaten, and rolled together; WEAVING, in which threads going one way *(weft)* are passed over and under threads going another way *(warp)* on a frame known as a *loom*; KNITTING, in which a thick cord of fiber *(yarn)* is knotted together in a series of stitches with the aid of two long needles.

Cloth can be colored by dyeing or printing it, or threads or yarn of different colors can be woven or knitted together in patterns. Dyes used to be made mostly from plant juices, but for over a hundred years they have also been made from the chemicals found in coal.

Felting, weaving, and knitting are all done by machinery in large factories today, but weaving and knitting are also hobbies. Knitting is especially popular, and yarn can be bought in stores almost everywhere. SEE ALSO: CLOTHES, KNITTING, SPINNING, TEXTILES, WEAVING.

CLOTHES

People have worn clothes from the very earliest times. Some primitive tribes believe that clothes are a magical protection against harm. Often the style of clothes shows whether someone is wealthy or has a special part to play in society. One kind of costume, the *uniform*, is used to show that the wearer is a policeman, an admiral, or something of the sort. And clothing, along with jewelry and other things worn, has long been used to make a person attractive to the opposite sex.

The first clothes were probably animal skins. We know of cave paintings that show these being worn. Also bone needles have been found from very long ago.

A Bedouin shepherd

Greek dress

15th century dress

Later, the WOOL of sheep, camels, and other animals was woven into CLOTH and used in different ways. A wool suit traps air in its cloth, and since heat does not easily pass through air such a suit is warm on a chilly day. But the Bedouin, the Arabs of the hot desert, also wear robes of wool. It keeps the hot sun off during the day, and holds in the body heat during the cold nights.

COTTON was used in India 2000 years ago. When the Spaniards came to Mexico in 1520, they found that the Aztecs were wearing cotton clothes. Cotton does not hold in the heat as wool does, and is good for summer clothing. Moths will not attack it. When ELI WHITNEY invented the cotton gin to take the seeds out of cotton fiber, it became a cheap cloth.

The ancient Egyptians and Greeks made clothing of LINEN, the fiber of the flax plant, and of wool. Linen is expensive; and some people prefer it to cotton and use it in the same ways, for bedsheets, underwear, handkerchiefs, shirts, and suits.

The Chinese have been using SILK for thousands of years. Its fibers come from the cocoons of the silkworm. Silk is light, strong, and pleasant to touch. It is rather expensive, and people often use man-made fibers such as RAYON or nylon in its place.

LEATHER and FURS are important too. Leather can be so thick and hard that it has been used for armor. Also it can be made into suede (pronounced swayed), which is flexible and soft. Many animal furs are made into linings for warm coats, or are made into the coats themselves.

Tailors have made these materials into many beautiful forms throughout history. Some of these will be discussed in the article on DRESS. SEE ALSO: CLOTH, COTTON, FUR, LEATHER, LINEN, RAYON, SILK.

197

CLOUDS

Clouds are made up of tiny droplets of water or very small ice crystals. These droplets are so small that more than 100 million would fill a teaspoon (5 ml). Each droplet usually forms around an even tinier speck of dust. Clouds are more likely to form if there are particles in the air to act as "seeds" for the water vapor to condense upon.

As the wind blows over the hill, the air is cooled and more clouds are formed. If they are cooled sufficiently, rain will fall.

Wind currents

Since cool air is dense, it cannot hold as much water vapor (an invisible gas) as

Cirrus

warm air. As a result, clouds usually form when warm air is cooled. Warm air rises and cools when blown by the wind against a range of mountains or hills.

When droplets of water are very tiny, they are able to float on the air currents which shape the clouds. However, as the temperature drops, the droplets increase more and more in size, until they become so large they fall as rain. If the air is very cold, they fall as snow, sleet, or hail.

There are four basic types of clouds: *cirrus*—thin, white, feathery clouds, four or five miles (6.4–8 km) high, which contain ice crystals; *stratus*—a wide gray layer of low cloud; *cumulus*—huge, fluffy white piles of rounded, fair weather clouds with flattened bases (heavy layers, however,

Cumulus

stratus

threaten rain); and *nimbus*—dark, ragged storm clouds.

Nimbus - the dark rain-cloud

Clouds at ground level are called mist or FOG. These droplets can form around dust and smoke in industrial areas, and the result is then called smog. Smog is very bad for people, especially those with allergies and heart and lung diseases. Acid, dirt, and other industrial pollutants in the air are now becoming a serious concern of the public. SEE ALSO: AIR, CLIMATE.

198

COAL

More than 600 years ago, MARCO POLO returned to Venice from China with the news that the Chinese burned a black rock for fuel. The black rock was coal.

Coal was formed during the "Coal Age," when much of the world was warm and giant FERN trees and other tall trees grew in great swamps.

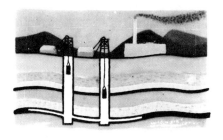

Upcast shaft-air is sucked up by a powerful fan

Water is pumped up from the bottom of the shaft

These fern trees grew quickly, then died, and were buried in the shallow swamps. More trees soon took their place and repeated the cycle. The swamps sank and layers of sediment and rock accumulated above the plant material. The pressure of the rock layers forced water out and helped change the plant material into coal. The first step in the formation of coal is *peat* or "unfinished coal." In time, peat under greater pressure hardens into a soft poor kind of dark brown coal called *lignite*.

Lignite is not a very old form of coal. It is very crumbly and burns with much smoke because it still contains a lot of moisture. It does not give off much heat. Lignite is compressed into bricks to reduce the moisture content. It is mined in North Dakota.

A harder form of coal, mined in the Rockies and Appalachians, is *bituminous* or "soft coal." This burns well but with a smoky flame. This shiny black coal is often used industrially because it is cheaper than

199

anthracite. Anthracite or "hard coal" is coal that has undergone tremendous pressure and heat over the longest period of time. It gives off more heat than the other forms of coal and burns with very little smoke. Almost all of this type mined in the United States is found in Pennsylvania.

Coal is sometimes called "black diamond," because DIAMONDS are made of carbon, as coal is.

Usually coal mining is shaft mining. From each shaft, which cuts through the various seams of coal, tunnels fan out in all directions into the various seams of coal. The seams are dug out either by machines or by miners with picks and drills. The loose coal is then carried away by conveyor belts and trucks.

Great safety precautions must be followed. As the seams are worked, the empty space must be supported with timbers and finally filled in with stony material to prevent a mine cave-in. Also, mining engineers must devise ventilation systems to rid the mine of dangerous gases and to provide oxygen. They also must rid the mine of unwanted water that might seep into the tunnels. The coal that is near

the surface can be simply dug out by removing the overlying layer of dirt. This is called *open-cast* mining.

There is a smokeless, high quality coal called *coke*. This is produced by heating coal in large ovens emptied of air. Gases and liquids are also given off. The gases are used as fuel, and the liquids, such as benzene and coal tar, are used in making dyes, plastics, fertilizers, and medicines. SEE ALSO: CARBON, DIAMONDS, FUEL.

Gas and coke are produced at the Gas Works

COAST GUARD

The United States Coast Guard keeps the coasts and inland waterways safe, making sure ships obey the navigation laws. It also helps vessels and persons in trouble at sea. It works to stop the smuggling of illegal goods (contraband) into and out of the country.

The Coast Guard operates LIGHTHOUSES, LIGHTSHIPS, weather ships, icebreakers, BUOYS, and radio navigation aids. In addition, very fast ships called *cutters* and rescue helicopters and airplanes are also widely used by the Coast Guard.

COCOA and CHOCOLATE

Cocoa (or coco) and chocolate are made from the seeds of the cacao tree. The cacao trees, grown in the tropical parts of the world, are only about 20 feet (6.2 m) tall. When the trees are four years old, they begin to bear pods about 10 to 14 inches (25–35 cm) long. Inside the pods are seeds or *beans*, which are harvested twice each

year. The beans are then roasted and crushed. Also, the husks are removed, leaving the kernels or *cocoa nibs*, which are then ground up between rollers. If cocoa is to be made, most of the fat or *cocoa butter* is pressed out. This cocoa butter is used in making candy, ointments, and soaps. However, if chocolate is to be made, extra cocoa butter with sugar and perhaps milk powder is added to the cocoa nibs. Then everything is thoroughly ground up and mixed together for a couple of hours in a special type of machine. The result is a delicious, sweet chocolate.

A chocolate kind of drink was made by the Aztecs of Mexico. The Spanish explorers brought it back with them to Europe. The Aztec drink was highly spiced with pepper, but the Spanish soon added sugar to it. By 1650, chocolate was being sold in shops in various European cities. The English began to make it with milk, instead of water, in the 1700s. In the United States, chocolate was first made in 1765 at a mill near Dorchester, in Massachusetts.

Today, cocoa and chocolate flavor many of our drinks, puddings, candies, cakes, pies, and ice cream. Much of the world's supply comes from Brazil and Africa.

COCONUT

The coconut is the seed of the coconut palm tree. Inside the seed is white edible meat and a milky liquid. The coconut palm trees grow throughout the tropical regions of the world. Because the seeds float, they are often carried by ocean currents thousands of miles from the parent coconut trees. The trees therefore establish themselves naturally in other tropical areas.

The coconut palm, which grows from 60 to 100 feet (19-31 m) in height, is a very useful tree. Besides the nut that provides food and drink, the dried kernel, called *copra*, has an oil that is used in soaps, candles, and margarine. The leaves are used for making baskets and thatch for roofs. The fibers from the husk are made into brushes, ropes, and mats. The trunk provides timber, called porcupine wood, that is hard and fine grained.

COFFEE

Coffee is made from the seeds or *beans* of a plant that grows in hot climates. It originated about 1300 years ago in Abyssinia (now Ethiopia) and Arabia. Although Arabian coffee is still considered the finest in quality, most of the world's supply comes from Brazil and Columbia.

Coffee trees are kept to a shrubby height of 5 to 15 feet (1.6—4.7 m), so that the fruit can be easily reached. The fruit, borne continuously throughout the year, looks like red cherries. However, each "cherry" contains *two* seeds or beans.

Sprig of coffee plant with flowers & berries

After the fruit is gathered, crushed, and washed, the beans are dried in the sun. Then the husks are removed. The coffee beans are later shipped to coffee roasters all over the world. They are roasted (browned and dried by heat), blended with other coffees, and ground just before being sold.

Coffee was introduced into England from Turkey in 1652. By 1700, coffeehouses were popular places for people to meet, do business, and have arguments. The French word *café* and the Spanish American word *cafeteria* come from words meaning coffee and coffee shop, respectively.

Coffee contains a substance, *caffeine*, which can keep some people awake. Some coffees have the caffeine removed.

A Coffee House

COLLEGE and UNIVERSITY

To gain admission to a college or university, a boy or girl must graduate from a high school, pass certain examinations, and generally show that he or she can do more difficult work in higher education. Many subjects such as English, history, physics, and psychology are studied. A student in a 2-year college can earn an *associate's degree* and in a 4-year college a *bachelor's degree*. A college graduate can then do more advanced study and earn a *master's degree* and a *doctor's degree* in his or her particular field, whether it be English, business, medicine, law, or any other.

There were universities of a kind—groups of people studying together—in ancient Greece and Rome. In the 9th century A.D., the first European university was founded at Salerno, in Italy. Around 1200, universities were set up in Oxford, Cambridge, Paris, and Bologna. Harvard University, founded in 1636, was the first institution of higher learning in the U.S.

Universities are usually larger than colleges and are allowed to award the doctor's degree. Many private colleges are, or have been, controlled by a religious group or church. Private colleges or universities depend on students' tuition and grants from wealthy individuals or companies. Public institutions of higher education are supported by local and state governments, with some loans and grants from the federal government, and by some tuition from the students. Many students win scholarships that pay part or all of the cost of going to college. Others work while they study or take educational loans from banks. SEE ALSO: SCHOOL.

COLOMBIA

Colombia is a large country in northwestern SOUTH AMERICA, with coastlines on the Pacific Ocean and the Caribbean Sea. Three high ranges of the Andes divide the country into different regions. The flat coastal areas are sometimes swampy, but some places are good for growing cotton, rice, tobacco, and bananas. The highlands near and in the Andes have very fertile soil, ideal for growing coffee and for raising cattle. The eastern part of Colombia consists of grassy plains, vast forests, and dense jungles. Colombia is rich in minerals. Oil, natural gas, salt, gold, iron, platinum, and emeralds are mined. The country has developed its hydroelectric power and its industries. The chief manufactured products are textiles, steel, chemicals, and food and rubber goods. Colombia has more than 25 million inhabitants, most of whom are of mixed European (mainly Spanish), Indian, and Negro ancestry. The capital and largest city is Bogotá, situated about 9000 feet (2790 m) above sea level in the Andes.

Ancient Indian tribes are said to have inhabited the region as early as 5000 B.C. In the 1500s, the Spanish conquered and settled the region, founding there a Spanish colony named New Granada. New Granada included parts of what are now Panama, Ecuador, and Venezuela, as well as Colombia. Finally, in 1819, SIMÓN BOLÍVAR led the people in their successful fight against the Spanish. In 1863, the republic of Colombia was established. Panama was a part of Colombia until 1903.

COLOR

The colors of different objects depend on the kind of LIGHT which is absorbed or reflected by them.

Sir Isaac Newton, a British scientist, discovered that sunlight, the whitest of lights, is actually made up of many colors (the SPECTRUM). As proof, he made a ray of light pass through a wedge-shaped piece of glass. The prism broke up the sunlight much like raindrops do when sunlight passes through them to produce a RAINBOW. A circular disc with all the colors of the spectrum will also appear white when spun very rapidly.

Glass prism

yellow

red

yellow and red

blue

yellow, red and blue

black

A red book, for example, appears red in daylight because the red dye of the book absorbs all the colors of the spectrum falling on the book *except* red which is reflected to the eye. Red glass appears red because all the colors of white light are absorbed by the glass *except* red which passes through it. A black object absorbs all the colors of white light; a white object reflects all the colors of light.

There are artificial lights that do not give off white light like sunlight. For example, a mercury vapor lamp gives off light minus the red rays. A person looks very strange in such a light: his lips are purple and his cheeks bluish because no red rays reach the eye.

Colored illustrations, like those in this book, are made by printing four colors (yellow, red called magenta, a special blue called cyan, and black) on top of each other. The various stages are shown to the left; the final result is on page 207.

COLORADO

Colorado is divided by the Rocky Mountains. This western state has more than 1000 peaks that rise at least 10,000 feet (3100 m), including the famous Pikes Peak. In the east are the high plains, while the Rockies make up the central region. In the west is the rugged Colorado Plateau. Denver, the capital, lies just east of the Rockies and is often called the "mile-high city." Colorado has great extremes in climate, as is typical of many mountainous areas.

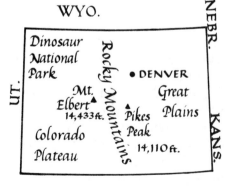

WYO.

NEBR.

Dinosaur National Park

Rocky Mountains

● DENVER

UT.

Mt. Elbert 14,433 ft.

Pikes Peak 14,110 ft.

Great Plains

KANS.

Colorado Plateau

N. MEX.

The state produces most of the world's molybdenum, which hardens steel and is used in rocketry. Oil shale, lead, zinc, and tin are also mined. Manufacturing and tourism rank high among the state's important industries. Cattle and poultry are raised on the plains, and wheat, sugar beets, and hay are grown.

In 1682, France claimed Colorado's eastern part, but Spain took control of the entire area in 1706. Explorers and settlers found many Indians already living there. The Utes were in the mountains, and the Arapahos, Comanches, Cheyennes, Pawnees, and Kiowas on the plains. The U.S. got eastern and central Colorado as part of the Louisiana Purchase in 1803, and the western part after the Mexican War in 1848. Men flocked to the area in 1858 when gold was found in Cherry Creek (now downtown Denver). Bloody battles occurred between whites and the Indians, whose hunting grounds were stolen. Peace was finally made, and most Indians moved onto reservations. Colorado became a state in 1876. Today its population is more than 2.5 million.

Christopher COLUMBUS (1451–1506)

Christopher Columbus was a skilled mapmaker and explorer who discovered AMERICA in 1492. He was really searching for a route to the "Indies," as Asia was then called. For centuries, historians thought that Columbus was the first to find America. However, historians now believe that LEIF ERICSON was probably the first European to reach North America.

He was born in Genoa, Italy, as Cristoforo Colombo. As a boy he went to sea and learned about navigation and maps, making many trips to the Gold Coast of Africa. Believing there was a shorter way to India by going west, Columbus tried to get money and ships from the King of Portugal but failed. For six years, he sought the same from Queen Isabella of Spain, who finally supplied money and three ships. The *Niña*, the *Pinta*, and the *Santa María*, commanded by Columbus, made a difficult voyage across the Atlantic. The men almost mutinied as they sailed farther and farther west. Columbus even had to promise his crew that he would turn back if land were not sighted within three days. On the third day, October 12, several islands were discovered.

Columbus named the land San Salvador, claiming it for Queen Isabella and Spain. He thought he had found the "Indies," but really he had landed on an island (now called Watling Island) in the Bahamas. He named the people there "Indians."

He then sailed on to Cuba and to Hispaniola (Haiti and the Dominican Republic), where the *Santa María* was wrecked on the north coast. Leaving men there to found a colony, Columbus hurried back to Spain aboard the *Niña*; the *Pinta* was lost on the way back.

After being hailed as "admiral of the ocean sea," he made a second voyage in 1493, this time discovering the Leeward Islands, St. Kitts, the Virgin Islands, PUERTO RICO, and JAMAICA. On a third expedition in 1498, he discovered Trinidad

and SOUTH AMERICA. Also he tried to administer his colony in Hispaniola, but in 1500 another governor was sent by Isabella to rule the colony. He sent Columbus back to Spain as a prisoner in chains.

After being set free in 1502, Columbus gathered together four ships for a fourth voyage to the New World and to find a passage to India. He touched CENTRAL AMERICA, but suffered terrible hardships which forced him to return to Spain.

Although his voyages and discoveries marked the start of American history, Columbus died in poverty, almost forgotten, in the village of Valladolid, in northern Spain. SEE ALSO: AMERICA.

COMET

Comets are heavenly bodies that travel around the sun on long, elliptical orbits. The earliest records of comets date back about 2500 years ago. Some comets come close to the Earth quite regularly. Halley's comet, first described in A.D. 684, comes in sight every 75 years. Encke's comet has the shortest orbit and appears every 3.3 years. These two comets are called short-period comets.

The head of a comet may be quite large, but it is probably not very solid. The tail of the comet, which may be millions of miles long, contains in 10,000 cubic miles (41,800 km³) less than a cubic inch (16.4 cm³) of solid matter. In fact, the Earth has occasionally passed through the dust and gas of a comet's tail.

COMICS

About 150 years ago, artists who worked for newspapers and magazines began to publish funny pictures. Sometimes they did a single cartoon, but sometimes they used several cartoons to tell a story. The idea of having the characters of the cartoons return day after day, week after week, came only in the 1890s. In 1897, an American newspaper publisher began to print a "supplement" (non-news part of a paper) in color. It had nothing but comics in it. This was published only on Sunday, but soon comic strips began to appear in daily papers. They were printed in black and white. Later there were comic books.

Comic strips have all sorts of ways of appealing to people. Adventure is the main one. The hero overcomes criminals, enemies of his country, or beings from outer space. *Satire* (laughing at foolishness) is also very popular. Some satirical comic strips are more for adults than children. *Fantasy* (letting the imagination go) is often found in comic strips. Some strips have to do with love or duty. Many are simply funny, and that is all.

Because comic strips are so interesting and easy to read, religious groups, advertisers, and other groups that want to bring people around to their way of thinking use the comic-strip form.

The comic strip is not just a set of drawings of a thrilling or funny situation. Some are good art too, beautifully drawn. Even famous painters have done comic strips.

COMMERCE

The selling of things is called commerce. People in commerce include merchants, salesmen, people in advertising, and so on. Their job is to see that those who want to buy goods (useful things) or services (useful activities) are told about them and have a chance to get them. When your neighborhood store sells you something, that is commerce, and when American manufacturers send goods to foreign countries by the shipload, that is commerce too. Commerce is also called *trade*. SEE ALSO: BUSINESS, INDUSTRY.

COMPASS

A compass is a direction finder. It is thought to have been invented in China and brought to Europe about A.D. 1100. Until the invention of the compass, sailors did not dare to venture far out to sea. A compass helped them to find their direction without having to rely upon the stars or sun.

A magnetic compass basically has a flat-pointed needle which pivots on the point of a short rod. The rod goes through a card which has printed on it N (north), S (south), E (east), and W (west). The needle is a MAGNET and it always points to the

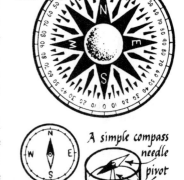

A compass card

A simple compass needle
pivot

Earth's magnetic north pole. The farther north one is, the farther from true north the compass needle points. Thus, navigators must use charts to correct their compass readings.

A more useful compass to navigators is the gyrocompass, which works on a different principle. Its wheel is set spinning and it points exactly to true north.

COMPOUND

When two or more elements chemically unite in a fixed proportion, they form a different substance known as a *compound*. For example, when hydrogen and oxygen (two gases) unite, the compound known as water is formed. A molecule of water contains two atoms of hydrogen chemically joined with one atom of oxygen. When the metal sodium unites with the poisonous gas chlorine, the compound sodium chloride (our common table salt) is formed. There are an estimated 4 million known compounds in the world, formed by combinations of about 100 elements.

CONCERTO

There are two kinds of concerto (pronounced concherto).

The kind we usually hear today is written for an orchestra and for a single performer whose playing stands out in contrast to that of the orchestra. His piano, violin, or whatever he is playing can be heard over the other sounds. Often he plays a *cadenza*, a complicated solo passage that shows his skill. Concertos have several movements, with contrasting speeds and melodies, like symphonies.

There is also the *concerto grosso*. A few players perform together, with no single performer standing out from the others. This sort of concerto was popular in the 17th and 18th centuries.

CONCRETE

Concrete is made by mixing together CEMENT, sand, gravel, and water. It is usually done in a mixer similar to the one shown here. Because of its great strength, durability, and cheapness, concrete is a major building material. Many highways, dams, and foundations of buildings, bridges, and piers are made of concrete.

The ancient Romans used concrete in the construction of their sewers. They also used it in many of their public buildings, including the Pantheon.

In the 20th century, concrete containing steel bars, strands, or mesh is used in much building construction. Known as *reinforced* concrete, it has allowed floors and roofs of large size to be built with few supporting pillars. It has made possible new architectural styles, too. Some barges and ships have even been built of concrete. SEE ALSO: CEMENT.

CONESTOGA WAGON

Eighteenth-century roads were bad in most places, and wagon builders along Conestoga Creek in eastern Pennsylvania built a special kind of freight wagon to handle the problem of travel. Their wagon had thick wheels that would not sink into mud, a floor that dipped toward the center so that the freight would not slide toward the ends on slopes and bumpy places, and a big canvas cover on hoops to shelter the load. Pulled by four or six horses, these wagons could carry six tons (5.5 metric tons).

Later, when the pioneers went westward, wagon builders supplied them with a similar but smaller kind of wagon called a *prairie schooner*.

CONFUCIUS (551-479 B.C.)

Confucius was one of the great Chinese philosophers and teachers. He lived around 500 years before Jesus.

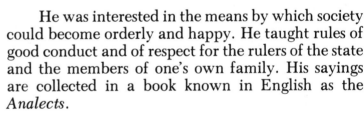

He was interested in the means by which society could become orderly and happy. He taught rules of good conduct and of respect for the rulers of the state and the members of one's own family. His sayings are collected in a book known in English as the *Analects*.

His teachings were not religious, but he was so highly regarded by the Chinese that a religion called Confucianism was developed.

CONGRESS

The Congress of the United States consists of a Senate and a House of Representatives. The Congress makes up the *legislative* branch of government (the other two branches are the *executive* and *judicial*). "To legislate" means "to make laws," which is the chief job of Congress. Members of the U.S. Congress meet in the Capitol building in Washington, D.C.

The Capitol

The powers of the Congress are divided between the Senate and the House of Representatives, both of whose members are elected by the people. There are 435 members of the House and 100 members of the Senate; the former serve for two years and the latter for six years before another election to office. The people in each of the 50 states periodically elect two Senators and a number of House members (depending on the population of that state).

The House of Representatives has the power through the CONSTITUTION to propose new *bills* (laws) concerning *revenue* (money from taxes and other sources). It can also *impeach* (bring charges against) the President or any other federal official for wrong-doing.

The Senate has some special powers like the *ratification* (approval) of all treaties with foreign governments. The Senate must also confirm the President's choices for CABINET members and SUPREME COURT justices. Like the House, it forms numerous committees to help in its work, such as in agriculture, health, energy, education, or foreign relations. The Vice President of the United States *presides* (exercises control) over the Senate.

Only Congress can declare war or raise and support an army or navy. It can set up federal courts and borrow money for the government, as well as give money to foreign nations. Also it can propose amendments to the U.S. Constitution. SEE ALSO: CONSTITUTION, PRESIDENCY, SUPREME COURT.

CONIFERS

Conifers are trees or shrubs that produce their seeds in cones. *Conifer* in Latin means "cone-bearing." Most conifers have long narrow needles as leaves and are evergreens. However, a few, such as the larch, are deciduous—that is, they shed their leaves annually. Other common conifers include PINES, FIRS, cedars, spruces, and cypresses. The SEQUOIAS of California are the largest conifers on Earth.

Conifers are mostly found in the highlands in the world's temperate regions. Many conifers grow quickly and produce a timber known as *softwood*. Also, the wood pulp from these trees is made into paper.

Spruce

Scots Pine

Seed

Spruce

Douglas Fir

CONNECTICUT

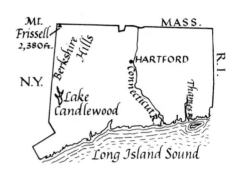

Connecticut factories make ball and roller bearings, jet engines, helicopters, nuclear submarines, chemicals, plastics, firearms, and electronic goods. Hartford, the capital, has many large insurance companies. The state's highly industrialized cities contrast sharply with its quiet villages nestled in the rolling hills. Connecticut has slightly more than 3 million people.

This region was inhabited by several Indian tribes, including the Mohegan, Wampanoag, and Pequot. The name "Connecticut" comes from "Quonecktacut," the Algonquin word for the Connecticut River, meaning "at the long tidal river." Adriaen Block, a Dutch explorer, sailed up this river in 1614. PURITANS from Massachusetts founded towns in Connecticut in the 1630s. They adopted the Fundamental Orders in 1639, which is said to be the first formal constitution ever written in the United States. During the American Revolution, Connecticut produced many patriots, such as NATHAN HALE, Jonathan Trumbull, and David Bushnell, who built the first submarine ever used in war.

The state has had numerous business pioneers, including ELI WHITNEY, who produced cotton gins and firearms in New Haven, Charles Goodyear, who developed the process of vulcanizing rubber, and Samuel Colt, who invented the revolver.

CONSERVATION

Conservation is the wise use and the preservation of natural resources.

When the settlers came to America and saw what appeared to be an unending supply of natural resources, they abused the land. Whole forests were leveled, and minerals were washed from eroding soil. Careless woodsmen often caused terrible forest fires. Buffalo were slaughtered, sometimes just for the delicate meat of their tongues.

The first protest against the devastation of America was made in 1864. However, the country was preoccupied with the Civil War. In 1871, California established Yosemite Park as a state recreational reserve. In 1879, President ULYSSES GRANT signed a bill establishing Yellowstone, in Wyoming, as the world's first national park.

However, America continued to squander its resources. In 1901, President THEODORE ROOSEVELT gave the idea of conservation his complete attention. Under his leadership, America's forestry conservation program developed. America's national forests became models to the world in the management and preservation of wildlife and wilderness.

By the time of World War I, however, America's rangelands had been overgrazed. Former drought-resistant buffalo and gama grasslands had been plowed under and replaced by vast wheat fields that could easily be eroded. Several severe droughts at that time caused many farmers to abandon their farms. Also, the war made greater demands for food, and thus more PRAIRIES were dug up to make wheat fields.

Kansas and Nebraska suffered terrible drought in the 1930s, and south central United States became known as the "Dust Bowl." This disaster caused a rebirth of the conservation movement in America. Farmers were helped by the newly formed federal Soil Conservation Service and the Grazing Service. When rain finally fell, the Dust Bowl area gradually began to recover. Farmers used wise methods of soil conservation.

Today, the American people are keenly aware of the need to protect our natural resources if future generations are to have clean air and water, as well as fertile land on which to grow food.

CONSTANTINE (A.D. 280?–337)

Constantine was the last of the great Roman emperors. He was also the first Christian emperor.

In A.D. 305, two Roman emperors ruled, one in the West and one in the East. Constantine's father was emperor in the West. During an expedition in Britain, his father died and the army proclaimed Constantine the new emperor. After several years, he was able to take complete control, defeating his enemies. During a battle, he had a vision of the Christian cross and believed it had brought victory. He decreed that Christianity be the official religion in the Roman Empire.

He founded a new capital city of Byzantium, renaming it in A.D. 330 the City of Constantine or Constantinople (now Istanbul). Rome remained the capital in the West, but Constantinople became more powerful. He was a tolerant and wise emperor who made legal, military, and religious reforms.

U.S. CONSTITUTION

After the American Revolution, the thirteen states tried unsuccessfully to live under the laws of the Articles of Confederation. Leaders of the new nation realized that a formal constitution had to be written if the states were to be united. In 1787, delegates from the states met at Independence Hall in Philadelphia. George Washington was chosen president of this Constitutional Convention. Some delegates wanted a strong central government, while others wanted to make sure the rights and powers of the states were respected. After much debate, a compromise was made.

The people of the United States would be represented in an assembly called the U.S. CONGRESS. The SUPREME COURT was established. The people would elect a President and not have a king. Each of these branches of government would check and balance the power of the others. Also, the states were left some powers. The writers of the Constitution—men like Thomas Jefferson, James Madison, Alexander Hamilton, and Benjamin Franklin—did not want the government to have absolute power. They believed that the people were entitled to basic freedoms and protections, too.

The U.S. Constitution was signed by the delegates on September 17, 1787, and *ratified* (approved) by the required number of states (nine) on June 21, 1788. Ten *amendments* (additions), called the BILL OF RIGHTS, became part of the Constitution on December 15, 1791. Later, other amendments were made, according to Constitutional law. SEE ALSO: BILL OF RIGHTS.

CONTINENT

A continent is a large area of land that is nearly or completely surrounded by oceans. The continents are Eurasia (usually regarded as two continents—EUROPE and ASIA), AFRICA, AUSTRALIA, Antarctica, NORTH AMERICA, and SOUTH AMERICA. The total area of the continents takes up about 30 percent of the Earth's surface. Asia is the largest continent, Australia the smallest.

Some scientists now think that all the continents were one huge land mass when the Earth was first formed. It slowly broke up, and its pieces drifted apart and still are drifting today.

CONVENTS

Originally a convent was a place for monks—that is, a MONASTERY. But women also wanted to live the quiet religious life. Some of the old *orders* (associations) of monks had branches for women, but women later started orders of their own.

A woman in a *convent* (monastery for women) is called a *nun*. She is under the same strict rules that monks obey. Nuns may leave the convent to visit the sick, or they may be teachers; then they are called *sisters*. Catholic families often send their children to schools taught by Catholic sisters. Parents may even send their children to a convent to live while they are being taught.

Captain James COOK (1728–1779)

Captain Cook was an English navigator and explorer who discovered AUSTRALIA and the Hawaiian Islands.

He was born in Yorkshire, England, and in 1755 joined the British Navy. He was an expert mapmaker, surveying between 1760 and 1767 the coasts of Newfoundland and Labrador and the St. Lawrence River. In 1768, he sailed to the Pacific Ocean, hoping to discover Antarctica. He did not go far enough south, but did visit Tahiti, NEW ZEALAND, and eastern Australia, claiming it for England.

During a second voyage, lasting three years and covering 70,000 miles (112,700 km), he reached the Antarctic Circle and discovered New Caledonia and the Cook Islands.

On a third expedition in 1776, he looked for a northern passage between the Atlantic and Pacific. He discovered HAWAII and surveyed the North American coast from Oregon to the ARCTIC. During a second stop in Hawaii, he was killed in a fight with some natives.

COOKING

Cooking has been going on for countless years. Perhaps it began when an animal meant for food was accidentally burned.

There are several reasons for treating food with heat in some sort of way. It kills germs and tiny animals in the food that are harmful to man. It helps slow down the spoiling of some foods. It can soften foods that are too tough and give firmness to foods that are too soft. It allows one piece of food to be made into different things; for instance, a piece of meat can be roasted as a main dish while its bone can be used for soup.

Roasting

Of course, we do not cook everything. Salads and many fruits and vegetables are eaten raw. So are some sea foods, such as clams and oysters.

Roasting, or *broiling*, is an easy way of cooking. The food is placed close to a fire or something equally hot without touching it. The rays of heat from the fire cook the food.

In *frying*, the food is placed on a surface that is heated. A buttery or oily substance is melted on the hot surface to spread the heat.

In *boiling*, the food is placed in a pot with water which is heated until it bubbles. Boiling is good for softening food.

Baking surrounds the food with something hot. Sometimes the heat from the walls of an old-fashioned oven does the cooking. Sometimes the hot air in an oven is used. And corn and cakes have been baked in hot ashes.

There are other ways of cooking, but these are the main ones. Every country has its own way of cooking, because certain foods are more available and because of local customs.

Boiling

Baking

Ways of cooking – as pictured in a medieval book

COPENHAGEN

Copenhagen (which means "Merchant's Harbor") is the capital of DENMARK. It was a small fishing village during the Middle Ages. Because of its good harbor and location at the entrance to the BALTIC SEA, it grew in importance. It is situated on the islands of Zealand and Amager, which are separated by an inlet from the Sound (Oresund).

It is a noted publishing center of books and periodicals. Fabrics, machinery, silver, and earthenware are manufactured there, and its commerce by railroads and ships is extensive. SEE ALSO: DENMARK.

Nicholas COPERNICUS (1473–1543)

Nicholas Copernicus, called the father of modern ASTRONOMY, was born in Poland. Copernicus studied the stars and recorded his observations. The people of his day still believed the ideas of Ptolemy, an ancient Greek scientist, who thought that the Earth stood still while the universe revolved about it. Being at the center of the universe made man feel important. However, Copernicus, after studying the heavens carefully, believed that the PLANETS, including the EARTH, circled about the SUN. He also believed that the Earth spun as it revolved about the sun and that the stars were immense distances away from us.

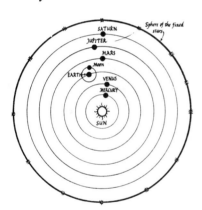

Many people urged him to write his ideas down in a book. Copernicus waited many years because he knew the Church would not approve and would feel it was a threat to religion. Finally, he wrote a book that was published in 1543. A copy of it reached him on the day he died. Although he was not the first person to suggest these ideas, he was the first person to put forth mathematical arguments. GALILEO with his telescope proved Copernicus was correct many years later. SEE ALSO: ASTRONOMY, GALILEO.

COPPER

Copper has been used since ancient times. Because it was often found in the pure state, copper was quite easy to discover, as gold was. By melting tin and copper together, early man produced BRONZE. Being harder than copper, bronze was very useful in making tools and weapons. Later, man discovered that melting copper with zinc produced BRASS.

Next to silver, copper is the best conductor of electricity. As a result, half of the copper mined is used for electrical machinery and wiring.

Copper not only polishes beautifully but it also conducts heat well. Therefore, pots, pans, and tea

Telephone wires are made of copper

kettles are made partly or completely of copper. Copper is very *malleable* (easily hammered) and can be easily molded into shapes, such as into tubes, sheets, coins, jewelry, and statues.

Today, most copper comes from copper ORES. It is usually joined chemically with sulphur, which is removed by roasting in large ovens. Large deposits of copper are in Utah and Montana. The greatest known copper deposit is in Chile.

CORAL

Coral consists of the limestone skeletons of tiny soft sea animals called *cnidarians*. These primitive creatures are shaped like cylinders and are related to the jellyfish. Different species produce different types of coral in many shapes and colors.

Coral itself is dead, yet it grows larger as the cnidarians continue to live on the outside edges and deposit coral around them. Coral grows about an inch (2.54 cm) per year.

Large masses of coral are called *reefs*. There are three types: coral fringes to islands; barrier reefs, which stretch for miles off the coast (for example, the Great Barrier Reef of Australia, is 1200 miles— 1932 km—long); and atolls, which are ring-shaped reefs or closely spaced coral islands enclosing a LAGOON.

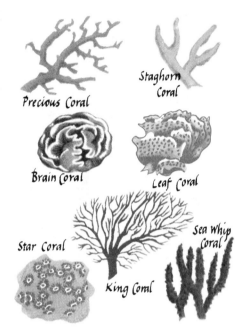

Precious Coral

Staghorn Coral

Brain Coral

Leaf Coral

Star Coral

King Coral

Sea Whip Coral

CORK

Cork is the outer bark of a special kind of oak tree, the *cork oak*, which grows in Mediterranean countries, such as Spain and Portugal.

Cork is extremely useful. It is strong, light, waterproof, elastic, and heat-resistant. Cork is used in making life jackets, coasters, bottle stoppers, inner soles, and hot pads. It is also ground up in linoleum and used as insulation in freezers. The Romans used cork for floats as early as the 1st century A.D.

When the cork tree is about 20 years old, the outer bark is removed carefully so

as not to injure the inner bark. Cork trees live 150 years; an 80-year-old tree produces 500 pounds (225 kg) of cork. Every 3 to 10 years, the cork is removed from the tree. Boiling removes the hard outer covering before cork products are made.

CORMORANT

The cormorant is a large water bird, related to the pelican. It is found mainly in coastal, temperate, or tropical regions.

Cormorants usually have dark feathers and green eyes; they grow to two or three feet (61–92 m) in length. With their webbed feet and long bill, cormorants are expert swimmers and "fishermen." In the Orient, they have been tamed and trained to catch fish. Cormorants generally build nests of seaweed on cliffs.

CORN

Corn is the only grain which originally grew in America. Corn is a variety of grass used in making CEREALS and BREADS. Indians raised corn long before Columbus discovered America. The Pilgrims were taught the value of corn by the friendly Indians they met. Corn is now an important crop in other parts of the world; such as South America, China, and South Africa.

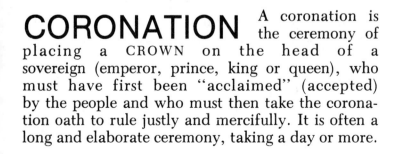

Corn is used to feed people, hogs, and cattle. It is also used in making flour, cornstarch, corn syrup, cooking oil, and margarine. Drugs, plastics, and wallboard are corn products, too.

In some parts of the world, such as England, corn is called *maize*.

CORONATION

A coronation is the ceremony of placing a CROWN on the head of a sovereign (emperor, prince, king or queen), who must have first been "acclaimed" (accepted) by the people and who must then take the coronation oath to rule justly and mercifully. It is often a long and elaborate ceremony, taking a day or more.

In England, since the coronation in A.D. 973 of King Edgar, the sovereign must also swear to protect the Church of England, as well as to administer a lawful government and justice. The pageantry of the English coronation is still like that of the Middle Ages. Lavish robes, scepters, rings, and thrones are used. Finally the crown is placed on the new sovereign's head, and he or she is given Holy Communion. Since 1066, English kings and queens have been crowned in Westminster Abbey by the Archbishop of Canterbury.

The picture shows the coronation of Queen Elizabeth II of England, which took place on June 2, 1953. SEE ALSO: CROWN.

Hernando CORTÉS (1485–1547)

Hernando Cortés (or Cortez) was a Spanish conquistador (conqueror) who seized Mexico during the early 1500s.

He sought adventure as a young man, sailing to the New World to conquer and become rich. After helping to conquer Cuba, he and 700 Spanish soldiers sailed to Mexico to find the reported gold of MONTEZUMA, the Aztec king.

He cut off any possibility of retreat by his men when he burned all his ships after landing. Then he marched inland, making friends with some tribes who thought he was a god. With them he reached Tenochtitlan (now Mexico City) and found a highly developed civilization. He captured Montezuma and soon conquered the whole country.

Cortés' route from Cuba to Mexico

On his return to Spain, he was coldly received by the king's court, which feared his popularity and ambition. After several other expeditions, he retired into solitude and died in relative obscurity. SEE ALSO: MONTEZUMA.

COSMIC RAYS

Cosmic rays are submicroscopic, electrically charged particles—largely protons of atoms—that travel through outer space at almost the speed of light. They originate somewhere in the universe beyond our solar system. Some happen to come into our atmosphere where they collide with atoms of air to produce

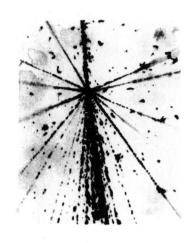

radioactivity. They travel with such force that they are able to penetrate hundreds of feet of water, despite being slowed down by the air.

Beyond our atmosphere, their penetrating effect is many thousands of times greater. This effect could prove to be a problem to space travel. On Earth, their effect on the human body is harmless, even though about one hundred of these cosmic particles bombard it per second.

Scientists have been able to learn a great deal about the ATOM by studying cosmic rays.

COTTON

Cotton is a very ancient plant. It was raised in India more than 3000 years ago. The Indians of Mexico and Peru made cotton cloth long before their countries were discovered by European explorers. The Egyptians were using cotton in 600 B.C. It remained, however, a rare luxury in Europe until the 14th Century or later. The United States is today the world's largest cotton producer. It is grown in the South, as well as in Arizona and California.

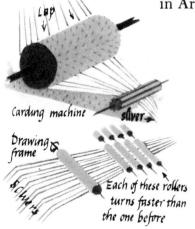

Carding machine — sliver →

Drawing frame

Slivers

Each of these rollers turns faster than the one before

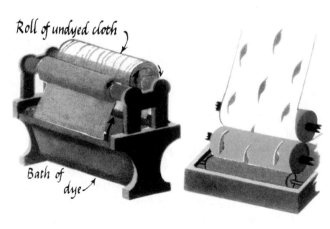

Roll of undyed cloth

Bath of dye →

The cotton plant grows about 3 feet (0.91 m) tall. When the cotton plants are ripe, the seed pods, or *bolls*, open. They are then picked by hand or machine. The seeds were removed by hand until 1793, when ELI WHITNEY invented the "cotton gin" to do this work.

The cotton is baled and sent to manufacturers who clean and spin the fibers into cotton thread, twine, and even rope. Cottonseed oil is used in making salad dressings and soaps. Cottonseed meal is good food for cattle.

Today, about three-fourths of the people of the world wear clothes made from cotton. The BOLL WEEVIL is a harmful beetle that does much damage to cotton plants by laying its eggs inside the bolls. When the larvae hatch out they feed on the contents of the bolls. SEE ALSO: BOLL WEEVIL.

COWBOYS

The name cowboy refers usually to any mounted herdsman hired by a rancher in the western United States to look after his cattle. The cowboy keeps the stock together, leads them to pasture, keeps them from mixing with other herds, protects them from cattle rustlers, brands them at the proper time, and drives them to their shipping point.

The tools of the cowboy's trade are his trusted horse, rope, saddle, spurs, and a branding iron. His costume includes boots, a Stetson hat, and a bandanna to protect his face from the dust and sun.

During the American Revolution "cowboys" were those who usually stole cattle and sometimes other property. These men operated on the roads east of the HUDSON RIVER between the British and American lines near New York. They claimed to be Tories (supporters of the British). Those who infested and plundered the same area and claimed to be Whigs (supporters of the Revolution) were called "skinners."

In the 19th century West, cowboys drove cattle across the open range to market towns. The coming of the railroad to bring cattle to market and the enclosure of the ranges with barbed wire ended the romantic era of the cowboy. He can still be found working on the modern-day ranches, and he can still be seen at events in RODEOS and other outdoor festivals in the West.

CRABS

Crabs belong to a group of animals called CRUSTACEANS. They have hard outer shells to which their strong muscles are attached. They also have five pairs of legs, the front pair being their pinching claws, and two feelers. Their two eyes are on the end of short, retractable stalks. The largest crustacean is the spider crab of Japan, which has been known to have a claw span of 11 feet (3.41 m). Some crabs live in shallow coastal waters; others live in deep ocean waters.

Many crabs are good to eat, such as the Alaskan king crab and the Atlantic blue crab. Soft-shelled crabs are "growing" crabs which have shed their outgrown shells. The hermit crabs lack a hard outer shell, and so they live in empty whelk shells for protection. Most crabs walk sideways. They feed on decaying plants and animals.

Hermit Crab

Edible Crab

CRANES

A crane is a machine for picking a heavy object up from one place and setting it down in another. Many cranes are *jib cranes*, which have a long arm for lifting. A *derrick* is a jib crane whose arm moves up and down. In a *cantilever crane* the arm stays level, and a little car runs along it to move the load. Factory buildings use *bridge cranes*. These have level beams that move on rails. Little cars move along the beam. The load can go anywhere in the building.

Cranes are also long-legged, long-necked birds that resemble herons.

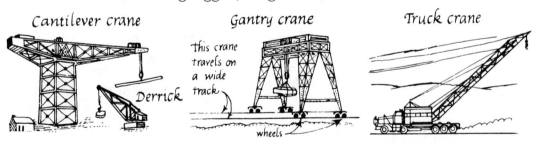

Cantilever crane

Derrick

Gantry crane

This crane travels on a wide track

wheels

Truck crane

CRATER

The crater of a VOLCANO is the hole through which lava, ashes, and burning gases are forced by pressures deep within the Earth. Active volcanoes have funnel-shaped craters; non-explosive volcanoes often have craters shaped like a shallow bowl. Japan's Mount Aso has the Earth's largest crater. It is 71 miles (114.3 km) long and 10 miles (16.1 km) wide.

A crater formed by the impact of a fallen meteorite is a bowl-shaped depression with a raised rim. The largest meteorite crater is in northern Arizona and is almost a mile (1.6 km) wide. It was formed long before Europeans came to America.

The craters on the moon are circular and have a deep floor usually containing a central mountain. They are always ringed with high walls. The largest discovered is more than 600 miles (966 km) in diameter.

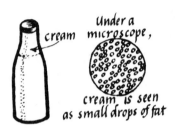

CREAM
Cream is the portion of whole milk that contains the fat. The fat in milk is evenly dispersed in the form of tiny droplets. When milk is allowed to stand for any length of time, these droplets gradually float to the top to form a layer of cream. It is from cream that butter is made. SEE ALSO: BUTTER, MILK.

CRETE
Crete is a long, mountainous island in the MEDITERRANEAN, just south of the AEGEAN SEA. It has extensive forests and a number of fertile valleys. The southern coast has few good harbors, but the northern has several inlets for ships. Crete is cool in summer and rainy in winter. It has rich deposits of iron, cobalt, manganese, and granite. Agriculture, however, is the chief occupation on the island. The language spoken there is Greek; the island belongs to GREECE.

Crete had one of the world's oldest civilizations, the Minoan Civilization, named after the legendary King Minos. Sir Arthur Evans, an English archeologist, began excavations in Crete in 1889 and learned much about the Minoans.

About 3000 B.C., a seafaring race, later named the Minoans, traded all over the Mediterranean. They were also an artistic people who erected large and splendid palaces on Crete, especially in their main cities of Cnossus and

Phaestos. Through the centuries, earthquakes and possible early invasions from MYCENAE on Greece destroyed many fine buildings, but the Minoans soon rebuilt them, adding more luxurious palaces.

Sacred ax

Golden statue

The walls of the palaces had colorful paintings of landscapes, birds, animals, and people. The Minoans were great metalworkers and ceramic artists, creating jewelry, stone and ivory figures, and beautiful vases decorated with drawings of plants and animals. The women had fashions then that looked quite modern, and the men dressed in a kind of short kilt.

The Minoans worshiped many gods that symbolized the powers of nature. They included a "snake goddess" and a "bull god" (probably the origin of the mythical Minotaur, a creature half bull and half man).

Their sports included a game in which young men or women grabbed a charging bull's horns and then somersaulted over his head, landing on his back before jumping to the ground.

About 1400 B.C. Cnossus was burned and utterly destroyed, possibly by invaders from Mycenae. Quite suddenly, the power of Crete collapsed, for reasons still obscure.

Later, Crete was conquered by the Greeks, Romans, and Turks. During one of the Crusades (1204), the island came under the rule of Venice until the Turks seized it. Because of a war in 1912 in the Balkans, Crete was annexed to Greece. SEE ALSO: AEGEAN SEA, GREECE.

Davy CROCKETT (1786–1836)

Davy Crockett was a typical unschooled pioneer, marksman, hunter, and trapper from Tennessee. In 1813, he served under General ANDREW JACKSON in a campaign against the Creek Indians. He served two terms in the Tennessee State legislature, and in 1828 became a member of Congress. He ran for a third term and was defeated, but returned to Congress in 1833. After again being defeated for reelection, he joined the troops in Texas fighting against Mexican rule.

He died in San Antonio defending the Alamo, a small chapel-fort.

During his career in politics, he became famous for his backwoods humor and peculiar ways. Popular pamphlets, called the "Crockett Almanacs," were published from 1835 to 1856. Along with the usual entries, these almanacs contained tall tales of the sayings and doings of Crockett and other frontier heroes, such as DANIEL BOONE and KIT CARSON. These publications played a very important role in establishing Crockett in American legend and folklore.

CROCODILE

The crocodile is a large flesh-eating reptile, covered with tough scales. It has very strong jaws, short legs, and a long flat tail. The crocodile's head is narrower and more pointed than that of the ALLIGATOR. Some crocodiles have grown more than 20 feet (6.2 m) long.

The American crocodile lives in the salt and fresh waters of southern Florida, the West Indies, Central America, and northern South America. The man-eating crocodile inhabits parts of Asia, Australia, and the South Pacific.

Female crocodiles lay about 20 to 70 eggs, the size of goose eggs. They hatch in the warm sand or in nests of reeds.

Oliver CROMWELL (1599–1658)

From 1649 to 1658, Oliver Cromwell governed England as Lord Protector. This period was the only time in English history when the country had no king or queen.

In 1642, a civil war erupted in England between the Roundheads, who opposed the harsh rule of King Charles I, and the Cavaliers, who backed the King. Cromwell was a Roundhead (the name was given to those who cut their hair very short). He led the army to victory and sat on the court that tried Charles I for treason. He also signed the death warrant of the King, who was beheaded in 1649. Cromwell was put in charge of a council of state that ruled over England as a commonwealth.

Cromwell dismisses Parliament

Cromwell gave religious freedom to the Puritans, Quakers, and Jews, but he had trouble with Parliament and was cruel in crushing rebellions in Scotland and Ireland. When he died, his government quickly fell apart, and Charles II was soon crowned as King to restore order.

CROW

The crow family includes rooks, ravens, jackdaws, carrion and hooded crows (pictured here), as well as the common crow. Crows are the largest of all perching birds. They are known for their intelligence.

In the United States, the common crow is a pest to farmers because it feeds largely on grain and corn. Some crows also attack smaller birds which are beneficial to the farmers. Crows, however, do eat large quantities of harmful insects.

CROWN

The crown of William the Conqueror

A crown is an official, circular head ornament. Sometimes it is merely made of leaves or flowers, but generally it contains precious stones and metals.

In ancient Greece and Rome, a wreath was

the crown of Henry IV

worn by victors in athletic or poetic contests or bestowed for an act of heroism or public service. In the Middle Ages, the crown of metal became associated with the king or queen. Among the most famous surviving crowns are the iron crown of Lombardy, the crown of CHARLEMAGNE, and the sacred crown of St. Stephen of Hungary.

William the Conqueror's crown was quite simple, as can be seen from the illustration on the preceding page. These old English crowns were destroyed under CROMWELL, and today English kings and queens use a replica of St. Edward's crown for the coronation (it contains 2783 diamonds, 17 sapphires, 11 emeralds, and 5 rubies).

Royal princes and princesses also wear smaller and simpler crowns, called coronets. Members of the nobility may wear similar ornaments, too.

CROWN JEWELS

These are the precious things worn by a king or queen when crowned, and on other formal occasions. They are not jewels only. Many of the gems are set into crowns, scepters, swords, and so on.

The most famous crown jewels are those of the United Kingdom, which are kept in the Tower of London. They are extremely precious, and include very large rubies and diamonds as well as fine pieces of goldsmith's work. Tourists usually want to see them when they go to London.

the Imperial State Crown

CRUSADES

PALESTINE was important to the Christians as the land of Christ. It was also important to the Muslims as the land of their prophets, Abraham and Moses. In the A.D. 600s, the Arab Muslims seized JERUSALEM in Palestine but allowed the Christians to visit their holy places.

In 1071, however, the area was suddenly captured by the Seljuk Turks, who murdered and enslaved the Christian pilgrims. The Pope proclaimed a Crusade, a journey to take back the Holy Land from Arab and Turkish Muslims. A preacher, Peter the Hermit, led thousands of peasants. Most of them were killed or lost along the way. Then, armies of knights started out from France and Italy and fought many bloody battles, until finally capturing Jerusalem in 1099. They also formed four states on the eastern Mediterranean shore.

About 50 years later, the Turks took back one of the Crusaders' four states. Two armies, one under the King of France and another under the

Emperor of Germany, were formed but were defeated by the Turks. In 1187, the Turkish leader, Saladin, retook Jerusalem and most of the Holy Land. During the Third Crusade, King RICHARD I of England, called "the Lion-Hearted," defeated Saladin in battle and made a truce with him, obtaining the right of Christians to visit Jerusalem.

Several other crusades took place in the 1200s, some to gain riches and trade, some to win back completely the Holy Land. Two armies of boys and girls, called The Children's Crusade, were organized in 1212 to march to Palestine, but most of the children never reached it, dying of hunger or cold, or being sold into slavery. In the end the Crusaders failed to conquer the area, but they brought back to Europe new ideas, trade, and learning. Arab knowledge about medicine, mathematics, and astronomy added greatly to later scientific discoveries in the West. SEE ALSO: JERUSALEM, SALADIN.

CRUSOE

Robinson Crusoe is the famous character created by Daniel Defoe in his story, *The Life and Strange Surprising Adventures of Robinson Crusoe*. Defoe wrote about a person, cast away all alone on an island, who lived on fish, fruit, goats' flesh, as well as by his own inventiveness. The story itself was based upon a true adventure.

Defoe had read the account, written by a British captain, of a Scottish sailor, Alexander Selkirk, who was put in 1704 on the uninhabited island of Juan Fernandez, off the coast of Chile. In the story created by Defoe, many of Selkirk's struggles are woven into an interesting adventure that includes an episode about a tribe of cannibals and Crusoe's fight to free their victim, a man named Friday. SEE ALSO: DEFOE, DANIEL.

CRUSTACEANS

Crustaceans are a type of ARTHROPOD. Like insects, all have jointed legs and are without a backbone. They all have two pairs of antennae. CRABS, shrimps, LOBSTERS, crayfish, and BARNACLES are crustaceans.

Most crustaceans live in salt water, but some live on land. The common crayfish lives in ponds; the wood louse and the sand flea live on land. Whether or not they live in water, all hatch from eggs, have a larval stage, and breathe with gills. Crustaceans have a tough, protective shell of *chitin*, which is really an outside skeleton. As the animal grows, the old shell is shed and a new one grows.

The smallest known crustacean is the water flea which is less than one-hundredth of an inch (0.25 mm) long. The largest crustacean is a Japanese crab with a claw span of more than 11 feet (3.41 m).

Amphipods, which are small crustaceans like the water flea, have been found at a depth of over 6 miles (9.7 km). Other amphipods have been found in the Andes Mountains of Ecuador at heights greater than 13,000 feet (4030 m). These small crustaceans, are important food for certain kinds of larger animals, especially some kinds of whales.

Lobster

shrimp

woodlouse

water flea (daphnia)

CRYSTALS

Crystals are solids which have orderly atomic structures. Each has a geometric shape consisting of flat surfaces. Crystals can look like cubes, prisms, and pyramids.

Nearly all minerals are found in nature as crystals. Many substances can be turned into a crystalline form. Water in a crystalline form is SNOW. The crystals of a particular substance take the same shape. Some crystalline forms are pictured here.

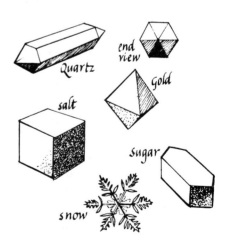

Quartz
end view
Gold
salt
sugar
snow

Crystalline rock is formed when hot rock deep within the earth cools. The slower it cools, the larger the crystal. The largest crystal recorded is made of quartz. It weighs 70 tons (63.7 metric tons) and is located in the Soviet Union. Gemstones—diamonds, emeralds, and garnets—are formed this way.

X-rays are scattered when they pass through crystals. Each scatter pattern helps scientists to learn about the structure of the ATOMS inside the crystal. X-rays are used in naming or identifying crystals when all other means have failed.

CUBA

Cuba is the largest island in the West Indies, about the size of Pennsylvania. Lying about 90 miles (150 km) south of Florida, Cuba is an independent nation with more than 9.5 million people. In the southeast, the land is wild and rough, especially in the Sierra Maestra Mountains. This area has large deposits of nickel, iron ore, manganese, cobalt, and chromium. Much of the island consists of fertile plains, suitable for growing sugar cane (Cuba's biggest crop), cacao, cotton, fruit, and tobacco. Cigars made in Havana, the capital, are world famous. Cuba also produces cigarettes, textiles, rum, and refined sugar.

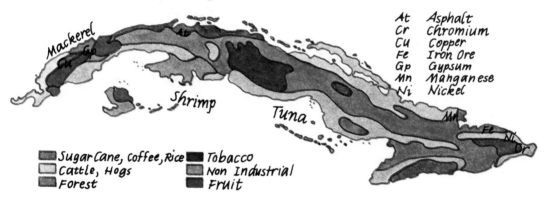

At Asphalt
Cr Chromium
Cu Copper
Fe Iron Ore
Gp Gypsum
Mn Manganese
Ni Nickel

Sugar Cane, coffee, Rice Tobacco
Cattle, Hogs Non Industrial
Forest Fruit

After COLUMBUS discovered Cuba in 1492, the island became a Spanish colony and a gathering point for Spanish treasure ships. French and British pirates often attacked settlements on its coast. Soon the native Arawak Indians died off and were replaced as slaves by NEGROES. In 1762, the British captured and briefly held Havana. Cuba, however, remained Spanish and grew wealthy from sugar and the slave trade. The people began to revolt against Spanish rule, which was often very harsh and cruel. The Spanish rulers put down several Cuban uprisings, but lost control of the island in the SPANISH-AMERICAN WAR of 1898. The U.S. ruled Cuba until 1902, when it became an independent republic. In the 1950s, Fidel Castro led a successful revolt against Batista, who was a dictator in Cuba at that time. Castro took control in 1959 and has since made Cuba into a socialist state, with strong ties to the U.S.S.R. and other Communist countries.

231

CUCKOO

Cuckoos are found in most parts of the world. The nesting habits of some of these birds are very unique and varied. New World cuckoos build nests and rear their own young.

But the European cuckoo lays its eggs in the nests of other kinds of birds. The particular species of foster parent is always the same for each specie of cuckoo. More than 50 species of birds are foster parents to the cuckoo's young.

The female lays 8 to 12 eggs, usually one to a nest. These eggs tend to resemble those of the foster mother. When the future foster parent is away from the nest, the female cuckoo replaces one of the eggs in the nest with her own. The cuckoo egg hatches first and the young cuckoo, naked and helpless, pushes the other eggs or newly hatched young over the edge of the nest. Thus, all the food brought to the nest by the foster parents goes to the young cuckoo which soon grows larger than they are.

The road-runner, which is Arizona's state bird, is a ground cuckoo that takes care of its own young. In the American tropics, several cuckoo species have an unusual habit: several females lay their eggs in one common nest and then all share the nesting duties.

CUNEIFORM

Many thousands of years ago, people in the Near East began to scratch pictures in slabs of soft clay to communicate with others. After a while, they saw that it was not necessary to show every line. The *stylus* (stick) used to draw the picture could be jabbed into the clay to make a pattern of wedge-shaped signs, each standing for a word. This was cuneiform (wedge-shaped) writing. Cuneiform began in Sumeria, then spread to Akkadia, Assyria, Babylonia, Persia and elsewhere in the Near East. It was used for about 3000 years.

Madame CURIE (1867–1934)

Madame Curie with the help of her husband, Pierre, discovered the radioactive element RADIUM. Radium is one of the Earth's rare elements.

Marie Sklodowska, born in Warsaw, Poland in 1867, came from a poor but happy family. She was very clever at science and eventually went to Paris to study physics and mathematics at the university there. In 1895, she married Pierre Curie, a French scientist and teacher, who was famous for his work with crystals and electricity.

They worked together studying all about URANIUM, which gave off rays that spoiled photographic plates even when they were encased in metal boxes. They called

this phenomenon *radioactivity*. Marie Curie searched for another radioactive substance and discovered that pitchblende contained something strongly radioactive. They treated more than six tons (5.5 metric tons) of pitchblende over a period of four years. At last, the Curies realized they had extracted pure radium. They returned to the laboratory one night and found radium glowing in the dark. For this discovery, they won one of the world's highest awards, the Nobel Prize for Physics.

In 1906, Pierre was killed but Marie continued research with radium and X-RAYS. In 1911, she was awarded the Nobel Prize for Chemistry. She died in 1934 from overexposure to radioactivity.

CURRANTS

Currants are seedless grapes which, when dried in the sun, become small raisins. Currants are grown in California, Greece, Lebanon, and Israel.

The tart red and black currants used in making jams and jellies are quite different. They look a little like currants but are related to the GOOSEBERRY.

Electric CURRENT

An electric current is produced when millions of tiny particles with negative charges, known as *electrons*, flow along a conductor such as a piece of wire or metal.

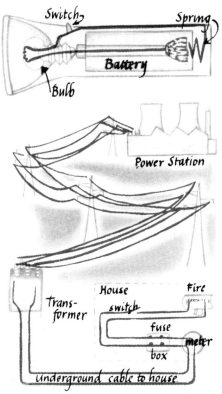

The top diagram shows the inside of a flashlight. The negative electrons are stored in the BATTERY, waiting to flow from one terminal to the other. When the switch is turned on, a gap is closed and the electric circuit is complete. The electrons can now move along the path shown by the red line. While the switch is on, 100 million billion electrons may flow through the bulb during one second. As they flow through the thin wire in the light bulb, the electrons make it white hot, thus causing light. The electrons move in one direction in this case, and the electric current is thus called *direct current* or *DC*.

In the bottom diagram, power stations generate electricity which flows through wires to our homes far away. This current moves backwards and forwards 50 times per second, and thus is called an *alternating current* or *AC*. For general use, alternating current is easier to control and more convenient than direct current. SEE ALSO: BATTERIES, DYNAMO, ELECTRICITY, GENERATOR.

CYCLONES and ANTICYCLONES

A *cyclone* is a widespread area of low air pressure surrounded by a circular wind system. Since air flows from high to low pressure areas, the winds blow toward the center. In the Northern Hemisphere, the spinning of the Earth gives the winds a counter-clockwise direction; in the Southern Hemisphere, the wind directions are reversed. Cyclones bring rain and unsettled stormy weather.

A region of high air pressure with winds blowing outward from the center is called an *anticyclone*. In the Northern Hemisphere, the winds blow clockwise; the reverse is true in the Southern Hemisphere. Anticyclones bring fine, hot weather in summer and crisp, cool weather in winter.

The word cyclone is often used loosely to describe areas where the pressure is so very low that the resulting winds reach a terrifying 100 miles (161 km) per hour or more. These violent storms are known as hurricanes or

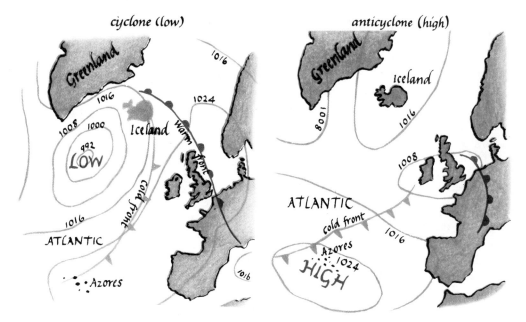

cyclone (low)　　　　　　　anticyclone (high)

TYPHOONS. The winds are sometimes so strong that houses, cars, and boats can be picked up and whirled through the air by them. SEE ALSO: BAROMETER, TYPHOON, WINDS.

CYCLOPS

A Cyclops, in Greek mythology, was an enormous giant, usually having one eye in the middle of his forehead. Cyclops in Greek means "round-eye."

Homer described the Cyclopes (spelled this way in the plural) as giant, cannibalistic shepherds. One of them, Polyphemus, captured and ate some of the sailors of ODYSSEUS, whom he had trapped in his cave. Later, Odysseus and the rest escaped by making Polyphemus drunk on wine and blinding him by burning out his one eye. Other Cyclopes in myth were sons of Heaven and Earth; others were blacksmiths of great strength who forged thunderbolts for ZEUS; and others were workmen who helped Vulcan, the god of fire, make weapons and armor for the gods.

CYLINDER

In geometry (the study of shapes) a cylinder is an object (or an empty space) that looks like a circle when seen from the end,

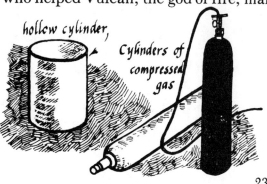

hollow cylinder

Cylinders of compressed gas

235

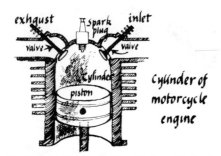

Cylinder of
motorcycle
engine

and like a rectangle when seen from the side. A grocery can is a cylinder; so is a straight length of pipe.

The strong steel bottles that hold gas under pressure are called cylinders. So are the round, closed chambers where the work of an ENGINE is done.

CZECHOSLOVAKIA

Czechoslovakia is a communist-controlled country in central Europe. It is somewhat larger than Pennsylvania and has no sea-coast. It is the homeland of two different peoples—the Czechs and the Slovaks—each with their own language. The Czechs live in Bohemia in the west, an area of hills, forests, and castles, and in central Moravia, an area of valleys and rolling plains. The Slovaks live in Slovakia in the east, a rugged land of mountains. Czechoslovakia's capital is Prague.

Other nations ruled these peoples for a long while. They finally gained their independence after the collapse of the Austro–Hungarian Empire. In 1918, Czechoslovakia was formed. During World War II, German troops occupied the country. Afterward Russia gained control, crushing in 1968 an attempt by Czechoslovakians to make the country more democratic.

Coal and iron are mined; wheat, sugar beets, and potatoes are main crops. It manufactures chemicals, machinery, and shoes.

DAMS

A dam is a high wall used to keep water from flowing down-hill as it naturally would. It can be used to store water for drinking or for spreading on farmland. It can create artificial lakes for fishing and boating. It can trap water and let it escape in a way that drives machinery. And it can hold water back in rainy seasons to keep land from being flooded.

Dams these days are usually built of concrete strengthened with steel, but in the past they were made of stone, brick, or earth. They are found in most parts of the world where man has settled. In the animal kingdom, beavers also build dams, using sticks and twigs.

236

DANCING

Moving the body in rhythms to show how a person feels, have a good time, or tell a story is one of man's oldest habits. Dancing is found in almost every part of the world.

The first dances may have had something to do with work. Many jobs are made easier if everyone moves together in time. Or it may have started with people stamping happily around an animal or enemy they had killed.

Many dances are magical or religious. Many tribes have had dances as part of the magic to get plenty of rain and good crops. The ancient Greeks and Romans used dancing as part of their worship. The choir-

boys at the Cathedral of Seville, Spain, still dance in front of the altar.

Some dances are performed when special things are happening. The coming of spring has its special dances in many places, as does the harvest. Warriors perform dances to put them in a fighting mood.

It is odd, but for most of history we can only guess at what dances were like. Dancing is an art of steady motion, and though we have paintings of dancers from very long ago we see them only at one moment of the

dance. We know that the Greeks loved dancing. It was used in their plays, and it was valued by ordinary people as exercise. The ancient Romans liked dancing much less. The upper class thought that it was undignified. During the Middle Ages, dancing was popular again, though the Catholic Church disliked some kinds of dancing.

Early in the 15th century, books on dancing began to appear. We have dance music from before that time, but only a vague idea of the dances themselves. But we do know about the dances after 1400.

There were two main kinds of dances in Europe, court dances and folk dances. *Court dances* were those of the upper class. They were usually slow and graceful, and people learned them from teachers. Folk dances were those of farmers and other ordinary people. Sometimes a good folk dance was turned into a court dance. The waltz is an example.

Over the centuries, the court dances came and went. Many were fashionable (done by everybody) for

only a few years, while others lasted more than a century. The branle, gavotte, minuet, and waltz are four of the famous ones. Some dance rhythms were often used in music not intended for dancing, such as symphonies. The waltz became fashionable about 150 years ago, and new waltzes are still being written. Many are not for dancing, but only for listening.

Folk dances stay in fashion

longer, and are often livelier, than the court dances. The Czech polka, the Polish mazurka, and the English country dance are folk dances that became court dances too. The English Morris dance, the Spanish flamenco, and the Scottish reel never became court dances but are famous folk dances all the same.

Modern *ballroom dances*, like the old court dances, are carefully taught rather than naturally learned as folk dances are. But they still borrow from folk dances, such as the South American rhumba and the tango. SEE ALSO: BALLET.

DANUBE

The Danube is a great river in central and southeastern Europe. It rises in the Black Forest in southern West Germany and flows eastward about 1750 miles (2818 km). Along the way it flows through Austria, along the border of Czechoslovakia, through Hungary and Yugoslavia, and between Rumania and Bulgaria, before finally reaching the Black Sea.

Tugs tow barges daily up and down the Danube, loading and unloading manufactured goods and oil, coal, and iron ore. The river is open to the shipping of all nations. A special commission controls commercial traffic.

DARK AGES

The Dark Ages is the name given to a period during the MIDDLE AGES when there was confusion and little learning. The period usually extends from the fall of the Roman Empire (A.D. 476) to about the time of WILLIAM THE CONQUEROR (1066). There are few written accounts about this period, which may be one reason it is called the "Dark Ages." Today, historians and archeologists are finding facts that give us a better picture of that time.

Saxon huts among Roman ruins

In Europe, large numbers of barbaric tribes pushed across the borders of the Roman Empire. In A.D. 410, the Goths under Alaric besieged and sacked Rome. Attila, leading the HUNS, invaded France and Italy, causing great destruction. Other tribes from the north and east broke up the Empire. There were Franks, Burgundians, Alemmani, Jutes, Teutons, Lombards, Magyars, and Bulgars; all were skilled warriors but uninterested in the western, Roman culture.

Saxon crosses at Sandbach, Cheshire.

In England, the ANGLO-SAXONS took control of many regions, driving the CELTS inland and west. Ireland was not affected by these invaders, and retained a high level of learning and civilization. With the coming of ALFRED THE GREAT in the 9th century in southern England, there was renewed interest in learning there.

During this "dark" era people lived in little huts close to a chieftain, who protected them. Farming was the chief way of life for most of them. It was a drab, routine existence that had little time for art. SEE ALSO: MIDDLE AGES.

Charles DARWIN (1809–1882)

Charles Darwin was an English naturalist and biologist who developed his own theory of EVOLUTION. As a young man, he went on a world-wide expedition on board a government ship. During the voyage, Darwin discovered new species and variations of plants and animals.

Charles Island (Galápagos)

He returned to England, and in 1859 published a very controversial book called  *The Origin of Species*. In this book, Darwin set forth his ideas about the origin of plant and animal species. He believed that only the fittest survive and the offspring inherit those qualities that make for survival. He theorized that plants and animals evolve (develop) after many, many centuries into higher forms of life. The same theory was advanced by another English naturalist, Alfred Russel Wallace, at the same time Darwin explained it.

Darwin studied the finches and huge turtles of the Galápagos Islands in the Pacific, off the coast of Ecuador. His idea of how they had arrived there and changed into different species was an important foundation stone in his theory of evolution.

In 1871, his book *The Descent of Man* suggested that man and apes had descended from one primitive type of animal. Darwin ignored what the Bible says about the creation of man, because he wanted a scientific way to explain how we were made. SEE ALSO: EVOLUTION, MAN.

DATES

Dates are the fruit of the date palm tree. Date palms grow in desert OASES, where they get water as well as bright sun. Dates do not grow properly if there is too much rainfall during the period of ripening. Date palms provide essential food for the desert peoples of Arabia and the Sahara. These trees are also grown in California and Arizona.

There are male and female date palm trees. The males furnish only the pollen; the females bear the dates. The trees can grow 80 feet (24.8 km) high. Each tree bears up to 200 pounds (90 kg) of fruit per year for at least a hundred years.

King DAVID (about 1000 B.C.)

David reigned as the greatest king of Israel, and in the Bible God promised to make one of his descendants the *Messiah* (deliverer) of the nation. God kept that promise when His Son, Jesus, was born in a family that descended from King David.

David began his life as a shepherd boy, watching the sheep of his father Jesse. He learned to play the harp while tending the sheep, and became skillful at it.

When King Saul of Israel became ill, he sent for David to play to him. When the Philistine giant Goliath threatened the Israelites, David went to fight him. He killed Goliath with a stone hurled from a sling and King Saul made him an army commander.

David's friendship with Saul's son Jonathan angered Saul, who sent David away. David became an outlaw, and when Saul and Jonathan were killed in battle, David became King of Israel. He made Jerusalem his capital. He was the father of SOLOMON.

Jefferson DAVIS (1808–1889)

Jefferson Davis, the President of the Confederate States of America during the U.S. CIVIL WAR, was born in Kentucky but moved with his parents to Mississippi. He graduated from West Point and fought in the Black Hawk Indian War in 1832. Then he became a Mississippi planter until 1845, when he was elected a U.S. Representative. He took part in the Mexican War and afterward served as U.S. Secretary of State and twice as U.S. Senator.

Davis believed strongly in Southern rights and in SLAVERY. Soon after Mississippi withdrew from the United States, Davis was made President of the Confederate government. His leadership was often criticized by other Southerners, who felt he did not raise enough money to fight the war and made bad military decisions.

He disapproved of the surrender by ROBERT E. LEE at Appomattox. Captured shortly afterward, Davis spent two years in prison, where he was charged with treason but never found guilty. SEE ALSO: CIVIL WAR.

Sir Humphry DAVY (1778–1829)

Sir Humphry Davy was a famous English chemist who discovered the elements potassium and sodium. He also discovered that "laughing gas" could be used as an ANESTHETIC.

By the age of 24, he was made professor of chemistry at the Royal Institution, in London, and a few years later he became President of the Royal Society. His interesting lectures became important social functions and greatly added to the public's respect for science.

Another important contribution was his invention of the miner's safety lamp, which is named after him. In those days, the exposed flames of miners' lamps often caused explosions from gases sometimes present in the mines. In his lamp, the flame is screened from the outside air by copper gauze. This gauze carries away the heat produced by the burning flame in order to prevent any gases from becoming hot enough to explode. Although electric lamps are now used, the Davy safety lamp is still used to detect the presence of dangerous gases. The flame in his lamp changes color when dangerous gases are present.

Davy also invented the arc lamp and explained the principles of electrochemical corrosion.

DAY and NIGHT

When talking about day and night, we use the word "day" to mean the period of time that the SUN is above the horizon and "night" to mean the period of time that the sun is below the horizon.

The Earth spins on its axis as it travels in an orbit about the sun. One complete revolution on its axis—a period of 24 hours—is also called a day. When one side of the Earth is facing the sun, it is having daytime. When that side faces away from the sun, nighttime occurs.

The Earth, however, spins with its axis at an angle to the sun. Therefore, each night and day is not 12 hours long, except daily at the EQUATOR and on the first day of spring and fall elsewhere.

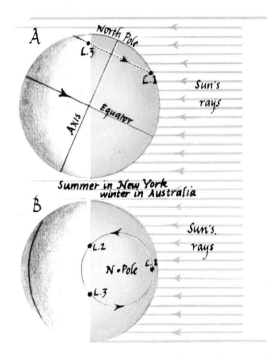

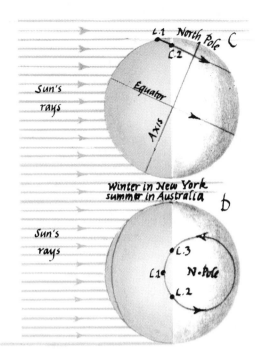

Diagram A shows how the northern half of the Earth tilts *towards* the sun during the summer months. Diagram C shows the Earth on the opposite half of its orbit when the northern half is tilted *away* from the sun in winter.

L.1 marks the location of London at noon in the diagrams; L.2 is sunset; L.2 to L.3, nighttime; L.3, sunrise; L.3 to L.2, daytime.

Diagrams B and C show the Earth as it might look from a space station far above the North Pole. Diagram B illustrates why the days are longer than the nights in summer. Diagram D illustrates why the days are shorter than the nights in winter. The farther north one goes, the longer the longest day is and the longer the longest night is. SEE ALSO: CALENDAR, SEASONS.

DEAD SEA

The Dead Sea is a salt lake on the border between ISRAEL and Jordan. It is about 45 miles (72 km) long and 9 miles (14 km) wide, and is in some places more than 1300 feet (403 km) deep.

The surface of the Dead Sea is 1300 feet below sea level (the lowest spot on Earth). The Jordan River and smaller streams flow into it, but no water flows out. Thus, the water is five times saltier than the ocean, and the shores have minerals like potash and bromides. It is mentioned quite often in the BIBLE. The Dead Sea Scrolls were found nearby in 1947.

The DEAF

Thousands of people in the United States cannot hear, or are hard of hearing. These people are said to be *deaf*. Even speaking may be hard or impossible for the deaf, since people imitate sounds they have heard when they speak. (People who cannot speak are said to be *mute*.)

A hearing aid often helps, but not all the time. Sometimes the deaf can lip-read; they watch the forms another person's mouth takes and learn the words he is saying. He can be taught by trial and error to form his words the same way and make the normal sounds.

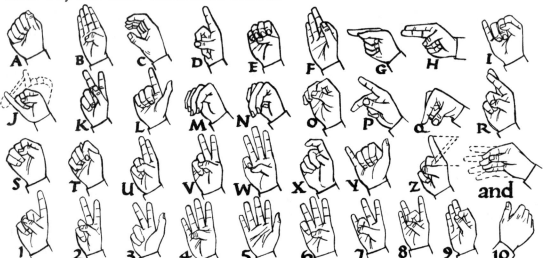

There is also an alphabet of hand signals, shown here. The deaf learn to use this.

A Spanish monk in the 16th century was the first person to train the deaf. Now there are many schools and colleges for them.

DEATH VALLEY

Death Valley is the lowest spot in North America. Most of it is 160 feet (49 m) below sea level, and the lowest part is 280 feet (86 m) below sea level. Death Valley is a hot desert region with very little vegetation, situated in southeastern California and southern Nevada. There are few water springs. Snakes, lizards, toads, foxes, rabbits, bobcats, and some birds are the principal animals living there. In summer, the temperature is extremely hot, sometimes above 120° F (49° C). The highest recorded temperature in the U.S. is 134.6° F (57° C), set in Death Valley in July, 1913. This burning desert has an annual rainfall of only 1.4 inches (3.55 cm).

Death Valley was named by the survivors of a group of gold prospectors who tried to cross it in 1849. Many others looking for riches have suffered or died of heat and thirst there. Death Valley was once the bed of a salt lake. It has large, valuable deposits of borax.

DECIMALS

Decimals are a way of expressing part of a whole amount. Decimals always deal with tenths, hundredths, thousandths, and on up. A decimal fraction is then one whose denominator is some power of 10. The word decimal comes from the Latin word *decem*, meaning "ten." Decimals are easier to use than common fractions, such as 3/4, 2/3, 4/7, etc. Since our number system is based on ten, adding, subtracting, multiplying, and dividing with decimal fractions is almost as easy as with whole numbers.

For example, in addition and subtraction, the decimal points simply need to be lined up exactly under one another. Then the problem is worked out the same way as in dealing with whole numbers.

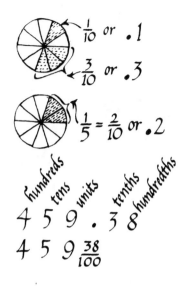

Decimals did not come into use until the late 1500s, and the decimal point was not inserted between the whole numbers and the fractional ones until the early 1700s.

DECLARATION OF INDEPENDENCE

As fighting at Lexington and Concord developed into the AMERICAN REVOLUTION, delegates from the Thirteen Colonies met in Philadelphia. Some wanted to come to terms with Britain without war; others said that the colonies would get their full rights only when they were free. On June 7, 1776, a Virginia delegate, Richard Henry Lee, made a resolution of independence. Several delegates were told to draft such a declaration, and THOMAS JEFFERSON was entrusted with the actual writing of it. JOHN ADAMS and BENJAMIN FRANKLIN helped Jefferson revise the first draft. On July 4, 1776, the final draft of the Declaration of Independence was adopted. Independence Day—July 4th each year—has since been America's chief patriotic holiday.

245

The Declaration states that all men are created equal, that men have certain rights that no government can take away, and that the people have the right to change or abolish a government that does not serve them. It explains how the British king has taken away the colonists' rights. It declares the colonies free from British rule, making them into the United States.

DEER

Deer are cud-chewing mammals that live in most parts of the world. Most deer live in forests where they eat small trees and plants. They have strong legs and can run as fast as 40 miles per hour (65 km/hr) and jump more than 20 feet (6 m).

Deer are the only animals with antlers. Antlers, unlike horns, are made of bone. The antlers drop off in the winter but grow back in the spring in time for the breeding season. The males, *bucks*, use their antlers to fight for mates or for leadership of the herd. A female, *doe*, gives birth to one or two young, *fawns*, each year. Most deer live for about 20 years.

The North American moose (top illustration) is the world's largest deer. The European REINDEER (middle) and its American cousin, the caribou, are the only deer where both males and females have antlers. In all other types of deer, such as the elk (bottom), only the males have antlers.

Daniel DEFOE (1660?–1731)

Daniel Defoe was born in London, England. He was a PURITAN and wrote about religion and politics. One of his writings, attacking the Church of England, caused him to be put in the pillory and then imprisoned. From 1704 to 1713, he wrote and published a *Review*, which was like our modern opinion magazines.

However, Defoe is best known as the creator of Robinson Crusoe. His novel, *The*

Life and Strange Surprising Adventures of Robinson Crusoe, appeared in 1719, followed by two sequels. Another of his novels, *Moll Flanders*, relates the adventures of a misguided young lady who wishes to get ahead in the world. SEE ALSO: CRUSOE.

DELAWARE

Delaware is the second smallest state in the United States. It lies near the big cities of New York, Philadelphia, Baltimore, and Washington, D.C. Because of this and the state's favorable incorporation laws, Delaware has become the home of about 73,000 firms, including some of the nation's largest.

The state is part of the Delmarva Peninsula, which separates the Delaware and Chesapeake Bays. Most of the land is low and flat. In the north are some rolling hills, and in the south are swamps. The climate is moderate, though quite humid in the summer.

The region was inhabited by the Lenni-Lenape (later called the Delaware) Indians when Henry Hudson discovered it in 1609. A year later, Captain Samuel Argall of Virginia named the bay for his colony's governor, Lord De La Warr. The Dutch made a settlement in Delaware in 1631, but the Indians destroyed it. Then the Swedes settled at present-day Wilmington. The Dutch captured this settlement, which was in turn seized by the British in 1664. Delaware fought as a separate state in the American Revolution and became the first state to ratify the U.S. Constitution.

Manufacturing is Delaware's biggest industry. It makes chemicals, canned and frozen foods, textiles, and machinery. Agriculture and fishing are also important, as well as the growing tourist trade. Delaware's capital is Dover, and its population is about 650,000.

DELHI

Delhi was the old capital of India when it was ruled successively by the Hindus, Afghans, Mongols, and British. Today, New Delhi is the capital. At least 15 different cities of Delhi are believed to have been located here at various times. Each conqueror destroyed his predecessor's city and built a new one on the plain near the old. Delhi thus changed location and name, but remained always in existence. The city of Old Delhi, on the Jumna River, is still enclosed by high stone walls.

This great metropolis, including Old and New Delhi, has many ruins of gardens, palaces, and mausoleums. Inside its old, solid stone walls are some of the finest carvings and buildings in the world. The Great Mosque, or Jamma Musjid, shows the Byzantine-Arabic style of architecture of the 17th century. Four miles (6.4 km) south of Old Delhi are the magnificent, new government buildings and the University, both part of the new city. Its bazaars (market places) are famous today for trading in fabrics, jewels, and metals. SEE ALSO: INDIA.

DELTA

The Greeks noticed the shape of the plain at the mouth of the NILE River and called it a *delta* because of its resemblance to the Greek letter D—△.

Since then delta has meant the fanshaped tract of land formed at the mouth of many rivers.

Rivers carry soil, sand, and mud that they deposit as silt or sediment at their mouths. However, deltas will not be formed if the coast is sinking or if strong ocean or tidal currents prevent any build-up of sediment. Islands are often formed at the delta, whose fertile plain is often subject to floods.

The Mississippi, RHINE, DANUBE, Volga, and EUPHRATES are rivers with large deltas. The delta formed by the GANGES and Brahmaputra Rivers is shown here.

DEMOCRACY

Democracy comes from a Greek word meaning "rule of the people." It is a political system in which people share in directing the activities of their government.

In ancient Greece, the citizens were members of the ruling assembly and participated directly in the making of all laws. This was a direct democracy, possible only in a small city-state.

Democracy has since changed, chiefly because democratic countries today have much larger populations than the city-states of ancient Greece. It would be impossible for all the citizens of the United States to attend a meeting, at which they could all speak and vote on the issues. Therefore, the U.S.A. is an indirect democracy. Its citizens usually vote to elect representatives, who then speak and act for them in legislative (law-making) assemblies. However, at the annual town meeting in some New England towns, the citizens (voters) elect directly the town officers and decide local issues such as the town tax rates. SEE ALSO: BALLOT, VOTE.

DENMARK

As you can see from the map, Denmark is almost entirely surrounded by water. The mainland consists of the Jutland Peninsula, and close by are most of the 400 Danish islands, such as Zealand, Funen, and Laaland. However, the Faëroe Islands in the north Atlantic and Greenland near North America are far from Denmark. It is about the size of Massachusetts and New Hampshire combined, with a population of about 5.25 million.

Danish soil is very fertile; its farms produce butter, cheese, and bacon. Fishing, shipping, and manufacturing are important industries. Its capital, Copenhagen, is an old and busy seaport. SEE ALSO: COPENHAGEN.

DENTIST

A dentist attempts to save teeth and the areas that surround them from decay and disease. People performed dentistry for thousands of years, though not too successfully. Around 1500, the barber, who was also the surgeon, was likely to be the dentist. In 1530, the first book on dentistry was published, in Germany.

By the 1790s, there were dentists in America. Some were good, but there was also much fakery. The first American dental school was begun in 1840. Dentists have gotten better year by year. They study dentistry for four years before they may practice. They help us keep our teeth longer than people once could.

DESERT

There are generally two kinds of deserts: barren, hot regions where lack of soil and rain prevent plants from growing; and barren, cold regions where the land is covered with ice and snow.

The hot, arid deserts extend around the Earth. The SAHARA, Arabian, Mexican, and Gobi Deserts can be found one belt north of the equator. And south of the equator are the Kalahari Desert in Botswana and southern Africa and the central deserts of Australia. Deserts are almost unknown in Europe. Smaller deserts are in North America (the Mojave Desert in California) and in South America (the Atacama Desert in Chile).

These hot deserts vary considerably in their surface; some are covered with hills of drifting sand that form dunes, and some consist of rocks and pressed gravel. Deserts can be made by prevailing winds that bring no moisture, by their distance from oceans, or by their isolation by mountains.

Small, thorny bushes and plants such as CACTI are able to survive and grow in many deserts because they need little water. Certain rodents, snakes, and lizards that require very little water to live are also

found in some deserts. Oases are sometimes formed in the desert because of underground springs. Wherever there is any water, desert soil may be fertile.

The polar regions of the Arctic and Antarctic are vast, empty wastelands. Mosses, LICHENS, and other small plants are found there, supplying food for wolves, seals, and reindeer. SEE ALSO: MIRAGE, OASIS, SAHARA.

Hernando DE SOTO (1500?–1542)

Hernando De Soto was a Spanish explorer in the present United States. At the age of 19, he took part in Spain's conquest of what is now Central America. Later, De Soto served under FRANCISCO PIZARRO, who conquered the Inca Indians of Peru.

In 1538, he was made governor of Cuba and sent to conquer what is now the North American continent. With an army of about 800 men, De Soto landed in 1539 near present-day Tampa, Florida. In search of gold, silver, and jewels, De Soto led his men north to the Carolinas. Then they turned south into what is now Alabama, where De Soto was wounded in a battle with Indians.

He found no treasure, but was so determined to continue the search that he did not tell his men that Spanish ships lay off the coast. He set forth again with his men and became the first white man to see and cross the Mississippi River. They traveled up the Arkansas River and as far west as Oklahoma. Finding no treasure, De Soto turned back to the Mississippi, where he died of a fever.

DETECTIVE

A detective is a special kind of policeman whose job is to investigate crimes. He usually spends much time gathering evidence that leads to the arrest of a suspect. A detective often works in ordinary clothes because he can gather evidence more easily if he is not recognized as a policeman. He is then referred to as a *plainclothesman*.

Some of a detective's work leads him into dangerous situations with desperate persons. However, much of his time is spent on dull, patient work, collecting clues or working in laboratories or searching for witnesses.

Some police detectives become private detectives who may be hired to find missing persons or to keep down theft in hotels or stores.

DIAMONDS

Diamonds are among the rarest and most prized of all precious gems. About one-fifth of those mined are used in making jewelry; the remainder are used in industry. Diamonds are actually CARBON crystals which have been exposed to tremendous heat and pressure. Probably the crystals were produced in molten rock deep within the Earth and were carried to the surface by magma. Because of their origin so deep within the Earth, they are the hardest substance known to man. Only a diamond can cut another diamond. Thus, those of poorer quality make excellent drills.

A diamond before cutting

The first diamonds were discovered in India more than 2000 years ago. Although diamonds are found in many parts of the world, the Kimberley Mines in South Africa are by far the largest. These mines were discovered in 1867 when a small boy found a "pretty pebble" in a river by his home. The "pebble" was a 21-karat diamond. It helped cause the "diamond rush" to that region in South Africa.

After being cut and polished, diamonds have a "fire" and brilliance unmatched by any other gemstone. Usually a diamond is cut to have 58 "faces" in order to produce the greatest amount of reflected light. SEE ALSO: CARBON.

Charles DICKENS (1812–1870)

Charles Dickens was a great English novelist. His family was poor and was living in one of the shabbiest districts of London when Dickens's father was imprisoned for debt. Dickens had little education and worked unhappily in a blacking warehouse. Later, he became a clerk and returned to school, learning shorthand to be a newspaper reporter.

His short "Sketches by Boz" were written for a newspaper and they brought him public attention. In 1836, his first novel, *The Pickwick Papers,* was praised for the humor and oddities of life he skillfully depicted.

Dickens soon wrote other novels, among them *Oliver Twist,* in which he attacked workhouses, and *Nicholas Nickleby,* in which he denounced cheap boarding schools. In all he wrote more than 15 novels, many of them appearing as serials, monthly parts in a periodical. *A Tale of Two Cities, A Christmas Carol,* and *Great Expectations* were first published as serial stories.

The names of his characters became common phrases and household words, such as the Artful Dodger, Uriah Heep, Mr. Micawber, Ebenezer Scrooge, and Mrs. Sarah Gamp. Dickens described poignantly the cold, hunger, cruelty, and injustices that the poor people of his time suffered. In this way, he created interest in social reform and helped improve the conditions of the poor.

DICTIONARY

A dictionary is a book of information. There are different kinds of dictionaries. The kind you are most likely to use is arranged alphabetically with words that you wish to understand. It shows you how to spell a word; tells you its history (words have histories); gives you its meanings; and lists other words that come from it. This is a *general language dictionary.* Other language dictionaries give the words in foreign languages that mean the same as English words. There are also *technical dictionaries*, which explain the words used by lawyers, doctors, and so on. And there are *glossaries* in books, which explain special words that are used there. SEE ALSO: ALMANAC, ENCYCLOPEDIA.

air′ pho′tog′raphy. See aerial photog′raphy.
air·plane (âr′plān′), *n.* **1.** a hea
kept aloft by the upward thrust e
air on its fixed wings and driven b
pulsion, etc. **2.** any similar heavie
glider or helicopter. Also, *esp. Brit.*
Gk āer(ó)nlan(os) wandering in air

DIGESTION

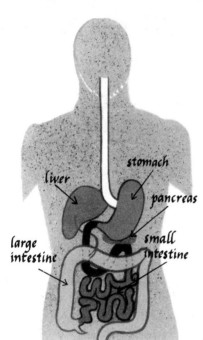

Every cell in our bodies needs food. However, the food we eat has to be changed into a liquid before it can be absorbed into our bloodstream. This breaking down of food is called *digestion*.

During digestion, the food mixes with several juices. The first juice is found in the mouth and is called *saliva*. Saliva begins breaking down starches into sugars. After the food is swallowed, it passes into the stomach where it is churned and mixed with *gastric juice* to form a kind of pulp. The pulp passes on to the small intestine where *liver bile* helps digest fats and *pancreatic juices* break up sugar and undigested starches. The small intestine is not really very small; it is 21 feet (6.51 m) long in an adult. This tremendous surface area for the absorption of the digested food into the bloodstream is increased by the *villi*, which are tiny projections along the intestinal passage. Whatever is not absorbed finally passes into the large intestine and then out of the body.

DIKE

Dikes are long mounds of earth and other materials that keep low-lying land from being flooded. The most important dikes are in HOLLAND, where much of the land is below the sea level. Some dikes carry canals that drain the interior of the country. A three-fold barrier of dikes keeps the sea out.

In the southern United States there are also dikes, which are called *levees*. Much of New Orleans is below water level and has to be protected by them.

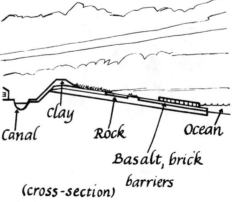

(cross-section)

DINOSAUR

Dinosaur is the name given to a variety of extinct REPTILES which existed during a time known as the "Age of Reptiles." This period ended 70,000 years ago.

The word *dinosaur* comes from the Greek words meaning "terrible lizard." The largest meat-eater that ever lived was *Tyrannosaurus Rex*, illustrated in the lower picture. This dinosaur was up to 47 feet (14.6 m) long and was almost 20 feet (6.2 m) high. Its weight was estimated to be 8 tons (7.3 metric tons). Its powerful jaws containing sharp teeth 5-inches (15.24 cm) long and its powerful claws on the back legs made this a fearsome dinosaur.

The *Diplodocus*, in the lower illustration, was the longest dinosaur. It wallowed in swamps of western North America and attained a length of almost 90 feet (27.9 m). It weighed over 11.5 tons (10.5 metric tons). This plant-eater may have lived mainly in water which supported its heavy weight, though many scientists believe it inhabited dry land.

Stegosaurus

Triceratops

Other smaller plant-eaters had protective armor as a defense against the fierce meat-eaters. The *Stegosaurus*, pictured at the top, had a double row of protective armored plates. *Triceratops*, in the top illustration, had a frill of bone and three sharp horns with which to defend itself.

Some dinosaurs were large, and some were only 2 to 3 feet (6.2–9.3 m) high. Some ran about on two legs; some, on four. There were many variations in size and shape. SEE ALSO: REPTILES.

Diplodocus

Tyrannosaurus Rex

Walt DISNEY (1901–1966)

Mickey Mouse and Donald Duck are famous the world over. Disneyland and Walt Disney World are visited by millions every year. A carpenter's son from Chicago, Walter Elias Disney, created all of these.

Disney was already drawing cartoons in high school, and had plans to become a commercial artist. In Kansas City he got interested in *animated cartoons*, which were shown in movie houses as advertisements. In every movie, many still pictures are shown every second so as to give an illusion of motion. This meant that even a short animated cartoon required many drawings, each a little different from the others. Disney and a friend drew all of these.

By 1927, Disney and his friend were in Hollywood, and in 1928 they introduced Mickey Mouse in the first animated cartoon to have sound. Donald Duck, Pluto, and the other famous Disney characters soon followed. The first cartoons in color appeared in 1932. Disney's work was very successful, and many artists came to work for him. In 1937, he brought out *Snow White and the Seven Dwarfs*, a full-length movie made with many thousands of drawings. He went on to make other "feature-length" movies of this kind, and movies that used photography along with or instead of drawings.

Disneyland, a gigantic amusement park near Los Angeles, was opened in 1955, and another park, Walt Disney World, was opened near Orlando, Florida, in 1971.

DIVING

For many centuries, all diving beneath the water was a simple matter of holding your breath, grasping a weight perhaps, and letting go or jumping off of a boat. Sponges and pearls were brought up by such diving.

But a diver who merely held his breath could stay down only a very short time. The *diving bell* was invented as one way of giving the diver more time. It was open at the bottom and airtight everywhere else. It was lowered into the water with the diver in it. Air was trapped inside for the diver to

breathe. Today, fresh air is pumped into diving bells through a hose.

The *diving suit* was invented early in the 19th century. It is a rubber suit with weighted shoes and an airtight helmet that fits around the head. Fresh air is pumped into the helmet through a hose. A diver in such a suit can go down about 300 feet(93 m) and stay for a good while. He must come up slowly, though. The pressure of the water can give him a crippling disease called the bends if he does not.

Scuba diving is replacing the diving suit. The diver takes his air with him under high pressure in bottles that fit on his back. He wears fewer clothes, and swims around as he wishes.

DOCTOR

A doctor treats diseases of the body and advises people on how to stay healthy.

Being a doctor is hard work, but some persons like it because they like to help others. Doctors are well respected by everyone, and are usually well paid.

To be a doctor, a person must be able to study long and hard, and to keep studying. New medicines and new ways of healing are constantly being invented, and a doctor must know about them. A doctor must not be upset by the sight of sick or dead people.

The person who wants to be a doctor must take *premedical* courses in physics, chemistry, and biology before he goes to medical school. At medical school he studies many subjects for three or four years. Then he goes into a hospital as an *intern*. He works with the hospital doctors for at least a year, treating the sick and learning about different illnesses. After his internship he may become a *resident* (hospital doctor) himself.

Many doctors are *specialists;* they treat certain kinds of illnesses or problems. A specialist will treat only skin diseases, for example, or something equally limited. *Surgeons* are doctors who operate on their patients, cutting away diseased parts of the bodies or binding up wounds. There are specialists among the surgeons too. One kind of surgeon heals broken arms and legs; a DENTIST is a surgeon who works on the teeth and gums.

DODO

The dodo bird became extinct nearly 300 years ago. Great numbers of these big, clumsy birds lived on two islands in the Indian Ocean. They were larger than turkeys, with down instead of FEATHERS. Their wings and tails were so short that they were unable to fly.

The dodo did not run from the men and animals who hunted it. The word *dodo* has since come to mean "one who is stupid."

DOGS

The dog was man's first domestic animal. Scientists believe the dog is descended from the wolf. The German shepherd and Siberian husky still show a resemblance to their wolf ancestor. The coyote of the western United States is sometimes called a wild dog. However, there are about 100 breeds today that an ancient cave man would not recognize as dogs.

Over the centuries, dogs were found to be useful in many ways. Some breeds were developed for their hunting ability. Terriers and dachshunds were bred to go down animal burrows. Greyhounds, which can run up to 41 miles per hour (66 km/hr), were originally bred to chase hares and rabbits. Spaniels and retrievers have soft mouths for gently carrying game birds.

The very highly developed sense of smell in the bloodhound is useful in locating lost persons. The huge jaws and pug nose of the bulldog were developed by careful breeding in order to make breathing easier for that breed when it held on to the hide of a bull. Guiding the blind is a quality recently developed in some breeds. The ancient Greeks developed the "lap" dog for the purpose of keeping women's stomachs warm. The smallest lap dog today is the Mexican Chihuahua which

when fully grown weighs 1 to 4 pounds (0.45–1.80 kg).

It is important to know the traits of a breed before selecting a pet. Some breeds are especially intelligent and affectionate; others are protective and high-strung; others are docile and good with young children. Some breeds are more trustworthy than others. Dogs have shown faithfulness to man and have always been thought of as "man's best friend."

DOLLS
A doll is a toy figure that resembles a baby. Children play with dolls in make-believe family games.

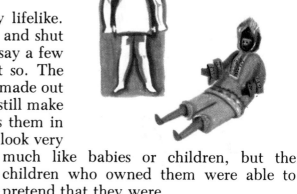

Modern dolls are often very lifelike. Some have real hair. Many open and shut their eyes, and walk. Some even say a few words. In the past, this was not so. The ancient Greek children had dolls made out of red pottery clay. The Eskimos still make dolls out of whalebone and dress them in fur costumes. Many dolls did not look very much like babies or children, but the children who owned them were able to pretend that they were.

Some dolls were not meant to play with. The Indians of the U.S. Southwest give children kachina dolls. They are carved from cottonwood or cactus plants, and have a religious meaning. They look like the beings that carry people's prayers to the gods.

Japanese girls—and also boys—use dolls. Some look like the Emperor and his family. Japanese girls often give parties in which they offer the dolls food and drink, while the boys prefer dolls that look like famous warriors or athletes. In Syria, girls hang dolls in the window when they are ready to be married.

DOLPHIN

Dolphin is the name given to a small type of WHALE. It is about 8 feet (2.5 m) long, with one fin on its back, and with 160-200 sharp teeth in its flattened beak. A dolphin is black above, white below. Like all whales, a dolphin is a MAMMAL. It gives birth to a single calf, which it devotedly nurses and cares for.

Dolphins have been known to sailors since ancient times. Their habit of following ships has gained them a reputation for friendliness. Dolphins swim in groups, called *schools*. They playfully leap and dive. They live on fish and often get caught in fish nets, much to the annoyance of fishermen. They are popular aquarium attractions because of their ability to learn tricks.

Their keen intelligence, their ability to communicate to one another with distinct sounds, and their sonar means of travel are reasons why scientists do much research on them.

DOMINOES

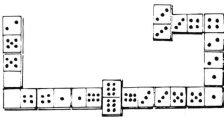

The game of dominoes is relatively new. There is no record of it before the 18th century in Italy and France. It is played by two or more persons, with 28 flat, rectangular pieces of bone, ivory, wood, or plastic. Each domino is divided into two halves, each half having either a blank or a number of dots—from 1 to 6.

The game begins by shuffling the pieces face down; then each player selects an equal number of pieces. Those extra dominoes are put aside. The player drawing the domino with the greatest number of dots lays it down. The second player sees if one of his dominoes can match the number of dots on either end of the first player's domino. He then puts his domino next to the first, and the next player tries to do the same, matching the dots on one domino half to that of the half already on the table. The first to play all his dominoes wins.

DONKEY

The donkey, a member of the horse family, was used as a beast of burden long before the horse. It is extremely hardy even in desert areas. The donkey can show patience, perseverance, and affection to a gentle master.

When a male donkey mates with a female horse (a mare), they produce a mule which is sterile (unable to reproduce).

DOVE

Dove is another name for pigeon. The turtle dove, the street pigeon, and the mourning dove are commonly known. Doves eat seeds and fruits. They are also fond of corn and do considerable damage to corn crops.

Although they have become the symbol of peace, love, and gentleness, doves often attack each other when they are kept in close confinement.

Pigeons have been tamed since 3000 B.C. They have for hundreds of years been used for carrying messages, especially during wartime.

DRAGONFLIES

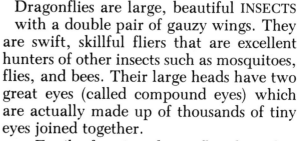

Dragonflies are large, beautiful INSECTS with a double pair of gauzy wings. They are swift, skillful fliers that are excellent hunters of other insects such as mosquitoes, flies, and bees. Their large heads have two great eyes (called compound eyes) which are actually made up of thousands of tiny eyes joined together.

Fossils of ancient dragonflies show that their wing span was 27.5 inches (69.85 cm). The largest dragonfly today is from Borneo with a wing span of 7.5 inches (19.05 cm). Most dragonflies, however, have wing spans of only 2 to 3 inches (5.08–7.62 cm).

Dragonflies are usually found feeding on insects near water. They dart rapidly about at speeds as fast as 40 miles per hour (64 km/hr). They lay their eggs on the underwater plant stems. When the eggs hatch, the young, wingless nymphs live in the mud at the bottom of the pond for 1 to 3 years. Here, each nymph feeds on water insects which it catches with its long, hinged underlip, which has pincers on the end of it.

After shedding its skin about a dozen times, the nymph crawls up a stem and comes out of the water. The skin is then shed for the final time, and the new wings dry in the sun. The new adult will live for several months.

Dragonflies are sometimes called "darning needles."

DRAGONS

A dragon is usually imagined as a great scaly lizard, breathing fire, flying on bat-like wings, and guarding treasures. Different peoples have had different ideas of the dragon, though.

Many peoples have seen the dragon as an evil creature. The Egyptians saw it as a serpent in the dark underworld. The Greeks and Romans thought of it as both good and evil. To the Greeks the dragon was the Hydra, with many heads, that Hercules killed. The Christians saw the dragon as a symbol of sin and paganism. Saint George is famous as a dragon-killer. So is Beowulf. Warriors sometimes used the dragon as a symbol of power.

The Chinese and Japanese dragon was friendly to man. To the Chinese he was a rain-maker. He is a national symbol of China. The Japanese dragon is supposed to change his size as he wishes.

Some real lizards of southeast Asia are called dragons. The dragon lizard can glide through the air like a flying squirrel. The Komodo dragon grows to be 10 feet (3 m) long.

Sir Francis DRAKE (1540–1596)

Francis Drake was an English navigator and admiral and was the first Englishman to sail around the world.

He left home as a young boy and became captain of his own ship at the age of 22. While on a slave-trading voyage to the West Indies in 1567, he was attacked by the Spaniards, who sank many English ships. Drake escaped but swore to take revenge. Between 1570 and 1573, he engaged in many acts of piracy against Spanish ships and settlements.

Drake set out in 1577 with five small ships and rounded the tip of South America, through the Straits of Magellan. Although the other ships turned back, his ship, the *Golden Hind*, sailed north, landing near San Francisco, and then proceeding homeward across the Pacific. Along the American coasts he looted many Spanish settlements. He returned in 1579 to England laden with treasure and was quickly knighted by Queen Elizabeth I.

Drake's ship   The 'Golden Hind'

In 1588, the Spanish Armada sailed into the English Channel, determined to crush the English once and for all. Drake, a vice admiral, conducted a brilliant offensive that routed the Armada.

During another expedition to the West Indies, he died of dysentery and was buried at sea off the coast of Panama. SEE ALSO: ARMADA.

DRAMA

When we talk of *the* drama we mean the art of writing and putting on plays in a theater. When we talk of *a* drama we mean a serious, rather than an amusing, play.

The drama began in ancient times as part of religious ceremonies. But nonreligious plays were written in ancient Greece and Rome, and never wholly disappeared. Most medieval plays were religious, but some were not.

By the time of Shakespeare, modern tragedies and comedies were being put on

A Greek open-air theatre

in special theater buildings. Other modern forms of acting that also tell stories, such as OPERAS and BALLETS, were just beginning to be written. SEE ALSO: ACTORS AND ACTING, BALLET, OPERA.

DREDGE

A dredge is used to bring up mud or other material from the bottom of a river, harbor, or other body of water. Most kinds of dredge use buckets to lift the mud. In some cases the bucket is on

the end of an arm and scoops up the mud. In others the bucket is lowered on cables and opens and closes. In another case, shown here, there is a "ladder" or chain of buckets constantly moving down and up again. There is also a suction dredge. In this, a nozzle is lowered to the bottom. It sucks up the mud and puts it into the scow that is waiting to carry it away.

DRESS

Egyptian   Greek

As you look around the world or study history, you will be surprised at the many forms CLOTHES can take. In some cases people's clothing is practical—comfortable and long-lasting. In other cases it is simply the sort of clothing that society has decided to be right. Such clothing may not be very practical at all.

Imagine a rich Italian. In Roman times he would wear a long, blouse-like tunic and then wrap himself in a large, sheet-like toga. In the 17th century, he might wear a very complicated and fancy costume of bright-colored cloth, looking very different. And today he would wear a suit not very different from that of an American businessman. An ancient Egyptian often went bare-chested and wore either a loincloth or a kilt, but today he would either wear a long white gown or a suit.

A woman in ancient Greece would wear a long dress, falling in natural folds and gathered in at the waist. A woman of 1860 would wear a much

Celt

Roman

Elizabethan   Victorian

263

fancier dress, whose skirt would be spread out by hidden hoops. A woman of 1900 would wear a dress that would go all the way to the ground, but a woman of 1925 would have a skirt whose bottom was just below the knee.

Such differences are mostly matters of fashion. Fashions come from many places. Often a king, a queen, or some other important person starts one. Henry VIII of England wore a new kind of collar one day, and this turned into the huge, crimpled ruff that was in fashion as a collar until after 1600. Louis XIV of France began to wear a wig, and wigs were fashionable all over Europe for 100 years. SEE ALSO: CLOTHES.

DRUGS

Drugs are chemicals from which medicines are made. Some drugs are obtained from plants. Penicillin comes from *penicillium*, a mold. Some drugs come from animals. Cortisone comes

from the glands of some animals. Some drugs, such as sulfur, are from the earth. Most drugs are made in the laboratory.

Drugs have different uses. Some deaden pain, such as aspirin, heroin, and ANESTHETICS; others, called tranquilizers, cause a relaxation of the nervous system; while antibiotics, like erythromycin, kill germs or prevent them from multiplying.

Drugs can prevent or cure disease. They can sometimes cause unpleasant side effects in certain people. When taken without prescription or in dosages not recommended by a doctor, they may be harmful, addictive, or fatal.

DRUMS

Drums are probably the oldest musical instruments. Most drums are struck with sticks but a few kinds, like bongos, are struck with the fingers. Some drums are rubbed rather than struck. Most drums have no special pitch but the kettle drum, used by orchestras, is carefully tuned.

Drums have been used in religious ceremonies in many places. In East Africa they are regarded as giving magical protection to tribal chiefs. In parts of the world, too, they have been used for sending messages. Also, armies everywhere have used them to beat time for marching and to send signals.

African drum

side drum

Kettle drum

Bass drum

264

DUCKS

Ducks are closely related to geese and the swans, but they have shorter necks and legs. Like their relatives, ducks have similar bills and are clumsy walkers, but they are powerful swimmers because of their webbed feet.

The oily coating on their feathers serves as waterproofing. To protect them from the cold, ducks have a thick layer of fluffy down under their feathers. This down is plucked from the breasts of the parent birds for lining the nest. The down from the Eider duck is used for stuffing pillows, quilts, parkas, and sleeping bags. The feathers of most male ducks become much more brightly colored during the mating season.

Ducks eat small water creatures, insects, grass, roots, seeds, and berries. Some ducks are fresh water ducks; some are salt water ducks.

The ducks illustrated here are the male (drake) and female mallard. This kind of duck feeds with its head dipped in the water. Other ducks dive underwater for their food.

Seasonal MIGRATION is common to many duck species. Some often nest in summer as far north as the Arctic Circle and then fly south in winter to regions that are temperate, sub-tropical, or tropical. SEE ALSO: MIGRATION.

DYE

A dye is coloring matter that becomes permanently fixed in the fibers of a material. A dye will not fade or run when the material is exposed to sunlight or water.

Dyeing has been practiced for thousands of years. Many of the world explorers were in search of new and cheaper dye sources. The beautiful royal blue, royal red, and royal purple colors were originally so expensive and difficult to obtain that only royalty could afford garments in those colors. The ancient Roman nobility wore garments dyed with Tyrian purple. This dye was prepared from the secretions of the murex, a small sea snail, which the Romans nearly exterminated. One pound (0.45 kg) of cochineal, a modern, expensive, crimson red dye, consists of about 70,000 dried bodies of a female insect that lives in Mexico.

Dr. Perkin

Through the centuries, the various sources of dyes have included: bark, flowers, berries, nuts, lichens, insects, nuts, and shellfish.

Many dyes need a *mordant* to "fix" chemically the dye to the fiber. Iron acts as a mordant. The thrifty, practical early American colonists sometimes used their rusty iron kettles for dye pots. Since iron tends to "sadden" colors, many of the early settlers' clothes were thus drab in color.

In 1856, the first artificial dye was produced. William Perkin, an English schoolboy, accidentally discovered that coal tar yielded a lavender (mauve) dye. Since then, scientists have been able to produce any color dye from coal tar. These dyes, called aniline dyes, are the most common dyes used today.

DYNAMITE

Dynamite is an explosive three times more powerful than GUNPOWDER. It has become the most widely used non-military explosive in the United States and in most other parts of the world. Dynamite is made from a dangerous substance called nitroglycerine. It was first tested by its discoverer, Alfred Nobel, a Swedish chemist, on a barge in the middle of a lake. In 1866, he mixed a kind of porous earth with it to absorb the shock and thus make it safer to handle.

It is now made in sticks about 8 inches (20.3 cm) long. About 75 percent of the dynamite made in the U.S. is used for blasting in quarries.

DYNAMO

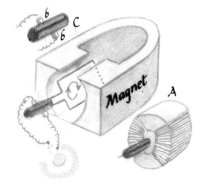

A dynamo or electric GENERATOR is a machine that converts mechanical energy into electrical energy.

In 1831, Michael Faraday, an English physicist, discovered that moving a wire between the poles of a MAGNET produced an electric current. This principle is basic to the working of the dynamo. An armature (A) is wound with hundreds of loops of wire. Next, the armature is turned rapidly between the poles of the magnet. The carbon brushes (b) which press on the commutator (C) collect the current. The commutator changes the frequency or direction of the current in the armature windings. SEE ALSO: CURRENT, ELECTRIC; GENERATOR.

EAGLE

Since 1782, the bald eagle has been the national emblem of the U.S. Eagles symbolize power and majesty. The ancient Romans considered the eagle as a symbol of power.

The eagle family is a large family of birds of prey which includes falcons, HAWKS, and VULTURES. The largest eagles have a wing span of over 6 feet (1.9 m). Males are somewhat smaller than females. Eagles have powerful wings, sharp claws and beaks, and keen eyesight. They feed on grouse, rabbits, mice, fish, and sometimes have been known to carry off a lamb or a fawn. In good light and in certain countryside, a soaring eagle can spot an 18 inch (45.7 cm) rabbit at ranges up to 2 miles (3.2 km).

An eagle's nest, called an *aerie*, is built on a high cliff or crag or at the top of a tall tree. Eagles have been known to return to the same nest for 20 years, rebuilding and gradually enlarging it. Two or three speckled, dull white eggs are laid in a nest.

Although these great birds of prey are protected by law, they are very much in danger of extinction. SEE ALSO: BIRDS.

EAR

The ear has three parts: the outer ear, the middle ear, and the inner ear.

The outer ear acts like a funnel to collect the sound waves of vibrating air. These are sent through a tube to the eardrum, which is a thin sheet of tightly stretched skin. Air must be present on both sides of the eardrum. On the inside, air is provided by the Eustachian tube, which connects the ear with the throat. Having a cold can block this tube and cause a temporary, partial deafness.

When the sound waves strike the eardrum, three tiny bones are set into

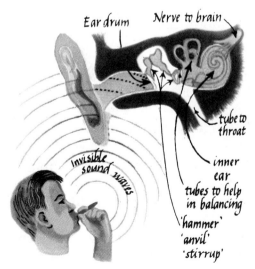

Ear drum   Nerve to brain

tube to throat

inner ear

tubes to help in balancing

'hammer'
'anvil'
'stirrup'

Invisible sound waves

motion to carry the sound to the inner ear. These tiny bones, named for their shape, are the hammer, anvil, and stirrup.

In the inner ear, nerve endings are located in an area shaped like a snail shell. These nerve endings carry the message to the brain. Nearby are three tubes shaped like horseshoes, which are filled with fluid for maintaining our balance. If a person with a serious disease of the inner ear closes his eyes, he is unable to stand or sit without swaying or falling. SEE ALSO: THE DEAF.

EARTH

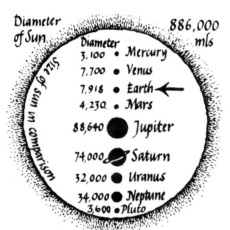

The Earth is a sphere which is slightly flattened at the North and South Poles. The distance around the EQUATOR is 24,902 miles (40,092 km), and the distance around the Poles is 24,860 miles (40,025 km). The Earth travels through space with its satellite, the MOON, which orbits the Earth once every 28 days (about a month). From 239,000 miles (384,790 km) away, the moon exerts a gravitational pull on the Earth and thus is responsible for our TIDES.

The Earth moves through space in three ways: (1) it rotates on its own axis once in 24 hours to produce DAY AND NIGHT; (2) it revolves around the sun once a year to produce the various SEASONS; and (3) it wobbles very slowly on its axis completing one turn every 25,800 years. The motions of the Earth can not be felt by those who live on it.

More than two-thirds of the Earth is covered with water. The Earth's greatest ocean depth is about 7 miles (11.2 km). The land and the sea rest upon a layer of rock, called *basalt*. Under this crust there is a *mantle* of hot solid rock. Below this is the core of molten iron and a small quantity of nickel. Surrounding the Earth is an "ocean" of AIR, called the atmosphere.

'Continental slope', where the land dips steeply down to the ocean depths

Ocean

Continental land mass.

Basalt

'Continental shelf' where the sea is shallow

Of the 9 PLANETS traveling in orbits about the sun, Earth is the fifth largest. It is the third planet in order of distance from the sun, and the only planet known to support life.

The surface of the Earth has undergone many great changes. It has become folded and wrinkled to form great MOUNTAINS, which gradually have been worn away as new ones have been formed. SEE ALSO: DAY AND NIGHT, MOON, PLANETS, SEASONS, SOLAR SYSTEM.

EARTHQUAKE

An earthquake is a shaking and a breaking of the Earth's crust. It is attributed to a sudden relieving of tremendous stress built up by uneven forces exerted on and beneath the Earth's surface. The break in the crust is called a *fault*.

The Earth's crust has a number of solid pieces called *plates*. These plates are separated by cracks because the plates move and rub against each other there.

It is thought that the plates move because very slow currents are moving in the Earth's hot mantle under the crust.

An earthquake may be caused by the slipping of the earth's crust along a fault line

Seismographs, which are very sensitive instruments for measuring these crustal movements and locating their source, record 500,000 quakes annually all over the world. Only one-fifth of these can actually be felt; about 1000 cause damage some place in the world each year.

Using reinforced concrete as a building material helps to reduce earthquake damage. Such buildings are able to shift without collapsing.

EASTER

At Easter, Christians celebrate the resurrection of Jesus after his crucifixion. Easter is one of the most important church festivals. It reminds Christian people that Jesus has promised them eternal life. So it is a time for joyful worship and hope. It is also a time to ponder the meaning of life and death. To the ORTHODOX CHURCH it is more important than Christmas. It marks the end of *Lent*, a time of fasting (going without many foods) that is begun on Ash Wednesday.

Easter is not held on any one date every year. A church council in A.D. 325 decided that it should take place on the Sunday after the first full moon in spring.

The use of brightly colored eggs at Easter goes back a very long time. Candy eggs, on the other hand, are an invention of our own times.

EAST INDIES

East Indies is the name formerly given to the area between the southeastern part of Asia and Australia. It consists of more than 3000 islands and stretches nearly 4000 miles (6440 km). Some large islands are located here: New Guinea (the second largest island in the world), Borneo (larger than Texas), and Sumatra and Java (parts of Indonesia).

Explorers like COLUMBUS and VASCO DA GAMA were attracted to the East Indies, then referred to as the "Spice Islands." Its rich spices include pepper, nutmeg, cloves, and mace. The area has vast resources, such as oil, tin, bauxite (from which aluminum is made), nickel, and coal, that are even more important than spices today. Rubber, tea, coffee, and tobacco are grown there and exported.

For more than 300 years, the Dutch controlled many of the islands of Indonesia. During World War II, the Japanese occupied the area, but afterward it gained independence. North Borneo is part of Malaysia, and eastern New Guinea is a new country called Papua New Guinea. Most of the rest is now part of Indonesia.

ECHO

Sound travels in waves. When these waves bounce off surfaces, like walls or cliffs, they reflect back on their course. The repetition of sound produced by the reflection of sound waves is called an echo. A sound echo that is reflected again and again from different surfaces, as in a tunnel, is called a reverberation.

Sound waves moving towards cliff face

Sound waves reflected back from cliff face to produce echo.

In order for an echo to come back to where the sound originated, the reflection of sound must be direct—that is, in a straight line. If not, the echo will not be heard by the one making the sound, but by another in a different place. Natural echoes are produced out-of-doors in certain valleys, mountains, and forests. Some places are famous for their echoes, such as a spot in Ireland, where 100 echoes have resulted from one note sounded by a bugle!
SEE ALSO: SOUND.

270

ECLIPSE

For thousands of years man has been amazed by eclipses of the moon and sun.

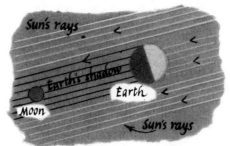

A lunar eclipse occurs when the Earth passes between the moon and the sun. Since the moon has no light of its own but merely reflects that of the sun, it ceases to shine when it passes into the Earth's shadow. A total eclipse of the moon lasts 104 minutes, and, as shown in the first diagram, it can be seen by half the Earth.

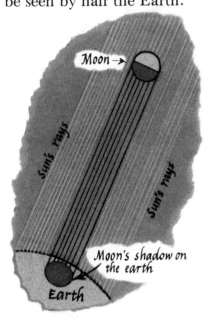

A solar eclipse is the most spectacular natural phenomenon. The moon passes directly in front of the sun, and daylight suddenly disappears and even stars may be seen. Solar eclipses last about 8 minutes and are seen only in those areas that lie within the 100 mile (161 km) shadow cast by the moon. The second diagram illustrates what happens when there is an eclipse of the sun.

Early civilizations did not understand this phenomenon. People thought an eclipse signalled disastrous future events. SEE ALSO: ASTRONOMY.

Thomas Alva EDISON (1847–1931)

Thomas Edison was born in Milan, Ohio, and attended school for only three months. When he was twelve years old, he was employed on the Grand Trunk Railroad, first as a newsboy and later as a telegraph operator. He spent his spare time experimenting with printing presses and with electrical and mechanical devices.

As a telegraph operator, Edison made his first important invention, a transmitter and receiver for automatic telegraph. In 1877, he announced his invention of a phonograph, and two years later produced the first practical incandescent electric light bulb. Other discoveries by him include the mimeograph; an alkaline, nickel-iron storage battery; and a motion picture camera. He patented more than 1000 inventions. Scientists in the research laboratory that he founded developed the earliest forms of TELEVISION and many other inventions that we take for granted today. Few great scientific discoveries can be credited to him, but he was a genius as a practical inventor.

EELS

Eels are fish though they look more like snakes. Sea eels are often 6 feet (1.9 m) long, but fresh water eels are only half as long.

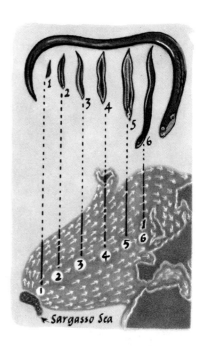

As eels drift to the east they slowly grow in size.

All eels pass through a lengthy larval stage during which the body is transparent. American and European eels from fresh and salt water migrate to the Sargasso Sea, in the North Atlantic near Bermuda. Here the adult eels spawn and die. The eggs float upon the water and hatch into flat, leaf-shaped LARVAE. It takes the European larvae about three years to drift 4000 miles (6440 km) back home. While drifting eastward, a transformation (change) in size and shape occurs, as shown in the picture. Since the trip is shorter for the American eels, the transformation only takes a year. When the young eels (elvers) reach home, they are about 3 inches (7.6 cm) long. The fresh water eels then leave the sea and head upstream to ponds and marshes to grow to full size.

Fresh water eels are a delicacy in Japan and Europe and are eaten either smoked or fresh. They are caught when they are rich in fats as they migrate toward the sea.

EGGS

The females of mammals, birds, reptiles, amphibians, fish, and arthropods produce eggs. Before an egg can begin to develop, it has to become fertilized by uniting with the sperm of the male. Eggs vary greatly in size. The human egg is 0.006 inches (0.152 mm) in diameter, and the ostrich egg weighs up to 4 pounds (1.8 kg) and is capable of supporting the weight of a 250 pound (112.5 kg) man.

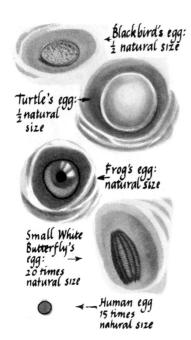

Blackbird's egg: ½ natural size

Turtle's egg: ½ natural size

Frog's egg: natural size

Small White Butterfly's egg: 20 times natural size

Human egg 15 times natural size

The eggs of mammals develop inside the female until the young are ready to be born. The exception is the strange duckbill platypus of Australia, which lays eggs but nurses its young like any other mammal.

Fish and amphibians lay eggs surrounded by a jelly-like substance. Some fish lay millions of eggs at once but many of the eggs get eaten by birds and other fish.

Reptile eggs are protected by a leathery shell; bird eggs, by a brittle shell. Arthropods have various ways of protecting their eggs: bees lay them in cells, and spiders cover them with silken threads.

The eggs of chickens, turkeys, ducks, and geese are a good source of protein and vitamins A and D. The U.S. alone produces about 70 billion chicken eggs each year.

EGYPT

Egypt occupies the northeast corner of Africa. The country is mostly hot and dry desert, but the NILE River makes a fertile strip of land, varying between 2 and 120 miles (3.2–193 km) wide from Sudan in the south to the delta on the Mediterranean. Here most people live and raise cotton, wheat, barley, rice, citrus fruits, dates, tobacco, and sugar cane. Some Egyptians work in textile, steel, automotive, cement, fertilizer, or glass factories, located in or near cities like CAIRO (the capital), Alexandria, Giza, or Suez.

The country has very little rainfall, and in ancient days the land was mainly watered by the annual flooding of the Nile. The Aswan Dam, completed in 1970, now holds back the Nile waters during the flood season, and releases them in the dry season. As a result, some Egyptian land can grow four crops a year and an extra 1 million acres of land can be cultivated.

The origin of the Egyptian people is uncertain, but ancient Egypt had one of the first civilizations in the world. Written records of its history date back before 4000 B.C. Ancient Egyptians developed a form of writing called HIEROGLYPHICS, made writing paper from the papyrus reed, and learned a lot about medicine. They built large temples, PYRAMIDS, and stone statues to honor their Pharaohs (kings) and gods.

They believed in life after death and also wrapped their dead in layers of cloth to preserve them as mummies, many of which can be seen in our museums today. It is from the mummies and the contents of the tombs that we have learned about ancient Egypt.

Peasants, called *fellahin*, make up three-quarters of Egypt's population (about 39 million people) today, and most of them live in poverty. There are also groups of Turks, Greeks, Syrians, and Armenians, as well as a few Europeans. Most Egyptians are followers of the religion of ISLAM. SEE ALSO: CAIRO, HIEROGLYPHICS, NILE, PYRAMIDS, SUEZ CANAL.

Albert EINSTEIN (1879–1955)

Albert Einstein was born in Ulm, Germany, and spent his childhood mainly in Munich, another German city. He became a professor of PHYSICS at the University of Berlin, but, when Hitler came to power, he moved to England and then later to the United States.

All his life was devoted to mathematical and physical research. In his *theory of relativity*, Einstein correctly predicted in 1905 that objects moving at almost the speed of light do not obey the laws of motion developed by Isaac Newton in the 1600s. Also, his theory showed that matter and energy are really two different forms of the same thing. His ideas were far ahead of his time and few could understand them.

Scientists today are still testing and marveling at his theories of gravitation. He is recognized as one of the greatest scientists of all time, one who changed man's ideas of nature and the universe.

Dwight D. EISENHOWER (1890–1969)

Nicknamed "Ike," Eisenhower grew up from humble beginnings on a mid-western farm to become a statesman, soldier, the supreme commander of the Allied forces in western Europe during WORLD WAR II, educator, and 34th President of the United States. He was the oldest man to hold the office of President and the second Republican to serve two full terms.

Born in Denison, Texas, on October 14, 1890, young Dwight moved with his family to the unfashionable section of the small, farming community of Abilene, Kansas. With his broad grin and easy manner, he became popular with all. Although his family was poor, they all accepted and thrived on hard work. Dwight and his five brothers grew vegetables and did odd jobs to earn money.

Dwight's mother belonged to a religious group that hated war. However, Dwight decided to take advantage of a college education at the United States Military Academy at West Point. He worked hard and got along with others. His many years of military experience—rather than a brilliant mind and a flashy personality—made him rise to become a great military hero.

The most important single decision he ever had to make changed the course of world history—the exact timing for the Allied invasion of France during World War II in 1944. Within a year, under his leadership, the Allied forces had ended the war in Europe by overrunning Germany.

In the late 1940s, General Eisenhower accepted the presidency of Columbia University. Late in 1950, President Truman asked him to become commander of the North Atlantic Treaty Organization. Two years later, he was elected President of the United States, as a Republican.

Eisenhower helped bring about the end of the KOREAN WAR, strengthened the social security system, urged the development of atomic weapons, and reached an agreement with Canada for U.S. participation in the building of the ST. LAWRENCE SEAWAY. Reelected President in 1956, Eisenhower used federal troops in Little Rock, Arkansas, to enforce school desegregation. He also sent U.S. forces to contain Communist aggression in the Middle East.

ELECTRICITY

Electricity has been known since the time of the ancient Greeks. They discovered that when certain materials, such as AMBER, were rubbed, they were able to pick up lightweight materials. This frictional or static electricity which they discovered was not a very useful form of electricity.

When you comb your hair with a certain kind of comb, electrons pass from your hair to the comb. Your hair becomes positively charged, and the comb negatively charged. They therefore attract one another, and your hair sticks out towards the comb.

Scientists later learned that when two substances are rubbed together, the electrons of one of the substances get rubbed off. When an object has more or fewer electrons than usual, it becomes electrically charged. If a substance loses electrons, it becomes positively charged; if it gains electrons, it becomes negatively charged.

Two substances which are oppositely charged attract each other. Two substances of the same charge repel each other.

Electrons always move from a negatively charged place to a positively charged place. Some metals, such as copper, allow electrons to flow easily along them. These metals are called conductors. When electrons move along a conductor, an electric CURRENT is flowing. Those substances through which electrons cannot pass are known as insulators. Wires that conduct electricity are wrapped with an insulating material, such as rubber or plastic, to prevent a person from getting a shock. SEE ALSO: BATTERIES; CURRENT, ELECTRIC; DYNAMO; GENERATOR.

ELEMENTS

Just as letters are the building blocks of words, elements are the building blocks of the world. When two or more different elements unite, they form a COMPOUND.

SALT is **not** an element, because it can be broken up into Sodium and Chlorine (a metal) (a yellow gas) These **are** elements, because it is impossible to break them up into simpler substances

The ancient Greeks believed all matter was made up of elements. However, they thought that the elements were earth, air, fire, and water. Their idea persisted until 1661, when Robert Boyle, an English physicist, suggested that there might be quite a number of elements. He defined an element as a substance which cannot be broken down into simpler substances. Scientists later accepted atoms as the substances that cannot be broken down.

There are over 100 known elements. Ninety-two elements occur naturally; the rest have been produced in laboratories. Some familiar elements are aluminum, copper, gold, silver, iron, mercury, oxygen, and uranium.

ELEPHANTS

Elephants are the largest land animals. They are native to Africa and southern Asia. The African elephant is twice as big as the Asian (or Indian) elephant. The African elephant weighs about 6 tons (5.5 metric tons), has much bigger ears and tusks, and is darker in color. The tusks, which are actually elongated upper teeth, consist of ivory.

Elephants are characterized by their unusually long nose or trunk. This awkward looking feature is really a very useful tool. It is not only an organ for breathing, but it is also used as a giant straw for sucking up water, which is sprayed onto the back or squirted into the mouth. The trunk is also used for obtaining food and for spraying and dusting itself.

The elephant's great strength for pulling and carrying and its ability to use its trunk for lifting heavy objects have made the elephant a beast of burden for agricultural, royal, military, and pageantry purposes for almost 4000 years. Asiatic elephants are the easiest to train for working and hunting. In captivity they usually live about 50 years.

Elephants are gentle in temperament if left undisturbed. The elephant is now protected by law because many have been killed by hunters for their ivory tusks. Growing towns and villages have also reduced their natural habitat.

ELEVATORS

For most of man's history, the height of buildings has been limited by two things: the difficulty of building very high, and the difficulty of climbing many steps. The SKYSCRAPER was made possible when these two problems were solved.

In 1850, landlords found it hard to rent space in buildings above the fifth floor. People refused to climb any higher. But in 1853, Elisha Graves Otis, an American, demonstrated the first passenger elevator. It ran by steam, and it already had a device to catch the elevator if the rope broke. A New York department store installed one in 1857, and elevators became increasingly popular.

Steam power had disadvantages, though, and other means were introduced late in the 19th century. The *hydraulic elevator* ran by water pressure, which either lifted the elevator at the top of a long rod or ran a winch that wound a hoisting rope in or out. The modern *electric elevator* is raised and lowered by a winch run by a motor.

The first elevators were open platforms, but these were unsafe. Passengers were in danger of being crushed between the platform and the floors. Elevator designers introduced enclosed cars made of fine woodwork or ironwork. At first the elevator shafts were open, but later they were enclosed to prevent danger from fire.

The *escalator* was invented around 1900. This is a staircase like an endless chain that rises, taking passengers with it. At the top, the steps pass over a drum and return, upside-down, to start over at the bottom.

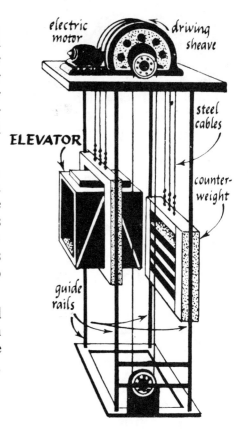

ELIZABETH I (1533–1603)

Anne Boleyn

Elizabeth was the daughter of Anne Boleyn and King Henry VIII. After her half-sister, Queen Mary, died in 1558, Elizabeth became Queen of England. For 45 years, she ruled the country, making it rich and powerful through exploration and trade.

Elizabeth helped settle England's religious problems for a while, although later new conflicts began between PURITANS and the Roman Catholics. She made many enemies abroad, mainly in France and Spain, but she managed to keep the country at peace for 30 years. She had trouble from MARY, QUEEN OF SCOTS, a Catholic who had a claim to the English throne. Catholics abroad and in England tried to make Mary queen. When Mary gave up the Scottish throne and fled to England for safety, Elizabeth kept her prisoner for 19 years and finally had her executed in 1587.

In the next year Philip of Spain sent more than 100 ships, called the ARMADA, to attack England. SIR FRANCIS DRAKE was one of the English admirals who, using smaller and faster ships, defeated the big and clumsy Spanish ships.

Elizabeth never married and so Parliament was worried about whom should succeed her. As she lay dying, she agreed to James VI, King of Scotland, as the new King of England, and·he thus became JAMES I of England. SEE ALSO: JAMES I, MARY QUEEN OF SCOTS.

ELM

The elm is a tall and graceful shade tree, with a vase-shaped crown of fine branches and twigs. It grows mainly in the Northern Hemisphere.

The American or white elm was once a common shade tree on streets, village greens, city parks, and college campuses. However, it was greatly

reduced in numbers by the fungus known as the Dutch elm disease. This disease, which was accidentally brought to the United States from Holland, was spread by two kinds of bark beetles. No effective control for it has yet been discovered. The common English elm (pictured here) has been successfully introduced into the United States.

The wood of the elm is tough, durable, and water-resistant. It is used in making furniture. The elm's outer bark is used in making dyes and medicines. Sometimes elm logs have been hollowed out for water pipes.

EMBROIDERY

The decoration of cloth with needlework is an art that goes back to ancient Egyptian times. The oldest embroideries we have are Coptic (Egyptian Christian) ones of the 4th century A.D. The Byzantines (who lived where Turkey is today) made very fine embroideries that included gold wire. China, India, and Persia have also done very good embroidered work.

One of the most famous works of art in English history, the so-called Bayeux Tapestry, is really a piece of embroidery. In true tapestry the design is woven into the cloth. In the Bayeux Tapestry the design is stitched on.

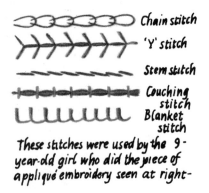

Chain stitch
'Y' stitch
Stem stitch
Couching stitch
Blanket stitch

These stitches were used by the 9-year-old girl who did the piece of appliqué embroidery seen at right-

In medieval Europe the English led all others in embroidery. "English work" was very popular for the vestments (ceremonial clothes) of bishops and other church officials in the 13th and 14th centuries.

Embroidery was easy to do, and was done in America from the earliest days. Most girls learned to make *samplers*, pieces of embroidery intended to show how much they knew. Alphabets, numbers, religious sayings, and pictures of things like houses made up such a sampler.

Ralph Waldo EMERSON (1803–1882)

Ralph Waldo Emerson, an American writer and PHILOSOPHER, was born in Boston, Massachusetts. He became minister of Old North Church in Boston in 1829. Because of his personal religious beliefs, Emerson left the church in 1832 and made a trip to Europe. There he was influenced by several English writers, such as WILLIAM WORDSWORTH, and developed a philosophy based on nature.

After his return to the U.S. in 1834, Emerson settled in Concord, Massachusetts, and began writing and lecturing. His first published essay, "Nature," showed his belief that God is in all things. Emerson also stated that man's instincts were essentially good and sound and could be depended upon as guides to life. This is not what the Bible teaches.

Emerson's lectures attracted wide attention. Audiences liked his pleasant manner and personality, as well as his ideas about individual freedom, self-reliance, and conscience, although some people disagreed with his beliefs. He influenced many other American writers and thinkers, like HENRY DAVID THOREAU and Walt Whitman.

ENAMEL

To make enamel, a craftsman coats a piece of metal with finely powdered glass. Then he heats the piece until the glass melts and sticks to it. Both artists and manufacturers use enamel. A sink or a bathtub may be of enameled cast iron, but enamel has also been used in many places for fine decorative work.

Where different patterns and colors of enamel are needed, a technique called *cloisonné* is often used. Little strips of metal (brass or silver usually) are attached to the piece to be enameled, so as to divide the surface into areas. Enamel glass of the right color is put into each area before firing. The Chinese and Japanese have done very beautiful cloisonné.

Many modern artists do enameling in the United States, and many people do it as a hobby.

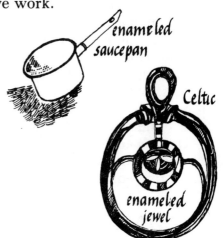

enameled saucepan

Celtic

enameled jewel

ENCYCLOPEDIA

You are now looking at an encyclopedia for young readers. It tries to give you important information about things that interest you.

An encyclopedia is different from a DICTIONARY, though they may have some of the same information. If you want to know what the word "medicine" means, go to a dictionary. But a dictionary will not tell you anything about medicine. If you want to learn the history of medicine, or know what has been happening in medical science in the last few years, you need an encyclopedia.

An ALMANAC, is also different from an encyclopedia. It comes out once a year and gives much information about what happened the year before. If you want to know who last year's bowling champions were, this year's almanac will tell you. If you want to know the rules of bowling, you are more likely to find them in an encyclopedia.

Almanacs, dictionaries, and encyclopedias are all useful. If you need to know about many things, you should be able to use them all.

The first encyclopedia was written in the 13th century, but encyclopedias were not published in large numbers until the 18th century. In 1750, the French scholar Denis Diderot published one of the greatest of all encyclopedias. It has good, large illustrations that tell us much about the 18th century. The most famous modern encyclopedia, the *Encyclopaedia Britannica*, was first published in Scotland in 1768. It is now published in Chicago. It is made up of 30 books, each with more than 1000 pages. It has been rewritten 15 times to include the new things the world has learned since 1768. SEE ALSO: ALMANAC, DICTIONARY.

ENGINEER

Engineering is one of the most interesting and important human occupations. Without engineers the modern world would be impossible.

There are two kinds of engineer. One engineer is a man who knows exactly how to design and put together something useful to mankind. Some kinds of engineers can be artists as well, but often the engineer's work is hidden from sight. There are *structural engineers*, who design the frames of buildings; *civil engineers*, who design bridges, roads, canals, and so on; *sanitary engineers*, who design sewer and drainage systems; *mechanical engineers*, who design machinery; and engineers who design lighting, heating, and ventilation systems. There are even engineers who see to it that audiences hear plays and concerts properly.

There is another kind of engineer, one who runs engines. Such engineers run locomotives and powerhouses. In television and radio studios they run the broadcasting equipment. They are very skilled at their jobs.

ENGINES

Engines are machines that give the power to run other machines. An engine can get its power from the pressure of steam, explosions of gasoline or oil, or the force of moving air and water. Gasoline and oil engines are often called *motors*. Engines can be driven by electricity too, but such engines are always called motors.

Air

Water

Steam

Gasoline

Rocket

One family of engines uses *pistons*, circular objects that fit snugly into CYLINDERS. These are round spaces in which the piston slides back and forth. Steam is let into one end of a cylinder, or else gasoline or oil are exploded there. This drives the piston away. The piston moves the machinery that the engine is driving, usually by cranking a shaft around. Then the piston comes back, forcing out the steam or gas that has done the work. Such engines are called *reciprocating engines*. A reciprocating engine that runs on explosions in the cylinders is called an INTERNAL-COMBUSTION ENGINE. Most reciprocating engines have several cylinders to help them run steadily and smoothly.

TURBINES are another family of engines. A turbine is rather like an electric fan, except that instead of moving a fluid (like air) the fluid moves it. Steam, water, and air can all be used to run turbines. A WINDMILL, for instance, is a turbine. So are some water mills that use water under high pressure.

Some engines, such as jet engines and ROCKET engines, use the principle of *reaction*. If gas or water is forced from one end of an object, the object tends to be forced the other way. When a rocket emits gas under high enough pressure, it rises.

Efficiency is usually considered very carefully when an engine is planned. The fuel (coal, for instance) or the moving fluid (such as water) has a certain amount of force in it. With coal, oil, and other fuels, this force is released by burning. Some of this force is wasted in any engine; the whole force can never be used to run machinery. Steam and gasoline engines are not very efficient; electric motors are. SEE ALSO: AUTOMOBILE, STEAM ENGINE, TURBINE.

ENGLAND

England is the largest of the four countries in the BRITISH ISLES. It is surrounded by water on the east and south and borders on Wales in the west and on Scotland in the north. The land in the west is the highest, and the central area has rolling hills and valleys. To the east the land is low and flat. In this nation, that is the size of Alabama, live about 46 million people.

An ocean current, the North Atlantic Drift, which flows from the equator past the coasts of England, helps to keep the climate mild. In winter, when the warmer winds blow from the current, temperatures seldom go below 20°F (–7°C).

England's natural resources are chiefly coal, iron ore, and oil (in the North Sea). It manufactures many goods to be sold to other countries, such as textiles, steel, machinery, jet aircraft, and whisky. Much of the land is used for farming, and yet the country must import half of its food. The large fishing industry supplies much food for the population, and also provides many jobs.

The name "England" comes from the Angles, an early tribe that seized a part of the country in the A.D. 500s. It was first made a single kingdom under Edward the Elder, the son of ALFRED THE GREAT. The English language

283

developed from Anglo-Saxon, which is a Germanic language; it contains many words from Latin (brought to England by the Romans), and from Norman French (brought by WILLIAM THE CONQUEROR).

Kings and queens once ruled the country with a strong hand, but the PARLIAMENT and the people now control the nation's government. The royal family is still honored today, but the English monarch is really only an adviser. SEE ALSO: ANGLO-SAXONS, BRITISH ISLES, GREAT BRITAIN, LONDON.

EQUATOR

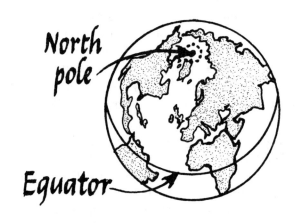

The equator is an imaginary line that divides the Earth into a Northern Hemisphere and a Southern Hemisphere.

Equator means "equalizer" in Latin. At the equator, which is 0° latitude on a map, the sun's rays almost always fall directly on the Earth, and therefore day and night are nearly equal in length. Because of the directness of the sun's rays, the CLIMATE of most places on the equator is always very hot, with heavy rainfall and dense jungles. However, Quito, Ecuador, which is on the equator, is 9250 feet (2868 m) above sea level, and the climate there is always very much like spring all year round.

Recent satellite pictures have revealed that the equator is closer to the South Pole, but the difference is so slight that it is still correct to say that the equator is halfway between the North and South Poles.

Leif ERICSON

Leif Ericson was a Norse or Viking explorer and is now acknowledged as the first European to reach North America. His father was Eric the Red, a Norse chieftain who left Norway and colonized Greenland.

Leif's boyhood was probably spent in Greenland. About A.D. 1000, he sailed back to Norway, where he was converted to Christianity. He was then sent by the Norwegian king as a missionary to GREENLAND. According to one account, Leif was blown off course on the return voyage and landed on the eastern coast of NORTH AMERICA. He called the place "Vinland," because of the wild grapes and fertile land he found there.

Historians agree that Leif Ericson landed in North America, but they cannot agree on the location of Vinland. Many say it is Nova Scotia, and others say it is Newfoundland, New England, or even Virginia. SEE ALSO: VIKINGS.

ESKIMOS

Eskimos are a people who live in northern North America, Greenland, and Siberia. The name Eskimo is an INDIAN name meaning "eaters of raw meat."

Eskimos have Mongoloid features—unusually wide faces, straight eyes, high cheekbones, and yellowish complexions — which suggest an Asian origin. Also, they are short to medium in stature.

Eskimos are among the most skillful hunters in the world. From hunting seals, walruses, whales, and caribous they used to obtain most of their food, clothing, cooking oil, tools, and weapons. Today, however, with money they obtain from fishing and from trapping (fox furs), Eskimos buy modern oil lamps, packaged food, and guns.

They generally live in small bands, under a leader known for his superior ability. In winter, their shelters are built of sod, driftwood, or sometimes stone. The snow hut, or *igloo*, is seldom used today. In summer, their huts are usually made of caribou skins or sealskins. The Eskimos use the dogsled for carrying heavy loads over long distances. Also a skin canoe, called the *kayak*, is used by them.

ETHIOPIA

Ethiopia is a mountainous country in northeastern AFRICA. Some of its mountain peaks have snow all year round even though they are located near the equator. It faces on the Red Sea, but its main rivers run into the Nile River. It is larger than Texas, Oklahoma, and New Mexico combined, with a population of 29 million.

The Ethiopians come from many different African and Asian tribes. They live mainly in rural areas, raising coffee, grain, sugar cane, and tobacco. Addis Ababa is the capital and largest city. Ethiopia was once called Abyssinia.

ETRUSCANS

Before the great days of ancient ROME, a people called the Etruscans lived in central Italy, in an area we now call Tuscany. They supposedly came from Asia Minor about 1000 B.C. and built in Italy several large cities that were all joined together in a league.

Many of their achievements have survived and show us the kind of culture they had. Etruscan underground tombs have colorful paintings on plaster. Etruscan sculptors with terra cotta, a ceramic clay, fashioned large and impressive figures. They made attractive black pottery known as *bucchero*; they were skillful in making jewelry, which the Etruscan women wore a great deal of. The beautiful furniture and household items in their palaces, as well as the Etruscan clothing, indicate a happy, gentle, and civilized people.

The Etruscans began the custom of giving everyone a first name and a family name. They designed their towns in a rectangular plan, which the Romans copied. The Romans copied also the Etruscan idea of public games and gladiator fights.

At the height of their power about 535 B.C., they ruled most of northern Italy and were trading in many parts of the western

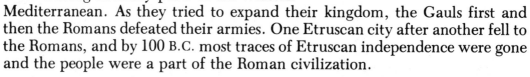

Mediterranean. As they tried to expand their kingdom, the Gauls first and then the Romans defeated their armies. One Etruscan city after another fell to the Romans, and by 100 B.C. most traces of Etruscan independence were gone and the people were a part of the Roman civilization.

Much of the Etruscan life remains a puzzle to historians today. Perhaps Etruscan religion is the best-known aspect. Many gods and goddesses were worshiped, many with the same names as the Roman ones. Etruscans believed they could foresee the future by studying the intestines of dead animals and the soaring flights of birds. Their language is difficult to understand and cannot be put into any known group of languages. SEE ALSO: ROME.

EUPHRATES

The Bible (Genesis) refers to the Euphrates as one of the four rivers of the Garden of Eden. It rises in eastern Turkey and flows southeast through Syria and Iraq, emptying into the Persian Gulf after a course of about 1700 miles (2737 km). The Euphrates through Iraq is generally parallel to the Tigris River; the two rivers join eventually to form the Shatt-al-Arab, which later separates into two arms.

The fertile Tigris-Euphrates valley was the location of Mesopotamia, the home of the ancient civilizations of SUMERIA and BABYLON. Many archeological excavations along the Tigris and Euphrates have furnished valuable historical information.

EUROPE

Europe is separated from the continent of Asia by the Ural Mountains and the Caspian Sea. It is surrounded by water on the three other sides: the Arctic in the north, the Atlantic in the west, and the Mediterranean in the south. Many islands around the continent are considered part of it, such as the Azores, Crete, the British Isles, and Iceland.

Europe consists of rugged, rocky highlands and mountains in the northwestern regions—Scotland, Norway, and Sweden. The great European plain lies farther south, stretching from southeastern England, through France, Belgium, Holland, northern Germany and Poland, curving through southern Finland and Russia to the Black Sea. Europe's longest river, the Volga, flows through this plain in Russia. The great European plain has rich farmland, dense forests, and many industrial cities with large populations. South of the plain are high, flat hills that extend through parts of Portugal, Spain, France, Germany, to Czechoslovakia. Here are located Europe's great deposits of coal. Still farther south are higher mountains—the Pyrenees between France and Spain, the ALPS of Switzerland and Austria (with the Apennines running into Italy), and the Carpathians stretching from Czechoslovakia to Rumania. Two major rivers—the RHINE and the DANUBE—begin in the Alps.

The climate of Europe is generally temperate—warm in the summer and cool in the winter. However, in the northwest, warm winds from the Atlantic bring rain all the year around. Here are forests and fertile pastures for cattle and sheep, and orchards and good land for cereals. In eastern Europe, the winters are bitter cold and the summers very hot. Enormous coniferous forests and grassy plains (called *steppes*) cover much of Russia. The Mediterranean countries usually have mild, wet winters and hot, dry summers, a climate fit for growing oranges, lemons, olives, and grapes.

Countries, cities, and physical geography of Europe

Mountain ranges

500 miles

Europe has been one of the great centers of civilization; modern western culture has its roots in Greece. The people of each country have their own particular characteristics. No common language is spoken in Europe, but usually English, French, or German are understood in every country. Most of the languages belong to the Indo-European family of languages. Europeans were among the first people to explore other lands and trade with the rest of the

Distribution of resources in Europe

288

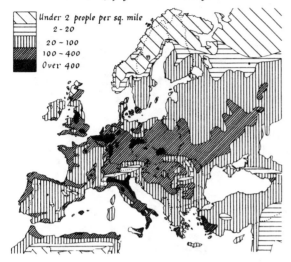

Distribution of population in Europe

Under 2 people per sq. mile
2 - 20
20 - 100
100 - 400
Over 400

world. Also, many Europeans left in search of political and religious freedom, going to North and South America, Australia, and Africa. Today the continent is one of the most densely populated areas of the world, having now more than 600 million people. At least 20 European cities have populations of more than 1 million. The largest are London, Paris, Rome, and Moscow. SEE ALSO: INDIVIDUAL COUNTRIES OF EUROPE.

EVAPORATION

Evaporation is the changing of a liquid into a vapor. For instance, water in a puddle on the road gradually *evaporates*—that is, it disappears as invisible water vapor into the air.

However, when the air becomes cooler, some of the water vapor may again turn into water, forming tiny suspended droplets. These droplets can form clouds, mist, and sometimes rain.

After rain, the pools on the road evaporate.
Many gallons of water evaporate each day from the leaves of a tree.

Evaporation occurs because some of the molecules (the tiniest particles of matter) on the surface of a liquid have enough heat energy to break away from the other molecules and to escape into the air. Heat increases the rate of evaporation because it causes the molecules to escape faster from the surface. Some liquids, like rubbing alcohol, evaporate much faster than others, often producing a tremendous cooling effect. Water is continually evaporating from our skin's surface and from the leaves of trees and bushes.

EVEREST

Everest, on the border of Tibet and Nepal, is the highest mountain in the world. It is one of the many high peaks in the HIMALAYAS, and is 29,028 feet (8998 m) above sea level. Called Chomo-Lungma by the Tibetans, it is in English named after Sir George Everest, a surveyor who in 1841 first worked out its location and height.

289

Climbers have made many attempts to reach the summit of Everest. Weather conditions allow only a short time each year when camps can be pitched and the climbers can become used to the thin, mountain air. British expeditions in 1922, 1924, and 1933 approached the summit from the north, but bad weather and avalanches prevented success. British attempts in 1936 and 1938 were also unsuccessful, and two Swiss expeditions failed in 1952.

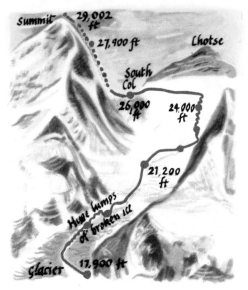

Two members of another British team—Sir Edmund Hillary, a New Zealander, and Tenzing Norgay, a Nepalese guide—finally reached the summit on May 29, 1953, after approaching it from the south side. The final stages of their ascent are drawn in the picture.

The EVERGLADES

This vast fresh water swamp covers most of the southern half of Florida. The Everglades was formed hundreds of years ago by overflowing waters from Lake Okeechobee to the north. This region is extremely difficult

to explore because of the dense, tall saw grass that blocks passage. Being only a few feet above sea level at its highest point, the Everglades is covered by several hundred square miles of water 1 to 6 feet (0.3–1.9 m) deep.

The Everglades is teeming with beautiful tropical and subtropical wildlife, including orchids, water lilies, palms, cypresses, pines, and giant ferns, as well as alligators, crocodiles, bears, panthers, wildcats, pelicans, herons, spoonbills, turtles, and snakes.

The Seminole Indians are perhaps the most familiar with the area, having hunted and fished there since 1834. Since 1906, canals have been dug from Lake Okeechobee to the Atlantic to divert the flood waters and reclaim land for farming.

The Everglades National Park, established in 1947, is in the heart of the Everglades.

EVERGREEN

As the name indicates, an evergreen is a tree or bush that remains green all year round. Evergreens shed their old leaves only after new ones have been produced. Apart from the larch, most CONIFERS are evergreen. Other evergreens also include: HOLLY, laurel, rhododendron, cedar, and some types of live oak and magnolia found in the southern United States.

EVOLUTION

Evolution is a theory that states that living plants and animals have gradually changed from very simple original forms to higher present-day forms. Theories of evolution attempt to explain development from the primitive to the complex.

The earliest ideas of evolution were recorded in ancient Greece about 2500 years ago. However, CHARLES DARWIN, an English naturalist, after making a five-year voyage around the world, was the first person to make a scientific study of evolution. His books, *The Origin of Species* (1859) and *The Descent of Man* (1871), earned him the title, "Father of Evolution." His books aroused much controversy because they seemed to contradict Christian beliefs in the creation of the world by God. Darwin pointed out that no two individual plants or animals are ever *exactly* alike.

According to Darwin, these differences may help plants and animals to get more food, and thus to become stronger and live longer. They would survive better than other plants and animals and bear more offspring. As centuries passed, the plant or animal would look extremely different from what it did originally. Also, Darwin believed that extreme changes in the environment might encourage some variations in plants or animals and might hinder others, making it more difficult for them to survive. SEE ALSO: DARWIN, CHARLES.

EXPLORERS

Modern exploration began with MARCO POLO, who in the late 13th century journeyed in caravans across Asia to China and returned to Italy with stories of the wealth of the Far East and the East Indies.

Europeans on the Atlantic were determined to find a route there. Because the Turks controlled Constantinople after 1453, explorers and traders had to find another way eastward. Prince Henry of Portugal encouraged exploration by ship, inspiring Bartholomeu Diaz to sail to the southern tip of Africa in 1488. Another Portuguese explorer, VASCO DA GAMA, sailed around Africa and reached India in 1498.

Marco Polo, 13th C.

Jacques Cartier, 16th C.

Captain Cook, 18th C.

Sir Henry Stanley, 19th C.

Hunting for the rich "Indies," COLUMBUS crossed the Atlantic in 1492. Five years later, CABOT landed on what is now the eastern coast of Canada, and Cartier in the 1530s explored and tried to colonize for France the St. Lawrence. Other men such as Giovanni da Verrazano, Sir Walter Raleigh, and HENRY HUDSON explored much of the east coast of North America.

In the mid-1500s, DE SOTO explored much of the southern United States, and Coronado penetrated into the southwest areas. The French explorers, MARQUETTE AND JOLIET, discovered in 1673 the headwaters of the Mississippi River, while La Salle descended to its mouth in 1682.

In 1513 BALBOA crossed the isthmus of Panama and saw the Pacific Ocean. Later, MAGELLAN was the first to sail around the world (1519–1521). In the 18th century, Captain COOK, an Englishman, explored the south Pacific, Australia, and the Antarctic Ocean. The northern Pacific areas were then being surveyed by the Danish explorer, Vitus Bering.

From 1849 to 1873, a Scotsman, DAVID LIVINGSTONE, discovered the Zambesi River and Victoria Falls and explored South Africa. John Speke, an Englishman, explored central Africa and searched out the source of the Nile. An American, HENRY STANLEY, after searching for and finding Livingstone in Africa, explored the Congo (Zaire).

The Arctic and Antarctic regions were not explored until the 1900s. PEARY reached the North Pole in 1909, and AMUNDSEN reached the South Pole in 1911, a month before SCOTT made it.

Exploration in other areas includes the first ascent of EVEREST in 1953 by Hillary and Tenzing and the descent in a *bathyscaphe* (pressurized capsule) to the bottom of the Pacific in 1960 by Piccard and Walsh. When Neil Armstrong became the first to set foot on the moon in 1969, space exploration became a reality for the brave explorers of the future.

EXPLOSIVES

Explosives are certain chemicals which are made to produce a sudden and enormous quantity of gases. The heat of these gases creates the force of the explosion. The blast of an explosion occurs when these hot gases and bits of material from the container escape from the close confinement of a shell or a bomb.

Some explosions are caused by explosives that burn very rapidly—that is, they rapidly unite with oxygen. The oxygen in an airtight container is supplied by a chemical, such as potassium nitrate in GUNPOWDER, which gives up its oxygen easily. Sometimes an explosion can be touched off by unstable compounds, such as nitrogen iodide, receiving a very delicate vibration.

DYNAMITE, nitroglycerin, and TNT are all explosives that contain nitrogen in the form of nitric acid. For each of these high explosives, the nitric acid reacts with a specific chemical to produce an explosion. These explosives are used mainly in mining, construction, and road building.

Atomic explosives produce colossal quantities of gas, light, and heat, causing dangerous radioactive fallout. These types of explosions are produced by the fission or fusion of atoms. SEE ALSO: ATOM, ATOMIC BOMB, GUNPOWDER, NUCLEAR ENERGY.

EYEGLASSES

(a) lens for near-sighted person
(b) lens for far-sighted person

People have worn eyeglasses since the Middle Ages, but we do not know if they were invented in Europe or in China. The first picture we have of a man in glasses was painted in Italy in 1352.

Many people are *near-sighted*, and cannot see objects clearly that are far away. Doctors prescribe glasses with *concave* (inward-bulging) LENSES for them. Other people are *far-sighted*, and they wear *convex* (outward-bulging) lenses so that they can read. Some people need *bifocals*, which have separate parts for near and distant vision. People who object to the look of glasses or who find them clumsy to use often wear *contact lenses*, tiny lenses that are set on the eyeballs themselves.

Glasses are prescribed by doctors called *oculists* or *optometrists*. They are made by experts called *opticians*, who grind the lenses to the exact form needed.

293

EYES

The eye is the organ which receives light waves and converts them to a pattern of nerve impulses that travel to the brain. The process of seeing is actually the function of the brain rather than that of the eye. In fact, if the portion of the brain involved with receiving nerve impulses is damaged or seriously diseased, then a person may be blind even though the eyeball itself is in perfect condition.

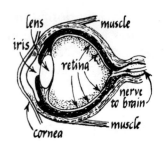

Section through a butterfly's eye

the butterfly's eyes are made up of thousands of tiny eyes

A frog's eyes

The eyes of an owl are large to help it to see in poor light

The fish's eyes are specially designed for seeing under water

the human eye — shown in section at the top of the page.

The entire eye is about 1 inch (2.54 cm) in diameter. Six muscles attached to the eye enable it to move in various directions. As shown in the diagram, the eye has three layers of tissue: (1) the tough "white" (*sclera*) of the eye covering the front has within it the colored portion called the *iris*, which surrounds an opening known as the *pupil*; (2) the *cornea* is the transparent window over the sclera; and, (3) the *retina* is the innermost and light-sensitive layer.

In bright sunlight, muscles in our eyes enlarge the iris to reduce the size of the pupil and hence the amount of light entering the eye. At night, the reverse happens: the pupil enlarges or dilates in order for more light to enter the eye.

Behind the pupil is a kind of magnifying glass through which the light passes. Actually the *lens*, as it is called, is filled with a special kind of jelly. It rests on a cushion of another kind of jelly which fills the inside of the eye. The retina behind all this gelatinous filling contains millions of nerve endings buried in the cells. These nerve endings join together to form the optic nerve which sends the message to the brain telling us what we see.

The eye is like a miniature camera. Light rays from the object viewed pass through the lens onto the retina. If the object is near, tiny muscles make the lens slightly thicker; if the object is far away, they make it thinner. In this way the eye brings the image of the object into clear focus.

Sometimes the muscles controlling the thickness of the lens of the eye do not adjust it to the right thickness, or the eyeball is too long or too short, or the cornea bulges too much. The image then is distorted. Fortunately, wearing eyeglasses or contact lenses will correct such eye defects.

294

FACTORY

A factory is a place devoted to the making or manufacture of goods. It includes the machines, buildings, and workers necessary for the manufacture or production of various things like clothes, radios, cars, food, or drugs.

Some factory-like systems in ancient Greece and Rome made pottery and glass and bronze goods to be sold to the public. These factories were merely large workshops where each person worked independently. However, the usual place of production was the worker's own home. By the

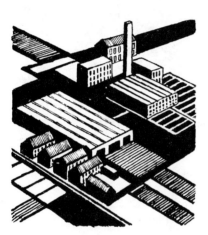

17th century, some factories with heavy machines, operated by water power, came into being in Europe, particularly in England. These factories became larger when steam began to replace water as power for the machinery. The invention of new machines increased production and marked the start of the INDUSTRIAL REVOLUTION. Factories were built close to towns and cities, where the laborers were plentiful and where a market existed for the manufactured goods. Industrial society began to rely on complex machinery rather than tools.

At the beginning of the 19th century, conditions in the factories in England were bad: wages were low; women and children, six or seven years old, worked all day in hot, dirty, dark factories. By the end of the century, the government had made laws, improving the sanitary conditions and ordering periodic public inspections. Organizations, called *unions*, were formed by many workers to fight for higher wages, better safety, and new social and economic reforms. In the U.S., the government now

regulates most factories, inspecting payrolls, plants, conditions, and employees to see if there are violations of safety, health, production, and employment. SEE ALSO: INDUSTRIAL REVOLUTION.

FAIRIES

Stories about fairies exist in almost every country in the world. Fairies are supposed to be small creatures, usually in human form, and very rarely seen. In folklore (beliefs and writing of a people), fairies are such beings as brownies, elves, goblins, trolls, pixies, dwarfs, and leprechauns.

Some of them are good and help people in trouble; others are mischievous and sometimes evil, especially if they are treated badly. Many of them have powers of magic and enchantment. These creatures supposedly live in an imaginary region called fairyland, but many people also believe they live in real valleys, hills, trees, lakes, and streams.

The belief in fairies has existed since ancient times. In country places and on farms, fairies are said to churn milk and drive horses. At night they supposedly come out and dance in the fields, forming "fairy rings"—really caused by certain fungi that grow in a circle. Craftsmen used to believe fairies cobbled shoes and built houses. Among seafaring people, fairies were mermaids or sirens who could be kind or wicked.

The characteristics and adventures of fairies have been written about by HANS CHRISTIAN ANDERSEN and the GRIMM BROTHERS.

FAIRS

Fairs are events at which people buy, sell, or show goods. In ancient Greece, Rome, and China a fair was a kind of religious festival and later became a market place for farmers and craftsmen. In the MIDDLE AGES, fairs were an important way of carrying on the trade of the country. Merchants would sell their goods in a common marketplace, traveling from village to village during the year. Gradually each place began to have its own annual fair on a particular day, and the merchants gathered then and there.

In France, the region of Champagne became famous for its fairs from the 12th to 16th century. Other well-known fairs were held in Brussels, Belgium, in Leipzig, Germany, and in Stourbridge, England. One of the largest was St. Bartholomew's Fair in London, England, which was the first fair known to have plays and other amusements, along with trade exhibits. These fairs were permitted by the king, who would collect taxes from the merchants.

By the 17th century, pleasure fairs with jugglers, ACROBATS, and showmen had became popular. When trading became easier and shops were established in towns, fairs survived as places of fun, with sideshows and lively entertainment.

In the 1800s in the U.S., farmers used annual fairs to show off their livestock and farming tools, as well as to demonstrate new ways of growing crops and breeding animals. Later, contests for the best vegetables and fruits, the tastiest jams and jellies and cakes, and the best cow and pig were included in the fairs. County and state fairs today have added other

amusements, like rides, games, races, and entertainers.

Today, another kind of trade fair, called the *exposition*, has developed. People from all over the world take part in it, exhibiting new and important achievements in the fields of industry, agriculture, science, or art. In 1976, the Bicentennial Celebration, honoring the 200th anniversary of the United States, was a kind of national fair with displays about history, technology, and art, as well as fireworks and parades.

FANS

Fans are usually for moving air or gases from one location to another. The earliest fans probably originated in China or India about 5000 years ago. Chinese hand fans consisted of large feathers like the peacock's mounted in the end of a handle. They were used to cool the body or to ward off insects. Large fans were often carried and worked by slaves.

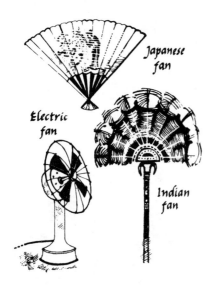

Japanese fan

Electric fan

Indian fan

About 1300, the folding fan developed in Japan. The slats (narrow strips of wood) were made of ivory, bone, mother-of-pearl, or tortoise shell and were delicately carved. The slats' framework was covered with parchment, paper, or silk. These fans were introduced into France and England about 1600. Folding fans of lace and silk were beautifully decorated with paintings by outstanding artists.

Today, mechanical fans with revolving, metal blades are often used for ventilation. They are also used in winnowing grain (blowing chaff away) and in removing dirt and waste material.

FARMING

According to archeological records, many ancient people knew nothing about farming, or AGRICULTURE. They were hunters who ate wild fruits, grasses, and roots when they could not catch animals. Early fishermen probably had bows and arrows, but no tamed animals, with the possible exception of the dog.

Later people learned to raise wheat, barley, and millet, and kept dogs, sheep, goats, and oxen. Hunters slowly changed their way of living to those of farmers and shepherds.

The people near the EUPHRATES River valley planted wild seeds in rows and learned to weed and water their fields regularly. To guard their fields, they built houses nearby. This is how communities, villages, and towns began.

By the time of Abraham, Egyptian farmers in the Nile valley were raising wheat, flax, millet, and barley, and they knew about onions, garlic, radishes, lentils, and beans. Here and in the Tigris-Euphrates valley, cattle grazed on grassy ranges; goats were kept for milk; sheep were raised for

wool; and camels and donkeys carried items and people.

Later the Greeks learned how to grow beets, cabbage, lettuce, turnips, and peas. The Greeks are believed to have been the first to spread manure on their fields. The Romans learned how to raise oats, rye, celery, and peaches; they also plowed and harrowed their fields and developed good methods of drainage.

During the MIDDLE AGES, peasants farmed strips of land owned by a lord or knight. Gradually some of them acquired their own farms.

However, the methods of farming remained very similar to those of the earliest times. Natural fertilizers and irrigation were used in Italy, Spain, Holland, and Belgium. The Chinese and the INCAS in Peru were also growing such crops as cotton and wheat, using all available ground.

After the middle of the 18th century, many improvements in farming occurred. Lord Townsend in England demonstrated the value of the proper rotation of crops. His system, known as the *Norfolk Rotation*, consisted of the annual rotation of wheat, turnips, barley,

Wheat
Barley
Oats
Kale
Potatoes
Rutabaga
Beet

and clover. This allowed for half of the land to be used for grain, while the other half produced fodder (feed) with which to fatten cattle and pigs. Thus, the land was not worn out by continuous use by one crop and was not lying fallow (at rest) and unproductive. Also, livestock raising was encouraged, and the product of the land was returned to it as manure.

Farming was also helped by the development of new FERTILIZERS. After the chemical composition of plants and soils became known around 1900, farmers started to use artificial fertilizers having potash, NITROGEN, and PHOSPHORUS. The land was greatly enriched and could produce more.

Since the dawn of history, farming has been done with simple TOOLS. Horses and donkeys were used to pull plows, to haul wagons, and to trample grain on the threshing floors. In the late 1800s, farmers had machinery like seeders, mowers, and reapers. After 1920, mechanical power exceeded horsepower on the farms. Gasoline tractors and trucks made it possible for farmers to work much larger areas. Large combines could harvest much grain, cutting and threshing in one operation.

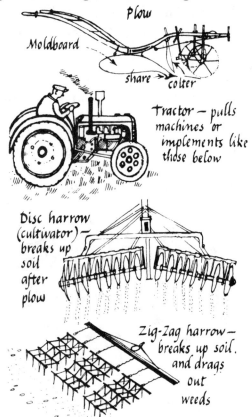

Plow

Moldboard

share — colter

Tractor — pulls machines or implements like those below

Disc harrow (cultivator) — breaks up soil after plow

Zig-Zag harrow — breaks up soil. and drags out weeds

Devon Red

Guernsey

Friesian

Today, the American farms in the midwest are growing more than enough food to feed Americans. Large surpluses of grain are exported to help other countries. However, farming has some problems to solve, such as water and air pollution, high operating costs, and new animal and crop diseases. SEE ALSO: AGRICULTURE, FERTILIZER.

FAUCET

This cutaway view of an ordinary household faucet shows how it works. Water comes in from the left. When the valve is closed, as it is here, it keeps the water from going up and across to the mouth of the faucet on the right. A padlike *washer* is screwed down to fit tightly on the opening the water must use. When the faucet handle is turned, the *spindle* is screwed up, raising the washer and letting the water through.

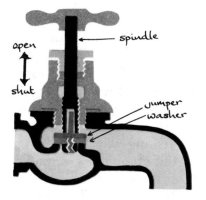

open

shut

spindle

jumper washer

To change the washer when it gets leaky, a person shuts off the water supply, then unscrews the whole top of the valve. The *jumper*, which holds the washer, can be removed to allow the washer to be replaced.

FAUST

A man named Faust is supposed to have lived in Germany in the 15th or 16th century. Details about his life occur again and again in many different stories. Goethe wrote the classic form of the life of Faust. It is said he was a magician, a doctor, and a student of theology and astrology. With the Devil he supposedly made a contract: the Devil would have his body and soul, if, for a time, the Devil obediently served him. At the end, the Devil possessed Faust.

FEATHERS

Birds are the only members of the animal kingdom that have feathers. Feathers are made of *keratin*, the same material that makes up claws, horn, hoofs, and fingernails. Feathers are similar in function to the hairs of mammals; they help to keep birds warm.

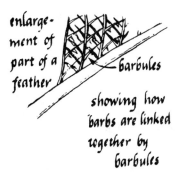

enlargement of part of a feather — barbules

showing how barbs are linked together by barbules

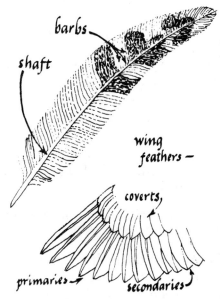

barbs

shaft

wing feathers —

coverts

primaries —

secondaries

The typical feather consists of a hollow quill which is embedded into a small sac in the skin. The opposite end of the quill passes into a thinner portion called the shaft. On either side of the shaft is the vane. This bladelike portion of the feather is made up of hundreds of tiny branches known as barbs which are hooked to one another by barbules. Some kinds of feathers have many unconnected barbs; others, called down feathers, are very fluffy because the barbs are all unconnected. Young birds mainly have down feathers that gradually get replaced by adult flight and body feathers.

All birds *molt* at least once a year—that is, their old feathers are pushed out by new ones. By mating time in the spring, the feathers, especially those of the male, are more colorful than the old ones. Birds keep their feathers in good condition by preening or "combing" them with their beaks.

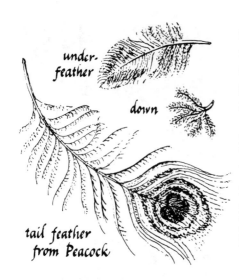

under-feather

down

tail feather
from Peacock

Feathers have been used by man in three basic ways: for costumes, as filling for mattresses, pillows, quilts, and chairs, and as writing instruments. The word *penna*, from which we get the word pen, is a Latin word meaning "feather."

Since many birds have been slaughtered for their feathers, several species have become extinct or nearly extinct. The United States has been particularly instrumental in passing laws and in forming organizations, such as the National Audubon Society, to protect birds.

FEDERAL BUREAU OF INVESTIGATION

The Federal Bureau of Investigation (FBI) is the investigative branch of the U.S. Department of Justice. It gathers information about and reports violations of federal laws. The FBI investigates crimes of espionage (spying), sabotage (destruction), kidnaping, and airplane hijacking. Most of its work, however, deals with federal bank robberies, interstate transportation of stolen goods, thefts from interstate commerce, and dishonesty and cheating against the U.S. government. Counterfeiting (making imitation money) and crimes relating to drugs, taxes, the postal service, and customs are not investigated by the FBI. Other U.S. agencies handle these matters. Because of national security, the FBI keeps records of organizations and persons (with their fingerprints) that are important to the U.S. government. FBI agents often work with local and state police in solving various crimes.

Organized in 1908, the FBI became an important law enforcement agency under John Edgar Hoover, its director from 1924 to 1972.

A person wishing to be hired by the FBI must pass difficult examinations. He or she must be a U.S. citizen and a high school graduate. If a person wishes to become a special agent, he or she must be between 23 and 35 years of age and a graduate of an accredited law school. College graduates with degrees in accounting, physical science, or language, or with special experience, may also become candidates for the FBI. The FBI sends all applicants to its schools in either Washington, D.C., or Quantico, Virginia.

FENCING

Fencing, or dueling with swords, was first developed as a sport by the Germans in the 14th century. Before then, it was a method of earnest combat, in which men killed each other for various reasons.

On guard

The lunge

The sport of fencing became popular in the 17th century when the heavy German sword was replaced by the light Italian rapier. Fencing schools sprang up in Europe, teaching gentlemen the art of dueling, which became the personal and honorable way of settling an argument. Many civilized countries outlawed dueling, and not until the late 19th century did fencing become an organized sport. It was included in the OLYMPIC GAMES in 1896.

Today, many people like fencing because it is good exercise. A fencer must be fast on his feet, coordinating his mind and his muscles. Using a light sword called a *foil*, opponents try to touch each other in the target area, which is from the neck to the groin. Fencers wear padded, canvas jackets and wire-mesh face masks for protection. Two of the many complicated moves in fencing are shown in the illustration.

FERMENTATION

Fermentation is an important and vital process in the changing of grapejuice to WINE and in the rising of BREAD dough. Milk turning to buttermilk and apple juice turning into vinegar are also brought about by fermentation.

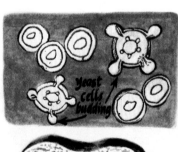

yeast cells budding

Fermentation is a chemical change caused by different kinds of yeasts, molds, and bacteria. These microscopic plants produce chemical substances, called *enzymes*. The enzymes in YEAST break down the sugar in bread dough to form alcohol and carbon dioxide. The carbon dioxide gas makes the dough rise. When the bread is baked, the alcohol evaporates. In wine-making, grape sugar (glucose) makes ethyl alcohol and carbon dioxide is given off.

Beer is made through a more complex fermentation process. Other foods that are products of fermentation include cider, sauerkraut, yogurt, and certain kinds of cheeses.

Our bodies' digestive enzymes, some in the saliva in our mouths, help to change starch into sugar, which is then absorbed into our blood to produce growth and energy.

FERNS

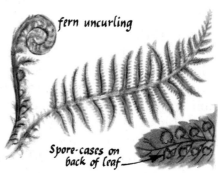

fern uncurling

Spore-cases on back of leaf

Ferns are among the oldest land plants known. Ancient ferns and other vegetation died and became fossils, forming the coal we use today. These plants vary in size from a tropical species, which grows to 60 feet (18.6 m) in height with leaves (fronds) 15 feet (4.7 m) in length, to a floating water fern, which is only 0.25 inches (0.64 cm) across. Because ferns produce no flowers, they have no seeds.

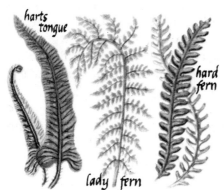

harts tongue

hard fern

lady fern

As a fern grows, the fronds unroll. Underneath each frond are many little brown swellings called spore cases, once believed to be the egg cases of an insect. When ripe, the spore cases burst and scatter the tiny spores, like specks of dust, on the moist ground.

A spore sends down a root and forms a flat, heart-shaped plant the size of a nickel. On the underside of this "leaf" are the microscopic male and female cells. When the male cells join with the female cells, a fern plant grows. This plant looks like the grandparent, not the parent plant. The many kinds of frond shapes are shown in the picture. SEE ALSO: COAL.

FERRET

The ferret is a small weasel closely related to minks, skunks, badgers, and otters, all of which have a characteristic musky odor.

The red-eyed yellow or white ferrets, which are about 1.5 feet (45.8 cm) long, have been semidomesticated in Europe and America for hunting rabbits and killing rats. In some parts of the United States ferreting (hunting

with ferrets) rabbits is illegal. However, the ferret never becomes truly tamed. It does not show affection to its master when raised in captivity and must be kept on a leash.

The black-footed ferret is a 2-foot (61 cm) long wild brown weasel inhabiting the plains of Kansas and Nebraska. It feeds upon prairie dogs and lives in deserted burrows.

FERTILIZER

Fertilizer replaces the minerals which growing plants have removed from the soil. The important elements supplied by minerals are nitrogen (for green leaves and tissue growth), potassium (for increasing starch production and for lengthening the growing season), and phosphorus (for improving the growth of roots, flowers, and seeds). The most balanced enrichment for plants, then, comes from mixed fertilizers.

Probably the most valuable fertilizer comes from the compost pile, made by mixing together leaves, grass cuttings, farmyard manure, straw, and vegetable scraps. The mixture is then allowed to decompose by the action of bacteria.

After World War II, when devastated lands were unable to meet the world's need for food, one of the most important international problems became the more effective use of natural and synthetic agricultural fertilizers. Today, large crop yields are produced by various modern methods of applying fertilizer.

FEUDAL SYSTEM

During the MIDDLE AGES, a special system of holding land developed in Europe. It was called the *feudal system* and was begun as a way to give protection to people. At that time there was no governmental authority to supply aid and protection.

The basis of the feudal system was the *fief*, a piece of land which a tenant (*vassal*) held from his lord. The lord protected the vassal in return for the vassal's help during war. Often a vassal had to supply a certain number of knights to fight battles. The lord had certain judicial and other rights over his vassal, who took an oath of loyalty and promised to serve him. The vassal could also, if holding a large fief, grant parts of it to others, who would then be his vassals and to whom he stood as their lord. Thus, complex relationships, based on fiefs, developed between landholders.

Each lord ruled over his large estate, called a *manor*, and over the common people who lived on the estate and worked for him. There were also *serfs*, who lived in villages outside the lord's manor. They were given strips of land to farm, and had to give the lord a portion of their produce. Beyond the fields was the common land, used for the grazing of animals. In case of any attack, the serfs and others could take shelter in the lord's fortified manor. SEE ALSO: MIDDLE AGES.

FIGS

Figs are the dried seed cases of the fig tree, which is native to southwest Asia and the Mediterranean.

The delicious Smyrna fig produces infertile pollen and cannot bear fruit unless provided with the pollen from the wild fig. Wild fig branches are suspended among or grafted to the branches of the cultivated fig trees. The pollination can only be done by a special kind of wasp. This wasp enters the fig through a small hole at the end of the fig and carries on its wings the pollen from the wild fig. Other types of figs can develop without pollination.

This wasp is the only insect that can fertilize the fig

Figs are sold dried, fresh, or canned. In very humid areas like parts of Texas, drying becomes difficult so the figs are canned. Most Mediterranean figs are dried before marketing. California produces large quantities of figs, such as the Kadota and Mission variety.

FINCHES

The finch family, with about 1200 different species, is the largest family of birds. Finches are found in most parts of the world. They are small birds with stout, conical beaks, used to crack open hard seeds. They are valuable to the farmer because they eat undesirable weed seeds, many harmful insects, and other garden pests.

306

Chaffinch
Goldfinch
finch's beak
Bullfinch
Greenfinch

Most finches, except the meticulous goldfinch, build sloppy cup-shaped nests in which four to six eggs are laid. Also, most finches fly in a rising and falling pattern that is difficult to follow.

Goldfinches, named for their bright yellow markings, are lovely and musical birds. Bullfinches, with reddish breasts and bluish-gray backs, are sometimes kept as pets in cages. Chaffinches are similarly marked but with a brownish back, wings, and tail. Other finches include the purple finches, the dickcissels, the redpolls, the grassquits (native to the Bahamas and Cuba), and the canaries. Buntings, grosbeaks, and cardinals are in the finch family.

FINGERPRINTS

Fingerprints are the impressions of the undersides of the tips of fingers and thumbs. They are made by placing a person's finger tips on an ink pad and then pressing them on a special card. Because the lines—arches,

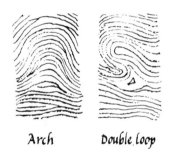

Arch   Double Loop

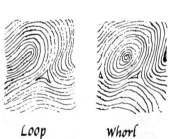

Loop   Whorl

whorls, loops, and composites—differ with each person, fingerprints are used for identification.

Realizing this, the Chinese around 200 B.C. used an inked thumb-print as a signature. In 1891, Sir Francis Galton, a British scientist, developed a system for comparing fingerprints. The Commissioner of London's Metropolitan Police, Sir E. R. Henry, used this system for the identification of criminals. In 1924, the FEDERAL BUREAU OF INVESTIGATION (FBI) in the U.S. adopted Sir Henry's filing methods for its fingerprint collection.

Today, police have fingerprints of every criminal. Should he commit further crimes, his fingerprints will be left on door knobs, windows, furniture, and so on, unless he wears gloves. The armed forces also fingerprint all their members, and aliens entering the U.S. have their fingerprints taken. Most hospitals make palm and fingerprints of newborn babies.

FINLAND

Finland is surrounded by Sweden, Norway, and Russia, in northwestern Europe. Ancient GLACIERS smoothed the land in the south and the central region, leaving thousands of hollows that formed into lakes. The north consists of high, flat hills.

Thick forests of pine, spruce, and birch cover about 70 percent of Finland. Timber is cut in winter, and the logs are left by the side of lakes and rivers. The Finns in the summer float these logs to large sawmills to be processed. Paper and wood products are the country's biggest exports. The best soil is along the southern coast, where farmers grow oats, wheat, and potatoes, as well as produce much butter and cheese.

Thick ice and snow cover the lakes and forests during winter, and the BALTIC SEA freezes, closing the country's northern ports to shipping. Icebreakers keep open Helsinki, the capital and largest port, situated on the Gulf of Finland in the south.

From 1154 to 1809, Sweden controlled Finland. Then Russia reigned over it, until Finland gained its independence in 1917. The Finns prevented Russia from seizing it during World War II, and they remain free and democratic today.

FIORD

Fiords, or fjords, are long, narrow, and deep arms of the sea, reaching far inland. They are found along the mountainous coasts of Norway (fjord is a Norwegian word), Iceland, Scotland, Greenland, British Columbia, Alaska, New Zealand, and in many Antarctic islands.

Fiords were probably formed by large GLACIERS that dug deep valleys into the sea. Sea erosion and faulting and uplifting in a particular region may have contributed to the formation of fiords. A fiord is different from most inlets because of its steep sides, often going far beneath the water surface. The Sogne Fiord in Norway is 4000 feet (1240 m) deep and more than 100 miles (161 km) long.

FIR

The fir tree belongs to the pine family. It is a tall, pyramidal-shaped evergreen, sometimes growing more than 200 feet (62 m) high.

A fir differs from a pine in that its short, flat needles grow singly on the stems and not in clusters. The soft wood of the fir is valuable in building houses. It is used for interior finishing, as well as for making crates and boxes.

Firs are found chiefly in the mountainous regions of the Northern Hemisphere. The balsam firs are popular as Christmas trees in the northeastern United States. The red, silver, and white firs are found in the Northwest.

FIRE

Fire has fascinated and mystified man for thousands of years. Many ancient civilizations actually worshipped fire.

Trees set aflame by lightning probably provided early man with fire. Then fire was kept continuously burning in man's caves and huts for cooking, warmth, light, and protection from animals.

The first friction MATCHES were invented in 1827. For the previous 3000 to 4000 years, fire had been produced by rubbing dry sticks together or by striking flint and iron together near a bundle of dry grass.

In 1783, Lavoisier, a French chemist, gave the first scientific explanation of fire. He explained that when a substance is burning, it is rapidly combining with the OXYGEN in the air. This process he called combustion. Some substances join very slowly with the oxygen in the air and do not produce any light or heat. Rusting is an example of the slow oxidation of iron. SEE ALSO: FLAME.

FIRE FIGHTING

Until the fire pump was regularly used for fighting fires, men formed *bucket brigades*, lines of men passing on buckets of water from a distant well, lake, or stream. As taller and larger buildings were built, more water was needed to extinguish the fire than before. Soon hand-operated pumps mounted on wagons were pulled to fires by horses or men. However, it was still necessary for a bucket brigade to fill the large tub from which the pump drew its water.

In 1840, the first fire pump operated by a steam engine was used in New York City. Soon large cities installed underground water pipes and outlets called fire hydrants to bring more water more quickly to fires. Today, gasoline or diesel engines operate all fire fighting equipment, such as pumps, hoses, ladders, and special platforms.

Water is still the most common material for quenching a fire. Gasoline or oil fires must be smothered; water would only spread the burning liquid. Chemical sprays or foams stop these fires by keeping out the air. Since water conducts electricity, chemicals must also be used to smother electrical fires, as in wiring.

FIREFLY

A firefly or lightning bug is a small beetle that has an organ for producing light at the end of its tail. The light is made when a substance called *luciferin* combines with oxygen. The firefly can regulate the oxygen supplied to the luciferin, and thereby it can control the brightness of the light.

The European glowworm is related to the firefly. The male glowworm has a weak light, but the wingless female has a bright, greenish light. There is an unusual South American glowworm that emits a reddish light from its head and a greenish light from the sides of its belly. These two lights can be flashed separately or together. In America a glowworm is the luminous larva of fireflies. The flashing lights in all species of fireflies attract the sexes. Each kind of firefly has its own special pattern of lights. The male firefly flies around flashing his lights. If it is the correct pattern, the female flashes back and the male lands beside her.

310

FIREWORKS

Fireworks were invented in ancient China. When European armies began to use gunpowder in the Middle Ages, they also began to make fireworks to celebrate victories.

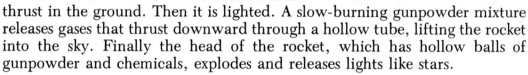

The main explosive of fireworks is gunpowder. To this are added chemicals whose burning gives the fire its color. Magnesium gives white, sodium gives yellow, calcium gives red, and copper gives blue and green. Other chemicals are also used for these colors. Steel filings produce sparks.

The most popular firework is the ROCKET. It is mounted on a stick that is thrust in the ground. Then it is lighted. A slow-burning gunpowder mixture releases gases that thrust downward through a hollow tube, lifting the rocket into the sky. Finally the head of the rocket, which has hollow balls of gunpowder and chemicals, explodes and releases lights like stars.

FIRST AID

The attention you give to a sick or injured person before a doctor or an ambulance arrives is called "first aid." However, you should only try to help someone if you know exactly what to do. A person may be hurt more seriously if you do the wrong thing.

Never move someone who is hurt very badly, otherwise you may do him further

harm. Just keep him warm and comfortable, and do not give him anything to eat or drink, as he may have a stomach injury.

Bleeding can often be stopped by pressing a clean pad against the wound. After the bleeding stops, wash the wound with clean, hot water and soap and cover with a clean kind of bandage. Go to a doctor or hospital at once if the bleeding does not stop.

You can treat a *first-degree burn*—a small burned area on the skin that has become red. Hold the burn under cold, running water. Never put any kind of grease like butter or margarine on any burn, as it may become rancid and collect bacteria. If someone's clothes catch FIRE, immediately roll him up in a rug or woolen blanket.

FISH

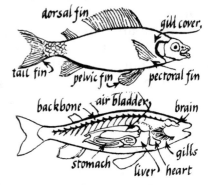

There are over 15,000 species of fish on Earth today. Fish are cold-blooded VERTEBRATES—that is, they have a backbone and their blood is able to adjust to the temperature of the surrounding water.

All fish have scaly skin and most breathe with GILLS. Water enters the mouth and is forced out through the gill slits on the sides of the body after the oxygen is removed by the gills.

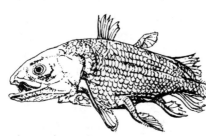

This coelacanth was caught near Madagascar in 1952.

The eye of the fish is designed for long distance vision. The pupil is large in order to take in as much light as possible in the dim surroundings. The fish's sense of taste is undeveloped, but it has a keen sense of smell. It has sensitive organs along its sides that detect disturbances in the water rather than vibrations of sound.

Some fish lay millions of jelly-like eggs at one time, such as the ocean sunfish which lays up to 300 million. Most fish leave the eggs to hatch and develop on their own, and most do not escape being eaten by larger fish. Therefore, it is important that fish lay tremendous numbers of eggs in order to insure the survival of their species.

Fish also feed on tiny water creatures, seaweeds, or plankton. Fish use their fins to enable them to swim quickly away from any predators.

Jellyfish, starfish, shellfish, whales, dolphins, and porpoises all live in the water, but none are truly fish. SEE ALSO: GILLS.

FISHING

From ancient to modern times, man has caught fish—by hand, club, spear, hook, or net. Fishing is a major way of life for many people, providing both food and work. Fishing as a sport or pastime is comparatively recent, although man has probably enjoyed catching fish for the fun of it since prehistoric days.

Boys and girls, using only a fishing rod or pole, a fishing line, and a baited hook, can easily catch freshwater fish such as catfish, sunfish, perch, and bass. Live bait (worms, insects, minnows) dropped into a pond or lake will attract fish to bite the hook. Often tied near the hook is a piece of lead, called a *sinker;* it keeps the bait from floating to the water's surface. On the fishing line is a float, or *bobber,* made of cork, wood, or plastic. It floats on the surface and "bobs" up and down whenever a fish nibbles on the bait. When the fish "bites" the bait, the hook will catch in its mouth, and then the fishermen can reel in their catch. There are other, more complicated ways of fishing like bait-

casting and fly-casting. A stronger rod and reel (metal spool for winding in the fishing line) is used for bait-casting, which is done chiefly in lakes and rivers. Fly-casting is fishing with a *fly* as bait. A fly resembles an insect but is made of colorful thread and feathers which hide the hook. Trout and salmon are often caught by fly-casting. For salt water fishing, heavier rods and reels of the bait-casting type are used to catch game fish like bonefish, marlin, kingfish, or sailfish.

line fishing

Along the coasts of the world, fishing is an important industry. Major fishing countries bordering the ocean and having not enough farmland to grow all the food they need include Japan, Peru, Iceland, England, and Norway. The United States, Russia, Canada, China, and Spain also have large fishing industries.

Commercial fishermen use special methods for catching large quantities of fish. In the shallow Grand Banks off the coast of Newfoundland, fishermen use lines and hooks to catch cod because nets would be torn by the rocks on the ocean floor.

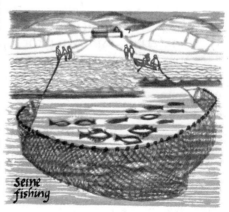

seine fishing

Nets are, however, the most common way to gather in a large school of fish. One kind of net, called the *otter trawl*, is used to catch crabs, lobsters, shrimps, and fish that live near the ocean floor, like flounder. Wheels on the bottom of the net keep it from catching on rocks, and floats at the top keep the net open for fish to swim into it. As the fishermen's boat, known as a *trawler*, moves through the water, the net, with pieces of wood attached to its side, is pulled wide open. Haddock, sole, plaice, and halibut are caught this way, too.

Herrings, sardines, and anchovies are caught differently. These fish generally swim in shoals (groups) and close to the surface. A *gill net* is stretched into the ocean like a fence. The bottom of the net sinks deep into the water, while the top stays up. These nets are often a mile (1.61 km) long. When the fish swim into the nets, their gills get stuck in the net's small holes.

Another method for catching cod and halibut is by means of a long rope, to which are tied short fishing lines with baited hooks. The rope is attached to buoys and may be several miles long, with several thousand fishing lines hanging down from it.

Another fishing method, called *seine* fishing, can be done from the shore. One end of the long, narrow net is fastened to the shore. A small boat sails out and around and back to shore, dropping the rest of the net, and carrying the other end to shore. The two ends of the net are then pulled in.

FLAGS

A flag is a piece of cloth, bunting, or other material displaying the special mark or sign of a country, region, armed force, or individual. A flag can show what country controls a particular place or where certain troops are in a battle, or it can indicate that an important person is present. Flags are a way, too, of showing pride.

Modern flags, made of cloth hung by one edge, date from the MIDDLE AGES. Many early ones had crosses of

United Kingdom

United States of America

U.S.S.R.

China

certain colors against backgrounds of other colors. The British flag combines three crosses that represent England, Scotland, and Ireland. The United States flag has stripes, which are also found in many other flags. Our thirteen stripes represent the original states, while the 50 stars represent the states now in the Union. Some other countries, like the U.S.S.R. and the People's Republic of China, also use stars.

FLAME

When a substance burns, it sometimes produces a flame. A FIRE can occur, however, without a flame; this happens when charcoal burns perfectly. A flame occurs when part of the burning substance, such as wood, turns into a gas that burns. A flame's inner part is filled with gas; its middle part produces light; and its outer part radiates heat. When a candle burns, the carbon in the hot wax joins with the oxygen in the air to produce light.

The heat of the flame melts the wax, which creeps up the wick and is burnt there.

FLAMINGO

The flamingo is a large pink or red water bird, related to the heron and stork. It has a long neck, long legs with webbed feet, and a unique down-bent beak. The flamingo, whose name means "flame," spends much of its time wading through shallow water in marshes and lagoons. It scoops up shellfish, frogs, and water plants from the muddy water.

In the spring, the female lays one or two eggs in a conical mud nest. The male takes turns with the female sitting on the nest with its legs folded on either side.

The American flamingo lives in Florida and the West Indies. The Bahama Islands have been a favorite nesting place for flamingoes, which like to live in large groups. A scarlet flamingo with black wing feathers is common in southern Asia and Africa.

315

FLAX

Flax is a slender plant that is grown for its fiber and seeds. The stalks of the flax plant produce the fiber from which LINEN is made. Linseed oil is made from the seeds.

The flax plant has been cultivated by man for many centuries. The ancient Egyptian mummies were wrapped in linen cloth made from flax. Flax was the main source of cloth fiber until the growth of the cotton industry around 1800.

The fibers for making linen come from the rind (outer coat) of the flax stalks. When the flax plants are ripe, they are pulled up, tied in bundles, and dried. The bundles are then "rippled" (the seeds are combed out) and "retted" (soaked in warm water to separate the fibers from the rest of the stalk). The fibers are combed, cleaned, and bleached so that they can be spun into yarn.

Linseed oil is made by crushing the flax seed. This oil is important in the manufacture of paints, varnishes, printer's inks, and linoleum. Most flax grown in the U.S. is made into linseed oil.

FLEA

The flea is a tiny, wingless, bloodsucking INSECT. It has a hard, flattened body and very powerful legs, enabling it to jump more than a hundred times its own height. The adult flea lives as a parasite on birds and mammals, feeding only on blood.

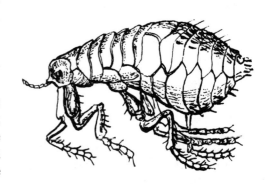

The human flea is found mainly in the warmer parts of the world. This species and the dog and cat fleas attack man. Certain rat fleas transmit typhus and bubonic plague (see BLACK DEATH) to man. Tularemia, a disease of rabbits that resembles the plague, is transmitted to man by another kind of flea.

FLINT

Flint is a hard rock usually embedded in CHALK deposits. It is made of silica (which forms sand), crystallizing around a nucleus of the microscopic remains of SPONGES. Lumps of flint range in color from gray to black but change to yellow or brown when exposed to the weather.

A flint quarry. The flints are embedded in the chalk

Primitive man in Europe and North America chipped the lumps of flint he found into sharp weapons and cutting tools, such as arrowheads, knives, axheads, skin scrapers, and spear points. The first flint implements were crude and simple; later flint tools were skillfully shaped.

Flint was also useful for starting a fire. When struck with iron or steel, it readily produces sparks. Flint therefore was used in igniting tinder and gunpowder until the invention of matches in 1827.

hand axe

Old Stone Age flints

Arrow head

New Stone Age flints

sickle

The finest flint in the world is found in the chalk cliffs of Great Britain and northern France; a poorer grade is found in the United States and elsewhere. Flint is used as an ingredient in making fine pottery.

FLORIDA

Florida, in the extreme southeast United States, is mainly a peninsula, separating the Atlantic Ocean from the Gulf of Mexico. This state varies from gently rolling, pine-covered hills in the north to steaming, tropical marshes and swamps in the south, where giant orchid plants sometimes grow for hundreds of years. Along Florida's coasts are sand bars, coral reefs, and keys (low coral islands), which are slowly creating new land out of the ocean.

Many centuries ago, this region was inhabited by Indians. In 1513, JUAN PONCE DE LEÓN, a Spanish explorer who was searching for the legendary Fountain

ALA. GA.
345 ft.
TALLAHASSEE
Atlantic
Ocean
Lake George
Cape Canaveral
Tampa Bay
GULF OF MEXICO
Palm Beach
Miami Beach
The Everglades
Florida Keys

of Youth, landed here and thought he was on a beautiful island. He named it Florida, meaning "Isle of Flowers," and claimed it for Spain. In 1565, the Spanish founded St. Augustine, the oldest city in the U.S. Spain, France, and England fought for control of the region, battling the fierce Seminole Indians, whose land was often stolen from them.

To Florida now come many vacationers, fleeing the winters of the North. Elderly people come here for a warm and comfortable retirement. Tourism is the state's leading industry, with major resorts in places like Miami Beach, Palm Beach, Fort Lauderdale, and Sarasota. Some of Florida's chief attractions are Disney World, Cypress Gardens, and the Everglades National Park.

The state grows a variety of vegetables and citrus fruits, notably oranges. Commercial fishing and mining, especially of phosphate, is also done. Tallahassee is the state capital, and Florida's population is about 8.5 million.

FLOWER

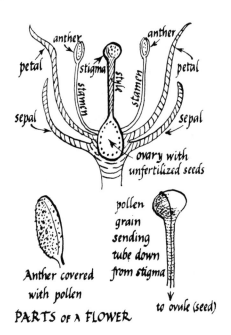

PARTS OF A FLOWER

Flowers contain the reproductive organs of the most highly developed PLANTS—the *angiosperms*. The function of the flower is to produce a fruit with seeds, from which a new plant can grow. Because of this complex, efficient method of producing fresh, vigorous offspring, angiosperms have become the dominant plant forms.

There are about a quarter of a million different species of flowers, and they have thousands of sizes, shapes, and colors. The largest flower is an Asian lily which is 3 feet (93 cm) across and weighs up to 15 pounds (6.8 kg). Some flowers are so small that they are hardly visible without a microscope.

The parts of a typical flower are illustrated here. The *sepals*, usually green, protect the developing petals and reproductive organs during the bud stage. The petals (as well as the flower's scent) attract bees, wasps, butterflies, moths, some kinds of flies, and birds, all of which help to *pollinate* the flower—that is, to transfer the pollen from the anther to the stigma.

The male organ is the *stamen*, capped by the anther in which rests the pollen grains, each containing a male cell. The female organ is the *pistil*, composed of a stalk, or *style*, and crowned with a bulbous sticky top called a *stigma*. The base of the style bulges to contain the *ovary*. The ovary has within it tiny female sex cells called *ovules*. When the microscopic pollen grains stick

318

to the stigma, they send very fine tubes down through the style to the ovules in the ovary. When the two cells join, fertilization occurs and a seed grows.

Some flowers have many pistils and stamens; some have one pistil and several stamens; others have the male and female organs in separate flowers.

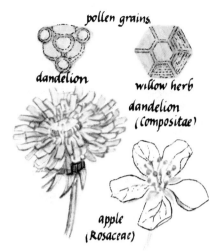

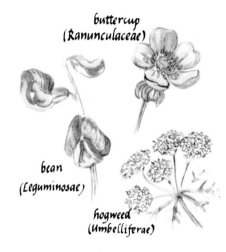

There are five basic families of flowers, and they are illustrated here. Those flowers, like the dandelion, which are actually a composite or cluster of a great many flowers are called *compositae*. Other families include *rosaceae* (rose-like), *umbelliferae* (umbrella-like), *ranunculaceae* (the buttercup family), and *leguminosae* (the pea and bean family).

FLUTE

The flute is called a *woodwind*, though metal flutes are commoner than wooden ones these days. A modern flute has three octaves above middle C, and is played by blowing across a hole at one end. The notes are determined by opening and shutting holes along the flute.

The *piccolo* is a small, high-pitched flute. An old-fashioned kind of flute is the *recorder*, still very popular and used to play music of the 18th century and before. SEE ALSO: WOODWIND.

FLY

Flies have been pests in the plant and animal kingdoms since the earliest times.

Most INSECTS have two pairs of wings, but a fly has only one pair plus a pair of short stalks or "balancers." These are vibrated 200 to 1000 times a second to produce the familiar buzzing sound. A fly has six legs, each of which has two claws and a sticky pad that enable a fly to walk on any surface—even upside down.

A fly's head has two large compound eyes (each made up of 4000 very small eyes) and between them three smaller ones. The tongue is long, with two pads at the end for sucking in liquids. If a fly wants to eat anything solid, it must first dissolve it with digestive juice sent down from its mouth through the tubular tongue.

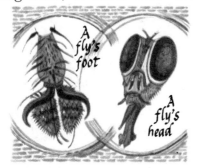

Flies breed quickly. About 150 eggs are laid at once and hatch in a day—bred usually on decaying garbage, rotting vegetable matter, or the skin of animals. In about a week the white maggots or larvae have grown to adulthood.

FLYING FISH

Flying fish are found in the warmer waters of the Atlantic, Pacific, and Indian Oceans. They do not actually fly, but their powerful tails propel them out of the water with a powerful lash. With their very large wing-like fins, they turn and glide in the direction in which the wind is blowing. They rise to a maximum of 35 feet (10.9 m) and glide as far as 200 yards (182 m). They leap and glide to escape their enemies or to follow smaller fish they want to eat. Many kinds of flying fish are eaten by man, as well as by marine fishing birds.

The Catalina flying fish is the largest known flying fish. They sometimes grow to 18 inches (46 cm) in length. They are found off the coast of southern California, where they are caught in large quantities for food. The sharp-nosed flying fish are found off the coasts of Central and South America. SEE ALSO: FISH.

FLYING SAUCERS

Flying saucers is another term for unidentified flying objects (UFOs). The first written account of a UFO dates back to 1500 B.C. in Egypt. Several hundred UFOs were recorded during the next three thousand years. In 1896 and 1897, there were many reports of cigar-shaped silver aircraft.

The term "flying saucer" was first used in 1947 when ten saucer-shaped objects were seen flying in formation over the state of Washington. Many of the reported sightings and photographs have proven later to have been hoaxes. Others were proven to have been atmospheric peculiarities, weather balloons, meteors, or misperceptions. However, some have remained unexplained and are under investigation by an Air Force study group. Some scientists believe that UFOs should be closely studied; others say they are explainable, scientific phenomena.

FOG

Fog is a mass of minute droplets of water condensed from the air. Fog, suspended near the Earth's surface, reduces visibility to half a mile (0.8 km) or less. A light or thin fog is often called a mist. As the droplets of water become larger, fog turns into a drizzle.

Fog is normally formed when a mass of moist, warm air comes in contact with cold land or water. The cold causes the invisible moist air to condense (become denser) and thus form a visible mass of fog.

FOOD

Food is the fuel for the body. It provides energy and strength as well as providing materials for the growth and repair of body tissues.

The burning of body fuel occurs as it becomes joined with oxygen. This oxidation process occurs so slowly that no flame is produced when this fuel burns, but heat is given off to maintain our body temperature.

Early man wandered in the wilds in search of food, such as fruit, meat, fish, and herbs. He often ate small grubs and caterpillars. At first everything was eaten raw, but later man discovered that cooking made food look and taste better, more digestible, and better preserved. Cooking also helped to kill GERMS that would otherwise have been harmful. Later, man stopped wandering for an uncertain food supply and settled in small villages which later grew into large communities. As centuries passed, cooking methods became more refined, and flavorings and garnishes were added to enhance the meal. Methods of preserving food—drying, salting, smoking, and chilling—added to the length of time foods could be stored.

Eating a well balanced diet is essential for good health. Scientists have learned that we need: (a) body-building foods (meat, fish, eggs, cheese), (b) energy-giving foods (fats, sugar, and breads), and (c) protective foods (fruits and vegetables for providing vitamins and minerals).

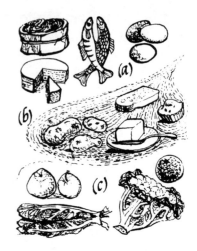

The greatest problem facing the world today is adequately feeding the millions of people in the developing countries, especially since, by the year 2000, the world's population is predicted to almost double what it is today. SEE ALSO: AGRICULTURE, DIGESTION.

FOOT

The part of an animal that touches the surface walked upon is called the foot. Cats, dogs, cows, and horses all walk on their toes, the heel being located higher up on the leg. Clams have a single foot that pulls them along the mud or sand, while snails slide along on a slimy flat foot. The squid and octopus are cephalopods, that is "head-footed."

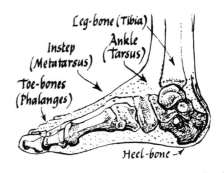

The human foot has 26 bones shaped into a strong arch. It is composed of three main parts: the ankle, the instep, and the toes. SEE ALSO: HOOF.

FOOTBALL

The game of American football is played by two opposing teams of 11 men each, on a level field, 100 yards (91 m) long and 53 yards (48 m) wide. At each end of the field stand H-shaped goal posts and lie end zones, 10 yards (9 m) wide.

Each team tries to carry or pass the football across the other team's goal line, thus scoring a *touchdown*, counting six points. The defending team tries to prevent this by tackling the man with the football or by intercepting a pass. Also, three points are scored by kicking the ball over the crossbar between the goal posts, called a field goal. After a touchdown, one point can be made by kicking the ball over the crossbar, or two points made by running with or passing the ball over the goal line. If a man is tackled with the ball in the end zone, the other team is awarded two extra points; this is called a *safety*.

Football is divided into two 30 minute halves, each having two periods, or quarters. Each half is begun by a kickoff, which also begins play after every score, except a safety. If the teams violate any of the rules of the game, officials mete out penalties.

Henry FORD (1863–1947)

Henry Ford was an American AUTOMOBILE engineer and manufacturer. In 1892, he built his first automobile by hand. In 1903, he organized the Ford Motor Company, which began to manufacture an inexpensive car that many people could afford. He pioneered the idea of "mass production," realizing it was cheaper, faster, and more efficient to produce large numbers of identical cars on assembly lines. Each worker on the assembly line did one job only, such as bolting on the wheels, before passing the car to another worker, and so on. The Model T Ford, nicknamed the "Tin Lizzie," became his most famous car.

Model 'T' Ford

FOREST

A forest is a large tract of land extensively covered with one or more kinds of trees. There are three main kinds of forests.

The thick jungle or tropical rain forests near the equator are broad-leafed evergreens. These forests are hot and steamy; the trees have to grow tall to reach the sunlight. As a result, the forest is dense and tall with much tangled undergrowth.

In the cold regions of the Northern Hemisphere, the forests are mainly CONIFERS, which are also evergreens. These trees grow quickly and conservationists are now replacing those cut down for TIMBER and wood pulp for PAPER.

In temperate regions, where the temperatures are moderate, and in tropical countries (like India and Burma) having a dry season, there are deciduous trees. These trees shed their leaves in winter and include hardwoods like maple, oak, and hickory.

Originally the United States had what appeared to be unlimited conifer and hardwood forests. The early settlers, therefore, paid little or no attention to CONSERVATION when they cleared the land for homes and farmlands. The forests began disappearing as rapidly as the country grew. Since 1900, scientists have realized the importance of forests. Forests prevent erosion and flooding. They supply not only timber, but also nuts, fruits, maple sugar, turpentine, and drugs, as well as a suitable environment for animals and smaller plants.

Diseases and insects are serious enemies of the forests. The American chestnut was destroyed by blight. A fungus disease known as the blister rust threatens to kill the white pines in the South. The Dutch elm disease has killed many elms in cities, parks, and forests.

Many kinds of insects attack forests. Some of the most destructive are the spruce budworms, bark beetles, and tussock moths. Forest rangers use various chemicals and sprays to control insects. SEE ALSO: CONSERVATION.

FOSSILS

Fossils are the remains of extinct plants and animals that have become preserved in the Earth's crust. The study of fossils is called *paleontology*.

Ancient forms of life were preserved in various ways. In every case, the plant or animal was buried suddenly and decayed over many years. The presence of hard parts such as bones, teeth, shells, or tough woody plant fiber helped to preserve the original shape of the animal or plant. Footprints and leaf prints made in soft mud were left to harden. Eventually the hardened mud turned to stone, preserving the imprint.

Some animals, such as DINOSAURS, and trees fell into tar pits and became engulfed in the ooze. Their bones or woody parts sank into the bottom and remained intact. California has famous tar pools that have yielded much valuable information about the Earth's past.

Insects were trapped in the sticky resin of ancient evergreen trees called CONIFERS. Over the years this resin became as hard as stone. Many forms were perfectly preserved in this clear golden material, known as AMBER.

Ice preserved the flesh of some wooly mammoths in Alaska and Siberia for centuries, keeping it "refrigerator fresh." Also, drifting desert sand *mummified* (dried and preserved) other forms of life.

Molds and casts are another common form of fossil. A mold is formed when the animal or plant imbedded in a rock is completely dissolved by water, leaving the original shape still in the rock. If the space is filled with minerals deposited by the water, then a cast is formed. SEE ALSO: DINOSAURS.

Ichthyosaurus

Fish

Sea Urchin

Fern

Lily

Cave man's foot-prints

Stephen Collins FOSTER (1826–1864)

A Pittsburgher was our country's first great songwriter. "Oh, Susanna," "Swanee River," "Old Black Joe," and "Beautiful Dreamer" are still familiar to Americans a century and a quarter after they were written.

Foster wrote two kinds of songs. He wrote songs, sometimes lively and sometimes sentimental, for the *minstrel shows*. In these shows, white singers and dancers blackened their skins and appeared as Negroes. Such shows were very popular around 1850. As a child, Foster heard much real Negro music, both religious songs and work songs. Foster also wrote the sentimental BALLADS that were sung in the home early in the 19th century.

Although Foster's songs were popular from the start, he himself was not very successful and led an unhappy life. He died poor when he was only 37.

FOUR-H CLUB

Four-H or 4-H is one of the largest youth organizations in the world. Four-H clubs were originally formed in the United States during the early 1900s to teach youngsters between the ages of 9 and 19 improved methods of FARMING and homemaking. The four Hs stand for Head, Heart, Hands, and Health. The 4-H pledge reads:

"I pledge my Head to clearer thinking, my Heart to greater loyalty, my Hands to greater service, and my Health to better living."

The original courses in canning, sewing, and raising crops and animals have been expanded to include projects to interest particularly the children of the inner city. Projects are offered in community service, citizenship, personal development, leadership, science, as well as food and nutrition. More than a half million city youngsters have joined 4-H. About 4 million members are from the United States, and about 10 million are from 80 foreign countries. Local agents representing the United States Department of Agriculture provide information and advice to local clubs.

FOWLS

There are many kinds of fowls or POULTRY: chickens, turkeys, ducks, geese, guinea fowl, pheasants, pigeons, and quail. They eat seeds, insects, and worms that they find by scratching the ground. Many fowls are raised for their meat and eggs. These birds usually have short wings and heavy bodies so they cannot fly well. Their feathers are often used to stuff pillows and winter clothes like down jackets.

Rhode Island Red
West Sussex
Buff Orpington

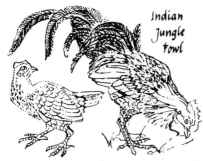

Indian Jungle Fowl

In the United States, chickens are a common type of poultry. They are the only birds with a "comb," a flap of red skin on the top of the head. Female chickens are called hens, males are called roosters or cocks, and babies are called chicks. Some poultry farmers use special breeding methods to produce chickens that have more meat and lay more eggs than other chickens. This is important because each American eats about 50 pounds (23 kg) of chicken and 280 eggs every year! Because chicken is less expensive and has less fat than beef or pork, some companies now use chicken to make hot dogs and cold cuts.

FOX

Foxes belong to the dog family. They characteristically have sharp-pointed ears and noses, and large bushy tails (called *brushes*). Foxes are found in most parts of the world except South America.

They are active at night hunting for rabbits, rodents, and other small animals.

They are famous for their raids on hen houses. The term "foxy" comes from this animal's reputation for being clever, crafty, and cunning.

Foxes live in burrows, called *earths*. The American gray fox is able to climb trees and often has its nest in a hollow tree. The word "fox" often refers to the male, while *vixen* refers to the female.

The white Arctic fox has a bluish or brown coat in summer. The silver fox of northern Asia and America has black fur with silver tips that brings high prices in the fur industry.

FRANCE

The largest country in western Europe is France, bordering the Atlantic on the west. In the south, mountains called the Pyrenees separate France from Spain. The French Alps form its border with Italy and Switzerland. The country also shares borders with Belgium, Luxembourg, and Germany. The Mediterranean Sea washes its southeastern coast, which is a favorite resort area. The island of Corsica in the Mediterranean is also a part of France.

Except for the south coast where the summers are hot and dry and the winters are warm and wet, most of France has a temperate climate. Warm, moist winds off the English Channel make the winters in northwestern France quite mild. Much snow falls in the ALPS, making this part of the country an excellent place to ski in the winter.

Most of her soil is rich, especially in the river valleys of the Seine, the Loire, the Garonne, and the RHÔNE. The chief crops are wheat, sugarbeets, potatoes, and a wide variety of fruits. France's vineyards produce more wine

than those of any other country in the world. The country also has large amounts of coal, iron ore, and bauxite.

One of the earliest recorded dates in French history is the founding of the port of Marseilles in about 600 B.C. CAESAR conquered France, then called Gaul, in 51 B.C. The Romans ruled the area until the 5th century A.D., when tribes from the north invaded. One of these, the Franks, gave the country its modern name. Later, CHARLEMAGNE united and ruled France, which eventually reached

great heights of civilization under King Louis XIV (1643–1715). However, the life of the common people was far different from that of the rich nobility. Finally, discontent led to the French Revolution in 1789. The people gained new rights. Shortly afterward, NAPOLEON made France the most powerful country in Europe.

France's buildings and cathedrals in PARIS, the capital, Reims, and Chartres, are world-famous. It has produced great painters and writers such as Cézanne and Renoir. SEE ALSO: PARIS.

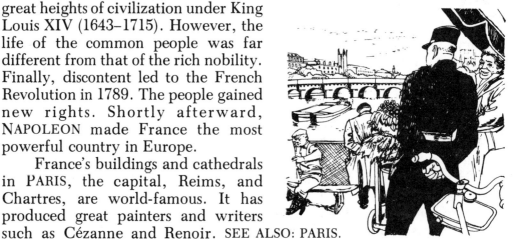

328

Benjamin FRANKLIN (1706–1790)

Benjamin Franklin was not only one of America's greatest statesmen, but he was also a great writer, publisher, patriot, and inventor. He even made an important scientific discovery.

Franklin was the fifteenth child of a Boston family. After working since the age of 10 for his father and brother, he ran away to Philadelphia to seek his fortune. He was hired by a printer, and within six years he ran his own shop, where he founded the *Saturday Evening Post* magazine. He also was the writer and publisher of *Poor Richard's Almanac*, which contained many popular, wise sayings. At the same time, Franklin made scientific investigations. The Franklin stove and bifocal glasses were among his famous inventions. His famous experiment, flying a kite with a key in a thunderstorm, proved that lightning is electricity. He also gave much time to serving the colony of Pennsylvania.

By the late 1740s, Franklin had spent many years in Europe as a representative of the colonies. However, he returned from England when he learned that the colonies wanted freedom. He was one of the authors and signers of the DECLARATION OF INDEPENDENCE. Later, he went to France and gained her support in the AMERICAN REVOLUTION.

After the war, Franklin returned home and, at the age of 80, helped write the U.S. CONSTITUTION.

FREEZING

Freezing occurs when a liquid substance is cooled enough to change it into a solid state. Most matter, when increasingly cooled, will pass from a gaseous state, to a liquid, and then to a solid. However, carbon dioxide and iodine never exist in the liquid state.

Water begins to turn into ice at 32° Fahrenheit (0° C), which is known as the "freezing point." The mercury used in our thermometers remains a liquid metal until the temperature drops to –63.8° Fahrenheit (–53° C).

This much water makes this much ice

The extra space taken up by the ice bursts the pipe

If a liquid has a substance dissolved in it, its freezing point may be substantially lowered. Antifreeze (ethylene glycol) added to the water of a car's radiator will prevent it from freezing under normally cold temperatures. Salt added to ice and snow will cause melting.

Most substances occupy less space when they are frozen. However, when water turns into ice, it takes up more space. This expansion is what causes pipes to burst when water inside them freezes in winter.

FRENCH AND INDIAN WAR

The French and Indian War refers to the struggle between Great Britain and France for control of North America. In the 18th century, these two countries were building their empires and were fighting each other for world domination.

The French moved southward from Canada and claimed the land in the Ohio River valley and west of the Appalachian Mountains. The British colonists felt threatened, especially when the French began to build forts to establish their control in western Pennsylvania. After Fort Duquesne (now Pittsburgh) was built by the French, the British colonists in Virginia decided to drive them out. A force of militia under GEORGE WASHINGTON, at that time a 22-year-old lieutenant colonel, attacked the fort in 1754. With help from the Indians, the French defeated Washington's small force.

The following year, General Braddock led British and colonial troops against the French at Fort Duquesne. The French and Indians, fighting from behind trees and rocks, badly defeated Braddock's small army. Afterward, the British lost several battles, but they began to use their stronger navy to block supplies from reaching the French.

In 1758, the British captured Fort Frontenac on Lake Ontario and at last seized Fort Duquesne. The French were also forced to surrender at Forts Ticonderoga and Niagara. The British then surrounded Quebec, the main French city and fort in Canada. The city was under attack for three months in 1859. Finally, the British under General Wolfe won a decisive battle against the French under General Montcalm. Both Wolfe and Montcalm were killed during this battle on the Plains of Abraham, near Quebec. The British now took Quebec. In 1860, MONTREAL fell to the British, and the war was over. All the territory between the Appalachians and the Mississippi River (except New Orleans) came under British control. The British also gained most of Canada.

FROGS

Frogs are AMPHIBIANS. Therefore, they spend the first part of their lives in water. Also, as adults, they live partly in the water and on the land.

When there is cold weather, frogs hibernate underground or in the mud underwater. At that time, they do not eat or breathe in their usual way. Instead, they take in oxygen through tiny openings in their skin. Since frogs are ectothermic, their temperature matches that of their surroundings.

They wake up from their winter sleep in the spring. The females then lay their eggs (each female may lay several thousand). These eggs are in a jelly-like mass, which is sometimes attached to a water plant. The male frogs fertilize the egg mass with sperm. The eggs then hatch and tadpoles (also called polliwogs) emerge.

Each tadpole has GILLS and a tail. During the next weeks, each develops back legs and then front legs. Soon the gills disappear and the tadpole develops lungs for breathing. Its tail is the last to disappear before it becomes a frog.

A frog's skin is smoother and slimier than a toad's. A frog also has longer hind legs for jumping and a quicker tongue for catching insects, such as mosquitoes.

FROST

When moist air is suddenly chilled below the freezing point of water (32° F or 0° C), frost forms. When these conditions occur, dew does not form because the water vapor of the air passes directly into the solid state.

In cold weather, beautiful feathery patterns of frost form on the *inside* of our windowpanes. The outside air chills the glass of the window. The warm moist air inside the house freezes when it comes in contact with the cold glass.

Although frost can be very beautiful to look at, it can cause serious damage to plants by FREEZING the water in the plant cells and damaging them. Frost warnings are important to farmers. Sometimes farmers light fires under fruit trees and cover small plants to keep them from being ruined by a late or early frost. SEE ALSO: FREEZING.

FRUIT

Fruits contain the SEEDS of a flowering plant. After the male sex cells in the pollen find their way to the female egg cells *(ovules)* in the ovary and unite with them, fertilization occurs. The ovules ripen into seeds; the ovary ripens into fruit.

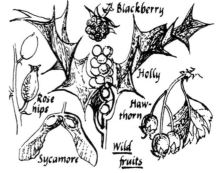

The fruit helps to distribute the seeds. For example, sometimes seeds (such as the

Cultivated fruits

dandelion, milkweed, and maple) are equipped with "parachutes" or "wings" to let them drift long distances on wind currents. Some, like nettles, have small hooks for latching onto fur and clothing, and they can travel great distances before being removed. Many seeds survive the digestive tract of birds and may fall with the birds' droppings many miles away.

Since some wild fruits are poisonous to man but not to birds, unidentified species are best left alone.

Scientists have been able to improve the size, flavor, and appearance of fruits. Sometimes the wild varieties, from which our familiar apples, pears, plums, peaches, and strawberries have developed, are hardly recognizable.

FUEL

For a substance to be a fuel, it must give off a great deal of heat. Fuels also supply us with steam power and ELECTRICITY as well as run cars, trucks, trains, and airplanes.

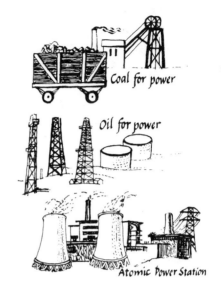

Coal for power

Oil for power

Atomic Power Station

Fuels may be solids, liquids or gases. Gases and liquids do not leave any ashes, but they may produce as much SMOKE as some solid fuels. Natural gas and coal gas burn without ashes or soot and are therefore widely used in stoves and furnaces.

Wood was early man's first fuel. Later he discovered charcoal which gave greater heat, especially for smelting metals. Today COAL is by far the most important solid fuel, providing two-thirds of all the world's power and heat. Liquid fuels are mainly derived from petroleum. One cubic foot (0.03 m³) of fuel OIL produces double the heat of the same volume of coal. Gaseous fuels are clean and reasonably cheap. Some can be produced from coal but natural gas is obtained from the Earth's crust.

Since the supply of the traditional natural fuels is limited, scientists have turned their attention to NUCLEAR ENERGY supplied by radioactive elements, such as uranium. Solar energy and tidal power hold out possibilities for solving our future fuel problems. SEE ALSO: COAL, GASOLINE, OIL.

Robert FULTON (1765–1815)

An American engineer and inventor, Robert Fulton was a professional painter of portraits and landscapes as a young man. At the age of 22, he left his home in Pennsylvania to study in England with Benjamin West, an American artist. West introduced him to many people, some of whom were interested in boats. At age 28, Fulton turned his full attention to mechanics and engineering. After obtaining several patents for his inventions, he went to Paris at the invitation of the United States minister to France. Here he invented a submarine and tried several experiments with steam-driven boats.

In 1807, he surprised a mocking, jeering crowd on the banks of the Hudson River by launching the *Clermont*, the first really successful steamboat. In the year before his death, he constructed the *Fulton*, the first steam-powered warship.

FUNGI

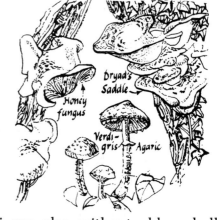

Fungi (singular, *fungus*) are primitive plants that have no seeds, flowers, roots, stems, or leaves. Most are small, and many are microscopic. They reproduce by means of *spores*, which are minute cells that grow into new fungi if they fall on moist soil, food, or other matter. Mold and mildew on food and clothing are caused by the action of these microscopic spores after falling on a suitable moist location for growth.

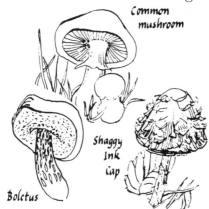

Fungi are also without chlorophyll, which is the green coloring matter needed by higher forms of plants in manufacturing their own food. Consequently, fungi must get their food from either dead or living plants and animals. MUSHROOMS, molds, YEASTS, smuts, rusts, mildews, and BACTERIA are all fungi. LICHENS are also part fungi.

Some fungi are beneficial and are used in making dyes and drugs. Penicillin, an important antibiotic, is made from a mold. Other fungi cause rotting and prevent dead animal and plant matter from accumulating. Yeast is used in the making of wine, some cheeses, and breads that rise. Beneficial bacteria live on our skin and in our digestive tract. Fungi that live off living organisms often cause serious disease, such as wheat rust, potato blight, ringworm, athlete's foot, and thrush.

334

Some mushrooms and puffballs are edible and are a fine source of nourishment; others are poisonous. The most poisonous fungus is the death cap toadstool, which produces vomiting, delirium, collapse, and death in 6 to 15 hours after tasting. Since poisonous and nonpoisonous varieties of fungi often look alike, they are best left unpicked.

FUR

The main function of fur is to maintain an even body temperature for a MAMMAL. The fur of some animals serves to camouflage them from their enemies. Fur can be bristled (stiffly erected) by a mammal as a warning to its enemy and also to make the animal appear larger and more fearsome.

The color of some mammals (such as the Arctic fox, ermine, and snowshoe rabbit) turns white in winter and dark in summer. Mammals grow thicker fur in winter and shed some of it when spring comes.

Fur skins probably supplied man with the earliest form of clothing, before weaving fibers were developed. Many explorers went in search of furs, which were so valuable that they were often a substitute for money.

Popular furs for the clothing industry include beaver, mink, muskrat, chinchilla, fox, rabbit, and ermine. Several species are becoming seriously endangered. Animals now protected include the tiger, leopard, and most seals.

FURNITURE

Furniture-making is an old art. The ancient Egyptians already had much light, graceful furniture. Oddly enough, though, they seem not to have used tables very much. We have a few pieces of Egyptian furniture from the tombs of the pharaohs. It is often covered with gold or ivory. Most Egyptian furniture was

made of wood. (Wood has always been the favorite furniture material.) The Egyptians even used plywood.

The ancient Greeks were also fine woodworkers, and their graceful designs are known to us from vases and sculptures. The Romans liked heavier and more highly decorated furniture.

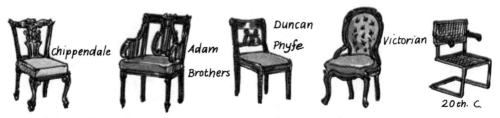

Chippendale *Adam Brothers* *Duncan Phyfe* *Victorian* *20th. C.*

Medieval furniture was simpler and more boxlike. Sometimes it was made of carved panels set in simple frames, and sometimes it was made of boards joined with iron straps. The Renaissance and Baroque periods introduced new designs, often heavy and ornate, that were meant to give a dignified, impressive effect.

In the 18th century, lightness, grace, elegance were desired rather than dignity. The 18th century is usually thought of as the greatest period for furniture. Upholstery and veneers (thin sheets of attractive wood) in patterns were much used. In the 19th century, ornateness was in fashion again. Modern furniture continues to be made of wood, but is also made of steel and plastic.

GALAXY

When you look up at the sky on a clear night, you can see a cloudy band that seems to run across the sky like a belt. This is the Milky Way, the *galaxy* to which our sun belongs. A galaxy is a large system of stars. It may be shaped like a pinwheel, a flat disc, a bubble, or a cloud. But each galaxy contains millions of stars.

Astronomers can see many galaxies when they use powerful telescopes. These stars are so far away that it takes years for their light to reach the Earth. SEE ALSO: NEBULA.

GALILEO (1564–1642)

Galileo is the common name for the famous Italian scientist, Galileo Galilei. By his persistent investigation of nature, he greatly enlarged man's idea of the world and laid the foundation of modern science.

When he was 17, he studied the swinging of a lamp in the Pisa Cathedral and suggested that a pendulum could be used for measuring time. Soon

Galileo became known through his invention of a liquid balance and his writings on gravity. He studied the speed of falling objects, discovering that solid objects fall at the same speed, whether they are light or heavy.

In 1609, he built the first complete astronomical telescope, with which he discovered that the moon had an uneven, mountainous surface and that the Milky Way had countless stars. He observed the phases of Venus and the spots on the sun.

Galileo

His investigations made him believe the theories of COPERNICUS concerning the SOLAR SYSTEM.

His discoveries contradicted the accepted teachings about the universe, which were based on the writings of ARISTOTLE. He was summoned to Rome, where the INQUISITION tried him in 1633. Galileo was imprisoned for his writings that said the Earth and other planets revolved around the sun. Later, he lived in seclusion in the country near Florence and continued, although he became blind, scientific studies until his death. SEE ALSO: SOLAR SYSTEM.

GANGES

The Ganges River flows southeastward across the great plain of northern INDIA. It begins in the HIMALAYAS, where it collects water from melting snow and glaciers. The river gathers additional water from its tributaries, such as the Jumna, Gandak, Son, and Kusi. After being joined by another great river, the Brahmaputra, the Ganges forms an enormous DELTA where it flows into the Bay of Bengal. Its length is 1560 miles (2512 km).

During the rainy season, great floods cover the lower river country and leave rich deposits of mud that fertilize the soil. Wheat, rice, sugar, and cotton are grown on the large and fertile plains.

Many great cities are situated on the banks of the Ganges, such as Calcutta, Patna, and Varanasi (Benares), where there are more than 1500 mosques and temples. The Hindus believe the Ganges is a sacred river, with waters that cure sickness and purify the soul. Millions make pilgrimages to bathe at holy places along its banks. SEE ALSO: INDIA.

GAS

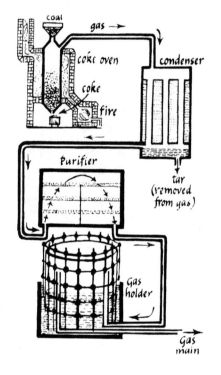

When scientists use the term "gas," they are referring to a state of matter that is neither solid nor liquid. Gases have no definite shape and expand to fill their containers.

As the volume of a gas increases, the pressure of the gas decreases. However, if the same number of gas MOLECULES is made to fit into a much smaller container, then the pressure exerted by that gas is increased. Robert Boyle, an English chemist, discovered this "law" in 1662. *Boyle's law* says this holds true as long as the temperature remains unchanged.

The molecules of a gas move freely. They increase their rate of movement when heated, and they move farther apart and cause the gas to expand with a resulting increase in pressure. The reverse happens when cooled. This law has been known, since its discovery in 1787, as *Charles' law*.

Most liquids (and a few solids, like iodine) become gases when heated sufficiently; the opposite is true when gases are cooled sufficiently.

Of the more than 100 known elements, only 11 are gases under ordinary conditions. These gases are: HYDROGEN, helium, NITROGEN, OXYGEN, fluorine, neon, chlorine, argon, krypton, xenon, and radon. All other gases are COMPOUNDS made up of at least two elements.

Gases can be poisonous (such as carbon monoxide) or non-poisonous (such as oxygen and helium); they can be life sustaining (such as oxygen for animals and carbon dioxide for plants) or life destroying (such as hydrogen in the destructive hydrogen bomb).

The picture illustrates how coal gas is produced from coal.

GASOLINE

Because gasoline and air form a highly explosive mixture, it is used as FUEL to drive the ENGINES of automobiles, boats, motorcycles, snowmobiles, power lawnmowers, and small airplanes. Gasoline is a by-product of petroleum which comes from OIL wells. It is separated from the other products by a process called refining.

The gasoline we buy also includes certain additives to keep the engine clean and to increase mileage. SEE ALSO: FUEL, OIL.

GEMS

Gems are cut and polished precious stones that are prized for their beauty and value. They are usually crystals that have been formed by great heat and pressure deep within the Earth's crust. These crystals are normally dull and rough, with a coating that makes them look like ordinary rock.

Polishing gems

Gems are divided into two main groups according to their beauty, value, rarity, and durability. *Precious gems,* which are treasured the most, are DIAMONDS, rubies, sapphires, and emeralds. Other stones of less value, such as topazes, opals, amethysts, jade, and garnets, are called *semi-precious gems.* PEARLS are also considered precious gems. Of much lesser value are certain other organic gems—jet (a kind of coal), AMBER (ancient petrified resin), and CORAL (skeletons of tiny sea creatures).

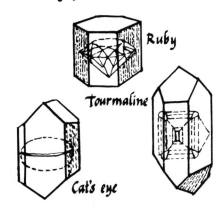

Cutting gems out of crystals

Ruby

Tourmaline

Cat's eye

Gems were known and used by the ancient Babylonians and Egyptians as engraved seals to stamp personal marks on various objects. The Greeks and Romans engraved many gems with beautiful figures of people and animals. After the Renaissance, the art of gem engraving was revived, and artists made beautiful jewelry with gems in settings of metal.

Today, synthetic (artificial) gems, such as diamonds, rubies, and sapphires, are made by special fast processes. Many differ from the natural stones only in that they are man-made and not by the slow work of nature. Many synthetic gems are used as cutting drills in industry. Because of their exceptional hardness, diamonds are very popular.

GENERATOR

A generator is a machine that produces power by converting mechanical energy to electrical energy. The term generator is used for DYNAMOS above a certain size, such as those used in power stations to produce thousands of units of electricity.

Steam turbines and electric generators in a power station

In large generators, a coil containing thousands of loops of wire is placed between two huge magnets. When this loop spins in the magnetic field, it produces a continuous electric current.

The rotating coils of wire are powered by steam or gas TURBINES or by water power, depending upon which source is cheaper and more readily available.

Wherever electricity is needed to produce power, light, and heat, there are generators. SEE ALSO: DYNAMO, TURBINE.

GENEVA

Geneva, a beautiful city in SWITZERLAND, lies in a gap between the Jura Mountains and the ALPS. It is situated on the western end of Lake Geneva, where the RHÔNE River flows from the lake. The inhabitants speak mainly French, but also German and Italian. Since Geneva is the headquarters of many corporations and of many international organizations, such as the Red Cross and the European United Nations, many foreigners speaking different languages meet in Geneva each year for conferences. After World War I, it was the seat of the League of Nations.

Geneva contains many beautiful parks, narrow, crooked streets, large hotels, quaint cafés, and broad boulevards. Its famous university was founded in the 12th century. John Calvin, the great Protestant leader, lived and taught here during the REFORMATION. Today, Geneva is an important manufacturing and banking center; its watches, jewelry, and musical instruments are exported around the world. SEE ALSO: SWITZERLAND.

GENGHIS KHAN (1162?–1227)

Genghis Khan or Jenghiz Khan is considered by many to be the world's greatest conqueror. This Mongolian leader's empire stretched from the China Sea to the Dnieper River of eastern Europe, and from the Persian Gulf to almost the Arctic Ocean.

Actually, Genghis Khan is a title, not a name. The title means "great khan of khans." A *khan* is a ruler or lord. Genghis Khan's real name was Temuchin. He lived in the Mongolian Desert of Asia. When Temuchin was 13, his father died, leaving the boy as tribal chief. The tribe did not want a boy leader and many of his subjects joined neighboring tribes or revolted against him. He was even captured by another tribe, but he managed to escape. Slowly, he rebuilt his tribe and demonstrated his bold leadership and military genius. By the time he was 45, he had conquered most of Mongolia and was hailed as Genghis Khan by his subjects.

He was possessed with a feverish desire to conquer more of the world. In 1211, he and his soldiers scaled the Great Wall of China, and after a series of bloody campaigns he finally captured China and then Korea. Next he invaded India and Persia, and then headed for Russia, looting, sacking, and plundering as he went. It appeared that Europe would also fall to him. In the midst of victory, however, Genghis Khan died. His empire was divided among his three sons who were unable to hold the territory which their father had conquered.

Genghis Khan's greatness in battle was matched by his excellent organization and discipline of his armies and his empire. It was claimed that travelers could go from one end of his dominion to another without fear or danger.

GEOGRAPHY

Geography is the study of the surface features of the Earth, especially how these features affect the human environment. Geographers do not explain how the oceans were formed; that is the science of GEOLOGY. However, geographers deal with the character and arrangement on Earth of such elements as climate, elevation, soil, vegetation, population, land use, industries, and countries. Maps are an important part of geography.

Geography can be divided into two branches: physical geography and cultural geography. Oceans, mountains, rivers, and many other land and water features are described and studied under physical geography. These geographers also map the climates of the world, the locations of mineral deposits, and the environments of plants and animals. Cultural geography studies nations, customs of people, lines of communication, transportation, buildings, and other human changes of the environment. All geographers make use of other fields in their studies, such as geology, history, economics, botany, anthropology, and sociology.

GEOLOGY

Geology is the study of the Earth's crust. Geologists study how, when, and where the various layers of rock were originally formed. FOSSILS in the layers give clues as to the early history of the Earth.

Geologists classify rocks according to their age and the way in which they

were formed. There are three basic types of rocks: *igneous, metamorphic,* and *sedimentary.* Igneous rocks, such as basalt, were once molten rocks that cooled and solidified. Because they were formed at the greatest depths and under the greatest temperature and pressure, they are extremely hard. Sedimentary rock, such as shale, sandstone, and limestone, is formed by layers of mud, sand, or sea shells. When igneous or sedimentary rock is changed by great heat or pressure, metamorphic rock, such as slate, results. This layer forms at an intermediate depth. Forces acting upon the Earth's crust, however, can cause the various layers to be shifted to entirely different depths.

Although ancient scholars attempted to explain tides, volcanic activity, earthquakes, and fossils, the study of the Earth's crust has only been truly scientific for the past two centuries. Even today, many basic geological questions remain unanswered. SEE ALSO: EARTH, FOSSILS.

GEOMETRY

Geometry, meaning "land measurement," is one of the most important branches of mathematics. Geometry is not a new science. The ancient Egyptians used practical geometry in dividing up the land before and after the annual flooding of the Nile River in order to determine their taxes.

The ancient Greeks Pythagoras and Euclid developed the geometric theories which are still the basis of elementary geometry today.

Geometry is the study of plane (or flat) and solid (or three-dimensional) shapes. Angles, lines, points, and their relationships play a major role in this study. Geometry is based on reasoning, and logic is used to prove or disprove statements about the shapes. Geometry is important in surveying, architecture, navigation, engineering, and designing.

Saint GEORGE

St. George is said to have lived in Cappadocia, in ASIA MINOR, in the 3rd century A.D. The most famous of the many legends that have grown up around him tells how he slew a dragon. A fierce dragon was tormenting a village in Libya, and the people offered first sheep and then themselves to satisfy the dragon. Finally, the daughter of the king was taken out to await the dragon, but St. George arrived and killed him with a magic sword. St. George converted the village to Christianity. In the 14th century, he became the patron saint of England.

King GEORGE III (1738–1820)

At the age of 22, George III became King of Great Britain and Ireland. He tried to gain back royal powers that he believed Parliament had taken away from the king. After the dismissal of several ministers who did not agree with him, King George found a loyal supporter in Lord North, who became prime minister in 1770. Lord North tried to carry out the King's wish to punish the colonists in America for the BOSTON TEA PARTY. The King's use of force finally led to the AMERICAN REVOLUTION in 1775, which ended six years later in independence for The Thirteen Colonies. King George reigned during the long war with Napoleon, the Emperor of France.

During his reign, King George suffered from mental illness. In 1811 he was declared insane, and Parliament voted to have his son rule in his place as regent. SEE ALSO: AMERICAN REVOLUTION.

GEORGIA

Georgia, in the southeast United States, has three main regions. In the north are the Appalachian Mountains; in the middle the Piedmont Plateau; and in the south the wide Coastal Plain, which slopes gently to the Atlantic Ocean. Along Georgia's border with Florida is the huge Okefenokee Swamp, where wild ducks, muskrats, opossums, wildcats, and alligators live. The state has about 5 million people.

Georgia has great hydroelectric power, valuable marble and gravel deposits, and vast forests of pine. It is the nation's largest producer of peanuts and poultry. Other crops include cotton, peaches, pecans, and tobacco. Atlanta, the capital and largest city, is the chief manufacturing and commercial center of Georgia.

Tourism is an important industry and is helped by such attractions as Chattahoochee and Oconee National Forests, Franklin Roosevelt's "Little White House" at Warm Springs, and Andersonville Prison Park, the site of the famous Confederate prison during the CIVIL WAR. The world's largest single piece of sculpture is the Confederate Memorial Carving, cut into the north face of Stone Mountain, near Atlanta.

In 1540, the Spaniard De Soto visited the region, which was inhabited by Creek and Cherokee Indians. Later, Spain and Britain fought over control. In

1733, JAMES OGLETHORPE established the first permanent settlement at Savannah as a place of safety for English debtors. Soon, NEGROES were brought to the region to work on the plantations, and Georgia grew as new immigrants arrived from Europe and settlers came from Virginia and the Carolinas.

GERMANY

The empire of CHARLEMAGNE included most of present-day Germany and France. After his death in A.D. 814, the empire was divided among his three grandsons. The eastern portion, which eventually became modern Germany, was ruled by kings who could never keep the region united for very long. Also, tribal chieftains controlled small kingdoms and warred among themselves for many centuries. In 1871, Germany became a united nation under the King of Prussia. The King's prime minister, Otto von Bismarck, unified the several German states, including Prussia, through industrial and military strength and success.

Then Germany tried to control Europe, which led to WORLD WAR I and Germany's defeat in 1918. ADOLF HITLER tried to make the nation great again by seizing territory, which brought on WORLD WAR II. Germany was defeated and became two countries. Today, East Germany has about 17 million people who live under the communist influence, and West Germany has nearly 62 million who live in a democratic republic with its capital at Bonn.

A great, flat plain stretches across the north of both countries (East Germany lies mostly in this plain). Large river ports, like Hamburg and Bremen, and many factories are situated here. This area has long, hard winters and warm summers. South of the plain are central highlands, through which the RHINE and other rivers flow. In central West Germany are huge coal fields and iron and steel industries. East of this factory region lies fertile farm land.

345

West Germany in the south has beautiful scenery. Rich farmlands are found in the many valleys between picturesque mountains, on which stand old castles. The Black Forest, thick with spruce and fir trees, has healthful mineral springs that many tourists bathe in each year. The Bavarian Alps on the border with Austria have famous summer and winter resorts.

Many great philosophers, writers, and musicians have come from Germany. Martin Luther was a leader of the Protestant REFORMATION; Hegel and Kant were great philosophers; Goethe was one of Europe's greatest writers; and BACH, BEETHOVEN, and Brahms became famous as composers. SEE ALSO: BERLIN, RHINE.

GERMS

Germs, or microbes, are *microscopic* plants and animals that produce disease in animals and people.

anthrax germs

Robert Koch

In 1876, a German doctor named Robert Koch demonstrated that a specific disease was caused by a specific microbe. He showed that anthrax, a disease that annually killed thousands of sheep and cattle, was caused by certain germs in the blood. Seven years later, he developed an anthrax *vaccine* (see VACCINATION). In

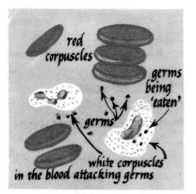

red corpuscles

germs being 'eaten'

germs

white corpuscles
in the blood attacking germs

1882, Dr. Koch discovered the bacterium that causes tuberculosis, and in 1905 he won the Nobel prize for his discoveries connected with this disease. Since then, scientists have learned that such diseases as pneumonia, diphtheria and whooping cough are all caused by germs that produce poisons in the body. Many germs are still to be discovered.

There are various kinds of germs, including bacteria and viruses. Viruses are so small that scientists must use a powerful *electron* microscope to study them. Their behavior and properties make it difficult to decide whether to group viruses in the animal or mineral kingdom. Viruses cause such illnesses as poliomyelitis, colds, smallpox, measles, and some forms of cancer. SEE ALSO: BACTERIA, VIRUS.

346

GERONIMO (1829–1909)

Geronimo was a famous American Indian leader of the Chiricahua band of the Apache Indians. His Indian name was Goyathlay, meaning "one who yawns," but the Mexicans nicknamed him "Geronimo."

In 1874, some 4000 Apaches were forced to live on a barren reservation in Arizona. Many Apaches, led by Geronimo, rebelled in anger and left the reservation to attack white settlements. The Indians burned homes and killed many whites. To avoid being captured, Geronimo and his band fled to Mexico.

In 1884, he surrendered to U.S. forces under General George Crook and was returned to the reservation. The following year, he left the reservation again. After more than a year of war and bloodshed, Geronimo surrendered and was promised that, after a short imprisonment in Florida, he and his band would be allowed to return to Arizona. The promise was never kept. Geronimo was moved to Alabama in 1888 and later to Fort Sill, in Oklahoma Territory, where he farmed. He published his life story in 1906.

George GERSHWIN (1898–1937)

One of America's most gifted songwriters was also a classical composer. George Gershwin is remembered for such songs as "Swanee" and "The Man I Love," and musical comedies such as *Of Thee I Sing*, but also for *Porgy and Bess*, the *Rhapsody in Blue*, and the *Concerto in F* for piano. A New Yorker of Russian Jewish origin, Gershwin had a marvelous gift for combining original melodies with ideas taken from east European music and from the ragtime and jazz amid which he grew up.

Gershwin began writing in 1916, but his first successful song was "Swanee," first sung in 1919. He became a very popular composer of songs during the 1920s, but wanted to be more. A jazz concert conducted by the popular band leader Paul Whiteman gave him the chance to write the *Rhapsody in Blue* (1924), a classical composition with a jazz feeling. Gershwin wrote several other classical works, and in 1935 finished *Porgy and Bess*, an opera about the Negroes of Charleston. This is regarded by many as the best American opera. Gershwin took his music very seriously, and tried to learn new methods for composing. He died when he was only 38, but left behind a great many works that will probably always be popular.

Battle of GETTYSBURG

From July 1st to the 3rd, 1863, a major and decisive battle occurred at Gettysburg, Pennsylvania. It is regarded as the turning point of the CIVIL WAR. Afterward, the war became mainly a test of endurance for the Confederacy.

Confederate General ROBERT E. LEE, hoping to make the North more weary of the war, marched his army of 75,000 men into southern Pennsylvania. At Gettysburg, he encountered the Union army under General George G. Meade.

GETTYSBURG BATTLE SITE

The first day of fighting brought heavy losses on each side. On the second day, many desperate attacks and counterattacks took place to gain strategic locations, like Little Round Top, Cemetery Hill, Devil's Den, Culp's Hill, and the Peach Orchard. Many Confederate and Union soldiers were again wounded or killed. On the third day, Confederate troops captured Cemetery Hill. However, there were no reinforcements. Also, Confederate troop formations were confused and under constant attack by Union troops and artillery. As a result, the Southerners fell back, having lost too many men. Lee now awaited a Union attack, which never came. That night, under cover of darkness and a heavy rain, Lee's army began its retreat to Virginia. Meade had won. The Union army, which had been larger than the Confederate army, had about 23,000 casualties (killed, wounded, captured, or missing). Confederate casualties were about 20,000.

On November 19, 1863, President ABRAHAM LINCOLN dedicated the battlefield at Gettysburg as a national soldiers' cemetery. He delivered there a great, moving speech, known as the Gettysburg Address. In it, Lincoln expressed deep personal sadness for the brave, dead soldiers and spoke of the spirit and hope of democracy. SEE ALSO: THE CIVIL WAR.

GEYSERS

Geysers are hot springs under the Earth's surface that spout hot water into the air. To produce a geyser, there must be hot rock close to the surface of the Earth's crust and a narrow, crooked tunnel filled with water leading from this rock to the surface. Under these conditions, hot water becomes bottled up and begins to boil, producing steam which pushes out the cold water at the top of the passage. The resulting release in pressure causes the hot water to change rapidly to steam and to shoot high up into the air.

Geysers are very rare. Most have unpredictable eruptions, but "Old Faithful" in Yellowstone National Park, Wyoming, erupts about every 66 minutes and sends up a gusher 90 to 180 feet (27–55 m) high. There are about 200 geysers in Yellowstone National Park. Others are found in Iceland and New Zealand.

GHANA

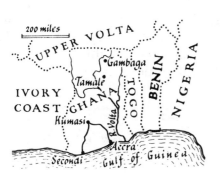

Ghana is a republic in west Africa that includes the former British colony known as the Gold Coast. In 1957, the country gained independence and joined the United Nations.

It has a tropical climate with as much as 60 inches (152 cm) of rain each year. Dense forests cover the southern region, and hilly grasslands lie inland. Ghana grows and exports more cacao than any other country. Large amounts of gold, diamonds, and bauxite come from the country's mines.

After the completion in 1965 of a huge hydroelectric dam on the Volta River, an aluminum plant was built about 10 miles (16 km) east of Accra, Ghana's capital. Today, more factories are being built because of abundant electric power. Ghana's population is about 10.5 million.

GIANT

People in almost every country in the world have told stories about giants—creatures who are unusually large and powerful. One of the most famous giants was Goliath, who led the Philistine warriors into battle against the Hebrews until he was killed by a shepherd boy named DAVID. Myths and legends also mention giants. Greek myths tell of Atlas, a giant who held the world on his shoulders. Greek and Roman myths often mention the Titans, giants who lived on the Earth before man. The one-eyed giant named CYCLOPS was a descendant

of one of the Titans. In American legend, the most famous giant is probably PAUL BUNYAN.

Indeed, there are people who grow extraordinarily large. For example, an American named Robert Wadlow grew in 1940 to almost 9 feet (2.7 m) tall. Today several circus giants are more than 7 feet (2.1 m) tall.

GIBRALTAR

On the northern side of the strait between the Mediterranean and the Atlantic Ocean stands the magnificent Rock of Gibraltar. The rock itself forms a peninsula that is connected to Spain by a narrow sandy strip of land. Gibraltar consists of the Rock and this strip of land. The town of Gibraltar lies on the west side of the Rock, which rises 1396 feet (433 m) above sea level.

The Arabs and later the Spanish occupied Gibraltar before the British captured it in 1704. The British turned it into a fortified naval and military base. Since 1964, Spain has made claims that Gibraltar is Spanish territory, not British. Many of the 30,000 inhabitants are of British and Maltese descent.

GILLS

All mammals, birds, reptiles, and most adult amphibians have lungs for obtaining oxygen from the air. However, fish, amphibians in the early stages of life, most mollusks, crustaceans, and aquatic larvae are among the animals that have gills as respiratory (breathing) organs for obtaining oxygen from water.

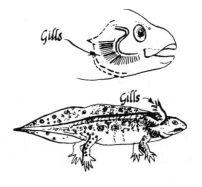

In fish, the water enters the mouth and then passes to the gills through slits in the back of the throat. The gills have extremely thin walls full of blood capillaries. Oxygen from the water passes into the blood in the capillaries. The water then passes out the gill slits located just behind the head. SEE ALSO: RESPIRATION.

GIRAFFE

The giraffe is the tallest animal, often standing 18 feet (5.6 m) high. Giraffes are well suited for the hot, dry plains of central and eastern Africa where they live. They can go long periods without water, and their long legs, neck, and tongue enable giraffes to eat the leaves off trees when grass is scarce. In order to reach drinking water or to eat grass, a giraffe must spread its long legs wide apart.

The giraffe's brown and yellow spotted coat blends in with the surroundings and conceals it from enemies. If forced to fight, the giraffe has long legs which can give a powerful kick. These long legs make giraffes swift but awkward runners. Giraffes have keen senses of sight, hearing, and smell.

The okapi, which has a shorter neck and legs, is a close relative of the giraffe.

GIRL SCOUTS

The Girl Scouts of the United States of America was founded by Mrs. Juliette Gordon Low in 1912. She had gotten the idea of a girls' organization from her British friend, Robert Baden-Powell, who had founded the BOY SCOUTS and Girl Guides in England. Today, there are about 90 countries in the world with Girl Scout groups (sometimes called Girl Guides).

Girls first belong to the Brownies, whose activities are aimed for girls age 7 and 8. Then they become Junior Girl Scouts from 9 to 11, Cadettes from 12 to 14,

and finally Senior Girl Scouts from 15 to 17. Adults serve as leaders of each Girl Scout troop, which usually has from 16 to 32 members. Good citizenship and community service are stressed in their activities, which include arts and crafts, music and dancing, first aid, nature study, sports and games, and homemaking. Girl Scouts may also collect clothing for needy people, work in nursing homes, or plant trees for their community. They believe sincerely in their saying, "Do a good turn daily."

GLACIER

A glacier is a great river or sheet of moving ice which is usually found in valleys between high mountains. The great weight of the ice gradually forces glaciers downward. The speed of a glacier depends on how steep the slope is and how large the glacier is. Some glaciers move less than a foot (0.31 m) a day; others, in Greenland move 60 feet (18.6 m) a day.

Glaciers begin in a *snowfield*, which has been formed by a buildup of unmelted snow over the years turning to ice. The ice gradually thickens and begins moving downward, breaking up into many glaciers.

Glaciers that flow down through valleys are called *valley glaciers*, such as in the Alps or Rockies. As they move, these glaciers carry earth and rocks that carve out a U-shaped valley. An ice sheet covering most of a continent is called a *continental glacier*. Greenland and Antarctica are covered by continental glaciers. When glaciers meet the sea, pieces break off to form ICEBERGS. As glaciers reach warmer regions and begin to melt, they often form the source of a river.

When a glacier melts, the deposited debris, or *moraine*, may be hundreds of feet thick. Long Island is a type of moraine formed by the last continental glacier that covered most of North America. SEE ALSO: ICEBERGS.

GLADIATOR

In ancient Rome, gladiators were armed men who fought each other in large public arenas. At first, they were slaves or captives who were compelled to fight for the entertainment of the spectators. Later Roman citizens trained to become gladiators, showing great strength and skill and winning large sums of money.

There were various types of gladiators. The *Samnites* were heavily armed with swords and shields. A Samnite might fight against a *Retiarius*, who battled almost naked, using a net and a trident (three-pronged spear), or against a *Thracian*, who used a curved dagger and a small, round shield.

Besides man-to-man contests, gladiators often fought wild beasts and sometimes rode on horses or drove chariots.

A defeated gladiator was usually killed by the victor. The spectators showed they wished him to die by turning their thumbs down. By waving their handkerchiefs, they could save him.

GLASGOW

Glasgow University.

Glasgow is Scotland's chief seaport and largest city. Situated on the river Clyde, it is known for its large shipyards and metal-works. Also, it manufactures chemicals, textiles, and tobacco. Much of the population comes originally from the Scottish Highlands and Ireland.

The city was founded in the 6th century A.D. and grew into a large commercial and industrial city because of its proximity to great iron and coal fields and its location on the Clyde. SEE ALSO: SCOTLAND.

GLASS

Because it's transparent and can be molded into any shape when heated, glass is one of the most useful materials known to man.

Glass is widely used in making windows, lenses, cookware, thermometers, bottles, and art objects.

Molten glass forced through small holes to produce very fine fibers is called fiberglass. Fiberglass can be woven into fabrics resistant to fire, water, and acid. Such material also absorbs heat and noise.

Made of glass

Glass can be etched, polished, cut, enameled, colored, and even made opaque. It can be made to withstand very high or low temperatures and to be stronger than steel.

Glass is made by heating sand, soda, potash, lime, and some other substances to very high temperatures in furnaces. The art of glass making is so old that no one knows when it began. We do know, however, that the Egyptians made glass beads and vases more than 5000 years ago. In those days, all glass vessels were made by blowing through a long tube with a mass of molten glass at the end. As a glass bubble formed, it could be shaped with tongs. Today this craft still survives but has been largely replaced by machines which mold and roll the various shapes in factories.

GLIDERS

Every airplane glides from time to time. That is, it shuts its power off and skims quietly through the air, coming down slowly as it does. This is what a glider does all the time. It is launched, either from an airplane or from the ground with the help of

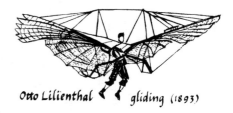

Otto Lilienthal gliding (1893)

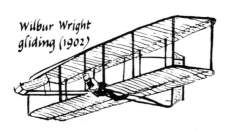

Wilbur Wright gliding (1902)

a fast car, a kind of giant slingshot, or some other means that supplies the power the glider itself lacks. It may seem as if only a low, short flight would be possible, but one glider came down from 46,267 feet (14,102 m) and another traveled 472.2 miles (760 km).

During World War II, gliders were very useful for carrying troops and supplies. Nazi commandos in gliders rescued Mussolini when he was held prisoner on a mountain. Today there are many glider clubs in Europe and America. People enjoy the sport of using the air currents to keep in the air. Some currents even help them to rise, so that they can go on for many miles.

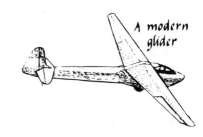

A modern glider

GLOVES

Whether intended for dress or protection, gloves go back to ancient times. They have been found in an ancient Egyptian tomb, and are often mentioned in Greek and Roman writings. Men of the upper class wore them in medieval Europe from the 13th century. Throwing down a glove or slapping someone with one became a way of challenging someone to a duel.

An Egyptian glove 3,300 years old

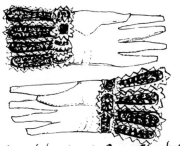
Gloves belonging to Queen Elizabeth I

The fashion of glove-wearing for ladies started in the 16th century.

The fashionable material for dress gloves has long been light-colored kid (young goat) leather, but many other leathers have also been used. Cloth gloves used to be made of woven linen, but now are usually made of knitted wool or cotton. There are working gloves too, made of rubber, asbestos, and other materials.

GLUE

Any substance that is used to make objects stick together is called *glue*. Glue can be made from sticky material in animal hides and bones, fish, milk, and some plants. Scientists use chemicals to make new types of glue that are stronger than the glue made from natural ingredients.

A very simple type of glue called *school paste* is made by mixing flour and water. Another common type of glue called *mucilage* is made from the gummy sap of certain plants.

Sources of Glue

GNAT

Gnat is the name given to several kinds of small flies, mosquitoes, midges, and buffalo gnats. They lay their eggs on stagnant water. The larvae hang head downward into the water and breathe through two tubes that project out from the "tail." These larvae feed upon tiny forms of life in the water. Only the female gnats have the piercing mouthparts that produce the "bite." SEE ALSO: FLY, MOSQUITO.

GOAT

Goats are hoofed mammals that are close relatives of sheep. Goats can be distinguished from sheep in several ways. Goats are thinner than sheep and their hair is longer and straighter. The male goat always has a beard. Also, the horns of goats always point back from the head, while the horns of sheep grow more to the side. Goats can thrive where the land is very steep, rocky, and sparse in vegetation.

Domestic goats are raised for their meat and sweet milk which can be made into cheese. Their hair is used to make mohair, and their skin to make morocco leather book bindings.

GODS

Egyptian god and goddess
Isis
Osiris
Viking god
Greek god
Zeus
Odin

In his desire to understand the Creator of the world, primitive man developed many gods. His ancient myths told of gods that could create and gods that could destroy, gods of war and of love, gods of cities, gods of commerce, and even gods of theft. A believer in such gods had a god or goddess for everything important in his life. Primitive man believed that the gods fought among themselves, tricked each other, and used human beings as they wished. All pagans tried to gain the favor of the gods to avoid trouble.

In creating such gods later civilizations like the Greeks and Romans were seeking to know the true Creator. The Jews came to know one all-powerful God who told men about Himself through the prophets. Christians learned more about God through His Son, Jesus Christ.

GOLD

Gold, one of our most precious metals discovered more than 5000 years ago, is an ELEMENT that does not react with very many substances. As a result, it does not tarnish but instead keeps its shiny yellow luster. Its lack of reactivity makes it ideal for dental work because it is not affected by acids in the mouth.

Gold cup from Mycenae

3,500 years old

Although it is one of the heaviest metals known, gold is very soft. For this reason, it is easily shaped into many forms and can be hammered to a four millionths of an inch (0.0001 mm) thickness to make gold leaf for gilding and lettering. When used in jewelry or coins, gold is mixed with other metals, such as platinum, copper, silver, or nickel to form a harder *alloy*. The purity of this gold alloy is expressed in *karats*. Pure gold is 24 karat (24 k), so 14 k is 14 parts gold and 10 parts other metals.

Gold may be found embedded in rocks or in the muddy beds of waterways. Most gold is obtained by crushing the rock and dissolving the gold in either mercury or a solution of potassium cyanide. About five tons (4.6 metric tons) of crushed rock produce one ounce of gold. Salt water in the world's oceans contains about 10 million tons (9.1 metric tons) of gold, but no efficient process has been found to extract it.

GOLD RUSH

The discovery of gold has usually set off a "gold rush" as people rush to the area to search for gold. One of the most famous gold rushes took place in California in 1849. The year before, gold had been found at Sutter's sawmill, near San Francisco. News of the discovery flashed across the U.S. Thousands of prospectors flocked to the area to stake a "claim" on which to dig for the precious yellow metal. Known as the "forty-niners," most did not find gold, but many helped in the settlement of America's West.

In the late 1850s, other gold rushes occurred in Colorado and Nevada. From 1860 to 1864, gold finds sent men rushing to the Snake River valley, in Idaho, and to Washington, Montana, and British Columbia. When gold was discovered in the Klondike, a region in what is now the Yukon Territory, a wild gold rush began in 1896, with thousands of men streaking there in order to get rich.

Other large gold rushes have taken place in Victoria, Australia (1851–55) and in Witwatersrand, South Africa (1884).

GOLF

Golf is an outdoor game that originated in Scotland before the 15th century. Players hit a small, hard ball with specially made clubs over a grassy course, which consists of 18 "holes," varying in length from about 100 to 600 yards (91–546 m).

The aim is to hit the ball from an original point, the *tee*, over a strip of land, the *fairway*, to the cup, or *hole*, which is placed in an area of closely cropped grass, the *green*, in the fewest possible strokes. To add to the difficulty of striking a small ball, a player must avoid *hazards* (ponds, trees, sand traps, and so forth). Each player may carry up to 14 clubs, each of which is designed for a different stroke. The Royal and Ancient Golf Club of St. Andrews, Scotland, founded in 1754, still controls the basic rules of the game.

GOOSE

A goose is a large, noisy, web-footed water fowl related to the DUCK family. Technically, the name "goose" refers to the female; the male is called a "gander."

Geese differ from ducks in several ways. Most are larger than ducks and have longer necks and legs. The male and female geese have identical plumage. Both wild and tame species mate for life, and the male assists in the care of the young.

At the end of the breeding season, geese molt, or shed, their FEATHERS, which were once used to make arrows and quill pens. In winter when they migrate to warmer climates, geese usually fly in a V-shaped formation.

GOOSEBERRY

Gooseberries are a bush fruit of the Northern Hemisphere closely related to CURRANTS. The name *gooseberry* comes from the Dutch word *kruisbe*, meaning "crisp berry." Gooseberries may be golden, green, or deep purple. After centuries of cultivation, varieties of the berry are now hairless. Gooseberries are used in making jams, jellies, and pies.

Like the currant, the American varieties spread the disease known as blister rust that attacks the white pine. For this reason, the planting of gooseberries is prohibited in some areas. SEE ALSO: CURRANTS.

GORGON

In Greek mythology, a gorgon was one of the three frightful sisters that were known as Stheno, Euryale, and Medusa. Instead of hair, these hideous monsters had a cluster of writhing snakes. Their bodies were covered with scales, and their teeth were like the tusks of wild boars. Anyone who looked at them was turned to stone.

Stheno and Euryale were *immortal* (they could not die), but Medusa could be killed, for she had once been human. With the help of the goddess Athena, the Greek hero Perseus cut off Medusa's head while looking at her reflection in his shield. PEGASUS, the winged horse, supposedly sprang from her blood, and Perseus used her head to turn his enemies into stone.

GORILLA

The gorilla is the largest of the APES. It is native to western equatorial Africa. The male gorilla may reach a height of 6 feet (1.8 m) and weigh more than 500 pounds (225 kg). His brain is, however, only about a third the size of man's.

The illustration compares the skeleton of a gorilla with that of a man. Man's arm bones are not nearly as long as the gorilla's. Also, the gorilla's jaw juts markedly forward and its forehead slopes backward from the ridges above the eyes.

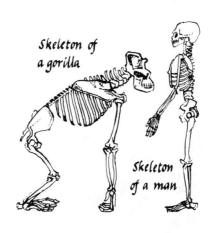

Skeleton of a gorilla

Skeleton of a man

Gorillas usually live on the ground, walking on all fours with their hands doubled under. They can stand erect on two feet more easily than other apes. They feed on various plants, such as bamboo and wild berries. Gorillas live in small groups among the jungle brush and trees. At night they build nests of leafy branches, either on the ground or in the trees. Gorillas are very shy and usually gentle, but can be dangerous when they are angered.

GRAND CANYON

The Colorado River has carved the Grand Canyon, situated in northwestern ARIZONA. In ancient times, this region was pushed upward. Afterward, the river cut through many layers of rock to form the deep gorge. Erosion from wind and rain have helped make the canyon with its many colorful cliffs, plateaus, and rock formations. The canyon is about a mile (1.6 km) deep, 4 to 18 miles (6.4–29 km) wide, and 217 miles (349 km) long.

GRANITE

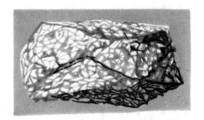

Granite is one of the most common rocks in the Earth's crust. It is usually classed as igneous rock, formed under great heat and pressure from the molten (melted) rock deep in the Earth's core. Granite is composed chiefly of quartz, feldspar, and mica crystals, which are large enough to see with the naked eye, as a result of slow cooling underground.

Because of its extreme hardness, granite is very resistant to weather. Therefore, it is a very suitable building material for buildings, monuments, and bridges.

Ulysses S. GRANT (1822–1885)

Ulysses Simpson Grant, the 18th President of the United States, was a graduate of West Point and served in the MEXICAN WAR. For a while he was a farmer near St. Louis, Missouri. After the outbreak of the CIVIL WAR, he was made colonel and then brigadier general of a regiment of Illinois volunteers. He won victories in Missouri, Kentucky, and Tennessee as a tough and aggressive field commander. President LINCOLN made him a major general, and Grant won important battles at Vicksburg, Mississippi, and at Chattanooga, Tennessee. Then Lincoln made him commander of all the Union armies on March 8, 1864.

Although Grant failed to defeat ROBERT E. LEE in several battles in Virginia, his larger armies enabled him to wear down the Confederates. On April 9, 1865, Lee surrendered to Grant at Appomattox Courthouse. Grant allowed the beaten Confederates to keep their horses "for the spring plowing."

As a Republican, Grant was elected U.S. President in 1868 and in 1872. Though he was honest, Grant's terms in office were marked by scandals, dishonest acts by public officials, and financial difficulties for the country. After his retirement from the presidency, he went into business and lost much money in a crooked banking company that failed in 1884. To provide money for his family, he wrote his *Personal Memoirs*. He died of throat cancer a few days after finishing the work. Grant's tomb is a granite mausoleum on Riverside Drive in New York City. SEE ALSO: CIVIL WAR.

GRAPEFRUIT

The grapefruit is a *citrus* fruit with a yellow rind and light yellow or pink pulp. Grapefruits were brought from Jamaica and introduced to Florida by the Spaniards in the 1500s. Florida produces half of the grapefruits grown in the United States; Texas, California, and Arizona are also grapefruit-producing states. Grapefruits are also grown in South Africa and Israel. Tangelos are a hybrid (mixed breed) of the grapefruit and the tangerine.

GRAPES

The grape was probably the first *cultivated* fruit. Water, wind, birds, and Phoenician sailors were responsible for carrying the grape westward from its origin in the region of the Caspian Sea. In order to grow, grapes need sun and warmth. In colder climates, they are grown in greenhouses. Grapes are used for making jellies, juice, WINE, and raisins. SEE ALSO: WINE.

GRASSES

Grasses are the most important flowering plants. Some animals eat nothing but grass, while others eat only those animals which feed on grass.

Grasses called CEREALS (such as wheat, oats, and barley) provide us with a well-balanced diet. We eat the grain of these grasses in breakfast cereals and bread. Sugar is made from another grass called sugar cane.

Other grasses make beautiful lawns, prevent erosion, and enrich the soil. In some parts of the world, grass is used in making skirts, straw hats, corn husk dolls, and mats. It even provides roofing and building materials (like bamboo) for making huts. SEE ALSO: CEREALS.

GRASSHOPPER

Grasshoppers are insects that have very powerful back legs for jumping. In fact, if a man could jump proportionately as high as a grasshopper, he could leap to the top of a church steeple.

Most male grasshoppers chirp by rubbing their wings together. One kind rubs its wings on the insides of the hind legs. Some grasshoppers have auditory (hearing) organs on their legs; others have them underneath their bodies.

Leaves and plant stems make up the grasshopper's diet. One type of grasshopper, the locust, will gather in swarms and devour all the plants, including grass, in its path. The largest swarm of locusts ever recorded numbered about 250 billion and covered 2000 square miles (5180 km²)

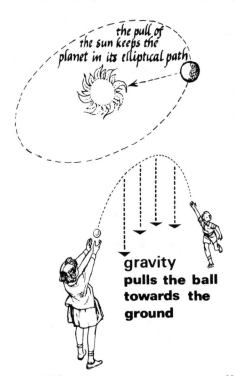

the pull of the sun keeps the planet in its elliptical path

gravity pulls the ball towards the ground

GRAVITY

Gravity is the attraction or pull of one object on another. Even the tiniest object has its own gravity. The strength of gravity depends on the *mass* (amount of matter of an object) and the distance between objects. Heavier objects have a stronger gravitational pull than light ones. As objects get farther apart, the gravitational force diminishes.

In 1665, SIR ISAAC NEWTON began his famous studies on gravity after watching an apple fall. GALILEO, an ancient Greek scientist, had proven earlier that all objects fall at the same rate of speed. However, it was Newton who realized that gravity is everywhere. He was able to prove mathematically how the moon is held in orbit by the gravitational pull of the Earth.

When astronauts in a satellite experience weightlessness, it is because they are falling to the Earth at the same speed the satellite is falling.

Without gravity, everything would float off in different directions. SEE ALSO: GALILEO; NEWTON, SIR ISAAC.

GREAT BRITAIN

The name Great Britain refers to England, Scotland, and Wales, which together make up one large island, and which are all governed by the same parliament.

England conquered Wales in 1282. England and Scotland were joined in 1603 when James I became King of England, and in 1707 the name Great Britain was officially given to these countries. When Ireland came under the same king and parliament in 1800, the name was changed to the United Kingdom of Great Britain and Ireland. In 1922, southern Ireland broke away and afterward became an independent republic, known as Eire. Northern Ireland remains today a part of the United Kingdom, and sends 12 members to the British House of Commons.

GREAT LAKES

The five freshwater Great Lakes—Superior, Huron, Michigan, Erie, and Ontario—lie between Canada and the United States.

French traders in the early 1600s were the first Europeans to see the Great Lakes, which were later fought over by the English and French. After the WAR OF 1812, Americans rapidly developed the commerce on the lakes. Today, large amounts of iron ore, coal, oil, steel, grain, and numerous manufactured articles are shipped from April to December. Winter storms prevent much navigation, and thick ice closes many lake ports. Many large industrial cities lie along the Great Lakes, such as Milwaukee, Duluth, Chicago, Cleveland, and Buffalo.

The ST. LAWRENCE SEAWAY connects the lakes with the Atlantic Ocean. The New York State Barge Canal links them with the Hudson River, and the Illinois River Waterway allows ships to go to the Mississippi River.

GREAT WALL OF CHINA

In 214 B.C., a Chinese emperor who feared the HUNS decided to connect some existing walls on his northern frontier with new ones. The result, the Great Wall of China, is believed to be the largest thing ever built. It is 1500 miles (2400 km) long and in most places is 30 feet (9 m) high, with towers 40 feet (12 m) high. It is made of stone, brick, and earth. Much of it was rebuilt in the 15th and 16th centuries.

GREECE

Greece is about the size of Alabama, with a population of about 9.3 million. It is part of the BALKANS, reaching into the Mediterranean with the Ionian Sea on the west and the Aegean Sea on the east. It is a mountainous country with a heavily indented coastline and hundreds of islands, including CRETE, Rhodes, Corfu, and Malos. Because the soil is poor, much work

is needed to grow its chief crops of olives, grapes, cotton, tobacco, and citrus fruits.

People lived in Greece more than 3000 years ago and developed a great civilization with widespread influence. ATHENS, the modern capital, was then the main city-state, and the Athenians developed a system of government known as democracy. Other Greek city-states became jealous of Athens. SPARTA, Corinth, and Thebes each had periods of greatness, and Greek colonies were scattered over the ancient world, especially in Sicily, Italy, and ASIA MINOR.

The Romans, Byzantines, and Turks successively controlled Greece until it gained independence in 1829. It has been ruled since by kings, dictators, and civilians. Greece is now a parliamentary republic. SEE ALSO: ATHENS.

GREENLAND

Greenland, the largest island in the world, lies off the northeast coast of Canada. It is three times the size of Texas and belongs to Denmark, with which most of its trade in whale oil, fish, furs, and aluminum ore is done.

The ice cap that covers much of the island reaches a thickness of more than two miles (3.2 km). Greenland's coast is very indented and rocky, with countless small islands offshore. Glaciers flow down to the surrounding oceans and drop off huge pieces of ice, called icebergs.

Greenland was discovered in the 9th century by Eric the Red, an Icelandic Viking, who called it "Greenland" to attract people to settle there.

However, only the southwest coast in summer shows much greenery; Godthaab, the capital, is located here. Most of Greenland's 60,000 people are of mixed descent—Eskimo, Danish, and Norwegian.

Edvard GRIEG (1843–1907)

Edvard Grieg was born in Bergen, Norway. His mother taught him at an early age to play the piano. At 15, he was sent to study music in Germany, where he began to compose songs.

On returning home, his music began to express the special spirit of his country and people. He used Norwegian folk song melodies in original ways, creating beautiful, lyrical piano pieces and songs. Two of his most famous compositions are the music for Ibsen's play *Peer Gynt* and the Concerto in A Minor. His manner of using short melodies to build larger pieces influenced later composers like Debussy, TCHAIKOVSKY, and Sibelius.

GRIMM BROTHERS

The Grimm brothers, Jakob (1785–1863) and Wilhelm (1786–1859), were born in Hanau, Germany, and became well-known for their books of fairy tales.

As students, they first became interested in the folk stories of the country people of Germany. They wandered

throughout the country, collecting and writing down many tales that had been passed down by word of mouth from generation to generation. Between 1812 and 1815, *Grimm's Fairy Tales* was first published in three volumes, which included such favorites as "Tom Thumb," "Cinderella," "Hansel and Gretel," and "Rumpelstiltskin."

Also the Grimm brothers wrote a number of scholarly books about the German language, explaining the way words change when they pass from one language to another. This became known as *Grimm's Law* and is today very important to philologists—those who study the history and meaning of words.

GROUND HOG

The ground hog or woodchuck is a stocky, burrowing RODENT closely related to the squirrel. Ground hogs have thick, reddish brown fur. They may grow to be 2 feet (61 cm) long.

Ground hogs spend summer days eating tree roots, grain, leaves and vegetables. They dig deep, elaborate tunnels to their *burrows* or *dens*. Because they often ruin vegetable gardens and lawns, ground hogs are considered pests.

By October, the ground hog is so fat it can barely waddle. At this point he is ready for HIBERNATION and sleeps curled up in his den, living off stored body fat. According to legend, on February 2 (Ground Hog Day), the ground hog comes out of his den. If he sees his shadow, he takes it as a sign that winter will last for six more weeks and goes back into hibernation.

GUILDS

The Guildhall at Thaxted, in Essex, England

During the MIDDLE AGES, many merchants or craftsmen joined together to form associations, called guilds. They discovered that they could do more business and make more money as a group. In the A.D. 1000s, the first merchant guilds were formed, with members agreeing on prices for their goods. Later, the merchants all agreed on the same wages for their workers and made strict rules for *apprentices* (young people learning the business).

In the 1100s, craftsmen like bakers, tailors, blacksmiths, and goldsmiths formed their own guilds with rules. Sometimes, craft guilds permitted only their members to practice a trade in a particular city. A young person learned a trade by joining the guild as an apprentice and by living with a *master* of a particular craft, who taught him and gave him room and board. After several years, the apprentice became a *journeyman*, who either stayed with the master and received a daily wage or started his own business, eventually becoming a master.

Today, LABOR UNIONS are similar in many ways to the old craft and merchant guilds. SEE ALSO: LABOR UNIONS.

GUINEA PIG

The guinea pig is not a pig at all but a medium-sized RODENT, native to South America. The guinea pig sleeps in its burrow during the day and feeds upon vegetables and grain at night.

The INCAS of Peru raised these animals for their excellent meat. Today, they are popular household pets that require little care or space. They are also raised in laboratories by scientists as experimental animals for testing drugs.

GUITAR

The traditional guitar is a wooden instrument plucked with one hand and fingered with the other. It was developed from older instruments in 16th-century Spain. The *Hawaiian guitar* has a sliding tone, caused by rubbing along the strings with a metal bar. The *electric guitar* has an odd shape, and plays through loudspeakers. There are still other kinds of guitar.

GULF OF MEXICO

This arm of the Atlantic Ocean borders five southern states of the United States as well as more than 1000 miles (1610 km) of Mexico. The southern states that have seacoasts on the Gulf of Mexico are Texas, Louisiana, Mississippi, Alabama, and Florida.

There are two great Gulf ports. They are New Orleans, Louisiana, near the mouth of the Mississippi River, and Houston, Texas.

When warm winds blow northward from the Gulf, they bring much rain to the eastern half of the United States. At times, hurricanes sweep across the Gulf and do severe damage to seacoast areas. Galveston, Texas, was almost demolished in 1900.

The Gulf is a busy shipping area. Ships loaded with oil, fruit, cotton, sulfur, and chemicals go to all parts of the world. Some are pleasure boats, many of which carry travelers to South America.

GULF STREAM

The Gulf Stream is a warm ocean current that begins in the Gulf of Mexico, passes around Florida, and flows northeastward, parallel with the U.S. coast. South of Newfoundland, it mixes with the colder Labrador Current and then flows across the ocean, creating the North Atlantic Current. Great Britain and northern Europe are warmed by the winds that accompany this ocean current.

The speed of the Gulf Stream is about 4 miles per hour (6.4 km/hr). At the start, its temperature is 80°F (27°C) but drops steadily as the stream moves north. About 800 miles (1288 km) east of New York, the Gulf Stream is no longer distinguishable from the general ocean drift.

GULLS

Gulls are sea birds which are mostly white with some gray or black on their backs and wings. Although the gull's diet includes small fish, clams, and mussels, it is the great scavenger of the bird world. Because gulls eat the food refuse of fishing fleets, beaches, farmyards, and garbage dumps, they help to reduce pollution.

Colonies of gulls usually build their nests on rocks or cliffs near the sea. However, many herring gulls—the most common gulls of North America—nest in inland lake areas where there is food to scavenge.

GUNS

A gun is a weapon that fires a bullet or some other missile. A gun usually fires by the force of an explosion, but compressed air or gas or a spring can also be the propelling force.

Pistols, rifles, and *shotguns* are hand-carried guns which are called *small arms.* Portable, automatic weapons that fire many rounds of ammunition per minute are called *machine guns.* Big heavy guns that move on wheels or stand on ships or in forts are called *cannons* or *artillery.*

The idea of shooting missiles from a strong tube by means of explosives first occurred to Europeans early in the 14th century. The explosive used for many years was gunpowder, a Chinese invention. Shells which carried their own explosives first became practical in the 19th century when rifling was introduced. Rifling was the cutting of swirling grooves in the barrel of a gun.

The grooves spun the shell, sending it point first. This made it possible for the shooter to aim more accurately.

The Pilgrims used the *matchlock* for hunting animals and fighting hostile Indians. Later, the *flintlock* replaced the matchlock and was used from about the time of the American Revolution until after the Civil War. In the late 1800s, the repeating rifle came into use; it held a number of *cartridges* (bullets) in a *magazine* (metal container) and could be fired rapidly. Probably the most famous American gun is the Colt *revolver* with its revolving storage chamber for bullets. It is often called the gun that "won the West."

17th century flintlock musket

British Sten Gun 1942

Rifles and pistols use ammunition measured in *caliber*, the inside diameter of a gun's barrel. A .22 caliber gun has a barrel with an inside diameter of 22 hundredths of an inch (5.6 mm). Shotguns, which scatter pellets over a wide area, are measured in gauges. A 12-gauge shotgun means that it takes 12 lead balls which fit the barrel of the shotgun to weigh one pound (.45 kg). SEE ALSO: CANNON, EXPLOSIVES.

GYMNASTICS

Gymnastics is a sport in which individuals perform special acrobatic events that show body coordination, balance, and strength. It grew out of *calisthenics*, exercises for health, that were done in Europe in the 1800s. Gymnasts demonstrate their skill on special gymnastic equipment—the vaulting and pommel horse, the horizontal and parallel bars, the uneven parallel bars, the balance beam, the flying rings—and during floor exercises.

Rings   Beam   Parallel Bars   Horse   Uneven Parallel Bars

369

In competition, girls and boys (women and men) compete separately. Individuals are judged and awarded points on how well they have executed the various gymnastic events. The winner is the one with the highest score for the event. Team competitions are decided on the basis of total points for all events. In international competition, such as the OLYMPIC GAMES, gymnasts have to compete in all events, and the one with the highest overall score is considered the best (champion) gymnast. One must go through intensive training in order to be a good gymnast.

GYPSIES

The word "Gypsy" is an old English form of "Egyptian." The Gypsies, however, are not from Egypt. These wanderers, who can be found in most of the world's countries, started out in India about a thousand years ago. They came to Persia around A.D. 1000, then split into two big groups. One went down through Egypt and the other went up into Europe.

The Europeans had no idea where the Gypsies began. Besides thinking of them as Egyptians they also called them Bohemians, as if they came from central Europe.

Because Gypsies often wander, and because they keep apart from the people of the countries they visit, they are often suspected of crime. The Nazis killed over 400,000 Gypsies because they believed the Gypsies were an inferior race.

Gypsies have made their living in many ways, the men as horse dealers, musicians, and metalworkers, the women as fortune tellers and entertainers. Gypsies have also been given unpopular jobs to do in every country.

Gypsies usually do not associate with *gadjes* (non-Gypsies). They move in wandering bands. Each band is governed by a *voivode* (chief) who is elected. The Gypsies call themselves *Rom*, and their language is known as *Romany*.

370

GYROSCOPE

A gyroscope consists of a heavy, spinning *flywheel* mounted in a circular frame. As it spins, the wheel is free to move within the frame.

This invention has been made into a toy which can be balanced on one's finger or even on a piece of string. The gyroscope is also an important device used by boats and aircraft in navigation (charting courses). Since the *axis* of a spinning gyroscope continues to point in the same direction, it makes an excellent COMPASS. Ships and submarines have huge gyroscopes which steady them in rough waters. SEE ALSO: COMPASS.

HADDOCK

Haddock, a type of fish, is closely related to cod. Haddock feed mostly on *mollusks* and *crustaceans* (shellfish) and are rarely more than two feet (71 cm) long.

Haddock are found in the cold waters of the North Atlantic and the North Sea. Very important to the fishing industry, haddock are caught in *trawling* nets. Half the weight of fish caught in the North Sea are haddock.

Haddock are often prepared for eating by smoking them over wood fires, but they may be cooked fresh, too. SEE ALSO: FISH, FISHING.

The HAGUE

the Royal Palace, The Hague

The Hague is the seat of the government of HOLLAND, whose constitutional capital is Amsterdam. Besides its beautiful royal government buildings, it has the Peace Palace, the Groote Kerk (Great Church), and the Mauritshuis Museum, where Rembrandt's finest paintings can be seen. The city has been an important meeting place for international congresses.

HAIR

Only MAMMALS—that is, animals that nurse their young—have hair, which provides warmth and protection. Hair is present to some extent in most mammals, even those which seem hairless, like the elephant and rhinoceros.

There are many types of hair. Sheep have kinky, matted hair called wool. Pigs have stiff bristles; porcupines have quills. When the hair is fine and closely spaced, it is called fur. Human hair varies widely, too. It can be dark or light; straight, wavy, or kinky; coarse or fine. However, all hair grows from the skin in the same way.

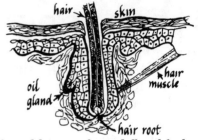

Hair is composed of *keratin*, the same substance constituting horn and fingernails. A hair has no blood vessels or nerves. It is embedded into the skin and held fast by a root. The root is fed by a

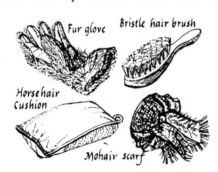

blood vessel and kept soft and flexible by oil glands. A tiny muscle attached to each hair enables it to bristle or "stand on end." Hair grows from the root, not from the tip. After a while, a hair falls out and is replaced by a new one. If there is root damage, however, no more hairs will grow in that spot. SEE ALSO: FUR, WOOL.

Nathan HALE (1755–1776)

"I only regret that I have but one life to give for my country." These were Nathan Hale's famous last words.

After graduation from Yale at the age of 18, Hale taught school in Connecticut for two years before the outbreak of the AMERICAN REVOLUTION. He joined the American army immediately as a lieutenant. Displaying outstanding leadership qualities, he was soon promoted to captain.

In 1776, General Washington lost the Battle of Long Island, and the British were in control of New York City. Washington had to know the enemy's plans if the colonists were to win the war. A volunteer spy was needed. Young Hale volunteered and did not listen to his fellow soldiers who tried to dissuade him.

Posing as a Dutch schoolmaster, he spent 10 days behind enemy lines. On his return, he was captured and his secret papers discovered in between the soles of his shoe. A confessed spy, he was hanged by the British the following morning, but his words live on as a great symbol of American patriotism to future generations.

HALLOWEEN

Halloween is the night before All Saints' Day (November 1). The ancient CELTS in Britain celebrated on October 31 each year an autumn festival. They believed that on that night the dead returned in the shape of cats, witches, and ghosts. Huge bonfires were lit to ward off these evil spirits. That day was the end of summer and the start of winter. Today, the old customs are seen in our scary jack-o'-lanterns and make-believe witches.

Alexander HAMILTON (1757–1804)

Alexander Hamilton was an important American statesman. He helped to establish the government of the United States, doing much to get the CONSTITUTION ratified (approved) by the states.

Born on the island of Nevis in the West Indies, Hamilton went to the North American colonies in 1772. There he studied at King's College (now Columbia University) and became very interested in the colonists' fight for independence. During the AMERICAN REVOLUTION, Hamilton was a captain of artillery and a military aide to General George Washington. Later, as a lawyer and a member of Congress, he pushed for the establishment of a strong central government, as a leader of the Federalist party.

In 1786, Hamilton became a delegate from New York to the Constitutional Convention. With James Madison and John Jay, he wrote articles urging the acceptance of the Constitution. As the first U.S. Secretary of the Treasury, Hamilton founded a national bank and wanted a strong tax system. Hamilton's political enemy, Aaron Burr, shot and killed him during a duel. Hamilton's portrait now appears on the ten-dollar bill.

HAND

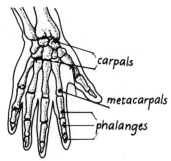

Man has been able to dominate his world because of his highly developed brain and hands. His brain has helped him invent tools, weapons, and machines for his hands to use.

The human hand has four fingers and a thumb, which can be used to grasp things tightly. In the tips of these fingers, the sense of touch is very sensitive.

There are 27 bones in each hand—eight wrist bones (*carpals*), five palm bones (*metacarpals*), and 14 finger bones (*phalanges*). *Tendons* connect these bones to the more than 60 muscles, mostly in the forearm, which control the movement of the hand.

George Frederick HANDEL (1685–1759)

George Frederick Handel was born in Halle, Germany, and learned to play the organ at an early age. As a young man, he studied for four years in Italy, where he wrote several operas in the Italian style.

In 1710, he became a musical director in Hanover, Germany, but two years later he settled in England, where he was employed by the King to compose music. In 1719, an opera company, the Royal Academy of Music, was formed, with Handel as one of the musical directors.

He played the harpsichord very well and composed 46 operas. He also wrote many oratorios (musical settings of words from the Bible). The best known is probably the *Messiah*, which tells about the coming of Jesus, his suffering, and his death. The *Messiah* uses Scriptures from many books of the Bible. Two of Handel's orchestral suites—*The Water Music* and *Music for the Royal Fireworks*—are very famous, too.

In 1753, Handel became totally blind but continued to conduct performances of his works on occasion. After he died, he was buried in Westminster Abbey in London.

HANDWRITING

Man first began to write by drawing pictures. The drawings helped him to show other people what he was talking about, and they helped him to remember things he did not want to forget.

At first, picture writing represented only the object pictured. Then it came to represent ideas that were associated with the pictures, and, finally, it came to represent sounds. In order to make writing easier and quicker, men agreed that certain ways of drawing lines would represent certain sounds. The new symbols were arranged in the form of an ALPHABET.

The alphabet and new writing tools made it possible for more people to learn to write. During the Middle Ages, handwriting became so elaborate and decorative that it was very hard to read. But during the 15th century, Italian scholars designed a new and beautifully clear handwriting similar to what we call *italic* (shown here). Today, we write either by printing, which looks like the words you see in this book, or by *cursive* writing in which we join together the letters in each word. Some of our typewriters type in a way that imitates cursive writing.

Some people, called *graphologists*, believe that a person's handwriting can be analyzed to show what kind of person he is.

In fact, handwriting is so individual that experts can identify a person by comparing one sample of his writing with something else he has written. This is one reason we are asked to sign legal documents, such as a driver's license, in cursive writing. Because our handwriting identifies us so well, it would be difficult for someone to claim a license was his when it really belonged to someone else. He would not be able to copy the signature well enough to get away with it.

Forgery (the copying of someone else's signature in order to secure money or other goods illegally) is often recognized because of some very small difference between the true and the false signatures.

HANNIBAL (247–183 B.C.)

Hannibal was the most famous general of ancient CARTHAGE, a city in North Africa. At the age of 26, he became commander of the Carthaginian army and captured much territory in Spain. The Romans thought that Carthage was seizing too much land, and in 218 B.C. they declared war. Hannibal decided to march into Italy and capture Rome. With thousands of men and many horses and elephants, he crossed the ALPS and descended into Italy. His superior cavalry helped him win a number of battles. At Cannae in southern Italy in 216 B.C., his soldiers surrounded and killed about 50,000 Romans. Hannibal fought for 15 years in Italy, but he was unable to capture Rome.

In 203 B.C., he was recalled to Carthage to stop a Roman invasion. At Zama in North Africa, Hannibal was defeated by the Romans. After peace was made, Hannibal became the chief minister of Carthage. Later, the Romans denounced him, and he fled to Syria. When he was about to be captured, Hannibal poisoned himself rather than become a Roman prisoner.

HANUKKAH

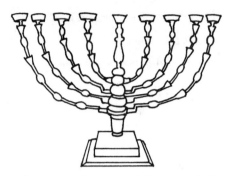

In 168 B.C., a Syrian king who hated JUDAISM desecrated (made unfit for religious use) the Temple in Jerusalem. A Jewish leader, Judas Maccabeus, defeated the Syrians and had the Temple rededicated to God. Hanukkah, also called the *Feast of Lights*, celebrates the rededication in 165 B.C. The lighting of the nine-branched candlestick, beginning with one and adding one candle per evening for eight days, celebrates a miracle. There was only enough sacred lamp oil for one day when the Temple was reopened, but the lamps burned for eight days, until more oil could be gotten.

Hanukkah is celebrated either in late November or during December. Like Christmas, it is a time for rejoicing and present-giving.

HARBORS and PORTS

When a ship comes in from the sea, it must have a place to load and unload cargo and passengers. Such a place should be free of high waves, which would make the work difficult and dangerous. It should have cranes, storehouses, and whatever is needed to handle the cargo.

Any town where passengers and cargo are transferred to and from ships is called a *port.* Oceans, large lakes, and large rivers all have ports. A place that is safe from the waves of an ocean or a lake is called a *harbor.* Some harbors are made by nature, for instance that of New York. Other harbors are man-made. They are protected by *breakwaters,* walls that face the open sea and take the force of the waves.

A ship will sometimes anchor away from the shore if it is too soon to unload it. When things are ready, it raises its anchor and ties up at a *quay* (pronounced key), a kind of roadway going along the shore. Or it may enter a *dock,* a body of water big enough for one or two ships. On either side of the dock are *piers* or *wharfs,* platforms built out into the water from the shore. Docks and piers allow a port to serve more ships than a quay does. The whole waterfront neighborhood of a city is sometimes called the docks.

Two types of men help load and unload cargo. *Stevedores* work on board the ship, while *longshoremen* work on the wharf or pier. Oil or other liquid cargo in tankers is pumped into storage tanks through hoses and pipes.

There is another kind of dock, called a *drydock.* When a ship enters it, this dock is pumped dry so that the underwater part of the ship can be repaired.

HARES

Hares are related to rabbits but usually weigh more and have longer hind legs and longer ears. Their long hind legs enable hares to run as fast as 45 miles per hour (72 km/hr). They are also good swimmers and have been known to swim a mile.

The most important difference between hares and rabbits is in their living habits. Hares live in hollows in the grass called *forms* instead of in *burrows.* Hares eat grass, vegetables, fruits, and the bark of young trees. Both animals give birth to several litters a year. Young hares are called *leverets.*

Hares are widely distributed over most of the world. In America, the "jack rabbit" and "snowshoe rabbit" are really hares, not rabbits. SEE ALSO: RABBITS.

HARP

Harps are frames that keep strings stretched so that each, when plucked, plays a note different from that of the others. On this frame is a light, boxlike object that vibrates with the strings and enlarges their sound.

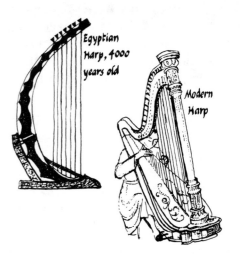

Egyptian Harp, 4000 years old

Modern Harp

Harps were used in ancient Egypt and Mesopotamia as far back as 3000 B.C. They have been used all over the world. Until the 16th century they were very simple, but at that time Europeans began to make them so that they could play more notes. A modern harp has two sets of strings, and pedals that alter their pitch.

HARPOON

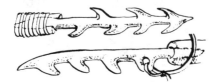

The spearing of whales and other large creatures of the sea is done with harpoons. They have barbs on their heads that hold the spear in the flesh of the victim. The other end of the harpoon has a long rope attached to the harpooner's boat. Modern whaling harpoons are shot from guns.

HARPSICHORD

The harpsichord was a popular musical instrument in Europe from about 1600 to 1800. Much of the music of BACH, HANDEL, and MOZART was written for it.

A harpsichord looks a little like a grand piano, but works differently and has a different sound. In a piano the strings are struck with hammers. In a harpsichord they are plucked by quills that rise when the keys are pressed. Some harpsichords have two or three keyboards, and all have at least two strings to each note. Harpsichords also have *stops*, which allow different combinations of strings to be used. This gives a choice of sounds and makes a rich effect.

Other keyboard instruments with plucked strings were the *virginal* and the *spinet*. These were simpler than the harpsichord, and not so rich in sound.

William HARVEY (1578–1657)

William Harvey graduated from Cambridge University in England and was granted a doctor's degree from the University of Padua in Italy. In 1616, he made known for the first time how the BLOOD circulates in the body. When his ideas on blood circulation were published in 1618, his practice was nearly ruined, and he had to continue his studies in secret because it was considered wrong to question traditional beliefs about the human body. He was also the physician to two Kings of England, and, in his later life, he received many honors for his work.

Battle of HASTINGS

Hastings is an old seaport, situated on the English Channel 54 miles (87 km) southeast of London. On October 14, 1066, the Battle of Hastings was fought on Senlac Hill, a few miles inland.

William with his Norman army of mounted knights, foot soldiers, and skilled archers invaded England and met Harold

Landing on the beach: unloading horses

Attacking the hill

with his Saxon army of foot soldiers and armed peasants. The Saxons stood firm behind a wall of shields and stakes and managed to drive back the Normans. However, Norman archers kept up a hail of arrows, which wounded and killed many English peasants. Harold was mortally wounded, and by nightfall William had broken the English defenses and secured victory for the Normans.

The Battle of Hastings was the first major triumph for the Norman invaders under WILLIAM THE CONQUEROR and marked the beginning of the Norman conquest of England. SEE ALSO: WILLIAM THE CONQUEROR.

379

HATS

There are two kinds of hats. One kind protects the head from the weather, from flying or falling objects, and so forth. The Mexican sombrero keeps the hot sun off the face. The soldier's helmet protects the top of his head from bullets, and the worker's "hard hat" keeps his head

Chinese   Arab   1400   1400

Stovepipe   18th Century   1900   Modern

Sombrero   Hard Hat   Royal Crown   Policeman's

safe from hammers, rivets, and other things that may fall by accident. The hood of the Eskimo parka protects the ears from frostbite.

The other kind of hat is intended to tell everyone what sort of person the wearer is. The crown of a king is a type of hat that is worn at ceremonies. So is

380

the tall, pointed mitre of a bishop. An army officer may show his rank by the insignia (badges) he wears on his cap. A policeman's cap is part of his uniform. Some men and women regard it as good manners to wear hats as part of their street clothes and on formal occasions. A hundred years ago, no man of any kind was seen out of doors without some kind of hat.

Some people wear hats for religious reasons. Some women feel that they should have their heads covered when in church. And Orthodox Jews often wear hats or caps indoors.

We speak of a *hat* when the thing worn is rather high and stiff. *Caps* tend to be low and soft.

HAWAII

Niihau　Kauai
Oahu
HONOLULU　Molokai
Lanai　Maui
Kahoolawe

Pacific Ocean

Hawaii　Mauna Kea
13,796 ft.

Hawaii, the 50th state to join the U.S., consists of a group of islands, situated in the Pacific Ocean about 2400 miles (3864 km) west of California. The islands have beautiful beaches, tropical rain forests, and rugged mountains, some of which are active volcanoes. There are eight major islands. Hawaii, the largest, has the highest point, Mauna Kea, an extinct volcano, 13,796 feet (4277 m) high. On Oahu, the most populous island, are Honolulu (the capital and largest city) and Pearl Harbor. The other islands are Maui, Molokai, Kauai, Lanai, Niihau, and Kahoolawe. Cool trade winds give the state a pleasant climate all year round.

During the eighth century A.D., Polynesians from the South Seas settled in Hawaii. The first European visitor was CAPTAIN JAMES COOK in 1778. A local chieftain named Kamehameha took control in 1782 and set up a kingdom. During the 1800s, many missionaries and traders arrived, and the Americans built large, profitable sugar and pineapple industries. In 1893, the Hawaiian queen, Liliuokalani, was overthrown and a republic was set up. By 1900, Hawaii had become a U.S. territory, and in 1959 it became a state. The present population of about 900,000 includes Japanese, Filipinos, Americans, Polynesians, and Chinese—many of mixed racial ancestry.

Hawaii is an important U.S. military base. Tourism is the biggest business, but agriculture and food-processing are also valuable sources of income.

HAWKS

Many small birds of prey are often referred to as "hawks." However, true hawks have short wings, long tails, and a wavy, unnotched edge to the upper beak. Falcons, also part of the hawk family, have long pointed wings and notched beaks.

The goshawk of America and Europe and its close relatives represent the typical hawk. This hawk was used for centuries in the ancient sport of *falconry*, in which it was trained to hunt, kill, and retrieve small animals for its master. Drawings found in Assyria show that falconry was popular in 700 B.C. The kings, knights, and nobles of the Middle Ages used hawks for hunting. Today, falconry is a rare sport.

The kestrel is a common small falcon. It always hovers with its head down against the wind before diving on its prey.

The buzzard is sometimes included with the hawks, although it is not a hawk. It is more like an EAGLE and has similar nesting habits.

Hawks fly only during the daytime and go after moving prey, such as small mammals, reptiles, insects, and chickens. The adult hawks fiercely protect their young.

(top) Goshawk (middle) Kestrel (bottom) Buzzard

Nathaniel HAWTHORNE (1804–1864)

Nathaniel Hawthorne was a famous American novelist and short story writer. From an early age, he devoted himself to writing. His short stories soon gained him some attention. Unable to earn a living by writing, Hawthorne worked at the Boston customhouse and later as surveyor of the port at Salem, Massachusetts, his birthplace. All the while, he continued his career as an author, writing such short stories as "Young Goodman Brown," "My Kinsman, Major Molineux," and "Rappaccini's Daughter." Hawthorne liked to write about the strange happenings in Puritan New England. His tales were about witchcraft, curses, sins, punishments, and death; they showed people in deep spiritual conflict.

In 1850, Hawthorne wrote his masterpiece, *The Scarlet Letter*. This novel and his next, *The House of Seven Gables*, brought him much fame. Hawthorne now wrote two books for children, several more novels, and many more short stories. He is said to have established the American short story as an art form.

HAY

Hay is mainly made up of grass, clover, and alfalfa. These plants are grown, cut, dried, and stored by a farmer to provide food for livestock during the winter.

Modern farmers have machines which cut, gather, bale, and stack the hay. There are machines which dry the plants in wet weather so that they can be cut.

Hay cutter   Hay elevator & rick

HEART

The heart is a powerful muscle, about the size of a fist, that circulates BLOOD through blood vessels, called ARTERIES AND VEINS. A tough skin, the *pericardium*, covers and protects the heart. The heart has four rooms or chambers—two upper receiving chambers, called *auricles*, and two lower pumping chambers, called *ventricles*.

The heart *contracts* to squeeze the blood out of the heart chambers and through the arteries. This action is felt as a *pulse*. The heart relaxes between these contractions, which normally occur about 70 times per minute. During strenuous activity, the rate of the heart may double. Two nerves leading from the brain to the heart automatically control the speed of the beat. When the heart beats faster, the rate of breathing must also increase to provide enough oxygen in the blood. Fear and other emotions can cause the heart to beat faster so that the body will have the additional oxygen necessary for a quick reaction.

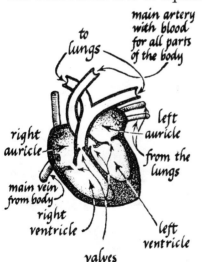

main artery with blood for all parts of the body
to lungs
right auricle
left auricle
from the lungs
main vein from body
right ventricle
left ventricle
valves

Blood enters the right auricle of the heart from two large veins coming from the upper and lower parts of the body. This bluish, *venous* blood carries

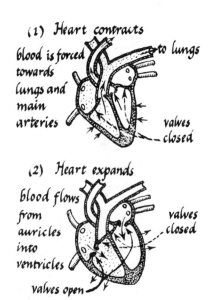

(1) *Heart contracts*

blood is forced towards lungs and main arteries

to lungs

valves closed

(2) *Heart expands*

blood flows from auricles into ventricles

valves closed

valves open

carbon dioxide, which has been given off by the body cells as a waste product of growth and repair. The blood passes through an opening *(valve)* to the right ventricle, which pumps the blood through *pulmonary* (lung) arteries to the lungs. Here the blood gives up the carbon dioxide to be breathed out. The *hemoglobin* in the blood picks up oxygen from the air breathed into the lungs, turning the blood bright red. Pulmonary veins send the blood to the left auricle, which sends it through another valve to the left ventricle. Here the blood is pumped out the main artery *(aorta)* and carried through the body by smaller arteries.

HEAT

Heat is the energy of molecules in motion. Molecules are in constant motion, or vibration, in all substances, even *solids*. The hotter the substance, the faster the molecules vibrate. Eventually, the force of vibration becomes greater than the forces which bind the molecules together. This is what happens when a solid substance melts, or becomes liquid. Molecular movement in substances can be increased by heating, by *friction* (rubbing), by chemical action, or by sending a current of electricity through them.

Heat energy moves from warmer to colder objects. The giving off of heat by a hot object is called *radiation*. The sun's heat travels through 93 million miles (150 million km) of space to reach us this way.

The flowing of heat from one object to another touching it is called *conduction*. Conduction occurs when the heat energy of one vibrating molecule activates the one next to it. The best heat conductors are metals. Substances that do not conduct heat are called *insulators*.

molecules vibrating at ordinary temperatures

molecules vibrating at high temperatures

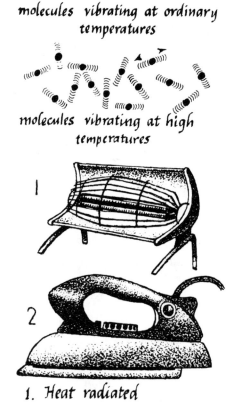

1. *Heat radiated*
2. *Heat conducted*

HEBREWS

The River Jordan in Judaea

The Hebrews were the Jews of the Old Testament, the first half of the Bible. They were wandering tribes that lived in the Middle East and believed there was only one true God. "Jew" first meant a member of the Hebrew tribe of Judah.

The Hebrews' first leader was ABRAHAM. God promised Abraham that he would bless the Hebrews and make them a great nation. Abraham's great-grandson, Joseph, led the Hebrew tribes to Egypt. After living there for many years, they were forced into slavery. Later, MOSES led the Hebrews out of Egypt into Palestine, where they settled in Canaan.

About 1000 B.C., the Hebrews founded a kingdom in Canaan and became a strong people under their kings, Saul, DAVID, and SOLOMON. Later the nation was separated into two kingdoms, Israel and Judah. In 721 B.C., the Assyrians destroyed Israel, and in 586 B.C. the Babylonians conquered Judah, taking the Hebrews of Judah into exile in Babylon. From then on, these Hebrews became known as Jews. Some returned to Canaan, or Judaea. SEE ALSO: JEWS.

HECTOR

The story of Hector, the bravest of the Trojan warriors, is told in the *Iliad* which was probably written by the poet HOMER.

Hector was the son of Priam, the King of TROY. The Greeks had besieged the city of Troy for nine long years, but the Trojans (men of Troy) had managed to hold them back. In the tenth year of the siege, Hector killed one of the greatest of the Greek warriors, Patroclus, who was the best friend of ACHILLES.

Achilles sought revenge. Before the walls of Troy, Achilles and Hector met in combat, which ended with the death of the valiant Hector. Then Achilles dragged Hector's body in the dust around the walls behind his chariot, refusing to allow the Trojans to give Hector an honorable burial.

Priam begged the Greeks for the body of his son. The body was delivered to Priam for ransom and buried in a great ceremony. Hector represented for the Trojans the good and noble man. SEE ALSO: ACHILLES, TROY.

HELEN of TROY

According to Greek legend, Helen was the most beautiful woman in the world. She was the daughter of ZEUS, the supreme god of the ancient Greeks.

Many men wished to marry Helen, but she chose King Menelaus of Sparta for her husband. Odysseus made each of her thirty suitors swear to defend the rights of Menelaus if ever there was need. When Paris, son of the King of Troy, carried Helen off, all the Greek princes and kings gathered in anger and sailed for TROY to bring her back.

Some stories say Helen was forced by Paris to go to Troy; others say she fell in love with him and went willingly. In the *Iliad* and *Odyssey*, both thought to be written by HOMER, Helen became the wife of Paris but always remained in sympathy with the Greeks. When Troy fell after a ten-year siege, Helen returned to Menelaus and lived a peaceful life in Sparta.

Many poets have used Helen as a subject, always describing her magical beauty and charm. SEE ALSO: TROY.

HELICOPTER

An airplane needs a long runway for its takeoffs and landings. This means that there are many places where it is not practical, because there is no space for runways or because buildings and other high objects would be in its way. The helicopter allows people to fly into such places because

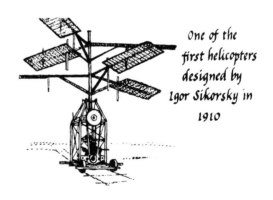

One of the first helicopters designed by Igor Sikorsky in 1910

it rises and descends vertically. It has a powerful *rotor* (propeller) that lifts it straight into the air. A smaller rotor on the tail is set sideways to control the way the helicopter faces and to give it a forward motion.

Helicopter-like toys were used in the Middle Ages. In the 15th century, LEONARDO DA VINCI, the great artist and inventor, designed a helicopter. None of these helicopters was practical, though. There was no way to give them the power for long flights until the gasoline engine was invented in the late 19th century.

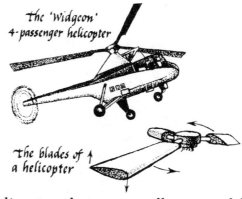

the 'widgeon' 4-passenger helicopter

the blades of a helicopter

In 1909, a Russian, Igor Sikorsky, built a helicopter that could lift itself. But it was not powerful enough to lift anything else as well. In 1923, Juan de la Cierva, a Spaniard, flew a type of helicopter called an *autogiro*. This was a cross between an airplane and a real helicopter. In 1940, Sikorsky built a helicopter that was really successful, and helicopters became important in World War II and the Korean War.

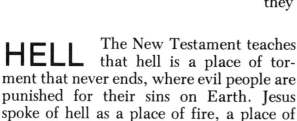

Today, helicopters are in widespread use. Many are used to taxi people quickly between airports and downtown areas. Others are used to watch for traffic jams and other forms of trouble. The army has helicopters powerful enough to carry tanks and other very heavy objects to places where they are needed.

HELL

The New Testament teaches that hell is a place of torment that never ends, where evil people are punished for their sins on Earth. Jesus spoke of hell as a place of fire, a place of never-ending death.

The myths and legends of ancient nations described other places which were like the hell that Jesus described.

One of the Greek words used for hell was *Hades*. Greek mythology used this

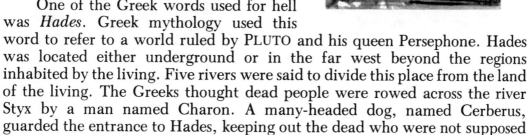

word to refer to a world ruled by PLUTO and his queen Persephone. Hades was located either underground or in the far west beyond the regions inhabited by the living. Five rivers were said to divide this place from the land of the living. The Greeks thought dead people were rowed across the river Styx by a man named Charon. A many-headed dog, named Cerberus, guarded the entrance to Hades, keeping out the dead who were not supposed to enter.

HENRY II (1133–1189)

Thomas à Becket disputing with Henry II
(from an old painting)

Henry II became King of England in 1154 and reigned prosperously until a long and violent quarrel arose with Thomas à Becket, the Archbishop of Canterbury. A large area of France came under his rule after Henry married Eleanor of Aquitaine, daughter of a French duke. He brought order to England, destroying many of the castles of the powerful barons. He strengthened the royal courts and set up a legal system that became the basis of the one in England and the United States.

When Henry tried to limit the power of the Roman Catholic Church, he clashed with Thomas à Becket, who was deeply devoted to the Church and refused to believe the state (king) was superior to the Church. In 1170, four knights murdered Thomas in Canterbury cathedral, and the Pope ordered Henry to walk barefoot to the tomb of Becket and to pray for forgiveness.

During his last years, Henry's sons plotted against him. When he died, his oldest son, RICHARD I, became king.

HENRY V (1387–1422)

Henry V   1413 – 1422

Henry V became King of England in 1413 and set out to regain lands in France that were once owned by his ancestors. He laid claim to Normandy and to parts of France never in English hands. Henry also claimed the French throne and led an English army to France in 1415. His soldiers captured the town of Harfleur, but many of them died from camp fever (typhus) so Henry decided to return to England. During the march across France to the port of Calais, his weary and hungry army encountered and defeated a huge French army at

Agincourt. The English archers with their longbows mowed down thousands of French soldiers. After his victory at Agincourt, Henry won the whole of northern France and married the daughter of the King of France. He was also named heir to the French throne, but he was never crowned.

HENRY VIII (1491–1547)

Henry VIII became King of England in 1509. He soon appointed Thomas Wolsey to high positions in church and state. For the next 20 years, England prospered under the strong administration of Wolsey, to whom Henry gave almost complete control.

At 19, Henry married Katharine of Aragon. Failing to have a son by her and being infatuated by a court maid, Anne Boleyn, Henry in 1529 asked the POPE to declare his marriage void. Wolsey was charged with obtaining the Pope's approval, but he failed to and was dismissed by Henry. Then Henry decided to make the King, not the Pope, the supreme head of the Church of England. Parliament helped Henry accomplish this, and afterward he married Anne Boleyn. Henry had the Bible translated into English and used in the Church of England. Also, he seized the property of many monasteries and enriched the national treasury. The Pope retaliated and excommunicated (banned from the Roman Catholic Church) Henry. Henry now concerned himself with increasing his own power.

Henry VIII 1509–1547

In 1536, Anne, who had given birth to a daughter, the future Elizabeth I, but no male heir, was charged with unfaithfulness and was beheaded. Ten days later, Henry married Jane Seymour, who bore him a son, the future Edward VI, and then died. Henry in 1540 married Anne of Cleves, but divorced her shortly and then married Catherine Howard, who in 1542 met the same fate as Anne Boleyn. Catherine Parr became Henry's sixth queen in 1543, and she survived Henry's death.

During Henry's reign, England became a powerful country with a large navy. Henry made Wales and Ireland a part of his kingdom and ruled as a popular, though sometimes cruel, king.

389

Patrick HENRY (1736–1799)

"Give me liberty or give me death." With these words said two centuries ago, Patrick Henry urged the American colonies to fight for independence from England. Shortly afterward, the colonies joined in the AMERICAN REVOLUTION and became a free nation.

Patrick Henry was a great American patriot. As a young boy in Virginia, he disliked school and went to work as soon as possible. He was unsuccessful at various jobs until he studied law. He was so interested in his studies that he became a lawyer after a short time. His special interest was government, and his speeches were very important in rousing the Colonial revolutionaries. Later, he became governor of Virginia several times. He also spent many years in the Virginia legislature. He worked to have the first 10 amendments (BILL OF RIGHTS) added to the CONSTITUTION.

HERALDRY

When he went into battle, the medieval knight was completely covered in armor. To make himself known, he painted his shield with a pattern easily recognized. This was the beginning of heraldry. The pattern became a symbol of his family, and each member of the family had his own version of the *escutcheon* (shield design). Gradually, other decorative features were added to the escutcheon to make a complete *coat of arms*.

To see that everyone used the coat of arms that was his and his alone, experts called *heralds* were appointed by the kings of various countries. Heralds designed new coats of arms when told to do so.

Heraldry is a complicated art, with its own language. British and American heraldry uses words from medieval French.

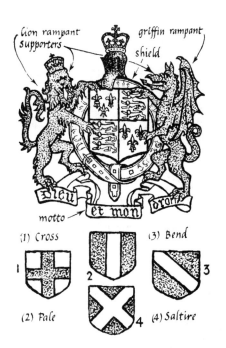

HERCULES

Hercules was the Roman name for the legendary Greek hero, Heracles, who was known for his extraordinary strength and courage. Roman myths said that his father was ZEUS, the king of the gods, and his mother was a human named Alcmene. The myths tell how Zeus' wife, Hera, hated Hercules because he was the child of her unfaithful husband.

The fifth Labor

When Hercules was born, Hera placed two snakes in his cradle to kill him, but the infant killed them with his hands. Hera later drove him insane, which caused him to kill his wife and children. Hercules felt great guilt for his wickedness, and for 12 years he performed nearly impossible tasks for his purification and freedom. These tasks were called the "Twelve Labors of Hercules," which consisted of (1) killing a lion and (2) the Hydra, a nine-headed monster; (3) catching a wild boar and (4) a very swift stag; (5) destroying man-eating Stymphalian birds; (6) cleaning the stables of King Augeas, where 3000 oxen had been kept for 30 years; (7) capturing the mad bull of King Minos of Crete and (8) the man-eating horses of King Diomedes of Thrace; (9) defeating the warrior-women called Amazons and seizing the queen's girdle; (10) killing Geryon, a monster with three bodies; (11) capturing Cerberus, the three-headed dog that guarded the entrance to Hades; and (12) obtaining the golden apples of the Hesperides.

Hercules went on the Argonaut expedition with JASON.

HEROD

At the time of JESUS, Palestine was an eastern province of the Roman Empire, ruled for the Romans by the Kings of Judaea, several of whom were named Herod.

Herod the Great (d. 4 B.C.) was governing at the time of Jesus' birth. He rebuilt many temples and many parts of his cities, especially JERUSALEM. Near the end of his reign, he became somewhat insane and executed many people. His son, Herod Antipas (d. A.D.39?), ordered the execution of John the Baptist and was king at the time of the Crucifixion of Jesus. SEE ALSO: JESUS.

391

HERODOTUS (484?–425? B.C.)

Herodotus was an early Greek historian who traveled throughout the Mediterranean, visiting Syria, Palestine, Babylon, Egypt, Italy, and Greece. Later, he returned to his native town of Halicarnassus in ASIA MINOR and began to write a HISTORY of these lands. In 443 B.C., he helped to establish the

Greek colony of Thurii in southern Italy, where he is said to have spent the rest of his life. There he wrote a narrative history about the war between the Greeks and the Persians. His writings contain much interesting—but often inaccurate—information about the ancient world. However, he was the first to attempt to write a comprehensive "history" and is often referred to as the "father of history."

HERRING

Herring is thought to be the world's most plentiful fish. They can even be found around the north and south poles. They have silvery-white sides and metallic, dark blue backs. They swim in large *schools* near the surface and can easily be caught in fishing nets.

In Europe, most herring are salted, pickled, or smoked as *kippers*. In northeastern North America, young herring are netted and canned as sardines.

The size of herring varies greatly. Herring in enclosed waters (such as San Francisco Bay) or in waters with a low salt content may be only four inches (10.2 cm) long when fully grown. Those found in the North Atlantic may exceed one pound (0.5 kg) in weight and 15 inches (38 cm) in length.

Among the most nourishing of all fish, herring make excellent food for animals and rich fertilizer. The once great herring industry has suffered in recent years due to over-fishing. SEE ALSO: FISHING.

HIBERNATION

In cold climates, some animals spend the entire winter in hibernation, a sleeping state. Cold-blooded animals hibernate because their blood temperature drops when when the outside temperature drops. Their body functions slow down to such an extent that they appear dead. Frogs and turtles burrow into the mud, while snakes go into holes in the grounds. Snails, butterflies, and other insects hibernate, too.

Dormouse and adder hibernating

The warm-blooded animals that hibernate probably do so because their food supply becomes scarce. Bears, ground hogs, and skunks are some of the mammals that store a supply of nourishment in their body fat and hibernate all winter. Others, such as the squirrel, sleep lightly, waking up on mild days to eat nuts stored in the fall.

Fish escape the cold by swimming to deeper waters, while many birds *migrate* or fly south to warmer weather.

Wild Bill HICKOK (1837–1876)

James Butler Hickok, nicknamed "Wild Bill," was an American soldier, Indian scout, and border marshal who became a legend during his lifetime.

Before the Civil War, Wild Bill was a stagecoach driver on the Santa Fe Trail and then on the Oregon Trail. As a driver, he battled many tough gangs of OUTLAWS. During the Civil War, he was a scout and spy for the Union army. Afterwards, he became a marshal stationed in the wild

Kansas border towns of Fort Riley, Hays City, and finally Abilene. He also served as an Indian scout for General George Custer, and in 1872 he toured the East with BUFFALO BILL. In 1876, he was shot in the back during a poker game by the notorious Jack McCall. Since then, the cards he held, which were a pair of aces and a pair of eights, have been called "the dead man's hand." After his death, Wild Bill Hickok became one of America's favorite folk heroes.
SEE ALSO: OUTLAW.

HIEROGLYPHICS

The ancient Egyptians cut and painted sets of pictures on their buildings as a form of writing. The Greeks called these hieroglyphic writing, and suggested that they were sacred carvings. Although the writing took the form of pictures, they probably represented sounds that the names of the

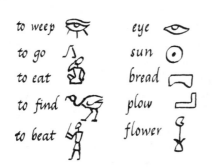

objects suggested, and were seldom intended to be pictures of the objects themselves.

Here are two sets of hieroglyphics that are encircled to show they are royal names. The first gives the sounds K, L, E, O, P, A, T, R, A (CLEOPATRA); ; the second gives P, T, O, L, M, EE, S ("of the Ptolemy family").

Writing on papyrus was done in two styles that were based on hieroglyphic writing but were much easier to write.

Hieroglyphics were a mystery until the discovery in Egypt in 1799 of the ROSETTA STONE, which has Greek and Egyptian versions of the same writing.

HIMALAYAS

The Himalayas are the highest mountain range in the world and have the world's tallest mountain—EVEREST. The Himalayas have 28 peaks that rise more than 28,000 feet (8680 m). Some of the mountains near Everest are so rugged that no one has been able to climb them to this day.

This range extends about 1500 miles (2415 m), forming a natural boundary between TIBET and INDIA. Parts of the Himalayas lie also in Nepal, Bhutan, China, and Pakistan. Melting snows and glaciers in these mountains feed three great rivers of India—the Brahmaputra, GANGES, and Indus.

Little of the Himalayan region is inhabitable. The southern areas have

Himalayan peaks

jungles and swamps. Grazing is possible on some of the gentler slopes, with farming in the fertile valleys. There is lumbering in the forests on the upper slopes. The region often has severe earthquakes, avalanches, and floods.

HIPPOPOTAMUS

In Greek, the word *hippopotamus* means "river horse." It does spend much time in the African rivers and lakes, but the hippopotamus is a much closer relative of the pig than the horse. It weighs up to four tons (3.6 metric tons) and has skin an inch (2.5 cm) thick. Its mouth is wide and the incisors and lower canines (teeth) are large ivory tusks.

The nostrils, ears, and tiny eyes are located high up on the head which allows the hippopotamus to remain mostly submerged underwater. The perspiration of a hippopotamus is red, and it looks like it is "sweating blood."

HISTORY

History is the story of man's past. It is specifically the written record of events in time, especially those concerned with the development of man, nations, institutions, arts, and sciences. History generally begins with provable dates; earlier times are said to be *prehistoric*. For understanding prehistory, the work of ARCHEOLOGY is very important. HERODOTUS is considered by many to have been the first historian.

From Cave-men to Space-ships

Learning about the past helps us to understand our own times better, and enables us to prepare for the future. By seeing how people lived and acted in the past, we realize how different from us, and yet how like us, they were. We try to understand how we would have acted during that period, under similar circumstances. This is how we learn the "lessons of history," realizing the mistakes of the past and trying not to repeat them.

However, our knowledge of the past is always changing, as we discover new evidence (old inscriptions, papers, coins and other objects). Also, certain things sometimes become more important than we first realized.

Adolf HITLER (1889–1945)

After WORLD WAR I, Germany had high unemployment and very little money. The German people were extremely unhappy. In 1920, an unknown Austrian house-painter named Adolf Hitler established the National Socialist German Workers (or Nazi) Party. The Nazis promised prosperity for Germany, and the people believed them.

In 1923, Hitler tried to sieze power but was arrested. In prison he wrote a book called *Mein Kampf* (My Struggle), which contained his political ideas. He also thought that "pure" Germans were superior

Hitler speaking at a Nationalist-Socialist (Nazi) Party meeting

to other people, especially JEWS, on whom Hitler blamed Germany's troubles. In 1933, the Nazi Party controlled the country, and Hitler became chancellor. Soon he had complete power and named himself "der Fuhrer" (the leader). He quickly built up Germany's armed forces and killed or imprisoned his opponents.

After seizing Austria and Czechoslovakia, he invaded Poland in 1939, which brought on WORLD WAR II. In 1944, some Germans tried unsuccessfully to kill Hitler, whose desire to rule the world was only bringing ruin to Germany. When Hitler saw that Germany was beaten, he committed suicide.

HOCKEY

Hockey is a game played on a field or on ice. A form of field hockey was played by the ancient Persians, who passed it on to the Greeks and Romans. The game was further developed by the English, who brought it to America in the 1800s. It is played by men or women, but is especially popular in girls' schools. The eleven players on each side hit a ball down a field with curved sticks. A point is scored when a team drives the ball into the other team's goal.

Ice hockey, though played on similar principles, is a faster and more rugged game. Six players on each side, wearing ice skates and padded clothing, move a hard, rubber disk *(puck)* up and down a smooth, ice surface *(rink)*. A team tries to score a goal by shooting the puck into the other team's goal *(net)*. Ice hockey is a popular boys' and men's sport, especially in Canada, where it originated.

HOLIDAYS

A holiday is a day set aside for the celebration of some important event. Holidays may be for religious reasons, such as CHRISTMAS, HANUKKAH, or EASTER, or for a patriotic observance, such as Memorial Day, Independence Day, or Washington's Birthday. Holidays may also be for rest and recreation, like New Year's Day and Labor Day.

Holiday recreation

Sunday is a traditional holiday in the United States and other Western countries, because most Christians honor Sunday as "the Lord's Day." In the U.S. legal holidays are decided by the separate states. Usually those holidays mentioned above are always celebrated, along with others such as THANKSGIVING Day and Veterans Day. On legal holidays, banks, schools, and many businesses are closed.

Holidays are observed throughout the world—for example, May Day (May 1) in the Soviet Union, and Bastille Day (July 14) in France.

HOLLAND

Holland is the common name for the country of The Netherlands. Its 14 million people are crowded into an area about twice the size of New Jersey.

Holland is a flat country in northwest Europe, bordering on Belgium and West Germany. It is protected from the NORTH SEA by many dunes, which have been strengthened by many artificial dikes. One part of Holland where the sea washed away

the dunes and flooded the land is the Yselmeer (ZUIDER ZEE). A 20-mile (32 km) DIKE now separates it from the North Sea. Inside this inland lake and in other parts of Holland are *polders*, lowlands reclaimed from the sea that now provide rich farmland.

There are many dairy farms that supply delicious butter and cheese for export. Dutch flower-bulbs are also shipped all over the world. Other industries are shipbuilding, machinery, textiles, chemicals, and fishing. AMSTERDAM (the capital), and ROTTERDAM, and THE HAGUE are important cities.

HOLLY

Holly is an evergreen with dark green, glossy leaves. Depending on the variety, the leaves may or may not have thorny edges. Holly will produce red berries when the female plants are pollinated by pollen from male plants nearby. These berries, which are eaten by birds, are poisonous to man.

Early Christians adopted from the Romans the custom of using holly to decorate their homes at Christmas. During the ancient, midwinter festival called Saturnalia, Romans gave their friends boughs of holly to accompany new year's presents.

Sherlock HOLMES

Sherlock Holmes is one of the most famous DETECTIVES in fiction (imaginative writing). He was created by Sir Arthur Conan Doyle (1859–1930), an English doctor and writer.

In 1887, Doyle's first story about Sherlock Holmes, "A Study in Scarlet," was published. Three years later, Doyle gave up his medical practice and began to devote himself to writing. Sherlock Holmes appeared in 68 of his stories, including "The Sign of the Four," "The Hound of the Baskervilles," and "The Valley of Fear."

Holmes is depicted as a tall, thin detective with a pipe. He has a brilliant mind that can draw the right conclusions from small bits of evidence. He usually puts Scotland Yard (London police that engage in criminal investigation) to shame. Dr. Watson, Holmes's friend, lives and works with him.

At one time, Doyle tried to end the stories by having Sherlock Holmes killed. His readers, however, insisted that the detective could not be killed, and Doyle was forced to write more stories about Holmes.

HOMER

Homer was supposed to have written the two greatest poems of ancient Greece—the *Iliad* and the *Odyssey*. No one knows for certain who Homer was or when he lived, though it is believed it was some time between 1100 and 800 B.C. HERODOTUS said that Homer was a blind old man who wandered about reciting his poems. Others have argued that these two long poems were composed by several wandering minstrels, who strung together many short stories to make two long ones.

Portrait of Homer Playing the Lyre

The *Iliad* is the story of the siege of TROY, which was captured and burned after ten years. It relates the fight between ACHILLES and HECTOR.

The *Odyssey* is the story of ODYSSEUS on his journey home from the Trojan War. It describes his battles with nature, men, monsters, and gods.

HONG KONG

Hong Kong is a mountainous little island that lies off the southeast coast of CHINA. In 1841, it was taken by the British and became a Crown Colony. The colony includes other nearby islands and the New Territories on the mainland of China. The capital is Victoria, which has a large harbor.

Almost all of Hong Kong's 4.5 million people are Chinese, many of whom live in dirty, crowded shanties. It has grown into a great international trading center, handling more than a quarter of China's foreign trade. Textiles, garments, and electronic products are manufactured there.

Hong Kong has about 2000 schools and two universities. Teaching is usually in English at the University of Hong Kong, but not at the Chinese University, founded in 1963. Radio and TV stations broadcast in English and Chinese.

HOOFS

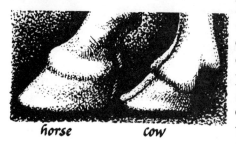

horse   cow

All hoofed animals are mammals that eat plants. They are called *ungulates* (from the Latin word *ungula* meaning a hoof). Some ungulates, including the horse, donkey, rhinoceros, and zebra, have only one solid toe or hoof. Others, including the camel, cow, deer, giraffe, goat, hippopotamus, pig, and sheep, have cloven (split) hoofs. The elephant has a small hoof on each side of its toes. Hoofs are adapted to the particular habits and ways of the animal.

HOPS

When dried, the ripe, scaly fruit of the female flowers of the hop vine produce a yellow powder. This bitter herb is used in flavoring beer and making *sedative* (soothing) medicines.

The twisting hop vine grows to a length of 15 to 25 feet (4.7–7.8 m). It

twines around ropes and along wires supported by tall poles.

In the summer, hops are harvested by pulling the vine down from the wires. Before being taken to *breweries*, the hops are dried in *oasthouses*.

England is famous for its hop fields. American hops are grown only in the Pacific states.

HORATIUS

Horatius was a Roman hero. During the 6th century B.C. before Rome became a great empire, he and two others held off an entire army of ETRUSCANS.

While the Roman army tore down the Sublician Bridge that connected Rome with the road westward, Horatius valiantly fought the Etruscans before the bridge. As the last timbers gave way, he plunged into the Tiber River and safely swam to the Roman side. According to the legend, he was rewarded with as much land as he could plow in a day.

HORN

Horn is the thick, hardened skin found in claws, hoofs, beaks, parts of feathers, fingernails, corns, and calluses. Only the outer layer of cattle and sheep horns are hard skin; bone forms the core. Ancient drinking horns were made from this outer layer of animal horns.

'A drinking horn.

Boiling water softens horn, which can then be split into thin sheets. Such sheets were used before glass as windowpanes. The pages of the old-fashioned *hornbook* (a book of lessons) for children were protected by a sheet of transparent horn.

French HORN

An old hunting horn

A French Horn

The modern French horn is a coiled-up, tapering tube of thin brass that, if straightened out, would be 11 feet (3.4 m) long. The old hunting horns on which it is based were "natural" horns, without valves and able to play only a few notes. In the 18th century, the French horn became part of the orchestra. Then it was supplied with "crooks," lengths of tubing that could be attached to change the length of the horn and thus change its pitch. Today the French horn has valves, like the modern TRUMPET.

The French horn can play very sweetly and softly, or it can produce loud, shuddering noises. The sound can be changed by putting an attachment called a *mute*, or the player's hand, into the bell (wide end).

HORNETS

Hornet is a name used for any large WASP. A very large wasp known as the European hornet is pictured here. The white-faced hornet of North America is called a "yellow jacket."

Some hornets, such as the white- and bald-faced hornets, construct papery nests made from partially digested wood. The European hornet's nest is brown, while the North American yellow jacket's is gray. Both may be found high up in trees, rafters, or other sheltered places; yellow jackets also build nests near or in the ground.

Hornets feed on larval and adult INSECTS and ripe fruit. SEE ALSO: WASPS.

HORSE

A horse is a hoofed mammal. It has strong, muscular legs for running and jumping. Each foot has one toe with a strong, hard hoof. The bottom of each foot has a rubbery pad that acts as a shock absorber. Horses have good eyesight and hearing.

There are many types and sizes of horses. Some weigh more than 2200 pounds (1000 kg). A male horse is called a stallion. A female is a mare. A baby horse, or colt, can walk and run within a few hours after it is born. Horses eat grass and hay.

The only wild horses in the world live in Asia. Wild mustangs in the United States are actually domesticated (tamed) horses that escaped and began to live in the wild again. Before cars and tractors were invented, horses were used for transportation and farming. Today, most horses are raised for racing or riding. They are also used in circuses, parades, and by some police departments.

Shire

Appaloosa

American Saddle

Arabian

HORSESHOES

During the American Revolution, both the American and British soldiers played the game of horseshoes. They tossed actual horseshoes at a stake driven into the ground, trying to make the horseshoe encircle the stake. That is still the object of the game today.

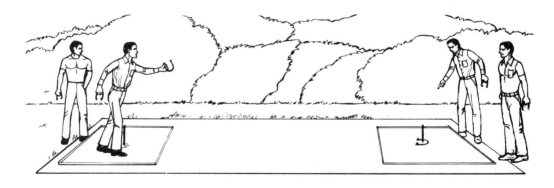

Horseshoes are now designed for pitching and each weighs 2.5 pounds (1.2 kg). There are two stakes about 40 feet (12 m) apart. When a player wraps a horseshoe around a stake, it is called a *ringer* and counts three points. When his opponent tosses one of his two horseshoes on top of it, those three points are canceled. A horseshoe leaning against a stake counts two points, and each horseshoe nearer the stake than that of his opponent is one point. A game is won when a player, or a two-man team, makes 50 points.

HOSPITALS

In the Middle Ages, a hospital was any place devoted to charity. Today it is a place where the sick are treated.

Many hospitals are large and complicated. Different illnesses need different kinds of treatment. *In-patients*, who are staying in the hospital, have to be housed in rooms or wards. *Out-patients*, who do not stay at the hospital, have to have a place to go. And there have to be rooms for taking care of emergencies, operating rooms, laboratories, and so on.

Hospital Ward

HOUSES

People have found many curious ways of taking shelter from the weather—and often from their fellow-men. In parts of the North African desert and of northern China there are few buildings, only large holes in the ground. These are the courtyards of underground houses, dug out of the earth. In South America, Africa, and other areas that have many rivers and lakes, people may build their houses over the water on wooden poles. These people depend on FISHING to provide their food.

Pit dwelling

Lake dwellings

In central Turkey there are gigantic cones of ash from volcanoes. Greek monks dug homes and churches out of these. They are still lived in, and some of the churches are still bright inside with color. In southern Italy some of the houses are cones of rough stone, with almost no windows.

403

Round huts

Until a hundred or so years ago, almost everyone built with the materials to be found close by. And most people built the kind of house that suited the weather of their country. In some cases, the house was a light shelter made of saplings and woven grass, with a roof of thatch or palm leaves. Such houses are common in central Africa, South America, and other hot places where plants grow well. In other places, the house is a solid mass of stone, mud brick, or some other earth material. Such houses are often found in lands with hot days and cold nights. The heat of the day stays in the walls to keep the house warm at night. Some of the Indians in our Southwest build groups of such houses, called *pueblos*. The Arabs, the Greeks, and the southern Italians build such massive houses too.

Houses built of mud bricks

The CASTLE is a type of house, intended to keep the inhabitants safe against enemies. Defensive towers are also to be found all across Europe. They are not as large or complicated as castles, but serve the same purpose.

But the house is not just a shelter. It is usually built in a way that the inhabitants enjoy. The Hausa people of Africa build mud houses with brightly painted fronts. The Turks like houses with living rooms on the top floor that have many windows looking out over the landscape. The Greeks, who live in the same part of the world, prefer houses with few windows. The Italian nobleman of the 16th century built himself a palace that was like a box, decorated with classical ornament and with an impressive doorway. An American millionaire of the 1920s often preferred a big, rambling house with many roofs and chimneys.

Building a hut in central Africa

Our house architecture is based largely on that of England. The first settlers of the present United States were forced at first to live in rough huts, even caves. But when they had the time and the materials to build as

A log cabin

they wished, they built the kind of houses they had known in England. The New Englanders usually put up a house made of heavy timbers, covered with clapboards. It was a big, weather-tight box with large fireplaces inside: a good house for the harsh New England winters. People in the South and in Pennsylvania usually preferred brick or local stone. These materials made the house cool in summer.

Once canals and railroads started, and once factories were built, Americans had more choice as to how to build. In New Orleans, where sitting on porches was popular, porches began to be made of cast iron in delicate patterns. In the Midwest and Far West, wood brought by train was the common building material for houses.

The earliest American houses were plain and rather medieval looking, with many gables. But the 18th-century house had much carved woodwork around its doorway and in other places. This was in a classical style also used in England. Around

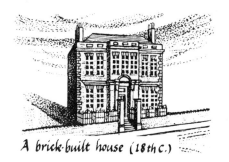

A brick-built house (18th C.)

1830, Greek architecture was fashionable; some houses even looked like temples. Later, many European styles were imitated, including the modern ones that use much plate glass.

Today, since our fuel supplies are running low, we are trying to use the heat from the sun and building so-called *solar houses*.

A modern house

HOVERCRAFT

When a hovercraft starts up, a powerful fan blows downward with enough force to lift it a little above the ground or water over which it travels. It can skim over rough ground, swampland, or a sea disturbed by the wind, smoothly and at almost 100 miles per hour (160 km/hr). Some can carry over 600 people or 40 cars.

Henry HUDSON (died 1611?)

The exact details of Hudson's birth, early life, and death are a mystery. In 1609, he sailed up the river named for him to present-day Albany. He was in search of a northern route to China in a small sailing vessel, the *Half Moon*, owned by the Dutch East India Company.

When he realized this route did not lead to the Pacific, he headed back for Holland with a weary and mutinous crew. On the way, he stopped in England, where his boat was seized. He was ordered not to return home and to explore unknown regions for England.

In 1610, he set sail in the English ship *Discovery* to look again for a northern route to China. After a stormy voyage, he and his rebellious crew reached what is now called Hudson Bay. Winter ice prevented their return to England. Food ran low. By spring, the crew mutinied, and on June 21, 1611, Hudson, his young son, and seven sick crewmen were set adrift in the bay and lost forever. SEE ALSO: HUDSON RIVER.

HUDSON RIVER

The Hudson is the major river of New York, situated in the eastern part of the state. The Adirondack Mountains are its source, and it winds 350 miles (564 km) through the Appalachian Mountain range to empty into New York Bay.

The river is navigable for 150 miles (242 km) to Troy, below which it is a half to one and a half miles (0.8–2.4 km) wide. Ocean-going vessels can travel as far as Poughkeepsie, 70 miles (113 km) north of NEW YORK CITY. This great waterway has been the historical reason for New York City becoming the world's most commercially important port.

The first European to see the Hudson was Giovanni da Verrazano in 1524. However, it is named for HENRY HUDSON who explored it in 1609. Settled by the Dutch, the valley was commercially and militarily important before the American Revolution.

The famous Hudson River School of landscape artists of the early 1800s captured the picturesque scenes of the river and the nearby Catskill mountains. SEE ALSO: HUDSON, HENRY.

HUNGARY

Hungary is a landlocked country, surrounded by Austria, Czechoslovakia, Russia, Rumania, and Yugoslavia. Most of the land is flat, but the Carpathian Mountains rise in the north and east. The DANUBE River flows through the central region, creating a fertile plain, on which wheat, corn, sugar beets, and fruits are grown. Hungary has 11 million people.

From 1600 to 1918, Hungary was part of the Austrian Empire. After World War II, the Soviets came and made Hungary a Communist country. In 1956, an anti-Communist uprising began in Budapest, the capital, but Soviet tanks and troops supressed it.

HUNS

The Huns were a savage people who had yellow complexions, short and strong bodies, flat noses, and eyes set deeply into the head.

They ruled a powerful state in Mongolia until about 80 B.C., when they moved westward. In A.D. 374, the Huns invaded eastern Europe. Under their greatest warrior, Attila, they overran much of Poland, Germany, and France, helping to destroy the Roman Empire. After Attila's death in A.D. 453, the Huns withdrew from Italy, which they had ravaged, and gradually pulled back east of the DANUBE River.

Attila, the Hun leader (from an old coin)

HYDROGEN

Hydrogen, a colorless, odorless, and tasteless gas, is the lightest element and has the simplest ATOM. It is also highly flammable. Hydrogen and oxygen gases in close confinement will unite explosively when heated. When hydrogen is burned in air or in oxygen, WATER is formed.

Hydrogen is the most common element in the universe. It is found widely in chemical combination in rocks and in all living things. Coal, oil, and natural gas all contain some hydrogen. Pure hydrogen is rarely found in the Earth's atmosphere. However, the sun and stars are mostly hydrogen.

Weather balloon (filled with hydrogen) being released.

parachute

radar reflector

instruments

Because of its lightness, hydrogen was once used in airships. However, after several airship explosions, it has been largely replaced by a safer gas, *helium*, which has almost as much lifting power as hydrogen.

Hydrogen is important in producing fertilizers, margarine, soap, ammonia, and synthetic petroleum. The devastating hydrogen bomb tested in 1954 was 750 times more powerful than the atomic bomb which destroyed Hiroshima, Japan, during World War II.

HYENA

This wolf-like animal of Africa and Asia is about the size of a large dog. Hyenas hunt at night for *carrion* (dead bodies of animals) and have a reputation for being cowardly. They have strong front legs and shoulders, and their bodies slope down to small hindquarters. Hyenas have extremely strong teeth and jaws. The well-known cry of the hyena sounds like a madman laughing.

HYMNS

A hymn is a song of praise to God sung by a congregation. The Old Testament of the Bible contains many hymns of the Hebrew people; these are called PSALMS. Saint Augustine wrote about hymns around A.D. 400. Some of the hymns of the Middle Ages are still sung.

When PROTESTANTISM began in the 16th century, hymns became even more important than they were under Catholicism. Martin Luther composed hymns. His *A Mighty Fortress Is Our God* is very well known. The Calvinists in Geneva translated the Psalms so that they could be sung.

The second book printed in English America was the "Bay Psalm Book," a hymnal (book of hymns). This was printed at Harvard College in 1640.

ICEBERGS

Icebergs are masses of floating ice that have broken away from GLACIERS or icefields, mostly coming from Greenland and Antarctica. Those from Greenland may rise 200 to 300 feet (62–93 m) above the water and measure a mile (1.6 km) across. As the picture shows, most of an iceberg lies under water, presenting great danger to ships. As they float toward warmer waters such as the Gulf Stream, however, icebergs slowly melt. The various shapes of blue, green, and white formed by the icebergs give them an unusual beauty. At night when mysteriously glowing they are especially impressive. SEE ALSO: GLACIERS.

ICELAND

A large geyser in Iceland

Iceland is the westernmost country of Europe, occupying an island in the northern Atlantic Ocean. Iceland's capital is Reykjavik, which is also the country's most important seaport. Most of the population (225,000) live along the west and south coasts, where the temperatures are fairly mild because of the North Atlantic Drift (see GULF STREAM). Most of Iceland, however, is uninhabitable, being covered with glaciers and volcanic ash. The steam and hot water from geysers throughout the country heat offices, houses, swimming pools, and greenhouses, where vegetables and fruits are grown. Many people make their living by fishing and processing fish, chiefly cod and herring.

Icelanders are descendants of Vikings who came from Norway in the 9th century A.D. The island first belonged to Norway and later to Denmark, from which in 1944 it broke its ties to become an independent republic.

IDAHO

Idaho is a rugged mountainous state that has beautiful canyons, swift-flowing rivers, peaceful lakes, and large forests of fir, pine, and spruce. The southern part of the state is dominated by the Snake River, which flows in a great curve through beds of lava deposited from volcanoes thousands of years ago. Much of the Snake River Basin is irrigated, creating extremely fertile farmland. Here are grown the famous Idaho potatoes, as well as sugar beets, wheat, and apples. The Snake River runs through Hell's Canyon, which at one point is 7900 feet (2449 m) deep, exceeding the Grand Canyon.

In 1805, the region was explored by LEWIS AND CLARK. Soon Canadians and Americans established fur-trading posts, buying animal pelts (skins) from the Indians, such as the Shoshones, Bannocks, and Nez Percés.

In 1861, gold was discovered, and men flocked to the region. Land was then stolen from the Indians for mining, farming, and ranching, and bloody battles occurred between U.S. troops and the Indians. In the 1880s, silver and lead were found. Violent fights often took place between miners and mineowners in this lawless area. The coming of the railroads in the 1890s brought new settlers and helped to build such cities as Pocatello, Idaho Falls, and Boise, the capital.

Today, agriculture is the state's biggest money earner. Manufacturing, lumbering, and mining are also important. Many tourists come to ski in winter, especially at Sun Valley in the Sawtooth Mountains. Others come in summer to boat, fish, and hunt. Idaho has about 850,000 people.

IDOLS

The Jewish and Christian religions forbid man to worship anything but the true God. They also forbid the worship of a picture or statue that is supposed to represent God. This kind of worship is called *idolatry*, and it is still popular in many countries of the world.

An *idol* is anything that is worshiped as if it were God. A person may be an idol. So may one's country, a political idea, or anything that takes a person's attention away from God.

Many pagan religions use statues to show their ideas of the gods. Some pagan worshipers do not believe an idol is a god itself. But other worshipers really believe that a god is in the idol.

When Moses came down from Mount Sinai with the Ten Commandments, he found that the Hebrews had begun worshiping a golden statue of a calf. The ancient Greeks had many statues of their gods, but most Greeks knew they were only works of art. Some central Africans make doll-like figures called *fetishes*, and worship them.

Most people in Europe and America do not worship pictures or statues; many do worship the idols of money or other things instead of the true God.

ILLINOIS

Illinois, one of the mid-western states of the U.S., consists mostly of rolling plains. In the north is CHICAGO, the largest city and one of the great transportation and business centers of the nation. More than half of Illinois's population of about 11.5 million live in or around Chicago.

The state's plains are very good for farming. Corn, soybeans, and wheat are the principal crops. Livestock is also raised. Illinois manufactures much heavy machinery. It has large deposits of soft coal, and mines most of the nation's fluorite, which is used in making steel.

Illinois was inhabited in ancient times by Indians who built earthen mounds as burial places or bases of temples. Many of these mounds are in Cahokia Mounds State Park. In 1673, Frenchmen from Canada, MARQUETTE AND JOLIET, explored the region. French priests founded the first permanent settlement at Cahokia in 1699. At that time, the main Indians of what is now Illinois belonged to six united tribes, called the "Illiniwek." The French changed this hard-to-pronounce Indian word to "Illinois." In 1763, Britain took control of the area. After the American Revolution, the U.S. government took over, making it part of the Northwest Territory in 1787. Settlers fought and defeated the Black Hawk Indians in the early 1800s. Illinois became a state in 1818.

Abraham Lincoln moved to Illinois at the age of 21. He worked in New Salem in the 1830s and later became a lawyer in Springfield, the state capital. Illinois has since been called the Land of Lincoln. SEE ALSO: CHICAGO.

IMPORTS and EXPORTS

Many countries can not produce all they need. They may need certain kinds of food for their people or certain raw materials for their factories. Because they are unable to grow some foods or to produce some materials, many countries must buy them from abroad. Products brought into a country are called *imports*. For example, the United States imports much oil from Saudi Arabia and Venezuela and much machinery and equipment from Canada, West Germany, Japan, and Britain.

Countries also sell things they produce to other countries. Products sent to other places for sale or exchange are called *exports*.

Thus, countries engage in international trade, in which they import from nations what they do not have or need, while they export to other nations what they have or produce.

INCAS

The Incas were an Indian people in South America who established a great empire in PERU. By the 14th century, the Inca empire extended thousands of miles along the Andes Mountains and far into the valleys of the AMAZON, in Brazil, and the Orinoco, in Venezuela. Their capital was at Cuzco, in southern Peru, but was moved to Quito, in Ecuador, in the early 1500s.

Inca ruins - the city of Machu Picchu

The Incas built a great network of stone roads that connected all parts of the empire. They erected bridges, AQUEDUCTS, and terraces along the mountain slopes, where they grew crops, including corn and potatoes, then unknown in Europe. The ruins of one of their cities, Machu Picchu, are shown here. Adobe bricks and stones were cut and fitted together to make large temples, palaces, and fortresses. They made metal tools, weapons, *ceramic* pottery and woven cloth. Gold was used for decoration and making jewelry.

Pottery figure of warrior

Using a number system based on 10, the Incas kept records of grain harvests, populations, animals, and historical events. They also charted the solar system, made medicines from herbs, and performed surgical operations. Their system of law and justice was stern, but fair, and their religion sometimes called for the sacrifice of human beings. They named their king the Inca, worshiping him as a Sun god.

The Incas were conquered in 1533 by the Spaniards, led by PIZARRO, who sought the Incas' gold.

INDIA

India is a very large country, with more than 625 million people. India is often referred to as the *subcontinent* of ASIA. From the HIMALAYAS in the north to the southern tip in the Indian Ocean, the country has several different regions and climates.

The northern states of India have generally a cool and dry climate. On the slopes of the hills and mountains, tea is cultivated

and cattle, goats, and sheep are raised. The capital city, New Delhi, is on the Jumna River, on whose banks further south stands the magnificent TAJ MAHAL at Agra. The Jumna flows into the GANGES, which has made a fertile plain ideal for growing rice, wheat, and barley. During the wet season, the Ganges often overflows and adds rich soil to the plain. However, in the hot season, the earth becomes hard and dry, with many cracks.

Hindu temples

A great plateau, called the Deccan, lies south of the Ganges and extends into the huge peninsula of southern India. The Deccan is separated from the coasts by mountains, called the Eastern Ghats and the Western Ghats. The Western Ghats are much higher than the Eastern Ghats, which slope gradually to the Bay of Bengal. Most of the Deccan is covered with forests, but there are small farms and pastures along the banks of the many rivers that flow eastward across the Deccan.

An Indian village

Oxen drawing plow

The climate of India is controlled by strong winds, called *monsoons*, which blow steadily in one direction for months at a time. From December to February, the winds blow from the northeast. It is cool and dry then, with only the southeastern tip of India having any rain. From March to June, the weather is hot and dry, and the sun is directly overhead. Then in June the temperature drops, and the air over the Indian Ocean, laden with moisture, is sucked in over the land. Monsoons from the southwest bring a hot, wet season when everything grows quickly. The heavy rains stop at the end of September, and during October and November the weather is warm and humid.

Cotton is grown in the southern and central regions of India. JUTE is raised for its fiber, which is used in making rope and sacks. Also, rubber, pepper, coffee, nuts, bananas, and citrus fruits are raised. India

Gathering tea

has coal and iron-ore mines; its factories produce aluminum, fertilizers, and machinery.

India, PAKISTAN, and Bangladesh formed the British Dominion of India until 1947, but they are separate nations today. Most Indians are Hindus; 1600 languages and dialects are spoken in India. SEE ALSO: DELHI, GANGES.

INDIANA

Indiana, a midwestern state of the U.S., is a land of rich prairies and rolling hills. It touches Lake Michigan in the northwest, where the city of Gary is situated—one of the greatest steel-producing centers in the world. Indiana's southern border is the Ohio River. Much of the state is in the basin of the Wabash River and its tributaries. The soil here is excellent for growing grain and raising livestock.

Indiana means "land of the Indians," for the region was inhabited by mound-building Indians long before the white man came. Later, the Miami Indians occupied the land and were joined by other tribes from the East. French fur traders and priests came to the area in the early 1700s. They founded the first permanent settlement at Vincennes on the Wabash River. The French lost control of the region to the British, who had to give up their claim after the American Revolution. Settlers in the region took land belonging to the Shawnee Indians. Tecumseh, the Shawnee chief, led several tribes on the warpath. The Indians were defeated at the Battle of Tippecanoe in 1811 and forced to move westward.

Indiana today has huge steel mills, oil refineries, and manufacturing plants. From its quarries comes much of the nation's building limestone. The state has about 5.5 million people and its capital is Indianapolis.

American INDIANS

When COLUMBUS reached the West Indies in 1492, he thought he had landed in India. Thus he called the people there "Indians." The ancestors of the American Indians crossed from northeast Asia to Alaska in ancient times. These people slowly spread east and south, into the plains and forests of North America.

The early settlers found Indians almost everywhere. Each Indian tribe had its own customs and way of living. Their shelters included tipis,

414

wigwams, lean-tos, and mud, clay, stone, and wooden houses. Indians got their food from hunting and fishing and raising corn, peanuts, pumpkins, squash, and other crops. Buffaloes were a major source of food and clothing for many Indians. Clothing was made of buffalo hides, deerskin, woven bark, and even cotton cloth. Some Indians were excellent weavers, painters, and musicians, and most all tribes lived by strict rules.

North American Indians were, however, less advanced than the Mayas and Aztecs of Central America and the INCAS of South America. Some famous North American tribes were the Mohican, Iroquois, Shawnee, Seminole, Apache, Sioux, and Shoshoni.

Wars with the white man and diseases caused the death of many Indians. For a while there were less than 250,000 Indians in the U.S. Today, with better health and education, they number about 700,000.

FAR NORTH
Naskapi

CALIFORNIA
INTER-
MOUNTAIN
Hupa

EASTERN
WOODLANDS
Iroquois

PLAINS
Sioux

INDUSTRIAL REVOLUTION

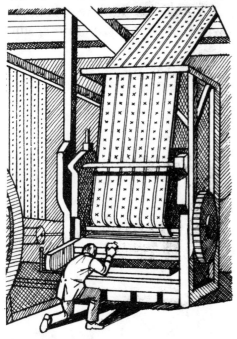

New England Power Loom, 1840s

For centuries, tools, clothing, and other goods were produced mainly by hand, either in the home or by skilled craftsmen. People also grew their own food on farms. About the middle of the 18th century, a great change occurred in people's work. Men began to make goods in large quantities in factories. They did not have time for their farms, and thus they started to buy their food in stores. This was the beginning of the industrial revolution, which changed many nations from an agricultural to an industrial economy.

Thomas Newcomen, an Englishman, invented a clumsy steam engine in 1711. Later JAMES WATT made it a workable, efficient engine. With this new source of power, machines for SPINNING and WEAVING were invented and placed in factories, where men, women, and even children made large amounts of clothing —the start of mass production.

When railroads were built in the 1800s, manufactured goods and raw materials were transported more easily to and from the factories. The invention of the BLAST FURNACE brought changes in the iron and steel industries. The telegraph was also invented, quickly speeding up communications.

Towns and cities grew as people left the country to work in the factories, hoping to make more money than they could on the farms. Many problems also arose concerning wages and working conditions. Soon people formed groups called LABOR UNIONS that worked to correct many of these conditions.

Today, industry has raised the standard of living, but it has also created many problems, such as POLLUTION of the air and water from the waste products of the factories. SEE ALSO: RAILROADS; WATT, JAMES.

INDUSTRY

Originally, "industry" meant either "work" or "willingness to work." But it has also come to mean any kind of activity that supplies *goods* or *services* (useful things or actions) in large amounts, that gives many people work, and that uses tools or machines to do so. This is only a general idea. Steelmaking is an industry, of course. Television has been called an industry whose product is entertainment and information. But agriculture, which uses machines, is usually not called an

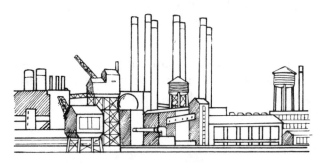

industry. And the work of a surgeon, though he uses tools, is called a PROFESSION. Transportation is sometimes thought of as COMMERCE because it takes goods to where they are sold, but it is an industry, too, because it sells a service.

INK

The earliest writing inks were made thousands of years ago by the Egyptians and Chinese. These inks were made by mixing charcoal or lamp-black (carbon collected as soot) with gum. India ink used today is made the same way.

The Romans made ink from *sepia*, a dark brown inky liquid squirted by cuttle-fish to hide themselves in the water when pursued by their enemies.

Modern writing ink is made from iron sulphate and the *tannin* in nutgalls. Nut-galls are round cases formed by oak trees around the eggs deposited by the gall fly.

Colored inks are usually made from dyes. Invisible inks used for secret writing are usually made from substances which are invisible until exposed to heat, such as milk or lemon juice.

INNS

The old-fashioned inns of Europe and colonial America were places where a traveler and his horse could find food and lodging for the night. They were also the places where a villager would go in the evening to meet his friends. Villagers exchanged and discussed news items at inns. Sometimes a play or a puppet show would be given in the yard of an inn by traveling performers.

At its best, the inn offered good food, drink, and lodging. It rented out horses, which travelers would leave at the next inn.

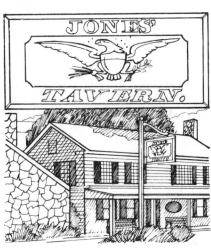

417

Some of the English inns of around 1800 became famous places for STAGECOACHES to stop. Other inns were bad in every way. Their landlords were often paid to tell bandits which travelers were worth robbing.

The railroad took much of the trade away from the inns, and many failed. But the inn became popular again when many people began to have automobiles. A large modern motel offers many of the things that the inn once did: rooms, restaurants, and entertainment.

INOCULATION

An inoculation injects bacteria (germs or viruses) into the body through a puncture in the skin. The inoculation produces a mild form of a disease and causes the body to produce *antibodies* which will kill similar bacteria should they enter the body later. A person who has been inoculated is *immune* (protected from the disease).

In the 1700s, a smallpox epidemic swept through Europe, killing more than 60 million people. Edward Jenner, an English doctor, discovered that the disease could be prevented by inoculating people with a cowpox *vaccine*. People receiving this vaccination had a mild form of the cowpox, but they did not get smallpox.

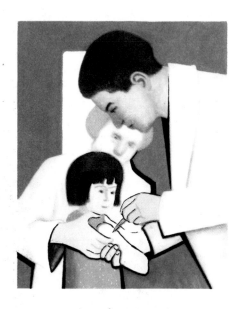

Inoculations Protect Children from Disease

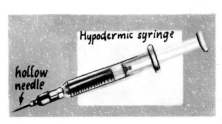

Today, in countries where smallpox vaccinations are required, the disease is almost nonexistent.

A Frenchman, LOUIS PASTEUR, learned in the 1800s that bacteria cause most diseases. He developed inoculations to prevent other deadly diseases, such as rabies, cholera, and anthrax.

Today, measles, poliomyelitis, scarlet fever, and whooping cough can all be prevented by inoculations. Typhoid fever and diphtheria, can be controlled by inoculation.

Inoculations of antibiotics such as penicillin are often given to help stop a disease.

418

INQUISITION

After the 6th century A.D., the Roman Catholic Church tried and punished some *heretics*, people who questioned the laws and beliefs of the Church. In the 13th century, special courts were founded by the Church for the purpose of examining and punishing heretics, and they were known as the Inquistion (inquisition means examination). They grew strong in Italy, France, Portugal, and Spain, but never in England or Germany. In the late 16th century, they were introduced into Mexico and Peru, in the Western Hemisphere.

A heretic is burned at the stake

The courts were especially powerful in Spain in the 15th century, when the king and queen used them to control the nobles and to harass and kill the JEWS and the MUSLIMS. At that time, victims of the Inquisition were whipped, imprisoned, hanged, and burned alive at the stake. The Grand Inquisitor was the chief officer and became so strong that he even defied the POPE, who was never in favor of these courts. The Spanish Inquisition was finally abolished in 1820.

INSECTS

Insects make up the largest class in the ANIMAL kingdom. There are at least 625,000 various kinds.

The adult insect body consists of three parts: the head, thorax, and abdomen.

On the head are two large *compound eyes*, each made up of thousands of very tiny eyes. Many insects may also have *simple eyes* as well. Most have ANTENNAE (feelers) on the head as organs for smell and touch.

Insects are ARTHROPODS, having six jointed legs. They may have up to two pairs of wings. Both the legs and the wings are attached to the thorax. A series of airtubes connected to holes in the skin of the abdomen serve as breathing organs.

1. Beetle 4. Fly   (a) head (b) legs
2. Ant   5. Mosquito (c) wings
3. Wasp   6. Bee   (d) thorax (e) abdomen

Most insects go through a *metamorphosis* (a change in body structure) as they grow to adulthood. The caterpillar and cocoon stages of a butterfly are examples of the *larval* and *pupal* stages of development. SEE ALSO: ARTHROPODS.

INSURANCE

Accidents happen to people, and when they do they can be very expensive. Suppose you need long and complicated medical treatment, or that your house burns down, or that your car is wrecked. If you have the right kind of insurance, you need pay little or nothing out of your own pocket.

An insurance company makes its living by taking *premiums* (regular payments) from people in return for promising to pay if accidents happen to them. The company figures that it is likely to make more money than it has to pay out. If you want to *insure* your life, so that some other person gets paid if you die, the company will want to know how likely you are to live a long time. It will probably have a doctor examine you. If you want to insure your house against fire, it will find out how it is built and how good your fire protection is.

If the company is satisfied, it will write a *policy*. This is a document that states what is being insured, what accidents the policy covers, what the premium is, and who the *beneficiary* (person who gets the money) is. If an accident happens, the beneficiary sends the company a *claim* for the money. The money paid by the company is the *settlement* for the claim.

INTERNAL-COMBUSTION ENGINE

An internal-combustion engine is so called because a mixture of air and gasoline or oil is exploded in its CYLINDERS to give the force that moves the pistons. The pistons move rods that crank the engine's drive shaft around. A heavy flywheel on the drive shaft helps the engine to move steadily. So does having the pistons in different places at any one time.

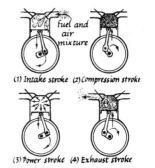

(1) Intake stroke (2) Compression stroke

(3) Power stroke (4) Exhaust stroke

There are different kinds of internal-combustion engines. The *gasoline engine* (see AUTOMOBILE) works on a mixture of gasoline and air that is shot into the cylinder, then exploded by a spark. The *diesel engine* runs by compressing air until it is so hot that oil, shot into the cylinder, explodes at once.

In most engines, four *strokes* are needed in any one cylinder. In the *intake stroke* the piston moves down, sucking air and fuel into the cylinder. In the *compression stroke*, the air and fuel are compressed as the piston moves up. In the *power stroke*, the fuel and air mixture explodes, driving the piston down to help run the engine. And in the *exhaust stroke*, the piston moves up, driving out the burned gases. This is a four-stroke *cycle*. Some engines have just a two-stroke cycle.

Internal-combustion engines are used in automobiles, motorcycles, and other road vehicles. They are also used in many ships and in some power plants. SEE ALSO: AUTOMOBILE, ENGINE.

IOWA

Iowa lies in the Great Plains of the mid-western United States. This state's western border is the Missouri River and the Big Sioux River, which flows into the Missouri. Its eastern border is the Mississippi River. Iowa has wonderful farmland, ideal for growing corn and soybeans and for raising pigs and cattle.

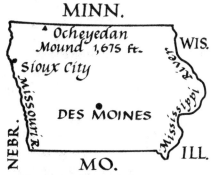

Prehistoric Indians, known as Mound Builders, lived in this area and built many earthen burial and temple mounds. When MARQUETTE AND JOLIET, French explorers, visited here in 1673, there were several Indian tribes, such as the Sauk, Sioux, and Fox. The Indians allowed Julien Dubuque to mine lead near the Mississippi—in the area of the city named after him. The U.S. obtained the region as part of the Louisiana Purchase in 1803. Fighting occurred between the white settlers and the Indians. Black Hawk, a Sauk chief, was defeated in 1832, and soon most of the Indians were pushed out of the area. Iowa became a state in 1846.

Settlers flocked to the state when news of its fertile farmland spread. They came with strong oxen, because they had heard that horses and mules could not pull plows through the tough grass-covered earth, known as prairie *sod*. Thus, the early farmers were called "sodbusters."

Iowa is one of the nation's chief agricultural states. It also produces much farm machinery and processes food. Each summer the state's farm and industrial products are exhibited at the famous Iowa State Fair, held in Des Moines, the capital. There are nearly 3 million people in Iowa.

IRAN

Until 1935, Iran was officially called PERSIA, and it is still widely referred to by that name. Today the country is only a small part of the old Persian Empire, but it is nevertheless very large—about the size of Alaska. Its population of more than 34 million consists mostly of MUSLIMS.

Situated in southwest ASIA, Iran has barren mountains, hot deserts, and grassy valleys where wandering peasants keep sheep, goats, and camels, whose wool and hair are used in the famous Persian carpets.

One of the gates of old Tehran

421

In the northwest and along the coasts are fertile lands suitable for growing cotton, sugar beets, rice, and fruits. The country has coal, chromite, copper, iron, and sulphur, but its wealth comes mainly from oil, which lies in vast amounts beneath the deserts.

Tehran, the capital, and Isfahan are great cities with many beautiful buildings, mosques, and palaces. SEE ALSO: PERSIA.

IRAQ

Iraq borders on Turkey in the north, on Iran in the east, on Saudi Arabia in the south, and on Syria and Jordan in the west.

An oil refinery, Iraq

The country's central area, between the Tigris and EUPHRATES Rivers, has rich soil suitable for growing dates, tobacco, cotton, and grain crops. Oil is, however, Iraq's most important natural resource.

Its population of 12 million are mostly MUSLIMS, who live on farms or in villages. Some work in industries in Baghdad, the capital, and in Basra, the chief port, near the Persian Gulf. The southwest, part of the Syrian Desert, supports a group of nomadic (wandering) shepherds, who raise goats, sheep, cattle, and camels.

The history of Iraq goes back 5000 years, to the time of SUMARIA, UR, and BABYLON. In 538 B.C., it was conquered by PERSIA, and later seized and ruled by several other conquerors. The Turks ruled it from 1638 until World War I, when the British took control. In 1932, Iraq became independent.

IRELAND

Ireland, often known as Eire (the Irish name for the whole island), has a flat central plain and massive granite cliffs and rugged headlands on the west coast, facing the Atlantic. Ireland has many lakes and rivers, and steady winds from the ocean give the country a moderate and moist climate.

Ireland lies west of GREAT BRITAIN, and is divided into two parts. The six northeastern counties form Northern Ireland (Ulster), which is part of the United Kingdom. The remaining 26 counties make up the independent Republic of Ireland, with Dublin as its capital.

The Irish people are mainly descendants of the CELTS that settled there more than 2000 years ago. *Gaelic* (the ancient Celtic language) is spoken by many Irish, who also use English. More than 90 percent of its 3.25 million people are Roman Catholics.

The lush pastures of Ireland support a large cattle and dairy industry. Irish beer, whisky, woolen goods, meat, and dairy products are valuable exports. Small industries and homes in Ireland burn peat (a soft form of coal) for energy and heat, and peat diggers with their ponies and carts are often seen on the roads.

For many years the English ruled the island. In 1949, they recognized the independence of the Republic of Ireland, but retained control of Northern Ireland. Today, the Irish Catholics continue to fight the English and the northern Protestants for control of Northern Ireland. This struggle has caused much bitterness, violence, and bloodshed.

IRON

Iron is a tough, hard metal that has been known for at least 3800 years. In its pure form it is a chemical ELEMENT. It is hardly ever found pure, though, except in meteorites (see METEORS).

Iron was probably discovered when a hot fire was lighted against a ledge of ORE-bearing rock. When first made, it was probably not fully melted. A charcoal fire, fanned by a blast of air, reduced the iron to a pasty lump, which was beaten to drive out the *slag*, or useless part of the ore, The result was called *wrought iron*. This was a tough iron that resisted pulling well and was useful for structural work of all sorts.

When the BLAST FURNACE was invented, it became possible to produce *cast iron*. The blast furnace produced *pig iron*, which was remelted and refined in furnaces called *cupolas*, and poured into molds to make castings. Cast iron is easier to make than wrought iron, and because molds are used, thousands of cast-iron objects can be produced, all exactly

423

ladle holding molten steel

ingot molds

alike. Delicate decorative work and heavy plumbing pipes can both be made of cast iron. It is very hard and resists wear very well. It does not resist pulling as well as wrought iron.

Pig iron can be turned into wrought iron through *puddling*. A special furnace introduces oxygen to the melted iron. This causes the impurities in the iron to separate from the iron in the form of slag.

Pig iron is also used for making STEEL. There are many kinds of steel, since different processes add or remove

different chemicals. Even the different ways of cooling hot steel are important in deciding what sort of steel it is going to be. Steel is really a form of iron. It has more carbon than wrought iron and less carbon than cast iron. It can be stronger than wrought iron, can be ground to a very fine edge, can be used to make delicate springs, like those in watches, or can be made to resist rusting. Wrought iron is not much used any more; steel has taken its place.

There are several possible ways of making steel. Almost all use pig iron from the blast furnace, but some also use steel scrap or refined ore. The first steel was made before 1200 B.C. by putting wrought iron in contact with hot charcoal. This increased the carbon content of the iron. In 1740, English steelmakers began to melt wrought iron in *crucibles* (fireproof pots) to create a high-quality steel. Around 1850, an American, William Kelly, and an Englishman, Henry Bessemer, invented a machine that turned iron into steel by blowing air through it to burn off impurities. They did not know of each other's work, and the machine is called the *Bessemer converter*. In 1864, the *open-hearth furnace* was invented. The iron was placed in a shallow basin under a brick roof, and a flame of hot air and hot gas played over it. Today the heat from an electric arc or from a fire into which pure oxygen is pumped is often used.

In every case, molten steel pours from the furnace into huge ladles, which carry it off to be cast. Usually the steel is poured into molds to make *ingots*, tall pieces of steel. The ingots are allowed to get solid, then are "soaked," that is, heated by gas jets until they are of the same heat through-out. Then they go to the rolling mill. There they pass between rollers that

424

squeeze them into various shapes that the steel mill's customers want: railroad track, structural beams, plates, rods, and many others. A piece of steel may be worked over many times before it takes its final form.

There is a new process called *strand casting*. The steel is poured from a ladle into a machine that turns it into a long steel bar.

Modern iron and steel making is a very scientific process, though it may not look that way at first. Chemists and other scientists have to watch everything that is done. SEE ALSO: BLAST FURNACE, STEEL.

IRRIGATION

In regions where there is little rain, land can often be made productive by bringing water to it. In ancient Mesopotamia, the Tigris and EUPHRATES Rivers brought water to the desert by a system of canals. Irrigation has been practiced for more than 3000 years in Egypt. The *shaduf* and the treadmill are two ancient methods of irrigation still used in Egypt.

A shaduf

Treadmill irrigation

Egypt, the United States, Russia, India, Africa, and China have constructed immense dams which reserve flood waters for use in irrigation. Pumps carry water from the reservoirs produced by these dams into canals, concrete channels, or specially-dug tunnels under hills and mountains. Pumping stations keep the water moving. Gravity may be used to allow the water to flow from feeder canals into the fields and rows of sprinklers may water the crops.

Irrigated farms yield about twice as much as the average farm. In combination with other modern techniques of soil management, the average farm production can be increased threefold.

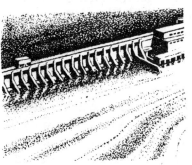

Washington IRVING (1783–1859)

Rip Van Winkle's long sleep and Ichabod Crane's attempt to flee from the headless horseman were incidents in stories created by Washington Irving about 150 years ago. The first American author to be honored abroad, Irving is known as "the father of American literature."

As a boy, he was a sickly child living in New York City. He loved to spend his hours listening to stories about the Dutch who settled New York. When he began writing, he used Diedrich Knickerbocker as his pen name.

Much of his adulthood was spent in Europe. Many of his stories are about Europe and Europeans, but his most famous books are about the stories he heard as a child in America. *The Sketch Book* contains his best works.

ISAIAH

Isaiah was probably the most famous of the Hebrew prophets in the Old Testament. He lived during the late 8th and early 7th century B.C. He had great influence over the Hebrew people and warned the four Kings of Judah about making unwise political treaties. Isaiah reminded the Hebrews that they were supposed to be the people of God. The kings paid little attention to his prophecies, and later NEBUCHADNEZZAR attacked and destroyed Jerusalem, taking the Hebrews into captivity. Isaiah kept a record of his prophecies, and it is now the Book of Isaiah in the Old Testament.

ISIS

Isis was a nature goddess of the ancient Egyptians. They believed that she worked with Osiris, the king and judge of the dead, and with Ra, the sun god and universal creator. Isis was the personification of the moon, and she was often represented with a cow's head or cow's horns. Gradually other people of the Mediterranean area began to worship Isis.

The head of Isis, showing her special headdress

The Greeks called her Athena and Demeter. Her worship became one of the chief religions of the Roman Empire, opposing early Christianity.

ISLAM

Six hundred million people belong to a religion called Islam. The people are called MUSLIMS.

Muslims believe in one god, who is called *Allah*. They accept Jesus as a prophet, but they believe the supreme prophet of Islam is MUHAMMAD. Muhammad was born in Arabia around A.D. 570. He lived in Mecca, an Arabian city where there was already a shrine to Allah called the *Kaaba* (see picture at right). Most Arabs were pagans, worshiping many gods, but Muhammad preached that Allah was the only god that really existed. He taught generosity and fairness as well as worship of Allah.

Muhammad became unpopular with the political leaders of Mecca, and he and his followers had to flee to Medina. Their flight is called the *Hegira*. It took place in A.D. 622, and the years of the Muslim calendar date from it.

In Medina, Muhammad became a political leader. He began to fight, and by the time of his death he had conquered a large part of Arabia.

The Muslims continued to conquer after his death. They were supposed to regard each other as brothers, but were allowed to attack non-Muslims. Sometimes they forced the people they conquered to become Muslims, but sometimes they allowed Christians and Jews to practice their own religions.

They rapidly overran all of North Africa and spread into Asia, converting such peoples as the Turks and the Mongols. They took over most of Spain, and in the 8th century got as far north as central France. The Turks moved westward into Europe. They were turned back from Vienna in 1683. There are many Muslims also in southeast Asia and in Pakistan. The Black Muslims in the United States are well known.

The history of Islam is very complicated. There is a major dispute over who was the rightful leader after Muhammad's death. Some Muslims believe in things that others do not. Some Muslims will do things that others will not.

All Muslims believe that Allah is the only god, and that Muhammad is his messenger. They believe that the KORAN, the holy scripture of Islam, was dictated to Muhammad by Allah. And they believe that a Muslim has five duties: 1) to state his belief in Allah and Muhammad; 2) to pray five times a day; 3) to give part of his wealth to the poor; 4) to go without food, drink, or tobacco from sunrise to sunset one month of the year; and 5) to make a pilgrimage to Mecca and the Kaaba. These are the Five Pillars of Islam.

427

ISRAEL

The country of Israel occupies part of the ancient land first called Canaan in the Bible and later called PALESTINE. Situated on the eastern shore of the Mediterranean, Israel is about the size of New Jersey and has a population of more than 3.5 million. Tel Aviv with its port at Jaffa is the largest city. JERUSALEM, the capital, is a holy city for Jews, Christians, and Muslims.

Oranges, grapefruits, grapes, olives, cotton, and grain crops are grown on the fertile coastal plain, where one type of farming community, called the *kibbutz*, is common. People live and work together on a kibbutz, sharing food, farm equipment, and money earned from the crops.

Israel was established in 1948, under the leadership of David Ben-Gurion, as a homeland for the Jews. Since then, it has had to defend itself against hostile Arab countries. During the "Six Days War" of 1967, Israel captured land from Syria, Jordan, and Egypt. In April, 1979, Israel signed a treaty with Egypt, attempting to end over 30 years of conflict in the Middle East. SEE ALSO: JERUSALEM.

ISTANBUL

Istanbul, the chief city and seaport of TURKEY, was founded about 660 B.C. and was called Byzantium until A.D. 330, when Emperor CONSTANTINE made it his capital and renamed it Constantinople. Its name was officially changed to Istanbul in 1930.

Istanbul was a crossroads for trade between east and west. Built on seven hills, the city on the Bosporus saw many ships with rich cargoes sail into its fine harbor, known as the *Golden Horn*. In the Middle Ages, Istanbul had more than 1 million inhabitants and was the richest, most splendid city in the world. For centuries, it preserved its ancient artistic and literary treasures and defended Christianity against the Muslim invaders. In 1453, it was sacked by the Turks, but the city soon flourished again under the sultans (Islamic rulers).

Many MOSQUES, palaces, monuments, baths, and fountains were erected or restored from former days.

Perhaps the most beautiful structure is Hagia Sophia, or Santa Sophia, a masterpiece of Byzantine architecture. Built in A.D. 532–37, it was an early Christian church until it was converted into a Turkish mosque in 1453; it is now a museum. SEE ALSO: TURKEY.

ITALY

The peninsula of Italy, extending 700 miles (1127 km) into the Mediterranean, is shaped like a boot. The ALPS are along Italy's northern border with France, Switzerland, and Austria. A little further south is the wide, fertile Po River valley, where farmers grow wheat, rice, flax, and grapes. The great industries of Italy are located here, too. In the cities of Milan and Turin and the ports of Genoa and VENICE are huge factories, producing machinery, automobiles, shoes, textiles, and chemicals. Much marble and alabaster is quarried in northern Italy.

In the rice fields, Northern Italy

The Apennine Mountains run down the center of Italy, and to the west of these is a fertile region where farmers cultivate olives and grapes for wine. Crops grow even on the lower slopes of the active volcano, VESUVIUS. Two famous, old cities in central Italy are Florence and ROME, the capital.

There are few cities south of Naples, and the people in the south are generally poor and work very hard to earn a living. Crops are often grown on steep hillsides, where the soil is poor. Little water is available here for irrigation, for most streams dry out during the hot summers.

429

Ponte Vecchio   *Florence*

From the 8th to 6th century B.C., the ETRUSCANS lived in central Italy. They conquered much land, but were unable to take over the entire peninsula. The Roman people later conquered the whole of Italy, and by 27 B.C. they ruled a vast empire, stretching from England to the Middle East. The Roman Empire survived for about 500 years, until many tribes from the north invaded. The country was split into several states, some of which, like Genoa and Venice, became rich and powerful. By 1860, Count Cavour, prime minister of Sardinia, had united most of northern Italy, and Giuseppe Garibaldi and his army had seized southern Italy. By 1870, the peninsula had been united as the Kingdom of Italy, and it had its first king. Later Italy's rulers became more interested in their power, and in the 1920s the Italian people accepted Benito Mussolini as their dictator. Mussolini organized a fascist government and signed a treaty with Adolf Hitler. Italy was defeated in World War II, and the people voted in 1946 to become a republic.

Italy has had a great influence on Western civilization. In the MIDDLE AGES, she produced great poets like Dante and Petrarch, and famous painters like Giotto. In the RENAISSANCE of the 15th and 16th centuries, some of the world's greatest painters, sculptors, poets, and architects lived in Florence. Michelangelo and LEONARDO DA VINCI, who was a scientist as well, created masterpieces as artists. In the early 1600s, the first operas were written and perfomed in Italy. SEE ALSO: ROME, VENICE.

IVORY

Ivory comes from the teeth or tusks of the HIPPOPOTAMUS, the WALRUS, the WHALE, and the ELEPHANT. Most commercial ivory is obtained from the tusks of the African elephant. Natives collect it from elephants who have died naturally.

Ivory has been prized for ornamentation since prehistoric days. Today, ivory is used in making piano keys, billiard balls, chessmen, and small pieces of jewelry.

Chinese artists have used ivory as a material for centuries. Delicate carvings of animals and flowers have been produced on Chinese fans, bird cages, boxes, and combs. The Japanese are also highly skilled in the art of ivory carving.

JACKAL

The jackal is a wild dog found in Asia, Africa, and southern Europe. It hunts at night, sometimes in packs, feeding mostly on small animals and carrion (dead flesh), but will scavenge for anything. Jackals have been known to follow or lead lions and other larger *carnivores* (meat-eaters) to their prey and feed upon their leftovers. The jackal is a menace to farm animals.

Jackals prefer high ground, hiding in burrows and caves during the day. At night their blood-curdling howls are often heard.

Andrew JACKSON (1767–1845)

Andrew Jackson, the seventh President of the United States, fought in the American Revolution when he was 13 years old. Though he had little schooling, Jackson studied and became a lawyer. He served briefly as a U.S. Representative and Senator from the new state of Tennessee. Afterward, he was appointed a judge in the Tennessee supreme court.

During the WAR OF 1812, he became a military hero. He won a decisive victory against the British at New Orleans. His soldiers named him "Old Hickory," because he was so tough. In 1818, he led a military expedition to Florida, where he put down an uprising of the Seminole Indians.

In 1824, Jackson ran for President and won the most votes, but not a majority (more than half). The election was decided by the U.S. House of Representatives, which chose JOHN QUINCY ADAMS. However, Jackson won easily in 1828 and became "The People's President," as a Democrat.

He gave many political jobs to his friends and fought the Bank of the United States, accusing it of favoring rich people. Many liked his noisy, rough ways. Jackson was reelected President in 1832.

Though "Let the people rule" was his slogan, he believed that the laws must be obeyed. When South Carolina refused to collect a federal tax on imported goods, Jackson ordered troops and warships to Charleston to enforce the law. SEE ALSO: WAR OF 1812.

JAGUAR

The jaguar is the largest and fiercest American wildcat. Found from southern Texas through South America, jaguars are especially plentiful in the dense forests of Brazil and Central America. Jaguars look like LEOPARDS but are heavier. Their yellowish brown fur with black spots *camouflages* them as they lie motionless along a tree branch.

Jaguars feed on deer, peccaries (wild pigs), monkeys, birds, turtles, fish, and any other animal they can find. They sometimes kill horses, sheep, and cattle. They rarely attack man but are a favorite target of big-game hunters.

JAM

Jam is slightly crushed fruit that is preserved by boiling it with sugar. *Pectin*, a chemical in ripe fruit, causes the hot syrupy liquid to set (jell) as it cools. Some fruits, low in pectin, such as strawberries and cherries, must have the substance added. Lemons, oranges, gooseberries, or currants may be used to obtain the necessary pectin. Liquid or powdered pectin can be bought to set jams.

Jams are also called preserves. *Marmalade* is jam made with small bits of oranges or lemons. When the crushed fruit is strained out, the remaining jelled liquid is called *jelly*.

If plain jam or jelly is stored in sealed jars, it can be preserved for at least a year.

1 lb fruit, 1 lb sugar, some water, makes 2 lbs jam.

JAMAICA

Jamaica is a mountainous island in the WEST INDIES, situated 90 miles (145 km) south of Cuba. It won independence from Britain in 1962, but remains part of the British Commonwealth of Nations. Its capital is Kingston, the largest city. Jamaica is about the size of Connecticut.

Along the coast the temperatures range from 80° to 90°F (27°–32°C), while in the high mountains they go down to 40°F (4°C). It has tropical

Home of a Jamaican peasant

jungles, where mahogany and other valuable kinds of wood are grown. Much of the island has fertile soil for the growing of sugar cane, bananas, coffee, and marijuana.

COLUMBUS visited Jamaica in 1494. The Spanish killed the Arawak Indians, the original inhabitants, and ruled the island until the British seized control in 1655. It became a haven for many pirates who roamed the Caribbean Sea.

Many of its 2.25 million people are descendants of the thousands of Negro slaves who were brought to Jamaica in the 18th century to work on the sugar plantations. Most are very poor. Recently, Jamaica's socialist government has moved to take control of the rich bauxite mines owned by foreign companies.

Jamaica

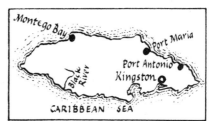

JAMES I (1566–1625)

James I was the son of MARY, QUEEN OF SCOTS, and a cousin of Queen ELIZABETH I of England. When his mother had to give up the throne of Scotland, he became King James VI of Scotland. Later, after Queen Elizabeth I died in 1603, he was crowned King James I of England, ruling both Scotland and England.

He believed that God, not the people, gave him, the king, the right to rule. His "divine right of kings" made him unpopular with the people. While he reigned, JAMESTOWN, the first permanent English settlement in America, was founded in 1607 in Virginia, being named after him. He also authorized a translation of the Bible into English, known as the *King James Version*.

Jesse JAMES (1847–1882)

Jesse James, the famous American OUTLAW, was born in Clay county, Missouri. At only 15 years of age, he joined a band of guerrillas that was raiding towns in Kansas and Missouri.

In 1866, Jesse James and his brother, Frank, organized their own band of outlaws. The "James gang" acquired a worldwide reputation for bold robberies of banks and trains. The gang killed many innocent people and terrorized the West. Finally, the governor of Missouri offered a reward of $10,000 for the capture of Jesse James, dead or alive. A member of his own gang turned traitor and shot and killed Jesse James in his home in Saint Joseph, Missouri. Many popular stories and songs have been written about James's reckless life as an outlaw.

JAMESTOWN

Jamestown was the first permanent English settlement in America. It was established in 1607 on a marshy peninsula beside what is now the James River in southeastern Virginia.

In honor of the English king, JAMES I, the colonists named their community "King James His Towne," which was later shortened to Jamestown. At first, food was very scarce there. Many would have starved if CAPTAIN JOHN SMITH, the colonists' leader, had not traded for food with the Indians. He also urged the colonists to grow their own food. However, during the severe winter of 1609–10, known as the "starving time," many died of sickness and hunger.

In April, 1610, Lord De La Warr arrived from England to find that the colonists were about to abandon the settlement. He persuaded them to stay and sent for supplies from England. Soon the colony began to prosper. Tobacco was first grown there by John Rolfe, who learned about it from the Indians.

JAPAN

Japan consists of four main islands and many smaller ones, lying off the coast of east Asia. The total area is about twice the size of Oklahoma, with a population of 113 million.

The coast of Japan is deeply indented, and the inland region is mountainous. There are about 50 volcanoes, most of which are inactive, such as Fujiyama, the highest mountain in Japan (12,388 ft. or 3840 m). It stands 60 miles (97 km) southwest of TOKYO, the capital, and the Japanese regard it as

434

sacred. Fujiyama is on Honshu Island. Many Japanese and foreign tourists climb to the top of the mountain each summer.

The climate of Japan varies from the north, where there are cool summers and cold winters, to the southernmost island, where a subtropical climate exists.

The Japanese grow much of their food, despite the little available land for farming. They have built special terraces on the lower slopes of mountains for growing rice and tea. They also cultivate SOYBEANS, wheat, and many kinds of fruit. The seas around Japan are rich with fish, which is a major food of the Japanese, as well as one of their chief exports.

Modern buildings in Tokyo

After WORLD WAR II, Japan became a great industrial power, despite having few natural resources. Much iron ore and coal are imported from other countries to be used in the production of steel. Most of its oil comes from the Middle East. Today, it is the largest shipbuilder, especially in the construction of supertankers, and the second largest automobile manufacturer in the world. Also, Japanese television sets, radios, cameras, and other electrical products are exported around the world.

MARCO POLO, who went to China in the 13th century, wrote about Japan in his

diaries. However, Portuguese sailors in 1543 were the first Europeans to visit the land. Later the Japanese rulers feared that Europeans might conquer Japan, and so they shut out many foreigners for more than 200 years. The emperors, who ruled Japan for thousands of years, were believed to be descended from the sun god. They had absolute power until after World War II, when they had to give up most of it. Today, Japan is a constitutional monarchy, having an emperor with no real power, a prime minister, and a legislature. SEE ALSO: TOKYO.

JAPANESE BEETLE

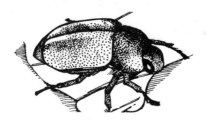

The Japanese beetle is an insect pest that was accidentally brought into New Jersey from Japan in 1916 and has since spread throughout the eastern United States. The adult beetles are a bright metallic green with coppery brown wing covers. Japanese beetles often attack a plant in great numbers and strip it of all its leaves and early ripening fruit.

The females lay their eggs underground in July and August. When the eggs hatch in two weeks, the white grubs feed on grass roots until they hibernate (sleep) for winter. These larvae can cause much damage to lawns and golf courses.

Biologists have discovered sprays and other methods to control this pest. Certain wasps which feed on the larvae are being brought here from Japan. There are also bacteria, fungi, viruses, and roundworms which can be introduced to infect the larvae with diseases. SEE ALSO: BEETLE.

JASON

Jason was one of the bravest men in Greek mythology. He was supposed to have been brought up by a CENTAUR, named Chiron, because his uncle had killed his father, the king, and seized the throne. Later, when Jason demanded his rightful kingdom, his uncle told him he could earn it by fetching the Golden Fleece—the wool of a magic, golden ram.

With other brave men, Jason was said to have sailed in a ship called the *Argo* to Colchis, on the shores of the BLACK SEA. His crew was called the *Argonauts*. After a dangerous voyage, they reached Colchis, where Jason with the help of Medea, the king's magical daughter, captured the fleece. Later Jason married Medea, but tired of her and married another princess. In great anger, Medea killed the princess and her own children. Jason, in grief, killed himself.

JAZZ

Jazz is an American art form known all over the world. There is no really good definition of jazz. It keeps changing as one creative musician after another tries new things. What is true of one kind of jazz may not be true of another. But it is more or less true to say that in jazz, soloists *improvise* (make up their own ways of playing) against a background of harmonies and rhythms decided on before a piece is played.

Jazz began with purely Negro music, old west African songs and the spirituals and work songs of the slaves in the South. When the slaves were freed after the Civil War, they also began to play white songs and dance music. All these things mixed together by the 1890s to become the first jazz.

In New Orleans around 1900, there were many Negro bands that played at weddings, funerals, and other such occasions. They played out of doors mostly, and the trumpet, which could be heard easily in the open air, became the most important instrument. Trumpeters would do solo improvisations on the tune the band was playing. The bands became popular, and started playing indoors in dance halls, bars, and other places. Out of this indoor playing grew jazz piano. New Orleans was the home of jazz until the First World War, when officials had many of the bars and other places closed so that the sailors and soldiers would not get into trouble.

After 1917, jazz musicians left New Orleans to look for work. Many went to Chicago, but some went to New York and even to Europe. Jazz was popular in Paris in the 1920s.

Before 1920, many people thought that jazz was not respectable. But it became popular all over the United States during the 1920s, and records of jazz sold very well. White musicians began to play it, and some bands began to use *arrangements*, in which every note was written down for the musicians. This was the time of Prohibition, and jazz was popular in the many illegal bars that were opened.

After Prohibition was repealed in the early 1930s, people could drink legally. Night clubs, dance halls, and other such places became popular. So did the so-called *big bands*, which played jazz arrangements to huge crowds. In the mid-1930s a special kind of jazz called *swing* was very popular, and stayed so until the Second World War. But some people felt that the big bands were not playing real, creative jazz. After the war, in the late 1940s, creative musicians introduced new forms, *bebop* and *progressive jazz*. New forms are still being invented.

The history of jazz is complicated, because the individual performers are so important. The history of jazz is, in fact, the history of people: famous soloists such as Jelly Roll Morton, Duke Ellington, Bix Beiderbecke, Benny Goodman, and Dizzy Gillespie, and many, many bands. Some of the things they did cannot even be written down musically, but must be described in the ordinary technical language of music or in the constantly changing slang of the jazz musicians themselves.

Thomas JEFFERSON (1743–1826)

Thomas Jefferson, the third President of the United States, was a brilliant student at William and Mary College, in Virginia. Later he studied law and was soon elected to the Virginia legislature.

In 1775, Jefferson was given the task of writing the DECLARATION OF INDEPENDENCE, which with few changes was adopted by the Congress in 1776. He then was a Virginia lawmaker until he was elected the state's governor. He wrote a strong law on religious freedom and tried to pass one that would gradually abolish slavery in Virginia and in the new lands added to the U.S.

Jefferson was minister to France (1785–89) and U.S. Secretary of State (1790–93). A firm believer in democracy, he wished to limit the federal government's powers to those that the CONSTITUTION specifically granted. He opposed ALEXANDER HAMILTON, who supported federal banking, and he preferred that the U.S. remain chiefly an agricultural society.

In 1796, he was elected Vice President under JOHN ADAMS. He fought for basic states' rights and the people's right to criticize their government. In 1800, Jefferson was elected President as a Democratic-Republican and reelected in 1804. While in office, he doubled the size of the U.S. with the LOUISIANA PURCHASE. He proposed the LEWIS AND CLARK EXPEDITION.

Jefferson was a man of many talents—an excellent horseback rider, musician, writer, and architect. He designed his beautiful home, MONTICELLO, in Virginia. He founded and designed the University of Virginia. SEE ALSO: DECLARATION OF INDEPENDENCE.

JELLYFISH

Jellyfish are not fish but primitive sea animals which have no backbone or brain. The transparent, umbrella-shaped jellyfish are 96 percent water and will dry up quickly and seem to disappear when washed ashore. However, when in the water, they swim very gracefully by contracting their bodies; at night, they glow faintly.

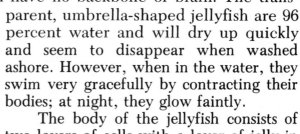

The body of the jellyfish consists of two layers of cells with a layer of jelly in between to keep it afloat. The tentacles hang down from the body and are used to sting its prey.

Some jellyfish are microscopic in size, while the largest are seven feet (2.2 m) or more in diameter with tentacles 120 feet (37.2 m) long.

The most poisonous jellyfish live in Australian waters and have a venom equal in strength to that of the Asiatic cobra, capable of killing a swimmer within three minutes.

Jellyfish lay eggs that hatch into *larvae*. The larvae attach themselves to the floor of the sea and grow into what looks like a pile of small discs. Each "disc" breaks loose and becomes a new jellyfish.

JERUSALEM

A mosque in Jerusalem

Jerusalem, the capital of ISRAEL, is built on the hills of Judea, about 35 miles (56 km) east of the Mediterranean. It is the most famous city in the Old and New Testaments of the Bible. It is a holy city for Jews, Christians, and Muslims.

About 1000 B.C., David, King of the Hebrews, made Jerusalem his capital. His son, King Solomon, built a great temple there. In 586 B.C., the Babylonians under Nebuchadnezzar took the city and seized the Hebrews. Jesus was crucified there while the Romans governed the city. Today, Christian pilgrims visit the Church of the Holy Sepulchre, where Jesus is thought to have been buried, before He rose from the dead.

Jerusalem was destroyed by the Roman emperor, Titus, who was angry because the Jews had revolted against the harsh Roman rule. In the A.D. 300s,

A street in Jerusalem

Constantine, the first Roman emperor who was a Christian, rebuilt Jerusalem and erected the Church of the Holy Sepulchre.

It was seized by Muslim Arabs in A.D. 637, who believed that Muhammad, their great leader, rose to heaven from where King Solomon's temple once stood. The Muslims built the Dome of the Rock, an important MOSQUE, on the site. Later, during the Middle Ages, the city was conquered by the Saracens (Muslim Turks), held by the Christians for a while during the CRUSADES, and then retaken by the Saracens. After the creation of the state of Israel in 1948, Jerusalem was partly in Jordan. In the war of 1967, all of Jerusalem became part of Israel and remains so today.

JESUS

Since the times of the prophets, the JEWS had been expecting a promised deliverer, whom they called the Messiah, a Hebrew word meaning the anointed (chosen) one, or the Christ. They believed that He would be a conqueror who would free their country from its enemies. Jesus of Nazareth claimed to be that Jewish Messiah.

Very little is known about the early years of Jesus' life. The New Testament of the BIBLE shows that He first came into the public eye at 30 years of age, when John the Baptist baptized Him in the Jordan River. Then Jesus went into the wilderness to meditate and pray. There Satan tempted

A head of Christ, from a medal presented by Sultan Bajazet to Pope Innocent VIII.

Him to disobey God, but Jesus did not yield to this temptation.

Jesus told simple stories (parables) to teach the truth about God. He taught that God forgave those who confessed their sins and gave eternal life to the people who had faith in Him.

People flocked around Jesus because He healed sick people. Often He spent periods of quiet times talking with His twelve closest disciples. Other religious leaders of His day grew jealous and thought He was trying to overturn their teachings. They began to plot His death.

Soon Jesus was brought to trial in Jerusalem. Jesus' enemies believed He was trying to gain too much power, and they charged that He was stirring up a rebellion against the Roman Empire. Pontius Pilate, the Roman governor, allowed the Jewish leaders to execute Him by crucifixion (being nailed to a cross).

The Flight into Egypt

After Jesus died, He was put in a tomb. Three days later, an earthquake opened the tomb and Jesus came back to life; Christians call this event His *Resurrection*. Afterward, He appeared to many of His disciples. Jesus was with them for forty days until His *Ascension* (when He rose from Earth to heaven). He told His disciples that He would return to Earth to take them to heaven too.

After His Resurrection and Ascension, Jesus' followers began to teach the *gospel* (from the Old English words *good spiel*, meaning "good news") of Jesus. They taught first in PALESTINE and later, with the help of PAUL, throughout the Roman Empire. The gospel is that Jesus gave His life to pay the penalty for sin, He rose from the dead to show His victory over sin and death, and those who trust in Him can have eternal life.

The calendar we use today is dated from the birth of Jesus, which we celebrate each year at CHRISTMAS. The calendar uses the letters "B.C." which means "before Christ" and "A.D.", which means *anno domini* (Latin for "in the year of our Lord"). SEE ALSO: APOSTLES, CHRISTIANITY, CHRISTMAS, EASTER.

Christ's body is taken down from the cross. (This picture is copied from an old painting)

JET ENGINES

The jet engine has replaced the old piston engine in large airplanes. The piston engine is a *reciprocating engine*; its parts move back and forth to produce a rotary (round) motion through cranks. In a jet engine, all parts turn around.

There are several types of jet engines. The simplest is the *ramjet*, which has no moving parts. Air is sucked through the front opening at high speed, is turned into hot gas (kerosene is the usual fuel), and escapes with great force through a narrow opening at the rear. A scientific law says that a force going

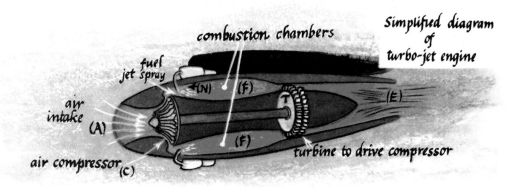

combustion chambers

Simplified diagram
of
turbo-jet engine

fuel
jet spray

(N)   (F)

air
intake   (A)

(E)

air compressor (C)

(F)

turbine to drive compressor

one way produces an equal force going the other way. The burning of the fuel gives the jet a great thrust that sends the engine forward. The trouble is that the engine must be moving already, or not enough air will be sucked into it.

Many planes therefore have *turbojet* engines. In these, a fanlike *compressor* moves the incoming air at a high rate of speed into a *combustion chamber* where it is burned. As the hot gas leaves the combustion chamber it drives

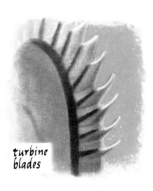

turbine blades

a TURBINE which runs the compressor. An electric motor is used to turn the compressor until the engine is running properly.

In a *fan jet*, part of the incoming air is not burned at all. This part is sucked into the engine, driven backward by a low-pressure compressor, and sent out of the engine either as a cold jet through special nozzles or through the same nozzle by which the hot gases leave. Fan jets are more economical than turbojets since they burn less fuel, but they are not so powerful.

part of propeller

compressor

turbine to drive compressor
turbine to drive propeller.

The *turboprop* engine is a propeller engine run by a turbine. Its exhaust is a jet, but is too weak to add much to the thrust of the engine.

JEWS

The early history of the Jews can be read about under the entry HEBREWS.

When the Persians conquered Babylon about 540 B.C., some of the exiled Jews returned to Judah, in south Palestine, and rebuilt Jerusalem. At this time, many Jews moved to other parts of the Mediterranean and Black Sea region. This great scattering of Jews to other countries outside Palestine was called the "Diaspora."

In Judah, the Jews were ruled successively by the Persians, Greeks, and Romans. In A.D. 70, the Romans destroyed Jerusalem, killed more than half a million Jews, and in A.D. 135 crushed Judah entirely. The Jews were scattered throughout the world.

In the centuries afterward, they were often harshly treated and persecuted. During the Middle Ages and the CRUSADES, Christians in Europe were sometimes very cruel to Jews, who were often forced to live in small, crowded areas, called *ghettos*.

In the 1930s and early 1940s, millions of Jews were killed in Europe because of the persecution incited by HITLER. However, after World War II, the state of ISRAEL was founded as a homeland for the Jews, many of whom live also in Europe and North America. SEE ALSO: HEBREWS, JUDAISM.

A Jew wearing a phylactery (a box containing sacred texts) on his forehead during worship.

JOAN OF ARC (1412?–1431)

Joan was the daughter of a farmer in northern France. She believed she heard voices and saw visions, directing her to lead an army against the English, who had controlled much of France since the time of HENRY V.

Although some people believed she was mad, she went to see the Dauphin (the French prince who had not been crowned), who was convinced Joan had powers from heaven and let her lead his troops. Joan saved the city of Orléans from the English. In 1429 the Dauphin was crowned King of France, and Joan was at his side.

A year later, the Burgundians, friends of the English, seized Joan and sold her to the English. To escape responsibility for putting her to death, the English handed her over to the INQUISITION, who tried her for heresy and witchery. Joan was found guilty and was burned at the stake.

Later the Roman Catholic Church reversed its judgment, and in 1920 declared her a saint.

JOHN

There were two early Christian leaders named John. John the Baptist was a Jewish prophet who predicted the coming of the promised Messiah. He used the ceremony of *baptism*, a washing that indicated that the baptized person wished to repent of his sins. He baptized JESUS in the Jordan River. When John the Baptist denounced King HEROD for marrying his own brother's widow, Herod had him killed.

John the Apostle wrote the fourth *Gospel* (book on the life of Christ), three *epistles* (letters to Christian congregations), and the Book of Revelation. All of these are included in the New Testament. John and his brother, James, were fishermen on the Sea of Galilee when Jesus called them to follow Him. John became Jesus' close companion, and the Bible calls him "the beloved disciple."

King JOHN (1167–1216)

King John reads Magna Carta

John was the youngest son of King HENRY II of England. He received no lands when his father died, being thus nicknamed "Lackland." However, his oldest brother, King RICHARD II, gave him much property. Later, when Richard was imprisoned in Austria on his way back to England after the Third Crusade, John plotted unsuccessfully to take the crown. When Richard died in 1199, John inherited the throne.

At this time, he fought a long war with the French king, who wanted John's nephew to be king. John is thought to have arranged the murder of his nephew. In 1204, John gave up most of his French possessions.

John also fought with the Pope, who sided later with John's enemies, the English *barons* (noblemen). The barons had been forced by John to pay much money to support the French war. In 1215, the barons forced John to sign the MAGNA CARTA, which took some power from the king and gave the barons certain rights.

Dr. JOHNSON (1709–1774)

Samuel Johnson became famous as an English writer. His most notable work was the *Dictionary of the English Language*, which was published in 1755. He also wrote poems and essays, a play and a novel, and studies of many English poets.

His good friend, James Boswell, kept an account of almost everything Johnson said and did. After Johnson died, Boswell wrote *The Life of Samuel Johnson, LL.D,* which appeared in 1791, and which is one of the finest biographies ever written. SEE ALSO: DICTIONARY.

444

JUDAISM

The religion of the Jews is Judaism. Its teachings have influenced Christianity and Islam.

The Jews believe in a single God, who created the universe and who has made a *covenant* (agreement) with *Israel*, the Jewish nation. They believe God has given Israel his *Torah*, a collection of important religious teachings. The Torah contains the first five books of the BIBLE and of ancient traditions handed down by word of mouth. It tells Israel to set an example to the world by its obedience to God's law. In return, God promised to protect Israel.

Many early *rabbis* (teachers) interpreted the Torah in order to solve the many problems of Jewish life. The rabbis' comments were written down, and over a thousand years ago they were collected into two books of many volumes called *Talmuds*.

Today, there are three main types of Judaism. *Orthodox Judaism* follows the ancient Jewish tradition very strictly. An Orthodox Jew will not eat dairy products and meat from the same dish. He will not carry money on Saturday, which is the traditional Sabbath. He will do no work on Saturday, because Jewish tradition forbids such things. *Reform Judaism* teaches that these ancient laws can be ignored without losing the true spirit of Judaism. *Conservative Judaism* is stricter than Reform Judaism and not so strict as Orthodox Judaism.

Jewish traditions call for religious exercises both at home and in the *synagogue*, the local center of Jewish worship. At home, certain prayers and blessings are to be recited. At the synagogue, the Jews recite other prayers and blessings, along with readings from the written Torah and the books of the Hebrew prophets. There are important holidays during the Jewish year. The year begins in autumn, with Rosh Hashana. This introduces a ten-day period of sorrow for disobedience to Torah that ends in YOM KIPPUR, the Day of Atonement. Other days recall important events in Jewish history, when God saved Israel from its enemies. The most important is Pesach, or PASSOVER, when God freed the Jews from their slavery in Egypt. SEE ALSO: HANUKKAH, PASSOVER, YOM KIPPUR.

JUDAS ISCARIOT

Judas Iscariot was the disciple who betrayed Jesus. For a reward of 30 pieces of silver, Judas told the soldiers that Jesus would be in the Garden of Gethsemane at a certain time. When the soldiers arrived, Judas showed them who Jesus was. He did this by giving Jesus a kiss.

Some reports say that when Judas realized what he had done, he was grief-stricken. He returned the silver and hanged himself. Other reports say that he fell headlong into a field and died. SEE ALSO: APOSTLES, JESUS.

445

JUDGES

Judges are people who make decisions based on rules. In baseball, the judge is called an *umpire* or, in other sports, a *referee*. It is he who settles disputes according to the rules of the game. Other kinds of judges decide who will win competitions such as spelling bees, beauty pageants, soapbox derby races, talent shows, and cooking contests.

The judges who have the most important decisions to make are the judges in our courts. They must see that every person who goes to court is treated fairly and is given a just decision.

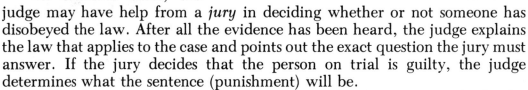

In criminal cases, the judge may have help from a *jury* in deciding whether or not someone has disobeyed the law. After all the evidence has been heard, the judge explains the law that applies to the case and points out the exact question the jury must answer. If the jury decides that the person on trial is guilty, the judge determines what the sentence (punishment) will be.

If the person who loses a case in one of the lower courts thinks the decision is unjust, he may ask to have his case reviewed by a higher court. If he is not satisfied with the decision of the higher court, he has the right to appeal his case again and again all the way up to the Supreme Court.

The Supreme Court of the United States is the highest court in the land. The nine judges (or *justices*) of the Supreme Court decide whether or not laws agree with the Constitution. If a law does not, it is declared *unconstitutional* and cannot be enforced.

The Supreme Court judges are appointed by the President, with the approval of the Senate. They are judges for life, unless they resign or are impeached.

Some famous American judges are John Marshall, Oliver Wendell Holmes, Jr., Benjamin Cardozo, Louis Brandeis, and Learned Hand.

One of the books of the Old Testament is known as Judges. It tells about the Hebrews in the Promised Land from Joshua's death to the time of Samuel.

JUNGLE

Jungles are tropical FORESTS found in parts of America, Africa, and Asia where the climate is extremely hot and wet. Burma, Malaysia, and West Africa have some of the densest jungles in the world.

Light can hardly penetrate the dense Amazon jungle

As much as 140 inches (356 cm) of rain may fall in a jungle each year. Due to the moist air, fast-growing, tangled under-growth covers the jungle floor. Some of the moss-and-vine-covered trees, in their struggle for light, grow as high as 300 feet (93 m), making the sky hardly visible. Some cleared jungle areas will become completely overgrown within a few years, and some plants bloom as often as four times per year.

Among the trees growing in jungles are the teak, ebony, mahogany, banana, and rubber. Monkeys leap and chatter among the treetops, and brilliantly colored birds and butterflies fly about. Mosquitoes and many other insects that often carry disease buzz among the foliage, and snakes slither under foot.

JUPITER

In Roman mythology, Jupiter, also called Jove, was the father of all the gods. He was also the god of the heavens and weather, particularly rain and thunder. His wife and queen of the gods was called Juno. The Greeks called him ZEUS.

Two of Jupiter's moons

Jupiter is also the name given to the largest PLANET. This planet, fifth away from the sun, is more than 1000 times the size of Earth. Jupiter takes about 12 years to orbit the sun but spins so rapidly on its axis that one day is about 10 hours long.

The illustration shows what Jupiter looks like through a telescope. It is divided into different-colored belts and has a red spot apparently floating on its atmosphere. Two of Jupiter's 14 moons or satellites are shown circling it.

The satellite Voyager I has revealed that a ring of rocky debris orbits Jupiter inside its innermost moon. It has also shown a tremendous amount of violent activity in the atmosphere of Jupiter. The red spot is a vast tornado-like region, and clusters of lightning flashes are visible in Jupiter's atmosphere. Voyager I also revealed an *aurora* (glowing lights) at Jupiter's North Pole.

447

JUTE

The tough fiber of the jute plant is used for making burlap cloth, sacks, rope, twine, and wrapping paper. This plant, which adapts well to a loamy soil in a hot, humid region, grows in Brazil, India, and Pakistan. The usefulness of this strong fiber has been known to the people of India for centuries.

Like FLAX, jute fibers are *retted* (soaked) to separate them. The fibers are then dried in the sun before being spun into yarn. Manufacturing centers for jute are Dundee, Scotland, and Calcutta, India. SEE ALSO: FLAX.

KALEIDOSCOPE

When you look throught the window at the end of this fascinating toy, you see what looks like a snowflake of many colors. Two mirrors inside, set at angles to one another, produce six reflections of bits of colored glass that move in front of a translucent window. By turning the kaleidoscope, you

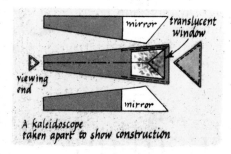

A kaleidoscope taken apart to show construction

can get an endless variety of patterns. This toy has been amusing children since it was invented by Sir David Brewster, a Scottish physicist, in 1817.

KANGAROO

Like the koala bear and opossum, the kangaroo is a *marsupial*—that is, the female carries her newborn in a pouch. Kangaroos are native to Australia, Tasmania, and New Guinea.

A baby kangaroo, called a *joey*, is only about an inch (2.5 cm) long at birth. It lives in its mother's pouch for three to four months before it begins to search on its own for food. Kangaroos are plant-eaters.

The largest kangaroos are five feet (1.5 m) long, with tails up to four feet (1.2 m) long. The strong tail provides balance while the hind legs enable a large kangaroo to jump more than 25 feet (7.8 m) and leap nine feet (2.8 m) into the air.

A small kangaroo, known as a *wallaby*, is no larger than a rabbit.

KANSAS

Kansas, a state in the central United States, has broad plains in the east and highlands and mountains in the west. It is often called the "Nation's Breadbasket" because more wheat is grown there than in any other state. Sorghum, corn, and rye are also grown, and much livestock is raised on the prairie land of Kansas. However, manufacturing earns more money than agriculture does. Aircraft, motor vehicles, and other transportation equipment are the state's chief industrial products. Most factories are in Wichita, Kansas City, and Topeka, the capital. Kansas has 2.5 million people.

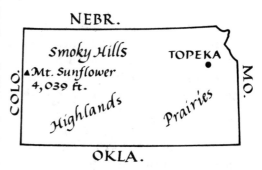

When the Spanish explorer Francisco Coronado visited the region in 1541, he came upon a number of Indian tribes, including the Pawnee, Comanche, and Kaw. The state got its name from the Kaws, who were also called the *Kansas*. French explorers claimed the area in the 1600s. The U.S. acquired most of what is now Kansas with the Louisiana Purchase in 1803. The U.S. government moved many Indians there from 1825 to 1842. Since the Santa Fe Trail and the Oregon Trail went through the territory, many settlers stopped and established farms there. During the years before the Civil War, many violent battles were fought over slavery in this U.S. territory, which became known as "Bleeding Kansas." In 1861, Kansas entered the Union as a free, non-slave state.

John KEATS (1795–1821)

John Keats became one of the greatest English poets. Trained to be a chemist and surgeon, he turned to writing poetry and joined a circle of literary men, including the English poets Percy Bysshe Shelley and Leigh Hunt. He wrote a

famous sonnet about his feelings on reading a translation of HOMER. He wrote other famous poems such as "I Stood Tip-Toe upon a Little Hill," "Ode to a Nightingale," and "To Autumn." His poetry is filled with a mysterious and strong sense of beauty and joy. "The Eve of St. Agnes" is a lovely poem about the elopement of two young lovers.

He fell passionately in love with a young girl named Fanny Brawne. The letters he wrote to her, his sisters, and his friends are among the finest and most beautiful letters ever written. He died of tuberculosis in Rome, Italy.

Helen KELLER (1880–1968)

At the age of two, Helen Keller became both blind and deaf from a severe illness. The doctors examined her, and there seemed little hope that the small girl would ever be able to hear and see again. How would Helen be able to understand and communicate with others? In 1887, the Perkins Institute for the Blind and Deaf in Boston sent a young teacher, Anne Sullivan, to help Helen.

Anne Sullivan began to use the manual alphabet—that is, she "spelled" the names of objects into Helen's hands. Anne would put her fingers in Helen's palm. The movement of Anne's fingers would mean ("spell") the certain thing that she was trying to communicate to Helen. When a stream of water flowed over Helen's hand, Anne spelled *w a t e r* into Helen's other hand.

In only three years, Helen had learned the manual and Braille alphabet and could read and write well. With Anne's help, Helen graduated with honors from Radcliffe College in 1904. She then devoted herself to helping the handicapped, traveling and lecturing throughout the world and writing many articles and books about the problems of the blind and deaf.

John F. KENNEDY (1917–1963)

John Fitzgerald Kennedy, the 35th President of the United States, came from a wealthy political family in Massachusetts. During World War II, he served as commander of a PT boat in the South Pacific. He heroically rescued an injured crewman when his boat was sunk by the Japanese. He was forced to leave the Navy because of an old back injury, which gave him pain for much of the rest of his life.

Kennedy was elected U.S. Congressman from Massachusetts in 1946. After serving three terms, he was elected U.S. Senator in 1952 and reelected in 1958. As the Democratic candidate for U.S. President, Kennedy defeated his Republican opponent, Richard M. Nixon, in 1960. Kennedy founded the Peace Corps, which sends Americans to work with people in undeveloped countries. He also urged the development of the U.S. space program and the passage of civil rights laws to help the poor and the blacks. In 1962, he successfully demanded that the Russians remove their missile bases in Cuba or risk going to war. The whole world mourned when Kennedy was murdered in Dallas, Texas, on November 22, 1963.

KENTUCKY

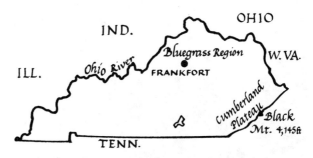

Kentucky was the first area west of the Applachian Mountains to be settled by American pioneers. In 1774, James Harrod established the first permanent settlement, Harrodsburg, in central Kentucky. The following year, DANIEL BOONE blazed the Wilderness Trail through the Cumberland Gap and founded Boonesboro. At first settlers were raided by Indians, such as the Shawnees, Wyandottes, and Cherokees. However, by the time the region became a state in 1792, the Indians had been defeated.

Kentucky extends from the Mississippi River in the west to the high Cumberland Plateau in the east. The state has good land for growing tobacco. It also has the famous bluegrass region, where thoroughbred race horses are raised. Many products are made in Kentucky, like whisky, machinery, and chemicals. Much coal is mined in the southeastern region.

Thousands of people come to Louisville each May to see the Kentucky Derby, one of the world's great racing events. Among the state's other attractions are Mammoth Cave, with 150 miles (242 km) of explored underground passages, Natural Bridge, and the birthplace of ABRAHAM LINCOLN.

Kentucky has about 3.5 million people, and its capital is Frankfort.

Captain KIDD (1645?–1701)

William Kidd, known as Captain Kidd, was a famous Scottish-born English pirate. Originally, he was a very wealthy shipowner and sea captain. During King William's War (1689–1697), he fought against privately-owned warships licensed to operate by the French government. Later, the British government hired him to put down piracy in the Indian Ocean.

By 1697, one-third of his crew had died of cholera. Those left were unpaid and threatening to mutiny, and his ship was leaking. He decided to attack the ships he had been hired to protect. He joined two of the pirates he had been assigned to capture. Arriving in the West Indies in 1699, Kidd learned that he had been declared a pirate by the British authorities. Promised a pardon, he docked at Boston where he was arrested. He was sent to London where he was tried and hanged for murder and piracy.

Afterwards, he became a legend in England and America. Contrary to popular opinion, his treasure buried at Gardiners Island, New York, was dug up by colonial authorities in 1699.

Martin Luther KING (1929–1968)

Martin Luther King, Jr., was an eloquent black Baptist minister who fought for civil rights and against racial discrimination in the United States. He won the Nobel Peace Prize in 1964 for his leadership in using nonviolent means in the fight for racial equality.

King was a well-educated man, with a Doctor of Philosophy degree from Boston University. In 1954, he became a minister of a church in Montgomery, Alabama. At that time, the black people of Montgomery had to sit at the back of the city's buses. King led the blacks in a successful boycott of the buses—that is, the blacks refused to use the buses until they could sit anywhere they wanted.

King gained national recognition and helped organize the Southern Christian Leadership Conference. This organization worked to end injustice against the blacks. Through King's efforts, the blacks received equal opportunity in schools, jobs, and housing. In 1968, King was shot and killed by James Earl Ray in Memphis, Tennessee.

KINGFISHER

The kingfisher is a bird found all around the world. It is known for its colorful *plumage* and unusual calls. Kingfishers can be found living in river-bank nests or trees. Depending on the *species*, the birds feed on everything from insects to fish to small mammals. The American Belted Kingfisher is chiefly a fish-eater, diving into the water for its prey.

Rudyard KIPLING (1865–1936)

The English writer, Rudyard Kipling, was born in Bombay, India, which was at that time a part of the British Empire.

He went to school in England as a boy and returned to India to work as a newspaper reporter. He began to write short stories about British life in India, and his first collections of stories were very successful. In 1889, Kipling returned to England, where he wrote more stories and poems about the life of

British soldiers in India, such as "Mandalay" and "Gunga Din." He married an American girl in 1892 and went to live in Vermont, where he wrote his two famous *Jungle Books* and *Captains Courageous.* Later, he went back to England and settled, and in 1907 he became the first Englishman to win the Nobel Prize in literature. Among his well-known books are the *Just So Stories* and *Kim.*

KITE

Kite flying is popular in many places. It is very popular in the Far East, where it often has a religious meaning as well as being fun. The Japanese used to fly kites that needed 200 men to get them off the ground. While our kites are usually in the form of diamonds or boxes, Far Eastern kites are often in the form of birds, fish, or flowers.

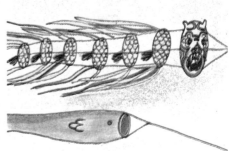

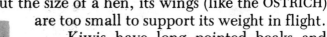

Scientists and others have used kites for practical purposes. Benjamin Franklin used a kite in 1752 to prove that lightning is electricity. Engineers have used them to get ropes across wide valleys. And scientists have used them for weather observation.

KIWI

The kiwi is a flightless bird native to New Zealand. Although a kiwi is only about the size of a hen, its wings (like the OSTRICH) are too small to support its weight in flight.

Kiwis have long pointed beaks and iron brown *plumage* that looks like hair. These *nocturnal* birds hide in burrows during the day, coming out at night to feed on worms and insects.

KNIGHTS

In the MIDDLE AGES in Europe, knights were mounted warriors who came from the upper classes. Knights were landowners who pledged allegiance (loyalty) to a lord—a prince or a king—who gave protection in return for the knights' services in battle. During the CRUSADES, religious orders of knights were formed, such as the Knights Templars and Knights Hospitalers, that fought to free the Holy Land from the Muslims.

At first, a young man became a knight after he proved he could ride a horse and use a sword. Kneeling before the lord, he was touched on the shoulder with the lord's sword, thus becoming a knight, with the title "Sir" before his first name.

Later, a young man was specially trained to be a knight. At seven or eight, he become a *page* at a lord's castle, where he learned riding, hunting, music, and good manners. At 14, he became a *squire*, an assistant to a knight who taught him to ride and fight in armor. At 21, if the squire had proved to be faithful and brave, he became a knight and made many solemn vows, kneeling in prayer before the altar of a church throughout the night. In the morning, he dressed in

armor and went before the lord, who touched him with a sword, dubbing him "knight." Then he would show his skill during a tournament with other knights. Wearing armor and carrying shields painted with their coats of arms (see HERALDRY), these knights fought each other, on horseback and on foot, with swords and lances. They were often wounded and sometimes killed.

Knights obeyed certain rules of behavior. They were kind, honorable, and helpful to women and people in distress. Often a knight wore his lady's scarf during his adventures and in battle. KING ARTHUR and his knights were legendary heroes of courage, courtesy, and duty.

Today, the king or queen of England bestows knighthood as an honor on one who has done service or something outstanding for the state.

KNITTING

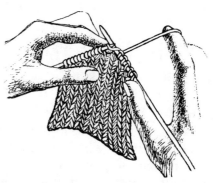

Knitting is the craft of making a piece of cloth out of loops that move in and out of each other. Usually only one piece of *yarn* (a kind of thick thread) is used. In hand work, knitting is done with two long needles. Knitted clothing can be done with all sorts of patterns, made either by putting stitches in certain places to build up the thickness of the cloth or by using yarns of various colors.

Many garments these days are knitted by machinery. Such garments are warmer and more moisture-absorbent than ordinary woven ones.

KNIVES, FORKS, and SPOONS

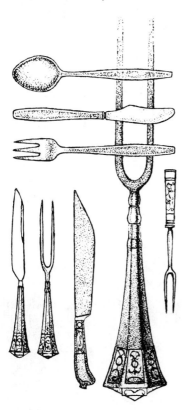

Knives were used in the time before recorded history. The first ones were made of chipped flint or sometimes of a natural glass produced by volcanos. These were probably used for cutting and sawing rather than for handling food. The Egyptians, though, had eating knives of flint. Later, bronze, silver, and steel knives were invented in various places.

Spoons are also very old. The earliest were made of baked clay, but later bone, wood, horn, bronze, and silver were used.

Forks go back to Roman times, but until the 17th century they were used in northern Europe only to serve food, not to lift it to the mouth. People used either pointed knives or their fingers. Eating with a fork was an Italian custom that reached England early in the 17th century. At first most of the English thought that table forks were ridiculous, but they were in widespread use by 1700.

We call knives, forks, and spoons for the table *silverware*, and in the past they were often of *sterling* (solid) silver or else were *plated* and had a silver coating over a less expensive metal. Today, much so-called silverware is really of stainless steel, which will not tarnish and is not expensive.

KNOTS

Knots are fastenings made with cord or rope. The art of tying knots has been known to sailors for thousands of years. There are innumerable knots used by sailors on boats and ships. One of the most useful for tying two pieces of rope or string together is the *reef*, or *square*, knot. The *bowline* forms a loop that will not slip. Sailors also often use the *half hitch* (for making a loop) and the *eye splice* (for any permanent loop).

1. *Reef knot* 2. *Clove hitch* 3. *Bowline*

Other commonly known knots include the *clove hitch*, which is used for tying a rope around a post. A *sheepshank* has a double loop with a hitch at either end; it is used for shortening a rope without cutting it. A special knot is the *honda*, a loop knot used for tying a bowstring to a bow (in archery) and for making a cowboy's lasso.

KOALA BEAR

A small animal resembling a teddy bear, the koala bear is not a member of the bear family at all. The koala (pronounced ko-ah-la) is a *marsupial*—that is, like the KANGAROO. The tiny newborn koala develops in its mother's pouch for about six months after birth. Then the young koala is carried on the mother's back until half grown.

Koalas feed on the leaves of eucalyptus trees, which grow mainly in Australia. This tree provides the koala with its only source of food, which it eats at night.

The slow-moving koalas were once sought for their thick, wooly fur. Now they are protected by law in Australia to prevent their becoming extinct.

KON-TIKI

The Kon-Tiki was a raft, built of balsa wood. It was sailed by the Norwegian explorer and anthropologist, Thor Heyerdahl, and five others from the coast of Peru to the Tuamotu Islands, in the south Pacific. Heyerdahl believed that the first settlers of Polynesia were of South American origin and that they traveled to this

area in the Pacific on rafts. To test his theory, he sailed 4300 miles (6923 km) across the Pacific in 1947. His raft Kon-Tiki was of primitive design, like the ones the South American Indians might have constructed for such a voyage. Later, Heyerdahl wrote about the daring trip in a book called *Kon-Tiki.*

KORAN

The Koran (also spelled Quran) is the sacred book of Islam. It is said to have been dictated to Muhammad, the founder of Islam, by an angel. It is divided into 114 surahs, or chapters. These discuss the nature of the god Allah, the universe, and man.

Tracing Koran texts in the sand

The Koran teaches that Allah is as close to man as the veins in his neck. He answers man's prayers, but demands that man obey him. According to the Koran, a person who obeys the commands of Allah goes to paradise, while the sinful person goes to hell.

The Koran is only one of the guides by which the Muslim leads his life. The *Hadith*, collections of the sayings of Muhammad, are very important, too. And there are teachings that scholars have created, based on the Koran and the Hadith. SEE ALSO: ISLAM.

KOREA

Korea, about the size of Kansas, occupies a peninsula in eastern Asia. China first ruled the land. For a while, it became a separate kingdom, called Chosen, but in 1910 it was seized by

Rice fields and irrigation canals

Japan. Since the end of World War II, the country has been divided into two parts: North Korea ruled by the Communists and South Korea ruled as a republic. About 1 million people died during the KOREAN WAR (1950-53) between the north and the south. Pyongyang is the capital of North Korea, a country that has 16.5 million people; Seoul is the capital of South Korea, which has 36.5 million people.

Much of Korea is mountainous, and about a fifth of the land is used for growing rice, barley, wheat, yams, and soybeans. Many Koreans work in factories, making steel, textiles, chemicals, and glass. Fishing is an important industry, too. SEE ALSO: KOREAN WAR.

KOREAN WAR

After World War II, KOREA was divided into two parts. North Korea was occupied by Russian troops, and South Korea had American troops. The United Nations then supervised elections in both parts, and two separate countries were set up. Rival governments were established.

On June 25, 1950, North Korean troops invaded South Korea by surprise. With the United Nations' approval, President HARRY TRUMAN immediately sent U.S. land, sea, and air forces to help the South Koreans. General DOUGLAS MACARTHUR was named commander in chief of all U.N. forces, which included troops of South Korea, Australia, the United States, Great Britain, Canada, and many other countries.

North Korean forces drove the U.N. troops into the southeastern corner of Korea. Soon U.S. soldiers began arriving and helped defend this small area, which included the important port of Pusan. Meanwhile, U.S. Marines landed at Inchon, farther north on the west coast. They moved inland and soon captured Seoul, South Korea's capital. Then U.N. forces under MacArthur pushed into North Korea. Pyongyang, the North Korean capital, was seized. However, the Chinese Communists joined with the North Koreans and attacked the U.N. forces, which had pushed into Manchuria (a region in northeast China). The new Chinese offensive drove the U.N. troops back into South Korea, below the 38th parallel that separated North and South Korea. MacArthur wanted to attack military bases in China and opposed Truman's orders. In April, 1951, Truman discharged MacArthur and made General Matthew Ridgway commander.

After a Chinese offensive was stopped near the 38th parallel, truce talks began in July, 1951, and continued for two years. During this time, many bloody battles were fought, but the battle lines changed very little. On July 27, 1953, an armistice (truce) was signed at Panmunjom. North and South Korea were divided almost like they were before 1950, and a buffer zone 2.5 miles (4 km) wide was established between the two countries.

KRAKATOA

Krakatoa, a small volcanic island in the EAST INDIES, erupted suddenly in 1883. Most of the island blew up, and the strait between the islands of Java and Sumatra was changed. This terrific volcanic explosion and the accompanying tidal wave killed more than 36,000 people in the area. New islands were formed from the lava, and debris was spread across the Indian Ocean as far as Malagasy, off the coast of Africa. No volcanic eruption since has been as great or powerful.

LABORATORY

Laboratory comes from a medieval Latin word meaning "workshop." Today, a laboratory means a place equipped to carry out scientific experiments in chemistry, physics, biology, engineering, and medicine. There are laboratories in many universities. There, professors and their assistants study and perform experiments, often trying to prove a new theory or idea. Biologists, chemists, and doctors sometimes use guinea pigs, mice, rats, dogs, and frogs in their research connected with the welfare of mankind.

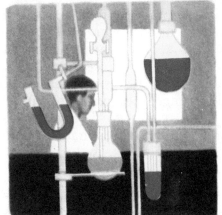

Many factories have laboratories where scientists and engineers discover and test new processes and products.

The first important chemistry and physics laboratories were established in the 1800s.

LABOR UNIONS

Workers often join together to form an organization, called a labor union, in order to obtain better wages, working conditions, and some fringe (side) benefits. Labor unions and company owners have representatives who meet to talk about the workers' demands. They engage in a process known as *collective bargaining*, during which they try to understand the other's point of view and to reach a fair decision. Sometimes a mediator or third party is brought in to help them come to an agreement. However, if no agreement can be reached, labor unions may decide to go on *strike*—that is, the workers walk off the job. Entire industries can be shut down until an agreement is reached. Company owners and government officials can seek a court *injunction* (order) to stop the strike. Firemen and policemen, whose services are needed for the public's safety, are sometimes forced by an injunction to go back to work. If they don't, they or their union leaders can be fined or put in jail. SEE ALSO: GUILDS.

LACE

Lace is a kind of decorative cloth made so that parts of it are left open. There are many ways of doing such openwork, but good lace is almost always either needlepoint or bobbin lace.

In *needlepoint*, a single thread is used. It is passed through a parchment on which the design is drawn, and is so knotted that when the parchment is removed a complete piece of cloth is left. In *bobbin lace*, the parchment is attached to a cushion with steel pins that outline the design. Threads

Lace making

wound on bobbins (little spools) are passed around the pins and knotted together.

Lace making developed around 1500, but no one knows whether Italy or Belgium was the first country to produce it. At that time, both men and women wore very fancy clothes, and lace was popular for these into the late 18th century. It was popular later for curtains and tablecloths. Lace-making machines were invented in the late 18th century. They are very complicated. Today lace is made of cotton rather than of linen as it used to be.

LADYBIRD

Ladybird (or ladybug) is the familiar name for a very useful family of *beetles*. Ladybird beetles are small insects, about a half inch (1.2 cm) long, and look like half of a small round ball. They are usually red or yellow and have black or white spots. The spots are either 2, 7, or 24 in number. They have small, delicate wings that can be tucked away under their hard, protective wing cases.

The ladybird beetles and grubs feed upon large quantities of plant lice and other small insects. Their usefulness is so great that they have been specially bred by biologists and sold to countries suffering from severe pest damage to crops. Organic gardeners prefer to use these beetles instead of toxic sprays for controlling garden pests. SEE ALSO: BEETLE.

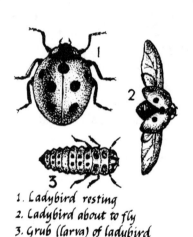
1. Ladybird resting
2. Ladybird about to fly
3. Grub (larva) of ladybird

Marquis de LAFAYETTE (1757–1834)

Marquis de Lafayette was a wealthy French nobleman and army officer. Hearing about the American colonists' struggle for independence, he sailed to America in 1777 and offered to serve in the Continental Army. He was made a major general and became a close friend of General GEORGE WASHINGTON. At Valley Forge, Brandywine, and Yorktown, Lafayette showed his military skill and courage, earning for himself the title "the soldier's friend." Lafayette also gave much money to help the colonists during the AMERICAN REVOLUTION.

In 1781, Lafayette returned to France and became a member of the French National Assembly and a commander of the National Guard. He helped write the French Bill of Rights. During the French Revolution (1792–1802), Lafayette became disappointed by the rebels' use of terror and murder. Declared a traitor, he fled to Austria but was captured and put in prison. Later he was freed by NAPOLEON, head of France's new government.

LAGOON

A lagoon is a shallow, quiet, saltwater body of water, separated from the sea by sandbars, barrier islands, or coral reefs. A narrow channel may join a lagoon to the sea.

Lagoons that lie between coastal barriers and the shoreline are usually long and narrow. Lagoons are often circular, as in the picture. In the south Pacific and Indian Oceans, reefs or islands of CORAL enclose shallow lagoons and form *atolls*.

An atoll is a ring-shaped coral island with a lagoon. The coral has grown up to form an enclosed lake, shutting off the water inside from the surrounding sea. Through the action of wind and waves, the coral is sometimes ground up and fills up the lagoon. SEE ALSO: CORAL.

LAKE DWELLINGS

Primitive people often built their houses over water in order to be safe from their enemies—wild animals or hostile people. These dwellings were built beside lakes or marshes in very ancient times.

Sometimes lake dwellers simply built huts on mounds of mud, stones, logs, and brush in the water. Sometimes they placed square log frames on the bed of the lake and drove long poles into the lake bottom within these frames, and then erected a platform with a hut on top of these long poles. Often the lake dwellers climbed ladders to get into their huts. When the ladder was pulled up, no enemy could get to them. Lake dwellings close to shore were sometimes reached by means of a narrow bridge. Canoes were also used by all lake dwellers.

Lake dwellings vanished when people used bronze and iron tools to build larger and stronger homes, and when they had better weapons against their enemies. Today, some people in the Philippine Islands and on the AMAZON River still live in huts built over water.

LAKES

Lakes are bodies of water surrounded by land. Most lakes contain fresh water, but some contain salt water.

Freshwater lakes have water running in and out of them all the time. Saltwater lakes only have water running in. Salt lakes do not overflow because they are found in dry regions, where the water evaporates quickly. Sometimes these salty lakes are called seas. The Caspian Sea is the world's largest salt lake. The GREAT LAKES of America are among the twelve largest freshwater lakes in the world, Lake Superior being the world's largest.

The hollow that contains a lake is known as a *basin*. Basins are formed in different ways. Glaciers gouged out many basins, such as the Scottish lochs and the lakes of Minnesota, "the land of 10,000 lakes." Some, like Lake Geneva in Switzerland, are formed when the Earth's crust splits. Some, like Crater Lake in Oregon, are the craters of inactive volcanoes. Some are formed when sediment (rocks and sand), lava, or dams block a river. Some are formed in depressions, where land sinks or soft rock gets washed away.

LAKE VICTORIA

In 1858, John Speke, a British explorer, discovered Lake Victoria, the largest lake in Africa. Bordered by Uganda, Tanzania, and Kenya, it is the second largest freshwater lake in the world; only Lake Superior is larger. The lake is about 3726 feet (1155 m) above sea level and has numerous islands and plenty of fish. Steamships travel between the lakeshore towns, including Entebbe, Musoma, and Mwanza.

LAMPS

Devices for producing light were first made many centuries ago. The earliest ones were simply hollowed-out rocks or seashells in which a little grease or oil was placed with a wick of moss or cloth. The purpose of the wick was to soak up the fuel and make it possible to light it.

The Egyptians, the Greeks, the Romans, and the Chinese sometimes turned lamps into works of art. They made them of pottery and bronze. Lamps were sometimes made like saucers in which the wick floated, and sometimes like shallow teapots, with the wicks coming out of the spouts. Such lamps used different kinds of animal fats and vegetable oils. But all these lamps were basically the same. They flickered and smoked in a draft of air, and gave only a dim light. Many people preferred candles if they could afford them.

In the 18th century, a Swiss man, Aimé Argand, invented a new kind of lamp. Its wick was hollow, and air came up through its center. This produced a much brighter light than had ever been known before. A little later someone put a glass chimney around an Argand lamp, and the light became brighter still.

In 1859, petroleum was first used for lamps. This new fuel was much less expensive than the others in use. By this time, too, many rooms and many streets were lighted by gas. Gas street lighting was introduced in London in 1807, and gradually replaced the old lanterns.

A kind of electric lighting began to be used in a few places in the 1850s, but it was very expensive until the *light bulb* was invented by EDISON and others late in the 1870s. Now electric lighting is used almost everywhere in the United States. SEE ALSO: LIGHT BULB.

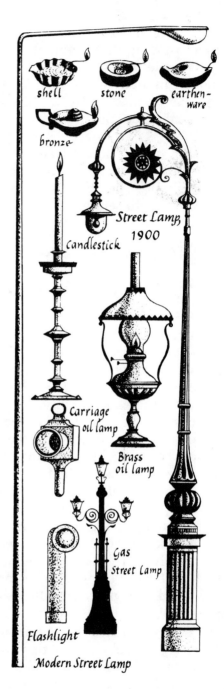

shell
stone
earthen-ware
bronze
Candlestick
Street Lamp 1900
Carriage oil lamp
Brass oil lamp
Gas Street Lamp
Flashlight
Modern Street Lamp

LANGUAGE

Because man uses language, he has a way of sharing information and ideas with others. Almost everything he has accomplished has been done thanks to the cooperation and understanding that language has made possible.

People communicate (share information, ideas, and feelings) with one another in many ways. A smile or a blush is a form of communication. So is a flag *signal* hoisted by a ship at sea, or the formula of a chemist or a mathematician. So, in fact, is a work of art that allows you to share the artist's feelings.

But none of these is language. A language is made up of two main things. One is a *vocabulary*, a supply of words for all the things you want to talk or write about. The other is a system of *grammar*, a set of rules for combining the words into sentences.

dog (*English*), **собáка** (*Russian*), **chien** (*French*), **hund** (*German*)

perro (*Spanish*), **狗** (*Chinese*), **canis** (*Latin*), كَنْبٌ ج كِلَابٌ (*Arabic*)

Learning a language can be very hard unless you are brought up speaking it. Languages grow naturally, picking up and abandoning words and *idioms* (special ways of saying certain things). Some words are oddly spelled or inflected (changed to show their exact meaning). Rules are useful in most cases, but there are exceptions. Spellings show you more or less how a word is pronounced, but you have to learn specially that "Taliaferro" is pronounced "Tolliver." You must know that "mis-" means badly, in order to know without being told that you say "mis-LED," not "MEEZ-led." In some languages, such as Chinese, written words are not even spelled. They are signs that used to be pictures of the things for which the words stand. In Chinese, too, the pitch of your voice when you pronounce a certain sound tells people what you are saying. One sound can mean several things.

But knowing a language well is worth the effort. People like to know exactly what you mean, and want you to know exactly what they mean. They think better of you when you speak and write your own language, English, well. And foreigners are often annoyed when Americans make no effort to speak their languages well.

You will learn grammar in school. But you will probably want a *dictionary* to help you with your vocabulary. It will tell you what words mean, as well as how to spell and pronounce them. Special dictionaries will give you the words in foreign languages that match words in English. You may even find a *thesaurus* useful. If you are looking for other words that mean the same thing as one you do not want to use, the thesaurus will make suggestions.

LARK

Of all the different kinds of larks, the most famous is the European skylark shown here. All larks are light brown and have long pointed wings with brown streaks on the feathers. They all nest on the ground in grasslands and other open areas. Many larks have a crest of feathers on the head.

Larks are often fine songbirds, the most famous being the skylark. It soars very high into the sky and sings as it flies, so that its long, sweet song is heard even though the bird is no longer seen.

Although it, too, is a bird of the grasslands, the American meadowlark is not a lark at all but is a member of the oriole-blackbird family. The only true American lark is the horned lark, which walks rather than hops. It has a black "necklace," a yellow face, and white outer tail feathers, and, like all larks, is brownish in color.

LARVA

Many insects and some other animals undergo a series of changes, called a *metamorphosis*, from birth to maturity. The early feeding stage in the development of insects is known as a *larva*. A larva may look very different from its parents. Thus, the larval form of a butterfly is a crawling grub, known as a *caterpillar*, not a beautiful winged creature.

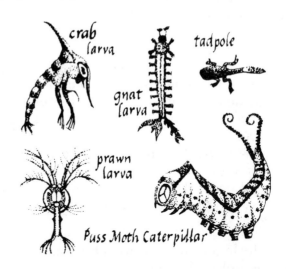

crab larva
gnat larva
tadpole
prawn larva
Puss Moth Caterpillar

After the larval stage, some insects then have a resting or *pupal* stage before developing into adults. The larvae of the dragonfly and the mosquito live in water before they develop into winged creatures. Some larvae spend their time in plants or in the soil. Some even live in men and animals. Larvae can cause diseases, like hookworm, and serious damage in plants. All larvae are continually eating.

Larvae appear only in the lower forms of vertebrates, such as eels, salamanders, and frogs. A frog's larval form is a tadpole.

LASER

A laser beam is a powerful and brilliant beam of intense light. Scientists have found a way to create this beam by using very special equipment to "pump" light into a tube of ruby until the light becomes so strong that it suddenly escapes.

The tube of ruby has a mirror at one end through which no light can pass. At the other end is a partial mirror through which some light can escape.

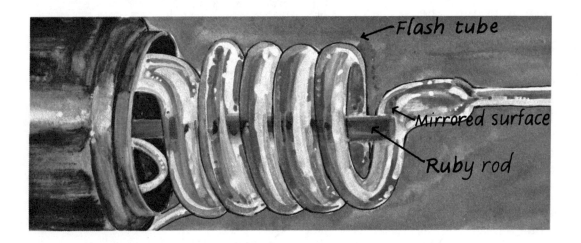

The atoms of ruby contain vibrating bundles of light energy called *photons*. When scientists have pumped as much light into the tube as it can hold, some of the atoms of the ruby release their photons. The mirrors at the ends of the tube reflect the photons back into the ruby many times. Each time, more and more photons are released and they become more and more active. Finally, the great number of photons and their excess activity in the overfull tube force the light to escape through the partial mirror as a tremendously powerful beam. Unlike light from the sun, which is made up of several colors and wavelengths, the laser beam is made up of one color and only one wavelength.

The letters in the word *laser* stand for Light Amplification by Stimulated Emission of Radiation.

A laser beam has many uses. It is powerful enough to cut through most materials, and can be used as a drill or cutter. In surgery, it can be used to cut away diseased tissue so quickly that surrounding healthy tissue is not harmed. In communications, laser beams can carry information, in the same way that a telephone wire does. Because they are so strong, laser beams can be used in lighthouses. Scientists are continuing to find new uses for the laser, which has become very important in the modern world.

LATEX

Latex is a milky fluid found in the sapwood just under the bark of certain trees. Usually latex is white, but sometimes it is yellow, orange, or red. It contains oil, starch, sugar, resin, protein, and RUBBER. Latex hardens when exposed to air and thus protects any wounds in the tree's bark. Some latex is bitter and poisonous and is thought to protect the tree from browsing livestock. Certain kinds of latex are used today to protect the wounds of human beings.

The best known latex product is rubber. The picture shows a woman in Malaysia, in southeastern Asia, collecting latex from a tree on one of the many rubber plantations. SEE ALSO: RUBBER.

LATIN

Latin was the language of the ancient Romans. It was first used by a central Italian people called the Latini, who lived in Latium, the area around Rome. As the Roman empire grew, Latin spread, and in time it was spoken all the way from Scotland to the Near East, as well as along the coast of North Africa.

When the Catholic Church began to spread from Rome, it too used a kind of Latin for its rituals and its official documents. Until a few years ago the mass was offered in Latin. During the *Renaissance*, scholars published their ideas in Latin, because so many people understood it.

Roman lettering

A medieval manuscript

Medical Latin
a. *acetabulum*
b. *femur*
c. *obturatur foramen*
d. *patella*
e. *tibia*
f. *fibula*
g. *digit*

rabbit's leg

The Spaniards, Portuguese, Italians, some of the French, and the peoples of the Americas south of the United States are also called Latins because they are descended from peoples of the Roman Empires. They speak *Romance* languages, everyday Latin influenced locally. The Rumanians in eastern Europe also speak a Romance language.

English is a *Germanic* language. Most of its words are of north European origin. But even so, a fourth of our words are taken from Latin. *Influence, people, vocabulary, language,* and *empire* are all words from Latin. And Latin is very widely used in the sciences even today.

467

LATITUDE AND LONGITUDE

The Earth is divided up into imaginary north-south and east-west lines to help mark exact locations on the globe. This method of pinpointing one's position is extremely important for navigators. For instance, there are no landmarks on many vast areas of ocean to use as guides by ships' navigators.

The Earth has an imaginary "belt," called the EQUATOR, that divides the globe into a northern half (*hemisphere*) and a southern half. This line is called zero degrees (0°) *latitude*. All the east-west lines or *parallels* north of the equator express north latitude; all those south of the equator express south latitude. The North Pole is 90°N (90 degrees north); the South Pole is 90°S (90 degrees south). Every degree is a 360th part of a full circle. The upper right illustration shows the Northern Hemisphere marked off in parallels, each 10° apart.

The north-south lines or *meridians* express longitude. All countries have agreed that the north-south line that passes through Greenwich, England, will be 0° longitude. This line, called the *prime meridian*, divides the globe into the Western and Eastern Hemispheres. However, 180° longitude, on the opposite side of the globe from Greenwich is neither east nor west.

The captain of a ship in trouble signaling for help would use the ship's COMPASS to indicate his position. A reading of 30°N and 45°W would mean that he is 30 degrees north of the equator and 45 degrees west of Greenwich, England. See if you can find where these two lines intersect

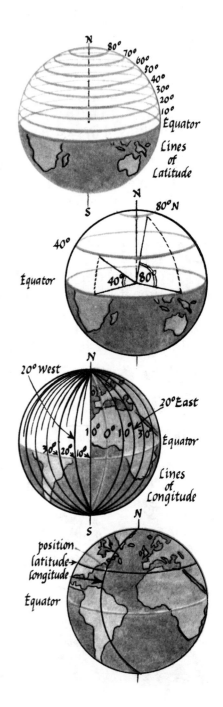

or cross on a globe and find his location. Any spot on Earth can be exactly pin-pointed because each degree of latitude and longitude can be subdivided into 60 equal parts called *minutes*, and each minute can be subdivided into 60 *seconds*. SEE ALSO: COMPASS.

LAVA

Lava is the melted or molten rock that pours out of the interior of the Earth when a VOLCANO erupts. Lava may have a temperature of more than 2200° F (1204° C). It sometimes flows down the sides of a volcano at one mile per hour (1.61 km/hr), covering, burning, and destroying roads, houses, and entire towns.

Hot lava becomes cool fairly quickly and forms either block lava or corded lava, also called *pahoehoe*. Block lava is made up of large fragments with rough surfaces; corded lava has a smooth and billowy surface.

Much of the rock on the Earth was once a semi-molten layer of lava under the Earth's crust. This hot layer was forced out through volcanoes and other openings in the crust. If the lava cooled rapidly, it created *basalt*, which sometimes split into six-sided columns, like the Devil's Tower in Wyoming. SEE ALSO: VOLCANO.

LAWRENCE of ARABIA (1888–1935)

Thomas Edward Lawrence was an English adventurer, soldier, and scholar. His early work in archeology in the Near East enabled him to know the ARABS very well. After joining the British Intelligence Service in World War I, he was sent to Arabia, where he organized and led the Arabs in their revolt against Turkish domination. He worked also to create independent Arabian states.

After the war, he sought anonymity (to be nameless and unknown) either because he felt he had betrayed Arab hopes for independence or because he disliked being treated like a famous person. He changed his name first to Ross and later to Shaw. He wrote *The Seven Pillars of Wisdom*, an account of his exciting life with the Arabs, and translated into English the *Odyssey* by Homer. For a while, he was a mechanic in the Royal Air Force. Later he was killed in a motorcycle accident in England.

LEAD

Lead is a heavy metal which has been used by man for at least 3000 years. The ancient Romans used it for water pipes, some of which are still in existence.

Shot Tower
Molten lead was poured from the top into water, forming small, round shot.

lead plates in a battery

Because lead melts easily, it can be poured into many shapes. Toy soldiers, printing type, and bullets are made of lead. A third of all lead produced is used in making the plates in *batteries*. Lead is mixed with tin for making solder. The early American settlers mixed it with tin to produce pewter.

Today, lead is used in special shields to protect X-ray technicians from radiation. It is also used in some kinds of glass, gasoline, and paint. However, long contact with lead is dangerous as it is poisonous to the body.

The United States, Russia, and Australia are the world's chief producers of lead.

LEAF INSECTS

Leaf insects are tropical insects related to the cockroach family. Their wing cases look exactly like the color, shape, and vein structure of small leaves. When at rest, with their wings closed over their backs, leaf insects blend easily into the background, often looking like parts of dead leaves, or stems. Their eggs are disguised to look just like seeds.

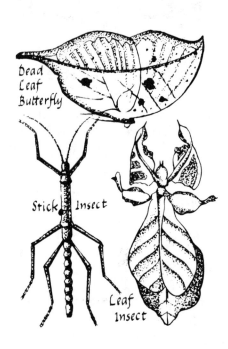

Dead Leaf Butterfly

Stick Insect

Leaf Insect

Leaf insects stay still during the day and feed actively at night. Only the males can fly.

Other members of this unusual family are the stick insects that look like twigs. Some species have green bumps on them that look like small bits of moss.

Protective animal *camouflage* helps creatures, like leaf insects, hide from their enemies by enabling them to appear like their surroundings. Many other insects, such as the Dead Leaf Butterfly, resemble leaves as well.

470

LEATHER

Leather is made from *hides* (skins of large animals) and the skins of small animals. The process of turning *rawhide*, the animal skin, into leather is called *tanning*.

First the rawhide is cleaned and preserved so that it will not decay. Usually it is dried. Often the rawhide is treated with lime to remove the hair.

Much modern tanning is still done with plant material, which contains a chemical called *tannin*. Tannin helps the leather to resist rot and other kinds of decay. Oils, minerals, and chemicals can also be used for tanning. Tanning is a long process, which can take up to a year. The hide is soaked in stronger and stronger tanning solutions. Each kind of solution produces a different kind of leather, so that different kinds of solution may be used together to get a special result.

Once tanned, the leather is cut into slices of desirable thickness, dyed, dried, and finished. The finish determines the feel of the leather and its resistance to wear. Ordinary leather has a rather dark brown, shiny appearance, since it is brushed with a special coating. But *suede* leather has a much softer feel and does not shine; it can be dyed in many colors. *Chamois* leather is treated with fish or whale oil and beaten soft. *Morocco* leather, used for binding books, is made of goat skin passed through rollers. *Patent* leather is heavily varnished.

Different animals provide different leathers. Shoes are made from cow, bull, and ox hide. Fine leather goods are often made from pigskin. Goatskin is used for other fine leather goods, including gloves. Leather of the horse family is used for some kinds of shoes, and also for belts. Even walruses, sharks, and ostriches supply leather for various purposes.

Processing Leather

hides

slaked lime bath

removing hair

softening – 'curing'

polishing

drying

471

LEAVES

Leaves are the main food-manufacturing organs of a plant. Also, a plant breathes (see RESPIRATION) through its leaves. Leaves absorb energy from the light rays of the sun. They then make sugar and starch, using carbon dioxide from the air and water from the earth. In order for this process to work, there must also be green coloring matter, called *chlorophyll,* in the cells of the leaves. Carbon dioxide is absorbed into the leaves through small pores, called *stomates.* There are about 100,000 stomates in an apple leaf.

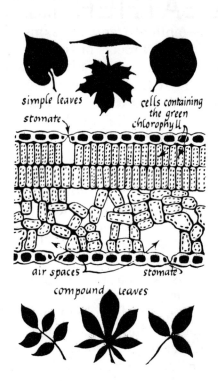

simple leaves
stomate
cells containing the green chlorophyll
air spaces
stomate
compound leaves

Because sunlight is needed if the food-making process, known as *photosynthesis,* is to occur, a plant's leaves are usually arranged in a way so that every leaf can get plenty of sunlight. Leaves grow on the stem opposite each other, alternate to each other, or in the shape of a spiral. Any gap in a plant's upper leaves are filled by a plant's lower leaves, which turn toward light.

Every plant has its own special shape of leaf that identifies it. Just as an animal's shape depends on the framework of its skeleton, a leaf's shape depends on the framework of its "skeleton" of veins. Leaves with very narrow vein skeletons are called *needles,* which are found on such trees as the pine, spruce, and hemlock. A leaf may be *simple* or it may be divided into leaflets, and in this case is called *compound.*

Leaves give off moisture, as well as store water. During winter, when the cold, frozen earth prevents the ROOTS from taking in water, certain kinds of trees (*deciduous* trees) shed their leaves.

Robert E. LEE (1807–1870)

Many historians consider Robert E. Lee the greatest general of the U.S. CIVIL WAR. His military skill, hindered though it was by lack of men and supplies, was a major reason for many Confederate victories.

Born in Stratford, Virginia, Lee was the son of Henry "Light Horse" Lee, a brilliant general in the American Revolution. In 1829, Robert graduated first in his class at West Point. He later served in the Mexican War, afterward becoming superintendent of West Point.

At the start of the Civil War, Lee declined Lincoln's offer to be field commander of the U.S. Army. Although he was not in favor of either slavery or Virginia's secession (withdrawal) from the Union, his loyalty and love of Virginia and the South came first. Soon he joined the Confederate army, becoming military adviser to JEFFERSON DAVIS and then a full general. He won great victories near Richmond and at Bull Run, Fredericksburg, Chancellorsville, Cold Harbor, and Petersburg, but lost key battles at Antietam and Gettysburg. In early 1865, Lee was made the commander in chief of all armies of the Confederacy, which had by then nearly collapsed. The Union army under General ULYSSES S. GRANT soon forced Lee's troops to retreat. On April 9, 1865, Lee surrendered to Grant at Appomattox Court House. Lee was made president of Washington College, at Lexington, Virginia. After his death the college was renamed Washington and Lee University. SEE ALSO: BATTLE OF GETTYSBURG, THE CIVIL WAR.

LEMONS

The lemon is a citrus fruit closely related to the orange, citron, lime, and grapefruit. It is thought originally to have been the result of a cross between the citron (a pale yellow fruit) and the lime. Lemon trees grow in the tropics and subtropics, especially in Spain, Italy, Portugal, California, and Florida.

The fruit is picked while it is still green and stored in dark rooms to ripen. The ripe fruit will keep for several months. The juice from the lemon is very high in Vitamin C and is made into a refreshing drink and used in flavoring. The lemon's yellow rind produces an oil that is used in the manufacture of PERFUMES.

Nikolai LENIN (1870–1924)

The people of the Soviet Union (U.S.S.R.) honor Nikolai Lenin as the father of their country. In November, 1917, he led a revolution that established a Soviet government.

His real name was Vladimir Ilyich Ulyanov, and he was born in the Russian town of Simbirsk (now Ulyanov). As a young man, he was exiled for three years to Siberia for revolutionary activity and for publishing illegal newspapers. Afterward, Lenin (who took this name to conceal his

473

real identity from the czar's police) lived in Germany and Switzerland. There he wrote pamphlets against the Russian government and organized the Bolshevik Party, a group of socialists who believed the poor people of RUSSIA would revolt and seize the government and the industries.

Red Square, Moscow

The Kremlin

Vasiliev Cathedral

Lenin's tomb

During World War I, the czar's government lost control over the people, and in March, 1917, a revolutionary group overthrew the czar. The new government demanded that Russia remain at war against Germany. However, the Bolsheviks wanted to get out of the war. Lenin returned to Russia in October, 1917, and took complete control. He established a Communist government and became the most powerful man in the new Union of Soviet Socialist Republics. He urged the Russians to work hard, thus enabling Russia to develop into a strong industrial state.

Lenin died of a stroke, and his body was placed in a large tomb in MOSCOW, to be viewed always by the Russians. Joseph Stalin succeeded Lenin as head of the Communist party.

LENS

A lens is an expertly ground and polished disc of glass or plastic that has one or two curved surfaces. Lenses that bulge outward are *convex*, while those that curve in toward the center are called *concave*.

When they pass through the lens, LIGHT rays are bent or *refracted* toward the thickest part. A convex lens makes objects look bigger. A concave lens makes objects look smaller.

The discovery that lenses bend and focus rays of light has led to the manufacture of CAMERAS, MAGNIFYING GLASSES, movie projectors, and EYEGLASSES. The arrangement of two or more lenses has made possible opera glasses, binoculars, TELESCOPES, and MICROSCOPES to extend man's view of the world about him. The natural lens of the eye causes it to focus.

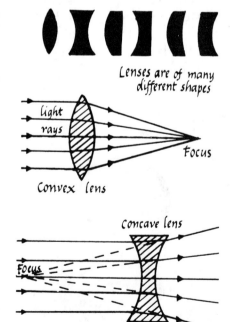

Lenses are of many different shapes

light rays

Focus

Convex lens

concave lens

Focus

LEONARDO da VINCI (1452–1519)

Leonardo da Vinci was one of the world's greatest geniuses. He was born in Vinci, Italy, during the time of the RENAISSANCE. He first studied painting in Florence, Italy, and painted many pictures for great Italian noblemen. He experimented also with different methods of painting and drawing.

Unfortunately, few of Leonardo's paintings remain today. His best known paintings are the *Mona Lisa*, a portrait of a smiling woman, and *The Last Supper*, a picture of Christ and his twelve apostles eating together for the last time. *The Last Supper*, painted on the wall of a monastery in Milan, was ruined by moisture and is in poor condition today.

Leonardo made hundreds of drawings, many of which are preserved in museums in Europe. These remarkable drawings show his great ability in the fields of science, engineering, architecture, sculpture, and art. He left many sketches for statues, elaborate plans for the dome of the Milan Cathedral, and thousands of notebook pages with advanced (for his time) scientific ideas and theories and drawings to go with them.

He was an early inventor in technology, imagining all kinds of useful machines that were not really understood until the 20th century. He made detailed drawings of water mills, explosives, military weapons, paddlewheels, and even a flying machine (though he could not find a source of power to make it work). For a long time, his theories were not known because many of his manuscripts were not easy to understand.

In anatomy, he made discoveries connected with the heart and the blood. He studied the action of the eye in vision. In geology and meteorology, he saw the effect the moon has on the tides and the way continents might have been formed. He understood, better than any man of his era, the importance of precise scientific observation.

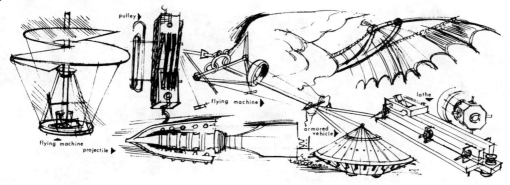

LEOPARD

The leopard, also called a panther, lives in Africa and southern Asia. Like the LION, TIGER, and JAGUAR, it is a member of the cat family and grows to about 4 feet (1.2 m) in length. The male leopard of India may be more than 7 feet (2.1 m) long.

The leopard lives in hill country. It can easily climb trees, where its yellowish body with black spots is easily camouflaged among the leaves. There the leopard hides, waiting to pounce down upon its prey. It is a very fierce hunter and attacks antelopes, birds, monkeys, cattle, sheep, goats, and sometimes even men.

Some leopards are completely black, and some, such as the Asian snow leopard that lives in Tibet, are white with black spots.

LEWIS and CLARK EXPEDITION

When THOMAS JEFFERSON became President in 1801, he proposed an overland expedition to find a good route to the Pacific Ocean. He wished also to strengthen American claims to the Oregon Territory and to gather information about the Indians. After Congress approved the plan, Jefferson appointed two army officers, Meriwether Lewis and William Clark, to lead such an expedition. Before it began, the LOUISIANA PURCHASE was made, increasing the value of Lewis and Clark's long journey.

The expedition, consisting of about 40 men, started up the Missouri River from St. Louis on May 14, 1804. After making the difficult ascent of the river

to what is now North Dakota, the group spent a winter with the friendly Mandan Sioux Indians. Lewis and Clark hired there a French-Canadian fur trapper, Toussaint Charbonneau, who brought along his Indian wife, Sacagawea, and their baby son.

The explorers next pushed westward into what is now Montana, following one branch of the Missouri as far as their canoes could go. Here Sacagawea, known also as "Bird Woman," helped them obtain horses from the Shoshoni Indians. They traveled west across the Bitterroot Mountains, part of the Rockies, and reached the headwaters of the Clearwater River. Canoes were built to carry the expedition down the Clearwater to the Snake River and then to the mouth of the Columbia River. Finally, on November 15, 1805, they reached the Pacific Ocean.

After spending a miserable, rainy winter in Fort Clatsop, which they built on the coast, the explorers began their return trip. On September 23, 1806, they arrived back in St. Louis, amid great excitement.

Lewis and Clark brought back diaries and maps that contained much information about the territory. Their journey had covered more than 8000 miles (12,880 km). They had encountered hostile Indians, accidents, sickness, lack of food, grizzly bears, and rattlesnakes, but only one man had died during the entire trip.

LIBERTY BELL

Outside Independence Hall in Philadelphia stands the modern shelter of one of the most famous bells in the world, the Liberty Bell. On its side is cast "Proclaim liberty throughout the land unto all the inhabitants thereof," a quotation from the Biblical book of Leviticus.

The bell was first cast in the famous Whitechapel Foundry in London, and was delivered to Independence Hall (then called the State House) in 1752. It was not well made, though, and had to be recast twice in Philadelphia.

It used to be believed that the bell rang on July 4, 1776, to celebrate the signing of the Declaration of Independence; this is not so, however. In 1777, it was taken to Allentown, Pennsylvania, to save it from the British. In 1846, while being rung on Washington's birthday, it cracked so badly that it could not be repaired, and has not been rung since.

LIBRARY

The ancient libraries were places where official records could be kept as well as books. The Near Eastern town of Nippur had a temple library, some 3000 years ago, full of the clay tablets that were used then as books. The Assyrian king Ashurbanipal (around 650 B.C.) had a library of 25,000 tablets. In ancient Greece, both temples and private scholars had libraries of papyrus scrolls. That of the philosopher Aristotle was famous.

The most famous library in the ancient world, that of Alexandria in Egypt, was modeled on that of Aristotle. Built early in the 3rd century B.C., it attempted to put all of human knowledge in orderly form. Pergamum, in Asia Minor, also had a large library.

The ancient Romans were very fond of reading, and a rich man often had a large library, which scholars were allowed to use. Julius Caesar would have founded the first public library if he had lived long enough, and one was founded about 40 B.C. in Rome.

The medieval monastery became the main place for both writing and storing books. Later, the great universities of Europe began to get their own libraries. Private collectors began, toward the end of the Middle Ages, to acquire large book collections again.

During the 17th and 18th centuries, there was a movement for the setting up of great national libraries and also of libraries for the general public. Since more people were learning to read, private rental libraries became common too. In the early 1890s a Scottish-American millionaire, ANDREW CARNEGIE, helped the public-library movement along by contributing money to build libraries in the cities and small towns of the United States.

Babylonian reading from baked clay tablets

Egyptian with papyrus roll.

chained library

Children's library

LICHENS

The strange patches of plant life seen growing on the bark of trees and bare rocks are sometimes primitive plants called *lichens* (pronounced like-ens).

Lichens

A lichen is actually two plants in one. Each lichen consists of a FUNGUS and an ALGA living together in an unusual partnership. The green alga produces food from the carbon dioxide in the air which feeds itself and the fungus. The threads of the fungus anchor the alga and soak up water from the fog, dew, and rain. The water keeps the fungus and the alga moist.

Lichens thrive where other plants cannot grow. The fungus produces an acid that gradually crumbles rock, turning it into soil in which other plants will eventually grow. Lichens also provide food for reindeer in winter. Some lichens produce a dye, such as litmus found in most chemistry sets. Others are used in the manufacture of some perfumes.

LIFEBOATS

Every ship must have a means of saving its passengers and crew if the ship sinks or has to be abandoned. Every vessel carries *life jackets* that allow people to float in the water until they are picked up. But more is needed at sea. When the *Titanic* sank, over 1500 people died. There were life jackets for everyone, but the water was very cold, and there were not enough lifeboats. Laws since then require more lifeboats, and part of a voyage today is a drill showing everyone how they are to be used.

A modern lifeboat contains air chambers that keep it from sinking even if it is filled with water. It is made so that it will turn right side up if it overturns. It has a diesel engine or a set of sails, and may have a supply of food and water. It also has some way of signaling for help. Certain crew members are assigned to each boat.

There are also lifeboats along the shore for use in shipwrecks. They are usually manned by sailors who volunteer their services.

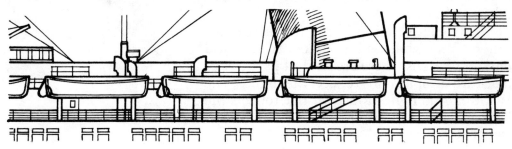

LIGHT

Light is radiant energy that is produced not only by the SUN and the stars but also by candles, fires, and electric light bulbs. Light enables us to see the various things about us because it is reflected by them to our eyes.

The nature of light has puzzled man for centuries. ISAAC NEWTON made many discoveries about its nature and demonstrated that light could be split up into the various colors of the SPECTRUM—violet, indigo, blue, green, yellow, orange, and red.

Later, it was discovered that light travels from the sun, 93 million miles (150 million km) away, to the Earth at the tremendous speed of 186,000 miles per second (299,460 km/sec). Light travels, however, more slowly through glass and water, and this decrease in speed causes *refraction,* or bending, of the rays. This is why a pencil that stands partly in water appears bent. Also, an object appears larger under a magnifying glass because of the refraction of light rays.

When light rays reach a mirror, the smooth surface bounces them all back exactly as they came, producing a reflection. The ability of mirrors to reflect light is put to use in periscopes and reflector TELESCOPES.

Colors we see exist only because of light. A beam of white light is actually made up of seven colors that merge together. Most objects absorb or take in some of the colors and reflect or throw back the others. Thus, a yellow buttercup absorbs all the colors of the spectrum except yellow, which it reflects to the eye. A white sheet of paper reflects all the rays of white light that fall on it, and black ink absorbs them all.

Astronauts beyond the Earth's atmosphere find that outer space is in total darkness because there are no dust particles or moisture droplets to reflect the light. The MOON has no light of its own but reflects the light shining on it from the sun. SEE ALSO: SPECTRUM.

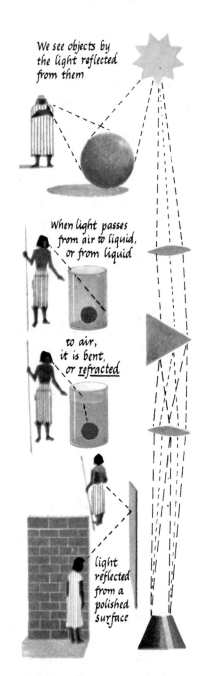

We see objects by the light reflected from them

When light passes from air to liquid, or from liquid

to air, it is bent, or _refracted_

light reflected from a polished surface

LIGHT BULB

When an electric light is switched on, the CURRENT enters the bulb through the two dabs of silver solder underneath it. The current then travels along the supporting wires (W) which are firmly held in a column of glass (G). Stretching between these wires is a very fine wire known as the *filament*. When electricity flows through it, the filament glows white-hot and thus gives out light.

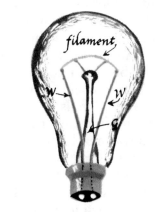

Finding a suitable material for the filament was the greatest challenge facing the early inventors, such as THOMAS A. EDISON. The filament had to last and not be burned up or melted away by the electrical current.

Tungsten, which melts at an extremely high temperature, is commonly used today in making filaments. To prevent it from burning away, the air is removed and replaced with a mixture of nitrogen and the rare gas argon, at low pressure.

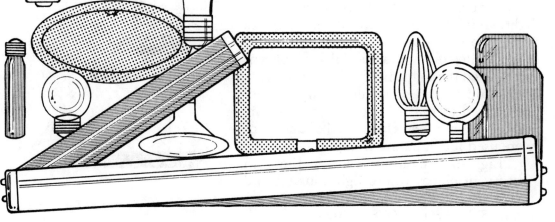

LIGHTHOUSES and LIGHTSHIPS

The work of the mariner would be much more dangerous without the lighthouse and its signals to tell him where he is. Some lighthouses show the way to a harbor. Some indicate a dangerous place that should be avoided.

The ancient Greeks lighted fires on hilltops as signals to ships. But as far as we know the first tower built to carry the fires was also one of the biggest: the Pharos of Alexandria, Egypt, which was about 350 feet (over 100 m) high. The Romans had 30 lighthouses in service at the end of their empire. During the Dark Ages there were no lighthouses, but by 1600 there were once again about 30.

Most of these early lighthouses were on shore, safe from the sea. When the first Eddystone Light was built on a rock in the sea of England, it lasted four years; then it was lost in a storm. In 1759, a Scottish engineer, John Smeaton, rebuilt the Eddystone Light in heavy stonework. Smeaton's way of building was used to erect other lighthouses that could withstand the force of the sea. Modern lighthouses are often built of steelwork or concrete.

Before 1800, most lighthouses used wood or coal fires. These gave a rather dim light. But the invention of the Argand LAMP made it possible to give a brighter light. Reflectors and a special kind of lens brightened the light still further. Revolving lights and glasses of different colors were introduced to make it possible to tell one light from another. Horns, bells, and guns were used for signaling in fog.

Lightships came into use in the 18th century in places where lighthouses could not be built. Many lightships are in use today. SEE ALSO: BUOYS, LAMPS.

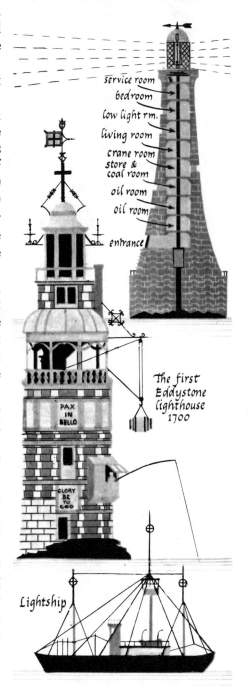

service room
bedroom
low light rm.
living room
crane room
store &
coal room
oil room
oil room
entrance

The first
Eddystone
lighthouse
1700

PAX
IN
BELLO

GLORY
BE
TO
GOD

Lightship

LIGHTNING

A study of ATOMS and ELECTRICITY teaches us that there is positive (+) and negative (–) electricity. These two opposite kinds of electricity are always attracted to one another.

Benjamin Franklin, an American statesman and inventor, discovered that one part of a thunder cloud becomes positively charged with electricity and another part becomes negatively charged as raindrops move through it. Eventually, there comes a point when the opposite charges of electricity can no longer be kept apart by the air between them. They then rush together in a flash of lightning. Several successive flashes, which may have more electrical energy than a large power station can generate, follow approximately the same path as the first flash in a few thousandths of a second.

The tremendous HEAT resulting from the flash of lightning causes the surrounding air to expand and contract very violently and produce the sound of thunder. Thunder may start as a sharp crack, but, as it becomes reflected from hills and buildings, it becomes a rumbling sound.

It is easy to figure out the distance between you and the flash of lightning. Light travels much faster than SOUND and reaches us almost immediately. Sound travels about 1 mile (1.6 km) in 5 seconds. Therefore, if you hear thunder 10 seconds after seeing the flash of lightning, then you know the flash was 2 miles (3.2 km) away.

Lightning rods, which are usually made of copper, protect buildings from damage by lightning. These rods intercept the flashes, diverting their electrical charges to the ground. Lightning rods are placed at the peaks of the buildings because lightning tends to strike the highest point. The rods are grounded (connected to the earth) by low-resistant, metallic cables.

LIMESTONE

Limestone is rock formed from the shells of tiny sea creatures which dropped to the ocean floor and became cemented together under tremendous pressure. Eventually, movements in the Earth's crust heaved the limestone layer up above the water to form cliffs and hills. Famous CAVES, such as the Carlsbad Caverns of New Mexico and the Luray Caverns of Virginia, are made of limestone.

483

CHALK is a soft type of white limestone. The famous White Cliffs of Dover on the southeast coast of England are made of chalk. MARBLE is a hard form of limestone and has been used by sculptors and architects since the days of ancient Greece and Rome. Some other important varieties of limestone are dolomite, oolite, and travertine.

Limestone is used in road construction, iron smelting, and in producing lime and CEMENT.

Abraham LINCOLN (1809–1865)

Abraham Lincoln became one of the greatest Presidents of the United States. During the CIVIL WAR, he prevented the North and the South from becoming two separate countries. He is also remembered for his intelligence, eloquence, and sense of freedom.

He was born in a log cabin in Kentucky. As a young boy, he helped support his family by splitting logs for fence rails and working at odd jobs. In his spare time, Lincoln educated himself and later studied law. In 1837 he began to practice law in Springfield, Illinois, where he married Mary Todd. He was elected to Congress in 1847, but did not run for a second term.

At this time, SLAVERY was legal in the southern states, where the work on the cotton plantations was done by the Negro slaves. Lincoln joined in 1856 the new Republican Party, which had been formed to fight slavery. In 1858, while running for the U.S. Senate, Lincoln and his Democratic opponent, Stephen A. Douglas, held debates in several Illinois towns. Lincoln was opposed to the Kansas-Nebraska Act, passed by Congress in 1854. This Act allowed slavery in the newly opened-up territories of the West. Lincoln lost the election but became nationally known for his speeches against slavery.

In 1860, he was elected President. Immediately several southern states seceded (withdrew) from the United States (the Union) and formed a new nation, called the Confederate States of America.

For four years, the North and South were engaged in the Civil War, and Lincoln fought all the while to keep the states together as one country. In 1863, he issued the famous Emancipation Proclamation, which freed the slaves, and gave his mighty Gettysburg Address, which defined democracy.

Shortly after Lincoln was reelected President in 1864, General ROBERT E. LEE surrendered and the South again became part of the Union. Five days later, Lincoln was fatally shot by John Wilkes Booth. SEE ALSO: THE CIVIL WAR.

Charles A. LINDBERGH (1902–1974)

Charles A. Lindbergh was the first person to make a solo, nonstop flight across the Atlantic Ocean. On May 21, 1927, he landed his small, single-engine plane called *The Spirit of St. Louis* at Le Bourget Airport near Paris, France. In 33 hours and 39 minutes, Lindbergh had flown from Roosevelt Field on Long Island, New York to Le Bourget, a distance of about 3600 miles (5796 km). Overnight Lindbergh became famous throughout the world.

Lindbergh was born in Detroit, Michigan, and grew up in the town of Little Falls, Minnesota. Before he was ten years old, he was taking apart, fixing, and assembling engines. He worked as an airplane mechanic and bought his own airplane in 1921. After becoming a flying cadet in the Army, Lindbergh served in the Air Force Reserve and later became an air-mail pilot. He was only 25 when he made his historic, transatlantic flight.

With his wife, Anne Morrow Lindbergh, he made several long flights. After their son was kidnaped and killed, they moved to England. He returned later to fly combat missions as an American pilot in World War II.

LINEN

Linen is made from the fibers of the flax plant. It has been used since prehistoric times; we have examples of fine linen from ancient Egyptian tombs. The Romans introduced linen weaving all over their empire.

Linen is a strong, good-looking cloth that can be bleached pure white. It is used for shirts, handkerchiefs, tablecloths, and other articles where comfort and attractiveness are important. It is also used for sails where strength is needed.

The great rival of linen is COTTON. In the early 19th century, cotton became a very important crop in the southern United States, and came to be used for many of the same purposes that linen is. It is cheaper to make than linen, though not as strong.

weaving linen damask on Jacquard loom

flax plant

linen sails

artists' canvas

LINERS

Until early in the 19th century, ships did not sail on a schedule. They left when they were full and went wherever people wished. Sailing ships that left on a definite day for a definite port were the first *liners*.

A ship called the *Royal William* became the first steam liner in 1827. In 1840 the Cunard Line, one of the most famous liner companies, began crossing between England and the United States in four paddle-wheel steamers. The trip was expensive, but it took only two weeks; a sailing ship would have taken at least six.

The transatlantic liner became the biggest and most highly developed of all ships. Cunard's first ships were made of wood and were about 200 feet (62 m) long.

'Mauretania' (1907)   780 ft   31,938 tons

Cargo liner   about 500 ft   9,000 tons

' Queen Elizabeth II ' (1968)   963 ft   58,000 tons

In 1843, the British engineer Isambard Brunel finished the *Great Britain*, which was longer, was made of iron, and used a propeller. Propellers were much more powerful than paddle wheels. Thanks to its durable iron construction, the *Great Britain* still exists in England. As new improvements were made and tested, they went into new liners that were being built.

Rival companies tried to win the Blue Riband, the prize for the fastest Atlantic crossing. By the mid-1870s, a fast liner crossed in seven days. In 1952, our own *United States* crossed in three-and-a-half days; this is still the record.

Liners began to sail to other parts of the world once places for the coal they needed were set up. Brunel built a gigantic ship, the *Great Eastern*, in 1858. It was supposed to carry enough coal for round trips to Australia, but was never used on the service.

Liners were usually safe, but the great liner *Titanic* sank on its first voyage in 1912, killing 1500 people. Later liners were much safer.

Early in this century, a great liner was called a floating hotel. It had everything necessary for a pleasant crossing. Artists decorated its rooms. The cooking was marvelous. If you traveled first-class, you were likely to see famous people. To cross the Atlantic on the *Mauretania*, the *Queen Mary*, or the *Normandie* was a great experience.

LINOLEUM

Linoleum was invented in 1860 by an Englishman named Frederick Walton. It is made from oil, gums, ground cork, and other materials that coat one side of a sheet of burlap or felt. Layer upon layer of this material is added until a thickness of up to a quarter inch (5 mm) is reached. After drying, the linoleum can be dyed or printed with a decorative pattern.

Linoleum is easily cleaned, cheap, durable, and will not burn. It is a favorite floor covering in kitchens and bathrooms. Some artists make prints with it, called *linoleum cuts* or *linocuts*. They carve away the parts of the surface they do not wish to have printed, then cover the smooth parts that remain with ink.

LION

The lion is often called the king of the beasts. Although the lion is one of the largest members of the cat family, it is by no means the largest animal. The lion has a kingly appearance, a powerful body, and a loud roar. When they are three years old, male lions grow a fine mane which covers their neck and shoulders.

Lions are capable of running at great speeds and leaping as far as 30 feet (9.3 m) in one bound. A lion pounces upon its prey and then kills it with his teeth.

Lions live in many parts of Africa. They used to live wild in many parts of Asia, but now they survive only in a game reserve in north-western India.

Like the domestic cat, lions hunt mostly at night. They feed on zebras, antelopes, wild pigs and only occasionally on men.

A pride of lions usually consists of one or two males, seven females, and their young. Each litter contains two or three faintly spotted or streaked cubs. The lionesses are affectionate mothers. They train their playful cubs, and do most of the hunting.

Joseph LISTER (1827–1912)

Joseph Lister was an English surgeon who radically changed surgical practices by introducing the idea of ANTISEPTICS.

Previously, the majority of people died when they had a serious operation. After LOUIS PASTEUR made his discoveries about BACTERIA, Lister realized that GERMS in the air caused blood-poisoning in many wounds, which often resulted in death. Lister disinfected the operating room by spraying it with carbolic acid. He used this germ-killing solution to clean his hands and arms, his surgical instruments, and the patient's wounds. He got his first successful results with the effect of carbolic acid in 1868. Many more of his patients began to recover.

Today, doctors use steam to *sterilize* (disinfect) their instruments. SEE ALSO: ANTISEPTICS, BACTERIA, GERMS.

LITERATURE

By literature we mean stories, poems, and other writings of widespread and long-lasting interest. Literature is the best writing a country has, the writing that it will always be proud of. Usually when we think of literature we think of *novels* (stories of book length) and poetry. But short stories can also be literature. So can *essays*, which give the writer's thoughts about something. So, sometimes, can history books, newspaper articles, and other writings of different kinds.

It is hard to know what causes a piece of writing to be literature, something out of the ordinary. Sometimes it is what the writer has to say; it may be something very important that no one else has said before. Sometimes it is the way the writer gets his ideas across. His writing is a pleasure to read. Every word is just the right word to use, and its combination with the other words he uses is just the right combination.

Literary critics (judges of writing) cannot agree on what is literature and what is not. One hates writing that another praises. In the long run, you must judge for yourself. Look for writing that makes you say, "How true!" or, "How well he says that!" If many others agree with you, the writing can be called literature.

LITHOGRAPHY

Grease and water will not mix. If one is put in the other, it will form a very small ball. This is the basis of lithography, which is a form of printing.

To do a lithograph, the lithographer roughens very slightly a slab of limestone or a sheet of metal. He then draws his design —in reverse, left to right, and right to left—on the surface, using a greasy ink or crayon. He then treats the surface with mild chemicals that remove everything but the grease. Next, he wets the surface; the water runs off the grease but coats everything else. Then he inks the surface with a greasy ink, which runs off the wetted areas but clings to the grease of his design. After this, he presses a paper over the surface. The design is printed by the greasy ink, and everything else is left blank.

Lithography was invented in 1796, but was not much used by artists until the

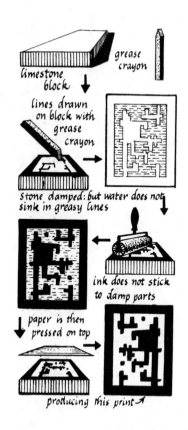

1820s. It became very popular after this, partly because it was easier than the engraving methods then in use, and partly because it was the only method then that would reproduce an artist's lines just as he had drawn them. French artists especially liked lithography in the 19th century. Advertising artists used lithography a great deal because thousands of posters, package wrappers, and other things that they designed could be printed from one drawing.

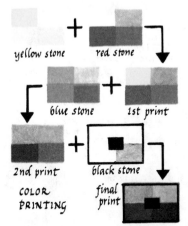

Around 1850, lithography in color (*chromolithography*) came into use. Black was printed from one stone, and each other color used in a chromolithograph needed a stone of its own. "Chromos" were very popular in the Victorian home. They could be used to reproduce famous paintings, but many were original art. The chromos of Currier and Ives, published in the late 19th century, are very highly prized today.

LITTLE LEAGUE BASEBALL

Little League baseball is for boys and girls aged 8 to 12. It is played on a field two-thirds the size of a major league field. Instead of the usual nine innings of a baseball game, a Little League game has only six innings. Each team has about 15 players, who are all taught the basic rules of BASEBALL and given a chance to play the game. There are generally four to six teams in each Little League. Winning teams compete in regional competitions to qualify for the World Series, which takes place each year in Williamsport, Pennsylvania.

Little League began in 1939 with three teams in Williamsport. Today, there are more than 60,000 Little League baseball teams throughout the United States and in 26 other countries. Little Leaguers can go on to play baseball in the Babe Ruth League (for players aged 13 to 15) and the American Legion Junior League (for players up to 18 years old).

David LIVINGSTONE (1813–1873)

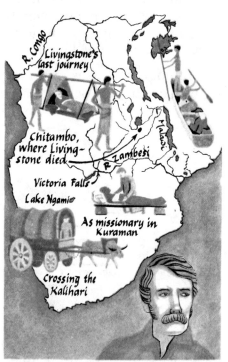

David Livingstone was a Scottish missionary and explorer in Africa. He first went to Africa in 1841, hoping to convert the Africans to Christianity. As he moved from village to village, he explored large areas of the continent. In 1849, he crossed the Kalahari Desert in southwest Africa and reached Lake Ngami. In 1851, he came upon the ZAMBEZI River. Following this river, he discovered Victoria Falls in 1855, situated on the border between Zimbabwe and Zambia. His *Missionary Travels in South Africa*, published in 1857, made him famous and aroused much concern about the African slave trade, which he opposed.

In 1866, he set out to find the source of the Nile. Nothing was heard of him for three years until HENRY STANLEY, an American adventurer, found him—sick and without food—on Lake Tanganyika in central Africa.

Despite his bad health, Livingstone refused to leave Africa, where he later died in the village of Chief Chitambo. His African friends cut out his heart and buried it in Africa and then carried his body 1000 miles (1600 km) to the coast; from there it was sent to England for burial in Westminster Abbey.

LIZARDS

Lizards are a type of scaly *reptile*. Most lizards have four legs, but a few are legless or run about only on their hind legs. Lizards are found mostly in warm climates. Some lay eggs, and others bear live young. The largest lizard is the dragon lizard of Indonesia which may be 10 feet (3.1 m) long and is capable of capturing a wild pig. However, most lizards range in length from a few inches to about 3 feet (92 cm).

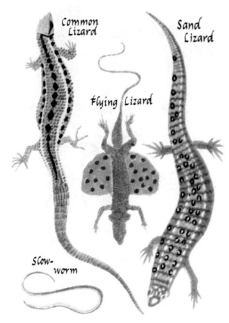

Common Lizard

Sand Lizard

Flying Lizard

Slow-worm

Of all the 3000 different species, only two lizards are poisonous: the Gila monster of the American southwest and the Mexican beaded lizard.

Many lizards have a very unusual way of escaping from their enemies, such as birds and snakes. If one is caught by the tail, it simply sheds its tail, only to grow a new one later. The CHAMELEON and some other lizards have the ability to change their color.

Most lizards are very useful because they eat INSECTS. A few lizards eat plants or animals. SEE ALSO: CHAMELEON, REPTILES.

LLAMA

Standing 4 to 5 feet (1.2–1.6 m) tall, the llama is the largest member of the CAMEL family living in the New World. It is a hoofed animal that lives in South America and is a distinct mammal species that has survived since ancient times. Llamas are usually white; some are solid black or brown, and others are white with black or brown marks.

Male llamas have been used as pack animals in the Andes Mountains of Bolivia and Peru for more than 500 years. These sure-footed animals can carry loads up to 150 pounds (67.5 kg) for 12 hours; llamas are never ridden. Like their camel relatives, when overloaded they lie down, refuse to move, and hiss and spit angrily at their drivers. The female llamas are raised for their milk and meat (which tastes like mutton). The long, soft and silky wool of the Alpaca llamas is woven into beautiful fabrics. Llama skins are tanned for leather.

The world *llama* should not be confused with *lama*—a word meaning a Buddhist priest of Tibet.

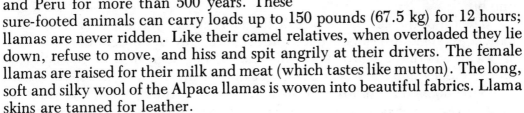

LOBSTER

Lobsters are a type of CRUSTACEAN found along the coastlines of the North Atlantic Ocean and the Mediterranean Sea. They are closely related to the CRAB, shrimp, and crayfish.

Lobsters have 10 legs, two of which are big claws. The larger of the claws is used for crushing prey; the smaller, for catching and holding their food. The flat shells of the lobsters' tails spread out like a fan and are used as a rudder when swimming. Their eyes are on stalks that can look in all directions. They locate their food mostly by their sense of smell, touch, and taste, rather than by sight. Lobsters are scavengers but also prey on shellfish and smaller fish.

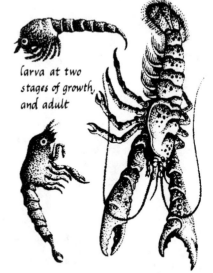

larva at two stages of growth, and adult

The lobster's hard shell is dark green in color. When boiled, the shell turns bright red. The lobster's flesh is delicious and nourishing to eat. Millions of lobsters are caught each year in traps, called lobster pots, and sold as seafood.

Lobsters shed or molt their shells once or twice a year as they grow. Without their shells, they are soft and helpless and are often eaten by other fish and even by other lobsters.

In summer, lobsters live in shallow water among the rocks close to shore; in winter, they move to deep water. The common American lobsters are found from Newfoundland to North Carolina, but especially along the coast of New England. A lobster is full grown in five or six years. The American lobster normally grows to a length of about 1.5 feet (46 cm).

LOCKS and KEYS

Most locks are still worked by keys. A key can consist of a *bow*, which is grasped by the fingers; a *shank*, which is a kind of stem; and a *bit*, the flat part of the key that does the actual locking and unlocking. In the ordinary Yale lock found on most modern doors, there is only a very short shank and a long bit.

The bit of the key has to be exactly the right one if the lock is to work. In many locks there are ridges called *wards*. If the key is the right one, the bit is cut away where the wards are. This allows it to turn, moving the bolt that holds the door shut. The wards will get in the way of any other shape of bit.

Some locks have *tumblers* instead of wards. A tumbler is a lever that the bit must raise to a certain height. When it does so, a projection on the tumbler will rise above a slot in the bolt so that the bolt can move.

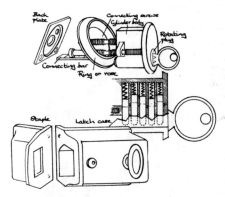

Many locks have *pins* instead of tumblers. The key has to raise a row of these pins to just the right height. In a Yale lock they are in a cylinder, and the key turns the whole cylinder once the pins allow it to turn.

There are also *combination locks*, which are turned by turning a dial to several numbers one after another. And there are *time locks*, which lock and unlock doors by clockwork at certain times.

LOCKS (on canals)

Some *canals* are at the same height from end to end. Many, however, are not. Canals with different levels are built stepwise with the aid of locks.

A lock is a section of the canal that can be closed off with high walls and two sets of watertight gates. Suppose a boat wants to go from a lower part of a canal to a higher one. When it enters the lock the lower gates are open and the upper ones are closed. The

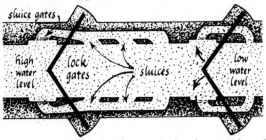

water in the lock is on the lower level, of course. The lower gates swing shut, and water is let slowly into the lock from the upper part of the canal through *sluices*. The water lifts the boat gently to the upper level. Then the upper gates swing open, and the boat goes on its way. If a boat is going downward, the opposite happens. Sluices drain water from the lock into the lower part of the canal.

barge entering lock

lock gates closed: water fills lock, lifts boat to upper level.

lock gates open, barge moves on

Locks are useful not only on canals. Some rivers have been "canalized." One such river is the Ohio. There is a great deal of navigation on the Ohio. Towboats push strings of barges up and down. Before about 1930, they could not do this all the time. They had to wait for enough rain to fill the river. Then the Army Engineers built *dams* to hold the water so that the river would always be deep enough. They converted the Ohio into a huge set of steps. In each dam they put locks for the towboats and their barges. SEE ALSO: CANAL.

LONDON

London, with a population of 7 million, is one of the largest cities in the world. It is the capital of the United Kingdom of Great Britain and Northern Ireland. London is situated in south central ENGLAND, on both sides of the THAMES River. Today, it is a bustling seaport and industrial and financial center, with modern warehouses and office buildings.

London began as a collection of huts in the time of the CELTS, who called it Llundain, which means "the stronghold by the pool." This wide part of the Thames River is still called the Pool of London, where many docks are located. In 43 B.C.,

the Romans landed in Great Britain and later built the first bridge across the Thames. After the Roman Empire fell apart and the Anglo-Saxons invaded the country in the 5th century A.D., London lay nearly deserted for the next 300 years. In the late A.D. 800s, Alfred the Great took over the city, rebuilt the Roman walls, and made it a trading center. William the Conqueror built a fortress to guard London Bridge. Later, this fortress became the Tower of London and was used as a royal palace and a prison.

Many Londoners died in the Great Plague of 1665 that swept through the city. The following year the Great Fire destroyed nearly the entire city, whose buildings were made of wood, with thatch (straw) roofs. Afterward, Sir Christopher

Wren, an English architect, helped rebuild the city. Stone and brick houses were then erected, as well as many beautiful new churches like ST. PAUL'S CATHEDRAL. Over the centuries, many squares, parks, and avenues were added.

During World War II, London was badly bombed and many buildings were destroyed. However, numerous historic buildings were saved. Today, visitors can see Buckingham Palace, where the Queen lives, the Houses of PARLIAMENT, and WESTMINSTER ABBEY, where the Kings and Queens of England have been crowned for centuries. London also has opera houses, theaters, art galleries, and museums, including the famous British Museum. SEE ALSO: ENGLAND, THAMES.

Jack LONDON (1876–1916)

One of America's best-known writers of adventure stories is John Griffith London, a man whose own life was full of adventure. He came of a poor family, and set out to make his own living when he was 14. For years he was a hobo, a sailor, and even a thief. But at the same time he wanted to write, and worked hard practicing different kinds of writing. He also tried to get the education that he had had to give up as a child. In 1897 he joined the rush to Alaska, where gold had been discovered, and his contact with the wild nature there gave him the inspiration for many of his best-known stories. He also sailed through the South Pacific.

Because London had seen much poverty and unemployment, he became a socialist. He believed that private business could not, or would not, allow the common man to live as well as he deserved. Today he is regarded in the Soviet Union, a socialist country, as one of the greatest American writers.

Henry Wadsworth LONGFELLOW (1807–1882)

One of the most famous American poems tells how a Boston silversmith traveled by night in 1775 to warn villagers near Boston that the British were marching to arrest two revolutionary leaders. "Paul Revere's Ride" was written in 1863 by Henry Wadsworth Longfellow, a language professor who was also the most popular poet in the United States during the last century.

Longfellow was born in Maine, and graduated from Bowdoin College there in 1825. In 1836, after years of travel and teaching, be became professor of modern languages at Harvard. He retired from teaching in 1854.

Among Longfellow's other well-known poems are "The Wreck of the Hesperus," *The Song of Hiawatha,* and the poems that make up *Tales of a Wayside Inn.* "Paul Revere's Ride" is one of these.

LOS ANGELES

Los Angeles, in southwestern *California*, is a very large city with more than 7 million people living in or around it. With an excellent harbor on San Pedro Bay, it is a major port of entry, served by railroads, airlines, and a complex system of freeways (express highways). Los Angeles leads the U.S. in the production of aircraft and aircraft parts. Other important industries include oil refining, food processing, printing and publishing, and the manufacturing of chemicals, electronics equipment, and clothing, especially sportswear. Since the early 20th century, Hollywood, a part of Los Angeles, has been the movie-making center of the U.S. More recently, the establishment of television studios has contributed to Los Angeles's prosperity.

In 1769, Gaspar de Portola led a Spanish expedition to the area. Two years later the Mission San Gabriel was founded. The city's official founding was in 1781, when the Spanish colonial governor brought settlers from Mexico to live on the west bank of what is now the Los Angeles River. SEE ALSO: CALIFORNIA.

LOTUS

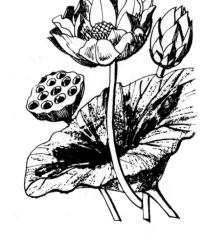

This name refers to certain unrelated plants. It is given to several kinds of water lilies, such as the Egyptian lotus or sacred lily of the Nile, whose white or pink petals float upon the water. Also, there is the Chinese lotus, whose petals and unusual round leaves stand above the water. The Chinese lotus is sacred to Buddhists and Hindus. The American, or yellow, lotus that is found in eastern North America is also called water chinquapin.

The ancient Greek poet Homer told of a magical lotus fruit which put the followers of ODYSSEUS in such a happy, irresponsible state that they did not want to journey home. This legendary fruit was probably the Mediterranean jujube shrub whose fruit is used for making wine.

The art of ancient Egypt frequently used the symbol of the lotus flower.

LOUDSPEAKER

When you hear a sound, your ear is receiving tiny quiverings of the air. A very low sound comes from the air shaking perhaps 50 times a second, while a very high sound is heard when the air shakes many thousands of times a second.

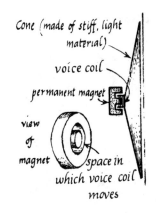

Cone (made of stiff, light material)

voice coil

permanent magnet

view of magnet

space in which voice coil moves

The purpose of a loudspeaker is to shake the air in such a way that "live" sounds (which have just been made) and recorded ones can be heard by more than one person. A microphone, a record, or a recording tape send out tiny pulses of electricity that enter a permanent magnet that is part of the speaker. The cone of the speaker, which actually shakes the air, has a coil of fine wire, the *voice coil*, at its center. The magnet causes the voice coil (also called the *motor*) to shake, and this shakes the cone. The cone is made of a light, stiff material.

There are often special speakers for high-pitched sounds (*tweeters*) and low-pitched ones (*woofers*).

LOUIS XIV (1638–1715)

At the age of 5, Louis became King of FRANCE. During his childhood, however, France was ruled by the powerful minister, Cardinal Mazarin. After Mazarin died in 1661, Louis took over the government and made himself an absolute monarch, with absolute power over his subjects. Although he picked able men to do his wishes, he made all the decisions. His word was law. "I am the State," he said.

Because the sun became his symbol of power, he was named the "Sun King." He loved splendor and extravagance. At his magnificent palace, which he built at Versailles, outside PARIS, Louis surrounded himself with artists, writers, musicians, and the French noblemen.

But his glorious reign faded. Louis led France into war with other countries. Determined to have more territory, he tried unsuccessfully to seize Holland. Louis fought other wars to gain power and land in Europe, but he was defeated and wasted much of France's wealth with his efforts.

LOUISIANA

Louisiana, a southern state of the United States, consists mainly of coastal plain. Part of the state is the delta of the MISSISSIPPI RIVER. There are numerous marshes, lakes, and bayous (sluggish streams) in southern Louisiana. In the north are low rolling hills covered with pine forests. Baton Rouge is the capital.

In the early 16th century, the Spanish explored this region. In 1682, a group of Frenchmen led by La Salle sailed down the Mississippi River and claimed all the land drained by the river for France. La Salle named the territory Louisiana in honor of his king Louis XIV For a while in the late 18th century, France lost control of the region but gained it back in 1800. Three years later, the U.S. bought the entire Louisiana Territory, which included all the land from the Mississippi River to the Rocky Mountains. The present-day state of Louisiana was carved out of this huge territory in 1812. Louisiana was the site of the Battle of New Orleans in 1815, when the British were defeated by the Americans under ANDREW JACKSON.

Today, Louisiana has almost 4 million inhabitants, some of whom speak a form of French, called Creole. Many work in agriculture, growing cotton, soybeans, rice, and sugar cane. Louisiana has large oil and natural gas fields, as well as deposits of salt and sulphur. It makes chemicals and food products, and has a large fishing industry. Muskrats are caught in the woods and swamps of Louisiana, and their fur is used in coats. There are also opossum, racoon, mink, and otter. The state manufactures paper, lumber, and many wood products.

LOUISIANA PURCHASE

The Louisiana Purchase, called the greatest land bargain in U.S. history, doubled the size of the United States. The Louisiana Territory extended from the Mississippi River to the Rocky Mountains, and from the Gulf of Mexico (where Louisiana is today) to the Canadian border. In 1803, this territory of 828,000 square miles (2,144,250 km²) was bought at less than three cents per acre.

The Louisiana Territory had been controlled successively by France, Britain, and Spain. In 1802, NAPOLEON, the French leader, regained the territory from Spain. Realizing that American trade depended on the use of the Mississippi River and the port of New Orleans, THOMAS JEFFERSON instructed Robert Livingston, U.S. minister at Paris, and JAMES MONROE, U.S. diplomatic agent, to try to buy New Orleans.

Napoleon offered surprisingly to sell not only New Orleans but the whole Louisiana Territory. The Americans accepted and signed a treaty, agreeing on the sale of the territory to the U.S. for a price of $15 million. About a fourth of this sum covered claims of U.S. citizens against France, which the

498

U.S. government agreed to pay off. The U.S. Senate, afraid Napoleon might change his mind, quickly ratified the treaty in 1803.

The exact size of the territory was not known. The LEWIS AND CLARK EXPEDITION set out to explore it and to establish its boundaries.

LUBRICATION

Oil is splashed
around inside a car engine

The inside of a ball-bearing (in
a bicycle wheel hub, for instance)
is packed with grease.

When two objects slide against each other, *friction* (rubbing) results. This friction may damage one or both of the objects. To avoid this damage is the purpose of lubrication. A *lubricant* is some sort of material—often a liquid—that keeps the two objects a little distance apart. Its rubbing against them is so light that it does no harm. Lubricants keep machinery running smoothly and efficiently. Even the body has lubricants in its joints.

Many kinds of lubricants are in use. Heavy machinery is often greased, while typewriters and clocks use a light oil. Locks are often lubricated with powdered graphite. Even compressed air can be used as a lubricant.

LUKE

Luke was a friend of the Apostle Paul and helped him on his mission of preaching Christianity. Paul calls him his "beloved physician," and he was probably a doctor.

He wrote the Gospel of Luke and the Acts of the Apostles, two books of the New Testament. His Gospel includes the Christmas Story and the stories of the Good Samaritan and the Prodigal Son. The Acts of the Apostles tells of his missions with Paul and of his accompanying Paul to Rome, where Paul was eventually executed by the government.

LUMBERING

Lumbering is the process of cutting down trees and turning them into useful pieces of wood. Most forests these days are planted rather than naturally grown. If the trees are planted for use as lumber, the owners often plan for some to be harvested, some to be allowed to grow, and new ones to be planted in any one year.

In *harvesting*, a tree is *undercut* on one side with a big wedge-shaped cut and *backcut* on the other side with a level slit. The tree falls in the direction of the undercut. Then its limbs are chopped off and it is stripped of bark and sawn into convenient lengths. It is dragged or trucked to a sawmill, usually, and is sawn into boards and square timbers. But some logs are left whole for use as telephone poles or other round objects. Some are turned against a broad knife to make *veneers*, large, thin sheets of wood that can be glued to make plywood or can be applied to less attractive wood to make an agreeable surface. And some trees are chopped up into small pieces that are pressed together to make different kinds of fiberboard or particle board. Wood is a very old material but still, in spite of new metals and plastics, a very useful one. In the United States, lumbering is one of the most important industries.

SAW MILLS

LUNGS

Lungs are organs of breathing or *respiration* for man and other land animals. In the lungs, oxygen from the air passes into the BLOOD, while at the same time carbon dioxide and water vapor (the waste products of body growth and repair) pass in the reverse direction.

In man, the two lungs occupy each side of the chest behind the rib cage, from the collarbone to the diaphragm. The air that man breathes in travels down the windpipe (*trachea*) and then on through two tubes, called *bronchi*. The bronchi branch out in all directions bringing air to all parts of the lungs.

500

The smallest branches are tubes ending in microscopic air sacs, called *alveoli*, which are supplied by a network of microscopic blood vessels called *capillaries*. There are more than 600 million alveoli in the two lungs. Here the gases between the air and blood are exchanged. The heart then pumps the oxygenated (treated with oxygen) blood to all parts of the body.

Chest muscles and a muscle underneath the lungs, the *diaphragm*, enable the lungs to fill and deflate in drawing air in and out.

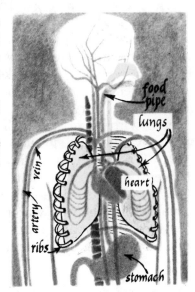

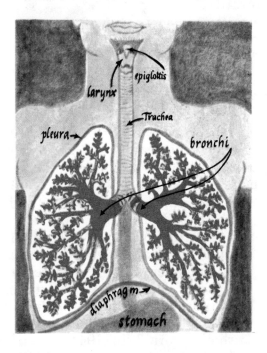

Each lung is enclosed by a kind of oil-filled sac, called the *pleura*, which forms an airtight cavity for each lung. An inflammation of the pleura results in the illness *pleurisy*; an inflammation of the bronchi is called *bronchitis*. If the lungs themselves are inflamed, the illness is called *pneumonia*. SEE ALSO: RESPIRATION.

LUTE Lutes are instruments with rounded backs and long stems, looking a little like mandolins. They usually have five or six pairs of strings along with one single bass string. The head, which contains the peg box for tightening the strings, is usually at an angle to the neck. The *lutanist* plucks the string with his fingers.

Lutes were possibly invented by the Arabs. They were very popular in Europe from the Middle Ages to about 1700, and are becoming popular again now that we have become interested in medieval and Renaissance music.

MACADAM

John McAdam was a Scottish merchant who around 1800 found a new way of making roads. Most roads of his time were very bad, more like dirt paths, so he invented a built-up road surface. It began with large rocks, which were covered with small stones. These, in turn, were covered with gravel, packed down tight. This made a compact road that allowed rain water to sift through. He also gave his road surface a *crown* (upward curve) so that the rain water would run off the sides. Macadam roads, now treated with tar or oil, are still being made.

Douglas MacARTHUR (1880–1964)

Douglas MacArthur, a famous American general, was born in Little Rock, Arkansas. After graduating from West Point at the head of his class, he served in the Philippines, Mexico, and Japan, and later fought in France during WORLD WAR I. From 1919 to 1922, he was superintendent of West Point. In 1930, he was made chief of staff of the U.S. Army.

After WORLD WAR II broke out, General MacArthur became commander of the U.S. forces in the Pacific. The Japanese forced him to withdraw from the Philippines, but MacArthur promised the people, "I shall return." In 1944, his troops landed on Leyte, an island in the central Philippines. By February, 1945, the Japanese had been driven from the islands. On September 2, 1945, MacArthur, as Supreme Allied Commander, received the formal surrender of Japan on board the U.S. battleship *Missouri* in Tokyo harbor.

In 1950, at the start of the KOREAN WAR, General MacArthur was put in command of the United Nations forces. For disobeying orders and making critical remarks, President Truman removed him as commanding officer.

NELSON'S
ENCYCLOPEDIA
FOR
YOUNG READERS

NELSON'S
ENCYCLOPEDIA
FOR
YOUNG READERS

EDITED BY

LAURENCE URDANG

CLIFTON FADIMAN

MILLICENT SELSAM

R. J. UNSTEAD

WILLIAM WORTHY

VOLUME II
MACKEREL -- ZURICH

THOMAS NELSON PUBLISHERS
NASHVILLE

Editor in Chief
Laurence Urdang

Managing Editor
George C. Kohn

Consulting Editors
Clifton Fadiman
Millicent Selsam
R. J. Unstead
William Worthy

Editors
Hope Gilbert
Walter C. Kidney
Lynne C. Meyer

Assistant Editors
Anthony J. Castagno
Janet Miller

ISBN 0-8407-5184-2

Library of Congress Catalog Card No. 80-14522

TO THE READER

This *Encyclopedia* will answer many of your questions about the world in which you live. It will guide you from very early times through the present day and point you toward tomorrow. It will take you to every major country of the globe and let you explore the depths of outer space. It will tell you how machines work, why nature behaves as it does, and when the important events of history occurred. You will find it fascinating.

The *Encyclopedia* is laid out in alphabetical order. If you don't find an article about a certain subject, check the index at the end of the last volume. The index may show that you can find the information under a different heading. Or perhaps you wish to find more information about a particular subject. Again, try the index; it may direct you to other articles that will give you the details.

Some words are printed in small capitals, like this: ABBEY. This means that the *Encyclopedia* has an entire entry on that subject, in case you want to know more about it.

We hope you enjoy using *Nelson's Encyclopedia for Young Readers*. The editors have prepared it with your special interests in mind. It will introduce you to many exciting ideas and will challenge you to learn more.

THE PUBLISHERS

MACKEREL

Mackerel are open-sea fish that are related to the tuna and bonito. They live on both sides of the North Atlantic and Pacific oceans. They travel in *schools* (groups) and often feed upon herring and squid. This fish is an important food because of its rich, oily flesh. Like herrings, they are caught with drift nets when they come close to shore to lay their eggs. Females lay about 600,000 eggs which float on the top of the water.

A mackerel is about 16 inches (40.6 cm) long and has silver sides and a greenish back with black wavy stripes.

The common mackerel has a large tail fin and is a fast swimmer.

James MADISON (1751–1836)

James Madison, the fourth President of the United States, was a short man with a brilliant mind. Frail and sickly as a boy, he studied hard and acquired a deep understanding of government. Until 1787, Madison served either in the Virginia legislature or in the U.S. Congress.

At the Constitutional Convention of 1787, Madison took a leading part in the writing of the U.S. CONSTITUTION. Because some of the Constitution's basic ideas were his, he is often called the "Father of the Constitution." He also kept a complete record of the convention's proceedings and helped to write *The Federalist Papers* with John Jay and Alexander Hamilton. This series of essays explained and urged the adoption of the Constitution, making clear the new government to the American people.

From 1789 to 1797, Madison was a U.S. Congressman and played a major role in preparing the first 10 amendments to the Constitution, known as the BILL OF RIGHTS. Later, after serving as Secretary of State under Thomas Jefferson, he was elected President as a Democratic-Republican in 1808. Immediately, he had to deal with attacks by France and Britain on American seamen and ships. He was unsuccessful, and the WAR OF 1812 broke out between the U.S. and Britain.

After the war, during Madison's second term as President, he approved a new national bank and built up the military and naval forces of the country.

MADRID

Madrid, the capital of SPAIN, is situated on the Manzanares River. The city lies in the center of the country, on a vast, open plateau more than 2000 feet (620 m) above sea level. As a result, it has extreme heat and cold throughout the year.

In the Plaza Mayor

Madrid is a fairly new city. After the 1890s, its trade and industry grew rapidly because of the railroads and modern highways. Today, it has large printing, publishing, and motion picture industries. Also, leather, tobacco, furniture, carpets, and jewelry are manufactured there.

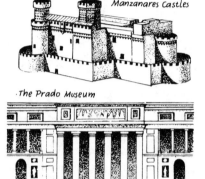
Manzanares Castles

The city was once a Moorish fortress and later a residence for Spanish kings and queens. In 1561, Madrid became the capital of Spain. One of the greatest buildings is the Royal Palace, which took almost thirty years to build and was completed by 1764. Another famous building is

The Prado Museum

the Prado, a museum which contains some of the greatest paintings in the world. There are also libraries, bullrings, parks, and a modern university in the city. SEE ALSO: SPAIN.

Ferdinand MAGELLAN (1480–1521)

Ferdinand Magellan was a Portuguese navigator who led the first expedition to sail around the world. Although he died before the end of the voyage, his determination inspired his crew to complete the trip.

Magellan wanted to find a shorter route to Asia by sailing around the Americas. The Portuguese king was not interested, but the Spanish king gave him 5 small ships and 265 men, and in 1519 Magellan set sail for the Molucca (Spice) Islands, in the EAST INDIES, going west instead of east.

He sailed down the east coast of South

America until he found the passage which is now called the Strait of Magellan. In 1520, his expedition, after a stormy trip through the strait, sailed into a calm ocean, which Magellan named the PACIFIC (or peaceful). After crossing the Pacific, he landed first on Guam Island and then on the PHILIPPINES, where he was killed by the natives. His men struggled on to the Spice Islands. Only one ship with 18 men managed to return to Spain in 1522.

MAGIC

Before men knew much science, they thought that by using special tricks and ceremonies they could change the weather and make crops grow, as well as make a person behave as they wished. This was magic. Later, when men saw that their magic did not always work, they began to believe in spirits, or gods, greater than themselves.

Most persons who practiced magic had secret words, special rites, strange dances, and odd costumes. They often believed they had power over a person if they obtained a lock of his or her hair. They also carried magical objects, such as stones, herbs, or claws, that helped them cast spells, or which kept away bad luck.

Such beliefs are still held by primitive peoples in Africa and the Pacific Islands. One kind of magic, belief in witches, still

exists in parts of the United States. Also, many people today believe in superstitions, such as a rabbit's foot is lucky and breaking a mirror is unlucky.

The word "magician" today means an entertainer who does tricks that seem impossible. He may saw a person in half, disappear from a locked box, or read someone's mind. All these tricks are done by quickness of hand or body or by mechanical help. One of the most famous magicians was Harry Houdini, who could escape from handcuffs, chains, ropes, and metal boxes.

505

MAGNA CARTA

The Magna Carta ("The Great Charter") was an agreement between the barons (noblemen) of England and KING JOHN. King John of England had forced the barons to pay higher taxes to support his war with France. Finally, the barons rebelled and drew up a list of their ancient rights. They then wrote them down and met with King John at a place called Runnymede. There, in 1215, the barons compelled King John to sign the Magna Carta.

This document gave less power to the English kings and granted certain rights to the English barons. The king would have to get permission from a council of barons and churchmen before he could raise taxes or make important decisions. The king must also rule according to the laws of the realm, and must recognize the rights of the council. This council was the basis of the English PARLIAMENT and the U.S. CONGRESS.

At first, only the barons were helped by the Magna Carta. As the years went by, however, the English people believed its rights applied to everyone, especially with respect to taxes and fair trial.

MAGNESIUM

Magnesium is a metallic element discovered by SIR HUMPHRY DAVY in 1808. It is extremely lightweight and is silver-white in color. When mixed with other metals, magnesium makes light and strong ALLOYS, which are used in the aircraft industry. It unites very rapidly with oxygen to burn with a bright white light. Magnesium is widely used in flash bulbs, flares, and fireworks. Some of magnesium's compounds are important in medicine (for example, Epsom salts and milk of magnesia).

MAGNET

A magnet is a piece of IRON or STEEL that has the power to attract objects made of the same material. It will also attract the metals NICKEL and cobalt, as well as their ALLOYS. Steel is an alloy of iron and is strongly *magnetic*.

The word *magnet* comes from Magnesia, a district in Turkey. Here men first noticed about 500 B.C. that certain black stones attracted iron. These stones were natural magnets and were an iron ore, now called *magnetite*.

It was soon discovered that a piece of magnetite or *lodestone* ("leading stone") suspended by a thread or placed on a scrap of floating wood, would always point north and south. A ship's compass is based on this unusual property of magnetized iron. The end of the magnetic needle or bar magnet that points north is known as the north *pole* (*N*) and the other end is the south *pole* (*S*).

In magnetic materials such as iron, the ATOMS themselves are like miniature magnets, all pointing in the same north-south direction. In a nonmagnet, the atoms are arranged in a haphazard fashion. When a magnet is near or touching an unmagnetized metal, it causes the miniature atom magnets to arrange themselves in orderly N-S lines and to become magnetized. Heating, hammering, or dropping a magnet can cause it to lose its magnetism because the atoms become disarranged.

Formerly, new magnets were made by stroking a piece of iron in the same direction with a magnet. Passing an ELECTRIC CURRENT around a piece of iron was later discovered to produce a magnet. *Soft* iron produces temporary magnets that keep their magnetism as long as an electric current is flowing. These *electromagnets* are very useful for electric motors, generators, and cranes that lift scrap iron.

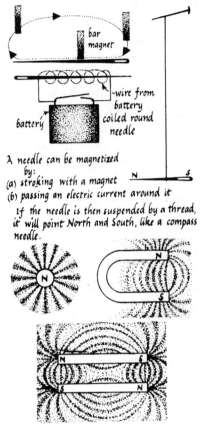

A needle can be magnetized by:
(a) stroking with a magnet
(b) passing an electric current around it

If the needle is then suspended by a thread, it will point North and South, like a compass needle.

The magnetic forces around magnets can be shown by placing magnets under sheets of paper, and sprinkling iron filings over them

MAGNIFYING GLASS

If we look at a fly, rays of LIGHT are reflected from the fly and come in straight lines to our eyes. The rays of light are brought together by our eyes to give a true image of the fly. However, if we look at the fly through a magnifying glass, it bends the rays of light as they pass through its double convex LENS.

Since light rays are bent toward the thickest part of the lens, they enter our eyes as if they had come from a much bigger fly. Therefore, the fly appears enlarged or *magnified*.

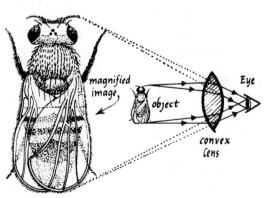

MAGPIE

The magpie is a member of the CROW family. It is about the size of a pigeon and has shiny black and white feathers with a long wedge-shaped tail.

Magpies are *resident* birds—that is, they do not migrate. In winter, they gather in large noisy flocks consisting of as many as 100 birds. The rest of the year, they are seen in pairs or small groups on farmlands, open rangelands, or the edges of woods.

A magpie's bulky nest is built in brush or at the top of a bush or tree. It is made of sticks, turf, and clay, and shaped to form a deep cup, plastered with earth and lined with fibers.

Although they eat insects and small animals that are harmful to crops, magpies are not liked by farmers, gamekeepers, and ranchers because they also feed on corn and on the eggs of gamebirds, as well as peck at sores on the backs of range animals.

MAINE

Maine, the largest of the New England states, lies in the extreme northeastern part of the United States. It has many thickly wooded areas, with mountains, lakes, and rivers. Its coastline on the Atlantic is long and rocky, deeply indented with bays and inlets. Many islands are scattered along the coast, too.

Winters are generally very cold in Maine, and summers are sometimes so cool that people must heat their houses. In spite of this and the rugged countryside, Maine attracts skiers, hikers, and campers to its many resorts, forests, and parks. Fishermen love its beautiful, inland lakes and streams.

In 1498, JOHN CABOT explored the coast and claimed the area for England. The British and French competed for control, establishing unsuccessful settlements in the early 1600s. Finally, several colonies were set up by the British in southern Maine, at Monhegan and York. The colonists lived peacefully with the Abenaki Indians, who often joined them to fight off the raiding Iroquois. In 1647, Maine became part of the colony of Massachusetts, but separated from it in 1820 to become a state.

Maine has a large fishing industry. Lobster, cod, sardines, flounder, mackerel, and haddock are caught in great numbers. From Maine's Aroostook region in the north come many potatoes. Farmers also grow sugar beets and blueberries for export to other states. Lumber, paper, and leather goods are manufactured.

Maine has slightly more than 1 million people. Its capital is Augusta.

MALARIA

Malaria is a disease caused when a tiny animal parasite enters a person's blood. In the past, this disease killed each year thousands of people in tropical and subtropical countries. Much of the credit for the control of malaria is given to Charles Laveran, a French doctor, who discovered in 1880 the parasite that causes malaria, and to Sir Ronald Ross, a British doctor, who discovered in 1898 the certain kind of mosquito that carries the parasite from one person to another.

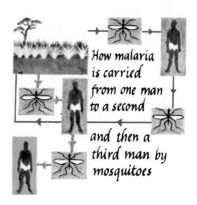

How malaria is carried from one man to a second and then a third man by mosquitoes

A person with malaria develops chills, high fever, headache, and profuse sweating. These attacks of fever can sometimes recur a few days or years later. Patients are now treated with the drugs of quinine, atabrine, and plasmochin. Also, since the mosquitoes' larvae develop in stagnant water, their growth can be prevented by pouring oil on the surface or by draining the water. SEE ALSO: MOSQUITO.

MALAYSIA

The country of Malaysia, occupying the southern Malay Peninsula in Southeast Asia and the northern part of the island of Borneo, was formed in 1963. The two parts are separated by about 400 miles (644 km) of the South China Sea. Malaysia is a little larger than New Mexico. Kuala Lumpur, on the Malay Peninsula, is the capital.

Tropical rain forests cover much of the country, which has fertile areas along the coast and mountains inland. The 12.5 million people of Malaysia have come from China, India, Pakistan, Sri Lanka, and England, as well as Malaysia itself. Many Malaysians work on the country's rich rubber plantations and in the large tin mines. Others grow rice, tea, coconuts, and fruits.

MALT

Grain (usually barley) that has been cleaned, soaked in water, and then spread on a floor until it begins to germinate (sprout) is called *malt*. When this occurs, the STARCH in the grain turns to malt sugar, called maltose, which is dried in a kiln, cured, and then mashed.

Because maltose is an easily digested sugar and good for body-building, it is used in the foods of infants and invalids. It is also used in malted milk shakes. The fermentation of malt by YEAST is important in the brewing of beer.

MALTA

Malta, lying in the Mediterranean about 60 miles (97 km) south of Sicily, is a small country with a long history. It comprises the islands of Malta, Gozo, and Comino, as well as two uninhabited rocks. Valletta is the capital. This country was ruled successively by the Phoenicians, Greeks, Carthaginians, Romans, and Arabs. St. Paul was

shipwrecked here. During the Middle Ages, the island was fought over, and in 1530, Charles V, the Holy Roman Emperor, gave it to the Knights Hospitalers, the last of the Crusaders, who later were called the Knights of Malta. The Knights held it until 1798, when it was surrendered to NAPOLEON. Two years later, the British ousted the French and set up important naval bases on the island. In 1974, Malta became an independent republic, which today has a population of about 330,000.

MAMMALS

Mammals are one group of VERTEBRATES (animals with backbones). Mammals have three important characteristics: (1) their young are born alive, (2) they nurse their young with milk from the mother, and (3) they are partly or completely covered with hair. Mammals are also warm-blooded— that is, the temperature of their body stays the same whatever the surrounding temperature. Mammals usually have four legs. The WHALE, however, has only flippers.

Elephant

Goats

giraffe

Kangaroo

Bat

Duck-billed Platypus

The duck-billed platypus and the porcupine anteater are two exceptional mammals because they lay eggs. They also have fur and nurse their young.

Man belongs to a group of mammals called *primates*. They have large brains in proportion to their bodies and hands that can grasp things. SEE ALSO: ANIMALS.

MAMMOTHS

Mammoths were ancient animals belonging to the ELEPHANT family. Unlike the elephant, they were covered with long, shaggy hair. Their long tusks curved upward.

The American mammoth was the

largest species identified. The remains of one found in Nebraska in 1915 had a pair of tusks weighing 498 pounds (224 kg) and each tusk was more than 13.5 feet (4.2 m) long. The animal stood about 14 feet (4.3 m) in height.

Mammoths used to live in the cold climates of SIBERIA, Europe, and North America. Drawings in caves show that man hunted them in very early times.

In 1806, the complete carcass of a mammoth was discovered perfectly preserved in the ice of Siberia. Part of the flesh, which was still in good condition, had been eaten by wolves and bears. This wooly mammoth was about the size of a modern Indian elephant.

MAN

Physically, man belongs to the group of MAMMALS called *primates*. Apes also are primates, but man is very different from apes. Man has a bigger brain and the ability to use LANGUAGE and express complicated ideas to another person. His brain can reason and solve difficult problems. Man's scientific name is *Homo sapiens*. Homo means "man" and *sapiens* means "wise." Man can choose to do good or evil, to love or hate, and by his actions determine his own future.

About a century ago, CHARLES DARWIN explained his theory of EVOLUTION. Darwin believed that human beings had evolved from a lower form of life. Today, anthropologists (scientists who study man's history) investigate the remains of early man to test Darwin's theory. SEE ALSO: LANGUAGE.

511

MANITOBA

Manitoba is known as the "prairie province" of CANADA. However, only a small area in the south is actually treeless grassland. The rest of the province consists of forests, lakes, rivers, and subarctic tundra (barren plains). Manitoba has nearly 400 miles (644 km) of saltwater coast on Hudson Bay in the northeast. WINNIPEG is Manitoba's capital and largest city. There are more than 1 million inhabitants of the province.

Manitoba's major source of income is from agriculture. Wheat, barley, flaxseed, and rapeseed are grown, and sheep, cattle, and hogs are raised. Fishing, lumbering, mining (copper, zinc, nickel), and fur farming (mink) are important industries. Manitoba's leading manufactured goods are dairy, meat, and other food products. There is abundant hydroelectric power for industry.

In 1670, the Hudson's Bay Company began setting up fur trading posts in the area, known then as Rupert's Land. Fur traders kept permanent settlers out until 1812, when a Scottish farming colony was established near present-day Winnipeg. The area became part of Canada in 1870.

MAPLE

There are about 150 varieties of maple trees—13 of which grow in North America. Most maple varieties are from Japan and China and include several red leafed kinds.

The tallest and finest types are native to North America. The big-leaf maple is the second most important hardwood of the Pacific northwest. It grows about 100 feet (31 m) tall and is valuable commercially for its use in furniture and flooring.

Among the hardwood species of eastern America are the sugar maple and the black maple. Both are important sources for timber and maple syrup. The sugar maple is also a popular shade tree. The red, or swamp, maple is a soft wood tree that grows rapidly and is also an excellent shade tree. It does not produce the high quality wood of the hard maples, but it produces the most spectacular autumn foliage of any type of tree.

The fruit of the maple is a double *samara*, which consists of two long, compressed wings that join the seeds at their bases. These winged fruits are dispersed by the wind. The leaves of most maples are simple and shaped like a hand with the fingers extended.

MAPS

A map is a drawing, usually on a flat surface, showing part or all of the features of an area. Some maps show the entire world, the heavens, or the moon, while others show a country, state, town, or city in detail. A world map that has been drawn on a sphere is called a *globe*. Maps often show the imaginary directional lines called LATITUDE AND LONGITUDE.

There are several kinds of maps. A *physical* or *relief* map shows land elevations and rivers. A political map shows man-made boundaries of towns, counties, states or countries. Maps for sailors are called navigational charts. They show the shape of the coastline as well as the depth of the waters. Some maps show average temperatures, rainfall, population, and types of farming, industry, or religion.

The *scale* of a map shows the amount by which actual distances have been reduced to fit them on the map. For example, a scale of "1 inch = 12 miles" means that 12 miles on the ground is represented by 1 inch on the map.

Road maps are especially helpful to the traveler. They give such information as the names of towns and cities, mountains, bodies of water as well as the sizes of the highways (and whether or not they are under major construction), route numbers, and the locations of auto ferries. Often such maps give descriptive listings of places to see and to stay overnight and the distances between major cities.

Contour lines shown on some maps indicate the height of the land above sea level. When these lines are close together the slope is steep. The number next to a contour line shows its elevation above sea level. For instance, "400" means 400 feet above sea level. North is often, but not always, at the top of a map. SEE ALSO: LATITUDE AND LONGITUDE.

MARATHON

About 26 miles (42 km) northeast of ATHENS is the famous plain called Marathon. There, in 490 B.C., the Greeks defeated the Persians, who lost more than 6000 men. Only 200 Greeks were killed.

A famous Athenian courier (messenger) named Pheidippides ran the 26 miles back to Athens to tell the Greek people of their victory. After announcing the news, he dropped dead.

The Plain of Marathon as it is today

Today we often call any long-distance race a marathon, honoring the great feat of Pheidippides. A marathon race is one of the events of the Olympic Games; it is exactly 26 miles and 385 yards (41 km 992 m) long. Each year thousands run in the Boston Marathon, another 26-mile race.

MARBLE

Marble is a type of LIMESTONE hardened ages ago under great heat and pressure. White is the color of pure marble. Black marble is produced by the presence of CARBON. Other impurities in the rock can add a greenish or reddish coloration.

When exposed to a moist, acid environment, marble crumbles readily, but it is very lasting in dry surroundings. Despite the fact that it does not resist weathering, marble has nevertheless been popular with architects and sculptors. Marble was widely used by the ancient Greeks and Romans. The famous marbles at Carrara and Siena, in Italy, were used by the Romans and the Italian sculptors of the Renaissance, such as Michelangelo. In the U.S., the finest marbles come from Vermont.

Marble takes on a high gloss. Its luster is due to the fact that light is able to pass a short distance into the stone and be reflected back by inner crystals. SEE ALSO: LIMESTONE.

Guglielmo MARCONI (1874–1937)

Guglielmo Marconi was an Italian electrical engineer who is considered the father of radio broadcasting.

As a boy, Marconi began to do experiments in electricity and telegraphy. When he grew older, he experimented with sending and receiving messages by means of electromagnetic waves in the air. In 1896, he went to England and set up the first wireless telegraph company.

At first his wireless signals were sent about a mile (1.6 km). He then began to set up his wireless equipment in lighthouses and ships, realizing how it could help ships in trouble. In 1899, a ship used Marconi's "wireless" and all aboard were saved. Two years later, he received in Newfoundland the first transatlantic radio signals, sent in MORSE CODE.

In 1909, Marconi received jointly with K.F. Braun the Nobel Prize in Physics for his work in radio telegraphy. After World War I, he turned his attention to short waves and later to microwaves.

514

MARCO POLO (1254–1324)

Marco Polo was a famous Italian adventurer and explorer. He was born in VENICE, and at the age of 17, he went with his father and uncle on a caravan trip to CHINA. In 1275, they reached Cambuluc (now Peking, China). Marco Polo soon became a favorite at the palace of Kublai Khan, the emperor of the Mongols.

Kublai Khan sent Marco all over his empire and even had him serve for a while as governor of a Chinese province. Marco learned Chinese well and visited also Burma, Tibet, and India.

After 17 years, the Polos left the Kublai's empire and returned to Venice in 1295. In spite of the rich silks and jewels they brought back with them, nobody believed the fabulous stories Marco told. Europeans could not believe an advanced civilization existed in China.

In 1296, Marco was taken prisoner by the Genoese during a sea battle, and while in prison, he dictated an account of all his travels. It became one of the best known travel books in the world, as well as a major Western source of information on the East.

MARGARINE

Margarine, also called oleo-margarine, is an inexpensive substitute for BUTTER. It was invented by a French chemist named Mège-Mouries in 1867 and was introduced into the United States in 1874. Beef fat, known as oleo, was the chief ingredient of margarine at first.

Today, margarine is a blend of skim milk and animal or vegetable oils. In the United States, lard or oil from corn, cottonseeds, peanuts, and soybeans is used. Other countries use whale fat or coconut and palm oils. Vitamins A and D are added to margarine so that it has the same food value as butter.

Margarine is white in color until mixed with a yellow vegetable dye to imitate the appearance of butter. SEE ALSO: BUTTER.

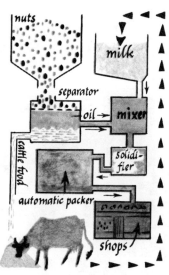

The Making of Margarine

515

MARK

Mark was one of the twelve APOSTLES of JESUS. He is the author of the Gospel of Mark. After the death of Jesus, he went on a mission to Asia Minor with PAUL and Barnabas. He may have written his Gospel after meeting PETER and getting information from him.

Mark is supposed to have founded the Christian church in Egypt, and is the patron saint of Venice. He is often shown with his symbol, a lion.

MARKETS

During the MIDDLE AGES, markets became very important throughout Europe. As towns increased in size and townspeople needed more than they could provide by themselves, merchants and peddlers congregated in one central area of a town, called a marketplace. Country people and fishermen also came from nearby districts to offer their goods for sale to the townspeople. Open air stands displayed meat, vegetables, and fruit, as well as pottery, knives, clothing, and so on. Later permanent shops became established in large rectangular marketplaces for year-round exchange and sale of goods.

Some towns in the Middle Ages got permission from the lord or king to hold very large markets. These were called FAIRS. Today, fairs still survive in many country areas, where farmers gather to show, buy, or sell animals and produce. Industrial fairs are held in large cities today.

In the 1800s, the general store replaced the public market with its stalls and booths. In the United States, the general store was a major institution of the country town. Later, independent stores developed, each with its own particular merchandise. In the 20th century, the independent store met stiff competition from chain stores, which were set up for the mass distribution of goods.

There are still, however, American towns that hold old-fashioned market days, when booths are set up once a year for selling handmade items. Many cities in the world still have marketplaces where one kind of goods is sold, such as leather items in Florence, Italy, or straw items in Nassau, in the Bahamas.

The stock market is a place where buyers and sellers come together to trade goods or securities.

MARQUETTE and JOLIET

Jacques Marquette (1637–1675) and Louis Joliet (1645–1700) were the first white men to explore the upper Mississippi River. They were also the first to report the existence of a water system from the Great Lakes to the Gulf of Mexico.

Marquette, a French missionary, and Joliet, a French explorer, were sent in 1673 on an expedition to find the direction and mouth of the Mississippi River. The governor of New France in Canada believed they would discover a route to the Pacific. With five other men, they set out in canoes across Lake Michigan, traveled up the Fox River in central Wisconsin, and portaged (carried boats and supplies overland) to the Wisconsin River. After paddling down the Wisconsin, they entered the Mississippi, which they followed to the mouth of the Arkansas River. Here, convinced that the Mississippi emptied into the Gulf of Mexico, they turned homeward by way of the Illiniois River. Their journals and maps were valuable for later explorers and settlers in central North America.

MARS

Mars was the Roman god of war and was said to be the father of Romulus and Remus. Romulus was the legendary founder of ROME in 753 B.C. Mars was thus worshiped as the father of the Roman people. March was his sacred month.

Mars is also the name of the next PLANET beyond Earth circling the sun. Because of its fiery red color, the Romans named it after their god of war.

In recent years, American and Soviet space probes have discovered that part of the surface of Mars has huge CRATERS like those on the moon. Another part of the surface has chasms and grooves, possibly worn away by erosion or caused by violent dust storms.

Since the very thin atmosphere of Mars is almost all carbon dioxide and a little water vapor, scientists feel that the advancing and receding polar "ice caps" on the planet are probably dry ice (frozen carbon dioxide) or a thin layer of hoar frost (frozen dew).

Parts of the surface undergo various seasonal changes. Although some astronomers suggest there is growth and decay of some form of plant life on Mars, a series of *Mariner* space probes have indicated to American scientists that there is a very unlikely chance of any life forms, especially since there is no oxygen and apparently no nitrogen in the atmosphere. SEE ALSO: PLANETS, SOLAR SYSTEM.

Thurgood MARSHALL (born 1908)

Thurgood Marshall is the first black justice of the Supreme Court of the United States. He was appointed to the court by President Lyndon Johnson in 1967.

Born in Baltimore, Maryland, Mr. Marshall became the lawyer for the Baltimore chapter of the National Association for the Advancement of Colored People (NAACP).

He has been allowed to plead cases before the United States Supreme Court since 1938.

He has won several cases for blacks and other minority people. His best-known case was called *Brown* v. *Board of Education*. The Supreme Court ruled in favor of Mr. Marshall's client in this case, and it ordered all public schools in the United States to open their doors to children of all races.

MARYLAND

Maryland is one of the Middle Atlantic states of the United States. The Appalachian Mountains are in the western part; the Piedmont Plateau in the central part; and the Atlantic Coastal Plain in the eastern and southern parts of the state. The coastal plain is divided by the long Chesapeake Bay, which is spanned by the Chesapeake Bay Bridge near Annapolis, the state capital. Maryland has about 4.25 million inhabitants.

In 1632, Great Britain gave land on Chesapeake Bay to Lord Baltimore, who was a Roman Catholic. He wanted to found a colony where Catholics and Protestants would have equal rights. He died, however, in 1632, but his son led 200 settlers to the New World in 1634. He established a colony called "Saint Marys" near the Potomac River.

Maryland was one of the original Thirteen Colonies. After the American Revolution, the state gave land to create the nation's capital, WASHINGTON, D.C. In the War of 1812, when the British tried to capture Fort McHenry in Baltimore harbor, Francis Scott Key composed *The Star-Spangled Banner*, the U.S. national anthem.

Today, Maryland is a manufacturing center, producing transportation equipment, chemicals, food products, clothes, and metals. Many people work in the wholesale and retail trade and government. Some Marylanders grow hay, corn, and tobacco and raise livestock. SEE ALSO: WASHINGTON, D.C.

MARY Queen of Scots (1542–1587)

Mary was the daughter of King James V of Scotland. Her father died six days after Mary was born. She then became queen of Scotland, and at 16 she

518

married the son of the French king. He died the following year, and Mary returned to Scotland, where she was still queen.

In 1565, Mary married her cousin, Lord Darnley, who soon became jealous of her Italian secretary, David Rizzio, and in 1566 had him murdered. Then Mary became fond of the Earl of Bothwell. In 1567, Darnley was found dead, and Bothwell carried off the Queen and married her. The Scottish nobles gathered an army against them, convinced they had killed Darnley. Bothwell fled to Denmark, Mary was imprisoned, and her one-year-old son became king. She escaped to England, where Queen ELIZABETH I then kept her a prisoner for 19 years. There were many plots to place Mary on the throne of England, and finally Mary herself was convicted of conspiracy and executed. Mary's son became King JAMES I of England. SEE ALSO: ELIZABETH I, JAMES I.

MASSACHUSETTS

Massachusetts is one of the New England states, situated on the Atlantic coast in the northeastern United States. The state's eastern part, including the Cape Cod peninsula and the islands of Martha's Vineyard and Nantucket, is a low coastal plain. In the interior are uplands separated by the fertile Connecticut River valley, and farther west lie the Berkshire Hills.

The name of the state, meaning "large hill place," comes from the Massachuset Indians. They lived in the hilly area south of BOSTON, the present-day state capital. In 1620, the PURITANS established the first settlement at Plymouth, and ten years later, John Winthrop and 900 settlers founded the Massachusetts Bay Colony to the north. British restrictions on the colonists finally led to the BOSTON TEA PARTY in 1773. Two years later, the American Revolution began at Lexington and Concord.

A great shipping industry developed in Massachusetts' ports in the 1800s. Whaling was very important in New Bedford. Large textile and shoe factories were built in eastern Massachusetts. Today, many of the state's nearly 9 million residents work in industry, producing such items as electronic equipment, food products, plastics, and metals. Some are farmers or fishermen.

Some of America's great persons have come from Massachusetts, including JOHN ADAMS, the second President of the U.S., PAUL REVERE, the American patriot, and Elias Howe, the inventor of the sewing machine. SEE ALSO: BOSTON.

MATCHES

During the 1700s, people used a tinder box to light a FIRE. A bar of steel would be struck against a flint stone and the resulting spark would fall upon and slowly ignite a piece of charred linen or dried fungus (the "tinder"). The glowing tinder then had to be fanned or blown upon until it burst into flame.

The fact that PHOSPHORUS and sulfur ignite at a low temperature was the basis for the fire-making inventions of the early 1800s. In 1805, the lucifer match was invented by a Frenchman. This match was a splinter of wood tipped with chemicals that would burst into flame when dipped into a bottle of acid. The first friction matches, like those we use today, had to be drawn across a piece of folded sandpaper.

Matches were not commonly used until 1833. The first ones contained yellow phosphorus that was dangerous to use and gave off poisonous fumes. Later, red phosphorus was discovered and proved to be safer. Today's "safety matches" have the phosphorus in the strip on the side of the box. They cannot ignite unless rubbed on this special surface.

Most matches are made of pine splints dipped in various chemicals. Factory machines are able to make about 1 million matches per hour. Much of the machinery for making household safety matches comes from Sweden, but book-match machinery is made in many countries, including the United States.
SEE ALSO: FIRE, PHOSPHORUS.

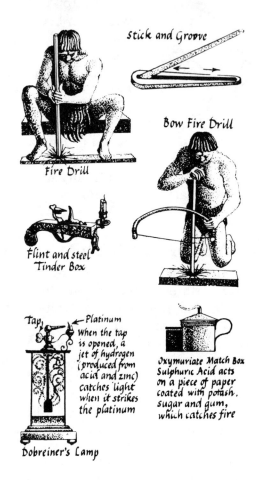

Stick and Groove

Bow Fire Drill

Fire Drill

Flint and steel Tinder Box

Tap — Platinum
When the tap is opened, a jet of hydrogen (produced from acid and zinc) catches light when it strikes the platinum

Dobreiner's Lamp

Oxymuriate Match Box
Sulphuric Acid acts on a piece of paper coated with potash, sugar and gum, which catches fire

Early English Matchbox

S. JONES
LUCIFER MATCHES
that IGNITE BY FRICTION produced by drawing the match briskly through a piece of SANDPAPER and are warranted never to impair by keeping.
Inventor of
the 'Prometheus' Self-acting Coffee Pot
LIGHT HOUSE, 201, STRAND, LONDON

520

MATTHEW

The people of New Testament times hated Jews who collected tax money for the Romans. Matthew, one of these hated tax collectors, worked on the important customs route between the city of Damascus and the Mediterranean coast. He became rich; but when JESUS called him to join His disciples, Matthew left his job and home to follow Christ. Jesus said that He had come to call sinners, such as tax collectors, to God.

Matthew wrote one of the Gospels, which gives a Jewish view of Jesus. His Gospel records the teachings of Jesus in five sermons.

MAYFLOWER

The *Mayflower* was the small ship that carried the PILGRIMS to America in 1620. It was a typical trading vessel of her time, with a straight bow and high stern, weighing 180 tons (164 metric tons) loaded and being 90 feet (28 m) long.

With the *Speedwell*, she set out from Southampton, England, but the little *Speedwell* soon proved unseaworthy, and the Pilgrims were forced to return. On September 6, 1620, the *Mayflower* left Plymouth alone, with 102 passengers and a crew of 44. The Pilgrims planned to start a settlement in Virginia, in America.

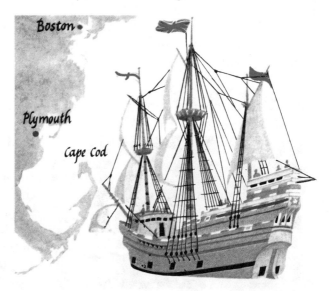

The voyage was terrible, for heavy seas drove the ship off her course and cracked her main beam. After more than two months, the *Mayflower* landed at what is now Provincetown, on Cape Cod. The Pilgrims then sailed across Cape Cod Bay and founded the colony of Plymouth, on the mainland of Massachusetts. Those passengers who were too sick to go ashore remained on board the *Mayflower*, which was anchored in the harbor for the winter. The ship sailed back to England in April, leaving a small colony of determined settlers. SEE ALSO: PILGRIMS.

Willie MAYS (born 1931)

Willie Mays was the first black "superstar" of baseball in the United States. Born in Westfield, Alabama, Mays joined the New York Giants in 1950. He later played for the San Francisco baseball team.

From 1951 to 1972, he broke several records of baseball's National League, including the League's home run record. The League chose him as its Most Valuable Player in 1954 and 1965. *Sporting News* magazine chose him as the Player of the Year in 1954.

MEAT

Long ago man learned to preserve meat by drying, smoking, or salting it. Now, it is also frozen or canned. Meat processing is one of America's leading industries. Americans mainly eat the flesh of cattle, pigs, sheep, and sometimes deer. *Beef* comes from bulls and cows; *veal*, from the calf. *Pork* comes from pigs; *bacon*, from the back and sides that have been preserved by salting. *Mutton* and *lamb* come from sheep, and *venison* comes from deer. The average American consumes about 150 pounds (67.5 kg) of meat in one year. The various cuts are shown in the diagram.

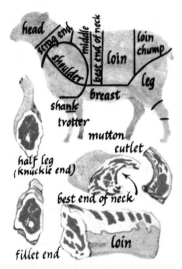

Only about half of an animal is meat. The blood, bones, glands, hair, and hoofs are now used in making fertilizer, glue, soap, animal feed, skin creams, plastics, and paints.

MECCA

Mecca, a city in Saudi Arabia, is famous as the birthplace of MUHAMMAD (he also died there). It is the holiest city of ISLAM, the religion of the MUSLIMS. Every year thousands of Muslims travel to Mecca to visit the large mosque, the Haram. Here is the famous shrine called the Kaaba, which is a small building, draped with a black carpet. The Kaaba encloses the Black Stone, which is the most sacred Muslim object because it was supposed to have been given to ABRAHAM by the angel Gabriel.

The Shrine at Mecca

Every Muslim tries to make a pilgrimage to Mecca once in his lifetime and to kiss the Black Stone. All Muslims face toward it when they pray. Also, after a Muslim has made his pilgrimage to Mecca, he may call himself *Hajji* ("pilgrim").

522

MEDICINE

Before the age of the Greeks, medicine, the study of healing, was a mystery. The Greeks were the first ones to study *symptoms* (signs) to try to discover the causes of illness. After the medical discoveries of Hippocrates, a Greek doctor about 400 B.C., and Galen, a Roman doctor about A.D. 175, there was very little medical progress until the 1600s. WILLIAM HARVEY then discovered the circulation of

the blood. The understanding of *anatomy* (how the body is constructed) and physiology (how the body works) was further aided by the invention of the MICROSCOPE. LOUIS PASTEUR contributed greatly to medical knowledge with his discovery that bacteria causes many diseases.

Medieval DOCTORS sought to cure most diseases by blood-letting, while doctors today have available thousands of useful DRUGS and vaccines to control disease. Modern doctors who treat disorders of certain parts of the body are called *specialists*. Those who operate on the body are called *surgeons*. A brain surgeon is a doctor who operates only on patients having a disease or disorder of the brain. SEE ALSO: DOCTOR, DRUGS.

MEDITERRANEAN

The Mediterranean is the largest inland sea in the world, surrounded by Europe, Asia, and Africa. The principal rivers flowing into it are the Elbro from Spain, the RHÔNE from France, the Po from Italy, and the NILE from Egypt. The water of the Mediterranean evaporates very rapidly and would likely vanish entirely to make a salt desert, were it not for the strong current that continually flows in from the Atlantic through the Straits of GIBRALTAR. Because the Straits are narrow, there is almost no tide in the Mediterranean.

The ancient Phoenicians, Egyptians, Greeks, and Romans thought that the Mediterranean was the middle of the world. Its name derives from two Latin words—*medius* ("middle") and *terra* ("land"). The Bible calls it "the Great Sea."

Herman MELVILLE (1819–1891)

Herman Melville, a famous American author, was born in New York City. At the age of 19, he went to sea as a cabin boy and learned much about sailing. In 1841, Melville joined the crew of a whaler and sailed to the South Pacific. He deserted the ship in the Marquesas Islands, but was captured by a tribe of cannibals. He managed to escape on an Australian ship, which he deserted in Tahiti. For several months, Melville worked as a field laborer on the island.

In 1843, Melville went to Hawaii and enlisted as a sailor in the U.S.

Navy. A year later, he left the Navy in Boston and settled down in Massachusetts to write novels about his adventures.

Melville became successful after *Typee* and *Omoo* were published. These books and others were full of action, describing life in the South Seas. After the publication of *Moby Dick* in 1851, Melville's popularity decreased. Readers did not understand this complex novel about a great white whale. Today, it is one of the great American novels.

MEMORY

There is still a lot unknown about how the human mind works. *Psychologists* (scientists who study the mind) do know, however, that memory is a concern of the entire BRAIN and not just a special section of it.

New ideas are remembered better if they are added to something we already know. Something that is understandable is also more interesting to remember. Before a new memory fades, it is helpful to recall it to your mind. This technique is helpful after studying a homework assignment. Also, things seen are often remembered better than things heard. It is often helpful to remember a new idea if you try to form a picture or diagram of it in your mind.

Sometimes a person's brain is injured in an accident, and he suffers from *amnesia* or loss of memory for a period of time afterwards. SEE ALSO: BRAIN.

Felix MENDELSSOHN (1809–1847)

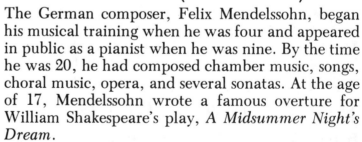

The German composer, Felix Mendelssohn, began his musical training when he was four and appeared in public as a pianist when he was nine. By the time he was 20, he had composed chamber music, songs, choral music, opera, and several sonatas. At the age of 17, Mendelssohn wrote a famous overture for William Shakespeare's play, *A Midsummer Night's Dream*.

Unlike many composers, Mendelssohn had a happy life. He wrote music in the romantic style, with rich melodies and deep emotion. He was also a great pianist and conductor. He gave many concerts while touring through Great Britain, Italy, and Germany. Mendelssohn also did much to make the music of BACH popular.

MERCHANT SHIPS

A ship that carries goods or passengers is called a merchant ship. All the merchant ships of a country make up its *merchant marine*.

LINERS used to be the most famous merchant ships because of their beauty, luxury, and speed, but few liners are being built these days. Instead of taking passengers on serious trips across the ocean, they are being used for cruises, round trips made purely for pleasure.

Tankers, which carry oil, gasoline, and other liquids are now the most famous and the largest merchant ships. *Supertankers* over 1100 feet (335 m) long have been built. Such tankers are causing many people to worry. If they are wrecked or have accidents, they can pollute large areas of the ocean.

Freighters carry dry cargoes, usually in containers. *Stevedores* put these in the *holds* of the ships. There are often five holds. A freighter that runs on a regular schedule is called a *cargo liner*. One that goes wherever there is a cargo to deliver is called a *tramp*. In spite of the name, tramps are often fine, up-to-date ships.

There are also *bulk carriers*, which carry iron ore, coal, grain, and other dry cargoes that come in small particles. There are many of these ships on the Great Lakes (where they are called *boats*).

New merchant ships are constantly being built. Some save stevedore costs by carrying truck trailers, railroad cars, barges, or huge containers full of cargo.

Various merchant ships from ancient to modern times are illustrated on this page.

MERCURY

Mercury was the Roman messenger of the gods. He was known to the Greeks as Hermes. Mercury was imagined as having wings on his sandals and helmet. He was worshiped as the god of trade and merchants.

Mercury is also the name of the smallest PLANET in the SOLAR SYSTEM. It is the planet closest to the sun around which it orbits once every 88 days. Mercury is a waterless planet without any atmosphere. Scientists once believed that Mercury always showed the same side to the sun, just as the moon does to the Earth. Radar observations have recently revealed, however, that it spins slowly on its axis making one complete revolution in 59 days.

Mercury is also an element often called quicksilver. In ancient days it was thought to be liquid silver. Mercury is a liquid metal at ordinary temperatures that breaks up into round beads when touched. It is the heaviest liquid known. When heated or cooled, Mercury expands or contracts rapidly at a regular rate for each degree of temperature change. Thus, it is an ideal liquid to use in THERMOMETERS and BAROMETERS. When mixed with silver, gold, and tin, it forms an ALLOY used by dentists for filling teeth. Mercurochrome and Merthiolate, familiar antiseptics in your family medicine cabinet, are mercury compounds. Mercury is widely used in industry and in scientific laboratories. Mercury vapors are poisonous to inhale.

METALS

The more than 100 elements can be divided into two groups: metals and nonmetals. Scientists admit, however, that some elements such as arsenic are difficult to put in either category and are therefore called *metalloids*.

Although they are usually hard and heavy, metals can be shaped by hammering. They are also good conductors of heat and electricity. *Precious metals*, such as GOLD, SILVER, and PLATINUM, are those few that keep bright for a long time. All the other metals are called *base metals*.

Most of the base metals are found in chemical combination with other elements and are mixed with gravel, clay, or stone. A great deal of modern technology is involved with extracting metals from these mixtures, called ORES. To obtain pure metals, the ore is crushed, washed, and smelted (heated). The most plentiful metals are IRON and ALUMINUM.

When two or more metals are mixed together, an alloy is produced. STEEL, BRONZE, BRASS, and pewter are alloys. New alloys are being developed by industry because they are stronger and better than any single metal used by itself.

METEORS

Once in a while, small pieces of matter enter the Earth's atmosphere and burn up. The resulting light that is seen is called a *meteor*. The small bits of iron and stone that burn are called *meteoroids*. They come from comets that have broken apart or from *asteroids*, which are pieces of what might once have been a small planet or moon that blew apart.

Meteoric storm

The friction as they speed through the air causes most of them to burn up completely. However, some are very large and manage to strike the Earth's surface. The meteoroids that land on Earth are called *meteorites*. The largest one known was found in Africa in 1920 and weighed 66 tons (60 metric tons).

The largest crater produced by a meteorite is located in Arizona. It is about a mile (1.6 km) across. The estimated weight of the meteorite that produced this crater is 2,240,000 tons (2,038,400 metric tons).

Burning meteoroids are often called "shooting stars." SEE ALSO: CRATER.

MEXICAN WAR

The Mexican War was fought between the U.S. and Mexico from 1846 to 1848. Many Americans in the early 1800s had settled on territory belonging to Mexico.

After TEXAS became a state in 1845, the U.S. claimed that the Rio Grande was the southern border of Texas. Mexico said the border was farther north, at the Nueces River. After failing to get a peaceful settlement and to buy western lands from Mexico, U.S. President James Polk ordered troops, under General Zachary Taylor, into the disputed Texan area. A Mexican army soon attacked Taylor's forces, and war was declared.

General Winfield Scott with many of Taylor's soldiers began an attack on Mexico City, the capital, from the port of Veracruz. General Santa Anna and his Mexican army attacked Taylor's small force on the Texas border. The battle at Buena Vista was a draw, and the Mexicans pulled back. Scott's army fought hard and captured Mexico City on September 14, 1847.

The war ended with the Treaty of Guadalupe Hidalgo. The U.S. received nearly all the land now included in the states of New Mexico, Arizona, Utah, Nevada, and California. Texas's southern boundary became the Rio Grande. Mexico received $15 million and no longer had to pay claims of Americans against it.

MEXICO

Mexico is a large republic, about three times the size of Texas, lying to the south of the United States. Most of Mexico is a huge tableland, which is separated from the narrow, coastal plains by two ranges of mountains, the Sierra Madre Oriental on the east side and the Sierra Madre Occidental on the west side. One of the highest peaks is the extinct volcano, Popocatepetl.

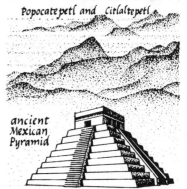
Popocatepetl and Citlaltepetl

ancient Mexican Pyramid

The seacoasts have a hot, humid climate. There are famous beach resorts on the Pacific, like Acapulco and Puerto Vallarta. The desert land in the north is hot and dry in summer, and often freezing cold in winter. The climate of central Mexico is not so severe, and the average, year-round temperature is about 65°F (18°C).

Aztec carvings
18th Century Church
Giant cactus
Village store

Mexico has rich silver, gold, copper, lead, and zinc mines. It has vast reserves of oil in Yucatan, a peninsula that juts into the Gulf of Mexico. Lumbering is also an important industry, and Mexico is one of the largest suppliers of sisal hemp, used for making ropes and rugs.

Despite these natural resources, most of the 65 million Mexicans live in considerable poverty. They are usually engaged in agriculture, growing corn, coffee, rice, tobacco, sugar cane, and bananas.

Before the birth of Christ, the Maya Indians had an advanced civilization in Mexico. The Mayas erected large stone pyramids and palaces and invented a calendar. Later, the Aztecs, another Indian tribe, had their own civilization, centered at Tenochtitlán, where Mexico City, the capital, now stands. HERNANDO CORTÉS, the Spanish conquistador, destroyed the Aztec empire in 1519. Since then, Spanish has been the language of Mexico.

MICA

This MINERAL can be split into very thin but tough, transparent sheets. Because of its transparency, mica has been used as windowpanes. Since it also resists heat, it is used for the windows of stoves and lanterns. In America, before the invention of clear plastics, mica was used for car windows.

Mica does not conduct electricity. This makes it valuable as insulation on electrical devices.

Another name for mica is *isinglass*.

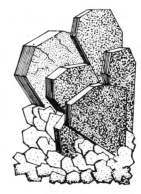

MICHIGAN

Michigan, a state in the upper mid-western part of the United States, borders four of the five GREAT LAKES. The word "Michigan" comes from an American Indian word meaning "big lake." The Straits of Mackinac, which link Lakes Michigan and Huron, divide the state into an Upper and Lower Peninsula. The Upper Peninsula has open land, swampy areas, and some highlands. Few live here, for the soil is poor and there are few industries. But, it is a wonderful region in which to go camping, fishing, and boating. The Lower Peninsula has woodlands with many small lakes. Most of Michigan's population of more than 9 million people live in the Lower Peninsula. Here also are the state's big cities like Detroit, Grand Rapids, Flint, and Lansing, the capital.

The major industry in Michigan today is manufacturing. Automobiles, machinery, metals, chemicals, and foods are the major products. Agriculture is also important. Cattle, pigs, and poultry are raised, and soybeans, wheat, and fruit are grown. Tourism is also important. People often visit the birthplace of HENRY FORD, America's pioneer in the manufacturing of automobiles.

When French missionaries and fur traders arrived in the 1600s, Michigan was inhabited by several Indian tribes, including the Ojibwa, Ottawa, and Potawatomi. Father Marquette established the first permanent settlement at Sault Sainte Marie in 1668. The French were driven out by the British, who later lost the region during the American Revolution.

MICROSCOPES

Microscopes are instruments that allow us to see things so tiny that they are invisible to the unaided eye.

The *optical microscope*, which was invented at the end of the 1500s, is a tube for holding a set of lenses so that they can be moved closer together or farther apart for focusing. Because the tube is usually vertical so that one can look down into it, the microscope has an adjustable mirror so that light can be reflected onto or through the object being viewed. The object is held on a platform or *stage* for viewing.

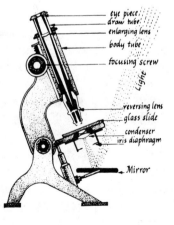

529

With a powerful microscope, it is possible to see BACTERIA, CELLS of living things, and other objects too small to be seen by the naked eye. The optical microscope enables us to see objects as small as 1/240,000th of an inch (0.0001 mm) in size.

An electron microscope works differently from an optical instrument. It focuses beams of ELECTRONS onto the object and enlarges, or amplifies, them electronically. Instead of viewing the image directly, the image is projected either onto a fluorescent screen or onto film. Because it is very much more powerful than an optical microscope, an electron microscope can be used to look at objects one millionth of an inch (0.000025 mm) in size.

MIDDLE AGES

The period of about a thousand years, between the end of the Roman Empire and the beginning of the RENAISSANCE about 1450, is referred to as the Middle Ages. Sometimes the first half of this period is called the DARK AGES.

In the A.D. 500s, northern tribes, such as the Goths, Burgundians, Franks, Angles, Saxons, Magyars, and the Huns, invaded and destroyed the Roman Empire. These "barbarians" were good warriors, but they were not interested in Roman culture. Eventually the Franks became the dominant tribe in Western Europe, and by A.D. 800 CHARLEMAGNE ruled much of the region, which was known as the Holy Roman Empire. After Charlemagne's death, there arose several separate kingdoms in Europe.

The Christian Church was the powerful force in men's lives at this time. Monks were religious men who lived in monasteries and who carried on learning, setting up libraries, schools, and hospitals. Monasteries spread to all areas of Europe, and CHRISTIANITY was carried everywhere by the monks, who saw the Pope in Rome as head of the Church.

Ignorance and superstition were common problems then, but knowledge began to advance after the CRUSADES, when new ideas were introduced into Europe from the East. Trade increased through the efforts of German merchants on the Baltic Sea. Art and literature also began to flourish in such cities as Florence and Paris, in stark contrast to the primitive knowledge of medicine that brought on the horror of the BLACK DEATH.

Medieval people lived under the FEUDAL SYSTEM, farming land owned by a lord in exchange for protection by that lord. At the close of the Middle Ages, many lived in towns, where merchants sold goods brought from other countries. Western Europeans were also exploring the world around them.

MIGRATION

When winter comes, some animals remain where they were living during the rest of the year. They are able to find food when snow is on the ground. Their fur becomes thicker to protect them from the cold. Some go into *hibernation*.

Many animals cannot live through the cold winter, so every year they travel toward warmer areas where food is not so scarce. This journey, which takes place twice each year, is called a *migration*.

Scientists are not sure why some animals migrate and others do not. For example, some kinds of birds fly to tropical climates, but others, like the house sparrow and the bluejay, remain in their wintry homes. Many people, knowing that food is hard to find in winter, provide birds with seeds and other food to help them survive.

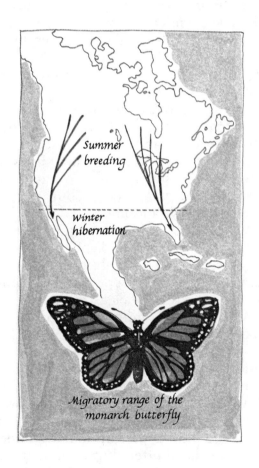

Summer breeding

Winter hibernation

Migratory range of the monarch butterfly

Many kinds of animals migrate. The monarch butterfly, which is seen all over the United States during the late summer, flies thousands of miles to Mexico where it spends the winter. Certain kinds of fishes migrate. The Alaskan fur seal swims from Alaska to the waters near the coasts of Japan and Mexico. It returns in the spring to Alaskan waters to give birth to its pups. Whales migrate to Antarctic seas to feed and to other areas to give birth to their calves. The Arctic tern, a small bird, travels 12,000 miles (19,320 km) in its migration from the Arctic to the Antarctic.

Scientists have studied how the animals know where and how to find the areas they go to every year. Present research indicates that many birds use the sun and stars as a compass, while many can find their way by landmarks.

MILK

MAMMALS are animals that produce milk to feed their young. By careful breeding, domesticated animals have been developed to produce milk for a longer period and in greater volume than those in the wild. A good milking cow may give milk for about 10 months after she has given birth to a calf and may produce as much as 5 gallons (19 liters) a day—enough for 80 cartons of the size used in a school cafeteria.

Milking by hand - and by machine

Vacuum Pump

Air

Milk

milk is weighed

The milk is next pasteurized and bottled

milk cooler

Although cow's milk is most common in the United States, goat's milk is very nourishing, easily digested, and widely used in many countries of the world. Other mammals around the world that supply milk for man are the camel, llama, yak, water buffalo, sheep, reindeer, donkey, and mare.

Milk is easily infected by germs, so a well-run dairy farm has to be kept very clean. The cows must be tested regularly for disease, the machinery must be kept spotless, and the milking shed has to be clean and airy.

At the dairy, milk is heated to a high temperature to kill harmful bacteria. We call this process *pasteurization*. Some milk is then fortified with Vitamin D before being cooled and bottled. Milk must be stored in sterile, refrigerated containers.

Milk is the best source of *calcium*, which is needed by babies and growing children for building strong teeth and bones.

Whole milk is used in making puddings, cream soups, and ice cream. Cheese, cream, butter, buttermilk, junket, sour cream, and yogurt are all milk products. SEE ALSO: MAMMALS; PASTEUR, LOUIS.

MINERALS

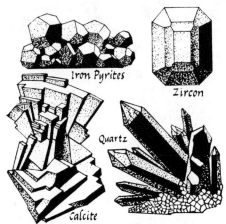

Iron Pyrites

Zircon

Quartz

Calcite

We can classify substances by listing them as animal, vegetable, or mineral. The mineral group is made up of substances that have never been alive, or are no longer alive. Minerals are obtained from the earth by mining.

There are about 1500 minerals known to us. Most of them exist in the form of CRYSTALS. Some rare minerals, such as diamonds, rubies, emeralds, and sapphires, are very beautiful when cut and polished. They are called precious GEMS.

Some rocks, like limestone, are made up of one mineral; but many, like granite, are made up of several minerals.

MINES

MINERALS are obtained from the earth in two ways: by *quarrying*, or digging from the surface, and by *mining*, or working underground.

Coal mines are the most common kind of mine. Other important mines give us salt, uranium, diamonds, and the ores of metals such as iron, copper, silver, tin, and gold.

Engineers find mineral deposits by drilling holes deep underground and bringing up a plug of rock which can then be tested.

If the rock shows that the mineral deposits are worth mining, a vertical shaft is dug. Horizontal tunnels are made to branch off from the shaft at various levels. Miners work along these tunnels, using picks or special machinery to remove the minerals embedded in the seams.

As the tunnels are dug, the roof and sides need to be braced to prevent a cave-in. Proper ventilation is especially important and is provided for by air shafts.

section of the Kimberley Diamond Mine

open pit

Diamonds are obtained from the blue rock in the 'pipe' (p) of an old volcano. They were at first dug out of an open pit, but are now obtained through shafts (s) and tunnels.

Water that accumulates in the mine must be removed by pumps or drains.

Sometimes minerals such as gold are found on the surface, in sand or gravel. Extracting the heavier mineral by washing away the lighter gravel is called *placer mining.*

MINNESOTA

Minnesota is in the north central part of the United States. This state is known as "The Land of 10,000 Lakes," but actually it has more than 15,000 lakes. About two-thirds of Minnesota is rolling prairie. There are also large woodlands. Winters are usually very cold, and summers are hot. The state has about 4 million people.

When a French explorer named Daniel Greysolon visited the region in 1679, the Sioux and Ojibwa Indians were already living there. Greysolon's title was Sieur du Luth. The city of Duluth on Lake Superior was named after him. After making friends with the Sioux, Greysolon claimed the region for France. The French, British, and Americans competed there in the fur trade. The U.S. government took complete control of the area in 1803. Fort St. Anthony was built in 1819 beside the upper Mississippi River; it later became the city of Minneapolis. Nearby an Indian village grew into St. Paul, the present-day state capital. Today, the two cities are side by side and are known as the "Twin Cities."

Much iron ore comes from the state's northern region, including the Mesabi Range. Minnesota's largest industries are food processing and machinery. Also important are lumbering and agriculture. Its dairy products—butter and milk—are very famous. Vacationers love the countryside, and fishermen and hunters come from all over to try their luck in Minnesota's lakes and forests.

MINOTAUR

The Minotaur, in Greek mythology, was a monster having the body of a man and the head of a bull.

King Minos of CRETE owned the Minotaur and kept it in a labyrinth (a system of complex passages designed like a maze). Because the son of King Minos had been killed by the Athenians, the King sought revenge by forcing the Athenians to send every ninth year seven boys and seven girls to be eaten by the Minotaur. When the third sacrifice came round, THESEUS volunteered to go. He slew the monster, and with the help of a ball of thread given him by Ariadne, the King's daughter, escaped from the labyrinth.

Archeologists have discovered wall paintings in Crete that show the sacred rite of bull baiting, which may partially explain this story.

MINSTREL

During the MIDDLE AGES, entertainers called *minstrels* wandered from place to place, singing and reciting poems. Often they composed their own songs, and played the harp skillfully. Sometimes a lord of a castle had his own minstrel, who was highly respected and given an important place in the household. After the evening meal, he sang and told long stories until his master's family went to bed. Minstrels who performed in taverns and inns generally received some sort of payment for entertaining guests. Then they moved on, carrying the news from village to village as they performed.

Eventually the Church denounced the minstrels because of their vulgar and irreverent speech and language. The state also came to dislike them, for they sang biting songs against people in authority and voiced the wrongs of the poor. Finally, with the coming of printing in the 15th century, the taste for listening to long poetic stories died out.

MINT

A mint is a factory for making coins. The first coins were probably made in Asia Minor around 640 B.C. Little "buttons" of a gold-silver alloy were cast in molds, then punched on the top with a figure of a lion. Most ancient coins were made of precious metal in this way. Eventually a lower *die* (punch) was used as well as an upper one, so that a coin had a design on both faces. Getting the two dies to line up properly was difficult, but many ancient coins are very beautiful. The Chinese did not use dies; they cast cheap

bronze coins with holes so that they could be held together by strings.

The need to get exactly the right amount of metal in each coin, and the need for large numbers of coins led to the development of machinery from the 17th century on.

In a modern mint, the metal for the coins is cast into *ingots* (small bars), which are rolled to just the right thickness. The sheets produced are punched so as to produce *blanks* about the size and shape of the finished coins. These are given a milled edge, then struck with dies in a coining press. Finally, the coins are weighed and counted.

The United States began coining its own money in 1792. There are United States Mints in Philadelphia, Denver, and San Francisco.

MIRAGE

Mirages were once thought to be the imaginings of weary, sick travelers on long journeys across deserts, oceans, or snow. Travelers across deserts sometimes see a lake of shimmering water just ahead of them. Sometimes, they see a town.

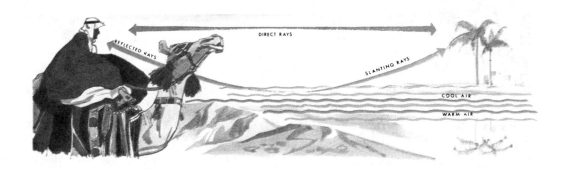

These illusions are produced by the bending of LIGHT rays as they pass from layers of hot air immediately above a hot surface into cooler layers of air above. The hot air layer acts like a mirror. The "water" illusion is actually a reflection of the blue sky. Since the layers of air are never quite still, the scene appears to quiver. SEE ALSO: LIGHT.

MIRROR

A mirror is a smooth, polished flat or curved surface that forms images by reflecting rays of LIGHT. From antiquity until the 1500s, most mirrors were made of polished metals—gold, silver, bronze, or brass. Crude glass mirrors were made in the 1300s, but smooth clear glass was not available until 300 years later.

A bronze Celtic mirror, over 2,000 years old

A modern driving mirror

Modern mirrors are made by coating one side of glass with a smooth layer of a bright substance containing tin, mercury, silver, or aluminum. It is this coating that gives the mirror its reflecting quality.

In addition to their everyday uses, mirrors are an important part of lighthouses' equipment, telescopes, microscopes, and cameras. SEE ALSO: LIGHT.

MISSISSIPPI

Mississippi, in the southern part of the United States, consists of two main regions. In the west is the flat and fertile delta area along the MISSISSIPPI RIVER, and in the east are grasslands and hills. The state touches the Gulf of Mexico in the south, where the Bay of St. Louis and Biloxi are situated. Jackson is the state capital. Almost 2.5 million people live in Mississippi.

In the 1500s, Spanish explorers came upon the Choctaw, Chickasaw, and Natchez Indians in the region. Later, the French brought settlers there, but in 1763 they gave it to the British. After the American Revolution, people established large cotton plantations there. Many Negro slaves worked the land until the Civil War. Then, with the abolition of SLAVERY, landowners hired workers, mostly Negroes. Today, agriculture is still the major business in the state. Cotton, soybeans, and sweet potatoes are the leading crops. Poultry and eggs are important, too.

Today, Mississippi manufactures clothes, chemicals, paper, and lumber. Also, oil and natural gas have contributed to the state's industry. Tourists bring much money to Mississippi. They come to the colorful state festivals, such as the Shrimp Festival at Biloxi. Other attractions include the elegant plantation houses around Natchez and Vicksburg. The Gulf coast beaches are becoming important winter resort areas.

MISSISSIPPI RIVER

The Mississippi is one of the great rivers of the world and is the longest river in North America. This great river divides the United States into two parts. Its source in the north is near the Canadian border, and it runs about 2500 miles (4025 km) south to empty into the Gulf of Mexico. Formerly, it was the western boundary of the United States.

Nicknamed "Father of Waters," the Mississippi has many branches. The main branches are the Missouri, the Ohio, the Arkansas, the Illinois, the Wisconsin, and the Red Rivers. With this vast network of inland waterways, the Mississippi stretches from the Appalachians to the Rockies. It covers an area of about 1,244,000 square miles (3,221,000 km²). Beginning at Lake Itasca, a little lake in northern Minnesota, the Mississippi starts as a small stream which is easily jumped across by a child.

As it flows southward, however, it is more than a mile (1.6 km) wide in places. Enormous volumes of water head for the sea and at times produce great floods. Great quantities of sand and mud are also carried along and deposited at its most southerly point to form a large DELTA. Its branches flowing through the delta are called the Passes.

In 1541, the Spanish explorer HER-NANDO DE SOTO crossed the Mississippi. A century later, the famous French explorers MARQUETTE, JOLIET, and La Salle explored it.

After ROBERT FULTON invented the steamboat, the river became a busy highway. The great steamboat period for passenger boats, cargo boats, and showboats was from about 1820 to 1865. The most important river cities that sprang up were New Orleans and St. Louis. Corn, wheat, pork, potatoes, cheese, and beef from the north and sugar, molasses, and cotton from the south were typical cargoes on the hundreds of freight boats traveling the river.

However, the railroads brought an end to this great steamboat era, and the river declined in importance. Nevertheless, it is still used today by barges for hauling bulky products like coal and lumber.

MISSOURI

Missouri is in the Midwest of the United States. In the state's rolling hills in the north and west much corn is grown and hogs, cattle, and sheep are raised. The Ozark Plateau in the south is famous for its good fishing, hunting, and scenery. The delta region (where the Mississippi and Ohio Rivers join) in the southeast produces soybeans, cotton, and melons. The great Missouri River forms part of the state's western border and then flows across the

state to join the Mississippi above St. Louis, the largest city. There are about 4.8 million people in Missouri. Jefferson City is the capital.

When the French fur traders came to the region in the 1700s, they encountered the tall, strong Osage Indians. The first permanent settlement was built at Ste. Genevieve in 1735. Later, the U.S. government received the entire area as part of the Louisiana Purchase in 1803. THOMAS JEFFERSON sent LEWIS AND CLARK westward up the Missouri River to explore the territory. Settlers soon came in great numbers. Many of them set out on the long journey over the Oregon Trail to the West Coast. Others traveled by paddlewheel steamboats on the rivers. The PONY EXPRESS was started in St. Joseph, Missouri.

Today, the state is a great manufacturing center, producing automobiles, airplanes, and food products. Also important are agriculture and tourism. Missouri has been the residence of many famous people, including MARK TWAIN, JESSE JAMES, and GEORGE WASHINGTON CARVER.

MISTLETOE

Mistletoe is an evergreen that is a PARASITE. Its white berries, which contain seeds, are eaten by birds. The seeds pass through the birds' digestive systems and are dropped on other trees. There they sprout, and their small roots enter the wood to draw nourishment from the sap of the "host" tree. In the western United States, leafless dwarf varieties of mistletoe have done great damage to CONIFER forests.

The Christmas custom of kissing under the mistletoe probably originated with the Druids, who were Celtic priests in the days before Christ. To them, the mistletoe was a sacred plant.

MOLECULE

A molecule of water (H_2O) consists of two ATOMS of hydrogen and one atom of oxygen. The molecule can be separated into its atoms, but once the molecule is broken up, it is no longer the original substance. The *molecule* is the smallest unit of a substance that still has all the properties of that substance.

Many molecules are too small to be seen even with a powerful electron MICROSCOPE.

Scientists, as they discover new ways to join atoms together, are able to create new molecules. SEE ALSO: ATOMS.

MOLES

Moles are rarely seen, although we often see the hills and ridges they make in lawns and gardens when they are digging their underground tunnels. Because they live underground and feed only at night, they are almost blind and avoid light.

These mammals are 5 to 6 inches (12.7–15.2 cm) in length and have a long snout, broad feet, and long, powerful front claws for digging. They dig burrows and tunnels close to the surface, one for escape and several leading to their feeding grounds.

Sensitive hairs on the fleshy nose and tail help them to locate the earthworms and insect LARVAE they like to eat. If they don't have food for ten or eleven hours, moles will die of starvation.

MONASTERY

Since the earliest years of Christianity people have avoided the every-day world in order to live the religious life more fully. Some, living alone, are called *hermits*. Others, grouped together in communities, are called *monks* if they are men and *nuns* if they are women.

A monastery is a community of monks. (A CONVENT is a community of nuns.) It belongs to an *order*, a monastic system founded by one person. The monks live according to a *rule*, which is in fact a set of rules telling the monks what they must and must not do.

A large, well-run monastery of the Middle Ages was a place of prayer and work. It usually had a large farm. It had a library where books were kept and a *scriptorium* where they were written. It had a school for *novices* (persons intending to become monks), an *infirmary* (hospital), a guest house for travelers, and an *almonry* where the poor were fed. The monks slept in a *dormitory*, ate in a *refectory*, strolled in a *cloister* (courtyard with covered walks), and had business meetings in a *chapter house*. Towering over everything was a large church, of course. A modern monastery is simpler.

A large monastery was ruled by an *abbot*, and was called an ABBEY. A small one was ruled by a *prior*, and was called a *priory*. A very small monastery ruled from a larger monastery was called a *cell*. SEE ALSO: ABBEY, CONVENT.

MONEY

One way of obtaining goods or services is to offer goods or services in return. But you may not be able to make a *barter* that satisfies the other person. If you offer enough money, you have a better chance of getting what you want. Everyone uses money, and most people have an idea of how much money something should cost.

People have used beads, seashells, bags of gold dust, coins, bits of printed paper, and many other things for money. Precious metals such as gold and silver have been very popular since their value is always high. But for coins of small value other metals, such as bronze or aluminum, are often used. Paper money has been in use for about 200 years. At first a *note* (piece of paper money) was a promise to pay so much gold or silver, but now it is "backed" only by the public's faith in the whole system of buying and selling.

Money should be easily recognized, thus enabling persons to tell its value quickly. Since money will pass often from one person to another, it should also wear well. Good money should be easy to carry around, too. The value of money in terms of buying power may vary. During times of inflation, money's buying power is reduced; during times of deflation, it increases. SEE ALSO: MINT.

MONKEYS

Monkeys are MAMMALS that inhabit the forests of South America, Mexico, Africa, and Asia. Like apes, they are *primates* having ten fingers and ten toes. Unlike apes, they nearly always have a tail. Their faces are short and narrow. Their arms are often longer than their legs.

Most monkeys eat fruits and insects; some species eat eggs and small animals. They are intelligent and are easily trained. They are very sociable and many live in large, well-organized units called "troops."

Recently, monkeys have been widely used in scientific research. Two monkeys, Able and Baker, went up in a Jupiter ballistic missile in 1958 to test the effect space travel might have on human beings. SEE ALSO: APES.

James MONROE (1758–1831)

James Monroe, the fifth President of the United States, fought in several battles during the American Revolution. He then studied law under his friend, THOMAS JEFFERSON, and later was elected to the Virginia legislature and the U.S. Senate. From 1794 to 1796, he was President Washington's minister to France, a country he greatly admired.

After Jefferson became President, Monroe was sent to Paris as a diplomatic agent to help Robert Livingston arrange the LOUISIANA PURCHASE. He also performed special diplomatic services in 1803 in England and in 1805 in Spain.

Monroe became governor of Virginia a second time in 1811, but was soon chosen by James Madison to be U.S. Secretary of State. Being a likeable gentleman, Monroe was easily elected President as a Democratic-Republican in 1816. At that time, the country was prospering, thanks to the developing industry in the North and the increasing settlements in the West. Monroe acquired Florida from Spain, settled boundaries with Canada, and restrained the Seminole Indians. His presidency was known as the "Era of Good Feeling." However, slavery was becoming a problem. In 1820, Monroe signed the Missouri Compromise, stating that, west of the Mississippi River, slavery was lawful only south of 36° 30' north latitude, except in Missouri.

Reelected to a second term, he established the MONROE DOCTRINE, which threatened war against any European nation that tried to set up colonies in the Western Hemisphere. SEE ALSO: MONROE DOCTRINE.

MONROE DOCTRINE

In 1823, Russia had several fur trading settlements on the northwest coast of North America. Also, many Spanish colonies in Central and South America had recently declared their independence. President JAMES MONROE, hearing that European nations might help Spain regain its former colonies, sent a message to Congress on December 2, 1823. It said that the United States would view with displeasure any attempt by European nations to set up colonies in the Western Hemisphere. It also announced that the U.S. would not interfere in European affairs and that Europe should not interfere in the governments of North and South America. This public statement became known as the Monroe Doctrine, developing into an important part of U.S. foreign policy.

Although Monroe wrote the central paragraphs of the message, his Secretary of State JOHN QUINCY ADAMS worked out many of the details. Adams had earlier sent a note to Monroe about Russian fur traders in the Northwest, stating that Europe should no longer make colonies in America.

MONTANA

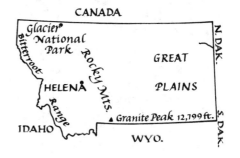

Montana is a large state in the western United States. It has the ROCKY MOUNTAINS in the west, and the high, gently rolling Great Plains in the east. Many of the mountains, below the timber line, are covered with thick forests of fir, pine, and spruce. More than 3 million Christmas trees come from Montana each year.

The first white men to visit the area were French fur traders from Canada in the 1700s. The Arapaho, Cheyenne, Blackfoot, Crow, and other Indian tribes inhabited the region then. Most of Montana was acquired as part of the Louisiana Purchase in 1803. Two years later, LEWIS AND CLARK explored the territory. Missionaries soon came to teach the Indians about farming and Christianity. During the Civil War, gold was discovered and prospectors flocked there. Then copper and silver were found, and mining towns like Butte sprang up over night. It was a tough, lawless area—part of the Wild West. As more settlers came, the Indians lost much land. After the 1850s, there were many Indian wars. At the famous Battle of Little Big Horn in 1876, U.S. General Custer and his 264 men were killed by the Cheyenne and Sioux Indians. However, the white men eventually beat the Indians, who were then forced to live on reservations.

Montana today raises many cattle and sheep and grows much wheat. Lumbering, mining, and manufacturing are important industries. The state capital is Helena. Montana has nearly 750,000 people.

MONTEZUMA (1466-1520)

Montezuma II was the last Aztec emperor of Mexico. He succeeded his uncle as head of the empire in 1502. In his early years as ruler, he successfully waged war against several tribes and enlarged the empire. However, his arrogant manner offended his subjects, whom he heavily taxed to support his luxurious style of living.

Montezuma captured many villagers to use for human sacrifice to the gods. Superstitions, prophecies by astrologers, and bad omens (such as

sighting a comet) gave Montezuma a feeling of powerlessness when CORTÉS and his men arrived in 1519. He sent the Spanish invaders lavish gifts, hoping to keep them from entering Tenochtitlán, his capital city (now Mexico City). However, these gifts made Cortés even more eager to enter the forbidden city. He had no trouble enlisting the aid of oppressed Aztec subjects to march against their emperor. Montezuma tried to bribe Cortés with jewels and other fine riches, but he was taken prisoner by the Spaniards. Montezuma stood on the wall to try to win back the allegiance of his subjects. However, according to the Spaniards, he was stoned by his own people. The Indians insisted that he was strangled by the Spaniards.

Afterwards, Montezuma became part of Indian legend and folklore. Even to this day, some mention him as a deity, although they do not worship him.

General MONTGOMERY (1887-1976)

In 1942, during WORLD WAR II, General Bernard Montgomery took command of the British Eighth Army in North Africa. Using heavy air and artillery bombardments, his army burst through the German lines at El Alamein, a town on the Mediterranean, 70 miles (113 km) west of Alexandria, in Egypt. His forces drove the Germans across North Africa, thus defeating the German general, Rommel. In 1944, General Montgomery was field commander of all troops during the Normandy campaign, which led to Germany's final defeat.

MONTH

"Thirty days has September, April, June, and November; all the rest have 31, except February, which has 8 and a score, until leap year gives it one day more." This is a familiar saying for remembering the number of days in the 12 months of the year. Originally, a month was the time between one new moon and the next. This is called a *lunar month*.

The ancient Egyptians had a calendar of 12 months, each with 30 days. The first Roman calendar had only 10 months. The Roman year began in March, named after Mars, the god of war. Then came April, from the Latin word "open"; May, from Maia, the goddess of spring; June, from Juno, the goddess of marriage; July, from JULIUS CAESAR; August, from Augustus Caesar; January, from Janus, god of beginnings; and February, from Februa, the festival of cleaning. Later, September, October, November, and December, meaning the 7th, 8th, 9th, and 10th month respectively, were added after August, for the Roman year had begun with March.

Certain stones have in ancient and modern times been associated with the months. They are known as lucky stones, or birthstones. The birthstones for the months are: January—garnet, February—amethyst, March—aquamarine or bloodstone, April—diamond, May—emerald or agate, June—pearl or moonstone, July—ruby or onyx, August—peridot or carnelian, September—sapphire or chrysolite, October—opal, tourmaline, or beryl, November—topaz, December—turquoise or zircon.

MONTICELLO

THOMAS JEFFERSON was not only a great United States president. He was also a great American architect. Traveling in France, he had seen not only what French architects of the late 18th century were doing but also the buildings left from the Roman Empire. He also got to know of the grand, elegant designs of the 16th-century Italian architect Andrea Palladio. In his own house, Monticello (Italian for "Little Mountain") he tried to  build as elegantly as conditions in the Virginia countryside permitted. He began the house in 1770 but revised it many times.

In it he included many clever things: a clock whose weights—cannonballs—told the day as they fell, a bed that rose out of sight to make an open doorway, and so on. After Jefferson's death the house was badly neglected, but later it was restored. It is now a museum. SEE ALSO: JEFFERSON, THOMAS.

MONTREAL

Montreal in QUEBEC is the largest city in Canada. Its urban population of about 3 million people is largely French, making it the second largest French-speaking city in the world. Lying at the foot of Mt. Royal, Montreal has a good harbor on the ST. LAWRENCE SEAWAY, which links the city with the industrial centers of the Great Lakes. Its chief industrial goods include clothing, foods, beer, plastics, steel, and electrical equipment. It is a large financial and transportation center. Montreal also has a well-known symphony orchestra, fine art museums, and large McGill University.

In 1535, the French explorer Jacques Cartier found a stockaded Indian village there. The French established Ville Marie de Montréal in 1642, which grew into an important fur trading center. The French gave the city to the British in 1760. SEE ALSO: QUEBEC.

MOON

The moon is a SATELLITE of Earth. It is about 239,000 miles (384.790 km) from the Earth about which it circles once in 29 and a half days (a MONTH). Because it takes as long to rotate on its axis as it does to circle the Earth, the same side of the moon always faces us.

The moon has no light of its own but reflects the light of the sun. Depending on the positions of the moon, the Earth, and the sun, the sun's light may appear to fall on only part of the surface of the moon visible to us. When the light falls on the whole surface, we see a full moon; when we can see only half of the lit surface, we see a half moon; and when we can see only a small part of the lit surface, we see a crescent moon.

Sometimes, the Earth passes between the sun and the moon, putting the moon into the Earth's shadow. This is called an *eclipse* of the moon. Other times, when the moon passes between the sun and the Earth, its shadow falls on a small part of the Earth, causing what we call an eclipse of the sun, or a solar eclipse.

Just as the Earth's GRAVITY influences the moon by keeping it in orbit, the moon's gravity (only one sixth that of Earth's) influences the Earth by causing the tides to rise and fall.

Normal life cannot exist in the waterless, airless environment of the moon. On its sunlit surfaces, the temperatures rise to 243°F (117°C); on dark surfaces, the temperatures drop to –261°F (–163°C). The lunar surface is strewn with rocks covered with powdery dust. There are fairly flat, great waterless "seas" and thousands of deep depressions or CRATERS, often with tall mountain peaks rising from the centers.

On July 20, 1969, the American *Apollo II* astronauts, Neil Armstrong and Edwin Aldrin, landed in the Sea of Tranquility, did some scientific tests, and collected 70 pounds (31.5 kg) of rocks for study. Twice more, manned Apollo missions were successful. In 1973, Russian scientists landed an automatic testing machine crawler to further investigate the surface of the moon. SEE ALSO: ECLIPSE, TIDES.

Sir Thomas MORE (1478–1535)

Sir Thomas More was a famous English statesman and lawyer. He became a Member of Parliament and also wrote a book called *Utopia*. Utopia was an ideal country where there was no crime and poverty. Everybody was equal and worked at what he did best.

After King HENRY VIII dismissed Cardinal Wolsey as his chief minister, he chose More to succeed him. King Henry expected More's support in his quarrel with the POPE over his divorce, but More did not believe that a king could disobey the Pope. More resigned from the king's court.

Later King Henry demanded that all men of importance sign an Oath of Supremacy, saying Henry was now the head of the Church in England. Sir Thomas More refused to sign, and King Henry had him beheaded for treason.

In 1935, More was declared a saint by the Roman Catholic Church.

MORMONS

The religious group we call the Mormons is really the Church of Jesus Christ of Latter-day Saints. This group calls the Book of Mormon its holy scripture.

Joseph Smith, a farmer in New York state, claimed in 1827 that he had received the Book of Mormon from an angel. He began to gather followers, whom he took first to Ohio and then to Nauvoo, Illinois. Smith was murdered there in 1844. One follower, BRIGHAM YOUNG, took most of the Mormons westward. They founded Salt Lake City, Utah, in 1847. This city is still the center of Mormon activities.

Not all Mormons followed Young. Some returned to Ohio, and some set up the Reorganized Church of Jesus Christ of Latter-day Saints in Independence, Missouri. The Mormons work hard to convert other people to their beliefs. They have strict rules for their personal lives.

MORSE CODE

The Morse Code was named after its American inventor, Samuel Morse (1791–1872), who was also an accomplished painter. Morse's interest in electricity stimulated him to perfect his own electric telegraph. In 1844, he demonstrated to the U.S. Congress his instrument and code by sending the famous message, "What hath God wrought!" over a wire from Washington, D.C. to Baltimore.

A	·—		N	—·
B	—···		O	———
C	—·—·		P	·——·
D	—··		Q	——·—
E	·		R	·—·
F	··—·		S	···
G	——·		T	—
H	····		U	··—
I	··		V	···—
J	·———		W	·——
K	—·—		X	—··—
L	·—··		Y	—·——
M	——		Z	——··

The Morse Code, which is still used today, consists of long and short sounds, known as dots and dashes, which stand for letters and numbers.

MOSAIC

Mosaic is a way of making designs by setting small tiles, colored stones, or other bits of material in mortar so that the mortar is entirely covered. Some of the very best mosaic is made of colored glass cubes with gold leaf behind them.

Mosaic is a very old art form, used in the Near East and in ancient Greece and Rome. Some of the very finest mosaics were set in the Greek Orthodox churches of Istanbul, and in the churches of Ravenna, Italy. Their colors are still beautiful and fresh, though they are over a thousand years old. St. Mark's church in Venice also has excellent mosaics. Artists are still working in mosaic today.

MOSCOW

Moscow is the capital and largest city in RUSSIA, having about 7.5 million people. It is far inland, but ships from the BALTIC, White, BLACK, Azov, and Caspian seas come there by way of the Moscow, Baltic-White, and Volga-Don canals, as well as the Moskva River.

In the center of the city is the *Kremlin*, the seat of government. Before the Kremlin is Red Square, where the famous May Day parades are held and where the tomb of NIKOLAI LENIN stands. Here also is the colorful Cathedral of St. Basil, with its onion-shaped domes. Moscow has a famous university, museums, and many theaters. Its Bolshoi Ballet tours around the world almost every year.

Moscow was at first a fortified village around 1100 and later became a political capital during the 1400s. The government was, however, transferred to St. Petersburg (now Leningrad) in 1712. After NAPOLEON occupied the city in 1812, a great fire, perhaps set by French looters or Russians who wished to drive out Napoleon, destroyed most of Moscow. Rebuilt, the city developed into a major industrial center, where today steel, tools, textiles, chemicals, and other items are manufactured. During World War II, HITLER reached within 20 miles (32 km) of Moscow. Since the Soviets (the governing communist officials of the U.S.S.R.) came to power in 1918, Moscow has been the capital and chief cultural center, with modern buildings, parks, and subways. SEE ALSO: RUSSIA, U.S.S.R.

Moscow - The Great Palace of the Kremlin

MOSES

Moses was born in Egypt at a time when his people, the HEBREWS, were slaves. The Egyptian Pharaoh believed the Hebrews were increasing in number too fast and ordered the death of all male children. Moses' mother hid him in the reeds by the NILE, where he was discovered and brought up by the Pharaoh's daughter.

As a young man, Moses received a special calling at the Burning Bush, where God told him to lead His chosen people (also known as the Israelites or Hebrews) from slavery. The Pharaoh refused to allow this, but after ten terrible plagues, he relented and Moses led his people in the 13th century B.C. out of Egypt. They crossed the Red Sea into the desert of Sinai, where on Mount Sinai, Moses received the Ten Commandments from God.

The Bible tells how the Hebrews became desert wanderers for 40 years, during which Moses made them into a nation with their own laws and customs. In his old age, Moses saw the Promised Land from Mount Pisgah. He did not enter it, for he died and was buried in Moab.

MOSQUE

A mosque is a house of prayer in ISLAM. It is a large hall, covered with huge domes or filled with many columns. The floor is covered with carpets. There is no altar, but a *mihrab*, an opening in one wall, shows the worshipers the direction of Mecca. They face this way when they pray. Beside the mihrab is a *minbar*, a raised platform from which parts of the KORAN are read.

Outside the hall of prayer is a courtyard with a fountain. Every Muslim must wash before he prays. There is also a *minaret*, a tall tower with a balcony. An official called a *muezzin* climbs it five times a day to call the Muslims to prayer.

MOSQUITO

Only the female mosquito bites people and animals to get the blood she needs to lay her eggs.

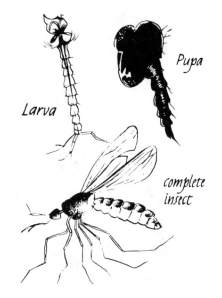

Larva

Pupa

complete insect

In summer, the eggs are laid on stagnant water. They hatch in a day or two into squirming larvae. Each larva pushes its long breathing tube out of the water. Many larvae are eaten by fish, but those that survive become *pupae*. In a few days, the skin of each pupa splits open and a mosquito emerges. It sits on the skin it has shed and suns itself for a few minutes before flying off as an adult mosquito. The adult mosquito lives about two weeks.

Mosquitoes are found all over the world. One type spreads a disease called MALARIA by sucking the blood of an infected person and passing the germs on to the other people it bites. Another mosquito carries deadly yellow fever. SEE ALSO: GNAT.

MOTHS

Although moths look very much like their close insect relatives the BUTTERFLIES, there are several ways in which they are different. The ANTENNAE of a moth are feathered and pointed at the ends; those of a butterfly end in a tiny knob. Unlike butterflies, moths generally fly at night and leave their wings open when at rest. The body of a moth is plump and often hairy looking. The body of a butterfly is slender.

Both moths and butterflies have four stages to their life cycle: egg, larva (grub), pupa (resting stage), and adult. Unlike butterflies, most moths spin a cocoon of silken threads in which to spend the pupal stage.

Many moths feed on the nectar of flowers. Some never eat anything in the adult stage and have short life spans. Moth CATERPILLARS do more harm than butterflies do by eating fruit, vegetables, leaves of trees, and fabrics. SILK comes from the cocoon spun by the caterpillar of the Chinese silkworm moth.

The Io moth is a large showy yellow moth with a circular dark purple eyespot on each hind wing. The larvae feed mainly on corn.

The adult of the small, brown common clothes moth does not eat. The caterpillars, however, chew wood, cotton, and fur.

The luna moths are collector's prizes. They are large and pale green with a purplish brown rimmed "window" on each hind wing. The hind wings each have an elongated "tail" that is half the length of the wing. The larvae feed mainly on sweet gum, walnut, oak, and beech trees.

The Cecropia moth of the eastern half of the United States is the largest species of silkworm moths with a wingspan up to 6 inches (15.2 cm). The wings are red, tan, and white. The larvae feed on numerous types of forest and fruit trees.

The gypsy moth was brought to the United States from Europe for experimentation in 1869. Shortly afterwards, it escaped and is now a serious menace to fruit and woodland trees in New England and eastern New York. Aerial spraying during blight years has helped to control its spread to other areas. SEE ALSO: ANTENNAE, BUTTERFLIES, CATERPILLAR, SILK.

saturnia mendocino
(U.S. California)

lymantria dispar
GYPSY MOTH
(E. America and Canada)

phragmatobia
fuliginosa
RUBY TIGER-MOTH
(Canada, N. U.S.)

platarctia parthenos
ST. LAWRENCE TIGER -
MOTH (Canada, U.S.)

phligophora iris
(Central & E. canada,
N. and N.E.U.S.)

MOUNTAINS

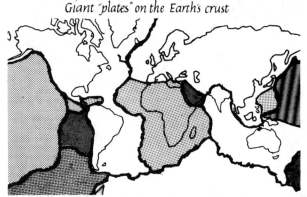

Giant "plates" on the Earth's crust

When the Earth was created it was very hot. Gradually, it began to cool and, as it did, a thick crust formed on its surface. The inside was still so hot that much of it was melted stone.

The Earth's crust has a number of solid pieces called *plates*. These plates are separated by cracks. Material from the hot mantle below the crust comes up and spreads out on the sea floor. This pushes the plates with the continents on them apart. In other places, the plates are pushed together. If this happens slowly, the crust buckles up and forms mountains.

The tallest mountains are the HIMALAYAS in southern Asia. Mount EVEREST, the highest mountain in the world, reaches almost 6 miles (29,028 feet or 8998 m) into the sky. The tallest mountain in the United States is Mount McKinley in Alaska, which is 20,320 feet (6299 m) high.

Not all mountains have their bases on land. The highest underwater mountain is Mount Pico, which forms part of the Azores Islands in the Atlantic Ocean. It is 23,615 feet (7321 m) tall; 7615 feet (2361 m) of it are above sea level.

MOUNT VERNON

The home of GEORGE WASHINGTON, now a museum, stands on the Potomac River 15 miles (18 km) from Washington, D.C. It is a large wooden house, two stories high, with a famous wooden porch as high as the walls. Washington inherited the plantation where the house now stands from his brother Lawrence in 1751. He first lived there in 1759, and spent 15 years enlarging and remodeling the house, which originally had been small. He was away for long periods while he was Commander-in-Chief during the Revolution and later when he was President of the United States. But he lived there the last few years of his life.

The house was neglected after his death, and it was in danger of being destroyed, but in 1858 a group of women purchased it and restored it to the appearance it had when Washington lived there. This was almost the first attempt to save any great American building.

MOUSE

The mouse is a relative of hamsters and rats. All are rodents, and all are MAMMALS.

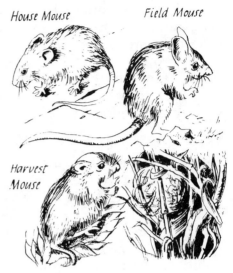

House Mouse

Field Mouse

Harvest Mouse

The best known mouse is the *house mouse*. His ancestors were wild and lived outdoors. When men first began to travel long distances and to settle in new places, these mice often accompanied them, though the men did not know it at the beginning of their journeys. It was not long before mice were living everywhere that men lived, even in men's homes.

Mice multiply rapidly because they have several litters of babies each year. There are so many mice that men often consider them pests. Mice destroy crops and get into food that is being stored; they chew wood and other materials that men use; they even carry disease. Cats, foxes, owls, and hawks are natural enemies of mice, and these *predators* help to control the mouse population.

Mice, however, can be helpful as well as destructive. For instance, they are favorite laboratory animals. Scientists have learned many things about our bodies and how to keep them healthy from experiments in which they have used mice.

Because mice are small and easily cared for, they are often kept as pets. Probably the best known and best loved pet mouse in the world is Walt Disney's cartoon creation, Mickey Mouse.

MOVIES

If many pictures of a moving object are flashed one after another in front of a person, for a split second each, the object will appear to move. The brain can record only so many new images each second, and retains each image for a short time after it has disappeared.

Early in the 19th century there were hand-painted toys that created this illusion of motion, but the real "motion picture" or *movies* depended on three things: film that could record fast-moving objects without blurring; long, flexible reels of film containing enough pictures to tell a story; and a *projector* that could flash the pictures on a large screen for an audience. These things were not available until around 1890. The first movies, as we know them today, were shown to audiences in France in 1895. They were made by Auguste and Louis Lumière.

For the first thirty years, movies had no built-in sound. Pianists, orchestras, or records gave musical or spoken accompaniments, but there was no way of recording directly on film what the actors were supposed to be saying. The first *sound track* on films, operating a LOUDSPEAKER through a photoelectric cell, was introduced in 1927.

Early movies were very short, and it took a while for their *directors* to realize that a movie gave them a chance to create effects never seen before. It was possible to show things happening in different places at the same time by showing *shots* (pictures) of one and then the other. By double exposure a length of film could show two things as if they were together, when each had really been photographed separately. A camera could swing around to show a whole landscape. It could show a scene as one person might see it. It took a few years for directors to develop all the techniques that we now enjoy at the movies. When movies first appeared, people doubted that they would ever be more than bad imitations of stage plays. By the 1920s, people realized that they were a great art form in their own right. Such actors as CHARLIE CHAPLIN and such artists as WALT DISNEY have remained famous even though they are no longer alive.

As an art form, movies are judged every year in many ways in many places. The persons who created and produced the best movies are honored. Awards are given for best acting, direction, photography, set decoration, and so on. In the U.S., the persons who have done the best work each year receive an Academy Award in the form of a gold statuette, called an Oscar.

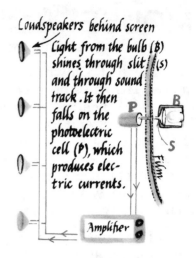

Loudspeakers behind screen

Light from the bulb (B) shines through slit (S) and through sound track. It then falls on the photoelectric cell (P), which produces electric currents.

Amplifier

The rotating shutter (S) cuts off the light while the film is being moved

lens

This moving claw jerks the film into position ready for the next picture.

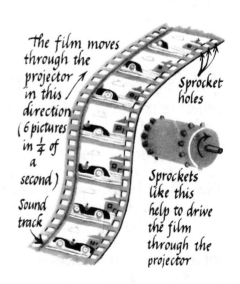

The film moves through the projector in this direction (6 pictures in $\frac{1}{4}$ of a second)

Sound track

Sprocket holes

Sprockets like this help to drive the film through the projector

554

Wolfgang Amadeus MOZART
(1756–1791)

Wolfgang Amadeus Mozart, born in Salzburg, Austria, became one of the greatest composers of MUSIC in the world.

Mozart's father saw his son's musical ability and began to give him lessons at a very early age. At five, Mozart began to write music, and at six, he gave his first public concert, playing the violin and the piano, in Vienna. His father displayed him and his older sister during a tour of Europe. Young Mozart's skill at playing the violin, organ, and piano caused a sensation. Kings, queens, and everyone liked the happy and friendly boy. Although Mozart never went to school, he learned many different musical styles from other musicians during his tours.

At 14, he was appointed concertmaster to the archbishop of Salzburg. Because he was poorly paid, he left in 1781 and went to Vienna, where he married. All the while, Mozart composed music of every kind: symphonies, CONCERTOS for piano, for violin, and for various wind instruments.

In 1787, Mozart became court composer to the Austrian emperor, but his salary was not very much. Until the end of his life, he had financial troubles. However, he was brilliantly clever and wrote more than a thousand compositions, which include the lovely OPERAS *The Marriage of Figaro*, *The Magic Flute*, and *Don Giovanni*. It was probably his hard and feverish work that caused his early death.

MUHAMMAD (570?–632)

Muhammad, also known as Mohammed or Mahomet, was the founder of the religion known as ISLAM. He was born in MECCA, a city in western Saudi Arabia, near the Red Sea. An orphan, he was brought up by his uncle. When he was 24, he married a rich widow and became an Arab merchant.

The Arabs then worshiped many gods, but at the age of 40 Muhammad felt that one had chosen him to be the prophet of true faith. He said that in the cave of Mt. Hira, north of Mecca, he was visited by an angel who commanded him to preach for the god Allah. Because he later preached against the rich and greedy merchants of Mecca, he was persecuted and forced to flee to Medina, a city 210 miles (338 km) from Mecca. His flight in A.D. 622 is known as the *Hegira*, and the Muslim calendar dates from that year. His new religion, which he called Islam, taught that Allah was all-powerful and merciful and that war for Islam was a holy war. In A.D. 630 Muhammad returned to Mecca and captured it. He destroyed its idols and converted the people to Islam. The new faith spread rapidly, winning converts throughout Arabia, North Africa, Persia, and much of India.

Muhammad's messages from Allah were written down and collected into the KORAN, which is sacred to the Muslims. SEE ALSO: ISLAM, KORAN, MUSLIMS.

MUSCLES

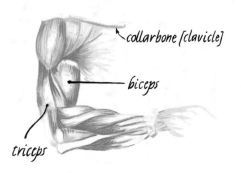

There are about 660 muscles in the human body, and they make up about 40 percent of body weight.

There are two types of muscles: *voluntary* and *involuntary*. The voluntary muscles work only on conscious command from the BRAIN. For example, when we want to write a word, our brain relays a message through the NERVES to the muscles, telling them to pull the arm and hand bones correctly for writing a certain set of letters. The involuntary muscles, such as those of the stomach, LUNGS, HEART, intestines, and ARTERIES, work automatically, without our thinking about it.

The *biceps* muscle that is located at the front of the upper arm, bends the arm at the elbow. The muscle at the back of the arm, above the elbow, is used to straighten the arm again. These muscles are made of bundles of fibers, each about an inch (2.5 cm) long. They are fastened to the arm bones by *tendons*.

Every time we move, we use one or more of the muscles in our bodies.

MUSHROOMS and TOADSTOOLS

A mushroom is a fungus (plural, FUNGI). There are about 38,000 varieties, some of which are so poisonous that they weaken the heart or dissolve the blood cells and cause death in 3 or 4 days. *Toadstool* is the name popularly given to inedible or poisonous mushrooms. A *puffball* is a ball-shaped mushroom that puffs trillions of spores out into the air like a thick cloud of smoke. Many times, only an expert can tell the difference between an edible mushroom and a poisonous toadstool.

Mushrooms grow best in warm, damp places. Commercially, mushrooms are grown in caves, abandoned coal mines, dark cellars, and other places specially designed for them. Mushrooms grow so fast that one may almost seem to pop up out of the ground after a summer shower.

Some mushrooms are small and brown, while others are huge and orange, red, or yellow. Many names are very descriptive, such as Shaggy Mane, Stinkhorn, Bird's Nest, and Witch's Butter. SEE ALSO: FUNGI.

MUSIC

When sounds are arranged in a pattern that means something special to the listener, the result is music. The beat of a military drum, a symphony played by a hundred musicians, or a recording of street noises arranged in a certain way all can be music.

The earliest music was probably no more than shouting or clapping in rhythm. But the Babylonians and their neighbors already had MUSICAL INSTRUMENTS 4500 years ago, and had a way of writing down music some time before 800 B.C. The Hebrews had their own musical tradition from 2000 B.C. The ancient Greeks and the ancient Chinese thought much about music, and saw it as a very important thing. Our own musical system is based on that of the Greeks and the Romans.

Gregorian Chant Notation

Modern Notation

The chants of the early Christians are the earliest music we actually know. The Gregorian chants of the 6th century A.D. are still sung sometimes. At first all singers sang the same melody, but by A.D. 900 *polyphony*, in which they sang in parts, each with its own notes, was introduced. By 1100, each part sang not only its own melody, but sang notes that were longer or shorter than those of the other parts.

After the early Middle Ages, music grew more and more complex in its sounds and rhythms. We know much of this old music from manuscripts, and much of it has been recorded. Many great composers revealed new possibilities for composing music, and inventors added new instruments. The public did not always understand what was happening, and many compositions that we know and enjoy today were hated at first.

Music today is very experimental. Electronic devices have added to the older instruments that composers can use. The public is still not always sure if it likes what is happening, but thanks to recordings it has almost 1500 years of music to choose from. SEE ALSO: MUSICAL INSTRUMENTS.

MUSICAL INSTRUMENTS

Most musical instruments can be divided into four groups.

Percussion instruments are struck. DRUMS, BELLS, cymbals, and castanets are all percussion instruments. So are gongs, xylophones, and maracas. Many of these instruments were first used either in parts of Asia or in Latin America. It may seem odd, but PIANOS are percussion instruments too. Their strings are struck by little hammers.

Wind instruments are played with the breath or with pumped air. Some instruments that are (or that used to be) made of wood are called WOODWINDS. These include FLUTES, piccolos, bassoons, clarinets, and oboes. *Brasses* are also wind instruments. These include TRUMPETS, trombones, FRENCH HORNS, tubas, bugles, and cornets. Woodwinds are used mostly in ORCHESTRAS, and brasses are used both in orchestras and BANDS. But there are other wind instruments not often found in either. Examples of these are BAGPIPES, mouth organs, and recorders. The pipe ORGAN is also a wind instrument, though it runs on pumped air rather than the breath.

There are two kinds of *stringed instruments*. Some are *plucked*, for instance the GUITAR, the LUTE, and the HARP. The HARPSICHORD has strings that are plucked mechanically. Other stringed instruments are *bowed*. Hair stretched tight and rubbed with rosin is drawn across the strings of the VIOLIN, the viola, the CELLO, or the double bass to make them sound.

Some musical instruments are outside all these groups. There are various modern electronic organs, for instance. Even tape recorders are being used as musical instruments these days.

MUSLIMS

Muslims are people who practice the religion called ISLAM. The first Muslims were Arabs converted by MUHAMMAD, but today there are Muslims on every continent of the Earth. Islam has always tried to make converts, regardless of their race or nationality. Many persons in the United States belong to the Black Muslims, a sect that began independently from true Islam. SEE ALSO: ISLAM, KORAN.

MYCENAE

Mycenae in southeastern GREECE was the site of an advanced, ancient civilization. The ruins of the city, near the modern town of Mikinai, show only the citadel (fortress), with its enormous rock walls. A German archeologist, Heinrich Schliemann, excavated in 1876 five shaft graves inside the walls. The treasures uncovered in those graves showed that Mycenae had a flourishing civilization during the second half of the second millennium B.C., long before ATHENS did. About 1400 B.C., the Mycenaeans invaded CRETE and traveled also throughout the AEGEAN SEA. Sometime after 1100 B.C., the supremacy of Mycenae came to a sudden end when the Dorians, a savage northern tribe, invaded and destroyed the city. Though later rebuilt, the city never regained its splendor.

Illustrated here is the Lion Gate, more than 3500 years old. It is believed that Agamemnon led his warriors through this gate to the Trojan War (see TROY).

MYTH and LEGEND

A *myth* is an imaginary story about gods or other supernatural beings. A *legend* is a story of heroes—human beings who may or may not have really existed and who have done great things. A legend may also illustrate how the supernatural characters of myths affect the lives of human beings.

Apollo pursuing Daphne, a myth

There are many myths about the creation of man. The VIKINGS, for instance, believed that once there was nothing but ice and fog, and that a cow, licking at the ice, uncovered the first man and woman. There are also myths about the destruction of the world, and even the destruction of the gods, for many primitive people felt that nothing could last forever.

An example of a legend is the Greek story of Aeneas, who fled from TROY after the Greeks had captured it. He sailed around the Mediterranean Sea with his followers as the gods dictated, and finally founded what eventually became the Roman Empire. There is also a Roman legend of Romulus, who is supposed to have begun the city of ROME.

NAMES

A *name* is a word that identifies a person, place, or thing. It sometimes helps us form an idea of whatever carries the name, and helps us talk about him, her, or it afterward. Some people have even felt that there was magic in names—that the name of God must not be spoken, or that knowing the name of a thing gives you power over it.

Most people have one or more *given names* (also called Christian names) and a *surname*. The given names are your very own, given you at birth or at a christening. The surname is your family name. People are usually known by their first given name, but sometimes prefer to be known by their middle names. President Woodrow Wilson's real first name was Thomas, for instance, but he was never known by it.

Surnames have not always been used. They came into being to help tell between two persons of the same name. The town a person came from (Lincoln), the trade he practiced (Mason), the fact that he was his father's son (Robinson), or a nickname might become the source of his surname, which would be handed on in his family. Most peoples put the surname after the given names, but the Hungarians and the Chinese do the opposite.

Place names give clues to the history of places. New York was named after the Duke of York. Three American cities are called Canton because their founders believed (wrongly) that they were directly across the globe from Canton, China. Pennsylvania means "Woods of Penn," since the land was given to William Penn in the 17th century. New Mexico, of course, is next to Mexico itself. Many of our state names are taken from words and phrases of local Indian languages.

NAPOLEON BONAPARTE (1769–1821)

Napoleon was born on the Mediterranean island of Corsica and was sent at the age of 10 to a military school in France. His small stature won him the nickname "the Little Corporal." In 1785, he became a lieutenant of artillery in the French army.

Later, Napoleon joined the revolutionary armies in France, fighting against the French king. He received military honors and was made a general at the age of 24. The revolutionary government of France then put Napoleon in charge of the French troops that were warring against the Austrians in Italy. He won several battles and returned to Paris as a hero.

Admired by his soldiers and the French people, Napoleon overthrew the revolutionary French government. He established a new government with himself as head. He also set up a new school system and gave France a unified body of law, called the Napoleonic Code, which became a model for other legal systems.

In 1804, "the Little Corporal" crowned himself Emperor of France. During the following years, he conquered almost all of Europe. With an army of 500,000 men, Napoleon invaded RUSSIA in 1812. The Russians retreated, destroying their crops as they went so that the French soldiers would have nothing to eat. By the time Napoleon got to MOSCOW, winter had arrived. The Russians had burned the city and gone to the country. Finding no food or shelter, the French army began the long trek back through snow and ice. Less than 100,000 men finally returned to France. Then Russia, England, Prussia, and Sweden formed an alliance that defeated Napoleon at the battle of Leipzig in 1813, and seized Paris the next year.

Napoleon was forced into exile on the island of Elba. In 1815, he escaped from Elba, and for a period called the "Hundred Days," he raised a new army. He was decisively defeated by the English and Prussian armies at the battle of Waterloo in 1815.

Napoleon surrendered to the British and was sent to the desolate island of St. Helena in the Atlantic. He died there, but his body now lies in Paris.

Carry NATION (1846–1911)

Mrs. Carry Nation led a strong campaign against the sale of liquor in the United States. Born in Kentucky, she married Dr. Charles Gloyd in 1867. Dr. Gloyd was a heavy drinker and caused a great deal of trouble for her. In 1877, she married David Nation. A few years later, she began her work with the Women's Christian Temperance Union (WCTU).

Mrs. Nation's efforts finally forced the United States Congress to amend the Constitution, banning the sale of liquor. She proved that women could have an important role in national politics.

NATIONAL PARK

A national park is land set aside by a country's government for the people to use and enjoy. These public lands usually contain much natural beauty, such as spectacular waterfalls, mountains, geysers, glaciers, volcanoes, caves, canyons, rock formations, and forests. National parks are also for the preservation of wildlife and wilderness.

Many parks provide outdoor recreation for visitors. Depending upon the rules of each park, there are sometimes facilities for camping, swimming, water skiing, hiking, boating, and even fishing. Also, national parks employ various guides, forest rangers, geologists, and historians to help the visitors and to take care of the animals, plants, trees, and scenic landscape. Some parks are mostly areas of important historic interest, such as birthplaces of famous persons, early settlements and buildings, and major battlefields.

In the U.S., national parks are established by Congress and run by the National Park Service, a branch of the U.S. Department of the Interior. The country has 38 national parks, such as Grand Canyon, Glacier, Everglades, Yosemite, and Yellowstone. Yellowstone National Park, established in 1872, is the oldest national park in the world. The U.S. has also more than 200 historical areas (monuments, memorials, military parks and battlefields, cemeteries, and residences). They include the birthplaces of Presidents Lincoln, Roosevelt (Theodore and Franklin), and Kennedy, Mount Rushmore in South Dakota, Gettysburg National Park (site of the Battle of Gettysburg), Grant's Tomb in New York City, and the Arlington National Cemetery (site of the Tomb of the Unknowns). There are more than 50 designated national recreation areas, including the seashores of Cape Cod, Cape Hatteras, and Canaveral, the Lake Mead and Golden Gate National Recreation Areas, and the Appalachian Trail.

Canada has 20 beautiful national parks, such as Baniff and Jasper, in Alberta, Fundy, in New Brunswick, and Wood Buffalo, in Alberta and the Northwest Territories.

NAVIGATION

Navigation is the science that tells you where you are and which way you are going, especially if you are in a ship or airplane. Birds are natural navigators, with excellent eyes and a good memory for landmarks that help them go where they want to over thousands of miles. Some animals navigate by smell. Man, however, has had to build up a complicated set of devices and methods to equal the accuracy of the birds.

Dead reckoning is the simplest form of navigation. If you know where you were at a certain time, and which way you have been going, you can tell more or less where you are now. To know just where you are, it is better to take a *fix*. This is done either by sighting on two visible objects, like a LIGHTHOUSE and a BUOY, or by finding the directions from which you get the strongest radio signals from stations whose locations you know. The *bearings* you take are like two lines; where they cross is where you are.

Celestial navigation, finding out the angle, from the horizon, of the sun or of a star at a certain time, is a good way of knowing how far north or south of the equator you are. A *sextant* is used to measure this.

These are only a few of the methods used in navigation. SEE ALSO: BUOYS, COMPASS, LIGHTHOUSES AND LIGHTSHIPS.

NAVY

A country's navy consists of warships, naval aircraft, officers, and enlisted men and women. It also includes naval docks, supply depots, and shipyards, where ships are built, housed, and repaired. During war, a navy protects a country's shore and also attacks the enemy's coastline and ships. A navy can carry ground troops and supplies on its transport ships.

A complete navy also has aircraft carriers, battleships (which are rarely used nowadays), cruisers, destroyers, submarines (many of which carry long range missiles and are powered by nuclear energy), and many auxiliary vessels, such as mine-layers, mine-sweepers, frigates and corvettes (both of which escort merchant ships), torpedo-boats, landing craft, dredgers, and icebreakers.

NAZARETH

In ancient times, the village of Nazareth was so small that it was not mentioned in the Old Testament of the Bible. The enemies of JESUS called him "the Nazarene" because he grew up there—in such a simple place.

Today the town has about 25,000 people. There are a number of shrines and churches; one is supposed to be a synagogue where Jesus preached.

NEBRASKA

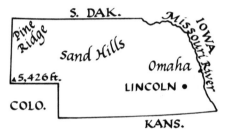

Nebraska is a state in the Midwest of the United States. It has wide prairies and rich farmland. The Sand Hills area in central Nebraska is an ideal place for rearing cattle and sheep. The state grows large crops of corn, wheat, oats, rye, sorghum, and alfalfa. Omaha, the largest city, is one of the world's great meat-packing centers.

In the 1700s, the Spanish and French visited the area. They found many Indians, such as the Omaha, Oto, Sioux, Cheyenne, Arapaho, Ponca, and Pawnee. The Pawnees were constantly battling other tribes, but were friendly to the white man. Great herds of buffalo roamed the plains and provided the Indians with meat, hides, and warm robes. The Sioux, Cheyenne, and Arapaho Indians fought the white settlers in the 1800s to keep their hunting grounds. After the Civil War, the U.S. government offered free land in Nebraska to those who would farm it. Gradually, settlers arrived and the Indian land was taken, but not without much bloodshed. Farmers there suffered droughts in summer and blizzards in winter. Slowly they learned how to work the tough sod (grassland), using irrigation and dry farming methods.

Agriculture is the state's chief occupation today. Many of the industries are related to farming. There are large meat-packing plants and canning factories. Tourists come to visit the Museum of the Fur Trade at Chadron and Pioneer Village at Minden. They also come to tall Scotts Bluff, a rocky landmark that once guided pioneers on the Oregon Trail.

About 1.5 million people live in Nebraska. Lincoln is the capital.

NEBUCHADNEZZAR (died 562 B.C.)

Nebuchadnezzar became King of BABYLON in about 605 B.C., when Judea was under Babylon's control. After the Egyptian Pharaoh, Necho II, defeated him in battle in 601 B.C., the Judeans revolted against his rule. Nebuchadnezzar crushed the Judeans in 597 B.C., but they started a new revolt in 589 B.C. Nebuchadnezzar then attacked Jerusalem and destroyed it entirely, taking the Hebrews into captivity in 587 B.C.

Nebuchadnezzar made Babylon a splendid city, with great temples, palaces, gardens, and canals. Because of his pride, he went mad at the end of his life. He finally surrendered to God who brought the king back to his senses. SEE ALSO: BABYLON.

NEBULA

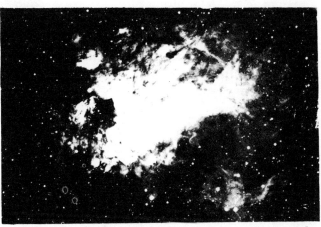

The word *nebula* comes from the Latin word meaning cloud or mist. We use it to describe objects of the night sky that look like clouds among the stars. Some *nebulae* (which is the plural of nebula) are clouds of gases and dust. Others consist of a single star surrounded by a huge cloud of gas. A third kind of nebula looks like a star to the naked eye. When looked at through a telescope, it can be seen to be an enormous group of stars, very much like the Milky Way, the GALAXY in which our sun is a star.

Some nebulae contain dark gases. We know that they are there only because we cannot see the light from the stars on the other side.

NEGROES

Negroes are one of the major RACES of mankind. They are characterized generally by brown to black skin, broad, flat noses, thick lips and wide mouths, and short, curly hair. Some anthropologists think Negroes may once have been more widely spread throughout the world, since the South Sea islanders, and some Asiatic peoples, have similar features.

The word "Negro" comes originally from the Latin *niger*, "black," but its use as a term for one of the main groups of the human race comes from Spanish-Portuguese term *negro*, "dark," dating from the start of the African slave trade in the 1500s. From AFRICA, slave-traders took large numbers of Negroes to America and the WEST INDIES. In the United States alone there are today about 23 million Negroes, who are usually referred to as Blacks.

African Negroes have lived in tribes under their chiefs for thousands of years. They have been farmers, herdsmen, warriors, and hunters; they have developed their own music, native art, and tribal customs and religion. After the Europeans settled in Africa, some Negroes found work as their servants, farm hands, and miners. During the 1800s, many white settlers forced Negroes to live

Louis Armstrong

Shirley Chisholm

Andrew Young

in separate communities, a practice known as *apartheid* in South Africa. And the Negroes often had no opportunity to gain skills and high positions in life. However, almost all former European colonies in Africa have become independent, and the "Blacks" have gained more control of their lives. SEE ALSO: AFRICA.

Horatio NELSON (1758–1805)

Horatio Nelson, English admiral, was one of the great heroes of English history. When he was only 12, he joined the Royal Navy as a midshipman. At 15, he went on a voyage of discovery in the Arctic; at 18, he served in the East Indies and almost died of fever. By the time he was 20, he was captain of his own ship. He lost an eye during a battle on shore in Corsica and an arm in a naval engagement near Santa Cruz de Tenerife, in the Canary Islands.

NAPOLEON had gone to war against the English, and Admiral Nelson pursued and destroyed the French fleet in the Mediterranean, at the battle of the Nile in 1798. Later, he prevented the Baltic navies from joining the French, who sought to invade England.

After an interlude of peace, war broke out again with the French in 1803. For 22 months, the English fleet, commanded by Nelson, blockaded the French fleet at Toulon, France. The French finally escaped. However, after pursuing the French across the Atlantic to the West Indies and back, Nelson in 1805 trapped and destroyed the combined French and Spanish fleets in the battle of Trafalgar, off the coast of Spain. He died from a wound received during the fight. After this great victory, the English navy was the strongest in the world.

NEON SIGNS

Neon is a chemical ELEMENT, a rare gas obtained by cooling air until it liquefies, then removing the helium and nitrogen that are found with it. Neon is so rare that 88,000 pounds of liquid air are needed to produce one pound of it.

Neon is used in some fluorescent tubes and in some other kinds of lamps, but we know it best from advertising signs. Scientists discovered neon in 1898, and soon showed that if an electric current were run through it, it would glow with an orange-red color. Other colors could be produced by adding chemicals; mercury and neon, for instance, produced blue. Neon signs were popular by the end of the 1920s.

NEPTUNE

Neptune is the eighth PLANET from the sun in the SOLAR SYSTEM. Because it is almost 3 billion miles (4.8 billion km) away from the sun, Neptune takes nearly 165 years to go around the sun just once. It receives little warmth from the sun, and

scientists think it is surrounded by frozen gases and liquids. Although it is about four times the size of the Earth, Neptune takes just 15 hours and 40 minutes to turn once on its axis. Neptune has two known satellites.

Like all of the planets except Earth, Neptune is named after a Roman god. Neptune was the Roman god of the sea. SEE ALSO: PLANETS, SOLAR SYSTEM.

NERVES

The senses of sight, hearing, smell, taste, and touch may start in the eyes, ears, nose, tongue, and surfaces of the body, but we are really made aware of them in the BRAIN. The "messages" to and from the many parts of our body are sent along pathways called nerves. These are two-way wire-like strings of cells that connect the brain with all parts of the body. When we touch something too hot, the sensitive nerve endings in a finger send a pain signal to the brain. The brain then sends a nerve signal back to the muscles in the arm that causes us to snatch the finger out of harm's way. All this takes place in an instant, so we know that the nerves are able to carry messages at lightning speed.

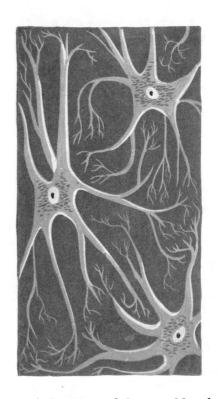

Through other nerve paths, the brain controls our eye blinking, breathing, heartbeat, digestion, and other bodily functions that we do not have to think about.

NEVADA

Nevada is a western state of the United States. Nearly all of the state is a vast desert highland, called the Great Basin. It is surrounded by mountains—the Cascade and Sierra Nevada Mountains in the west and the Rockies in the east. Nevada has numerous alkali *sinks*—that is, places in which rivers have dried up. Even the state's longest river, the Humboldt, goes into a sink, after flowing about 300 miles (483 km) across northern Nevada. Carson City, near Lake Tahoe, is the capital. There are more than 600,000 people in Nevada, half of them living in or near Las Vegas and Reno. Both these cities are famous gambling and resort centers.

The Paiute, Shoshone, and Washoe Indians once roamed the Great Basin. They caught rats and lizards and dug roots for food, for the region was too dry to grow crops and to support animals. The Spanish explored there in 1776, and fur traders came in the 1800s. KIT CARSON and John Frémont, two American frontiersmen, explored the Great Basin and the Sierra Nevada in the 1840s. After the Mexican War, the U.S. obtained the area. The MORMONS built the first permanent settlement in 1851—a trading post at what is now Genoa, Nevada. Later, silver, gold, and other metals were found, and many people came to "strike it rich." Outlaws robbed many who did.

Mining and manufacturing earn much money for Nevada today, but tourism is by far the most important industry. More than 20 million visitors go there each year. In 1977, almost $2 billion was spent by tourists.

NEW BRUNSWICK

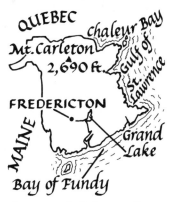

New Brunswick is a maritime province of CANADA, having a lengthy seacoast on the Atlantic Ocean. The Bay of Fundy, which separates New Brunswick from NOVA SCOTIA in the south, has the highest tides in the world. Much of the land is rocky and hilly, with some fertile river valleys and many forests of red spruce, white birch, balsam, and Canadian maple. Saint John is the capital and largest seaport of New Brunswick. Almost 700,000 people live in the province.

Manufacturing is the chief industry. Paper, lumber, and fish products bring in the most money. Also important is the mining of soft coal, lead, copper, and silver.

In 1604, the first white settlement was built at the mouth of the St. Croix River by de Monts and Champlain, two French explorers. The French and British fought over the region, which was later settled by many loyal British colonists who fled from New England during the American Revolution. In 1867, New Brunswick (formerly called Acadia by the French) joined three other colonies to form the dominion of Canada.

NEW ENGLAND

New England is a region in the northeastern United States. It includes the states of MAINE, NEW HAMPSHIRE, VERMONT, MASSACHUSETTS, RHODE ISLAND, and CONNECTICUT. The region is said to have been named by CAPTAIN JOHN SMITH, English colonist in America. He supposedly thought the area looked like the coast of England. From the Green and White Mountains in the north and the Berkshire Hills in the west, the land slopes toward the Atlantic Ocean in the east and Long Island Sound in the south. The region has many lovely mountain and shore resorts. There are numerous short, swift rivers; the Connecticut is the longest river, flowing 380 miles (612 km) from north to south.

After the PILGRIMS established a colony at Plymouth in 1620, other colonies were formed throughout New England. During the colonial period in America, New England was a great shipbuilding center and carried on much foreign trade. New England was the main area of struggle against the British before the AMERICAN REVOLUTION.

NEWFOUNDLAND

Newfoundland is a rugged island that lies off the east coast of CANADA, at the entrance to the Gulf of St. Lawrence. Its coast is rocky, with many inlets. Newfoundland's soil is poor for farming, but its vast forests of spruce and pine make lumbering an important industry.

The province consists also of Labrador, situated on the mainland of Canada. Labrador is a barren region that has severe winters. Rich iron ore is mined there, as well as some other minerals. The capital of the province is St. John's, in Newfoundland, which has about one-fourth of the 550,000 people that live on both the island and the mainland.

VIKINGS from Norway discovered Newfoundland and made a settlement there about A.D. 1000. Later, in 1497, JOHN CABOT claimed it for England. It remained a British independent colony, along with Labrador, until it was united with Canada in 1949. Most of the inhabitants are of British, Irish, and French descent. Many make a living catching cod on the Grand Banks, a large fishing ground southeast of Newfoundland.

NEW GUINEA

New Guinea is the second largest island in the world, situated in the southwest Pacific Ocean. The island has a tropical climate and is covered by mountains and dense jungle. It is divided into two parts—the western half, called Irian Jaya, is part of Indonesia; the eastern half is the nation of Papua New Guinea.

Parts of New Guinea have never been fully explored—particularly jungle areas, where there are all kinds of wildlife. Birds of paradise, unique species of butterflies, sloths, crocodiles, pythons, and wild boars live there.

People live along the coasts, such as in Port Moresby, the capital of Papua New Guinea and the largest city on the island. Most of the 4 million people who live on New Guinea are Melanesians —natives of this Pacific region. There are also some people from Malaysia, Australia, China, and Europe. Except for residents of the cities, most people live by hunting and fishing and by growing coconuts and bananas. Some tribes in New Guinea still use stone axes.

NEW HAMPSHIRE

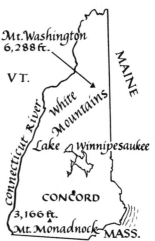

New Hampshire is one of the six New England states, situated in northeastern United States. It has many scenic lakes, swift rivers and streams, and thickly wooded regions. The White Mountains in the north contain the highest peak in the Northeast— Mount Washington, 6288 feet (1949 m) high. The mountain slopes provide excellent skiing in winter, and the lakes and streams furnish great fishing for trout, perch, bass, and whitefish. There is good farmland in southern New Hampshire. Here is situated Concord, the state capital. About 850,000 people live in the state.

The Abenaki Indians once lived there, as well as several other tribes. The first explorers from Europe were Captain Martin Pring, an Englishman, in 1603, and Samuel de Champlain, a Frenchman, in 1605. About 20 years later, the first permanent colony was established at Dover. Then the towns of Portsmouth, Exeter, and Hampton were founded. New Hampshire was part of Massachusetts until it became a separate British colony in 1679. But, in 1776 it declared itself independent of Britain. Soon, cotton mills and shoe factories were built, and the state became an important manufacturing center.

Today there are numerous factories along the Merrimack and Connecticut Rivers and in the seacoast area. Some of New Hampshire's chief products are machinery, textiles, paper, shoes, and chemicals.

NEW JERSEY

New Jersey is a Middle Atlantic State. It is an important manufacturing area, producing chemicals, paints, clothes, machinery, rubber, plastics, and food items. There are large oil refineries around Newark, the state's largest city. New Jersey also grows large amounts of vegetables and fruits, such as tomatoes, asparagus, spinach, apples, and peaches. Many of the state's factories process (can, freeze, or package) these farm goods. New Jersey's nickname is "The Garden State."

The region was inhabited by the Lenni-Lenape Indians when the first European, Giovanni da Verrazano, arrived in 1524. Henry Hudson explored there in 1609. Later, the Dutch made what is now New Jersey part of their colony of New Netherland (now New York). The British seized the land from the Dutch in 1664, and Sir George Carteret named it "New Jersey," after the Isle of Jersey in the English Channel. Many large and small battles occurred there during the American Revolution. For a while, Morristown was George Washington's headquarters. After the war, Alexander Hamilton started the first planned factory town in the U.S.A.—Paterson, New Jersey. Waterpower helped the growth of industry, until today the state is an industrial giant.

New Jersey has had many famous people live and work there, including THOMAS EDISON, the inventor of the electric light, and THOMAS PAINE, an American patriot and writer. Today there are about 7.5 million people in the state. Its capital is Trenton.

NEW MEXICO

New Mexico is a state in the southwest United States. It is a rugged place, with deserts, canyons, mesas (flat tableland with steep sides), and mountains. Large areas of the state have been made fertile by irrigation through dams and reservoirs on rivers, such as on the Rio Grande and the Pecos.

In the 1540s, Francisco Coronado, the Spanish explorer, searched there for the legendary Cibola (seven cities of gold) but found no treasure. The Pueblo, Navaho, Comanche, and Apache Indians lived in the region. The Spanish built the first white settlement at San Juan Pueblo in 1598. Twelve years later, Santa Fe, the present-day state capital, was founded. Missionaries came to teach the Indians, who often rebelled and went on the warpath. Mexico took control in 1821 but lost most of the region to the U.S. during the MEXICAN WAR. In 1853, the land along the state's southern border was bought from Mexico, as part of the Gadsden

Purchase. Then, white settlers and soldiers pushed the Indians off their lands and onto reservations. During the 1880s, the mining and ranching industries became very important.

Today, oil, natural gas, and copper are the three most valuable minerals found in New Mexico. Also high in value are potash and uranium. Manufacturing is growing in importance in New Mexico. Tourists come to ski, hunt, and fish, or to visit the ghost towns and dude ranches. The state has almost 1.25 million people.

NEWSPAPERS

Newspapers are very important in a country like ours. Without them, people would not have enough information for voting and making other decisions.

The ancient Romans posted bulletins to inform the public what was happening. The Chinese began to print a kind of news-paper over a thousand years ago. And other publications of news appeared now and then in Europe from the late Middle Ages on. Some were *newsletters*, full of infor-mation for businessman or other special kinds of person. The first real newspaper, appearing frequently and  with news of all sorts, may have been published in Antwerp, Belgium, from 1605 on. The first English newspapers were published in 1621. With the spread of public education and the development of high-speed power-driven presses in the early 19th century, newspaper reading became common everywhere.

One problem for "the press" (as newspaper people call themselves) has often been that of *censorship*. If the government of a country does not publish its own papers, it may at least forbid certain things to be said. Our freedom of the press is guaranteed by the First Amendment of the Constitution; it was first established by a lawsuit against a newspaper publisher in 1735. Many countries still have censorship.

A large newspaper is a complicated thing to make. Under the *publisher*, who owns the paper or represents those who do, is an *editor* in charge of everything that gets printed. There are other editors in charge of the various departments of the paper. *Reporters* gather local news. *Correspondents* send in news from outside the local area. *News services* send news to many papers all over the country. *Columnists* write their opinions of things. *Sports writers* write about sports, and *feature writers* writer about the theater, fashions, home-making, and many other things. The *advertising department* sells the advertising the paper needs for income. In the *press room*, everything is set in type and printed.

Sir Isaac NEWTON (1642–1727)

One of the most notable traits of great scientists is their immense curiosity. They observe simple events of everyday life and wonder how and why certain things happen. An apple falls from a tree. Why? What made the apple fall to the ground instead of up into the air or off the side? The tides rise and fall regularly in the seas. Why?

These particular questions puzzled the Englishman, Isaac Newton. They led him to discover the laws of GRAVITY while he was still in his twenties, to develop calculations of the orbits of the planets around the sun, and to study the part the moon plays in creating tides on Earth.

Newton's fascination with *light* resulted in his experiments with glass lenses and with triangular bars of glass called *prisms*. These experiments led to his work on the SPECTRUM and his invention of a reflecting TELESCOPE. These areas of knowledge had never been examined before with success, and Newton had to invent his own system of mathematics to describe his discoveries. That system is still used by engineers and scientists today.

A true genius, Newton solved problems that had confused scientists for centuries. His main work, *Principia*, was written only after his friends succeeded in persuading him to overcome his modesty. "If I have seen further than most men," he was once heard to say, "it is by standing on the shoulders of giants." The giants he meant were all those scientists who had come before him in history.

NEWTS

Newts are a kind of small AMPHIBIAN common to Europe and parts of Asia and to North America north of the tropics. The largest is about 6 inches (15 cm) long.

All species live in the water during breeding season and when they are LARVAE. Some go ashore to live after breeding while others, like the red spotted newt of North America, are always *aquatic*. Newts feed on insects and other small animals.

During the breeding season, male newts have brighter coloration and higher crests on the back and tail.

The Japanese fire-bellied newt is a popular aquarium pet. SEE ALSO: AMPHIBIANS.

NEW YORK

New York is the leading manufacturing state of the United States. This is primarily due to NEW YORK CITY, which is the nation's financial capital and largest city and port. The head offices of many great companies are also there. The state's major industries are clothing, printing and publishing, instruments, machinery, and food items. There are about 18.5 million people in New York.

Much of the state is hilly or mountainous, with numerous lakes and forests. However, the plains along the GREAT LAKES and the HUDSON RIVER provide excellent farmland. Here many dairy cattle are raised, and hay, potatoes, apples, and grapes are grown in large quantities. Much of the grape crop is used to make New York State wines. The state's highest mountains are the Adirondacks in the north. They and the Catskill Mountains in the southeast have many summer and winter resorts.

In 1609, HENRY HUDSON discovered the river that was later named for him, and Samuel de Champlain explored what is now Lake Champlain, in upstate New York. The Dutch in 1624 built a settlement called Fort Orange, which is now Albany, the state capital. The next year, they settled New Amsterdam (now New York City) and set up the colony of New Netherland. The British captured the region from the Dutch in 1664, giving English names to almost everything. During the American Revolution, many battles were fought in New York.

New York has had numerous famous residents, among whom were WASHINGTON IRVING, short story writer, HERMAN MELVILLE, novelist, and THEODORE and FRANKLIN ROOSEVELT, both Presidents of the U.S. SEE ALSO: NEW YORK CITY.

NEW YORK CITY

New York City, situated in the southeast corner of NEW YORK State, has about 7.5 million inhabitants. It has five boroughs: Manhattan, Bronx, Brooklyn, Queens, and Richmond (Staten Island). Because it has a natural harbor at the mouth of the Hudson River, New York City is the largest port in the United States.

The Dutch first bought the island of Manhattan from the Indians for $24 worth

of beads, shells, and other small objects. A Dutch settlement, called New Amsterdam, was then established and grew into a trading center. In 1664, the settlement was captured by the British, who renamed it "New York." Since then, Italians, Germans, Russians, Irish, Jews, Blacks, and Puerto Ricans have joined the original Dutch and British as permanent New Yorkers.

Today, great international banks have their headquarters there. Some of the famous sights of the city are the World Trade Center, the Empire State Building, the UNITED NATIONS, the STATUE OF LIBERTY, Broadway, Fifth Avenue, and Central Park. SEE ALSO: NEW YORK.

NEW ZEALAND

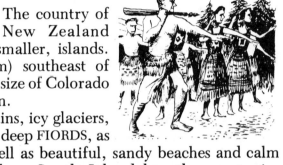

The country of New Zealand consists of two large, and several smaller, islands. Lying about 1300 miles (2093 km) southeast of Australia, New Zealand is about the size of Colorado and has a population of 3.25 million.

The country has snowy mountains, icy glaciers, boiling GEYSERS and volcanoes, and deep FIORDS, as

well as beautiful, sandy beaches and calm lakes. South Island has the most picturesque scenery, with a large range of mountains called the Southern Alps. Here also are the famous sheep pastures of Canterbury Plain. South Island is separated by Cook Strait (named for CAPTAIN JAMES COOK) from North Island, which has the best farmland and the chief ports of Auckland, the largest city, and Wellington, the capital.

New Zealand exports wool, meat, and dairy products to many countries. In the 1960s, it began to develop its natural gas and oil fields and also built its first steel mill and aluminum smelter.

The original inhabitants of New Zealand were the Maoris, a dark-skinned people who now have equal rights with the British colonists. In 1907, New Zealanders were granted their independence from Great Britain.

NIAGARA FALLS

The Niagara River connects two of the GREAT LAKES, Lake Erie and Lake Ontario. About 18 miles (29 km) from Lake Erie, the river becomes a series of rapids, divided by Goat Island. Here the two channels of the river plunge over a high cliff, forming Niagara Falls.

The border between Canada and the United States passes through the falls. The Canadian side has the Horseshoe Falls, named for its great curve 2600 feet (806 m) long, with a drop of 158 feet (49 m). They are a more majestic sight than the smaller American Falls. Though they are higher (167 feet or 52 m), they are much less wide (1000 feet or 310 m). About 95 percent of the water from the Niagara River plunges over the Horseshoe Falls, which is wearing away at the rate of more than 3 feet (about 12 m) each year.

Visitors can go aboard boats that go almost directly under the falls or ride a cable car above the spectacular Whirlpool Rapids. The Welland Canal enables ships from the ST. LAWRENCE SEAWAY to bypass the falls. Several hydro-electric plants nearby generate power for the region.

NICKEL

Nickel is a hard, whitish METAL. Prehistoric man fashioned tools with meteoric iron which contains up to 15 percent nickel. Nickel, however, was not isolated as a pure ELEMENT until 1751.

Steel is sometimes mixed with nickel to form an ALLOY that resists rust. Automobile engine parts, coins, and eating utensils are some of the the things made from alloys containing nickel.

Many metals were once nickel-plated to prevent them from tarnishing, but today chrome is seen more widely because it is cheaper and easier to use.

NIGERIA

The country of Nigeria has a population of about 67 million—more than any other country in Africa. Nigerians belong to 250 tribal and linguistic groups, including the Hausas, the Ibos, the Fulanis, the Yorubas, the Ibibios, and the Ijaws. In 1967, the Ibos of eastern Nigeria formed their own state of Biafra. The move plunged the country into bitter civil war until 1970, when the "Biafrans" surrendered. Nigeria

has since been ruled by military leaders, who have tried to develop the country's rich natural resources of oil, coal, lead, and iron ore.

There are wide mangrove swamps along the coast. Farther inland are tropical rain forests, where palm, cacao, and mahogany trees grow. In central Nigeria, cotton and peanuts are cultivated in this drier plateau region. Here there are also rolling grasslands and open woodlands—plains known as *savannas*.

Great tribal kingdoms once existed in Nigeria. Between the 15th and 17th centuries, the Portuguese and British developed the slave trade (see NEGROES) in Nigeria. The British occupied Lagos, the capital, in 1861, and slowly established control over the entire country. In 1960 Nigeria gained its independence.

NIGHTINGALE

The nightingale is a rather ordinary-looking bird that is related to the robin. The two are about the same size. The nightingale lives in Europe, however, except during the winter when it flies to North Africa.

The remarkable feature of the nightingale is its song, which is so beautiful that poets have described it for thousands of years. Kings and queens have kept nightingales as pets, just to hear them sing.

Florence NIGHTINGALE (1820–1910)

Florence Nightingale was born in Florence, Italy, and received the kind of education that was considered proper for a rich young lady in the 1800s. Her family was shocked when Florence decided to be a nurse. At that time, NURSING was considered a lowly job. Against her family's wishes, Florence visited hospitals abroad and became a nurse in France and Germany. In 1853, she became superintendent of one of London's few hospitals.

When the Crimean War between England and Russia began in 1854, Florence immediately agreed to go the Russian battlefront with medical supplies and 38 women nurses. Despite strong opposition, she founded hospitals at Scutari, near Istanbul, and at Balaklava, on the Black Sea in Russia. Above all, she showed the need for trained nurses and sanitation in the care of the sick and wounded soldiers.

After the war, Florence was a legend and spent the rest of her life establishing a properly trained hospital service. Throughout her life, she taught that nursing was a nobel profession for women.

NILE

The Nile flows about 4150 miles (6682 km) and is the longest river in the world. It begins in Rwanda, a little country in central AFRICA, and flows over rapids and waterfalls and through canyons to Lake Kyoga, in central Uganda. From there, it goes over Murchison Falls and into Lake Albert, on the border of Uganda and Zaire. It then proceeds through a swampy region and into the desert of Sudan.

As the White Nile, it flows north then for about 500 miles (805 km) to Khartoum, the capital of Sudan. Here it is joined by the Blue Nile from Ethiopia. Farther north, at Atbara, the main Nile receives its last great tributary, the Atbara River. The Nile then winds northward, broken by 6 cataracts (waterfalls). As it approaches Egypt, the Nile widens into a man-made lake 300 miles (483 km) long that was created when the Aswan High Dam was completed in 1969.

For the last 1000 miles (1610 km), the Nile passes ancient Egyptian temples, statues, and pyramids. It then reaches CAIRO, where the DELTA begins, and at last flows into the Mediterranean.

NITROGEN

Almost 80 per cent of the Earth's atmosphere is nitrogen, a colorless, odorless, tasteless gas.

Most life would be impossible without nitrogen. Plants generally get their nitrogen from the soil, and scientists have learned that FERTILIZERS must contain nitrogen in some form to make crops and other plants grow better. Some plants, like peas and beans, take nitrogen directly from the air. Animals get their nitrogen from eating plants.

When animals or plants die and decay, their nitrogen is returned to the soil. Also, a certain amount is added from the nitrogen compounds formed by lightning in the air and washed down by the rain.

NOAH

Noah was a righteous man whom God told to build a great ARK (ship). God warned Noah that a great flood would cover the Earth, killing all human and animal life on account of man's wickedness. Noah survived the flood with his family and animals. Then God made a covenant (agreement) with Noah, promising that a flood would never again destroy the Earth. The story of Noah is found in the Book of Genesis in the Bible.

NOBEL PRIZE

The Nobel Prize is probably the greatest honor a person can receive for his or her work. Each year Nobel Prizes are awarded to those who have most benefited mankind in the fields of physics, chemistry, medicine or physiology, economics, literature, and peace.

The Nobel Prizes were established by Alfred B. Nobel, the Swedish inventor and manufacturer of dynamite. He acquired great wealth but also worried about the possible misuse of dynamite. At his death in 1896, he left a special fund, whose annual income would be divided into prizes.

Various groups of outstanding scholars select the winners, who receive gold medals, certificates, and cash awards. The Nobel Prizes are awarded on December 10, the anniversary of Nobel's death. The Peace Prize is presented in Oslo, Norway, by the Norwegian king or queen. The other prizes are presented in Stockholm, Sweden, by the Swedish king or queen.

NORMANS

Norsemen from SCANDINAVIA began to raid the mainland of Europe in the 8th and 9th centuries A.D. They soon built settlements in northern France. In A.D. 912, one of their leaders, Rollo, was given a large area of France by the king,

Charles the Simple. This area was called Normandy. The descendants of the Norsemen who lived there became known as Normans. These people became good Christians, farmers, and builders, but they kept their love of adventure and fighting.

In 1066, the Normans invaded southern England because their ruler, who was later known as WILLIAM THE CONQUEROR, had been promised the crown of England. The invaders conquered England and seized much land from the ANGLO-SAXONS..

The Norman French language was soon used by the ruling lords of England. The FEUDAL SYSTEM of the Normans became the usual way of holding land in return for service. The Normans also erected many castles and churches that had solid pillars and round arches.

NORTH AMERICA

North America is the third largest continent in the world; only Asia and Africa are larger. North America consists of CANADA, the U.S.A, MEXICO, CENTRAL AMERICA, and the WEST INDIES.

The high ROCKY MOUN-
TAINS extend down the
western side of the continent
from Alaska to Panama. In the
northern and eastern area of
Canada are rounded moun-
tains called the Laurentian
Plateau, which stretches
around much of Hudson Bay.
Along the eastern part of the
United States are the Appalachian Mountains, running
from Maine to Georgia.

East of the Rockies, the
land becomes plains and
prairies, where winding rivers
have deposited fertile soil. The

GREAT LAKES in the plains are the largest
freshwater system in the world. In the
United States, the MISSISSIPPI RIVER flows
from near the Canadian border to the Gulf
of Mexico. Other great river systems that
drain the central plains include the
Missouri and the Ohio, both of which are
tributaries of the Mississippi. In Canada,
the Red River, Saskatchewan, and Nelson
system drain the plains, flowing into
Hudson Bay.

The climate of the far north is polar,
and only low shrubs, lichen, and moss grow
in northern Canada and Alaska. Here live

ESKIMOS, trappers, and
fishermen, as well as in-
creasing numbers of people
around the oil fields near
Prudhoe Bay in Alaska, and in
mining centers for gold,
copper, and uranium in the
Northwest Territories in
Canada. The climate of the
interior of North America is
fairly dry with extremes of

temperature. South central United States stretching into Mexico has a dry climate. The Mexican coasts, Central America, and the West Indies have warm, tropical weather, with both a wet and dry season during the year.

Canada has great forests of spruce, larch, fir, pine, and hemlock, which lumbermen use for paper, timber, and rayon. Some of the thickest forests are also in Washington, Oregon, and northern California.

In Saskatchewan, Manitoba, Montana, North and South Dakota, there are wide wheat fields, as well as enormous grazing areas for cattle. In central United States, corn is abundantly grown, and pigs are raised for slaughter in industrial cities like Chicago, Illinois, or Omaha, Nebraska. Along the Mississippi River are grown tobacco, cotton, and fruit

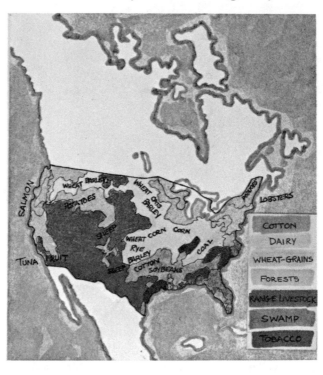

crops. New Orleans is the chief port of the south in this region. In Oklahoma, Texas, and Louisiana there are rich oil fields.

Along the Mexican coast on the Gulf of Mexico, large oil and gas deposits have recently been discovered. Mexico is the largest producer of silver in the world. Here and in Central America, sugar cane, rice, coffee, bananas, and pineapple are cultivated to be exported abroad.

The largest cities in Canada are Toronto and Montreal, both situated in the east. The three largest cities in the U.S. are New York, Chicago, and Los Angeles—all with more than 7 million urban residents. Mexico City, Mexico, is the largest city on the continent, with almost 10 million people.

North Americans have come from all over the world. The English left their customs and language in much of the U.S. and Canada, where there is also

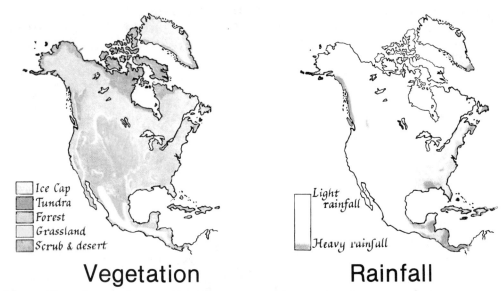

Ice Cap
Tundra
Forest
Grassland
Scrub & desert

Light rainfall

Heavy rainfall

Vegetation   Rainfall

a large French-speaking population, mostly in Quebec. Spanish is the first language in Mexico, Central America, and Cuba, on account of the early Spanish exploration and conquest in these areas. Numerous Indians throughout the continent still retain their old ways and language. However, since the time of COLUMBUS, the continent has attracted foreigners from every land, and so today you can find there Chinese, Japanese, Africans, Russians, and Europeans of all kinds, living next to one another, mixing old ways with new ones. SEE ALSO: AMERICA, CENTRAL AMERICA, INDIVIDUAL COUNTRIES OF NORTH AMERICA, WEST INDIES.

NORTH CAROLINA

North Carolina is a large state lying along the Atlantic coast. It has low coastal plains in the east, with Cape Hatteras jutting into the ocean. Many ships have been wrecked on this CAPE. Inland is the Piedmont Plateau, an area of low hills and forests, streams, and lakes. To the west are the scenic Blue Ridge and Great Smoky Mountains, part of the Appalachians.

The first English colony in America was established by SIR WALTER RALEIGH on Roanoke Island in 1585. However, it failed. About 1660, settlers from Virginia built the first permanent colony in North Carolina, on the Chowan River. It was named Carolina in honor of King Charles II (in Latin "Carolus") of England and later covered all the land that is now North and South Carolina. Colonists fought then with the Tuscarora and Cherokee Indians. In 1775, they drove out the British governor, and the next year voted for independence. One of the final battles of the American Revolution was at Guilford Courthouse in 1781. North Carolina joined the other southern states during the Civil War.

The state today grows much tobacco and manufactures many cigarettes. It also produces textiles, furniture, food items, and electronic equipment. Tourists are attracted because of the golfing, fishing, hunting, and skiing. More than 5.5 million people live in North Carolina. Raleigh is its capital.

NORTH DAKOTA

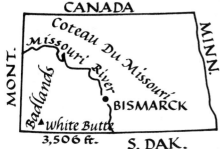

North Dakota is a state in the north central United States. It has vast fields of wheat, barley, oats, and flaxseed. On its central plains graze large numbers of cattle. Near the Montana border are the Badlands, where much of the land is bare. However, this area has startling scenery, with beautiful rock formations. North Dakota has dry, hot summers and long, cold winters.

French fur traders came to this region in about 1740. They found several Indian tribes, including the Mandan, Cheyenne, Chippewa, and Sioux. Later, British traders arrived. In 1803, France sold the southwestern half to the U.S. LEWIS AND CLARK explored there the following year. The other half of what is now North Dakota was given to the U.S. by Britain in 1818. Many homesteaders took land from the Indians and slaughtered the buffalos. The Sioux, led by Sitting Bull, fought back but were defeated by U.S. troops in 1881.

Besides agriculture, North Dakota has manufacturing industries, the largest of which is the processing of food. Mining is also important. Oil, natural gas, and lignite coal lie underground in vast amounts. Oil refining is a growing industry in the state. Tourists come to hunt deer, grouse, and waterfowl or to fish for trout, bass, and northern pike. Others visit the Theodore Roosevelt National Memorial in the Badlands or the many wildlife reserves, where buffalo, bighorn sheep, and elk wander freely. North Dakota's population is about 650,000. Its capital is Bismarck.

NORTHERN LIGHTS

People who live in the northern parts of the world can sometimes see a colorful light show in the night sky. Long, wavy fingers and bands of colored light seem to move up into the sky from the horizon to the north. This display, called the *aurora borealis*, is caused when electrified particles, sent out by the sun, are attracted by the Earth's magnetic poles. Scientists have noticed

the northern lights appear to be brighter during times when, using special equipment, they have observed great storms on the surface of the sun.

In America, the northern lights can be seen at certain times from the states closer to Canada.

There are similar lights, called the *aurora australis*, that occur at the South Pole. They can be seen only by people in the far southern parts of the world.

NORTH POLE

The North Pole is the northernmost point on the Earth's surface. It is located in the Arctic region, on a vast ice cap that floats above a deep sea. About 1000 miles (1610 km) away, near Prince of Wales Island in the Northwest Territories of Canada, is the North Magnetic Pole. This is the northern spot to which the needle of a compass points.

As early as the 16th century, men were interested in finding a NORTHWEST PASSAGE by sea. Explorers such as HENRY HUDSON, Sir Martin Frobisher, John Davis, Willem Barents, and CAPTAIN JAMES COOK made unsuccessful attempts, but they added to our knowledge of the area. It was not until ROALD AMUNDSEN accomplished the feat in 1906 that men stopped risking their lives in the attempt. However, during the search for the passage, various explorers also tried to reach the North Pole itself.

A Norwegian, Nansen, made a remarkable trip by sled to reach the Pole, but failed. A Swedish engineer, Andrée, tried to cross the Pole by balloon, but disappeared with his two companions. In 1909 ROBERT PEARY, an American explorer, finally became the first man to reach the North Pole. Not until 1969 did an overland expedition succeed in crossing the entire polar ice cap. SEE ALSO: ARCTIC AND ANTARCTIC.

NORTH SEA

The North Sea lies between Great Britain and the European continent. To the south, it is connected to the ATLANTIC OCEAN by the English Channel. To the north, it opens into the North Atlantic. In the east, a narrow channel links the North Sea with the BALTIC SEA.

The mixing of these waters brings sudden changes in temperature and tides to the North Sea, along with gale winds and heavy fogs. Nevertheless the North Sea is one of the busiest areas for shipping. Here are some of the largest ports in the world, such as Rotterdam in Holland, Antwerp in Belgium, and London in England.

The North Sea is fairly shallow in many parts (100–400 feet or 31–124 m). This makes it rather easy to explore for oil. Large amounts of oil and natural gas are now being pumped from oil fields off the coast of Norway and Scotland.

The sea is rich in codfish, which several countries catch in large amounts. Cod fishing is especially good off the northeast coast of England, at a place called the Dogger Bank.

NORTHWEST PASSAGE

After CHRISTOPHER COLUMBUS discovered that America blocked the sea route to the East, many explorers began to search for some way to sail through or around the American continents. FERDINAND MAGELLAN found a route around the southern tip of South America in 1520. Most important, however, was the search for a "Northwest Passage" around North America.

Jacques Cartier, Sir Martin Frobisher, and SIR FRANCIS DRAKE were explorers in the 1500s who always had a great desire to find and to prove the existence of a passage. In 1610, HENRY HUDSON discovered what is now called Hudson Bay during his search for a short route to Asia. For almost the next three hundred years, men such as Alexander MacKenzie, Sir William Parry, and Sir John Franklin explored great sections of the Arctic and proved that a Northwest Passage did exist.

—— the 1969 "Manhattan" route
– – – – the 1906 Amundsen route

It was not until 1906 that the first trip from the Atlantic to the Pacific through the Arctic passage was made. A Norwegian, ROALD AMUNDSEN, completed it in his small ship *Gjoa*.

In 1969, the American oil tanker, the S.S. *Manhattan*, with the help of a Canadian icebreaker traveled the Northwest Passage from the Atlantic to the Alaskan oil fields (see illustration).

NORTHWEST TERRITORIES

The Northwest Territories occupy more than one-third of CANADA. This region is mainly a vast wilderness and wasteland, extending north from 60°N latitude to the Arctic Ocean. The Northwest Territories are divided into three administrative districts—Keewatin, west of Hudson Bay; Mackenzie, east of the YUKON; and Franklin, in the northern section. In the Mackenzie district are two of the world's largest lakes—the

Great Slave and the Great Bear, which connect with the Arctic Ocean through the Mackenzie River, about 1120 miles (1803 km) long. In the desolate Franklin district are many islands, the largest of which are Baffin, Ellesmere, and Victoria. Farming is nearly impossible in the entire region. There are large softwood forests in the west and south. Also, the region has abundant mineral wealth—oil, copper, silver, gold, zinc, lead, and uranium. Yellowknife is the capital and largest town. The Northwest Territories has about 40,000 people. The ESKIMO and Indian inhabitants earn money from fur trapping, fishing, and hunting (seals, reindeer, and caribou).

NORWAY

Norway lies in northern Europe, in the western part of SCANDINAVIA. It has rugged mountains, forests, glaciers, and a coastline deeply indented by inlets, called FIORDS. Its capital, Oslo, is on a large fiord in the south.

Many of Norway's 4.25 million people are descendants of the old Norse Vikings, who often raided the coasts of Europe and America. Today, Norwegians earn a living from farming, lumbering, mining, fishing, and manufacturing. Norway mans one of the largest merchant fleets in the world and operates many offshore oil wells in the North Sea. In the Arctic region of the country live the Laplanders, a dark-haired, nomadic people who follow their reindeer herds.

Norway is a constitutional monarchy, with a king, a prime minister, and a parliament (the *Storting*).

NOVA SCOTIA

Most of Nova Scotia, a province on the east coast of CANADA, is a long peninsula with a rocky coastline on the Atlantic. A narrow *isthmus* (strip of land) connects the province with NEW BRUNSWICK. There are fertile plains and river valleys inland, where farmers raise cattle, hogs, and chickens and grow hay, vegetables, and fruits, especially apples. Nova Scotia's capital and largest city is Halifax, one of Canada's chief seaports. About 850,000 people live in the province.

Atlantic Ocean

Since the 1600s, coal has been mined there, especially in the northern part of Nova Scotia—Cape Breton Island. Gypsum, zinc, and salt are also mined. Fishing is a major industry, with great fleets catching huge quantities of cod, haddock, and lobster along the coast and on the Grand Banks. Lumber, pulp, and paper come from the province's forests.

In 1497, JOHN CABOT landed on Cape Breton Island. For a long time France and Britain fought bitterly for control of the region. Many Scottish colonists settled there, naming it "Nova Scotia" ("New Scotland"). In 1867, it joined three other colonies to form the country of Canada.

NOVEL

A novel is a long, continuous story. It is written in prose and is usually fictional (imaginary). However, the novel's characters, setting, plot, and conflicts may be based in some way on real life. A novel may be funny, like *Alice in Wonderland*, or adventurous, like *Tom Sawyer* or *Huckleberry Finn*. Some novels are a complicated series of events (the plot); others are simple to follow. Whether a novel is happy, sad, romantic, historical, or a mixture of all, the novelist

(writer) usually wants to make the story believable—true to life. It can be said that a novel is about people, even if those "people" are animals or robots.

NUCLEAR ENERGY

The center of an ATOM is called its *nucleus*. The nucleus contains particles called *protons* and *neutrons* that are locked together by tremendous forces. No one has ever seen any atomic particle, even with the most powerful microscope, because they are all so tiny.

If the nucleus could be split apart in some way, then enormous energy would be released. This energy could be used to drive an engine that would have many uses.

Scientists have discovered that there are several ELEMENTS in which the particles in the nucleus are not so tightly bound. Such an element is said to be *unstable* or *radioactive*. URANIUM 235 (U-235) is an unstable element.

It has also been learned that if a *neutron* escapes from the nucleus, it is possible to make it bump into other neutrons and particles and cause all of the particles to fly apart. If this happens all of a sudden, the result is an explosion. It was this knowledge of how to create such an explosion that led to the invention of the ATOMIC BOMB.

However, if the escaping particles can be slowed down and controlled, they can be made to boil water to create steam. The steam can then be used to drive machines called *turbines*. These turbines can be used to generate electricity or to drive engines. The device that uses nuclear energy in these ways is called a *nuclear reactor*. One pound (.45 kg) of U-235 can provide as much energy as 3 million pounds (1.35 kg) of coal.

Today, nuclear energy is used to generate electricity in some areas of the world where waterpower and other sources of energy are not available. Nuclear reactors are used to drive submarines, which need not come to the surface for air.

Great care must be taken in the operation of nuclear reactors, for they can be very dangerous. After use, their fuel remains radioactive for thousands of years. Radioactive materials can cause bad burns that lead to cancer and death in almost all living things. For that reason, nuclear waste must be buried deep underground to keep it away from people, animals and plants.

Scientists believe that in the future nuclear reactors will be the source of most of our energy. If we can make and keep them safe to use, they will be very important to mankind as COAL, OIL, and other sources of energy are exhausted.

SEE ALSO: ATOM, ATOMIC BOMB, ELECTRICITY, GENERATOR, URANIUM.

NUMBERS

Many centuries ago, people kept track of things (like sheep) by naming them. Today we use names like "one," "two," and "three" to count things.

Early man used pebbles, shells, or sticks as counters (see ABACUS). The most common counters were the fingers. Number names are much more convenient counters than small objects or fingers, especially for numbers above ten. But some primitive tribes still have no names for numbers above 3 or 4.

People have developed many different systems of writing numbers. Early man made tally marks on stone or on the ground in the following manner:

$$| \quad || \quad ||| \quad \text{and} \quad ||||$$

Most systems of counting are based on 5 (the number of fingers on one hand) or on 10 (the number of fingers on two hands).

The Chinese made strokes for numbers up to 5 (|||||); 6 was made by marking with a horizontal bar:

$$\top \ (6) \quad \overline{\top} \ (7) \quad \overline{\top\top} \ (8) \quad \overline{|||} \ (9)$$

One horizontal stroke stood for 10, two horizontal strokes stood for 20, and so on:

$$— (10) \quad = (20) \quad \equiv (30) \quad \overline{\equiv} (40) \quad \overline{\overline{\equiv}} (50) \quad \perp (60) \quad \underline{\perp} (70) \quad \underline{\underline{\perp}} (80)$$

The ancient Hebrews and Greeks used their letters with a little mark after each to show they represented numbers. For example,

a' = 1, b' = 2, j' = 10, ja' = 11, k' = 20, l' = 30, lc' = 33

However, this system was awkward to use for large numbers.

Roman numerals made arithmetic very complicated, but we still use them today on clocks, tombstones, and to number the chapters of books:

I	II	III	IV	V	VI	IX	X	XI	XX	XL	L	LX	C	D	M
1	2	3	4	5	6	9	10	11	20	40	50	60	100	500	1000

The numbers most commonly used today are called *Arabic numerals* because they came to us from the Arabs in about A.D. 1000. They probably originated with the Hindus in India. This system uses only ten signs, the numerals, *1, 2, 3, 4, 5, 6, 7, 8, 9,* and a new sign, *0,* called *zero.* For the first time, the *position* of the numbers gave information about their value: for instance, *35* is different from *53,* and *7348* is different from *3847.* SEE ALSO: ARITHMETIC.

NURSERY RHYMES

Nursery rhymes are short verses, poems, or songs that young children often learn. Many of these little jingles and rhymes are hundreds of years old and have been passed down from generation to generation of children. An old, popular rhyme is used in "counting-out" games, such as "Eenie, meenie, mini, mo." Another kind of rhyme is used to teach counting,

such as "One, two, buckle my shoe; three, four, shut the door; five, six, pick up sticks;" and so on.

The most famous of nursery rhymes is the Mother Goose collection, which was first published in 1765 as the *Mother Goose Melody*. Its original 50 rhymes have since become several hundred.

Nursery rhymes include tongue twisters, like "How much wood would a woodchuck chuck, if a woodchuck could chuck wood?" They can be funny, entertaining, comforting, and wise. Generally, they are fun to recite and easily remembered—if they are repeated long enough!

NURSING

For many centuries, the Church took care of the sick, injured, and helpless. Then old women attended to these nursing duties. Not until 1846 was there any real hospital training school for nurses. The work of a German hospital and of FLORENCE NIGHTINGALE helped establish proper training for nurses.

Today, a person must be examined and licensed by the state to work as a *registered nurse* (RN). A student nurse undergoes a rigorous course of study of anatomy, drugs, disease, surgery, nutrition, and the proper care of patients. The nurse studies these while gaining actual hospital experience.

The biggest group of nurses work in HOSPITALS, where they do "general duty," keeping charts of each patient's treatment, condition, and progress. Hospitals also have *pediatric* nurses who are specially trained to care for children. There are *psychiatric* nurses, as well, who know how to care for patients with mental and emotional disorders. Special *surgical* nurses help surgeons in operating rooms. Nurses assist doctors in their offices, making appointments, keeping patients' records, and often examining the patients.

OAK

Oak trees are found in almost every part of the world. There are at least 75 kinds in the United States.

Oak trees are very sturdy, and their wood is very hard and resistant to rot. Oak is good for furniture, flooring, and shipbuilding. The bark of some oaks is used in tanning LEATHER. CORK comes from the inner bark of the cork oak of Spain.

The oak tree, which may live to be 1000 years of age, matures slowly and does not produce seeds till after 20 years. These seeds, called acorns, provide food for many different kinds of animals.

Annie OAKLEY (1860–1926)

Born in Ohio, Annie Oakley learned to shoot a rifle while she was still a young girl. She had great skill in hitting targets. Eventually, she joined a traveling Wild West show that was owned by Frank E. Butler.

Annie Oakley would dress herself in fancy Wild West clothes and shoot at targets while riding on her horse. Her fame drew thousands of people to the show.

Forty years after her death, there appeared on Broadway a hit musical based on her life entitled, "Annie, Get Your Gun."

OASIS

Most people think of a DESERT as a sandy waste where there is no life at all. But here and there in the deserts of the world are small areas where the water, which is elsewhere very deep underground, comes nearer the surface. Such a place is called an *oasis*, and it is often marked by PALM trees. Larger oases may have towns built around them. Some provide enough water to support orchards and even cornfields.

Recently, wells of great depth have been drilled in the deserts of Tunisia and Algeria, in North Africa. Thousands of feet below the surface, water has been found and brought to the surface. If enough water can be brought up and if the soil is of the right kind, the deserts may become fertile enough for farming.

OBSERVATORY

One kind of observatory is a building with telescopes, cameras, and other equipment for observing the STARS, PLANETS, and other heavenly bodies. Other observatories have equipment for studying EARTH-QUAKES, VOLCANOES, or WEATHER.

The earliest known observatories for watching the stars and planets were built by the Chinese and Babylonians about 4300 years ago. They were probably high platforms that gave a full view of the heavens. About 300 B.C., the most famous ancient observatory was built in Alexandria by the Egyptians, almost 2000 years before the first European one was established at Nuremberg, Germany, in 1471.

Originally, people were interested in the movements of the stars and planets because they thought that through them they would be able to foretell the future. Later, they became important to determine the right time to plant and harvest crops.

The observatory in Greenwich, England, was built in 1675 mainly to provide accurate information about time, which is essential to proper navigation.

One of the most famous American observatories is at Mount Palomar in California. With its 200-inch (508 cm) mirror, it had the largest *reflecting* telescope until 1976, when the Soviet Union constructed a larger one. The world's largest *refracting* telescope was built at the Yerkes Observatory in Wisconsin in 1897. Experiments are now under way to launch an astronomical observatory into orbit around the Earth, outside of the atmosphere that prevents our getting a clear view of the sky.

The observatories where earthquakes are studied have equipment sensitive enough to detect a tremor thousands of miles away.

Weather observatories are often at the tops of tall buildings where temperature, wind speed, rainfall and snowfall, and other features are recorded and used to predict the weather.

OCEANS

Almost 75 percent of the world is covered by oceans. There are three great oceans—the ATLANTIC, the PACIFIC, and the Indian; the Arctic is also considered an ocean. The average ocean depth is 2 miles (3.2 km), which is more than five times the average height of land surfaces. The greatest ocean depth is in the Marianas Trench in the northern Pacific where the water is nearly 7 miles (11 km) deep.

Sunlight and warmth can only penetrate about 0.25 mile (400 m) into the water, so most of the water is icy cold and dark. Strange fish exist in these black waters. Most are phosphorescent—that is, they have cells in parts of their bodies that produce a cold light much like that of the FIREFLY.

Plankton, which consists of tiny animal and plant life, exists in tremendous quantity in the upper 600 feet (186 m) and provides food for WHALES and all sea creatures that do not prey on others.

Great currents flow through the oceans, like rivers. Some, like the Humboldt and Japan currents, encircle the vast Pacific Ocean. The GULF STREAM is a current that begins near the Caribbean Sea and flows north along the eastern coast of America, warming the water as it flows and carrying it as far away as northern Europe.

The Angler Fish (lower right) and other deepwater fish carry their own lights.

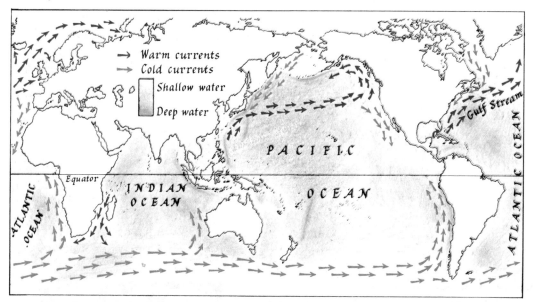

Part of the Aleutian current in the northern Pacific forms an eddy (backward-circling current) in the Gulf of Alaska. The other part flows south as the cold California current, which may be traced as far as lower California.

The seas are the least explored part of the world: man knows more about the surface of the moon after only a few years than he has learned about the surface of the Earth under the sea in thousands of years.

Only recently man has discovered oil beneath the seas. He must still learn how to mine the wealth of minerals and other resources that the oceans contain.

OCTOPUS

The word *octopus* comes from a Greek word meaning "eight-footed." An octopus is a sea creature with eight tentacles, which are like long, flexible arms. They are equipped with powerful suction cups underneath for seizing prey and sweeping it into the parrot-like jaws of the octopus. The octopus particularly likes to eat crabs and lobsters.

This animal creeps along the ocean bottom or swims by using its tentacles and propelling itself backward by sucking in water and forcing it out in sudden jets. The octopus is very timid and protects itself by squirting an inky fluid to darken the water and conceal itself from an attacker. The octopus of the American Pacific coast is about 14 feet (4.3 m) from tip to tip of its tentacles; however, most are no bigger than a baseball.

In China and the Mediterranean, the octopus has long been considered a table delicacy, and many restaurants in America now offer it as well.

ODIN

Odin was the supreme god in the mythology of SCANDINAVIA. He is said to have created the Earth and to have established the laws that governed the universe. His court was Valhalla, the hall of heroes, in the land of Asgard. He was attended by wolves, two ravens, and the Valkyries, beautiful maidens who carried the souls of brave warriors to Valhalla.

Odin was known as a god of war, as well as a god of learning, poetry, and magic. His German name was Woden, or Wodan, from which we get Wednesday, or Woden's day.

ODYSSEUS

The *Odyssey*, probably written by HOMER, the Greek poet, tells the story of Odysseus' journey back to Ithaca, in Greece. After the fall of Troy, Odysseus, who was the King of Ithaca, set sail with his men for home. However, he offended Poseidon (Neptune), the god of the sea, and was afterward blown constantly off course.

During his wanderings, he met and blinded the one-eyed CYCLOPS, named Polyphemus. He outwitted the beautiful sorceress, Circe, who had turned his men into animals. He evaded death at the island of the Sirens, who sang such enchanting songs that sailors were lured there. He escaped from the cannibal giants, and he eventually left the lovely Calypso, on whose island he had been shipwrecked. Calypso had offered him eternal youth if he remained with her.

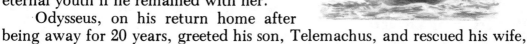

Odysseus, on his return home after being away for 20 years, greeted his son, Telemachus, and rescued his wife, Penelope, from the wretched suitors who wished to marry her.

The Romans referred to him as Ulysses.

James OGLETHORPE (1696–1785)

James Edward Oglethorpe, the founder of GEORGIA, was born in London, England. In 1722, he was elected to PARLIAMENT and became interested in prison reform and in helping English debtors.

In 1732, Oglethorpe proposed the establishment of a new colony in America, where English debtors recently released from prison could go to get a new start in life. He and 19 associates were soon granted a charter for a colony of Georgia, between South Carolina and the Spanish in Florida.

Oglethorpe led 116 English colonists to the New World in early 1733 and founded the town of Savannah, in Georgia. He made friends with the Creek Indians and built forts as a defense against the Spanish. In 1740, Oglethorpe tried unsuccessfully to capture the Spanish town of St. Augustine, in Florida. Later, on St. Simons Island, in Georgia, he defeated the Spanish in the battle of Bloody Marsh in 1742. The colony was now safe. The following year, Oglethorpe returned to England and resumed his career in Parliament, never to return to Georgia. SEE ALSO: GEORGIA.

OHIO

Ohio lies in the Midwest of the United States. This state has rolling plains and highlands. The climate is usually moderate, but it is sometimes marked by extremes and sudden changes. Ohio's capital is Columbus, and its population is almost 11 million people.

Mound Builders once lived in the region. They were followed by a number of Indian tribes, chiefly the Iroquois, Ottawa, Shawnee, and Miami. In 1669, La Salle, the French explorer, visited the area, providing a basis for France's claim to it.

American and British fur traders soon arrived, and the French tried to drive them out. At the end of the French and Indian War in 1763, the British gained possession of the region. But, the U.S. took control after the American Revolution. The first permanent settlement was established at Marietta, where the Muskingum River joins the Ohio River. The next year, Cincinnati was founded, also on the Ohio River. Then, the white settlers took much land from the Indians, who united and went on the warpath. In 1794, General Anthony Wayne and his soldiers defeated the Indians at the battle of Fallen Timbers, near present-day Toledo. Settlers came in large numbers to the territory. Ohio became a state in 1803.

Today, Ohio is one of the nation's leading industrial states. Its products include automobiles, airplanes, tires, machine tools, household appliances, plastics, and metals. The state also raises many milk cows, hogs, and sheep, and grows corn, wheat, tomatoes, and soybeans. Coal, gravel, sand, oil, and natural gas are mined in Ohio.

OIL

The technical name for the oil we get from the earth is *petroleum*. Chemists have found hundreds of different products that can be made from petroleum. Gasoline and diesel oil are used as fuels for most of the car and truck engines in the world. Special fuels made from petroleum are used in jet engines and in some rockets, and many electrical generators use a petroleum product as fuel. Other products are lighter fluids, kerosene, fertilizers, grease, detergents for washing laundry and dishes, and many plastics.

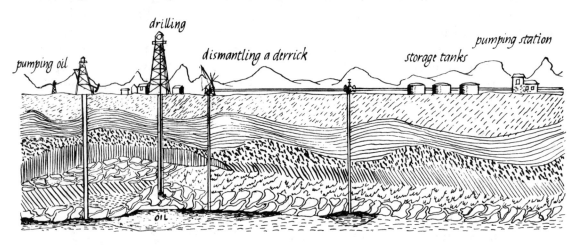

Petroleum is a *fossil* fuel—that is, like coal, it is a natural fuel that was created when certain areas of the sea and some large lakes were covered by rock. Trapped under the rock were millions of tiny plants and animals. They died and gradually decayed and left oily deposits. Later, more rock and soil covered these areas so that, today, they may be as far as three miles (4.8 km) under the surface.

About 100 years ago, men developed ways of drilling down into the earth to reach the underground pools of oil. They were able to pump it up to the surface. In recent years, huge deposits of petroleum have been found under the oceans, in the North Sea, in the Gulf of Mexico, and elsewhere. Although it is hard to see how we could manage without petroleum to heat our homes, offices, factories and to supply other needs of everyday life, scien-

tists tell us that we may use up all of the world's supply of oil in less than 100 years and that we must soon turn to substitutes.

Other kinds of oils are animal oils, which come from fish and from WHALES, and vegetable oils, which come from PEANUTS, OLIVES, coconuts, cottonseeds, flax, SOYBEANS, and other plants. Some of the many uses of these oils are for a source of vitamins (cod-liver oil), for cooking (olive and cottonseed oil), steel-making (cottonseed oil), making margarine (corn and other oils), and manufacturing paint (linseed oil from flax).

A whale being hauled up into the ship

OKLAHOMA

Oklahoma is a large state in the south-central United States. It consists largely of rolling plains, on which are vast fields of wheat and broad grazing lands for cattle. Parts of the state are mountainous. There are also pine and hardwood forests. About 2.8 million people live in Oklahoma.

Indian tribes such as the Wichita, Plains Apache, and Osage hunted buffalo there before the first European, Spanish explorer Coronado, passed through the region in 1541. Most of what is now Oklahoma became part of the United States with the Louisiana Purchase in 1803. In the 1820s, the U.S. government made it the home of the "Five Civilized Tribes"—Cherokee, Choctaw, Chickasaw, Creek, and Seminole. These Indians, who had been living in the southeastern U.S., were forced to resettle in the Oklahoma territory. Many Indians died from hunger, cold, and disease on the long, westward journey, known as the "Trail of Tears." However, later, white settlers seized much Indian territory, especially when the land was opened for homesteading by *runs* (races for a claim at a specific time). Some people went ahead of time to claim land and were known as "sooners." They gave Oklahoma its nickname, the "Sooner State."

Oklahoma is rich in oil, natural gas, and helium. It grows large crops of wheat, hay, and sorghum and raises many hogs and cattle. Much of the state's manufacturing is based on processing farm and mineral products. Much industry is in or around Tulsa and Oklahoma City, the state capital.

OLD IRONSIDES

The frigate *Constitution*, famous in the War of 1812, is called Old Ironsides because it resisted attack so well. As a matter of fact, it is made of wood. It was launched in Boston in 1797 as a full-rigged ship with 44 guns (it ended up carrying over 50). It fought the pirates of Tripoli in 1801–05. On April 19, 1812, it fought and sank the British frigate *Guerriere*. Later it had several other victories. The Navy wanted to break it up in 1828, but Oliver Wendell Holmes wrote a poem, "Old Ironsides," that caused the public to demand that it be saved. Much repaired, it survives as a Navy ship in Boston harbor. The public is allowed on board.

OLIVES

Olive trees, which are said to live for as long as 1000 years, have been cultivated in the Mediterranean region for many centuries. Although we eat pickled olives, both the unripe green ones and the ripe black kind, as a relish, the main use of olives has long been for oil, which is obtained by pressing. Olive oil has been so important for cooking and as a fuel that some people believe that the ancient Greek and Roman civilizations could not have developed without the olive.

The ancient Greeks thought the olive tree was sacred, and even today we recognize the olive branch as a symbol of peace.

OLYMPIC GAMES

In ancient Greece, athletic contests or games were held during religious festivals, honoring ZEUS. The first Olympic Games supposedly took place in 776 B.C. on the plains of Olympia in the southwestern part of Greece. The

Pentathlon was the most prized win during the games. It consisted of five events: running, jumping, discus and javelin throwing, and wrestling. The winner received a wreath of olive leaves, as well as valuable gifts and privileges. Later, the Olympic Games were held in a magnificent stadium in Olympia and included boxing, chariot racing, horseback riding, and even a contest for trumpeters.

When Greece was conquered by the Romans, the Olympic Games became more elaborate, with processions, banquets, and new honors for the victors. They were held at four-year intervals, an *Olympiad*, until A.D. 394, when the Roman emperor, Theodosius, abolished them.

In 1896, the Olympics were revived and developed into an international sporting event, staged every four years in the summer in various cities throughout the world.

The Olympics include every kind of sport, from archery to cycling and fencing, from gymnastics to shooting and yachting. After 1924, winter sports became part of the Olympics, adding skiing, figure skating, bobsledding, and more events. In the Winter and Summer Olympics, winners receive gold, silver, or bronze medals, depending on whether they place first, second, or third respectively in their event.

ONTARIO

Ontario is the second largest province in Canada. Northwest and central Ontario are part of the Laurentian Plateau, a region of mineral-rich rock covered with forests, lakes, and rivers. Much of Canada's nickel, uranium, platinum, iron, copper, and gold is mined in this area. Lumbering is also a big industry. Southern Ontario borders the GREAT LAKES. Here the soil is good for growing vegetables, fruits, and tobacco. Most of the province's industry is concentrated in the southeast area, especially in and around the cities of

Hamilton and TORONTO, Ontario's capital. Steel, automobiles, aircraft, machinery, processed foods, and pulp and paper products are manufactured. Almost 8.25 million people live in Ontario today.

In 1611, HENRY HUDSON sailed into what is now Hudson Bay, which bounds Ontario on the north. Samuel de Champlain and Étienne Brûlé explored and made French claims about 1615. The region was the home of the Huron Indians, who were always attacked by the Iroquois. The French and British competed for the valuable fur trade in the region, building posts and forts and making friends with the Indians. The British took control of the area in 1763. By 1791, this British colony had its own government and was known as Upper Canada (Quebec was Lower Canada). It was one of the four British colonies that joined together in 1867 to form the independent nation of Canada. The capital of Canada, OTTAWA, is in Ontario. SEE ALSO: OTTAWA, TORONTO.

OPERA

An opera is a play that is sung. The use of many songs in a spoken play is very old. Our *musical comedies* still carry on this tradition. The first opera, a play to be wholly sung, was put on shortly before 1600 in Florence, Italy.

An opera usually begins with an *overture*, an orchestral piece that sets the mood of the story. Some operas have *preludes* instead; these are shorter. In Italian opera, which is the best known, ordinary conversation is sung in *recitative*. Now and then the leading characters sing *arias* to

mark important points in the story. An aria is a song, and may be sung even when the opera is not being given. Sometimes a BALLET is part of the opera, and the orchestra sometimes plays *interludes* between scenes.

Opera is divided into *grand opera*, whose mood is often serious and which is elaborately presented, and *light opera*, which is intended for amusement. Light opera is much like musical comedy.

ORANGES

Oranges will not grow where it gets very cold. That is one reason why Florida and California are such important orange-growing states.

Oranges grow on evergreen trees. These trees usually bloom in the spring. Orange blossoms, which are white, are so beautiful and sweet-smelling that they are often used for making perfume or for decorations at weddings or other special celebrations.

Oranges taste good, and they are especially good for us. Eating oranges or drinking orange juice is one way to be sure that our bodies get enough Vitamin C, the vitamin that protects us from *scurvy*. Our bodies need new supplies of Vitamin C every day.

Oranges are thought to have grown first in southeastern Asia. It was Columbus who planted the first *sour orange* seeds in the West. He brought them with him on his second voyage and planted them on the Caribbean island of Haiti. The *sweet orange* was brought to the western world by Spanish and Portuguese explorers in 1500s. By the 1800s, oranges were being grown around the world.

Oranges keep well. They are not expensive. They are nutritious, and people like the way they taste.

ORCHESTRA

Originally the orchestra was the singing and dancing area of an ancient Greek THEATER. It is now the main floor of a theater *auditorium*, the place for the audience.

But when we say "orchestra" today we usually mean a large group of musicians that includes players on stringed instruments. A group without

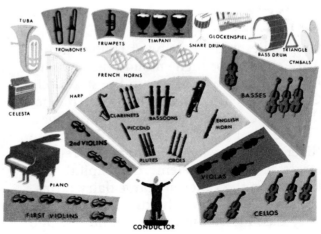

strings is a BAND. The modern orchestra began around 1600, when composers began to write for certain instruments. Before then, any group of instruments might play any piece. When composers wanted the qualities of sound that only a violin or a trombone could give, a group of players had to have the whole range of MUSICAL INSTRUMENTS that a composer might want. Orchestras became larger and more complex, and new instruments joined the strings, brasses, and woodwinds that were traditional. New percussion instruments and instruments such as the celesta and the saxophone were among the additions. By 1900, an orchestra might have more than 100 players. SEE ALSO: MUSICAL INSTRUMENTS.

ORE

Embedded in the minerals and rocks of the Earth are many kinds of METALS. A mineral containing one or more metals that can be taken from it is called an ore. Frequently, an ore contains more than one metal.

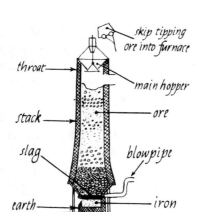

Some metals, like GOLD and SILVER, occur in a pure state in nature. To obtain most metals, however, the ore must be washed, heated, or treated by a complicated chemical process. For example, when a metal is in chemical combination with other ELEMENTS, like ALUMINUM, it may be difficult to extract. Iron ore, on the other hand, may be heated in a very hot fire to make the melted iron run out. This process is called *smelting*. Another method is used to extract MERCURY, or quicksilver, from its ore. SEE ALSO: BLAST FURNACE, IRON AND STEEL, METALS.

OREGON

Oregon lies in the northwest United States. This state has high mountains, plains, fertile valleys, and immense forests. Along Oregon's Pacific coast is the Coast Range, the lowest of the state's mountain ranges. To the East is the beautiful Willamette River valley, where Portland, Oregon's largest city, and Salem, the capital, are located. In the valley are large dairy farms, orchards, and green fields of crops. The lofty Cascade Mountains lie on the east side

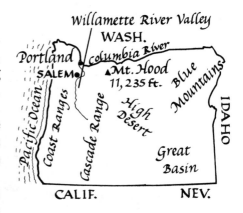

604

of the valley. They contain some of the highest peaks in North America, like Mount Hood, 11,235 feet (3483 m) high. East of the Cascades is some desert, then highlands, where much wheat is grown. The thickly wooded Blue Mountains cover the state's northeastern section.

The Tillamook, Kalapuia, and Chinook Indians were living in the area when an American captain, Robert Gray, sailed into Oregon Bay in 1787. Later, he went up a great river and named it after his ship. Today, the Columbia River is part of Oregon's border with Washington. Fur traders arrived in the early 1800s, and then settlers in covered wagons by way of the long OREGON TRAIL. In 1846, Britain gave the U.S. the territory, which then included Washington. Statehood was granted in 1859.

Lumbering is today the principal industry, and agriculture is second. Oregon mines some stone and nickel. Its fishing industry sells much salmon, tuna, halibut, sole, and cod. Tourists come to ski, hike, or just to enjoy the wonderful scenery. Slightly more than 2.25 million people live in Oregon.

OREGON TRAIL

The Oregon Trail was an overland route used by the American pioneers. It began in the vicinity of Independence, Missouri, and led northwestward through the valleys of the Platte, the North Platte, and the Sweetwater Rivers. Then it crossed through the Rocky Mountains to Fort Bridger, in Wyoming. Continuing northwest, the trail followed the Green River and then the Snake River, between Fort Hall and Fort Boise, in Idaho. From there, it went north across the rugged Blue Mountains to Fort Walla Walla, on the Columbia River. Pioneers then proceeded down the Columbia into the fertile Willamette Valley, where early settlements were built.

The end of the Oregon Trail shifted with new settlements, until Tumwater, now in the state of Washington, became the "final" end. This trail, about 2000 miles (3220 km) long, was heavily used by settlers in covered wagons and prospectors seeking gold in the mid 19th century.

ORGAN

There are electronic organs today that transmit sound through LOUDSPEAKERS, but the traditional organ is a wind instrument.

In the traditional organ, the sound is created by opening a valve by pressing a key. The valve sends air across an opening near the bottom of a pipe or across a vibrating *reed* so that the air is caused to vibrate. This vibration is what reaches our ears. There is only one note, and one kind of sound, for each pipe or reed. To give different sound effects, more than one pipe or reed is necessary for each note. There

may be as many as a hundred of them for each note in a large organ. *Stops* keep air from reaching the ones that are not supposed to play. If the organist "pulls out" a stop, the pipes or reeds it controls can receive air. To help with the complicated effects possible on a large organ, the organist may play on more than one *manual* (keyboard), and also play on *pedals* with his feet. Several stops can be combined for especially rich effects.

The world's largest pipe organ is the Auditorium Organ at Atlantic City, New Jersey. It has 12 manuals, 1477 stops, and 33,112 pipes. It is the loudest musical instrument in the world. Even a small organ today may have about 370 pipes, however.

ORPHEUS

According to legend, Orpheus was a Greek musician, who was given a lyre (harp) by the god APOLLO. He played so sweetly that everything and everyone stopped to listen to his music. Later, Orpheus married a beautiful young woman named Eurydice. While fleeing from a pursuer one day, she stepped on a snake and died of its bite. In his grief, Orpheus went down to Hades, the kingdom of the dead, and played before PLUTO, the king of this underworld. Pluto, charmed by the music, agreed to let Orpheus lead Eurydice to the upper world, though he must not glance back at her until they had passed out of Hades. But Orpheus forgot, and Eurydice was lost to him forever.

Afterward he wandered sadly. He was killed by the Maenads, women who believed in Dionysus, the god of wine and joy. They had been offended by his inattention and his loyalty to Eurydice.

ORTHODOX CHURCH

The Orthodox Church is the church of the Greeks, Russians, and other peoples of eastern Europe, the Near East, and North America. Actually, it is not one church under a single rule, but an association of 15 different churches, each having a head who is called a *patriarch*, *archbishop*, or *metropolitan*. The man who represents the whole Orthodox Church (but does not govern it) is the Patriarch of Constantinople (Istanbul, Turkey).

At first there was only one Christian Church, with each congregation as important as all the others. But in the early centuries of the Christian Era, the congregation of Rome began to dominate all the others. As the congregation of Constantinople became important in eastern Europe, it began to dominate congregations near it. By 1054 it was clear that there would be two Christian churches: the Roman Catholic Church and the Eastern Orthodox Church. The Turks captured Constantinople in 1453, and went on to capture most of the lands where the Orthodox Church was established. When the Turkish Empire broke up, each of the liberated nations started its own church. So did east Europeans who came to America.

An Orthodox church is governed by its *bishops*, who meet for that purpose. The *patriarch* is the bishop who heads the council, but his personal power is no greater than that of the others. The bishops are elected, sometimes by the congregations as well as by the priests. Unlike Roman Catholic priests, Orthodox priests are sometimes married.

Orthodoxy places great emphasis on the gathering-together of Christians. Its religious services are beautiful, with much singing and praying. The congregation is kept from seeing the altar by a high screen covered with *icons* (holy pictures), through which the priests pass at certain parts of the service. The Orthodox keep icons in their homes and in public places.

OSTRICH

For many years, people believed that ostriches hid their heads in the sand when danger was near. Careful observation has shown that they do not really bury their heads but lay them on the ground, closing their eyes because they are afraid of a lion or other animals that may kill them.

More often, these huge birds, which are about 8 feet (2.5 m) tall and weigh about 300 pounds (135 kg), run away from danger. They can run at speeds as high as 40 miles per hour (64 km/hr). When cornered, they use their powerful legs to kick an attacking animal.

Ostriches live in the grasslands and deserts of Australia, western Asia, and southern Africa, feeding on leaves, seeds, fruits, insects, and small reptiles. Like some other kinds of birds, they swallow pebbles which help to grind up food in their *craws*. They are used to life in dry areas and have been known to go without water for several days.

Ostrich eggs were once prized as decorations. Whitish in color, they are the largest eggs laid by any animal, and weigh about 3 pounds (1.35 kg) each. An ostrich hen may lay up to 15 eggs, which are tended by male and female birds.

For many centuries, beautifully plumed ostrich feathers were very popular for fans and as decorations on hats and other clothing. Most of the ostrich feathers we see today are those remaining from the olden days.

OTTAWA

Ottawa is the capital of CANADA, situated 125 miles (201 km) west of MONTREAL, in the province of ONTARIO. It is at the junction of the Ottawa and Rideau Rivers, where waterfalls supply hydro-electric power for industrial use by the city.

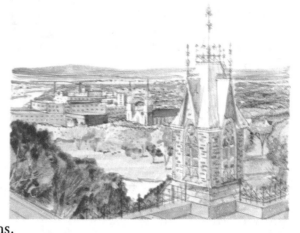

In 1826, a small settlement grew up here near a camp of several British Army engineers who were constructing a canal. It was called Bytown, in honor of their commander, Colonel By. In 1854, the name of the settlement became Ottawa, after the river and territory of the Ottawa Indians.

Pictured here are the Parliament buildings, constructed of sandstone in the Italian-Gothic style of architecture. Other handsome buildings in the city include two cathedrals, several museums, libraries, and colleges. Ottawa has many fine parks and avenues, too.

The Rideau Canal divides the city into an Upper Town and a Lower Town, where many of the people speak French. Paper milling and woodworking are big industries, supplied by the timber forests of eastern Canada.

OTTER

Otters are *aquatic*, which means they live in or near the water. Their nests are built in a burrow in a riverbank or nearby. There may be from 1 to 5 cubs in a litter, and many people are surprised to learn that otters must be taught to swim and hunt.

A fully grown otter may be 4 feet (122 cm) long, including tail about 18 inches (46 cm) in length. It has webbed feet, and a tapered and flattened tail which helps in swimming. A thick fur coat protects the otter from the cold water. Otters eat fish and other animals that live in or near the water, like shellfish, frogs, birds, and small mammals.

Except in northern Canada, otters are rare in North America because so many were trapped and killed for their valuable FUR. They are now a protected species.

OUTLAW

In ancient England, certain wrongs or crimes put a person outside the protection of the law. Such a person was called an "outlaw" by the community, and he lost his property and goods. He was also likely to be killed on sight. An outlaw would then make his home in the woods and live by hunting and robbery. ROBIN HOOD, who robbed the rich to help the poor, was a famous legendary outlaw in England. Gradually the law changed, and an outlaw was no longer

deprived of the protection of the law. After 1300, the free killing of an outlaw was forbidden, and law courts were set up to decide the punishment for outlaws. Today, an outlaw refers to someone who persists in crime—a habitual criminal.

In the 1800s, laws were not yet established on America's western frontier. Many outlaws wandered from town to town, robbing innocent people, banks, and stagecoaches. There were few sheriffs to keep the peace.

After the discovery of gold in California in 1848, many people moved to the territory. Taking advantage of the lawless conditions in the West, many men became outlaws and often roamed about in gangs. Expert sharpshooters were hired to protect banks, stagecoaches, and trains. Vigilantes (groups of private citizens who banded together to keep peace in their communities) fought and killed many outlaws. In 1866, Frank and JESSE JAMES organized a gang of outlaws that terrorized the West for the next 16 years. One of the West's worst outlaws was Billy the Kid, who killed several men and led a gang of cattle rustlers. Butch Cassidy and the Sundance Kid robbed banks all over the West. As outlaws, they were known to be friendly and happy-go-lucky.

As law and order was enforced, the number of outlaws became less. However in the 1900s, gunmen or gangsters like John Dillinger and "Pretty Boy" Floyd robbed banks and murdered people. They and the modern hijackers, kidnapers, assassins, and terrorists are the common outlaws of today.

Jesse OWENS (born 1913)

Jesse Owens was an outstanding black American athlete of the 1930 OLYMPIC GAMES. Born in Oakville, Alabama, he spent his boyhood years on a farm. In college, he proved to be an excellent athlete in track and field events. He competed in the 1935 National Intercollegiate Track and Field Championships, where he established new records in broad jump and track.

Mr. Owens won four gold medals at the 1930 Olympics. President Franklin Roosevelt appointed him as the National Director of Physical Education for Negroes. From 1942 to 1946, Mr. Owens served as director of personnel for the Ford Motor Company.

OWL

Owls are birds of prey that hunt during the night. There are two groups of owls: the barn or "monkey-faced" owls, which have heart-shaped faces and no ear tufts, and the typical owls, which usually have big "ears" or "horns." Actually, these are only tufts of feathers; their real ears are hidden beneath these FEATHERS. Some owls are small, like the elf owl, which is only 6 inches (15 cm) tall. Others are large, like the great gray owl of North America, which is nearly 3 feet (92 cm) tall.

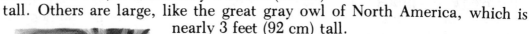

Owls have an unusual arrangement of feathers in their wings that makes their flight noiseless. That way, the mice, beetles, and other small animals that they capture for food cannot hear them. They are active at night and have very large eyes that enable them to see in the dark. Also, unlike most birds, whose eyes are at the sides of their heads, owls have their eyes in the front, and their vision is very keen.

They can hear very well also.

Most owls lay their white eggs in a hollow tree, belfry, barn, or abandoned house. Usually they make no nest at all, although the long-eared owl often uses an old MAGPIE or SQUIRREL nest.

The screech owls and hoot owls get their names from the sounds they make. The barred owl, also a hoot owl, gets its name from the different colored bars of feathers it has.

OXFORD

Oxford, a city in England, is famous as the seat of Oxford University, founded in 1167. Oxford is about 50 miles (81 km) northwest of LONDON. Besides its handsome university buildings, there are a number of historical structures, such as St. Michael's Church, dating from 1070, and His Majesty's Prison, on the site of an old castle probably built by the ANGLO-SAXONS.

Today, Oxford has automobile factories and large printing and bookbinding industries.

OXYGEN

One-fifth of the AIR we breathe is oxygen. Eight-ninths of water is oxygen by weight.

Without oxygen, very little of the animal and plant life on Earth could survive. When we breathe, tiny blood vessels in our lungs capture the oxygen and carry it to all parts of our bodies. It combines with other elements to provide warmth and energy.

When people travel to places where oxygen is scarce, like the top of a tall mountain, or to places where oxygen is not available, like under water, or into space, they must carry oxygen with them in tanks to stay alive. Fish and other marine life are specially equipped to enable them to get oxygen from water.

When we light a match or burn wood or paper in a fireplace, we actually start a rapid process by which oxygen combines with a substance. A slow process by which iron combines with oxygen is called *rusting*. SEE ALSO: AIR, BLOOD.

611

PACIFIC

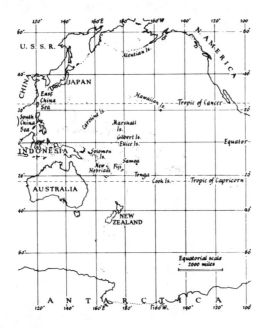

The explorer BALBOA was the first European to see the Pacific. In 1520, MAGELLAN named this ocean the Pacific (peaceful) because he had calm winds on his voyage across it. However, the Pacific has great storms like any other ocean; TYPHOONS are common in the China Seas.

It is the largest and deepest of the oceans and covers one-third of the world's surface. The ocean floor has several underwater mountain ranges. Peaks and volcanoes jut above the surface of the water to form atolls, islands of CORAL surrounding a LAGOON.

Many coral reefs, small islands, and island groups are in the central and western Pacific. The central islands are called *Polynesia*, which includes Samoa, Hawaii, and Tahiti. The southern chain of islands, near New Guinea and Australia, are *Melanesia*, and the northern islands, which include the Phillippines and Guam, are known as *Micronesia*.

Thomas PAINE (1737–1809)

Born in Thetford, England, Thomas Paine immigrated to America in 1774. With letters of introduction from BENJAMIN FRANKLIN, whom Paine had met in England, he began work as a journalist. In January, 1776, Paine published a pamphlet entitled *Common Sense*, which urged the Thirteen American Colonies to declare their independence from Great Britain. In it, Paine also said that independence would unite the colonies and would be seen as an example of freedom and democracy for other people living under immoral and corrupt kings. *Common Sense* was widely read by the Americans and helped turn public opinion in favor of the DECLARATION OF INDEPENDENCE.

In the AMERICAN REVOLUTION, Paine wrote a series of 16 pamphlets called simply *The Crisis*. These did much to encourage the patriots during the war.

After the war, Paine traveled to England and France. In 1791 and 1792, he wrote *The Rights of Man* in support of the French Revolution. In 1794, he was put in prison for his ideas. He returned to the U.S. in 1802 and died in poverty seven years later.

PAINTING

The oldest paintings we know were painted in Spanish and French caves and show animals that the cave men hunted. They have a wonderful way of suggesting the movement of the animals.

Cave paintings

Most peoples have wanted to show in pictures the things that mattered most to them: their gods, stories from their myths, or simply the things they enjoyed. The ancient Egyptians, for instance, might show a soul being judged by the gods after death, but they might also show a duck hunt. The Greeks represented the battles of heroes on their pottery, but they also enjoyed painting bunches of grapes that looked real enough to touch. The Romans enjoyed landscapes and pictures of legends.

During the Christian era, painters did pictures mostly of the saints and of Biblical scenes. In the 14th century, though, they began to take an interest in new subjects and new ways of painting, and this interest went on through the RENAISSANCE and up to the present. Painters will probably always try new ways of painting.

Here are just a few of the types of painting we know today, and just a few of the ways of making them. *Landscapes* are pictures of scenes in the country or city. PORTRAITS are pictures of people; they try to show what sort of people they are. *Still lifes* are pictures of objects, for instance objects on a table. *Genre* paintings are pictures of everyday life. There are also historical paintings, paintings that show Biblical scenes, paintings that show the sea, and many others. Some of these paintings are *naturalistic*, and try to show things exactly as they look. Some, on the other hand, are *abstract*, and give just the bare outlines of the objects. There are also *non-objective* paintings, which are not pictures of anything at all but are just designs made with paint.

It is possible to paint with color put into oil; this is *oil painting*. A few hundred years ago, many painters used *tempera*, which was color mixed with raw egg. *Murals* (paintings on walls) are often done in *fresco*, color that soaks into fresh plaster. *Water color*, colored water that soaks into paper, has been popular for many years. These are just a few of the *mediums* in which a painter can work.

Of course it is possible to make pictures without being a painter. The stained-glass artist makes colored windows. The artist in MOSAIC uses small cubes of glass, tile, or stone. And you can be a painter without making large pictures, by painting on dishes, pots, pieces of furniture, or the pages of books. Painting, you can see, is a large and complicated subject. Go to an art museum some time and see how many kinds of painting there are.

PAKISTAN

When Britain granted independence to India in 1947, the MUSLIMS decided that northeast INDIA and part of Bengal would be a separate country called Pakistan. The country was divided into two parts, East and West Pakistan, that had little in common. In 1971, the parts went to war, which ended when India helped East Pakistan become a separate country, called Bangladesh.

Pakistan borders India on the east, Iran on the southwest, Afghanistan on the northwest, and the Arabian Sea on the south. Rice, cotton, and wheat grow in the Indus River valley, and copper and iron ore are found in the mountains.

The capital used to be Karachi, the largest city and chief port, but it is now Islamabad, a much smaller city with beautiful parks and gardens. The majority of the 75.3 million Pakistanis come from the Punjabi tribe.

Bangladesh, on the Bay of Bengal, is a flat land that is flooded by the GANGES and Brahmaputra Rivers. Rice, jute, and tea are grown there. Its capital is Dacca and its population is 82.7 million.

PALESTINE
A small territory on the eastern shore of the Mediterranean, Palestine was a crossroads for traders and a battleground for many invaders. The HEBREWS lived in Palestine after they escaped from Egypt in the 13th century B.C. Later it was ruled by the Romans, and for centuries it was fought over by the Christians and the MUSLIMS, especially during the CRUSADES. In 1517 Palestine became part of the Turkish Empire, but it was still regarded as the homeland of the JEWS. In 1917 the British Legion finally liberated the land from the Turks.

The League of Nations in 1923 gave Palestine to Great Britain for administration under a mandate. Afterward, thousands of Jews settled there and were bitterly scorned by the Arab inhabitants. The conflict became so great that in 1947 the United Nations voted to divide Palestine into a Jewish state (ISRAEL) and an Arab territory (part of Jordan). The holy city of JERUSALEM was also split into two parts. In 1967, Israel decisively defeated Egypt in a six-day war and occupied much of the Arab section, all of Jerusalem, and the Sinai Peninsula. In 1973, Egypt recovered part of the territory it had lost.

PALMS

Palm trees, which grow in the tropics and subtropics, are of two main kinds: *feather palms* and *fan palms*. Feather palms, such as the DATE palm and the COCONUT palm, have leaves like ostrich plumes. Fan palms have huge leaves like fans. One or two of these leaves are often big enough to cover the entire roof of a native hut.

Palms come in many sizes and grow in many ways. Many have tall, straight trunks that grow 100 feet (31 m) tall. The rattan palm has long, climbing vines that are sometimes 600 feet (186 m) long. Its canes are used in making baskets and furniture.

Climbing a Date Palm in Iraq

Coconut Palm, Friendly Isles.

Palms are among the most useful trees in the world. They provide us with dates, coconuts, and other food; palm oil for margarine and soap; palm sugar; timber and roof thatch for building; imitation ivory; wax, furniture, and fans. Mats, hats, rope and clothing are made from palm fiber. SEE ALSO: COCONUT, DATES.

615

PAN

In Greek mythology, Pan was the son of Hermes, the messenger of the gods. He was a noisy, ugly god, with goat's legs and horns. The country was his home—the fields, forests, and mountains. Because he was supposed to make the flocks fertile, he was the god of shepherds, herdsmen, and hunters.

Pan was always in love with one woodland nymph or another, but was always rejected because of his ugliness. In one famous story, he pursued the nymph Syrinx. But before she was caught by Pan, her sister nymphs changed her into a reed bed, out of which Pan made his seven-reeded flute (pipes), called a *syrinx*. Pan later used his flute to defeat APOLLO in a musical contest.

Pan was known to startle unwary travelers at night. Hence sudden fright came from Pan and was called *panic*.

PANAMA CANAL

In 1881, Ferdinand de Lesseps, the Frenchman who built the SUEZ CANAL, began to dig the Panama Canal, which connects the Atlantic and Pacific Oceans. The project stopped in 1889 after 16,000 workers had died in Panama from yellow fever and malaria.

From 1904 to 1914, the canal was built by an American company, headed by Colonel George Goethals. The malaria-carrying mosquitoes were destroyed by spraying their breeding waters with oil.

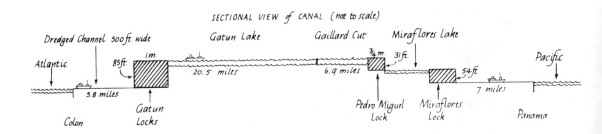

SECTIONAL VIEW of CANAL (not to scale)

616

From the Atlantic, ships are raised by a set of locks to Gatun Lake, which is 85 feet (26 m) above sea level. The ships then proceed into Gaillard Cut—the most dangerous part of the canal. At the Pedro Miguel and Miraflores Locks, they are lowered to sea level in the Pacific. Each lock, which is 1000 feet (310 m) long and 110 feet (34 m) wide, can be filled with water in 15 minutes. Ships are pulled by electric "mules" through each lock, and they usually take 7 to 8 hours to make the 50-mile (81 m) trip through the entire Panama Canal.

PANTOMIME

Today, we call pantomime any kind of acting without speaking. BALLET is a kind of pantomime, for instance. And even a play with spoken words can use pantomime, since the actors may use movements of their bodies or the looks on their faces to tell the audience things they do not put into words.

Pantomime is a very old art, found in many parts of the world. It was popular in ancient Greece and Rome, and became popular in the 18th century in England and France, when only a few actors were allowed by law to speak their parts. Characters from old Italian comedies were the best known at that time: the lovers Harlequin and Columbine, Columbine's foolish father Pantaloon, a crazy servant called the Zanni, and so on. Later, the English began to prefer Mother Goose characters and characters from fairy tales, while the French developed Pierrot, a gentle clown.

Most famous for solo pantomime or mime is Marcel Marceau of France.

PAPER

The thin, flat sheets or tissues we call paper come from plant fibers, which are minute threads found in trees, grasses, and other plants. Most of the paper used for newspapers, magazines, and books comes from the fibers of cone-bearing, evergreen trees. Paper can also be made from rope, jute, straw, esparto grass and bamboo. Some of the finest paper is processed from cotton and linen rags.

Linen & Cotton rags

Esparto Grass

Spruce

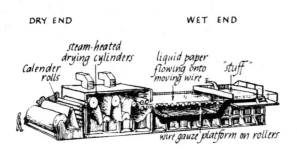

DRY END   WET END

Calender rolls / steam-heated drying cylinders / liquid paper flowing onto moving wire / "stuff"

wire gauze platform on rollers

Most paper is made from *wood pulp*. The wood or grasses are ground up and sometimes boiled. Water and chemicals are mixed in and then the pulp is washed, bleached, screened, or beaten. The pulp or "stuff" is fed into a papermaking machine and passes over wire screens. As water from the pulp drains through the screens, layers of fibers form and mat together. This wet, flabby material is passed through a stack of iron cylinders or rollers, pressing, drying and smoothing the "paper." The calender rollers smooth the surface of the paper. Fillers, usually clay or starch, are added to improve the printing, texture, and strength of the paper. Colored paper is made by adding dye to the pulp; good glossy paper is made by coating the paper with a layer of clay, mixed with adhesives. Waxed

paper comes from passing paper through a solution of paraffin.

papyrus plant

papyrus roll

The word *paper* derives from the Latin word *papyrus*, which is a tall, aquatic plant growing in the Nile valley. The ancient Egyptians made a paperlike material from the plant by pressing together thin strips of the pith (the tissue in the stems) of the papyrus. Papyrus was used to write on until about A.D. 1000. Then *parchment* and *vellum* were made from the skins of sheep, goats, calves, and kids. The monks and scribes of the Middle Ages used these materials for manuscripts and documents.

Paper itself is believed to have been invented in China around 100 B.C. Chinese paper was a mixture of hemp and bark. Papermaking was introduced into Europe through Spain. It was first done in America by William Rittenhouse of Philadelphia (1690).

PARACHUTE

A parachute is a device for coming down safely through the air from a great height. It has a large piece of light, strong cloth from which cords hang. These hold a harness that supports the person or object that is to be dropped.

Leonardo da Vinci designed the first parachute in 1514, but it was only in 1783 that one was really used for the first time. Yet parachuting from balloons was already common at fairs around 1800. In 1912, the first jump from an airplane was made, but most World War I aviators did not use parachutes. Before 1919, the parachute was attached by a "rip cord" to the aircraft, but in that year an aviator opened his own "chute" after he had fallen some distance. Parachutes were used in World War II to drop invasion troops and their supplies as well as to save life. Today, they are even used to bring re-entering space capsules down safely.

In addition to the old umbrella-like parachutes there are now chutes of many forms. Some use jets of the air they trap to send the parachutist in any direction he wishes.

Skydiving, falling great distances before opening a parachute, has become a popular sport. It is closely regulated to keep it safe.

PARAGUAY

Paraguay is a landlocked country in SOUTH AMERICA that is slightly larger than California. Most of its population of about 3 million are poor *mestizos*, people who are a mixture of Spanish and Guarani Indian.

The eastern part of Paraguay is made up of high, forested plateaus and fertile plains. Here are large plantations where cattle are raised and cotton, rice, and tobacco are grown. Western Paraguay, called the *Chaco*, is mostly dry scrubland where few people live.

Ships travel all the way from the Atlantic Ocean to the busy port of Asunción on the Paraguay River. This port is also the capital and by far the largest city in Paraguay.

The country was settled as a Spanish colony in 1537 and finally gained its independence in 1811. During a bitter war from 1865 to 1870 against Brazil, Argentina, and Uruguay, Paraguay lost nearly all its men. It has since been ruled by dictators or popularly elected presidents.

PARASITE

Parasites are plants or animals that live on or in the body of another (called the *host*). If it is not healthy enough to overcome the parasite, the host may weaken and finally die. However, not all parasites are harmful, and some hosts could not be healthy without the parasites that live in or on them.

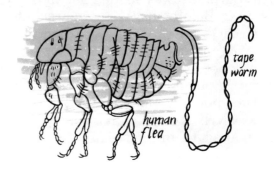
tape worm
human flea

MISTLETOE and many jungle vines are parasites on trees. Certain kinds of parasitic FUNGI must be controlled by man lest they kill crops and fruit. Some insects, like FLEAS and lice, are parasitic on man and animals and may carry dangerous diseases like the *plague*. BACTERIA are parasites that cause diseases such as tuberculosis and pneumonia. SEE ALSO: BACTERIA, FLEA, FUNGI, MISTLETOE.

PARIS

Paris is one of the most beautiful cities in the world. It is the capital of FRANCE, situated on the SEINE River, about 100 miles (161 km) from the English Channel. Most of the city is on a level plain, around which rise low, rolling hills.

A series of splendid avenues called *boulevards* radiate from the center of Paris. Other boulevards circle the city, for they were built where defense walls once stood. Thirty-two bridges cross the Seine River, which divides Paris into the Left (south) Bank, popular with students and artists, and the Right (north) Bank, the business center.

Many visitors come to Paris each year to see the Gothic cathedral of Notre Dame, the Louvre art museum, the Sacré Coeur church on the highest point

Arc de Triomphe

Eiffel Tower

Church of Sacré Coeur

Paris Street Scene

in the city, the artists' quarters, the expensive fashion shops, the open-air cafés, and, of course, the Eiffel Tower and the Arc de Triomphe, built to honor Napoleon's victories.

Paris also has one of the world's oldest universities, the Sorbonne. It has many modern buildings and factories, particularly in the growing suburbs, where most Parisians live and work. SEE ALSO: FRANCE.

PARLIAMENT

The word "parliament" derives from the French word *parler*, meaning "to talk." It was the name given to an assembly of lords, knights, and townsmen in the MIDDLE AGES. Thus, parliament became a place to speak and debate, especially about customs and laws. After the British Parliament originated in 1295, it became a model for lawmaking bodies (legislatures) in Canada, Australia, the United States, and many other countries.

The British Parliament in a part of London called Westminster consists of two chambers, the House of Commons and the House of Lords. Members of the House of Commons are elected by the British people and each represents a particular district in Great Britain. Members of the House of Lords are British *peers*, people with titles of nobility, and important churchmen.

Parliament discusses new laws and matters of national policy. Legislation is passed if a majority of members votes in favor of it.

621

Parliamentary laws or procedure applied originally to the customs and rules under which business was conducted in the British Parliament. Gradually, these parliamentary laws spread to America and other places and were used always to keep order at governmental meetings. Around 1800, THOMAS JEFFERSON, when presiding over the U.S. Senate, prepared a manual of parliamentary law based on the practice of the British House of Commons. Today, the usual guide for running meetings is H. M. Roberts's book, *Rules of Order*, published in 1876 and based on the procedures of the British Parliament and the U.S. CONGRESS.

PARROTS

Except for a few species, parrots are tropical birds. Most live on nuts, fruit, honey, and seeds, though some, like the sheep-killing kea parrot of New Zealand, also eat flesh. Most parrots have brilliant plumage. The African gray and the blue-fronted Amazon parrots have the unusual ability to imitate human speech, though there are others that can "talk," also.

Parrots live in large, noisy flocks and nest in holes in trees. They lay 1 to 12 white eggs in banks of earth. Some kinds have been known to live for more than 50 years.

Parakeets, which are common as pets in America, belong to the parrot family, which has more than 300 varieties. Lovebirds, usually seen in pairs, are another popular kind of parrot.

Red and Blue Macaw

Hyacinthine Macaw

Tricolored Macaw

African Grey Parrot

Blue-fronted Amazon

Red Lory

Carolina Parrakeet

Great White-crested Cockatoo

PASSOVER

When the Jews were still held captive in Egypt, God sent plagues to punish the Egyptians. The Jews marked their doorways with lamb's blood as a sign that they were His people and the Lord had "passed over" them, leaving them unharmed. The festival

of Passover celebrates this event. It is celebrated for seven or eight days in Judaism. A celebration called the *Seder* takes place in the Jewish home, with a recitation of verses appropriate to the occasion. In memory of the Jewish flight from Egypt, certain foods are forbidden. Bread made without yeast is the only bread allowed, and certain bitter herbs have to be eaten. In most synagogues, the Song of Solomon is read. The last supper Jesus had with His disciples was probably a Passover feast.

PASSPORT

A passport is a certificate of identity granted by a country's government, allowing the holder to leave the country he or she is in or to enter a foreign country. It supposedly gives the holder safe and free passage, as well as all lawful aid and protection.

In the U.S. a passport may be obtained by applying to any passport agency of the Department of State. A person must show proof of citizenship, present two identical photographs of him or herself, and pay a fee. A U.S. passport is valid for five years from the date of issue. Under certain conditions, vaccination against smallpox, cholera, or yellow fever may be required to enter certain countries.

Also, sometimes a foreign country's government requests a *visa*—special permission—for a traveler to enter and remain in that country for a certain period of time. A visa is usually in the form of a stamped notation on a person's passport.

Louis PASTEUR (1822–1895)

Louis Pasteur was a French scientist who studied the many different kinds of microscopic BACTERIA. Bacteria live inside of foods and in all living things, including people. Pasteur found that many bacteria are harmless and actually help us to digest our food; but he also discovered that some kinds can cause disease.

Pasteur discovered that bacteria present in wine turned the wine sour. He learned that heating the wine to a certain temperature destroyed the bacteria and made the wine safe to drink. Later, he used

the same method to kill bacteria in milk, and today we call the process *pasteurization*.

At the time Pasteur lived, silkmaking, an important industry in France, was in danger because the silkworms were dying. He found that the silkworms were infected by another kind of organism and thereby saved the silk industry. He also found that rabies, a disease that killed people who were bitten by mad dogs, was caused by an organism that recent research has shown to be a *virus*. He was able to create a *serum* that saved many lives.

Saint PATRICK (A.D. 389?-461?)

About 1600 years ago, Saint Patrick brought CHRISTIANITY to IRELAND and later became the country's patron saint.

His family lived in ancient England. When Patrick was 16, he was seized by pirates and sold as a slave in Ireland. There he looked after the castle of an Irish lord, but escaped after six years and went to France to become a monk. He supposedly had a dream in which the poor people of Ireland asked him to come back.

As a bishop, many years later, Patrick led a group of monks to Ireland. While converting the pagan Irish to Christianity, he founded churches and monasteries throughout the country. Patrick stayed the rest of his life there. One Irish legend says that Saint Patrick killed all the snakes in the land by driving them into the sea.

Saint Patrick's Day is celebrated each year on March 17th.

PAUL

Paul, who was also called Saul, was an educated Jew with Roman citizenship. He was born in Tarsus, a city of Asia Minor. He was a Jewish rabbi at the beginning, although he worked as a tentmaker for a living. At first he persecuted the followers of Christ, but then had a miraculous vision, while traveling to Damascus, that turned him into the greatest Christian missionary. For years he traveled around Asia Minor, Greece, and other countries of the eastern

Mediterranean, preaching and establishing churches. Other missionaries such as Barnabas, Timothy, and MARK, went with him on some of his trips. He was often sick, often attacked, was imprisoned and shipwrecked, but kept on in his work of organizing the small, scattered Christian groups into a church. He was probably killed in Rome at the orders of the Emperor Nero around A.D. 63. He wrote some of the Epistles of the New Testament, and his work is described in the Acts of the Apostles.

PEACH

Peach trees may have been cultivated by the Chinese thousands of years before they were brought to Europe in the centuries before Christ. Spanish explorers brought the peach to Mexico, and explorers, settlers, and Indians carried it to other parts of the Western Hemisphere.

The peach is a close relative of the APRICOT, PLUM, and almond. Its fruit is fleshy and juicy and surrounds a hard pit or stone. Inside the pit is one seed. The varieties in which the flesh is firmly attached to the pit are called *clingstones*; those in which the flesh separates freely from the pit are called *freestones*.

Nectarines are a fuzzless and smooth variety of peach, but most peaches have skins that are velvety.

Peach trees grow best in the warm climate of California and southern Europe. But the state of Georgia has so many peach orchards that it is commonly called the "peach state."

PEACOCK

The peacock is a relative of the PHEASANT. Native to Sri Lanka and India, it is considered sacred by some castes (social classes). It has been brought to other countries as an ornamental bird to grace the lawns of fine estates and palaces.

Usually the peacock refers to the crested male, with his bright, iridescent (rainbow-like) color. The male's long tail stands erect and spreads like a fan when he displays himself to the smaller and less brilliant female, called the *peahen*. Both the peacock and the peahen have small fan-like crests of feathers on their heads. These feathers are exported from India in great amounts for ornamentation. However, there is a superstition about the eyespots on the tail, saying they are unlucky for the wearer.

PEANUT

The peanut is also known as the ground nut, earthnut, monkey nut, ground pea, and goober. It is native to tropical South America. Today, India, China, western Africa, and the southern United States are the largest producers of peanuts in the world.

The plant is a low-growing annual that is a member of the pea family. After pollination, the flowers soon wither and an unusual structure, called a *peg*, is thrust from the base of the flower to penetrate eventually the soil. The characteristic fruit or pod develops underground from the fertilized ovules at the tip of each peg. The fruits function partly as roots, absorbing minerals directly from the earth. The roots need sufficient calcium for adequate development of the pods.

In peanut-producing countries other than the United States, the peanut is grown mainly for its oil, which is used in cooking and soap manufacturing. In the U.S., half the crop is made into peanut butter, while the other half is for roasted and salted nuts, and for use in candies and pastries, with 10 percent being crushed for oil. Southern farmers use the tops of the peanut plants as feed for their livestock.

GEORGE WASHINGTON CARVER, son of poor black slaves, discovered after years of careful research more than 300 different products—including milk, cheese, ink, and soap—which could be made from peanuts.

PEAR

The pear is the name of a fruit tree that is known for its sweet and juicy fruit, also called the pear. Pear trees were cultivated by the ancient Greeks and Romans. Today, pears are grown in temperate climates all over the world. Several varieties of pear, such as the Bartlett and Seckel, are grown on the Pacific coast and in the Great Lakes region of the United States.

The pear tree is neater and more upright than the apple tree, which is thought by some botanists to be closely related to the pear. The fruit is more easily bruised and more perishable than the apple. Pears are picked when they are hard and green and then placed in a cool place until they are ready to be sold and eaten. In Europe, a pear cider called *perry* is very popular.

PEARLS

Pearls are deposits of lustrous calcium carbonate secreted by oysters and other mollusks as a means of encasing an irritating foreign particle (such as a grain of sand or a tiny worm) inside the shell. A pearl is made of the same mother-of-pearl material that lines the inside of a mollusk's shell. Pearls are white and pink, and on rare occasions, black.

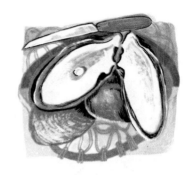

The most famous pearl fisheries are in the Persian Gulf, around the South Sea Islands, and off the coasts of Lower California and Australia. In these warm waters, divers go down 50 or 60 feet (15.5–18.6 m) to the oyster beds and bring up oysters in a net. If necessary, a diver uses his knife to protect himself from sharks. Sometimes boats dredge up oysters. Afterward the shells lie in the sun to allow the oysters to decay. They are then opened and searched for pearls. The largest pearl ever found weighed over 14 pounds (6.3 kg); it was discovered in the shell of a giant clam at Palawan in the Philippines. The estimated value of the pearl is well over $4,000,000.

"Cultured pearls" are man-made. A tiny seed pearl is placed inside each oyster to force the production of the protective coating. After several years in the sea, these oysters are examined for pearls. Only an expert can tell the difference between real and cultured pearls.

Imitation pearls are produced by coating glass beads with material made from fish scales.

Robert PEARY (1856–1920)

Robert Peary was an Arctic explorer who became the first man to reach the NORTH POLE.

After leading several unsuccessful expeditions to reach the Pole, Peary set out in 1908 for his last attempt at it. He sailed his ship, *Roosevelt*, to Cape Columbia, about 500 miles (805 km) from the North Pole. There he planned to make a quick trip over the ice floes (large flat masses of floating ice) of the Arctic Ocean, in the middle of which was the North Pole.

Most of Peary's men went only part of the way, clearing a route, building igloos, and storing supplies. With his black fellow explorer, Matthew Henson, and four Eskimos, Peary made the final dash for the Pole, using five sledges and forty dogs. On April 6, 1909, they reached it and hoisted the American flag at the top of the world for the first time. SEE ALSO: NORTH POLE.

PEGASUS

Pegasus was a beautiful winged horse in Greek mythology. He sprang full-grown from the body of Medusa, a GORGON, when she was slain by Perseus. He then immediately flew to the top of Mount Olympus, the home of the gods, where he was used by ZEUS to convey thunder and lightning through the heavens.

Bellerophon captured Pegasus when the horse was drinking at a spring and tamed him with a golden bridle given by Athena, goddess of wisdom. Pegasus carried Bellerophon in his successful fight against the monster Chimaera. Later, when he tried to ride Pegasus to Mount Olympus, the gods sent a gadfly to sting the wonder horse, thus killing Bellerophon when he fell to Earth. Pegasus then flew off to dwell among the stars.

Another myth says that Pegasus stamped his feet near the summit of Mt. Helicon, starting the sacred spring from which musicians, artists, and poets and poetesses (the nine Muses) received their inspiration.

PEKING

Peking is the capital and most famous city of CHINA. It is about 80 miles (129 km) west of the Gulf of Chihli, an inlet of the Yellow Sea.

The city was the capital for Kublai Khan, who led the Mongols from central Asia into China and established a large empire in the 1200s. It was called Cambuluc when MARCO POLO lived there in the late 1200s. Later, two

dynasties of Chinese emperors, the Mings and the Manchus, erected palaces in the city, which they named Peking, meaning "northern capital." From 1928 to 1949, when the capital of China was transferred to Nanking, Peking was called Peiping. The name Peking was restored by the Chinese Communists.

Peking is really several cities in one, all formerly surrounded by great walls. The

Tartar City is old Peking and contains the walled Imperial City, within which lies the purple Forbidden City. This was the palace and court of the former emperor. The finest building here is the famous Temple of Heaven.

Today, visitors can enter the Imperial and Forbidden Cities and other beautiful temples, palaces, and pagodas throughout the city. The Communist Chinese have built new buildings and cleaned up the streets. There are large industries throughout, producing iron and steel, chemicals, and textiles. SEE ALSO: CHINA.

PELICANS

Pelicans are large birds with enormous pouched beaks that serve as a fishing net. Large flocks live near lakes, rivers, and swamps. Pelicans feed on fish in the southern parts of America, in southeastern Europe, and in areas of Asia and Africa. One kind—the white pelicans—works together as a group to drive the fish into shallow water.

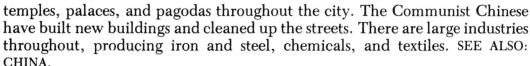

Their nests are untidy and built on the ground in the reeds. The female pelican lays 3 or 4 white eggs. The young are fed partly digested fish that the female regurgitates into the pouch. The pouch serves as a feed bucket for the young.

Pelicans are the largest web-footed birds. On land they are clumsy, but they are very capable fliers.

The legend that the pelican feeds its young with blood plucked from its own breast is untrue.

PEN

The modern pen has a variety of ancestors. The ancients often used a *stylus*, which was simply a pointed rod. With this the Babylonians did CUNEIFORM writing 5000 years ago on their tablets of clay, while the Greeks and Romans used it to cut letters in tablets covered with wax.

Another forerunner of the pen was the *ink brush*, which the ancient Egyptians used, and the Chinese and Japanese still use, for writing and painting on paper.

The first real pen was a bird's feather (*penna* is the Latin word for feather), which was sharpened to a point and split at the end. This *quill pen* was in use from Roman times until the middle of the 19th century. The Romans, however, sometimes also used pens with metal *nibs* (writing points), and around 1800 nibs of steel began to be sold in England. In 1884, a New Yorker named Waterman began to sell the first *fountain pen*, which carries an ink supply in its barrel and needs filling only at long intervals.

A few decades ago, the *ballpoint pen* was invented. This type of pen supplies ink to a tiny metal ball, which lays down a track of ink as it rolls along the paper.

A Babylonian writing

A Roman stylus

using a quill pen

A Victorian fountain pen

PENCIL

Pencils are rods of graphite and clay protected by casings of wood or some other material. Graphite used to be regarded as a type of lead, though it is really a kind of carbon. For this reason people talk of the "lead" of a pencil.

The first pencils were made in the 16th century, and by the 17th century, artists were using them. These early pencils had pure graphite, but in 1795 a Frenchman, Conté, began to mix graphite and clay to make pencils of different kinds. The more clay there was, the lighter the line it made. Today, we have a wide choice of pencils. Hard ones make very light lines, while soft ones will make broad, dark lines.

Stages of manufacture

wood

graphite rod

Graphite pressed out

PENDULUM

One day in 1583, the Italian scientist, GALILEO was in the cathedral of Pisa. He noticed a lamp, stirred by the breeze, that was swinging back and forth, taking the same time for each of its swings. The fact that the swinging was constant proved to be important in the study of PHYSICS. Scientists found that the weight of the object that swung had nothing to do with the time each swing took. This was important in learning the nature of gravity.

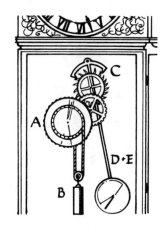

The lamp was a pendulum. A pendulum is a weight (called a *bob*) that hangs from a cord or a rod in such a way that it can swing freely. If well made, such a pendulum will swing back and forth in the same two directions throughout the day. It can show how the Earth rotates.

Most of our large clocks for 300 years have used pendulums. A Dutch scientist, Christiaan Huygens, first used a pendulum on a clock in 1657. In the diagram, A is a wheel turned by a chain that holds a falling weight, B. The wheel moves gears whose turning is controlled by a hooked device called an *escapement*, C. The gears move the escapement, which in turn moves the pendulum, D. The pendulum, in its turn, moves the escapement in such a way as to stop the gears for a moment until the pendulum has swung back to its original place. The shorter the pendulum, the faster it moves. The clock can be made to go faster by raising the bob of the pendulum with a screw, E.
SEE ALSO: GALILEO.

PENGUINS

These strange-looking black and white birds of the Southern Hemisphere, chiefly Antarctica, live in regions near cold ocean currents. The emperor penguin is over 3 feet (0.9 m) tall; the blue penguin is only 19 inches (48 cm) high.

Penguins are unable to run or fly. They waddle about on land but are graceful swimmers and expert divers for fish. Thousands gather on lonely breeding islands. The females lay 1 to 3 eggs. The emperor penguin rests her 1 egg on her feet to keep it up off the cold ice. Some penguins nest on high cliffs, to which they laboriously waddle and from which they toboggan comically downhill on their chests.

PENICILLIN

In our BLOOD, there are red and white blood cells (corpuscles). The job of the white corpuscles is to fight GERMS resulting from illness or injury. If the white corpuscles win the battle, the patient gets better. However, white corpuscles are also killed by many drugs and ANTISEPTICS, which are used to kill the germs.

In 1928, a Scottish bactcriologist Alexander Fleming noticed a greenish mold or fungus contaminating bacterial colonies of staphylococcus that he was growing in the laboratory. He noticed that the contaminating mold caused the staphylococci to disappear. After much experimentation, Fleming produced enough of this mold to make a liquid which he called *penicillin*. He proved that penicillin would kill the streptococcus BACTERIA that caused such diseases as pneumonia and diptheria without disturbing the white corpuscles.

Professor Florey and a team of others at Oxford University, in England, helped to discover how to produce penicillin in powder form in 1941. During World War II, British and American chemists were able to make enough of the "miracle drug" to save thousands of soldiers and civilians. Penicillin acts by killing bacteria that are growing and reproducing. It is especially useful to those patients who have bad side effects to sulfa drugs or who suffer from infections caused by strains of bacteria that have become immune to the action of sulfa drugs. SEE ALSO: ANTISEPTICS, BACTERIA, GERMS.

PENNSYLVANIA

Pennsylvania is one of the Middle Atlantic States. Most of the state is a highland, part of the Appalachian Mountains. There are lowlands beside Lake Erie in the northwest and along the Delaware River in the southeast. The Allegheny Plateau is in western and northern Pennsylvania. Harrisburg, the state capital, lies on the long Susquehanna River that flows south through the state. Pennsylvania has almost 12 million people.

The first settlers were the Swedish, who built a fort on Tinicum Island on the Delaware River in 1643. The Dutch seized the fort in 1655, but soon lost it to the British. In 1681, William Penn, an Englishman, established a settlement near what is now the city of PHILADELPHIA. It was named Chester and was a place where his religious group, the QUAKERS, could worship freely. The colony came to be called Pennsylvania, meaning "Penn Forest Land." In the western region, Frenchmen built Fort Duquesne in 1754. When the British took it four years later, they renamed it Fort Pitt, which is now Pittsburgh.

Pennsylvania is a great industrial state. Many of the country's largest steel plants are near Pittsburgh. The state mines nearly all of the hard coal and much of the soft coal of the United States. It makes machinery, chemicals, textiles, and food products. Tourists come to see historic sites, like Valley Forge, where, during the American Revolution, Washington's small army spent the bitter winter of 1777-78. SEE ALSO: PHILADELPHIA.

PEPPER

Pepper was one of the most precious SPICES brought to Europe by Venetian ships during the Middle Ages. It was used to flavor the tough, salt meat which the people used to eat in winter. It is still widely used for flavoring and in cooking.

Pepper grows in Sri Lanka and the East Indies on a vine-like shrub, *Piper nigrum*.

Black and white pepper come from this same plant. When the entire berries are ground it is black pepper. When the outer coating of the berry is removed, the product is white pepper. Cayenne or red pepper comes from *Capsicum*, a tropical plant. SEE ALSO: SPICES.

PERFUME

Perfume is an agreeable scent produced either naturally or artificially. The natural perfumes are produced by some plants and animals, the ones of animal origin being the longer lasting.

Some plants contain perfume in the petals, leaves, roots, seeds, or gum. Some perfume is contained in the rind of oranges and lemons, and some in bark, such as, cinnamon, cedar, and sandalwood.

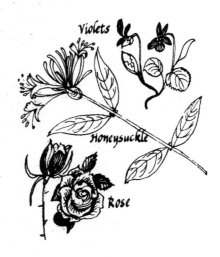

Violets

Honeysuckle

Rose

Heather

Lilies of the Valley

Various scents come from the glands of certain animals. *Civet* derives from the civet cat, *musk* from the musk deer, musk ox, and muskrat, *castor* from the beaver, and *ambergris* from the whale. These scents are disagreeably strong but in tiny quantities they make valuable perfumes.

The center of the natural perfume industry is Grasse, in France. However, nearly all modern perfumes, except for a few expensive ones made from flowers, are made artificially in laboratories.

PERICLES (495–429 B.C.)

After the defeat of Persia, ATHENS reached a cultural climax under the leadership of Pericles. As a youth, Pericles studied with the leading thinkers of his time and later went into politics as a representative of democracy. He made Athens the strongest city-state in Greece and made peace with SPARTA.

With the help of Phidias, the great Greek sculptor, Pericles erected the temples of the ACROPOLIS. Their greatest accomplishment was the majestic Parthenon, the temple of the goddess Athena. Pericles encouraged scholars, artists, and dramatists (writers of plays) to live in Athens, which was filled with beautifully decorated public buildings and statues.

Statue of Pericles

He wished to spread knowledge and well-being among the Athenians, whom he urged to serve in the law courts and to attend the theaters. The Age of Pericles is considered the peak of ancient Greek civilization, the so-called "classical period."

PERISCOPE

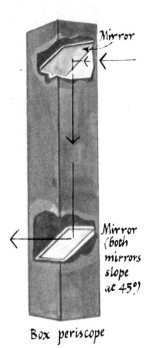

Mirror

Mirror
(both
mirrors
slope
at 45°)

Box periscope

A SUBMARINE can operate beneath the water, unseen by ships and safe from gunfire, only because it has a periscope. This is a long tube that rises above the surface of the sea. It has reflectors at the top and bottom that allow the view over the waves to be seen by those in the submarine. It may have lenses to magnify the view and a sighting device to help the submarine to aim torpedoes. Tanks and other army vehicles often have periscopes to help their crews steer and aim.

Making a simple periscope is easy. You need two mirrors and a long cardboard tube, put together as is shown on the left.

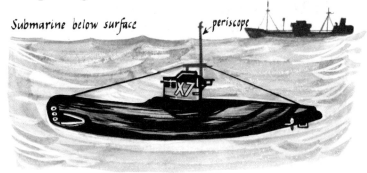

Submarine below surface   periscope

PERSIA

Persia was once the center of a great empire. Today, it consists of the country of IRAN, which lies between the Persian Gulf and Caspian Sea in southwest Asia.

Persia was originally settled by nomadic tribes from central Asia. The people who went to live in the valleys became known as the *Persians*; those who settled in the mountains were called the *Medes*. In the 500s B.C., Cyrus the Great united the Persians and the Medes to form a nation. Cyrus's son later conquered Egypt. The Persian Empire reached its greatest extent under Darius I, who controlled most of the area from India in the east to Greece in the west.

The Egyptians and Greeks rebelled under Persian rule, which finally came to an end when ALEXANDER THE GREAT overthrew Persia in the 330s B.C. The country was overrun by the Arabs in the A.D. 600s, and was conquered by the Mongols under Genghis Khan in 1251.

The ancient ruins of the magnificent cities of Susa (the old capital), Persepolis and Ecbatana can still be viewed today. SEE ALSO: IRAN.

PERU

Peru, on the Pacific coast of SOUTH AMERICA, is divided by the Andes Mountains into three regions. The coastal strip is almost rainless. Here lies Lima, the capital, about 6 miles (9.6 km) from Peru's chief seaport, Callao. There is also a 250-mile-wide (402 km) mountain belt and an inland region of tropical forests.

The Spanish, led by Pizarro, conquered the magnificent Inca civilization in the 1530s, and the INCAS became

slaves in the silver and gold mines. About 350 years later, Spain finally recognized the independence of Peru, which is now ruled by military leaders. The influence of Spain can be seen in the buildings and the use of the Spanish language.

Half of Peru's 16.3 million people are engaged in agriculture, growing cotton, sugar, coffee, tobacco, and grains and raising livestock. Many also work in the fishing industry and in the rich iron, copper, and silver mines in the mountains.

PETER

A fisherman named Simon was one of the three closest disciples (students) of Christ and a leader in the Christian church. After saying that JESUS was the Son of God, Simon was given the new name of Peter (meaning *rock* in Latin).

Peter's brother Andrew introduced him to Christ. Peter was an emotional man, acting quickly and speaking without always thinking through his actions. It was Peter who got out of a boat and walked on the water of the Sea of Galilee toward Jesus. When the soldiers came to capture Jesus, it was Peter who struck one with a sword, cutting off his ear. And it was Peter who three times denied that he knew Jesus.

Peter worked hard as a leader in spreading the new faith. He traveled widely, brought new converts to the Church, and settled disputes among its members. A tradition says that he was finally imprisoned in Rome around A.D. 65 by Nero and was crucified head down.

PETS

Pets are animals that are fun to have around and care for. The dog is most likely man's earliest pet, partly because of his hunting and guarding abilities, and partly because of his faithful and intelligent nature. Dogs want plenty of affection and daily exercise and need their own bed and one meal a day.

Cats are more independent than dogs. Cats have been pets for thousands of years, probably long before they were regarded as sacred by the ancient Egyptians.

Lambs, kids, monkeys, otters, and lion cubs are fun when they are very young, but few make good pets when full grown.

Rabbits, white mice, guinea pigs, hamsters, and gerbils are popular pets and are tame and harmless; however, they do require faithful tending.

Aquarium fish and cage birds, such as parakeets, canaries, and parrots, need the right kind of food and temperature. Special pet care books give important advice to the owners of these pets.

A turtle can forage for itself in your garden, but, in winter, extra green food and warmth have to be provided by its owner.

All pets need care and attention regularly. Their diet should be the same or nearly the same as it would be in the wild.

PHARAOH

The word *Pharaoh* really means "big house." The ancient Egyptians spoke of their king that way, much as we say "White House" when we mean the President of the United States or the people close to him.

Ancient Egypt was formed from a number of small kingdoms around 3100 B.C. For a long time the king was simply called the king. People began to speak of "the pharaoh" only around 1500 B.C., and the name became official only a few hundred years later.

The kings of Egypt had great power, and the whole life of the kingdom was supposed to depend on them. Their wishes were regarded as law. Some pharaohs, though, were weak, and other people in the kingdom or even foreigners were able to manage things. The book of Genesis, for instance, says that the Hebrew Joseph was made an important ruler in Egypt.

Egypt was conquered several times, and foreigners either ran it from their own countries or came to Egypt as pharaohs. When Cleopatra killed herself in 30 B.C., Egypt became a Roman province and the long reign of the pharaohs was finally ended.

PHEASANT

The pheasant is a ground bird, related to the grouse, the PEACOCK, and the partridge. It is native to Asia, chiefly India. The ancient Romans brought the pheasant to England. Today, large numbers of pheasants are raised on game preserves in England, Canada, and the United States.

Although they are ground birds, they are capable of roosting in trees. They eat grain, berries, seeds, and insects and like open countryside with some brush cover. Cocks (males) are magnificent in color and have an elaborate courtship ritual. The hens build nests in hollows in the ground, where they lay from 10 to 14 eggs.

The hybrid ring-necked pheasant is a common game bird in the northern United States. It is usually about 3 feet (.91 m) long. The Reeves pheasant, found in the Himalayas in Asia, grows to 8 feet (2.5 m) long, including its beautiful tail.

PHILADELPHIA

Philadelphia is in southeastern PENNSYLVANIA, at the junction of the Schuylkill and Delaware Rivers. It is the largest freshwater port in the world and a great industrial center. It produces textiles, clothing, chemicals, instruments, and food items. Oil refining, printing, and publishing are also important. Philadelphia has nearly 5 million people living in and around it.

In 1682, William Penn established a colony for QUAKERS here and named it "Philadelphia," meaning "city of brotherly love." The DECLARATION OF INDEPENDENCE was signed in Independence Hall. It was the American colonial capital during and after the American Revolution and the U.S. capital from 1790 to 1800. The first bank of the U.S. was established here.

Among the city's great historic attractions are the LIBERTY BELL, the Gloria Dei (Old Swedes') Church, and the Walnut St. Theater, the oldest in America. Also important are the University of Pennsylvania, founded in 1740 by BENJAMIN FRANKLIN, and large Fairmont Park, containing the museum of art and zoological gardens. SEE ALSO: PENNSYLVANIA.

PHILIPPINES

The Philippines is an archipelago of 7107 islands, situated in the western Pacific Ocean. The largest islands are Luzon in the north and Mindanao in the south. The eleven main islands are mountainous, with some coastal plains, wide valleys, hot springs, and volcanoes. The Philippines sometimes are hit by earthquakes and typhoons. Quezon City is the capital, and Manila is the biggest city and major seaport. About 45 million people, called *Filipinos*, live on this island nation.

The islands have rich deposits of silver, chromite, copper, gold, iron, manganese, coal, nickel, and zinc. The chief agricultural products are rice, sugar cane, coconuts, fruits, and Manila hemp (used for making rope or a coarse fabric). Manufacturing is growing in importance, producing appliances, clothing, pharmaceuticals, and paper products. Many tourists come to visit the islands.

In 1521, MAGELLAN visited the islands, and Spanish explorers named them after Philip II of Spain. The Philippines were a Spanish colony until the U.S. took control after the SPANISH-AMERICAN WAR. The U.S. Congress granted the islands independence in 1946.

PHILISTINES

The Philistines, who originally came from CRETE, settled in the lowlands of PALESTINE, on the Mediterranean coast. They were a civilized people, devoted to agriculture and trade, and possessed great skill in warfare. They were also expert at forging iron and were worshippers of a corn god, named Dagon.

The Philistines came in conflict with the HEBREWS (the Israelites), who began to occupy the Promised Land in about 1200 B.C., after their flight from Egypt. The territory of the Philistines consisted of five principal towns—Ashkelon, Gaza, Gath, Ashdod, and Ekron. Saul, the first King of Israel, died fighting the Philistines, despite the feats of SAMSON and the killing of Goliath. DAVID and SOLOMON fought against them and later seized their territory.

Although the Philistines rebelled against the Hebrew supremacy, they never again achieved great power. Excavations are slowly revealing more about the civilization of the Philistines.

PHILOSOPHER

Philosophy is the study of reality and the search for truth and wisdom. A philosopher, then, is a person who loves to think deeply about life and spend his or her time and energy in search of wisdom. In Greek, philosophy means "love of wisdom."

The ancient Greeks were particularly fond of discussing ideas. They wished to explain beauty, truth, the universe, and values through observation and reasoning. They asked such questions as: What is knowledge? Why is man born? What is goodness or happiness?

The most important sources of philosophy in the Western world are the Greek philosophers, such as PLATO, ARISTOTLE, and SOCRATES, and the BIBLE.

PHOENICIANS

The Phoenicians lived along the eastern coast of the Mediterranean, in what is now the country of Lebanon (ancient Phoenicia). They were the first great seafarers and traders.

Around 1500 B.C., they had become wealthy city dwellers in ports like Tyre and Sidon. Phoenician traders sailed all over the Mediterranean and into the Atlantic as far north as England and Scandinavia. They traded in gold, silver, copper, and tin, as well as in spices, pearls, linens, and

slaves. Phoenicians became well-known for a purple dye made from a type of mollusk and for their ALPHABET, which was copied by the Greeks. They also founded trading ports and colonies on distant shores, including Cadiz in Spain and CARTHAGE in North Africa.

After 700 B.C., the Assyrians and then the Persians conquered the Phoenicians, who were eventually ruled by the Romans after the 1st century B.C.

PHOENIX

The phoenix was a legendary fabulous bird that ancient peoples once worshipped. It was similar to an eagle but with red and golden plumage.

According to myth, the phoenix lived in Arabia. When it reached the age of 500, it flew from the Arabian desert to Heliopolis, the sun-city in Egypt. There the phoenix built its own funeral pyre (a kind of burning altar), on which it placed itself and burned to death, fanning the flames with its wings. From its ashes, a new young phoenix arose.

The phoenix was a sacred symbol in Egyptian religion, representing the sun that dies each night and rises each morning.

PHONOGRAPH

In 1876, the TELEPHONE appeared. This turned the vibrations of sound into electrical waves, then back into sound vibrations again. The next year, EDISON invented the phonograph, which allowed sound to be preserved.

In a modern phonograph, or *record player*, sounds are reproduced in the form of wiggles in a spiral groove on a disk called a *record*. The more wiggles in any part of the groove, the higher the pitch of sound. The record turns on a *turntable*, and a *stylus*, or needle, in the groove wiggles as the groove itself does, sending bursts of electricity along the *pickup* or *tone arm* (which holds the stylus) to an *amplifier*,

cylindrical record

A phonograph made in 1897

grooves in record →

needle/stylus

where the electricity gets enough strength to run the LOUDSPEAKERS or other devices that repeat the original sounds.

Today, sophisticated electronic equipment allows sound to be reproduced very precisely. Some systems use specially prepared tapes instead of records. Some split up the sound for *stereophonic* reproduction, which needs two loudspeakers, or *quadraphonic* reproduction, which needs four. SEE ALSO: EDISON, THOMAS ALVA; LOUDSPEAKER.

PHOSPHORUS

Yellow phosphorus is a waxy element that is never found free in nature but usually in compounds called phosphates. Phosphorus means "light giving"; it ignites spontaneously in air and burns with a greenish white light. It therefore must be kept under water. Being poisonous and caustic (burning body tissues), it makes a good rat poison. When it was originally used in MATCHES, it caused "phossy jaw," a disease of the jaw and teeth. Red phosphorus, made by heating ordinary phosphorus, is nonpoisonous and less dangerous than yellow phosphorus; it is thus used today in the manufacture of safety matches.

Phosphorus is important for plant and animal growth. Plants get it from the soil; animals get it from eating plants. We get phosphorus from lean meat, eggs, and cheese. It is important for building strong bones and teeth. To enrich the soil with phosphorus, farmers add manure and bone meal fertilizers.

PHOTOGRAPHY

Early in the 19th century, several people began to be interested in the fact that light would darken certain chemicals. At that time there was already a device called the camera, which used lenses to project scenes on a background so that they could be drawn exactly. If the camera could project its images on a surface treated with one of these chemicals, and if the image could be "fixed," that is, kept from disappearing when exposed to ordinary

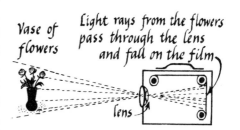

Vase of flowers

Light rays from the flowers pass through the lens and fall on the film.

lens

light, a new way of making pictures would be invented. The first photograph was made in France in 1826. It was very blurred, but soon inventors found ways of producing pictures so sharp that some artists felt that drawing and painting would become lost arts. They did not, but photography itself became an art form as well as a very useful way of gathering information about the look of things.

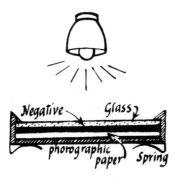

Negative   Glass

photographic
paper   Spring

The article CAMERA tells how a camera works. Once the roll of film is *exposed* completely, so that it has all the photographs it can hold, it is unloaded in a *darkroom*, where the only light is of a sort to which film is not sensitive. It is bathed in a *developer*, which determines how dark the dark areas are going to be in the final picture. The film is a *negative*; that is, it shows the dark areas of the final picture as light and the light areas as dark. The

Negative

photographer watches the development of the negative so that he can take it out of the developer at just the right time. Then he bathes the film in *hypo*, a chemical that fixes the images.

Once the images are fixed, he is ready to *print*. He puts the film under a strong white light over a chemically treated paper and makes a *positive*, which is really a negative of a negative. In this positive (also called a print), light areas arc light and dark areas are dark. This print is the photograph you actually see. By using lenses the photographer can make *enlargements*. The image on the film is very small, but enlargements may be big enough to cover part of a wall.

There are many tricks that the photographer can use in the darkroom to get just the special effect he wants, either to make the photograph clearer or for artistic reasons. Even the *cropping* of the picture, the leaving-out of parts that are not wanted in the prints, is important in deciding what effect the final photograph will have. SEE ALSO: CAMERA.

Positive

PHYSICS

Physics is a science that studies and investigates matter and energy. It deals with mechanics, SOUND, LIGHT, HEAT, ELECTRICITY, MAGNETISM, X-RAYS, cosmic rays, and NUCLEAR ENERGY.

Physics is so closely linked to chemistry, biology, geology, and astronomy that special branches of these sciences are called physical chemistry, biophysics, geophysics, and astrophysics. Some of the great persons who have won the Nobel Prize in physics are Wilhelm C. Roentgen, the German discoverer of X-rays, ALBERT EINSTEIN, the great theoretical scientist, and Enrico Fermi, the physicist who experimented with radioactivity and helped develop the atomic bomb.

PIANO

Around 1709, an Italian, Bartolomeo Cristofori, invented a keyboard instrument he called a *pianoforte* (Italian, meaning "loud-soft"). Unlike the HARPSICHORD and most other keyboard instruments of the day, its strings were struck with hammers rather than being plucked. By the mid-18th century, the piano was popular. Inventors added improvements over the years, and gradually the modern piano, able to be played very loudly and with a wide range of pitch, evolved.

The machinery for striking the wire string of a piano is called an *action*. Actions, as the diagram shows, are very complicated. Every note, except for the low ones, has two or three strings tuned the same way so that the note will be loud enough. The harder the pianist strikes the keys, the louder the sound he gets. Most pianos have three pedals, so that the pianist can control the sound quality with his foot. The left pedal allows only one string to be struck, so that the sound is quiet. The middle allows the strings to vibrate longer than usual when they are struck. The right-hand pedal allows all the strings to vibrate as long as it is down. SEE ALSO: HARPSICHORD.

PIED PIPER of Hamelin

According to legend, the Pied Piper rid the town of Hamelin in Germany of a plague of rats by luring them into the river with his magic flute playing. When the townspeople refused to pay the price agreed upon, the Pied Piper charmed away their children with his music, leading them into a mountain cave, from which they never returned.

Many believe this story is based on the Children's Crusade of 1212. About 20,000 German boys and girls followed a youth named Nicolas, but many died of hunger or disease before reaching JERUSALEM. Others were sold into slavery during this most disastrous of CRUSADES.

PIGS

Pigs usually have long mobile snouts, heavy, short-legged bodies, bristly hides, and small tails. Pigs are sometimes referred to as hogs or swine.

Pigs are descendants of the wild boars that used to be commonly found in the forests of Europe. Wild boars are fierce, lean animals. Their razor-sharp tusks are capable of ripping open a dog or horse. It is thought that the modern American pig descended from this European boar and from a smaller Asian boar that had been tamed in China.

Pigs are often grouped as meat-type or lard-type pigs and bacon-type pigs. Pigs raised for BACON, pork, ham, and sausage are longer and leaner; they are fed chiefly on alfalfa, barley, and skim milk. Pigs raised for meat and lard are also fed corn. The corn belt of the Midwest is the main pig-raising area in the United States.

Because pigs like to wallow in the mud to avoid the heat and insects, people tend to think of them as dirty animals. However, pigs thrive best in clean, well-ventilated barns and pens. It is also important that they have some sunlight and are permitted to exercise in grazing pastures.

One of the world's fiercest animals is the wild boar of India, a distant relative of the American domestic pig. There is also the pygmy pig of India, which is slightly larger than a fox terrier. Probably the ugliest pig of all is the wart hog of Africa, which has a bristly mane and a long tail. In some parts of North and South America, wild, hoofed pigs, called *peccaries*, live in herds and can sometimes be dangerous.

Besides being valuable for their flesh, pigs provide other products, such as leather gloves and footballs (sometimes called "pigskins"). Some bristles for brushes are taken from pigs. SEE ALSO: BACON.

PIKE

The pike is a fierce and greedy fish, sometimes called "the river wolf." It attacks and devours all kinds of fish, frogs, ducklings, and water rats.

This freshwater fish is native to the rivers and lakes of North America and Europe. The adult pike is 2 to 5 feet (61–153 cm) long and weighs up to 40 or 50 pounds (18–22.5 kg). Since they put up a tremendous battle when hooked, pikes provide good sport for fishermen. Pikes are a bony fish though a delicious tasting one.

PILGRIM

A pilgrim is someone who travels to a certain place for religious reasons. From early Christian times, people made pilgrimages to the Holy Places of JERUSALEM, BETHLEHEM, and NAZARETH. Many made trips to visit the shrines of local saints. In the Middle Ages, pilgrims became a familiar sight on the roads of Europe and in the southern ports, where they often took ships to PALESTINE. Many men who went on the CRUSADES thought of themselves as pilgrims.

Crusaders

A palmer

Pilgrims made these long and perilous journeys in the hope that pardons could be obtained for their sins or that sicknesses might be cured. Some were merely wanderers, whom kind people helped along the way with food or alms (money or other donations). Many pilgrims wore broad-brimmed hats and rough cloaks. Often they carried a staff (walking stick) and scrip (pouch), which were blessed by the priest before they made their pilgrimage. If a pilgrim visited Jerusalem, he was called a "palmer," because of the piece of palm in his hat.

Every year thousands of Jews make a pilgrimage at Passover to the Temple of Jerusalem. Once during his life, every Muslim tries to visit Mecca, the birthplace of Muhammad. Christian pilgrims go to such places as Rome, the Holy Land, and Canterbury (England). Hindus in India and Buddhists in China also make annual pilgrimages to holy places in their part of the world.

The PILGRIMS

In American history, the Pilgrims were the groups of English men and women who founded in 1620 Plymouth Colony in Massachusetts. The Pilgrims included members of a sect of PURITANS called Separatists, because they had broken away from the Church of England.

The Separatists had been persecuted in England and had fled to the city of Leiden in Holland. But their leaders decided to seek homes in America, where they could practice their religion in peace.

In 1620, they were among the 102 Pilgrim settlers who set sail on the MAYFLOWER to start a permanent colony in America. The voyage was very stormy, and many died of illness. In November, the Pilgrims finally landed on Cape Cod, far north of their original destination of Virginia. They then proceeded to the mainland, where they founded the settlement of Plymouth. John Carver was elected the Pilgrims' first governor and led them through the first winter, when cold, hunger, and illness killed half of the Pilgrims.

Carver made peace with the INDIANS, who later taught the settlers how to grow corn, squash, and other crops. Carver died, however, before the first plentiful autumn harvest. William Bradford, who succeeded Carver as governor, invited the Indians to a great feast, called the first THANKSGIVING. The Pilgrims had established a colony that later grew into a new nation—the U.S.A. SEE ALSO: MAYFLOWER.

PIN

Pins have been used for many thousands of years. They are useful for fastening pieces of cloth together for a short while, and in ancient times they were used in the way that we would use buttons today.

Early pins were very plain, being nothing more than thorns and small bones. But later they were often very decorative. Egyptian pins with golden heads have been found in tombs. The Greeks and Romans used *brooches*, rather like modern safety pins, to hold their clothing together when it was being worn. These brooches were highly decorated. The rich in the Middle Ages had pins of ivory, silver, and gold with decorative heads.

The ordinary modern pin is a sharp piece of stiff wire with a small, plain head. Wire has been used for pins since the 15th century, but pins today are made by machinery invented in the last 150 years. This machinery makes the wire, gives it points and heads, polishes the pins, and packs them ready for use.

early bone pins

Ancient Greek fibula

Greek hairpins

Ivory hairpin (Roman)

Anglo-Saxon brooches

PINE

Pine is a cone-bearing evergreen closely related to the larch, spruce, and FIR. This hardy tree is widely distributed from the Arctic Circle to tropical mountain slopes. Because it is able to thrive in poor, sandy soil where no other trees can grow, it is often planted on shifting sand dunes where the roots help bind the soil together.

The very slender leaves are known as pine needles. They grow together in clusters of 2 to 5 and are held together by little papery sheaths. The cones hang downwards. The soft wood makes excellent lumber for the interiors of houses and for furniture. The trees also produce RESIN, TAR, pitch, and TURPENTINE. SEE ALSO: CONIFERS, EVERGREEN.

PINEAPPLE

The pineapple is a tropical plant that grows an edible, juicy fruit. The fruit, also called the pineapple, looks like a large pine cone surrounded by a crown of broad, spiny leaves; hence, its name. The fruit has a hard, rough, and reddish skin and a yellow and sweet edible part inside. Pineapples are grown in large numbers in Hawaii, the West Indies, Spain, and North Africa.

PIRATES

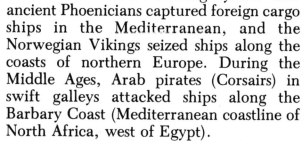

Pirates are robbers on the high seas. They have raided shipping ever since man started trading by sea. The ancient Phoenicians captured foreign cargo ships in the Mediterranean, and the Norwegian Vikings seized ships along the coasts of northern Europe. During the Middle Ages, Arab pirates (Corsairs) in swift galleys attacked ships along the Barbary Coast (Mediterranean coastline of North Africa, west of Egypt).

Often English, French, and Italian seamen became pirates when their countries were at war. Merchant vessels were always threatened by mutinies, when the sailors took over the ships and turned into pirates.

Piracy was greatest from the 16th to 18th century. Large Spanish treasure *galleons* (ships), loaded with gold, silver, and other riches from the New World, attracted pirates from many countries. SIR FRANCIS DRAKE, the Englishman, raided many foreign ships on the Spanish Main (West Indies), seizing goods with the full approval of the English queen. Later, pirates (also called buccaneers) such as CAPTAIN KIDD, BLACKBEARD and Morgan had hide-outs in the West Indies and Madagascar (in the Indian Ocean) from which they preyed on many merchant ships.

Gradually piracy became unprofitable because of strong navies, armed merchant ships, and better communications between ships. It still exists, however, in some Far Eastern waters.

PISA

The Italian city of Pisa was once a great commercial and artistic center, rivaling VENICE, Genoa, and Florence.

Visitors come to Pisa to see several famous buildings. The great cathedral, built in the 11th century and enlarged in the 12th century, is crowned by a large cupola. Its interior has fine sculptures, tombs, and paintings. Nearby is the famous Leaning Tower of Pisa, built from the 12th to the 14th century. It is a white marble campanile, or bell tower, 179 feet (55 m) high. After the first three of the Tower's eight galleries had been built, it started to tilt, and it now leans about 16.5 feet (5 m) from the perpendicular.

Francisco PIZARRO (1476?–1541)

In 1510, Francisco Pizarro sailed with other Spanish adventurers to America. For a while he settled in what is now Panama, but returned to Spain in 1528. Four years later, Pizarro led an expedition back to Panama and soon set out to find the gold in South America.

Landing on the coast of Peru, he and his men marched inland and killed the leader of the INCAS, Atahualpa. They then captured Cuzco, the capital city of the Incas. In 1535, Pizarro built the present capital of Peru, Lima. However, a quarrel began between Pizarro and Almagro, another Spanish conquerer in South America. It concerned the limits of the conquered territories. In 1538, Almagro was defeated in battle and put to death. Later, friends of Almagro plotted against Pizarro and killed him in his palace in Lima. SEE ALSO: INCAS.

PLANETS

Planets are heavenly bodies moving about the SUN or other stars. The word *planet* comes from a Greek word meaning "wanderer."

Nine planets move about the sun, each in its own path or *orbit*. Only 6 of these planets were known in ancient times: Mercury, Venus, Earth, Mars, Jupiter, and Saturn. Uranus was discovered in 1781; Neptune, in 1846. Pluto, a great distance from Neptune, was only discovered in 1930.

Since the planets vary greatly in their distances from the sun, the lengths of the various orbits and the times to complete one trip about the sun vary considerably. The sizes of the planets also vary tremendously. Mercury is very small; Venus and Earth are about the same size; Mars and Pluto are smaller than Earth; but Jupiter is 1300 times and and Saturn is 763 times larger than

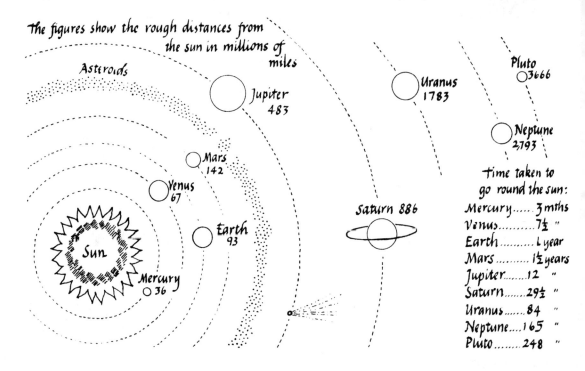

The figures show the rough distances from the sun in millions of miles

Asteroids

Jupiter 483

Uranus 1783

Pluto 3666

Neptune 2,793

Mars 142

Venus 67

Earth 93

Saturn 886

Sun

Mercury 36

time taken to go round the sun:
Mercury...... 3 mths
Venus...........7½ "
Earth ....1 year
Mars ....1½ years
Jupiter.......12 "
Saturn.......29½ "
Uranus.......84 "
Neptune.....165 "
Pluto........248 "

Earth. Unmanned rockets and space probes launched by the United States and Russia have investigated both Mars and Venus.

Between Mars and Jupiter is a belt of hundreds of small planets called planetoids or asteriods. The planets, their moons, COMETS, and METEORS are all part of the sun's family, the SOLAR SYSTEM. SEE ALSO: INDIVIDUAL PLANETS.

PLANTS

Without plants we could not survive, since even the animals that provide our meat live on plants or plant-eating animals. Plants also supply us with paper, medicines, furniture, clothes, coal, and plastics.

All living things are either plants or animals. The differences between plants and animals are not always that obvious. However, most plants cannot move about to obtain their food but instead get their nourishment through their leaves and roots.

Primrose

Section through leaf (magnified)

The roots absorb moisture and minerals from the soil, and the leaves take in carbon dioxide from the air through tiny openings on the undersides of the leaves. In the leaves are thousands of cells containing green coloring matter called *chlorophyl*. All green plants manufacture their own food. For this process, called *photosynthesis*, to occur, carbon dioxide, sunlight, water, and chlorophyl must be present.

In winter, many plants shed their leaves and live on food in the form of starches and sugars stored in their stems or roots. Maple sap is the stored food of the maple tree and can be boiled down to form delicious maple syrup.

Plants are found everywhere. CACTI inhabit the desert; LICHENS and mosses live in cold, rocky regions; MUSHROOMS AND TOADSTOOLS, in dim caves; waterlilies and watercress, in fresh water; and seaweed, in salt water.

The tallest plant is the California redwood, which can grow more than 350 feet (108.5 m) tall. The smallest plants are the microscopic bacteria. All plants struggle to reproduce their own kind, usually by means of SEEDS and spores, but sometimes by sending out runners, like the strawberry, or by forming little BULBS from the old bulb.

The study of plants is the science of BOTANY. SEE ALSO: BULB, LEAVES, ROOTS, SEEDS.

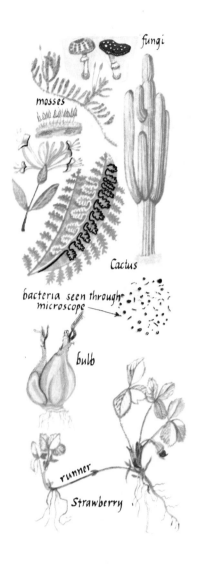

PLASTICS

Plastics is the name for various synthetic or natural organic materials that can be shaped through the use of heat or pressure or both. The word *plastic* comes from a Greek word meaning "moldable." Plastics are molded when soft and then hardened. Some plastics can again be softened by heat and remolded; others can not. Plastics include many kinds of resins, cellulose derivatives, polymers, and proteins, mixed with substances like dyes, fillers, plasticizers, and solvents.

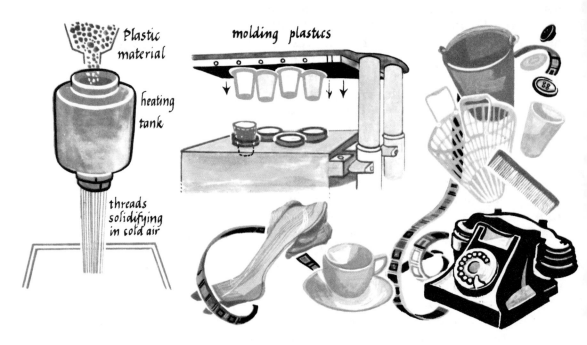

During the manufacturing of plastics, they are, at some stage, in a liquid form. This hot, plastic liquid can then be molded into many different items, such as buttons, combs, drinking cups, plates, toys, records, telephones, electrical equipment, and packaging material. In order to make tubes or threads, the hot liquid is forced through a special nozzle or group of holes, from which the molten plastic flows in continuous form. It is then cooled and later cut into certain lengths or coiled onto reels.

Celluloid, invented in 1869, was the first important synthetic plastic. It was widely used as a substitute for ivory, amber, bone, tortoise shell, hard rubber, and glass. However, not until the invention of *bakelite* in 1909 did plastics come into modern industrial use. Bakelite is a hard, infusible plastic, made from such materials as cotton, asbestos fibers, and wood pulp. Other plastics were soon discovered. *Rayon* was made from wood pulp treated with various chemicals. Thin, fine threads of rayon were woven into fabric. *Nylon*, a by-product of coal, was made from coal, air, and water. Today, nylon is probably the best known plastic used in hosiery, thread, fabrics, netting, rope, gears, and bearings.

New uses for plastics are continually being discovered. Lenses for eyeglasses, false teeth, musical instruments, building panels, automobile parts, and radio and TV housings are often made of plastic. Plastic products are generally cheaper, easier to clean, more colorful, and lightweight.

PLATEAU

A plateu is a stretch of flat land high above sea level. Because a plateau looks somewhat like the top of a great, high table, it is often referred to as "tableland." Plateaus are sometimes bordered by mountains and gouged with valleys and canyons. The Colorado River has gouged the GRAND CANYON in the Colorado plateau of the southwestern United States.

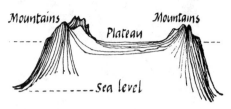

Australia is mainly an enormous plateau rising from the ocean floor of the Pacific. In South America, large regions in Ecuador, Peru, and Bolivia are notable plateaus, all situated in the Andes Mountains. The world's highest plateau is Tibet, a country north of the Himalayas. Called the "roof of the world," Tibet has an average elevation of about 16,000 feet (4960 m).

PLATINUM

When the Spanish explorers were conquering Peru, they discovered little nuggets of a gray metal while panning for gold. They did not realize these were rarer and more precious than gold. About two centuries later, this gray metal was given the name "platinum," which comes from the Spanish word, *platina*, meaning "little silver." Since it is usually found with gold, miners call it "white gold." This ELEMENT is generally found in small grains mixed with other precious rare metals, such as palladium, osmium, and iridium.

Sometimes called "the king of metals," platinum is easy to work. It is rust- and acid-proof, and it is able to withstand tremendous temperatures. It is also capable of being drawn into a tough wire so fine that 25,000 strands equal the thickness of a human hair. Platinum is widely used in making expensive jewelry and special laboratory and surgical equipment.

The largest amounts of platinum are found in Canada, the Soviet Union, South Africa, and Colombia, in South America.

PLATO (427?–347 B.C.)

Plato was a great Greek PHILOSOPHER. He was born in Athens, Greece, and was very good at sports as a young man. At 20 Plato became a pupil of SOCRATES, who influenced him very deeply.

After spending time in other lands such as Egypt and Italy, Plato returned to Athens in 387 B.C. and founded a school called the Academy. Here Plato gave famous lectures on philosophy, teaching the importance of ideas, deep thought, and beauty. One of Plato's greatest pupils was ARISTOTLE, another Greek philosopher.

Plato wrote down his ideas on politics, law, science, education, and art. They were mainly in the form of *dialogues*, or discussions, between Socrates and one or more friends. One of his dialogues was *The Republic*, a book which describes an ideal, or perfect, country whose citizens are educated to be good and just.

PLOW

The farmer cannot expect much of a crop if he scatters seeds on the bare ground. He must turn up the soil and bury his seeds. The earliest farmers used digging sticks and hoes to do this, working on their fields bit by bit. But some farmer thought of a better idea, that of hitching a pointed tool to an animal or a man that would drag it along, making a long furrow in the process. This was the first plow.

The ancient Romans used a light plow with an iron *share*, a blade that divided the soil. In some cases the plow also had a *colter*, a blade that ran in front of the share to make the first cut. Such light plows were useful in the Mediterranean countries where the soil was light. To deal with the heavy soils of northern Europe, a wheeled plow was invented. The wheel kept the plow from digging too deeply into the soil. At some point, too, other improvements were added. By the end of the 18th century, plows had *mold-boards*. The colter would make the first cut in the soil, the share would widen the cut, and the moldboard, coming after the share, would turn the soil to one side. Because the moldboard

Deer's antler used as hoe by early man

Ancient Egyptian hoeing

Handles fixed and then yoked to oxen

Roman Plow

beam

colter

moldboard

colter

Saxon plow with moldboard

Wheeled plow (14th century)

single furrow
horse plow

colter

moldboard

share

normal
share
(fits on
moldboard
here)

tended to push the plow out of a straight line when it thrust against the soil, a plate called a *landside* was put next to it. This braced the plow against the side of the furrow that was not receiving soil from the moldboard.

Early plows were mostly of wood with cutting parts of iron. Dirt tended to cling to the iron and to break the plow, and when the Midwest was settled its very heavy soils called for yet a new kind of plow. John Deere, in the middle of the 19th century, solved the problem by making a share and moldboard from a single piece of cast steel. The steel did not hold the dirt as iron did, and the plow went easily through the soil.

Today there are many kinds of plows, almost always pulled by tractors. The farmer can choose the type best suited to the soil on his property. Some plows are

made in the form of a row of sharp-edged disks that take the place of the old share and moldboard. Some are shovel-like, or have knives that turn in and out of the soil. Many plows not only turn up the soil but plant the seeds in it.

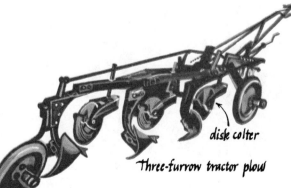

disk colter

Three-furrow tractor plow

657

PLUM

The plum is related to the rose family. It is a widely cultivated fruit of temperate countries. It is a close relative of the PEACH but has a smooth skin and an unwrinkled pit. Inside the pit is a single seed.

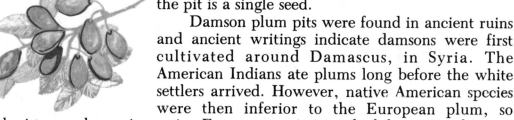

Damson plum pits were found in ancient ruins and ancient writings indicate damsons were first cultivated around Damascus, in Syria. The American Indians ate plums long before the white settlers arrived. However, native American species were then inferior to the European plum, so colonists soon began importing European varieties, which have since become dominant commercially in the United States.

Prunes are dried plums from varieties having a high sugar content. SEE ALSO: PRUNES.

PLUTO

In Roman mythology, Pluto was the god of the underworld. After the defeat of the Titans, Jupiter and his brothers Neptune and Pluto divided up the universe. Pluto received the dreary Kingdom of the Dead, the underworld, where he ruled with his queen, Proserpina (also called Persephone in Greek).

Pluto is also the name for the PLANET in our SOLAR SYSTEM that is ninth from the sun. It takes about 248 years for Pluto to make one complete orbit around the sun. In 1930, this planet was discovered by Clyde Tombaugh at Lowell Observatory in Arizona. Photographic plates showed Pluto's existence and location. SEE ALSO: PLANETS, SOLAR SYSTEM.

POCAHONTAS (1595?–1617)

Pocahontas was the favorite daughter of Powhatan, chief of the Chickahominy Indians in Virginia. Her real name was Matoaka; Pocahontas, meaning "playful one," was her nickname.

According to legend, Pocahontas saved the life of CAPTAIN JOHN SMITH when he was captured by the Indians. In 1613, the colonists captured her, holding her as a hostage for English prisoners in the hands of Powhatan. At JAMESTOWN, Pocahontas was converted to

Christianity and baptized as "Rebecca." John Rolfe, a colonial settler, fell in love with her and married her in 1614. Their marriage brought peace with the Indians.

Pocahontas went with her husband to England in 1616. There she was treated as a princess and met the king and queen. As she prepared to return to her homeland, Pocahontas fell ill and died of smallpox at Gravesend, England. She bore one son, Thomas Rolfe, who later came to Virginia and became quite rich. SEE ALSO: SMITH, CAPTAIN JOHN.

POETRY

Prose, our usual way of talking, is like a machine built to do a certain job. If a machine is well designed, every part works well with every other part, and there are no more parts than are necessary for the job the machine is designed to do. In good prose, every word, sentence, and paragraph works well with the others to convey information, opinions, or feelings to the listener or reader.

Most prose, like most machinery, is valuable only for the work it does. Just as a machine may be ugly, so a good prose sentence may be boring to read and yet do its job well. But imagine a machine that not only does a very good job but that is beautiful to watch as it works. Imagine that each part is handsomely made, and that the parts, as they move together, form a lovely sight. That is like poetry. In poetry, the thing that the poet is saying and the way in which he says it are both important to the whole effect the poem has.

Poetry is built up of *verses*, which are lines put separately on a page. A verse is usually different from a sentence. A sentence in a poem, for instance, may be written in two-and-a-half verses. The purpose of a verse is to guide the person who reads the poem aloud; at the end of one verse, he pauses briefly before reading the next. Some poets, like E. E. Cummings, have very special ways of putting their words on paper, partly as a guide to special ways of reading their poems aloud, partly because the very look of the poem helps it to say what the poet wants it to.

Much poetry is written in *rhyme*. That is, the sound at the end of one verse is echoed in other verses here and there so as to make a pattern throughout the poem. Ancient poets did not use rhyme, and many modern poets do not, but most of the poems we know are written in rhyme.

Most poetry is written in *meter*. That is, certain parts of each verse are more heavily accented than others when they are being read. These accents also form patterns that help give a form to the poem.

In this verse,

> "The time has come," the Walrus said,
> "To talk of many things:
> Of shoes—and ships—and sealing wax—
> Of cabbages—and kings—
> And why the sea is boiling hot—
> And whether pigs have wings."

659

the second, fourth, and sixth verses rhyme, while the first, third, and fifth do not. The meter is very simple; every other syllable is stressed:

"The *time* has *come*," the *Wal*rus *said*, so that the poem has a sound all its own, very different from that of prose. And the poem, Lewis Carroll's "The Walrus and the Carpenter," is in fact one that many people remember. This particular *stanza* (group of verses that join with other such groups to make a long poem) is especially well known, because it is a delightful piece of nonsense.

POISONS

Many common and helpful substances may also be very poisonous when improperly or carelessly used. Some acids, bleaches, disinfectants, and pills found in every household may cause serious, permanent injury or even death, if they are accidentally swallowed.

Deadly Nightshade

Yew berries

Bryony

Foxglove

Wild Arum

Improperly canned foods, such as meat, shellfish, and soup, can produce a deadly food poisoning known as *botulism*. All overdoses of drugs are poisonous to a person's system. Valuable drugs, such as arsenic, strychnine, and atropine (made from the belladonna plant and called *Deadly Nightshade*) are extremely dangerous. Common aspirin can kill a person if taken in too large amounts.

Also, it is very foolish to eat unfamiliar fungi, berries, seeds, and leaves. There are many poisonous varieties growing in the woods, in gardens, and near houses.

POLAND

Poland is a country in north central Europe, bordering on the Baltic Sea in the north. It is about the size of New Mexico and has almost 34.7 million people.

In the past centuries, wars with Russia, Germany, and other powerful neighbors resulted in continual changes in Poland's borders. The country has, at different times, been conquered, divided, and even removed from the map of Europe.

During World War II, Poland suffered terribly from invasion and occupation by Germany and Russia. Afterward, the Russians set up a Communist regime there, which has since ruled the country.

Its terrain is mostly fertile lowlands, with forests that yield good timber. In southern Poland, there are mountains that have rich deposits of coal, iron, and other minerals. Besides growing potatoes, sugar beets, and grains, the people work in factories owned by the state, making machinery, textiles, and chemicals. The largest cities are Warsaw, the capital, Lodz, Cracow, and Poznan.

POLICE

Police are uniformed men and women whose job is to protect the lives and property of people in a community. They enforce laws, catch criminals, and in general try to keep everything orderly.

Since ancient times, some kind of police protection has usually developed wherever people have lived together in groups. Roman emperors sometimes had a special police force to keep order in Rome. CHARLEMAGNE organized a police force when he came to power in France in A.D. 800. In England during the Middle Ages, families grouped together and appointed a leader and protector, called a sheriff. Each sheriff had an area that he watched over; he could also organize the men in that area into a police force whenever necessary.

The sheriff system was brought to the United States by the English colonists. In 1838, Boston had a small police force that worked in the daytime and was paid. Seven years later, New York City formed a large force that was on duty 24 hours a day.

Today, small towns have police departments of two, twelve, or twenty men and women. Large cities may have several thousand policemen or women. The head of a police department is known as the police chief. Below him are inspectors, captains, lieutenants, sergeants, and patrolmen.

The police departments in big cities have many separate divisions for different kinds of police work. There may be a traffic division for processing traffic tickets, a crime laboratory for studying evidence, and a detectives' bureau for investigating criminal suspects.

If a person wishes to become a policeman or woman, he must have a high school diploma (sometimes a college degree), must pass a civil service examination, and must have no criminal record. He then goes through rigorous training, learning what the laws are, how to use many weapons, and how to administer first aid. SEE ALSO: DETECTIVE.

POLITICAL PARTY

A political party is an organization of people that works to elect officials to run the government. A party writes down its viewpoints, goals, and programs of action in what is called a party *platform*, which may differ from that of another party or group of people. Thus, a political party usually competes with other political parties in furthering its ideas and programs. Political parties nominate candidates who stand for their programs and who will work for them if elected to office. These candidates try to persuade the people to vote for them, often giving speeches and participating in debates. On election day, the people will choose that candidate or candidates whose ideas and programs they are told or convinced will best serve them.

People in the United States have found that DEMOCRACY operates effectively with competing political parties. The public will and interests must always be kept in mind if the candidates of the various political parties are to be elected to office and to remain in control of the government.

In the U.S. today, there are two major political parties—the Democrats and the Republicans. Some smaller parties do exist that stand for other viewpoints. People can run for office as an unaffiliated (independent) candidate if no party supports them.

The two-party system also exists in Canada, New Zealand, and Australia. Some countries like Great Britain, France, Italy, and Sweden have several major parties. Russia, China, and some countries in Africa and Latin America have only one political party.

POLLUTION

Pollution is the contamination or dirtying of the Earth's air, soil, or water with harmful substances (*pollutants*) by an individual or a corporation (*polluters*). Pollutants—gases, liquids, and solids—are introduced into the environment, making it unfit for the various purposes for which it was normally intended.

The definition of pollution has been broadened to include also noise pollution, unsightliness caused by litter, and other nuisances and annoyances that can cause people to become emotionally, mentally, or physically

impaired. For example, workers subjected to long periods of hearing loud, high-pitched sounds may develop headaches, deafness, nervous tension, fatigue, poor concentration, ulcers, and other problems.

Overexposure to radiation can have an influence on a woman's ability to have healthy babies and can produce radiation burns and various forms of cancer, all without a person feeling the damaging rays. Harmful radioactive particles resulting from nuclear explosions encircle the Earth. X-ray technicians, nuclear power plant workers, and all those dealing with radioactivity need to be on guard with special instruments that detect levels of radiation exposure.

Industrial smokestacks give off *coal* and coke dust and choke the air with unhealthy gases unfit to breathe. Heavy smog (*smoke* and *fog*) in industrial cities is particularly harmful to those with lung, heart, and allergy conditions. Often those seriously ill with these health problems die when exposed to prolonged, severe smog pollution. The sulfur dioxide given off in burning most fuels becomes sulfur trioxide when exposed to the ultraviolet rays of sunlight. This then combines with the water vapor of the air to produce dilute sulfuric acid in the atmosphere. Such air produces effects ranging from runs in nylon stockings to stinging eyes and skin to the corrosion of marble statues.

Pollution of water and soil by sewage, industrial wastes, sprays, or garbage can cause not only disease but also the loss of wildlife, fish, and recreational areas.

POMPEII

Pompeii was an ancient town in southern Italy, lying beside the Bay of Naples. In A.D. 79, Mount Vesuvius, a volcano several miles to the north, suddenly erupted and poured out black, hot ashes. Pompeii and the nearby towns of Herculaneum and Stabiae were completely buried under cinders and ashes. At least 2000 people died. The disaster changed the countryside so much that no one knew where Pompeii lay.

In 1748, Italian peasants uncovered a buried wall, and this led to the total excavation of Pompeii. Archeologists found people and animals covered with ashes that had dried around them.

Today, visitors can walk through the streets and footpaths and into the public buildings, shops, and private houses of ancient Pompeii. They can read advertisements on walls and view rare and beautiful examples of Roman art. The way of life in Roman times was magnificently preserved under the layer of volcanic ashes.

Juan PONCE DE LEÓN (1460?–1521)

Juan Ponce de León served in the Spanish army and accompanied COLUMBUS on the second voyage to America in 1493. He helped conquer Higuey (now the Dominican Republic) and was made governor there. Hearing about gold on Boriquén (now called PUERTO RICO), Ponce de Léon conquered the island in 1508.

Later, the Carib Indians told him about a wonderfully rich island called Bimini which had a legendary Fountain of Youth—waters that would keep one young forever. In 1513, Ponce de Léon set sail from Puerto Rico and landed near what is now St. Augustine, Florida. He claimed the land for Spain and named it "Florida." He explored the coastal regions and then returned to Puerto Rico.

In 1521, Ponce de León returned to Florida—probably near what is now Tampa Bay—with the hope of colonizing it. However, his expedition was attacked by fierce Indians, and Ponce de León was wounded by an arrow. The expedition immediately sailed to Cuba, where Ponce de León died.

PONY EXPRESS

In 1860 and 1861, the mail was carried regularly from St. Joseph, Missouri, to Sacramento, California, by Pony Express. This route covered about 2000 miles (3220 km), much of it through hostile Indian territory. Outlaws, storms, and floods were also a threat to the riders of the Pony Express.

This private overland mail system was the idea of William Gwin, a U.S. Senator from California. A freight company was formed, charging five dollars for each half ounce of mail (this was later reduced to one dollar). Relay stations, where the riders changed ponies, were about 10 to 15 miles (16–24 km) apart. The first trip across the country took ten and a half days; later trips

took only 8 to 10 days. The fastest time ever made was 7 days and 17 hours—when copies of President Lincoln's inaugural address were delivered in Sacramento in 1861. Some of the great, tough riders of the Pony Express were WILD BILL HICKOK and BUFFALO BILL. The Pony Express stopped after coast-to-coast telegraph service was established in October, 1861.

POPE

The Pope is the bishop of Rome and the head of the Roman CATHOLIC CHURCH. Catholics regard him as having the same supreme power over Church affairs that Jesus gave to Peter. Whatever he says about religious matters must be believed by all Catholics.

He is advised by the *cardinals*, a group of bishops who form part of the Curia, the Pope's governmental organization. A pope is elected for life by the cardinals, and when new cardinals are to be chosen it is the Pope who chooses them. He is also supposed to be advised by all the BISHOPS of the Church, and some people believe that he has no right to say anything on religion unless the bishops agree with what he says. SEE ALSO: CATHOLIC CHURCH.

POPULATION

The total number of people in a town, city, country, or any area is known as its population. Most countries take a *census* every ten years—that is, they count the number of people living there.

One of the most startling facts of the modern world is the rapid increase in world population during the last one hundred years. The world's population grew very slowly until about 1850, when it finally reached one billion people. It then took only 80 years more for the population to grow to two billion people. Today, there are more than four billion inhabitants in the world. Scientists predict that the population will double again—if the present rate of growth remains unchanged—by the year 2000.

This rapid population increase can be attributed to fewer diseases and plagues, more food and better houses, so that people are living longer and fewer babies are dying. However, many scientists are worried that eventually there will not be enough food for everybody.

This population explosion has caused many people to support an idea called Zero Population Growth (ZPG). They want parents to have no more than two children, who would simply replace their parents when they die. Thus, the population would remain the same.

The annual rate of population increase is greatest in Africa, Asia, and Latin America. The largest growth is reported from Central America, where the birthrate is about 45 per 1000, and the death rate is about 10 per 1000.

Population also changes because of migration—the moving of people from one place to another. In the United States, a recent census shows that many people are moving to the South and Southwest. Also, farming areas in the Midwest are losing population and large cities have fewer inhabitants. But suburban areas are continually growing.

PORPOISE

Porpoises are MAMMALS belonging to the same family as WHALES and DOLPHINS. The porpoise is found in the northern Atlantic and Pacific Oceans, but it prefers the waters of inlets and river estuaries instead of the open sea.

They are about 6 feet (1.9m) long and look like small black whales, with a blowhole between their eyes. Great numbers of porpoises gather in *schools* to frolic and feed upon salmon, mackerel, and herring.

PORTRAIT

A portrait is a picture of a person or of a group of persons such as a family. Every portraitist gets a good likeness of his *subject*, the person he is doing a picture of, so that the subject is recognized by people who know him. But a good portraitist will also tell you what kind of person the subject is. The expression of the face will tell you that the subject is stubborn or kindhearted. If he is holding the plan of a building in hand, it may show that he is an architect. If you see a cannon in the background, it hints that the subject is an army man, and if he is in uniform you may be able to see just what kind of army man he is. Often a portrait is "posed," so that the subject stands still in a way that he would not usually, but some portraits show people acting as they do in everyday life.

Most portraits are paintings, but photographers also make portraits. Some have become very famous, for they capture a momentary look on the subjects' faces that shows their personalities very well.

PORTUGAL

Portugal is a country bordered by SPAIN on the north and east and by the Atlantic Ocean on the west and south. The Azores and Madeira Islands also belong to Portugal.

Lisbon, the capital, lies at the mouth of the Tagus River and has one of the finest harbors in the world. Near Lisbon is the famous beach resort of Estoril.

Much of Portugal is mountainous, with slopes thickly covered with pine, chestnut, oak, and cork trees. The country leads the world in cork production. In fertile valleys cut by rivers, corn, olives, and oranges are cultivated, as well

as sweet black grapes from which delicious port wine is made. Oporto, Portugal's second largest city, exports much port wine, to which the city gave its name.

Most of the 9.7 million Portuguese descended from the Lusitanians, Romans, and Arabs, who successively ruled the land. In 1185, Portugal became an independent kingdom and later was a great sea power with a vast empire. Today, it is rather poor, with some political and economic problems.

POSTAL SERVICE

The postal service is an arrangement made by a government for the exchange of letters, periodicals, and packages—the mail. Postal service first began as a messenger service for kings and lords. Messengers on foot or on horseback were used by the ancient Persians, Greeks, and Romans. Offices or inns were set up along the roads so that messengers could rest and maybe relay their letters to another messenger. These spots along the various routes were identified by special posts, from which comes our term "post office." Many private systems for conveying the mails operated during and after the Middle Ages. In the 1600s, governments took over the job.

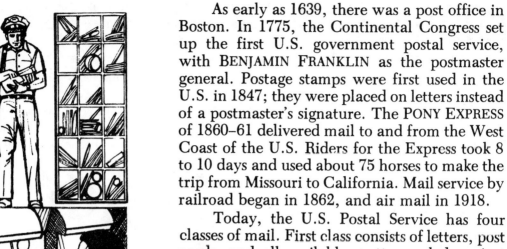

As early as 1639, there was a post office in Boston. In 1775, the Continental Congress set up the first U.S. government postal service, with BENJAMIN FRANKLIN as the postmaster general. Postage stamps were first used in the U.S. in 1847; they were placed on letters instead of a postmaster's signature. The PONY EXPRESS of 1860–61 delivered mail to and from the West Coast of the U.S. Riders for the Express took 8 to 10 days and used about 75 horses to make the trip from Missouri to California. Mail service by railroad began in 1862, and air mail in 1918.

Today, the U.S. Postal Service has four classes of mail. First class consists of letters, post cards, and all mailable matter sealed against inspection. Second class includes magazines and newspapers. Third class includes printed material and merchandise not over 16 ounces (.45 kg). Fourth class (called also parcel post) is for packages exceeding 16 ounces. The class of mail, the weight, and the distance the item is sent determine the cost of mailing. All mail should have a zip code number, which helps post office workers sort letters and packages and speed up their delivery.

The Universal Postal Union, an agency of the UNITED NATIONS, regulates the mail between countries.

POTATO

Native to the Peruvian Andes, the potato arrived in Europe in the 1500s with the returning Spanish explorers. Since then, its cultivation has spread rapidly throughout the temperate regions of the world, arriving in New England with Irish immigrants in 1719.

Potatoes are a particularly valuable crop because they produce a high yield in a small area.

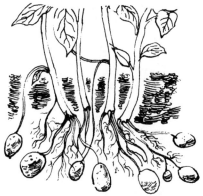

The potato is considered to be the most important vegetable in America and Europe. Because more than 75 percent of the dehydrated weight of a potato is carbohydrate, the potato is an important high energy food and a valuable source of alcohol, adhesives, potato meal, flour, and feed for livestock.

The potato is actually a swollen underground stem, called a tuber. Here in the tuber, food is stored by the plant. Potatoes are grown from "seed potatoes" that have "eyes" or buds. Since this method eventually reduces the quality of the new plants, new varieties are grown from the seed by careful cross pollination and selection.

Idaho and Maine are the two states in the U.S. most famous for their potatoes. Germany, Poland, and Russia grow large quantities of potatoes.

POULTRY

The term *poultry* includes chickens, ducks, geese, and turkeys. However, poultry farming usually refers to raising chickens for meat and for eggs.

Chicks are either hatched by a broody hen or are purchased from a hatchery as "day olds" and raised in an artificial "brooder." At the age of 6 weeks, the chicks are moved into a larger house with a run (an enclosure that allows the birds some freedom to run around). Male birds are called cockerels

until they are a year old and then called cocks or roosters. A capon is a castrated cockerel. Pullets are young female birds. When a pullet becomes a year old, it is called a hen. Hens need careful attention with plenty of fresh air, clean water, and a balanced diet, including greenstuff and grit. At the age of 5 to 7 months, they begin to lay eggs, producing 150-200 a year, though a good layer improves the second year. SEE ALSO: FOWLS.

PRAGUE

Prague is the capital and largest city of CZECHOSLOVAKIA. It is on the Moldau River, about 150 miles (242 km) from Vienna, Austria. It is an old city with many fine Gothic buildings, palaces, and churches. Thirteen bridges, including the famous Charles Bridge built in 1357, span the river which separates the scenic Old Town from the modern.

Prague was occupied by the Germans from 1939 to 1945, when American and Russian troops with help from the citizens liberated the city. SEE ALSO: CZECHOSLOVAKIA.

*Old Town Square
and Tyn Church*

PRAIRIE

The settlers heading westward in the 1800s went over mountains and rivers and through hundreds of miles of forests. When they came to the Mississippi valley, they were surprised to come upon vast stretches of flat, treeless grassland as far as the eye could see. This extensive grassland or plain came to be called prairie. In French, the word *prairie* means "meadow."

Seeing no trees, the pioneers at first thought the land must have poor soil. Later, they discovered the soil was rich. Today, grain-producing farms and cattle ranches cover the prairie. Most of Illinois, Indiana, Iowa, Missouri, Wisconsin, Ohio, Minnesota, Michigan, Kansas, Oklahoma, Texas, Nebraska, and western North and South Dakota are prairie lands.

In South America, Argentina's vast grassland is called the *pampas*. In the Soviet Union, the higher elevated prairie land is called the *steppes*. Three of Canada's provinces are known as prairie provinces.

Until John Deere invented his famous steel plow in 1837, the pioneers had great difficulty breaking through the dense sod (tough grassy soil) with their wooden and iron plows. The early settlers were thus called "sodbusters." They used chunks of sod to make their huts because lumber was so scarce. When the railroads finally ran across the prairies, the people were finally able to send their produce to market and get lumber and other necessities not available otherwise.

By the 1930s, the prairies had become overgrazed range lands and powder dry wheat fields. Years of drought and poor farming methods had turned the area into what was called the "Dust Bowl." This natural disaster was one of the major reasons for the establishment of our country's present policy of CONSERVATION.

PRAWNS

Prawns are CRUSTACEANS that look like shrimp. They differ from shrimp in being larger and having a sharp spine projecting out from the top of the head. They are pale in color and turn bright pink when boiled. Many live in shallow coastal waters, but some live at great depths in the open sea. Most prawns scavenge for dead plants and animals. Many fish, as well as people, find prawns good to eat. SEE ALSO: CRUSTACEANS.

PRESIDENCY

The President of the United States is the highest officer in the government. He or she is elected to a four-year term and cannot serve more than two terms. A candidate for the presidency must be a native-born citizen, at least 35 years old, and a resident of the U.S. for 14 years before running for the office.

The CONSTITUTION states that the President is head of the executive branch of government, which consists of his CABINET and many independent agencies. He is commander in chief of the nation's armed forces and can make treaties with foreign countries. He can recommend new legislation to CONGRESS, as well as veto (overrule) legislation passed by Congress.

The President has great economic power, regulating much money through the Federal Reserve System and interstate commerce through the Interstate Commerce Commission. Also, he annually presents a national budget to Congress and makes a report on the State of the Union. He appoints the justices of the SUPREME COURT. If the President dies or leaves office before the end of his term, the VICE PRESIDENT of the U.S. becomes President.

PRIME MINISTER

Countries that are governed by legislative assemblies or parliaments usually have a group of important government officials. Often the head of these officials is the prime minister, or premier.

The term "prime minister" was first used in Great Britain, where Sir Robert Walpole became the first prime minister in 1721. Today, the prime minister is the leader of the majority party in the House of Commons, in PARLIAMENT. He or she picks a special council, or *cabinet*, of ministers, who give him advice. If more than half of the House of Commons votes against the prime minister, he must resign or call for a new election, or do both.

Countries such as Canada, Australia, and India—all once belonging to Great Britain—have parliamentary governments headed by a prime minister. Countries such as Italy, France, and Spain have similar governments and have a chief minister called a premier.

PRINCE EDWARD ISLAND

Prince Edward Island is the smallest province in CANADA. It lies in the Gulf of St. Lawrence, separated on the south from NOVA SCOTIA and NEW BRUNSWICK by the Northumberland Strait. It has many bays, inlets, red sandstone cliffs, and white sandy beaches. On the south shore is Charlottetown, the capital and largest city. About 120,000 people live on the island.

With fertile soil and a pleasant climate, Prince Edward Island is often called the "Garden of the Gulf." It produces many potatoes, beautiful flowers, and many dairy products. Fishing is important on the island, producing for markets in Canada and abroad lobsters, oysters, cod, halibut, mackerel, and herring. Silver foxes and minks are raised for their fur on special farms. The island is a favorite summer resort.

Jacques Cartier, a French explorer, discovered the island in 1534. The French colonized it, but the British took control in 1758. It was later renamed for the father of Queen Victoria. Prince Edward Island did not become part of Canada until 1873.

PRINCE of WALES

The Prince of Wales is the title conferred upon the heir to the throne of Great Britain. It was originally bestowed upon the ruler of WALES, a peninsula on the west coast of ENGLAND.

During the early history of Wales, many chieftains or princes grew strong enough to claim the title. When the King of England conquered Wales in 1284, he conferred the title on his son. Later, the English kings or queens bestowed the title on their oldest son, who was also called the Duke of Cornwall.

Since the 1300s, it has been the custom for the oldest son of the English king or queen to become the Duke of Cornwall at birth and to be given the title, Prince of Wales, whenever the king or queen wants to bestow it.

The present Prince of Wales is His Royal Highness, Prince Charles, who will become King of England when Queen Elizabeth II dies. SEE ALSO: WALES.

PRINTING

Thanks to printing, which was introduced in Europe at the end of the Middle Ages, we have an abundance of books, newspapers, and posters. If each single one had to be done by hand, there would be very few indeed.

There are many ways of printing, each useful for certain purposes, but there are only three basic kinds.

Letterpress printing is the oldest. The first printed works were done from slabs of wood. The artist cut down the parts of the block that he did not wish to hold ink, so that the raised portions alone were reproduced. When

Printing cylinder

ink roller

"movable" type was invented in the mid-15th century, each letter was cast as a raised surface on its own piece of metal. And when *halftone* printing was invented in the late 19th century, raised dots of different sizes reproduced the shading found in photographs. All these ways of printing from raised surfaces were examples of letterpress printing.

In *engraving*, exactly the opposite happened. The engraver cut thin grooves into a smooth plate, usually of steel or copper. The plate was then inked, but the surface was wiped off so that the ink stayed only in the grooves the engraver had cut. Then a thick paper was forced down on the plate so that it touched the ink in the grooves.

Planography is less than 200 years old. Here, lettering or pictures are put on the surface of a metal plate or, as in LITHOGRAPHY, on a special kind of stone. The printing surface is treated in such a way that a special ink will cling only to the letters or to the lines or dots that make up the pictures.

The process of printing text (that is, words but not pictures) goes this way. The first stage is *composition*, in which the letters are assembled for printing. Today this is done by machinery, though for centuries it was done by hand, letter by letter. When the text is composed, a *proof* is made. A proof is a trial print intended to show that the right letters have been used and that the text is clear everywhere. Proofreaders look at the proofs to check them. There may be more than one proof for a given piece of text to show that corrections and necessary adjustments have been made. Once the proofs are all right, the printing begins. Usually, several pages are printed on one sheet of paper, which then has to be folded, cut, and sometimes bound to make the newspaper, magazine, or book that you read. SEE ALSO: LITHOGRAPHY.

674

Composition

Making a Proof

Printing

PRISON

A prison is a special building enclosed by fences and walls and used for the confinement of persons accused or convicted of crimes. Confined persons (prisoners) lose their freedom to come and go as they please and are restrained in other ways.

For centuries, the penalty for serious crimes was death or mutilation, such as cutting off an ear or a hand. Those committing minor crimes were often punished by whipping, by fines, or by being placed in the STOCKS. After 1500, more and more lesser criminals—thieves, burglars, debtors, and others—were sentenced to prison for punishment. Men and women of all ages were crowded into small, dirty prisons, where they were poorly fed, sometimes beaten, and often made to do hard work.

Criminals in England were chained up and sent to America in the 1600s and 1700s. Later, England sent its prisoners to Australia. While awaiting the trip to another land, they were herded into the "hulks," prison ships anchored in the Thames River or off the English coast.

Gradually, public attention became focused on the filthy conditions in prisons and the brutal treatment of prisoners. In the United States, Dorothea Dix helped stop the mixing of criminals and the insane. She did notable work in *penology*—the science of the punishment of crime and the management of prisons.

In the 20th century, much has been done in the United States to improve prisons. Some prisons have schools where prisoners can take high school or college courses. Prisoners also can learn a trade if they wish; they can work in laundries, printing plants, laboratories, and other work areas. Sometimes they receive pay for their work. If a prisoner behaves well for a

long time, he may be put on *parole*. This means he is released before the end of his prison term, on the condition that he continues to be good.

Juvenile delinquents are usually sent to reformatories or camps, where they are encouraged to become trustworthy.

PROFESSION

A profession is an activity that needs much training and thought on the part of the *professional* who performs it. It is always done for money; anyone who does not charge for his services is an *amateur*. Professionals are usually better trained than amateurs. Doctors, lawyers, teachers, and architects are all professionals. They are highly trained, and are supposed to think for themselves when they face problems. Most professionals are paid with *fees* (payments for each job), but teachers usually get *salaries* (steady payments).

Most professionals work with their minds rather than their bodies, but athletes such as football players or golfers are called professionals if they are paid for their playing.

PROMETHEUS

The Greek myth about Prometheus has fascinated poets and writers for many centuries. He was a noble, good man, who suffered terribly for his generosity.

ZEUS deprived man of fire, because Prometheus had tricked him into choosing a bag full of bones rather than the delicious meat of a sacrificial ox. Then Prometheus stole some fire from Mount Olympus and gave it to man. This so enraged Zeus that he then plagued man with Pandora, the first mortal woman, and her box of evils, and he chained Prometheus to a rock on Mount Caucasus. Every day an eagle came to feed on Prometheus' liver, which grew again at night. Finally HERCULES took pity on him, shot the eagle with an arrow, and broke Prometheus' chains.

Prometheus is often represented as wiser, but less powerful, than Zeus. He is also used as a symbol of rebellion.

PROPHET

Many people think that a prophet is someone who predicts the future. He may do that, but a prophet is really a person who is supposed to be inspired by a god to say certain things. He may preach a new religion, as Muhammad did. He may preach against wrongdoing, as Isaiah or Jeremiah did. Or he may interpret the will of the gods, as the priests of many religions have done.

When we think of prophets, however, we usually think of the Hebrew ones whose words are recorded in the Old Testament of the BIBLE. The Israelites had prophets from a very early period. MOSES was the greatest Hebrew prophet. Samuel and Elijah were among the early

A prophet preaching

Moses

prophets. Elijah tried to purify Judaism, which was beginning to accept the false god Baal. Amos and Hosea, in the 8th century B.C., carried on this work. Isaiah, again in the 8th century, warned the Israelites that they had turned against God and that all but a small portion of the Jewish nation would be destroyed. When the Jews were taken to Babylon as captives in the 6th century B.C., prophets gave them courage by saying that God would create a new nation of Israel, better than ever. Jesus Christ came to fulfill their predictions. SEE ALSO: MOSES.

PROTESTANTISM

A Protestant is any Christian who does not belong to the Roman CATHOLIC CHURCH or to any of the ORTHODOX CHURCHES of eastern Europe or the Near East. There are many different Protestant *denominations* (religious groups), each with its own beliefs and ways of worshipping God. Episcopalians, Presbyterians, Methodists, Baptists, and Quakers are all different, but all of them are Protestants.

In the 14th century, some people began to be dissatisfied with the Catholic Church, which then was the only religious group in western Europe. They felt that too many of the priests were interested only in wealth and power. They thought that any man who followed the teachings of the Bible could appeal directly to God without the help of the priest or without having to go to mass. They wanted to reform the Catholic church, but failed.

Early in the 16th century, though, other reformers succeeded in breaking away from the Church. Martin Luther in Germany began the Lutheran Church, which soon became the church of northern Germany and of Scandinavia. John Calvin founded the Reformed Church in Switzerland; soon this church was established also in the Netherlands and in Scotland. Henry VIII of England, who had been refused a divorce by the Pope, broke away and started the Church of England, from which the Episcopal Church was later formed. Other Protestant denominations, like the Methodists, the Baptists, and the Puritans, began as reformations of the Church of England. The QUAKERS also broke away from the Church of England. Instead of having a religious service, they worship in silence unless they feel that God has inspired them to speak to other worshippers.

There are many Protestant denominations because of a general feeling that every person must decide religious matters for himself. Protestants have persecuted other Protestants, in 17th-century England or Massachusetts for instance, but the persecuted people have moved away to where they would be free to worship as they chose. Many of the settlers of the United States and Canada were members of such persecuted denominations.

PRUNES

Prunes are the common name for dried PLUMS, which have a firm flesh and a high sugar content. The ripe plums are gathered after falling from the tree or picked from the tree. Without removing the stones, plums are placed in lye solution to prevent fermentation. They are then dried on trays in the sun or in special kilns (ovens). Afterward they are "glossed" in a boiling solution of glycerine or fruit-juice. The prunes are then steamed, redried, and finally packed.

In the United States, most of the commercial prunes come from California, Oregon, and Washington. Prunes are also produced in large quantities in Spain, Portugal, Yugoslavia, and Australia. SEE ALSO: PLUM.

PSALMS

The Old Testament contains 150 poems called psalms, which are printed in five groups. These are hymns of praise to God or appeals to God for help. Many of them were sung in the great Jewish temple in Jerusalem.

Many of the psalms were written by DAVID, the king and musician. Others were written by Asaph, the sons of Korah, and Moses.

The twenty-third psalm, "The Lord is my shepherd . . . ," is probably the most famous of them all.

PUERTO RICO

Puerto Rico is an island in the WEST INDIES, about 880 miles (1417 km) from Florida. It is a self-governing commonwealth that receives military protection and economic aid from the U.S. Puerto Ricans are U.S. citizens, but cannot vote for President or members of Congress. The population of more than 3.2 million people includes descendants of the early Spanish colonists, Indians, Africans, and many with mixed racial ancestry. San Juan is Puerto Rico's capital, largest city, and chief port.

The island has highlands and mountains in the central region. Its fertile coastal plain and interior valleys are excellent for growing sugar cane, coffee, tobacco, and many kinds of fruit. Manufacturing is, however, the main source of wealth. Puerto Rico produces textiles, chemicals, machinery, and electrical equipment. Puerto Rican rum is famous. Tourists come to the island because of the tropical climate and beautiful, sandy beaches.

COLUMBUS visited the island on his second voyage to the New World in 1493. PONCE DE LEÓN claimed it for Spain in 1508, and a Spanish settlement was founded on the site of present San Juan in 1521. At that time, the Arawak and Carib Indians were living there. Spanish colonists brought Negro slaves from Africa in the 1700s and 1800s. After the Spanish-American War in 1898, Spain gave the island to the U.S.

PUFFIN

The puffin is a seabird that lives mostly in the polar regions of the world. It has a dumpy body, short, orange-colored legs, and small wings. Its feathers above are black; those below are white. It is a clumsy bird on land and in flight, but its webbed feet make it an expert swimmer. Its wings are important in diving for fish and for swimming underwater. The puffin's large, yellow, blue, and scarlet-colored bill can carry several fish at one time; it has also earned for the puffin the nickname of sea parrot.

Puffins do not build nests. The females lay their eggs (each female lays one white egg) in rock crevices and burrows dug in the ground on the tops of cliffs. Puffins nest in colonies, and the males fiercely defend the nesting sites. The Atlantic puffins migrate as far south as Long Island; the Pacific puffins as far south as California.

PULLEYS

A pulley is a very simple, useful machine for lifting weights. It consists of a grooved wheel for guiding a rope. The wheel is housed in a case or block that can attach to a beam or wall. A pulley enables a heavy weight, attached to the pulley rope, to be easily lifted by pulling down on the rope. The wheel reduces the friction and makes the work easier.

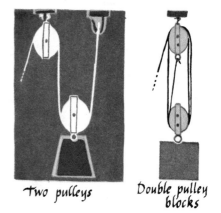

Two pulleys

Double pulley blocks

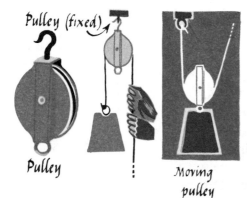

Pulley (fixed)

Pulley

Moving pulley

For heavier weights, a combination of a fixed and a movable pulley is used.

Since double blocks (that is, cases with two wheels in each) lift with four ropes, a very heavy weight can be raised with one-fourth the energy force. This combination of pulleys and ropes is called "block and tackle" and is useful in doing heavy lifting jobs, such as unloading cargo and lifting heavy fallen trees.

PUMA

The puma is a wildcat of the Western Hemisphere, ranging from southern Canada to Patagonia, in southern Argentina. It is generally smaller than its relative, the jaguar, and is usually reddish or grayish brown in color. The adult male puma may grow to be 8 feet (2.5 m) in length. In various areas, the puma is known as the cougar, mountain lion, catamount, deer tiger, and panther.

Pumas can jump amazing distances. They prey on deer, sheep, horses, cattle, and llamas. Very rarely do they attack man, who has occasionally been able to tame them.

PUMICE

Pumice, often used to remove stains from hands, is actually a piece of volcanic LAVA. It is full of tiny spaces or pores formed from bubbles of gas trapped when the lava was cooling. Since it is made up of pockets of trapped air, pumice floats on water.

PUMPS

A pump is a machine that moves or puts pressure on a fluid such as air, water, or oil.

There are many kinds of pumps. A *vacuum pump* pulls air or some other gas from a closed space so that the amount of gas in the space is decreased. A *suction pump* also creates a vacuum, but in such a way that

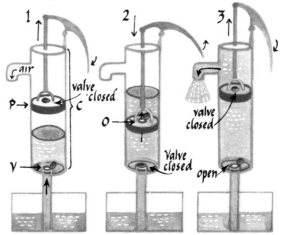

atmospheric pressure on a liquid forces it into the place where the vacuum exists. The purpose of such a pump is to move the liquid. A *lift pump* simply raises a liquid by pushing up from below, while a *force pump* pushes any fluid in any direction.

Such pumps often work with *pistons*, disks that fit tightly into cylinders through which they slide back and forth. Many pumps, though, are *rotary pumps*, in which whirling parts do the work. A *gear pump*, for instance, has two parts with teeth like those of gears. As the teeth mingle, they force a fluid in the direction they are whirling. A *centrifugal pump* has something like a fan that hurls liquids away from its center.

The pump shown here acts as a suction pump in getting water into the pump chamber, and as a lift pump in getting it up to the spout. P is the piston of the pump.

PUNCH and JUDY

English children enjoy the escapades of Punch, a hooknosed, hunchbacked puppet who abuses his wife Judy and gets into trouble with his landlord, the police, a hangman, and the devil himself but usually manages to get free unharmed.

Old Italian PANTOMIMES had such a character, whose name was Pulcinella. He became so popular that people used to dress like him, huge nose

and all, at carnival time. When Italian puppeteers came to England in 1660, they brought a miniature version of Pulcinella with them. The English first called him Punchinello, then shortened the name to Punch. Judy was an English invention. She is like a favorite character of medieval English plays, the bad-tempered wife of Noah who has to be dragged on board the Ark when the Flood comes. SEE ALSO: PUPPETS.

PUPPETS

Puppet theaters can be found in most parts of the world, for many kinds of people have found something appealing in the little, almost real, figures moving about their stages. The ancient Greeks had puppets 2300 years ago, and there are very old traditions of *puppetry* in Asia and among the American Indians.

There are many kinds of puppet. The simplest is the *finger puppet*, a kind of cloth doll that fits over

Javanese puppet early 13th Cent:

two fingers. Naturally, it is not very lifelike, though it can nod and bow. The *glove puppet* fits over all five fingers. It has arms that can move, but no legs. Such a puppet can do more things than a finger puppet can, but it has a lopsided appearance, since the little finger that moves one arm is much longer and thinner than the thumb that moves the other one. It is an easy kind of puppet to use, though. One *puppeteer* can handle two glove

A glove puppet

puppets, and they can move quickly across the stage. *Rod puppets* are more lifelike, but each one needs one or more people to handle it. Each arm has a rod to move it, and another rod supports the head.

String puppet

Marionettes are different from other puppets. Instead of being held directly by the puppeteer's hand, a marionette hangs from strings. There may be as many as nine strings to support or move different parts of the puppet's body.

Oriental puppets are different. The people of Java and China use flat puppets whose shadows are cast on a screen by a light behind them. Such *shadow figures* are also popular in Greece and Turkey. The Japanese have a kind of puppet that is almost life-size. Their puppets are controlled by a system of strings inside that moves not only the arms and the legs but also the eyes and even the eyebrows, so that the effect is very lifelike.

In the past, great playwrights and musicians wrote for puppet theaters. Today, puppetry is still respected as an art, especially in eastern Europe, where the old as well as the young enjoy the performances. SEE ALSO: PUNCH AND JUDY.

PURITANS

About 400 years ago, there were some English Protestants known as Puritans, because they wanted to "purify," or cleanse the Church of England. The Puritans wished to remain in the Church if they could, but they hoped to do away with the Church's elaborate rituals. They particularly disliked the priestly robes, set prayers, pictures, images, and music in church. Influenced by such religious leaders as John Calvin in Switzerland and John Knox in Scotland, the Puritans developed a simple church service and practised strict behavior in everyday life.

Because all English people were supposed to worship God in the manner decided by the Church and the king, the Puritans came to be persecuted for

Thomas Hooker

their different beliefs. Many of them dressed in black, cut their hair short, and led sober lives. One sect of Puritans called the Separatists sailed to America with the PILGRIMS in the MAYFLOWER.

The English king gave one group of Puritans land not far from Plymouth, Massachusetts. They made a community there and named it Boston. Other Puritans left Massachusetts and started new settlements, such as Roger Williams, who founded Providence, in Rhode Island, and Thomas Hooker, who founded Hartford, in Connecticut.

Puritans who stayed in England supported Lord CROMWELL, who ruled after the beheading of King Charles I in 1649. The Puritan government established under Cromwell was very strict about religion and behavior in public. In 1660, a king was put back on the throne, and thus the Puritans lost power and were persecuted again. Many years went by before they gained complete freedom to worship as they pleased and to speak and act in their own way. SEE ALSO: THE PILGRIMS.

PUTTY
Putty is a substance used to fill up holes in woodwork and to hold window panes in place. It is soft when fresh but soon gets very hard. Most putty is a mixture of whiting (powdered chalk) and boiled linseed oil, but other mixtures are also sold as putty. Some are poisonous, and should be handled carefully.

PYGMIES
Pygmies who live in the jungles of AFRICA rarely grow taller than 5 feet (1.5 m). Female pygmies are usually no taller than four and a half feet (1.3 m). Their shortness is inherited, as well as their slightness of stature and brown skin color.

They are a primitive, friendly, peaceful people, who live in bands of about 20 families and move from place to place in search of food. They gather fruit, wild honey, and vegetables and use nets to trap animals, which they kill with spears and bows and arrows, often poison-tipped. Their huts are made of leaves and branches.

Another group of pygmies live in southeastern Asia, in remote parts of MALAYSIA, NEW GUINEA, the PHILIPPINES, and the Andaman Islands. Some live permanently in one place, farming and sometimes hunting with a blowpipe and poisoned darts.

PYRAMIDS

A pyramid is a solid object with sloping triangular sides that meet at a point. But when we think of pyramids, we usually are thinking of the huge tombs that some of the kings of ancient Egypt built for themselves.

The oldest pyramid was built in steps rather than with flat sides for a king named Djoser. But the most famous of the pyramids are the flat-sided ones at Giza, not far from Cairo. The Great Pyramid at Giza was built in the 26th century B.C. for a king named Khufu. It is smaller than it used to be, but is still one of the largest buildings in the world. No man-made thing used more material until a dam was built in our West around 1950. It is built of solid stone. When built it was 481 feet (147 m) high and 775 feet (236 m) long on each side of its base. Its outer surface, smooth and sloping, was made of fine stone with a tip of gold and silver. It was taken away long ago. There are two other pyramids, smaller but still very big. There is also the famous Sphinx, a huge statue of a lion with a human head. This is 187 feet (57 m) long. Around these are smaller tombs and temples. Later Egyptian kings and queens were usually not buried in pyramids.

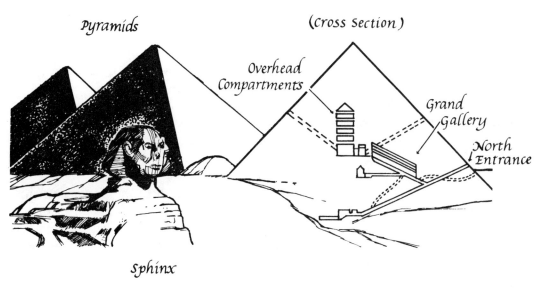

Pyramids   (Cross Section)

Overhead Compartments

Grand Gallery

North Entrance

Sphinx

PYTHON

The python is the largest and most powerful SNAKE in the world and it is not poisonous. Like a boa constrictor, the python kills its prey by wrapping itself tightly about it to cause strangulation. The python's huge, loosely hinged jaws allow it to swallow animals the size of a goat. The female incubates her eggs by coiling her body about them.

This snake is found in the tropics of Africa, Asia, Australia, the islands of the South Pacific, and Mexico. It often grows to be 30 feet (9.3 m) long. SEE ALSO: SNAKES.

QUAKERS

In 17th-century England, a number of people were unhappy with the teachings of the Church of England and the other churches that existed then. Some of these joined together and called themselves Friends. But, because they said that man should tremble before God, their enemies called them Quakers, and this is the name by which they are usually known.

Some Quakers today worship in churches and have services and ministers just as most Protestant denominations do. But the traditional Quaker has none of these. He believes in an "inner light," something of God in every man that can tell him what to do and to believe. Instead of going to a church service, he goes to a *meeting*. There the Quakers sit in silent worship unless one feels that God has inspired him to speak. Some Quakers are thought of as more inspired than the others, and tend to dominate the meetings, but they are not thought of as clergymen.

The Quakers are famous for their simple ways and their kindly attitude toward all people. Until a few years ago some still dressed in very simple clothes and had an old-fashioned way of speaking. Many refused to play music or dance. The Quakers have usually been opposed to slavery, war, and other harmful things, and have done much to help war and disaster victims, convicts, and other people in trouble.

QUARRY

Most stone used for building or for industrial purposes is taken from man-made pits called quarries. If there is a great deal of useful stone, these pits can be very large.

Much of the stone that is quarried is needed in small, irregular pieces. These are put into cement to make concrete or are used unmixed to make driveways, the foundations for railroad tracks, and so on. Such stone is broken up first by explosives, then by crushing in a machine. Some stone, though, is used in large pieces for building or for sculptures. MARBLE, LIMESTONE, and GRANITE are often used for these purposes. These large pieces of stone have to be split away from the rock with drills, wedges, and saws, using natural divisions between the layers of rock if possible. Then they can be cut up into convenient sizes.

Granite Quarry

QUEBEC

Quebec is the largest province in CANADA. The capital of the province is also named Quebec.

The St. Lawrence River flows through southern Quebec and into the Gulf of St. Lawrence. To the north are rolling hills and some mountains and many forests, lakes, and rivers. The province stretches to Labrador and Hudson Bay, where temperatures are far below zero in the winter. Snowfall of more than 100 inches (254 cm) is quite common in most parts of Quebec during the winter. Summers can be warm, especially in the south.

Quebec has good farming land and its forests supply much newsprint and lumber. Throughout the north country, there are rich deposits of iron ore, copper, zinc, and gold. A great deal of the world's ASBESTOS is found there, too.

687

The French explorer Jacques Cartier discovered Quebec in 1534, and another Frenchman, Samuel de Champlain built a trading post in 1608 at the site of Quebec city. In 1759, the British took control of the province and ruled until 1867, when Quebec became part of the new nation of Canada.

The French citizens of Quebec, many of whom live in MONTREAL, have kept their own religion, customs, and language. Also many want the province to form its own separate nation in Canada. SEE ALSO: MONTREAL.

RABBITS

Although they are appealing little animals, wild rabbits are classed as pests because of the tremendous damage they do to crops. They eat a great deal. They reproduce rapidly. For example, the cottontail doe (female) of the eastern United States has up to 8 litters a year with as many as 10 young in each.

The buck (male) helps the doe to build a new burrow which is lined with leaves and fur from the doe's body. The babies are born blind, furless, and helpless.

The American jack rabbit and the snowshoe rabbit are actually HARES. Hares look very similar to rabbits, but there are many differences in size, appearance and habitat.

As pets, rabbits are affectionate, gentle, clean, and easy to care for; they can be kept indoors and out. SEE ALSO: HARES.

RACES

The people of the world may be divided, on the basis of certain physical features, into a number of large groups, called races. Races differ because of head shape, hair texture and color, skin color, and other physical features such as eyes, lips, and height.

A common error about races is the

Australoid

belief that a number of pure "breeds," or strains of men, like breeds of dogs, became mixed over long periods of time. We all had a common ancestor, and experts in the field of ANTHROPOLOGY say that any physical characteristic in men can differ in countless ways. People in any community isolated for a long time in a particular climate would probably begin to show similar physical features.

Experts have grouped not only races, but peoples—that is, groups that are set apart from each other to some degree by less obvious physical features and by cultural differences like language, religion, and customs.

Illustrated on these pages are several main groups of people in the world. They are the *Australoid* type, who have crinkled hair, flat noses, jutting jaws, and dark skins. The ABORIGINES of Australia and parts of southern India belong to this race. The *Negroid* race has brown to black skin, thick lips, and wooly hair. NEGROES are from Africa and parts of Indonesia and New Guinea. The *Mongoloid* race has yellow or reddish-brown skin, straight black hair, high cheekbones and flattish faces, with almond shaped eyes. This large group includes the Chinese, Japanese, ESKIMOS, and American INDIANS. The *Nordic* people of northern Europe are tall, fair-haired, and blue-eyed and have now settled throughout the world. The *Mediterranean* racial type is of medium height, with long heads, narrow faces, and dark eyes and complexions. They are found in southern Europe, North Africa, and the Middle East to India. *Alpine* people are short, with broad heads and much hair, and live in central Europe to Russia. Most anthropologists use the term *Caucasoid* race for those with white skin color, as opposed to yellow, brown, or black. The United States has people belonging to most of these racial types, for different peoples have moved there during the last 200 years.

RADAR

Radar is a made-up word meaning *radio detection and ranging*. Its purpose is to locate objects that cannot be seen and to tell how fast and in what direction they are moving.

Radio waves travel about 1000 feet (300 m) every millionth of a second. If they hit something solid (called a *target*), some of them bounce off the object and return to the radio transmitter. Since the speed of a radio wave is known, it is fairly easy for modern equipment to take half the time between the sending of a radar *pulse* (very short signal) and its return and calculate the

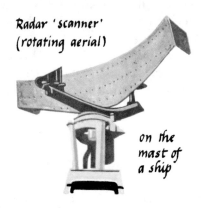

Radar 'scanner' (rotating aerial)

on the mast of a ship

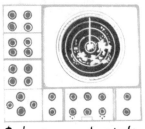

Radar screen and controls

distance of the object the outgoing signal struck.

Most radar sets work this way. A *scanner*, rotating on a mast, sends out thousands of pulses in all directions. Between pulses, the sending apparatus shuts off long enough to allow any *echoes* to come back. The locations of the objects that bounce back the waves are shown on a circular television tube at the correct distances from the center of the tube. The center represents the location of the scanner. Since radio waves travel along the Earth's surface, the radar can detect things beyond the horizon. The television tube is thus like a map of part of the world, with all solid objects shown on it in their right places.

The basic principle of radar was discovered in the 1880s, but it took a long time

Radar 'pulses' sent out to the 'plane, & reflected from it

to realize its usefulness and develop the equipment that allowed it to be useful. The first real radar set was made in the late 1930s, and its widespread use came only in World War II.

RADIO

Radio is a very important means of sending and gathering information. There is more to it than just the broadcasting of sound. The pictures seen on TELEVISION are often transmitted by radio waves. So are some TELEPHONE messages. So are RADAR signals.

690

James Clerk Maxwell, an English physicist, predicted in 1864 that radio waves would be discovered one day. Heinrich Hertz, another physicist, demonstrated in 1888 that Maxwell was right. Guiglielmo Marconi, an Italian, was the first person really to use these discoveries. He began to make radio equipment and to send messages around 1897. His equipment grew more and more powerful, and in 1901 he succeeded in sending messages across the Atlantic. An American, Lee De Forest, contributed greatly to the improvement of radio. By 1910, radio equipment was in use in many places. The radio signals of the sinking ocean liner *Titanic* in 1912 brought several ships to the rescue.

Early radio was a kind of telegraph system, and was often called the *wireless telegraph.* In 1915, the first radio transmission of the human voice was made, and in 1920 the Pittsburgh radio station KDKA became the first commercial broadcasting station in the world. Marconi's company began to transmit long-distance telephone messages in the mid-1920s.

RADIUM

Radium is a radioactive element that was discovered in 1898 by MADAME CURIE and her husband, two scientists working in Paris. It occurs with URANIUM in the mineral pitchblende. The powerful gamma rays given off by radium are used in treating several diseases, especially cancer.

RAILROADS

The first railroads were rough tracks of wood or metal, laid in the European mines from the 16th century on. The heavy mine carts of coal and ore, hauled by animal power, could move much more easily on such tracks than on the rough floors of the mine shafts.

The modern railroad, though, could not come to be until the STEAM ENGINE was invented and until boilers were strong enough to deliver high-pressure steam. The first steam locomotive that actually worked was built by the Englishman Richard Trevithick in 1803. It was too heavy, though, and the first really practical locomotive was built in 1812. The first railroad as we know it today, with passenger and freight trains pulled by locomotives, was the Liverpool and Manchester Railway, opened in 1830 in England. George Stephenson's locomotive *Rocket* was so successful that it remains famous as a great locomotive. In the 1830s, there was a huge amount of railroad construction in England. The steam railroad was proven convenient, and did much to change the way of life for many people. The French, the Germans, and the Austrians soon began their own railroads, but the Russians waited until about 1850 before they built many miles of track.

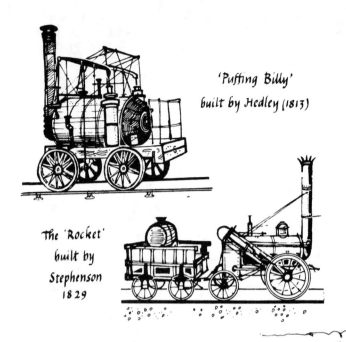

'Puffing Billy'

built by Hedley (1813)

The 'Rocket' built by Stephenson 1829

In North America, the railroad was quickly appreciated for its usefulness. Roads were very bad, and CANALS were slow and expensive to make. The United States was largely settled because of its thousands of miles of quickly built track. This track was much rougher than that in Europe, but American engineers developed new locomotives that could run on it easily. The first American locomotive was built in 1825, and the first passenger-carry-

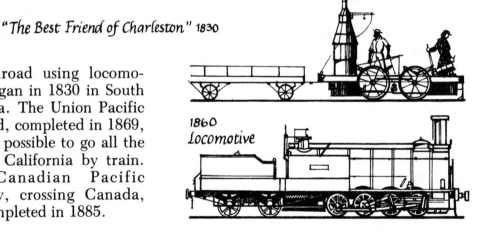

"The Best Friend of Charleston" 1830

1860 Locomotive

ing railroad using locomotives began in 1830 in South Carolina. The Union Pacific Railroad, completed in 1869, made it possible to go all the way to California by train. The Canadian Pacific Railway, crossing Canada, was completed in 1885.

For a hundred years after 1830, the railroad was very important in the lives of millions of people. It allowed people who might otherwise never travel to move quickly over great distances. It allowed people to buy and sell between distant places. It may have been the reason that the Union won the Civil War. People were thrilled to see the great trains pass by, or to hear the deep, distant whistle of the locomotives. Engineers built great bridges and tunnels and designed bigger and better locomotives. Railroad cars became more and more luxurious, and people were delighted to travel on some of the famous trains.

1900 Locomotive

"Bigboy" 4-8-8-4

Victorian Pullman

Diesel-Electric Locomotive

By 1930, the railroad began to become less important to the public. Airliners offered faster travel. Many people had their own automobiles. Buses and even trolley cars went from town to town. Still, glamorous streamlined trains ran between distant cities until World War II. After the war, passenger railroading became too expensive to pay for itself, and railroads made their real income on freight. Some railroads went bankrupt. Today, the U.S. government is paying railroads to run passenger trains, and some good trains are in service.

RAINBOW

When light passes through drops of moisture in the air, it is *refracted* (bent), reflected, and refracted again as it leaves the droplet. When this happens, each drop of water acts like a tiny prism and breaks the white LIGHT up into its SPECTRUM of colors, each of which travels at different speeds in the

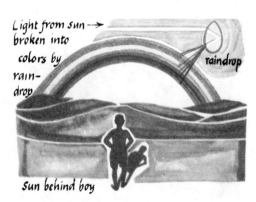

Light from sun → broken into colors by raindrop

raindrop

Sun behind boy

water. The broad arched band of colors seen consists of red at the top, followed successively by orange, yellow, green, blue, indigo, and violet. Rainbows often appear while the sun is shining after a rainstorm in the late afternoon.

RAINFALL

Everyone is familiar with "steamed up" windows in a bathroom that result when the warm air in the room strikes the cold glass.

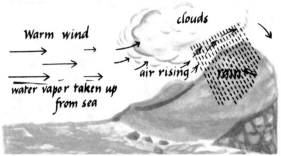

Rainfall is due to the cooling of rising warm moist air. When this happens, gaseous water vapor that forms a cloud *condenses*—that is, changes back to the liquid state. When these tiny droplets of water become too heavy to be held up by the air, they return to Earth as rain, snow, sleet, hail, dew, or frost. These forms of moisture are called *precipitation* by *meteorologists* (weathermen).

The wettest place on Earth is Mount Waialeale, Hawaii, with an average annual rainfall of over 451 inches (11.5 m). Calama, Chile, on the other hand, is on record for having had no rainfall for 400 years.

At weather stations, meteorologists set out rain gauges that are marked in inches and centimeters to determine the exact amount of daily precipitation.

In areas where there is a desperate need for rain, sometimes when conditions are just right, scientists have been able to "seed" the clouds with dry ice (frozen carbon dioxide) or silver iodide crystals. This procedure gives the droplets a nucleus to condense upon, but, unfortunately it is often unsuccessful. SEE ALSO: CLOUDS, FOG, SNOW.

Sir Walter RALEIGH (1552–1618)

Sir Walter Raleigh was an English soldier, explorer, colonizer, and writer. He founded one of the first settlements in North America.

As a young man, he fought in France, Holland, and Ireland and was rewarded with land and rich posts in England. Queen ELIZABETH I made him a knight and sent him to seek new lands for England in America. After a first, unsuccessful attempt to found a colony in North America, he organized another expedition in 1584 to explore Virginia. The next year Raleigh sent about 100 men to Roanoke Island, in Virginia, but they returned to England

694

in 1586. Raleigh sent more colonists the following year. When supply ships came in 1591, the colonists were gone. The "Lost Colony" remains an unsolved mystery today. Raleigh did, however, introduce tobacco and potatoes to Europe from America.

In 1595, Raleigh explored Guiana in South America, and in 1596 and 1597 he fought the Spaniards at Cádiz and in the Azores.

When King James I came to power, Raleigh fell out of favor and was imprisoned for treason. For about 13 years, he was a prisoner in the Tower of London, where he wrote a book called the *History of the World*. At long last, he was released and instructed to find El Dorado (the legendary city of gold) for the king, provided he and his men would not fight the Spanish. His men, however, disobeyed, and because of this, Raleigh was beheaded by order of the king.

RASPBERRY

The raspberry is closely related to the blackberry but has few or no prickles. This juicy fruit is small, usually red or black. The fruit separates from the core, which remains on the stem when it is picked. Raspberries like good soil and plenty of manure. New shoots (suckers) are taken from the roots and trained on wires. After bearing fruit, the canes (stems) are cut to ground level to allow for next year's new growth.

RATS

Rats are not native to North and South America. They came ashore from the ships with the early colonists from Europe. These unpleasant rodents are carriers of many diseases, such as typhus fever and bubonic plague (see BLACK DEATH), which are very dangerous to man. Because rats *contract* (catch) many of man's diseases, *albino* (white) strains of

the black and brown rat have been bred for scientific research that deals with diseases, medicines, and questions of growth, heredity, and learning. Although usually larger than mice, rats are closely related and are similar in habits and appearance.

Rats are bold and clever. If they are cornered, they become aggressive fighters. To avoid being seen, rats generally move about at night. At the age of five months, females begin to have litters about five times a year, each containing 8 to 15 young.

Rats will eat almost anything and can live just about anywhere. Like man himself, rats are one of the few animals that will aggressively kill their own kind. The brown rat is today much more common than the black rat, perhaps because it is bigger and fiercer.

Other rodents of the rat family are also called rats, such as the cotton rat, muskrat, African giant rat, and pack rat. The pack rat of the southeastern United States collects objects, especially shiny ones, which it stores in its burrow.

RATTLESNAKE

The rattlesnake is a poisonous American SNAKE with all but one species in North America. Rattlesnakes are 2 to 8 feet (0.6–2.5 m) long and have large fangs. Their bite can cause death, though man is rarely attacked. The rattling sound from the end of their tails comes from a series of dried, hollow segments. Their tails are vibrated as a warning when enemies approach. Most enemies are frightened off by the sound.

Rattlesnakes are at home in tropical forests, on hot deserts, and on cool mountains. In winter, hundreds of rattlesnakes coil up together during HIBERNATION.

RAVEN

The black common raven is the largest type of CROW. It is found everywhere in the Northern Hemisphere. The raven is the largest perching bird, and the one found furthest north. Shunning man, the raven prefers living in wild areas, such as seacoasts, mountaintops, deserts, and Arctic tundra.

It feeds upon dead, weak, newborn, or injured animals, mice, birds, eggs, snakes, insects, fruits, and seeds.

Ravens are intelligent and crafty and can be easily tamed. Some ravens can be taught to mimic (imitate) human speech. They seem to mate for life. Ravens construct a nest of sticks on rocky cliffs or in a large tree. The loud, harsh caw of these long-lived birds is a familiar sound in areas where they live. SEE ALSO: CROW.

RAYON

Rayon is made from *cellulose*, a substance found in soft woods and the fibers that cling to cotton seeds. The cellulose taken from these materials is dissolved until it forms a viscous (syrupy) liquid. This is forced through a *spinneret*, a kind of strainer with tiny holes, and comes out in the form of small threads. These are twisted together to make a yarn.

The commonest kind of rayon is called *viscose*, and was invented in 1892. It is easily dyed and has a glossy appearance. It can be dry-cleaned without harm, and can stand temperatures of up to about 365° F (185° C). It is used for clothing, carpets, and industrial goods. If specially treated, it is very strong.

Threads being pressed out of spinneret

RED CROSS

In 1859, a Swiss banker named Jean Henri Dunant was very disturbed by the suffering he saw at the Battle of Solferino, in Italy. Three years later, he wrote a book about forming a group of volunteers to help the wounded during war.

Red Cross Volunteer   *Red Cross In War Zone*

As a result, at a conference in GENEVA in 1864, twelve nations agreed to form such a society, which soon was known as the Red Cross. In honor of Dunant's nationality, a red cross on a white background—the Swiss flag reversed—was chosen as its symbol. Since then, the Headquarters of the International Red Cross has been in Geneva, and rules have been made concerning the sick and wounded on land and sea, as well as about prisoners of war (POWs), civilians, and refugees.

CLARA BARTON organized the American Red Cross in 1881. It now offers aid during all kinds of disasters and assists the armed forces and their families during war or peace. It also gives training in FIRST AID and runs a blood program—the collection of blood from donors to be given to needy patients.

At all times, the Red Cross represents neutrality and merciful behavior toward all nations and their peoples. It has done amazing work in times of war and peace, from ambulance-driving and stretcher-bearing to the care of children, the handicapped, and the old.

REFORMATION

The Reformation is the name of a period of time (mostly in the 16th century) when several European countries broke away from the Roman Catholic Church and adopted some form of Protestant belief.

JOHN KNOX

The main leaders of the Reformation were Martin Luther in Germany, Ulrich Zwingli and John Calvin in Switzerland, and John Knox in Scotland. All of them wanted a simpler religion based on the BIBLE. Their beliefs spread quickly in northern Europe, but Italy, Spain, Portugal, and much of France remained faithful to Rome and the rule of the POPE. In England, the separation from the Roman Catholic Church began with Henry VIII, but the final break with Rome occurred during the reign of Queen Elizabeth I.

REFRIGERATOR

In an ordinary modern refrigerator, a long tube passes into the *refrigerator compartment*, where the food and ice are kept, then out again. In this tube is a liquid that turns into a gas at certain points.

When the fluid enters the refrigerator compartment, it is mostly gas and is cold. It passes through many coils that allow it to absorb a great deal of the heat that is in the food or that has leaked into the compartment. Then it is sucked out of the compartment by a pump, which forces it, under pressure, into a condenser. The pressure heats this material so much that it becomes a liquid. It then passes through other coils so that it gives off its heat either to the open air or to water surrounding the coils. Then, still a liquid, it passes through a narrow opening into a tube. On the other side of the tube, the

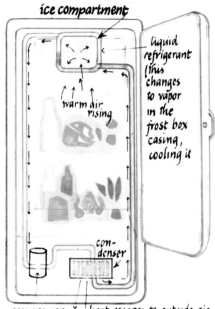

ice compartment

liquid refrigerant (this changes to vapor in the frost box casing, cooling it

warm air rising

condenser

compressor   heat escapes to outside air

pressure drops suddenly, and the liquid turns into a cool gas that can then go into the refrigerator compartment to absorb more heat from the food. The refrigerator compartment has a thermostat, which shuts off the pump when the compartment is cold enough and turns it on again when it gets too warm.

The first successful refrigerator was made in 1834, but home refrigerators could not be made until this century, when electric motors and proper cooling fluids were available.

REINDEER

Reindeer are mammals of the deer family, found in Norway, Sweden, Siberia, Canada, and Alaska. Wild reindeer in North America are known as caribou. Reindeer are the only kind of deer in which both the males and females have antlers.

Many centuries ago, the reindeer was tamed in Lapland (a region in northern Norway, Sweden, and Finland). The people there, called Lapps, have since kept large herds of reindeer, which provide them with meat, milk, cheese, and clothing. Reindeer are also trained by the Lapps to pull sleighs long distances. After reindeer were introduced in Alaska in 1891, they became important to the life and economy of the ESKIMO.

Wild reindeer grow larger than tame ones. They feed on various grasses, mosses, and LICHENS. During the winter, they become quite lean because of lack of food. Often they make a mass migration to the seacoasts where they feed on seaweed. The broad hooves of reindeer enable them to move easily over ice and snow. Reindeer are not bothered by extremely low temperatures and can be seen swimming in icy waters. Unfortunately, they have been greatly reduced in number by greedy hunters. SEE ALSO: DEER.

RELIGION

People everywhere have always wondered about themselves and the universe they live in. Scientists and philosophers offer answers to some of man's questions, but not all of them. The word *religion* refers to a system of belief in a god or gods, as well as the practice of worshiping, obeying, and serving that god.

Egyptian Gods

Most people believe the universe was created by someone; they believe it is affected by unseen forces. What does the

Christian altar

Creator want men to do? How can the unseen forces be understood? Religion is man's looking for answers to these questions by reaching for a god.

There are many kinds of religion. Some imagine an unseen being in every hill and every tree; they imagine that these GODS control everthing done in the world. Thus they teach that there may be a god of marriages or a god that controls traffic; there is a special god for every home.

Some ancient people, like the Egyptians, Greeks, Romans, and Vikings, imagined their gods were more human. Their gods received sacrifices and prayers in ceremonies conducted by priests. PROPHETS would go into trances and pretend to speak with the voices of the gods. This belief in many gods was called *polytheism*.

The Hebrews, on the other hand, believed that God is a single being who created the world, cares about it, and often influences what happens in it. This belief in one God is called *monotheism*. Christians also worship the God of the Hebrews. Islam is monotheistic and so is Hinduism, the religion of India. Hinduism seems to have many gods, but many Hindus believe there is really one god who appears in many forms.

So what sets JUDAISM and CHRISTIANITY apart from other religions? Other religions teach that man seeks God and attempts to understand him. But Judaism and Christianity teach that God sought to give man answers to his questions—first through the Hebrew prophets and then through Jesus Christ, whom Christians believe to be God Himself.

700

Some religions have no "god" in the sense of spiritual being. Buddhism, which is found in many parts of the Far East, is concerned with man and the way that he can learn to escape the miseries of existence. According to Buddhism, the most important thing is the training of the mind to understand the reality behind the world. Taoism, an old Chinese religion, is similar. Man is encouraged to put himself in harmony with a force through which all things happen. According to Buddhism and Taoism, the force is not a god; it wants nothing and does nothing. But nothing can go against it.

Because religion tries to answer the most important questions people can have about themselves, a person may feel very strongly about his religion. Because religion deals with matters that are supernatural—matter that cannot be measured with our five senses—religious beliefs cannot be proven scientifically.

Buddha

Because people disagree about religion and because religious beliefs cannot be proven scientifically, some people say religion is troublesome. But it is only through religion that man has been able to look beyond himself to God. SEE ALSO: BUDDHA, CATHOLICISM, GODS, ISLAM, ORTHODOX CHURCH, PROTESTANTISM.

REMBRANDT (1606–1669)

Rembrandt Harmenszoon van Rijn is one of the famous of the "Old Masters," a Dutch painter known especially for PORTRAITS that tell us much about the personalities of their subjects.

The son of a miller, Rembrandt was first sent to the University of Leiden, then to study painting. His talent was recognized at once, and he went on to become rich and successful. Although he later lost most of his money and had family troubles, his painting became better and better. His portraits, religious paintings, and landscapes are today regarded as some of the best pictures ever painted.

RENAISSANCE

In 14th- and 15th-century Italy, scholars and artists began to have a new curiosity about things. They were both interested in the modern world they knew and in the accomplishments of the ancient Romans and Greeks, which seemed so much greater than any accomplishments of the MIDDLE AGES. *Humanists*, scholars interested in the great thoughts of mankind and the things that mankind might accomplish in the future, studied the writings of the ancients. Architects were inspired by Roman ruins to create new buildings that used Roman ornament. Painters, who had worked mostly for the Church, now began to do portraits, landscapes, and other pictures of worldly subjects. They also began to study perspective, which helps the painting to look like a window showing a real scene. Sculptors studied the beauty of the human body. Scientists investigated the world of nature. Other persons wrote about principles of government and other matters of public importance.

The Renaissance spread to other lands, where scholars and artists were inspired by it. Much of what we know or take for granted today is due to the Renaissance, with its great curiosity about everything.

REPTILES

Reptiles are ectothermic—that is, the temperature of their blood is the same as that of their surroundings. Therefore, they cannot live in cold, icy regions but instead in warm or hot climates. In temperate (mild) areas, reptiles *hibernate* (sleep all winter).

Reptiles have dry scales. They lay leathery eggs, usually hatched by the warmth of the sun. A few LIZARDS and SNAKES bear their young alive. Although many live in or near water, reptiles have lungs and not gills like

Tortoise

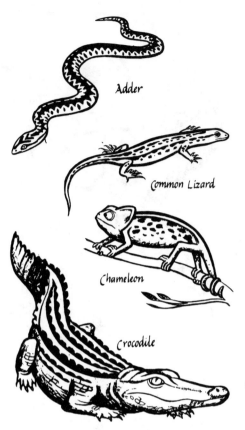

Adder

Common Lizard

Chameleon

Crocodile

those of fish and immature amphibians. The word *reptile* comes from a Latin word meaning "to creep." Creeping is their chief means of locomotion.

There are 5 basic groups of reptiles: CROCODILES and ALLIGATORS, the largest of the reptiles and inhabitants of only hot countries; TURTLES AND TORTOISES, living in fresh and salt water and on land in warm countries; snakes; lizards and CHAMELEONS; and the tuatura, now the last of a primitive group found only on some small islands near New Zealand.

A few reptiles are eaten and the skin of some is used for purses, shoes, and belts. However, as a group, they are of far less importance than the fishes, mammals, and birds.

Tuatura (New Zealand)

RESIN

Resin is the clear, sticky gum sometimes seen on pine and fir trees. It usually oozes out of a cut or wound in the bark. Sometimes chemicals are used to extract resin from wood.

AMBER is fossilized resin. Hard resins are used in making varnish. Soft resins are used in making TURPENTINE and frankincense, and they can be used as disinfectants and ointments. Frankincense is also used as an incense, a perfume ingredient, and a fumigating (smoking) preparation.

Rosin, used by violinists to coat their bows, is made by distilling the turpentine from crude pine resin.

RESPIRATION

Earthworm

Sea Anemone

All animals and plants need OXYGEN for *metabolism*, the build up and break down of body tissues for growth, repair, and energy. This oxygen is obtained by *respiration* or breathing. The oxygen is absorbed by the body cells, and carbon dioxide is given off.

703

Man, other mammals, birds, reptiles, adult amphibians, and some fish have LUNGS to aid this process. The oxygen of the air breathed in is carried by the blood to all parts of the body.

Oxygen also dissolves in water, and those animals with moist bodies, such as the earthworm, are able to absorb oxygen through their skins. Some aquatic animals, such as the sea anemone, also breathe this way, but most fish and young amphibians have GILLS for absorbing oxygen into their bloodstream.

Insects have air passages, the openings of which are called *spiracles*, which take the oxygen directly to their body cells.

Most plants breathe through their ROOTS and through little pores called *stomates*, on the underside of their leaves.

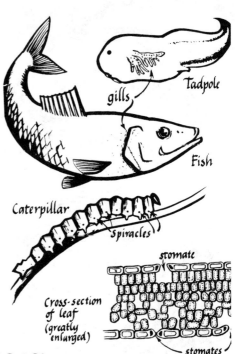

Tadpole

gills

Fish

Caterpillar

Spiracles

stomate

Cross-section of leaf (greatly enlarged)

stomates

Paul REVERE (1735–1818)

Born in Boston, Massachusetts, Paul Revere became a master silversmith. He designed and made many beautiful silver, gold, and copper pieces. He also turned his hand to other skills—engraving, printing, dentistry, and bell and cannon casting. He designed and printed the first Continental money.

As an active American patriot, Revere took part in the BOSTON TEA PARTY. He made several long trips on horseback for causes connected with the colonial struggle for freedom. On April 18, 1775, Revere found out that the

British planned to seize the patriots' guns and ammunition at Lexington and Concord. When the red-coated British troops began their "secret" march, Paul Revere, William Dawes, and Samuel Prescott set out on horseback to warn the countryside that the British were coming. The colonists in Lexington were warned, but on the way to Concord, Revere was captured by a British patrol. Dawes escaped, but turned back. Prescott sped on through the darkness to warn Concord. Later, Revere was released. SEE ALSO: AMERICAN REVOLUTION.

RHINE

The Rhine River is one of the chief waterways of Europe. It begins in the Alps Mountains and flows northward for about 820 miles (1320 km). The Rhine empties into the North Sea near ROTTERDAM in Holland.

Ocean-going ships bring raw materials like oil, coal, and iron ore to Rotterdam. Here, smaller vessels and barges carry these materials up the Rhine to industrial areas like Düsseldorf in West Germany. Barges are also towed by tugs all the way to Basel in Switzerland. Ships bring Swiss and German manufactured goods down the Rhine to be exported abroad.

Between the cities of Bonn and Mainz, the Rhine flows through a picturesque region. The steep hillsides are covered with vineyards that produce the famous Rhine wine. Many old castles and quiet villages are situated here. Lords in these castles once levied tolls on all boats that passed by. Today, there is no toll for travel on the Rhine.

RHINOCEROS

Rhinoceros comes from two Greek words meaning "nose" and "horn." A rhinoceros is a massive animal found in Africa, India, and Southeast Asia. The African species has two horns on its nose; most Asian species have only one horn. The horns are made of hard, compressed hair.

The rhinoceros is a MAMMAL, with a thick hide that is almost hairless. Though clumsy, it can move at a fast trot when disturbed. Its sense of sight is very poor, and it depends instead on its keen sense of smell or of hearing. The white rhinoceros of Africa has bird companions which warn it of danger. Despite its poor eyesight, a charging rhinoceros can be extremely dangerous.

Like the HIPPOPOTAMUS, this animal is fond of wallowing in the mud and water to get relief from the hot sun and the insects. The rhinoceros is the third largest land animal; only the ELEPHANT and hippopotamus are larger.

705

RHODE ISLAND

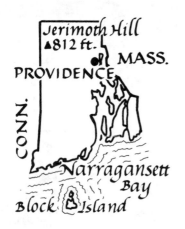

Rhode Island is the smallest state of the United States. It is not an island, although many islands lie in Narragansett Bay, which extends inland from the Atlantic about 28 miles (45 km). Also part of the state is Block Island, which is 10 miles (16 km) out to sea. The land consists of coastal plains and low, rolling hills. Providence is the state capital. There are nearly 1 million people in Rhode Island.

In 1524, an Italian explorer, Giovanni da Verrazano, visited the area. Adriaen Block, a Dutch navigator, explored there in 1614, but no settlements were established until 1636. At that time, some PURITANS from Massachusetts, led by Roger Williams, founded Providence, the state's first colony. Two years later, Williams set up the first Baptist church in the U.S. Rhode Island offered religious freedom to many people; Quakers settled there in 1657, and Jews from Holland in 1658. Colonists fought and defeated the Wampanoag and Narraganset Indians. They prospered, thanks to a three-cornered trade. Rum from Rhode Island was shipped to Africa and traded there for slaves who were then taken to the West Indies. The slaves were sold for molasses that was carried back to Rhode Island for making rum. Industry developed in the state after Samuel Slater built in 1790 the first cotton-textile mill in the U.S., near what is now Pawtucket, Rhode Island.

Textiles are still manufactured in the state today, along with jewelry, silverware, metal products, tools, and machinery. Rhode Island is famous for its poultry, notably the Rhode Island Reds.

Cecil RHODES (1853–1902)

The Englishman Cecil Rhodes worked at 16 in the diamond mines in Kimberley, South Africa. Afterward he studied at Oxford University in England, but returned to South Africa. Soon Rhodes controlled all of the South African diamond mines and formed the DeBeers Consolidated Mines Company.

He wanted to increase the power of his homeland, Great Britain, and used his economic power to gain large territories in Africa for Britain. The British took over Bechuanaland (now called Botswana). He

established the British South Africa Company (another mining company) in the present countries of Zambia and Zimbabwe. Until 1979, Zimbabwe was called Rhodesia, which was so named in honor of him.

Rhodes was Prime Minister of Cape Colony, in South Africa, from 1890 to 1896. After an unsuccessful attempt to seize the Transvaal, a colony of the Dutch, he resigned and later died during the Boer War between Great Britain and the Dutch colonists in South Africa.

Rhodes left his enormous fortune to found the Rhodes Scholarships at Oxford which are awarded each year to students from around the world.

RHÔNE

The Rhône River begins in the Rhône glacier in Switzerland and flows west to enter Lake Geneva. Leaving the lake at GENEVA, it enters France and is joined by the Saône River at the city of Lyons.

From here, the Rhône flows south for another 230 miles (370 km) through the fertile Rhône Valley, which is covered with vineyards and fruit and vegetable gardens. The river passes old towns like Avignon and Arles, where it separates into two branches before entering the Mediterranean. Because there is much mud and silt at its DELTA, a canal was built connecting the Rhône with the French port of Marseilles.

The river is an important commercial waterway, navigable to Lyons. A series of canals links it to the RHINE and to the rivers of northern France and Belgium.

RICE

Rice is a type of GRASS that has been raised in some areas of the world for more than 4000 years. It is rather closely related to wheat. From a distance, a rice field looks like a wheat field. Rice is the chief food for about one third of the world's peoples. Millions in the crowded lands of China, India, Japan,

Southeast Asia, and the Philippines live on little else. These people eat the unpolished rice, because the brown seed coat or husk contains vitamins and minerals. Those who live only on white, polished rice often come down with a disease called *beriberi*, caused by a lack of vitamin B₁.

Rice needs more warmth and water than most other crops. While the rice crop is growing, the rich mud of the rice paddies is usually flooded. At harvest time, the rice

paddies are drained. Rice is then threshed by bullocks (bulls or oxen) trampling round and round. If the husks are to be removed, the grain is pounded and then slowly poured to the ground from baskets at shoulder level, enabling the wind to carry away the husks. The starchy grains of rice are made into a flour that is used in making thin cakes like crackers. A strong Japanese wine called *saki* is made from rice, too. Rice straw can be woven into hats, shoes, and rugs.

Provided there is enough water and warmth, a rice crop yields more food per acre for the peasant of Asia than any other crop. In the United States, rice is grown in the fertile delta of the Mississippi River, as well as in parts of Arkansas, Texas, and California.

RICHARD I–III Kings of England

Richard I (1157–1199) became King of England when his father, HENRY II, died. With an English army, Richard went to the Holy Land to free Jerusalem from the Muslims (see CRUSADES). While returning home, he was taken prisoner by the Duke of Austria. After three years, he was released for a ransom and returned to England. He then started a war with the French king, seeking to recover his French lands lost during his absence. He died during a battle.

Because of his bravery and generosity, Richard I was nicknamed "Richard the

Lion-Hearted." His brother, JOHN, succeeded him as king.

Richard II (1367–1400) became the English king when he was only 11 years old. At 14, he faced an armed mob of peasants who were revolting because of severe taxes and won their loyalty. When he grew up, he constantly fought against the great English noblemen, who wished for more power. In 1399, his cousin, Henry of Bolingbroke, made him a prisoner in Pontefract Castle, where he either starved himself to death or was murdered.

Richard III (1452–1485) became King of England through treachery and murder. When Richard's brother, who was king, died in 1483, Richard was named protector of his brother's two young sons. He then locked them in the Tower of London, where their skeletons were discovered years later. Richard declared himself king, but was later defeated and slain at the Battle of Bosworth Field.

RIO DE JANEIRO

Rio de Janeiro, the second largest city in BRAZIL, has one of the most beautiful natural harbors in the world. Surrounded by low mountain ranges, Rio, as it is commonly called, is the financial, commercial, and cultural center of the country. It is famous for its healthful climate, fine sandy beaches, beautiful parks and palm-lined drives, and modern buildings. Rio's huge harbor allows the world's largest ships to dock near the center of the city.

Tourists like Rio's fashionable Copacabana Beach, in the shape of a crescent, and the lively Mardi Gras Carnival, celebrated every year before Lent. The *cariocas*, the citizens of Rio, are great sports lovers; Rio's sports stadium is the largest in the world. Rio's famous landmarks are Sugar Loaf peak, at the entrance to its bay, and Corcovado peak (2310 feet or 716 m), on which stands a giant statue of Christ. SEE ALSO: BRAZIL.

RIVERBOAT

Early in the 19th century, American roads were poor and there were no RAILROADS. CANALS connected some parts of the Eastern states, but they were slow to make and slow to travel. In many places, rivers were the best way to get around. On wide rivers like the Hudson, sailboats carried freight between New York and Albany. On the western rivers, rafts, keelboats, flatboats (which had no keels), and even sailing ships drifted downstream to New Orleans with merchandise from western Pennsylvania and the Midwest. At New Orleans, the river craft were sold for their lumber, while the sailing ships went on to Europe. Usually these boats could not go upstream.

The river boat as we know it was made possible by the STEAM ENGINE. The first American efforts to build *steamboats* were made late in the 18th century, but it was only in 1807, when Robert Fulton began to sail the *North River Steamboat* (usually called the *Clermont*) on the Hudson, that a real steamboat traffic

began. The first steamboat on the Mississippi was the *New Orleans*, which started from Pittsburgh in 1811, went down the Ohio, then into the Mississippi and all the way down.

By 1850, there were steamboats on many rivers in the East and Midwest, and boats that ran along the New England coast. The Eastern boats were all *sidewheelers*, with paddle wheels at the sides outside the hull. These boats were often very large and grand looking, and people enjoyed traveling on them. Similar boats were used on the Great Lakes. Such boats could not easily be used, though, on the Mississippi or on the Ohio and other rivers that fed into the Mississippi. Around 1815, a special type called the *western river boat* was developed for these rivers. It had a broad, flat hull suited to the very shallow water found in many places, and a lightly built upper part with space for engines, fuel, cargo, passengers, and crew. Travel on these boats was risky, for they often exploded, burned, or sank. But they were faster than any kind of land transportation, and were often very luxurious. They, too, were often sidewheelers, but *sternwheelers*, whose paddlewheels went all the way across the rear of the boat, became popular not long before 1900. *Towboats*, which pushed barges, were always sternwheelers.

Railroads, automobiles, and buses finally gave passenger steamboating too much competition, and almost all lines were closed down by the beginning of World War II. Today, towboats powered by diesel engines still push barges on the western rivers, and a few pleasure boats still run, but the day of the grand sidewheeler is past.

RIVERS

Most rivers begin far up in the hills or mountains, with melting snows, a GLACIER, or a SPRING as their *source*. As a river flows downhill, other streams or rivers, called *tributaries*, may join and make the river larger. A river and all its tributaries is called a river system.

When a river first descends the hills, it is in its *upper course* where steep slopes make it rush along. It may bound down rapids and waterfalls, carrying sand, soil, stones, and boulders. Its swift current cuts a straight, deep channel as rocks scrape its bottom. This scraping action is called *erosion*. Such erosion creates a gully, a gorge, or a canyon, such as the Grand Canyon of the Colorado River.

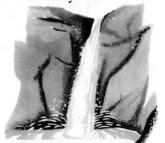

A river reaches its *middle course* when it enters a valley. The slope here is gradual and the river is wider. Since the current is more slow, there is less

711

erosion and rocks are often dropped at the bottom of the river, called the *riverbed*. Now the river cannot carry away obstacles, but must flow around them in broad loops or curves, called *meanders*. On the outer side of these curves, the water moves faster and wears away the river bank. The inner bank is lower, often with a small beach of sand and pebbles.

The *lower course* of a large river is usually across a *flood plain*. Here the river's current is very slow, and grains of soil, or *silt*, are left on the riverbed. The river becomes shallower and may meander all over the plain. During rainy seasons, the river overflows its banks and spreads rich mud, called *alluvium*, over the plain. Silt can form a low plain, or DELTA at the mouth of the river—where it flows into the ocean. If strong sea tides carry away the silt, a wide, deep inlet, or *estuary*, is sometimes created—an ideal harbor for ships.

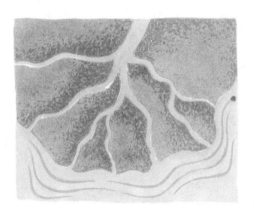

The world's rivers provide natural highways for boats and barges. Some provide drinking and cooking water; others supply water for irrigation of fields. Dams on rivers have made reservoirs and supplied water power for huge hydroelectric stations.

ROADS

Road-making is natural to man. People from a savage tribe make a path through the forest to exchange things with other tribes. Military commanders move armies along roads to attack other countries or defend their own. Ordinary travelers cross the continent on interstate highways for business or pleasure.

In ancient times there were already good roads, built to help carts and chariots move easily or to help armies march swiftly. Caravans crossed the

known world, exchanging goods between Asia and Europe. Towns where goods were bought and sold rose where the caravan roads met. The ancient Romans built the best of these ancient roads. Some can still be used.

After Roman times, European roads were not very good. Until the late 18th century, they were usually scraped from the earth. Farm laborers worked sometimes to keep them smooth, but they were dusty in dry weather and muddy in wet weather. Around 1800, John MacAdam found a way of making good roads out of small stones, and other British engineers also designed good roads. Conditions began to be better.

In America, early roads were usually dirt roads. Where there were plenty of slender, straight trees, some people built *log roads* or *plank roads*, which made vehicle travel fairly easy. Most of such roads were *toll roads* or *turnpikes*, built by private companies that charged people to travel on them. But most Americans preferred to travel by RAILROAD, by CANAL, or by RIVERBOAT if they could. Even city streets were often bare dirt, perhaps with sidewalks made of boards.

The automobile helped change things. It was heavy, and it quickly wore down old road surfaces. New types of roads, paved with bricks, stones, concrete, or asphalt had to be built for the growing numbers of automobiles early in this century.

Today, though there are still dirt roads in farm areas, most roads are paved. Towns, counties, states, and the United States Department of Transportation all contribute to a system of highways. The most important roads in the United States are called *interstate roads*. They have numbers with a letter I in front of them. Such roads are specially built to allow military units and equipment to travel along them in times of national emergency. SEE ALSO: MACADAM, ROAD SIGNS.

ROAD SIGNS

Along a road there are many kinds of signs that are important to drivers. These take many forms and colors. A red octagon carries the word STOP. A yellow diamond carries an arrow that curves in the direction the road turns. A bridge aross a high-speed road carries a green sign with the name of the next exit. Black-and-white signboards with arrows point to towns that can be reached from a crossroads and tell how far they are. Some signs give the motorist useful information, and some are like laws, telling the motorist what he must do. Here are some signs that motorists often see.

1. stop
2. winding road
3. exit
4. merging traffic
5. telephone
6. cattle crossing
7. railroad crossing
8. two-way traffic
9. pedestrian crossing

ROBIN

The robin is a typical thrush. This bird is only distantly related to the robin of the Old World. When the early American settlers first saw the bird, it reminded them of their robin redbreast, so they named it a robin.

The robin lives all over North America and is often the first bird American children recognize by name. The robin lives all year round in the southern states. Those living in the northern states migrate south for the winter. The return of the robin to the north is regarded as one of the first signs of spring.

The robin seems to like people and often builds a sturdy nest of sticks, grass, leaves, and mud close to a house or on a porch. Three to five beautiful blue eggs are laid by the female. Later, the parents are seen bringing worms and insects to their helpless young ones, which leave the nest two weeks after being hatched. Robins also eat fruit, much to the annoyance of farmers.

ROBIN HOOD

Robin Hood and his merry band of outlaws are said to have lived in Sherwood Forest, near Nottingham, England.

No one is certain if Robin Hood ever lived, but according to legend he came from a noble family and lived during the 12th century. It seems very likely that Robin Hood was a local hero who fought against the Norman lords and their forest laws. He may even have been a Saxon who lost his land when the NORMANS conquered England, and afterward robbed the rich (the Normans) to help the poor (his countrymen).

Stories about his adventures and his skill at shooting arrows have been handed down through the centuries. Robin's band included Little John, Friar Tuck, Will Scarlet, and Alan-a-Dale. Maid Marian was his lady love, and the Sheriff of Nottingham was his constant enemy. Robin Hood was the hero of many English ballads (romantic, narrative poems). The earliest mention of him is in *Piers Plowman*, a poem written about 1377.

John D. ROCKEFELLER (1839–1937)

John Davison Rockefeller grew up on a farm near Cleveland, Ohio. At 16 years old, he went to work as a bookkeeper. He saved his money and later became a partner in a grain business during the Civil War. In 1863, he established an oil refinery with his partners. By 1870, Rockefeller had become president of the Standard Oil Company of Ohio. By enlarging his business and buying out rival companies, he soon secured a monopoly (complete control) in America's oil refining industry. Rockefeller's numerous companies were tied together into an oil trust (holding company). However, in 1911, Rockefeller's oil trust was dissolved by order of the U.S. Supreme Court.

Rockefeller retired with a fabulous fortune, valued at more than one billion dollars. He then turned his attention to philanthrophy (giving money for socially useful purposes). His gifts helped establish the Rockefeller Institute for Medical Research, the General Education Board, the Rockefeller Foundation, and the University of Chicago.

ROCKETS

It is a scentific law that for every force that pushes one way there is another force that pushes as hard in the opposite way. This is the principle of every kind of rocket. A fuel that burns very quickly releases a huge amount of energy that is sent in one direction. The rock is sent in the opposite direction.

All rockets used gunpowder until about 100 years ago. They were probably invented by the Chinese and introduced into Europe in the 13th century by the invading Mongols from east Asia. Europeans used them occasionally in warfare in the next centuries, though CANNONS and GUNS interested them more. People preferred to use rockets only for FIREWORKS on great occasions. Still, the Bristish used them in the War of 1812, as the phrase "the rockets' red glare" from *The Star-Spangled Banner* shows.

Rockets were also useful for saving lives from shipwrecks and for catching whales. A rocket could carry a rope to a wrecked ship, or it could be fired into a whale's side, where it would explode.

Inventors still hoped to use the rocket for various purposes. An American, R. H. Goddard, did important experiments with rockets from 1916 on. He invented liquid rocket fuels and various steering devices that were important in improving the way rockets performed. He also predicted flights to the moon. The Germans were very interested in rockets for military purposes from the early 1930s on. During World War II they sent the first guided missiles, self-propelled flying bombs, against the Allies. Both sides in the war had rockets that could be fired from vehicles or hand-held tubes. Our *bazooka* was a open-ended tube held by a soldier; it could fire a rocket able to stop a tank.

Today there are many kinds of military rockets. They can be launched from hand-held tubes, vehicles, special structures, airplanes, or even submarines. Some of these are *free-flight missiles*, whose flight is not controlled once they are launched. Many are *guided missiles*, which can change the direction of their flight as guided from the ground. Others are *ballistic missiles*, which can be guided until their fuel runs out; after this they continue in free flight.

Rockets have made possible the launching of SATELLITES and *space-exploration vehicles*. From the time that the Soviet Union's SPUTNIK I was launched, in 1957, many satellites have gone into space on rockets to inspect different parts of the Earth and its atmosphere, transmit radio and television signals, and give out navigational information. The Soviets began sending up manned space vehicles in 1961. The United States was the first country to put a man on the moon, in 1969. SEE ALSO: SATELLITE, SPACE TRAVEL.

ROCKY MOUNTAINS

The Rocky Mountains stretch from Alaska to Mexico, in the western part of NORTH AMERICA. Numerous separate mountain ranges make up the entire Rocky Mountains.

In the U.S., the Rockies are highest and broadest in Utah and Colorado, where 55 peaks are more than 14,000 feet (4340 m) high. The Canadian Rockies are mainly in British Columbia, where the Canadian Pacific Railway goes through Kickinghorse Pass at 5320 feet (1649 m) above sea level.

Rich deposits of coal, lead, copper, silver, and gold are found in the Rockies. The scenery is beautiful, and several large parks are open to the public, such as Yellowstone and Glacier National Parks in the U.S. and Banff and Jasper National Parks in Canada.

RODENTS

Rodent comes from a Latin word meaning "to gnaw." Rodents are MAMMALS with teeth especially adapted for gnawing. Their large front teeth continuously grow, but the constant gnawing keeps them the proper size. Since the hard enamel is only on the front of the teeth, the dentine at the sides and back wears away faster and produces a sharp, chisel-like edge, enabling rodents to gnaw through wood and tree bark.

Most rodents are vegetarians, although the MOUSE and RAT will eat almost anything. Most live on land; however, the muskrat and BEAVER are mainly aquatic. The harvest mouse is the smallest rodent, weighing as little as 0.15 of an ounce (4.2 g). The largest is the capybara or water hog of tropical South America, weighing up to 174 pounds (78.3 kg). Other rodents include SQUIRRELS, gerbils, hamsters, guinea pigs, and chipmunks.

Skull of a rodent

Mouse

Rat

Rabbit

Squirrel

Beaver

RODEO

A rodeo is a public exhibition in which COWBOYS show their skill in various activities. Events include the roping, tying, and "bulldogging" (throwing to the ground by seizing the horns and twisting the head) of steers. Also, there is the riding of wild horses (broncos) and wild bulls—bareback and with saddles. Cowboys may demonstrate expert use of the lasso (a long rope) and of the gun.

Rodeo comes from the Spanish word for "roundup." In the 1800s, after cowboys rounded up, or brought in, the cattle from the range, they competed just for fun in riding and roping contests. About 1890, these contests drew large crowds, and competing cowboys began to charge an admission fee to perform. Prize money was then given to those cowboys winning the events. Today, professional cowboys earn money in traveling rodeos. Also, each year, great rodeos are held in Cheyenne, Wyoming, in Pendleton, Oregon, and in Calgary, Alberta.

ROME

According to legend, Rome was founded by twins named Romulus and Remus in about 753 B.C. Romulus became Rome's first king and ruled from the Palatine Hill—one of the seven hills of Rome. The city, situated on the banks of the Tiber River in central ITALY, prospered and developed because of its natural strongpoint. The Romans overcame the neighboring ETRUSCANS and then the Greeks in the south, becoming masters of all Italy by about 250 B.C.

Rome fought three wars with CARTHAGE, which was destroyed in 146 B.C. Rome's mighty armies conquered Spain, Greece, Macedonia, Egypt, Babylon, and Persia. Romans were relentless fighters with excellent weapons and strong discipline. They moved into Gaul

(France) and Britain, making Rome the ruler of an empire that stretched from Scotland to Persia.

Rome had several ruthless kings until they were overthrown in 509 B.C. Afterward Rome became a republic, ruled by two men called *consuls* and an assembly called the *senate*. In 70 B.C., the Roman Empire was led by a *triumvirate* (a government by three officers), until JULIUS CAESAR became the sole leader. After his death, his great nephew, Augustus Caesar, was the first of a line of Roman Emperors, some good, some cruel or mad. They ruled from Rome until CONSTANTINE, in A.D. 330, moved the government to Contantinople (now ISTANBUL).

Barbaric tribes had threatened the Romans for centuries, and finally in A.D. 410 Rome was captured and sacked by the Visigoths. Then other tribes, such as the Vandals and the HUNS, invaded and laid waste the great empire.

During their days of greatness, the Romans copied much of the learning and art of the Greeks. They were great builders, engineers, lawmakers, and soldiers. Some of Rome's famous poets are Virgil, Horace, and Ovid.

After the collapse of the empire, Rome became the center of Christianity. Today, as the capital of Italy, Rome has modern buildings and industries that stand beside the ancient ruins. During the RENAISSANCE, many foundations, squares, buildings, and churches were built, such as St. Peter's Church in the Vatican City, the home of the POPE. SEE ALSO: ITALY.

Eleanor ROOSEVELT (1884–1962)

Most wives of American Presidents are not very active in politics. But Eleanor Roosevelt was different.

Born into the wealthy Roosevelt family of New York, she married her cousin, FRANKLIN D. ROOSEVELT. A severe case of polio crippled him in 1921, and so Mrs. Roosevelt assisted his work in politics. He was elected as President of the United States for four terms. Mrs. Roosevelt visited several foreign countries for him during World War II.

After President Roosevelt died in 1945, Mrs. Roosevelt helped to establish the United Nations. She became a strong leader in American politics.

Franklin ROOSEVELT (1882–1945)

Franklin Delano Roosevelt was the only U.S. President to serve more than two terms. He was elected in 1932, 1936, 1940, and 1944. Less than three months after the start of his fourth term, he died of a cerebral hemorrhage (broken blood vessel in the brain).

The 32nd President came from a wealthy family. After becoming a lawyer in 1907, he developed a keen interest in politics and won election in 1910 to the New York State Senate. Woodrow Wilson made him assistant secretary of the Navy from 1913 to 1920. In 1921, Roosevelt was crippled by polio and was never fully able to use his legs the rest of his life. His interest in politics continued, and in 1928 he was elected governor of New York and reelected in 1930. Roosevelt belonged to the Democratic party.

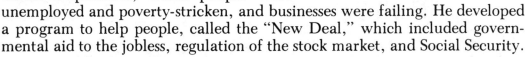

When Roosevelt was elected President in 1932, the U. S. was in a period called the Great Depression, when people were unemployed and poverty-stricken, and businesses were failing. He developed a program to help people, called the "New Deal," which included governmental aid to the jobless, regulation of the stock market, and Social Security.

America's foreign policy became important during Roosevelt's second and third term. He established the Good Neighbor policy of not interfering in the affairs of Latin American countries. He got Congress to allow military equipment to be sold to nations fighting Germany. After the U.S. entered WORLD WAR II, he mobilized the whole country against the Axis powers (Germany, Italy, and Japan). He worked with WINSTON CHURCHILL of Britain and Joseph Stalin of the Soviet Union in defeating the Axis powers and in planning for peace.

Theodore ROOSEVELT (1858–1919)

Theodore Roosevelt, the 26th President of the United States, suffered from asthma as a boy in New York City. Through exercise and determination, he built up unusual strength. As a young man, he studied law but turned to politics as a career. He was elected to the New York legislature at the age of 23.

After the deaths of his mother and wife, he spent about three years on his

ranch in North Dakota, where he developed into a skillful rider and hunter. After remarrying, T.R., or Teddy, as he was often called, served as a member of the U.S. Civil Service Commission and later as head of the New York City police board.

During the SPANISH-AMERICAN WAR, he organized the first volunteer regiment, known as the Rough Riders. He and his Rough Riders led the famous charge up San Juan Hill near Santiago, Cuba.

As a military hero, Roosevelt was first elected governor of New York and then U.S. Vice President under William McKinley. After McKinley was killed in 1901, Roosevelt became President as a Republican and was elected to that office in 1904. His motto was a "square deal" for everyone. He fought "big business," saying it was destroying politics and free competition. He took steps to conserve the nation's natural resources. He threatened to use force ("the big stick") when German and British forces disregarded the MONROE DOCTRINE, and he recognized the new Republic of Panama, making possible the PANAMA CANAL.

After leaving office, Roosevelt went big-game hunting in Africa. Later, he organized a third party, the Bull Moose Party, and ran unsuccessfully for U.S. President in 1912.

ROOTS

Roots anchor a plant firmly to the SOIL and absorb water and mineral salts. Some plants, like dandelions, have a long main or taproot, while others, like the GRASSES, have a mass of fibrous roots. Tiny root hairs near the end of each root absorb the water and minerals that the soil provides.

Roots also store food for such plants as carrots, beets, parsnips, and turnips, called "root crops" by the farmer. The tubers of the potato are not really roots but modified underground stems. However, some of the large fibrous roots of the sweet potato do swell up to store food.

ROPE

Rope is made from the twisted strands of strong fibers. The best fiber is considered to be Manila hemp; COTTON, JUTE, FLAX, and SISAL also make good rope. Nylon rope has proved highly successful in mountain climbing and towing. Rope is usually lightweight and very strong. It does not shrink when wet.

Ropes are now made by machine. They used to be made by hand in long passageways called "ropewalks," where one man handed raw fibers to another, who turned a wheel with hooks that spun the fibers into rope.

Wire ropes are made by twisting steel wire over a hemp core. These extremely strong cables are generally used for cranes and ships' derricks, where great strength is needed.

Ropes have been used by man for thousands of years. Some have been found in ancient Egyptian tombs and elsewhere. In some primitive parts of the world, bridges are made of rope.

ROSES

Roses belong to the *rosaceae* family of flowering plants which include the apple, plum, pear, almond, raspberry, and strawberry. Roses grow wherever the climate is rather mild; they prefer a stiff, rich soil, not a thin, sandy soil.

Roses from China, Japan, and Persia have helped breeders produce the many colors and varieties, four of which are shown here. Rambler, climber, and bush roses have been developed from wild roses all over the world. Wild roses have five petals, but most cultivated roses have more than five petals.

Most rosebushes are raised from branches. Rosebush seeds cannot be relied upon to reproduce the parent plant.

Roses, aside from their decorative use, are valued for their oil which is used in making perfumes and in masking foul odors of some medicines.

Dog Rose

Burnet Rose

'Ena Harkness'

'Peace'

ROSETTA STONE

For many centuries people did not know how to read ancient Egyptian HIERO-GLYPHICS. But in 1799, a Frenchman found a slab of basalt near the town of Rosetta in Egypt. It was carved with hiero-glyphics, demotic writing (another kind of ancient Egyptian writing), and Greek. If all three writings said the same thing, it gave scholars, who knew Greek already, a chance to understand hieroglyphics. The British, invading Egypt, captured the stone in 1801 and took it to the British Museum in London. There a Frenchman, Jean-François Champollion, and an English-man, Thomas Young, discovered enough to give scholars their first understanding of hieroglyphics.

The stone lists the good actions of a pharaoh who came to the throne of Egypt in 205 B.C. Since Greeks were very influential in Egypt then, and since many Egyptians did not understand hieroglyphics, the stone had to be written in three kinds of writing.

Betsy ROSS (1752–1836)

American folklore says that Betsy Ross made the first American flag. We do not know whether this is true, but many facts support the legend.

Born in Philadelphia, Pennsylvania, she married John Ross in 1773. At the Friends School in Philadelphia, Mrs. Ross developed a great skill for sewing and embroidery. General George Washington's army was based at Philadelphia early in the AMERICAN REVOLUTION, so he may have asked Mrs. Ross to design a flag for them.

The Continental Congress selected the nation's first official flag on June 14, 1977. The Congress did not say who had designed the flag, but the story of Betsy Ross became the popular explanation.

ROTTERDAM

Rotterdam is one of the busiest ports in the world. It is in HOLLAND and lies on both banks of the Maas River (the mouth of the RHINE). Rotterdam is connected to the NORTH SEA by a 20-mile (32 km) canal that is wide enough for ocean-going ships.

Rotterdam's chief industries include shipbuilding and ship repair, machinery production, and oil refining. The city also manufactures foods, beverages, tobacco, textiles, and furniture.

In World War II, German air bombardment destroyed the center part of the city, including the birthplace of Erasmus, the famous Dutch theologian and writer.

ROUND TABLE

There are many legends about KING ARTHUR and his Knights of the Round Table. The legendary table, at which they all took their special seats, was in King Arthur's palace and court, Camelot. Often the knights rose from a banquet at the table to ride to the aid of someone in trouble.

The origin of the Round Table is not clear. The King of Cornwall, the father of Arthur's wife Guinevere, is

said to have given it as a wedding present to King Arthur, who needed a table large enough to seat 150 of his best knights. Merlin, the magician, is also said to have made it at the request of Arthur to prevent quarrels among the knights. Since the table was round, every knight was equal in rank, with none sitting at the head—the seat of honor. Among those celebrated knights were Sir Lancelot, Sir Gawain, Sir Gareth, and Sir Galahad.

An old round table hangs now in the castle at Winchester, in England. It has places for 25 persons—a king and 24 knights.

RUBBER

When the Spanish first came to the New World, they found the Indians playing with balls that bounced. These balls were made from the milky juice, called LATEX, from the rubber tree. The Spanish, in search of gold and treasure, did not take any interest in the substance. Two centuries later, Frenchmen exploring the AMAZON River noticed that the Indians also made shoes, bowls, and bottles out of this same material. They brought some back to Europe, but it aroused little interest since it got sticky in summer and brittle in winter. However, Joseph Priestley, the English scientist who discovered oxygen, found that this substance from South America would rub out pencil marks; he called the substance "rubber."

Aside from being used for raincoats and rubber bands, rubber did not have a significant impact on industry until 1839. At that time, Charles Goodyear, an American, added sulfur to rubber and heated the mixture. The process, called *vulcanization*, made rubber easy to use: it was no longer brittle or sticky. Around 1900, an Englishman recognized the growing importance of rubber and planted many little rubber trees in Southeast Asia. The rubber plantations were a success, and by 1932 they were producing almost the entire world supply of rubber.

On the plantations, the first slanting cut ("tapping") is made halfway around the trunk of a rubber tree when it is about four or five years old. A spout at the base of the cut guides the latex to a cup, which is regularly emptied. At the factory, acid is mixed with the milky sap, which is then rolled into flat sheets and dried in wood smoke. The crude rubber is shipped to the United States and Europe, where it is vulcanized and molded into tires, toys, hot water bottles, rubber gloves, and many other things.

Artificial rubber was made from petroleum and alcohol during World War II, when there were shortages of natural rubber. Some products are better when made with artificial rubber. Other products are better when made with a mixture of natural and artificial rubber.

Peter Paul RUBENS (1577–1640)

This great Flemish painter, who was born in Flanders (now part of BELGIUM), studied the works of the great artists of Europe. He became Court painter at Antwerp and traveled frequently to France, Spain, and England, painting for kings and noblemen.

The paintings of Rubens are full of glowing color and the joy of life. The abundant energy and warmth of Rubens' nature is seen in his many portraits, nude figures, battle scenes, landscapes, and religious paintings. More than 2000 paintings are attributed to Rubens' studio. Here his assistants sometimes painted the lesser details on his huge canvases, and Rubens applied the finishing touches.

RUMANIA

Rumania, or Romania, is a country in southeastern Europe, bordering on the BLACK SEA. Bucharest is its capital and largest city.

The Transylvanian and Carpathian Mountains enclose a plateau in the northwest that is covered with thick forests. The rest of Rumania is drained by the DANUBE River, which flows along the southern border. Here the rich soil is ideal for growing corn, sugar beets, and wheat and for raising cattle. There are large oil and natural gas fields near Ploesti, in south central Rumania.

Many of the 21.6 million Rumanians descended from the Romans, who once settled there. Modern Rumania consists of three major areas: Moldavia, Wallachia, and Transylvania. It is a socialist republic controlled by the Communists.

RUSSIA

Russia is the common name for the Soviet Union or the U.S.S.R. (the Union of Soviet Socialist Republics). Russia is the largest country in the world, stretching from the Baltic Sea to the North Pacific. It is so vast that a train usually takes 10 days to go the 6000 miles (9660 km) across it. Russia's northern border is along the Arctic Ocean; its southernmost border touches Afghanistan—about 4000 miles (6440 km) from the Arctic. This enormous area is ruled by the Supreme Soviet (a "soviet" is a council) in MOSCOW, the capital.

Part of Russia makes up the eastern half of Europe. Here the land is a vast plain, with the Ural Mountains separating European Russia from Asian Russia. Several great rivers, such as the Volga and the Dnieper, flow over this plain. South of the plain are the BLACK SEA and the Caspian Sea (the largest

726

inland and saltwater lake in the world). These seas are divided by the Caucasus Mountains.

East of the Urals is the plain of SIBERIA. through which three great rivers—the Ob, the Yenisei, and the Lena—flow northward into the Arctic Ocean. Further east is a mountainous region that stretches to the Pacific Ocean. Along Russia's southern border with China and Mongolia are several high mountain ranges.

Because Russia is a large land mass, it has mainly a continental climate—that is, very hot summers, long cold winters, and moderate rainfall.

Since World War II, Russia has developed its natural resources. Huge amounts of grain are grown on its plains; much lumber comes from the great forests

in the north; coal and iron ore are mined in the Ukraine and Siberia; and oil and natural gas are abundant in the Caucasus region. Great hydroelectric plants have been built on many Russian rivers, which are also used for travel and transporting raw materials and manufactured goods. Industry and science have changed Russia, which today has one of the most modern educational systems in the world.

Russia contains many different peoples, with their own customs and language. There are Slavs, who are the real "Russians" and who live mainly in the European part, as well as Armenians, Ukrainians, and millions of Asiatics who look like the Chinese rather than any Western race.

The first Russian state was in Kiev in the 9th century A.D. The Mongols (Tartars) later overran the country. It grew under the dukes and princes of Moscow, and by 1480 freed itself from the Mongols. Ivan the Terrible, the first czar (emperor) in 1547, conquered new lands and ruled severely. In the early 1700s, Peter the Great added new territory and built Russia into a mighty empire, with its capital at St. Petersburg (now Leningrad). Since the RUSSIAN REVOLUTION of 1917, the country has been ruled by the Communist Party that says the state owns everything.

The RUSSIAN REVOLUTION

For about 500 years, RUSSIA was controlled by the czars (emperors), the nobility, and the rich landowners. The common people lived and worked under hard conditions and with little freedom. In the 1800s, secret revolutionary groups became active in Russia, seeking to make life better for the people and to reform the government. The czars, who had complete power, were often surrounded by corrupt officials, who prevented any reforms. Thus, there grew a strong spirit of unrest and anger, especially among university students and intellectuals. Many were influenced by Karl Marx, the German originator of Communism. He urged all workers to rebel and overthrow the wealthy classes. All property afterward would be owned by the people, who would also run the government. A rebellion in 1905 was unsuccessful, like many earlier ones.

Rasputin (1871 - 1916)

When WORLD WAR I began in 1914, Czar Nicholas II sent Russian soldiers to fight against Germany. Though they fought bravely, the soldiers were badly led and equipped; many returned home after many defeats on the battlefield. At home, the Russian court was under the spell of Rasputin, "the Mad Monk," who had charmed the czar's wife and totally confused the government. The sufferings of the people became worse. In March of 1917, a major revolution broke out that forced the czar to give up the throne. The revolutionaries set up a moderate government, headed by Kerensky and Prince Lvov, the czar's brother.

Lenin (1870 - 1924)

A group of Russian exiles, called Bolsheviks (Communists), now returned from Switzerland and demanded more complete change. Led by Trotsky and

LENIN, they overthrew Kerensky's government and took control in November, 1917.

Stalin (1879-1953)

Lenin, who became head of the Communist government, then made peace with Germany. The czar and his family were murdered, and the Russian workers seized the factories and the peasants grabbed the land. While the Communists gradually rebuilt the country according to their own ideas, Russia was plagued by famine and a bitter civil war broke out.

Lenin's death in 1924 brought on a struggle for power among the leaders of the Communist Party. Trotsky was exiled, and Stalin emerged as the dictator. Under him Russia, developed into a powerful Communist state.

RUST

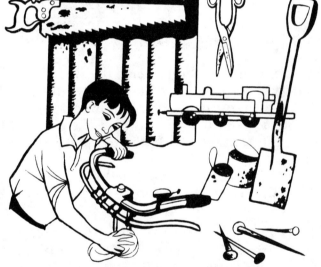

Rust is the reddish-brown coating that forms on IRON when it is exposed to the weather. It is formed when the oxygen of the air chemically joins with the iron to form iron oxide. Moisture, salt, and acid help the process; that is why iron rusts quickly in coastal areas near salt spray and in industrial areas with acidic sulfur dioxide fumes in the air.

The compound iron oxide is weak, so rusty nails, for example, no longer have the strength of iron and may soon break. The rust absorbs moisture from the air and the rusting process is speeded up more and more.

Rust can be prevented by coating iron or steel with plastic, paint, or tin- or zinc-plating. Also, iron can be mixed with corrosion-resistant metals to produce ALLOYS, called stainless steels.

Like burning, rusting is an oxidation process; however, since the iron joins with oxygen slowly, there is no heat or light given off.

Babe RUTH (1895–1948)

George Herman Ruth, better known as "the Babe" or "the Bambino," was born in Baltimore, Maryland. He attended St. Mary's Industrial School, where he developed into a good baseball player. In 1914, he joined the Baltimore Orioles, a team then in the International League. As a good left-handed pitcher, he soon attracted much attention and was bought by the Boston Red Sox of the American League.

With the Red Sox, Ruth became a successful pitcher, winning 87 games and three World Series games (one in 1916, two in 1918). However, his strong hitting ability made the Red Sox shift him to the outfield. In 1920, Ruth was bought by the New York Yankees and played with them until 1934. He hit the most home runs for several seasons, reaching a peak in 1927 with 60. His feats at bat and his pleasant personality brought him many fans. In 1935, the Yankees traded him to the Boston Braves, with whom he played one season.

In 22 seasons between 1914 and 1935, Ruth hit 714 home runs. Only Hank Aaron has hit more home runs in a lifetime.

RYE

Although rice and wheat are more important cereal grasses, rye is much hardier and can withstand poorer soil and colder temperatures. Russia grows half of the world's rye. Much rye is also grown in northern Europe.

The seeds or grains of rye are used in making rye flour for rye bread and crackers. The entire rye plant is often fed to farm animals. The straw from the dried stems is woven into mats and is also used as a packing material for china and glassware.

SAHARA

The Sahara is the largest DESERT in the world. It stretches from the Atlantic Ocean to the Red Sea across northern AFRICA. The NILE River flows through part of the eastern Sahara.

Much of the Sahara is a rocky plateau, about 1000 feet (310 m) above sea level. There are shallow valleys throughout the desert filled with stones and sand. The soft

sand of the Libyan Desert, a part of the Sahara, blows into massive dunes that constantly shift and change shape. In different spots, mountain ranges stick out and underground springs rise to the surface, creating an OASIS, where the land is green. Dried up riverbeds (wadis) and the ruins of ancient villages indicate that some of the Sahara once had fertile soil.

In the desert's interior, temperatures during the day may reach 130°F (54°C). However, they fall quickly at night. In winter (from December to January), it is quite cold and sometimes icy. Powerful wind storms often occur and very little rain ever falls.

Merchants with camel caravans (trains) cross the desert, following numerous stony trails and stopping at oases for rest. At places like Timbuktu, they trade in dates, salt, ivory, cloth, and rifles. Tough jeeps, trucks, and airplanes are now replacing the camel as the chief means of travel in the Sahara. There are also plans to build a railroad across it.

The different peoples that live there are the Arabs in the north, the Moors and Berbers in the west, the Tuaregs, the nomadic (wandering) Bedouins, and the black Tibus and Negroes in the south. Most are traders or herdsmen who drive their goats and camels from one spot to another.

Much of the Sahara was once controlled by France. Today, it is divided among the countries of Morocco, Mauritania, Algeria, Libya, Tunisia, Egypt, Sudan, Chad, Niger, and Mali. Recently, rich deposits of oil and natural gas have been discovered, especially in the northern regions. Copper and uranium have also been found, and engineers think there are other valuable minerals there. SEE ALSO: DESERT.

SAILS

Wind moves against one face of a sail in such a way that a low pressure is created on its other face. The effort of the air to make the pressure of the air equal on both faces is what moves a sailing SHIP.

There are many forms of sail, but a few types are common. A *square sail* normally extends across a ship

and hangs from a level pole called a *yard*. A *fore-and-aft* sail is more or less triangular and hangs either from a mast or from a tilted pole called a *gaff*. Its foot is often extended by a level pole called a *boom*. A *lateen sail* is triangular and hangs from a long, tilted yard. A *lugsail* is tall and four-sided, and hangs from a short, tilted yard.

The great full-rigged ships and barks of the 19th century were *square-rigged*, with mostly square sails though with a few fore-and-aft ones. Schooners and other smaller craft were usually *fore-and-aft rigged*. Lateen sails were used mostly in the Mediterranean Sea, while lugsails were used only in small boats.

The earliest European ships had only one sail, a square sail close to the deck called a *course*. As ships became more complicated, they added masts and sails.

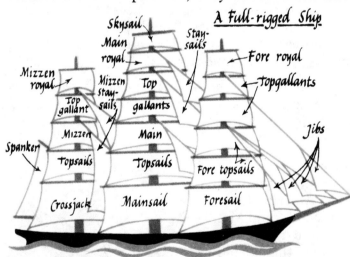

A Full-rigged Ship

The *mainmast* was the tallest mast, but in front of this might come a *foremast*, or behind it might come a *mizzen-mast*. Some ships had even more masts. Above the course came one or two *topsails*. Next there might be *topgallants*, and above those *royals*. A few ships had even higher sails. For a while some ships carried *studding-sails*, which hung from booms attached to the ends of the regular booms. These were given up in the late 19th century, when speed in sailing ships became less important than before. SEE ALSO: SHIPS.

732

SAINT

A saint is a person who lives a religious life so perfectly that other people respect and admire him in a special way. In the Roman Catholic, Orthodox, and some other Christian churches, a saint is frequently believed to have performed miracles and is officially recognized as being in heaven and able to go to God on behalf of sinners. Most Protestant churches, however, believe that the New Testament teaches that anyone who has become a Christian is a saint.

ST. LAWRENCE SEAWAY

The St. Lawrence Seaway is the largest inland waterway in North America. It is specifically the system of canals, locks, and dams built along a 182-mile (293 km) stretch of the St. Lawrence River between MONTREAL and Lake Ontario. However, the entire system of natural waterways, LOCKS, and CANALS from the Atlantic Ocean through the GREAT LAKES has come to be known as the St. Lawrence Seaway. It allows large ocean-going ships to go inland as far as the Lake Superior port of Duluth, Minnesota—a distance of 2342 miles (3771 km).

Jointly built and operated by the United States and Canada, the seaway was opened to shipping in 1959. Ships that use it pay tolls, which help pay back the cost of construction. Large hydroelectric power plants have been built along the seaway and provide much electricity to New York, Vermont, and Ontario. The seaway's 9500 miles (15,295 km) of navigable waterways have created a "fourth seacoast" for the U.S. and Canada.

SAINT PAUL'S CATHEDRAL

The city of London, England, had a great fire in 1666, in which the medieval cathedral of St. Paul was destroyed. Christopher Wren, an architect and scientist, drew plans for rebuilding the burned city and its cathedral. His plans for the city were not used, but he did build St. Paul's.

The cathedral is large and richly decorated, with a large dome like that of the United States Capitol. This is really a combination of three structures: an outer dome tall enough to be seen far away, an inner dome that is not too high for the interior, and a cone of brick between the two that carries a decorative construction of stone on top of the outer dome. The cathedral was finished in 1710.

733

SALADIN (1137?–1193)

Saladin became one of the great leaders of his time. As the sultan of Egypt and Syria, Saladin seized much land in north Africa and Arabia and constructed canals, irrigation systems, colleges, and mosques throughout his empire. In 1187, he captured JERUSALEM, and by 1190, he had taken most Christian strongholds that had been established during the first CRUSADES.

In 1191, King RICHARD I of England defeated Saladin in several battles, but was unable to recapture Jerusalem. Later, a truce was made between Richard and Saladin, who became famous for his valor and generosity.

SALMON

Salmon are fish that spend part of their lives in salt water and part in fresh water. The Pacific and Atlantic salmon travel from fresh water to salt water and back, but their journeys are not alike.

Pacific salmon spend most of their time growing up in the sea. When the time comes for the females to lay eggs, they start up river. The males go along

to fertilize the eggs so they will hatch. The journey to the spawning grounds may be as long as 2000 miles (3220 km). The salmon have to fight their way upstream over falls and rapids. Man-made fish ladders built around dams help the salmon in their exhausting travels. They do not eat but live on stored body fat. When they reach their spawning grounds, they are thin, tired, and no longer bright in color. Most die on the trip back. The baby salmon travel downstream to lakes and may remain there for a year or two before they proceed to the Pacific Ocean. They will mature and live in the ocean until it is time to spawn.

Atlantic salmon make several trips back to fresh water to spawn. The young salmon remain in fresh water for two years before journeying to the sea.

Both types of salmon return to the river where they were hatched to lay their eggs. Scientists have evidence that the salmon's sense of smell guides it back to the waters in which it spawned.

The Columbia River and Alaska are famous for their salmon. Salmon fishing with rod and line is a highly skillful sport. Most salmon are canned. They are also available fresh or smoked.

SALT

There are salt mines in areas where salty seas once existed. These seas eventually dried up and later other rocks covered the layers of rock salt, called *halite*. Today, large deposits of rock salt are in Michigan, New York, Ohio, and Texas. India, China, Russia, Poland, and Germany also have much salt.

Since early days, salt has been important as a seasoning and a preservative. In ancient Ethiopia and Tibet, cakes of salt were also used as money. Our word "salary" comes from *sal*, the Latin word for "salt." Part of a Roman soldier's pay was in salt.

With the use of modern mining machinery, salt has become very plentiful. There is enough salt in the ground to last for millions of years. Salt is dug out of underground mines in blocks or obtained by evaporating the brine (saltwater) from salt springs near salt mines. Besides being used for flavoring and preserving, salt is used in making steel, dyes, drugs, soap, and glass. It is also good for melting ice on sidewalks.

SAMSON

The story of Samson is told in Judges, one of the oldest books of the BIBLE. He was one of God's leaders and helped the HEBREWS in their struggle against their enemies, particularly the Philistines. Because he had taken the vows of a Nazarite, Samson was forbidden to cut his hair or to taste wine.

He had extraordinary physical strength, which enabled him to tear a lion apart with his hands. He was also able to slay 1000 Philistines with the jawbone of an ass. To escape from Gaza, he lifted up the gateposts and carried them away.

Samson fell in love with a Philistine woman called Delilah, to whom he revealed the secret that his great strength lay in his hair. She told this to the Philistines, who cut off his hair, and blinded and chained him in their temple. He regained his strength as his hair grew back. One day when the Philistines were making fun of him, he grabbed two large pillars of the temple and pulled them with all his might. The roof caved in, destroying Samson and his enemies.

SAND

Sand comes from the breaking up of rocks, mostly quartz, into tiny grains. Sand is found on the shores and bottoms of lakes and oceans and on DESERTS and also mixed with soil. It is therefore one of the most common substances in the world.

Sand is used in making CEMENT, CONCRETE, GLASS, and sandpaper. It is also used in filtering water and for casting molds in foundries.

SAN FRANCISCO

San Francisco, the second largest city in CALIFORNIA, is one of the most beautiful cities in the world. It is situated on a hilly and narrow peninsula, with the Pacific Ocean on the west and large San Francisco Bay on the east. More than 3 million people live in or around the city.

Golden Gate Bridge

Cable car

Coit Memorial Tower

San Francisco is known for its mild climate, dense fog, high hills, cable cars, fine restaurants and shops, and many foreign communities. Because its residents have a great interest in art, music, and theater, San Francisco is a major cultural center in the U.S. It is also the financial center of the West. Many of the imports and exports of the U.S. pass through the port of San Francisco.

The city was founded in 1776, when a Spanish mission was built. The GOLD RUSH to California brought many settlers after 1849. In 1906, San Francisco was destroyed by a great earthquake and fire. Quickly rebuilt, the city attracted many new residents and new businesses. SEE ALSO: CALIFORNIA.

SAP

Sap is the watery juice that circulates in plants. Besides water, it contains various mineral substances and salts absorbed from the soil by the root hairs of the plant.

Water with these dissolved substances flows up through the stem in tubes to the leaves. (These tubes can be seen clearly when a stalk of celery is placed in some water tinted with food coloring for a few hours.) Water is pulled upwards chiefly by *transpiration*. As water evaporates through the leaf cells, the leaves pull up more sap through the stem to replace the lost water. The ROOTS in turn absorb more water from the earth. Root pressure helps force the sap up, too. In aging trees, the sap can not flow through the

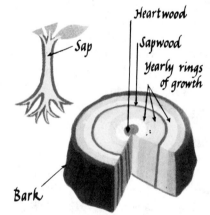

Heartwood

Sapwood

Yearly rings of growth

Sap

Bark

hard heartwood but instead moves through the lighter colored "sapwood" near the bark.

The sap of the tropical evergreen sapodilla tree is called *chicle*, a main ingredient of chewing gum. Some plants, such as sugar cane, sugar beets, and sugar maples, contain sugary sap that is commercially important. Rubber trees produce a special kind of sap called LATEX.

SASKATCHEWAN

Saskatchewan is a large province in central CANADA. The southern two-thirds of the province consists of vast, rolling plain. The land here is devoted to the growing of wheat, oats, barley, rye, and flax. Saskatchewan's northern part is a desolate, rocky country, with large forests and many lakes and rivers. Uranium is mined in the region north of Lake Athabasca. Saskatchewan's other mineral resources include oil, natural gas, coal, copper, potash, and zinc.

Vast buffalo herds roamed the central plains when fur trappers of the Hudson's Bay Company established posts there in the 1700s. The Assiniboin, Cree, and Chippewa Indians hunted and lived at that time in the region. With the building of the railroad and the offer of free land for farming, many settlers came in the late 1800s. In 1905, the province of Saskatchewan was created by the Canadian government.

Regina is the province's capital and largest city. Here are situated stockyards, meat-packing plants, flour mills, and automobile assembly plants. Saskatchewan has nearly 1 million inhabitants.

SATELLITE

A satellite is an object caught between two forces in the neighborhood of a planet. One force pulls the satellite toward the planet, while the other pulls it away. The two forces are equal, so the satellite keeps moving around. The Earth has one natural satellite—the MOON. Mars and Neptune have two each, Uranus has five, Saturn has nine, and Jupiter has twelve.

Since the Russian launching of *Sputnik I* in 1957, many man-made satellites have been launched.

A man-made satellite is sent up by a rocket that carries it through the Earth's atmosphere. It would move in a straight line, except that the Earth's gravity keeps pulling it down. The satellite keeps falling toward the Earth. But the Earth is round and the ground curves downward where the satellite is falling. The satellite maintains the same distance above the Earth and keeps going around and around. A man-made satellite reflects radio transmissions from the Earth to distance receivers on the Earth or gathers and transmits information about conditions in outer space. It usually spins, as a gyroscope does, to keep its antennas pointed toward the Earth.

SATURN

Saturn is the second largest PLANET in the SOLAR SYSTEM and the sixth in orbit around the sun. It revolves around the sun in a period of about 30 years, and its surface temperature is near –240° F (–151° C). Most of this yellowish planet and its atmosphere consists of hydrogen, helium, and the poisonous gases methane and ammonia; therefore, it is so light that it would float on water.

Saturn's three shining rings, bright as the planet itself, are made up of tiny moonlets that may be what remains of a moon that came too close to it and split into pieces. Saturn also has 9 moons, one of which, named Phoebe, travels in an opposite direction to the others.

SAXONS

The Saxons were a tribe that inhabited the northern part of Germany during the early Christian era. Later, they made settlements along the coasts of Gaul (France) and Britain. About A.D. 450, the Saxons joined with the Angles and Jutes—two northern tribes—and conquered a large area in Britain.

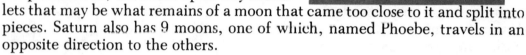

As the centuries went by, it became usual for the Christians in the country to call themselves Saxons. However, the country was soon known as England in

honor of the Angles. The Saxons under ALFRED THE GREAT fought the Danes, and a Saxon army led by Harold fought the Normans at the BATTLE OF HASTINGS.

The Saxons were skillful in making embroidery and jewelry of enamel, ivory, and silver. Saxon monks built solid churches of wood and stone, a few of which still stand, and decorated their books with beautiful illuminations. SEE ALSO: ANGLO-SAXONS.

SCANDINAVIA

Scandinavia consists of the countries of NORWAY, SWEDEN, and DENMARK. It sometimes includes ICELAND, an island about 550 miles (885 km) west of Norway, and FINLAND, a nation east of Sweden. Except for the Lapps in the north and the Finns in the east, the Scandinavians speak a closely related group of languages that developed from Old Norse; most belong to a Nordic people (see RACES).

SCHOOLS

Schools include all places of learning of any kind, from kindergarten to the university level. Education in the earliest times was conducted mainly by the parents and was generally religious in character. The ancient Greeks maintained a school system for all, teaching elementary subjects as well as advanced courses in philosophy, science, and language. In the Middle Ages,

schools were run by monks or priests in monasteries or churches. Gradually the idea grew that it was the duty of the state to educate the child—at least, to instruct him in elementary reading, writing, and arithmetic. But many still believed instruction should be left in the hands of the Church.

Schools in the United States are public, private, or church-related. The public schools are financed by local, state, and federal taxes. Each state controls its own public schools, and each city and county in a state has its own school system. Private schools are supported by groups of people or organizations, and by tuition (money) paid by the parents of the students who attend.

There are successive levels of schools in the U.S.—nursery schools, kindergartens, elementary schools, middle or junior high schools, senior high schools or vocational and technical schools, junior or community colleges, colleges and universities. Most schools operate from September to June each year, but many have summer sessions.

Children three and four years old learn through play and informal teaching in the nursery schools. Kindergarten begins to teach some basic skills. Elementary schools stress reading, writing, and arithmetic and have some science, history, and geography, as well as art, music, and drama. In junior and senior high schools, students usually go from class to class, being taught by different teachers. Each year they study more advanced subjects, such as algebra or English literature. Vocational schools instruct students for work as mechanics, carpenters, stenographers, and so on. Colleges and universities educate young men and women to be engineers, doctors, lawyers, businessmen, and so on. People also attend college just to learn more about the world, enriching their own lives in the process.

Franz SCHUBERT (1797–1828)

Franz Schubert lived most of his life in VIENNA, where he studied singing at a choir school. He was not considered a good student because he spent much of his time composing music.

At 14, Schubert began to write songs and a year later composed his first symphony. By 1816, he had completed three symphonies, four operas, three masses, a cantata (choral piece), and about 200 songs. This was the beginning of Schubert's incredibly productive, but short, life.

When he died of typhus at the age of 32, Schubert had composed more than 600 songs. Also, some of the world's finest orchestral, piano, and chamber music (for small groups of instruments) was composed by him. During his life, he earned little money from his music and gained little recognition, though BEETHOVEN admired his musical talent.

Albert SCHWEITZER (1875–1965)

Born in Kayersberg, a town then in German Alsace, Albert Schweitzer began piano lessons at the age of five and organ lessons at the age of eight. He studied religion and philosophy at the University of Strasbourg and at the Sorbonne (the University of Paris). After becoming a Protestant minister, Schweitzer was appointed head of Strasbourg's religious school and undertook much charitable work. By this time, he was an excellent organist and an authority on JOHANN SEBASTIAN BACH.

However, at the age of 30, Schweitzer decided to devote himself to the direct service of mankind. For six years, he studied medicine, becoming a doctor in 1911. Two years later, Schweitzer and his wife left for Lambaréné, French Equatorial Africa (now Gabon). As a medical missionary there, he established a hospital and dedicated the remainder of his life to helping others. He wrote several books about his philosophy ("reverence for life") and religious faith. From lectures and organ-recital tours, Schweitzer received money to enlarge and equip his hospital with drugs and medical supplies. He received the Nobel Peace Prize in 1952.

SCIENCE

Science comes from the Latin word meaning "to know." Science is a branch of knowledge dealing with facts or "truths" that have been logically arranged in a special system. If a scientist discovers something, it is usually the result of many experiments. His discovery is also the result of careful checking and the comparison of facts and findings of other scientists.

There are many branches of science. Some of the most important are astronomy, geology, botany, zoology, chemistry, physics, biology, geography, meteorology (the atmosphere, climate, and weather), psychology, and medicine. Most of these sciences are listed and explained in this encyclopedia.

The "pure" sciences, such as physics, chemistry, and botany, observe and explain nature and the universe. The "applied" sciences, such as engineering, medicine, and agriculture, put the findings of pure science to work in practical ways.

SCORPIONS

Scorpions belong to the SPIDER family. They vary in length from 1 to 4 inches (2.5–10.2 cm), but all have powerful pincers, that look like those of a lobster, and a curved and pointed stinger at the end of the tail. The poisonous sting is sharp and painful, although usually not fatal to man.

Scorpions come out at night to feed on insects. In desert areas, they can go without water for many months; in hot, moist areas, they can live without food for more than a year. The female carries her young on her back until they can care for themselves.

SCOTLAND

Scotland lies in the northern part of GREAT BRITAIN. It has a jagged coastline with many islands and deep inlets, or *firths* (see FIORDS). The country also includes the Hebrides Islands to the west and the Orkney and Shetland Islands to the north. Edinburgh, near the Firth of Forth, is its capital.

The Scottish Highlands in the north are an area of mountains and valleys, called *glens*. The highest peak—Ben Nevis, 4406 feet (1366 m)—is located here, in the Grampian Mountains. Many beautiful lakes, or *lochs*, rest in the Scottish glens.

South of the Highlands is a good farming region called the Lowlands. Most of Scotland's 5 million people live here. In Glasgow, Scotland's largest city, many work in shipbuilding along the Clyde River. Most of Scotland's other industries are in the Lowlands, such as the manufacture of whiskey, woolens, and tweed textiles. Oil in the North Sea has become a major industry and source of wealth for the Scots.

The Romans called the country Caledonia. In the A.D. 400s, an Irish tribe called the Scots settled on the west coast, and by the A.D. 900s the whole country was ruled by the Scots. The English kings often tried to take control of Scotland. In 1603, the son of MARY QUEEN OF SCOTS was crowned King JAMES I of England, and Scotland and England were ruled by the same royal family—the Stuarts. The two countries were officially united in 1707, and Scotland now sends representatives to the British Parliament in London. Many Scots want to make their country entirely independent from Great Britain.

Robert SCOTT (1868–1912)

Robert Scott was a British naval officer and explorer. In 1901, he went to the Antarctic region and spent the next four years surveying, exploring, and doing scientific research.

In 1911, he led an expedition to reach the SOUTH POLE. With four other men, Scott battled severe storms and finally reached the Pole on January 18, 1912. But they discovered that a Norwegian explorer, ROALD AMUNDSEN, had beaten them by about one month. On their return journey, the heroic expedition was hit by blizzards, lack of food, frostbite, and sickness. All five men died. The following spring, a search party found the bodies of Scott and two others only 11 miles (18 km) from their base camp. Later, Scott's diaries, records, and valuable scientific information were recovered.

Sir Walter SCOTT (1771–1832)

Sir Walter Scott was a famous Scottish poet and novelist. He was born in Edinburgh, Scotland, and spent much time as a young boy studying old legends.

In 1792, he became a lawyer, but soon turned his attention to writing. First he collected the old ballads and tales of the border region between England and Scotland and later wrote a long poem *The Lay of the Last Minstrel*. His success made him turn to a long series of romantic and historical novels. *Waverly, Rob Roy, The Bride of Lammermoor, Ivanhoe, Quentin*

Durward, and *The Talisman* are only a few of the books he wrote at great speed. *Ivanhoe* concerns the struggle between the NORMANS and the SAXONS, and ROBIN HOOD is one of the characters in the novel. Scott also wrote many popular lyrics and ballads, such as "Lochinvar" and "Proud Maisie."

After 1825, Scott had financial troubles and tried to pay off his debts by writing more and more. His health became poor, and he later died at his home, Abbotsford, in southeastern Scotland.

SCULPTURE

Today there are many kinds of sculpture, so that it is hard to say what sculpture really is. It is best to define it as art in three dimensions—that is, art that has height, width, and depth. A painting is not sculpture because it is flat. A building is not sculpture because it is meant mostly to be used, not looked at. A vase is not sculpture for the same reason.

Until this century it was easy to say what sculpture was. The *sculptor* carved stone or wood, shaped clay, or made castings of bronze to create figures of gods, men, animals, or plants. He made *statues* of people, showing their full figures, or *busts*, showing them from the chest up. He put these on stands called *pedestals*, as the Romans did, or in *niches*, openings in a wall, as the medieval sculptors did.

Statues and busts were usually done "in the round," showing all sides, but sculptors also did *reliefs*, in which the individual figures were raised from a background. In *high relief* the figures almost stand free of the background surface. In *low relief* they stand out very little, so that the relief is like a picture.

In this century, sculptors have tried many other forms of their art. They have simplified the natural forms they used to copy, or have created forms that do not copy anything in nature. They have made *kinetic sculptures*, which move. They have made sculptures out of wires, out of sheet metal, out of pieces of junk and other unusual things. They have

Easter Island (Pacific)

Egyptian (Queen Nefertiti)

Totem pole (N. American Indian)

Greek

Modern (Henry Moore)

Gothic (Medieval) Chartres

744

used new materials such as plastics. They have created *environmental sculptures*, like rooms through which people are supposed to walk. Even empty space can be used for sculpture rather than the solid materials that sculptors always used. Some sculptures have been made to be touched rather than seen.

Sculptors are still experimenting with new ideas, and yet statues and busts of people are still being made. The art of sculpture has never had so much variety as it has today.

SEA ANIMALS and SEA PLANTS

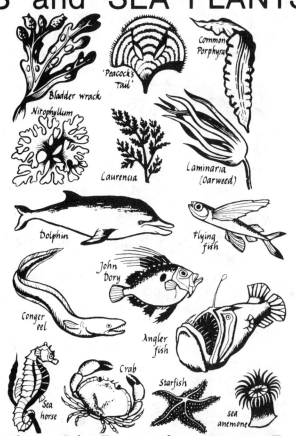

There is still much for marine biologists to learn about the strange life forms beneath the sea. Hundreds of varieties of red, brown, and green seaweeds anchor themselves to rocks by means of tough, flat suckers. Some are buoyed up by air bladders.

In the deep oceans, there are countless microscopic plants, such as algae and diatoms, and tiny sea animals that help to make up *plankton*, the food of many creatures, including the whale.

Sea animals are more varied. There are hideous fish, such as the angler fish of the cold, dark ocean depths, and pretty fish, like the tropical rainbow fish. Others are the large SHARK and cod families, flat fish, EELS, and oddities, such as the lungfish, sea horse, John Dory, and FLYING FISH. Even more numerous are those that are not fish at all: the mammals—WHALES, PORPOISES, and DOLPHINS; the crustaceans—shrimps, LOBSTERS, PRAWNS, and CRABS; the soft-bodied shell creatures called mollusks, such as the oyster, clam, squid, and OCTOPUS; and the simple sea animals, more like plants—the sea anemones, sea lilies, and SPONGES. CORAL is formed from the skeletons of tiny sea animals. Most sea animals prey upon each other, but some feed upon the rich supply of plankton.

SEALS

Seals are warm-blooded MAMMALS that live mostly in the sea. They are divided into three groups: eared seals, earless seals, and WALRUSES.

Fur Seal

Common Seal

The eared seals, named because they have little, external ears, include fur seals and sea lions. Fur seals spend the winter roaming the ocean. In the spring, they group together on their breeding grounds—the Pribilof Islands in the Bering Sea. To get there they often swim thousands of miles. The males (bulls) arrive first, and each establishes his own territory among the rocks. When the females (cows)

Young Common Seals

arrive, each bull claims about a dozen cows for himself and guards them ferociously. The young males are driven off. These eared seals used to be killed for their soft fur, but now they are under govenment protection. Sea lions, found in the Pacific and South Atlantic, are much larger and more agile on land than fur seals. They are favorite performers in circus acts because they are intelligent and easily tamed.

The earless or true seals include the elephant and harbor seals. An elephant seal has a big nose. An adult male may be 18 feet (5.6 m) long and weigh thousands of pounds. The much smaller harbor seal is often seen on shore. True seals are hunted for their oil and leathery skins.

Walruses live in the North Atlantic and are bulky creatures with ivory tusks that are used for prying shellfish from the rocks. SEE ALSO: WALRUS.

SEASONS

The EARTH takes one year to make one complete trip around the SUN. As it travels this annual journey of 600 million miles (966 million km), it spins on a tilt. It is this tilt of the Earth that causes the four seasons of the year.

The diagram on page 747 shows the position of the Earth's axis in relation to the sun at four different times of the year.

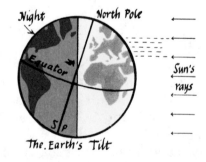

Night

North Pole

Equator

Sun's rays

S.P.

The. Earth's Tilt

In December, the North Pole tilts away from the sun. The Arctic gets no light at all, and northern countries are cold because the slanting rays of the sun spread the heat over a larger area with less heat in each part. Days are short.

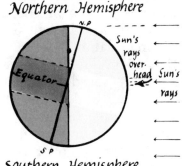

Northern Hemisphere

As winter progresses, days grow longer and warmer. By March, it is spring.

In June, the North Pole points towards the sun, and the Northern Hemisphere receives more direct rays from the sun. Days are long; the Arctic becomes "the land of the midnight sun," having light even at midnight. Summer has arrived.

By September, the days are cooler and shorter. It is now autumn.

Southern Hemisphere

The seasons are reversed in the Southern Hemisphere. Christmas in Australia would be in hot weather, for December is in their summer season.

The dotted lines in the top diagram represent the TROPICS. The area between them, on both sides of the EQUATOR, is always hot because the sun is almost always overhead there. The tropics have only slight variation between summer and winter, whereas, the poles have only summer and winter.

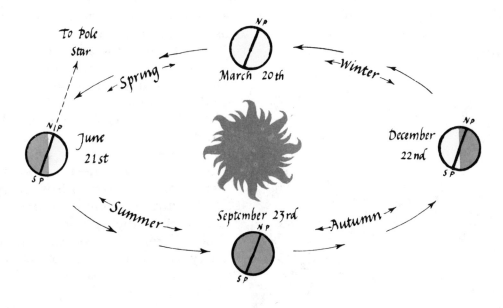

The Earth's Axis

in Relation To The Sun

SEEDS

More than 50 percent of all the world's PLANTS grow from seeds. Seeds vary greatly in size. The largest seed in the world is a type of coconut that weighs 40 pounds (18 kg). There is a type of orchid that has such a small seed that 35 million seeds weigh one ounce (28 g). Seeds may also vary greatly in color and shape. However, they are all alike in three ways: (1) they all contain a baby plant, (2) they all contain stored food for the baby plant, and (3) they all have a seed coat to protect the baby plant and its food.

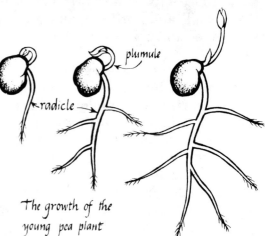

The growth of the young pea plant

Warmth and moisture cause the seed's tiny root (the *radicle*) to push downward and a shoot (the *plumule*) to push upward through the soil.

Some seeds, including bean, pea, maple, oak, and most flowering plants, have *two* special "seed leaves" (*cotyledons*) to nourish the seedling. These plants are called *di*cots. Another group, including daffodils, crocuses, tulips, and grasses have seeds with only *one* cotyledon. They are called *mono*cots.

If all of a plant's seeds fall beneath the plant, few will grow. But many seeds are carried away from the parent plant by wind or animals or water. The wind disperses many seeds. Some seeds may be light, like those of the poppy, and others may have "wings," like those of the maple and sycamore,

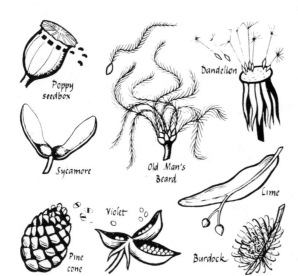

Poppy seedbox

Sycamore

Old Man's Beard

Dandelion

Lime

Pine cone

Violet

Burdock

or "plumes" or "parachutes," like the Old Man's Beard, milkweed, and dandelion.

The burdock and nettle produce barbed seeds that stick onto fur and clothing and get carried over a wide area before being brushed off. Birds carry seeds in their beaks, stomachs, claws, or on their muddy webbed feet. Water has been known to carry the seeds of coconuts for thousands of miles before they wash ashore.

Simple plants, such as mosses, ferns, mushrooms, and seaweed, do not produce seeds but living cells called *spores*.

SEINE

The Seine is an important river in FRANCE. It flows about 480 miles (773 km) toward the northwest and empties into the English Channel. Its course is through fertile farmland. Among the chief tributaries of the Seine are the Oise, Marne, Aube, and Yonne Rivers. It is connected with the Loire, RHINE, and RHÔNE Rivers by a system of canals, which allows the passage of many boats and barges from the east and the south.

The Seine flows through PARIS, where it is quite broad. Small ocean-going vessels can dock at the city's wharves, where there are many flatboats and barges waiting to transport cargo further inland.

Down river is the historic city of Rouen, built on both banks of the Seine. Here the river has been deepened so that Rouen is now a large seaport, with immense wharves. At the mouth of the Seine is Le Havre, the most important transatlantic port of France.

SENATE

In ancient ROME, the assembly of elders that met to advise the king was called the "Senate," meaning "council of old men." Originally it was composed of 100 members of noble families. When the Roman kings were overthrown, the Senate was directed by two Consuls who were elected each year from its members.

The Roman Senate grew to 300 members during the time of the Republic and had enormous power. It was constantly in conflict with the common people, who were excluded from membership. The Roman dictator Sulla increased the Senate to 600 and JULIUS CAESAR enlarged it to 900, reducing its power by filling the seats with his friends and supporters.

Today, a senate refers to the upper branch of the legislature in states and countries. The U.S. CONGRESS consists of two branches—the Senate and the House of Representatives. The Senate's presiding officer is the Vice President, and Senators, two from each state, are elected to serve for six years. SEE ALSO: CONGRESS.

SEQUOIA

Sequoias are gigantic CONIFERS that are the tallest trees on Earth. There are two species: redwood and "big tree." The sequoia is named after Sequoya (1770?–1843), a Cherokee Indian scholar who developed the first alphabet used by his tribe.

Redwoods are native to the fog belt of California and the coastal mountain ranges of southern Oregon. These trees exceed 300 feet (93 m) in height, with trunks so thick that a roadway has been cut through at least one of them.

California "big trees" are the largest in bulk of all trees. They are second only to the bristlecone pine as the oldest known living tree on Earth. These trees often grow more than 8000 feet (2480 m) above sea level on the western slopes of the Sierra Nevada. "Big trees" may live as long as 6000 years. One seed of a "big tree" weighs only one six-thousandth of an ounce (4.7 mg). The mature tree's weight may therefore be some 250 billion times greater than that of its seed.

Elizabeth SETON (1774–1821)

The Roman Catholic church named Elizabeth Seton as the first American SAINT in 1976. The daughter of a wealthy family from Maryland, Miss Seton became a Catholic when she visited Italy in 1803. She returned to the United States to open a boarding school in Baltimore. She began a new order of Catholic nuns, and called it the Sisters of the Charity of St. Joseph.

Between 1814 and 1821, Miss Seton opened several orphanages and schools in New York City and Philadelphia. Pope Paul VI praised her work with poor children when he named her as a saint.

The SEVEN WONDERS
of the WORLD

In the 2nd century B.C., a Greek named Antipater of Sidon made a list of seven magnificent works of art, which became known as the Seven Wonders of the World. They were:

1. *The Pyramids of Egypt* at Gizeh, built about 2500 B.C. as tombs for the Egyptian pharaohs (kings). Of all the Seven Wonders, only the PYRAMIDS survive today.

2. *The Hanging Gardens of Babylon*, built by NEBUCHADNEZZAR for his queen.

3. *The Colossus at Rhodes*, a bronze statue of APOLLO, more than 100 feet (31 m) high, at the harbor's entrance.

4. *The Pharos at Alexandria*, in Egypt, built by Ptolemy I about 270 B.C. It was a lighthouse, made of marble and about 400 feet (124 m) high, with fires at the top to guide ships into the harbor.

5. *The Temple of Diana at Ephesus*, in ASIA MINOR, made from white marble.

6. *The Statue of Zeus at Olympia*, made of gold and ivory by Phidias.

7. *The Mausoleum at Halicarnassus*, the large, splendid tomb of King Mausolus of Caria (now a part of Turkey).

SEWING

Many of the things we use are made of pieces of material joined with thread. Not only dresses and shirts, but shoes, automobile seat covers, and even books are sewn together.

Most sewing is *plain sewing*. It is intended to join pieces of cloth rather than to be decorative. The threaded needle is passed in and out of both pieces, which are laid flat against each other. The pictures show some of the stitches used in plain sewing.

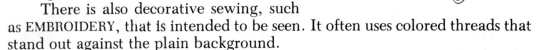

There is also decorative sewing, such as EMBROIDERY, that is intended to be seen. It often uses colored threads that stand out against the plain background.

For years hand sewing used a sharp needle to join the cloth and an evenly sharpened pair of shears to cut it. But *synthetic* fabrics, which use man-made threads rather than "pure" (natural) ones such as cotton, wool, or silk, require new tools: ball-pointed needles that separate the threads without the risk of cutting them, and shears ground so as to give the edge small teeth. While natural fabrics are *basted* (temporarily joined with widely spaced stitches), synthetics should be pinned.

Many women sew well, and are proud of their work. There are books to show you how to do the various stitches, from the simple ones shown here to the most complicated ones.

SEWING MACHINE

Sewing machines were the first machines to be important in the home. The first ones were made in France in 1841, but an American, Elias Howe, patented the first really efficient sewing machine in 1846. Howe's idea of putting the needle eye at the point was very important. A thread passed through the eye goes through the cloth and is knotted with a thread on the other side that is moved back and forth by a shuttle. This produces a *lock stitch*.

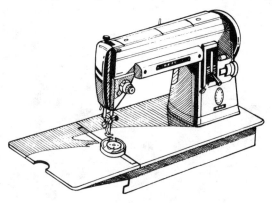

The first machines were run with a hand crank, but soon they were made to run by foot power. Today they are usually run with electric motors. SEE ALSO: SEWING.

Sir Ernest SHACKLETON (1874–1922)

Sir Ernest Shackleton was a famous British explorer in the Antarctic region. During his first voyage to the region, as a member of the 1901 expedition led by ROBERT SCOTT, Shackleton gained valuable experience. From 1907 to 1909, he commanded a polar expedition that climbed Mt. Erebus, located the south magnetic pole, and made a sledge journey within 97 miles (156 km) of the SOUTH POLE.

In 1914, he made another trip to the Antarctic. However, his ship was crushed in the tremendous ice and abandoned. Shackleton led his men to safety on Elephant Island. Then he and five companions made a heroic voyage in an open boat and across unknown territory to seek help on the island of South Georgia. During another trip to the area in 1922, he died and was buried on South Georgia Island.

William SHAKESPEARE (1564–1616)

William Shakespeare was a great English poet and dramatist (writer of plays). Son of a well-to-do merchant, he was born in the town of STRATFORD-ON-AVON and attended the local grammar school. At 18, Shakespeare married Anne Hathaway, but he left her and their three children in 1585 and went to London. This is about all that is known about Shakespeare's early life.

He worked in London as an actor and a playwright, joining a THEATER company or group called the Lord Chamberlain's Men. After a few years, he became a good enough actor to perform before Queen ELIZABETH I. He also wrote new plays for his theater company and became quite successful. In 1599, he and his acting company began their own theater—the Globe. Shakespeare seemed to prosper through his playwriting, and returned in 1597 to Stratford-on-Avon to buy New Place, the best

house in town. His company was able to take over the Blackfriars Theater in 1609. He retired about 1603 and spent his last years in Stratford-on-Avon, where he died and was buried in the chancel (space about the altar) of the church.

Shakespeare's plays show his extraordinary ability in the use of the English language, his complete mastery of stagecraft, and his skill in presenting notable characters. He based his plots on history, romance, legend, and folk tales. His total work is so overwhelming that some people can not believe that it was done entirely by Shakespeare—a man of moderate education and modest background.

His 38 plays include historical dramas, like *Julius Caesar* and *Henry V*, powerful tragedies, *Macbeth*, *Hamlet*, *Othello*, and *King Lear*, and comedies, of which *As You Like It* and *A Midsummer Night's Dream* are very popular. Shakespeare's tragic play *Romeo and Juliet* has many comic and historical parts and is rich in lyrical poetry. His sonnets (14–line poems) are among the best ever written. SEE ALSO: DRAMA.

SHAMROCK

The shamrock, national symbol of the Irish, is the wood sorrel. Legend says that St. Patrick, patron saint of Ireland, chose this three-leafed plant to illustrate the existence of God as a Trinity of Father, Son, and Holy Ghost.

SHARKS

Sharks are the flesh-eaters of the sea. However, the whale shark and the basking shark, which are the largest species, are so gentle that they will not attack even when harpooned. Although normally timid, the white shark and the blue shark are dangerous man-eaters when they smell blood.

Sharks live in every ocean of the world, but they are mostly found in warm

Hammerhead Shark

Blue Shark

Basking Shark

waters. Most sharks are gray with a spiny skin that feels like sandpaper. Most have a long snout with a mouth on the underside of the head. Their rows of teeth slope inward; as a shark's tooth wears out, a new one grows in its place.

A leather, called *shagreen*, is made from sharkskin. Oil, rich in vitamins A and D, is obtained from the sharks' livers; glue, from their heads; and fertilizer and dried food, from their flesh. In the Orient, shark fin soup is considered a great delicacy.

SHEEP

There are many different wild and domesticated (tamed) sheep. The male is known as a *ram*, the female as a *ewe*, and their offspring as a lamb.

Wild sheep, found in the mountainous regions of North America, Europe, and Asia, are nimble rock climbers with large, curving horns. Most wild sheep do not bear WOOL. Unlike wild sheep, domesticated sheep have short legs, long tails, and usually short horns. These sheep are bred for their wool, meat (mutton or lamb), and skins. In some parts of Europe and Asia, they are raised for their fat and milk, from which cheese is made.

Australia, Argentina, and Russia are the main sheep-raising countries. In the United States, the most important sheep-raising states are Texas, Wyoming, and California. Some of the chief breeds of sheep are the Cotswold and Leicester (both long-wooled breeds), the Merino (best wooled breed), and the Southdown (mutton breed). SEE ALSO: WOOL.

Cheviot ewe

Black-faced mountain ram

Welsh mountain ram

SHELLS

Shells are the hard coverings of the soft bodies of more than 75,000 sea animals, called *mollusks*. They are found not only at the seashore but also in dry places once covered by ocean.

Mollusks take lime from the water and build, layer by layer, the material of the growing shell. The outside of the shell is often rough, while the inside is smooth and pearly.

There are two main classes of shells: the single ones (*univalves*), such as the spiral snail shells, conches, and welks, and the double ones (*bivalves*), with the two shells being hinged together, as with oysters, clams, scallops, and mussels.

Shells have been used as money in many parts of the world. *Wampum* was the shell money of the American Indian. Buttons, jewelry, and knife handles can be made from shell. Oyster shells are fed to chickens to help them digest their food. Crushed shell is used in making porcelain and in keeping soil from becoming too acidic. When billions of ancient shells fall to the bottom of the sea and become cemented together by pressure, LIMESTONE is formed after a long, long time.

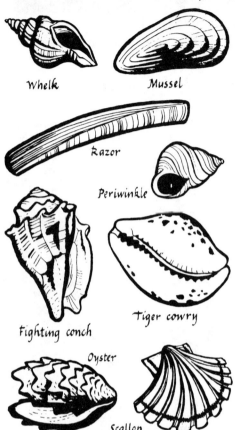

Whelk

Mussel

Razor

Periwinkle

Fighting conch

Tiger cowry

Oyster

Scallop

SHIPS

Some of the earliest ships were built at the eastern end of the Mediterranean Sea. The Egyptians had very little timber, and built their first ships of bundles of reeds. Other Mediterranean builders had enough trees and were able to use logs and planks.

The ancient Greeks and Romans had both *galleys*, rowed ships which were up to 150 feet (45 m) long, and merchant ships that used one square SAIL alone. The galleys were slender and fast, and were used especially for warfare. They had sharp

Coracle

Roman Galley

Crusaders' Ship

Tudor Ship

rams for sinking other ships. The merchant ships were shorter and broader.

In northern European waters, other kinds of ships were built. The Vikings built strong, shallow, open vessels with high bows and sterns. These were well suited to the condition of the sea around their countries. The *long ship* was their war vessel, long and narrow. It could be either rowed or sailed.

By the 15th century, new types of ships had evolved. Most of the older ships had only one mast, but the *carrack* of the 15th century had three. It sailed in north European waters, but it had the triangular lateen sails that

were popular in the Mediterranean. In the 16th century, the famous *galleon* came into being. It had both square and lateen sails on as many as five masts. Galleons were the largest ships so far, and the Spaniards especially used them for trading in the different parts of their world-wide empire. They were slow, but were often used as warships as well as merchant ships. They were heavily armed as a defense against pirates.

HMS Victory 1765

Great Britain and the Netherlands had Eastern colonies in the 18th century, and a new type of large merchant ship, the *East Indiaman*, connected the colonies with the mother countries. The galleons had high *forecastles* and *sterncastles* (structures at the bow and stern), but the sides of the East Indiaman were almost level, and were high above the water. Like the galleon, it was a heavily armed ship.

S.S. Britannia 1840

Americans had been building ships since the 18th century, and by the War of 1812 they had become very skilled. The frigates *Constellation* and *Constitution* (known as OLD IRONSIDES) were faster and more heavily armed than many European frigates. Beginning in the 1830s, American shipyards turned out a new kind of sailing ship, the famous *clipper*. This was built to take freight and passengers as quickly as possible rather than to carry large amounts of freight. The clippers were most popular in the 1850s, when they could sail much faster than any steamship of the time. The British began building them too, to carry tea and other cargoes from the Orient. By 1870, though, the competition from steamships was too great, and shipowners preferred slower sailing ships that could carry large cargoes.

Steamboats were first tried out in the late 18th century, and in 1801 the first really successful one, a Scottish canal tugboat, began service. In 1807, Robert Fulton started the first steam RIVERBOAT service, on the Hudson River, and in 1819 the American ship *Savannah* made an Atlantic crossing in which it used a steam engine part of the time. In 1840, Samuel Cunard, a Nova Scotian, began his famous LINER service with four ships. A few passenger ships had crossed the Atlantic in the 1830s, but the Cunard Line was the first to last more than a few years.

The early steamships ran with *paddle wheels*, but by 1870 ocean-going ships were usually built with *screw propellers*, which pushed the ship at the stern. By 1910, a ship might have four propellers. Liners became bigger and more luxurious, while even freighters, carrying cargo and few passengers, became larger and faster over the years. Ships were usually built with wood before 1850, but iron and steel became popular after that time.

tanker Opawa

Warships and merchant ships looked much like each other before 1850, but new inventions late in the 19th century such as armor and gun turrets turned the warship into a special kind of vessel with an appearance all its own.

USS United States

Most passenger-travel across the oceans is by airplane today, but freight ships are still very important, and new types are being invented. Some freighters still carry a few passengers. SEE ALSO: SUBMARINE.

SHOES and BOOTS

The first shoes were probably pieces of LEATHER held on the foot by strings or straps. These were *sandals*, and gave no protection to the upper part of the foot. When an upper part was added, true shoes and boots came into being. The illustrations show just a few of the kinds of shoes and boots that have existed in the last 1000 years. Fashions have had a great influence on the forms shoes have taken: people have always wanted to wear the same kinds of things that others of their time did.

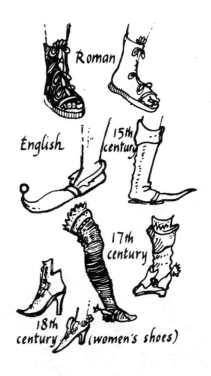

Before the 19th century, shoes were made wholly by hand. By 1900, they were almost all made by machinery. Machines soften the leather (calf or sheepskin) for the upper part, and stamp it out in the proper shapes. The sole (often of tough cowhide) is shaped by still other machines. Machines sew the parts together.

New materials are being used for shoes these days. RUBBER has been in use more than 100 years, of course, but many leather-like and rubber-like materials have been invented to be used, especially for soles and heels, as substitutes for leather.

SIBERIA

Siberia, a part of RUSSIA, is a vast region in northern ASIA. It is larger than all of Europe, stretching from the Ural Mountains in the west to the Bering Sea and the Pacific Ocean in the west. In the north are the *steppes*, vast grasslands, and the bleak *tundra*, frozen desert whose surface thaws only in the short summer. To the south are more steppes and the *taiga*, great wooded areas. To the east are remote uplands, plateaus, and mountains. Siberia has several great rivers and many lakes, of which the most important is Lake Baikal, the world's deepest lake (5715 feet or 1772 m).

Several million Ukrainians, Russians, and Mongol tribes live in Siberia.

Some are farmers, hunters, or fishermen, but many have been educated and put to work in the Soviet mines and factories of Siberia.

The Soviets are exploiting the vast natural resources of the area: coal, iron ore, gold, timber, and cereal grains. They are building huge hydroelectric plants and are today producing much of Russia's goods and machinery in Siberia.

SICILY

Sicily, part of ITALY, is the largest island in the MEDITERRANEAN. The land is mostly mountainous, but along the southern coasts it is generally flat. Cotton, corn, tobacco, flax, and vegetables are grown in the valleys and on the plains. Its mountain slopes are covered with orange, lemon, and olive groves and vineyards. Fishing for sardines, tunny, sponges, and coral is done

along the coasts. Sicily has earthquakes from time to time, and the volcano, Mt. Etna, rising 11,870 feet (3680 m), is still active.

At various times, Sicily has been invaded and settled by the Phoenicians, Greeks, Carthaginians, and Romans. After the A.D. 400s, barbarian tribes overran it, until the Saracens conquered it in A.D. 827. Sicily was ruled by the Normans from 1072 to 1194, and later it belonged to the kingdom of Naples. For a short time, France owned it, and then Spain controlled it for several centuries. It joined with Italy in 1860. During World War II, Sicily was occupied by the Germans until the Allies drove them out in 1943.

There are ancient ruins throughout the island, showing Greek temples and theaters, Roman amphitheaters and aqueducts, and Saracen and Norman buildings and churches. Three famous remains are the Greek theater at Syracuse, the Roman theater at Taormina, and the Norman cathedral at Palermo, Sicily's capital and largest city.

SIGNALS

Today we have the radio and telephone, which allow us to speak over great distances, but we still have many other ways of transmitting information or warnings for special purposes. ROAD SIGNS are an example. Such signs do not change from moment to moment, but we also use a great many signs that do change. These are called signals.

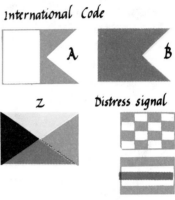

International Code

A

B

Z

Distress signal

A traffic light, for instance, is a signal that tells drivers to stop, go ahead carefully, or go as fast as the law allows. Many railroads use similar lights, colored red, yellow, and green, for *block signals*. The track is divided into separate lengths called blocks. When a train is in one block, the block's signal turns red to warn other trains not to enter. When the train leaves the block, the signal turns first yellow, then green as the train goes further away. Some railroads use *semaphores*. These are arms hinged at one end. Their

Lamp signal

positions say Stop, Caution, and Go just as the lights do. Semaphores were also used as telegraphs before the modern telegraph, which works by electricity, was invented.

Ships often display flags to send

messages. These can say that they need a pilot, are carrying mail, are about to sail, and many other things. Ships also use blinker lights, which flash on and off to send messages in MORSE CODE. Rockets serve as distress signals for ships. The sailor is guided also by signals from the shore. The special flash of a LIGHTHOUSE lamp tells him where he is, and the Coast Guard's signal flags tell him what kind of storm may be approaching.

Most signals are intended to be seen, and may be useless at night or in fog. Bells, gongs, guns, whistles, and horns have been used in various ways to help signal when the signaler cannot be seen.

The electric telegraph was the first means for signaling over very long distances without delay. Samuel Morse first demonstrated his telegraph, which uses a magnet to make a clicking noise, in 1844. The clicks spelled out the messages in Morse code. Early radios also used this code.

SILK

When certain caterpillars, called *silkworms*, are ready to become moths, they emit thin streams of a fluid that hardens in the air and becomes a fiber. They wind as many as 3000 feet (900 m) of this fiber around themselves until they are completely wrapped in a *cocoon*. When they have turned into moths, they break out of the cocoon.

Thousands of years ago, the Chinese discovered that such fibers could be spun and woven to make a light, strong, shiny cloth. They began to grow silkworms, feeding them on mulberry leaves. Once the cocoons were spun, the silkworm growers would kill the worms with heat, since in breaking out of the cocoons they would tear the fibers. The Chinese would twist enough fibers together to make thread, then make cloth out of them.

Silk was already known in ancient Europe, where the Romans were eager to buy it. For hundreds of years there was a famous Silk Route that went from China 4000 miles (6400 km) across Asia to the ports of the Mediterranean Sea. Caravans moved westward with silk and other Chinese products, and brought back

woollen goods and precious metals from the Roman Empire. When the Italian merchant Marco Polo went to China in the 13th century, he traveled along the Silk Route.

During the Middle Ages, European countries learned the secrets of silk-making. China, though, continued to be important as a source. Silk was a luxury material, suitable for the rich. In 18th-century Venice, noblemen were expected to wear it.

Today, RAYON, nylon, and other synthetic fibers often take the place of silk. They are shiny, light, and strong like silk, and are cheaper to make.

SILVER

Silver is a precious white shiny METAL known since ancient times. It is found in pure form and in ores in the earth. Though harder than GOLD, it is too soft for everyday use and, therefore, is usually mixed with COPPER to make an alloy for coins, jewelry, and tableware. Sterling silver is an alloy containing 92.5 percent silver and 7.5 percent copper.

Silver is unaffected by moisture, fruit juices, and most foods and has thus been used for bowls, plates, and eating utensils. Silver, however, is affected by sulfur from coal gas and eggs, which causes the silver to tarnish or blacken.

Silver can be made into wire that is finer than a human hair. It can be rolled into sheets 0.0001 of an inch (0.0025 mm) thick. Sometimes cheap metal objects are given a thin layer of silver—a process called silver plating.

Silver is found in Peru and Norway, and in the United States in Utah, California, and Arizona. It is much used in electrical and photographic industries, as well as in medicine.

Tetradrachm of Athens   Silver coin of Alfred

Elizabeth I   Crowns of   Elizabeth II

Cream jug   1780

SINGING

In different parts of the world people may sing in different ways, because their customs and their reasons for singing are different. In some places, *soloists* sing alone, or against the background of other singers in a *chorus*. In other places, several people sing at once, each with his own melody or even his own rhythm. In yet other places, people may sing only in chorus.

Some styles of choral singing use *harmony* a great deal; everyone sings the same song basically, but at each beat one part of the chorus sings a different note from the ones the other parts are singing. This produces *chords*, which give a richer sound than singing in *unison* (that is, with everyone singing exactly the same note) can do. In other styles of singing, *counterpoint* is common. In counterpoint, each section of the chorus has its own melody, which is woven with the melodies of the other parts of the chorus to give a rich, intricate effect.

Even the way that one person sings may be different from place to place. Most of our singing is still based on a rather loud, clear style developed for OPERA in the 17th century. It was intended to make the words of a song clear to the audiences of a large opera house. Our style of singing is also influenced by that of central Africa, with its strong rhythms. This is important in popular music such as JAZZ. SEE ALSO: SONGS.

SIPHON

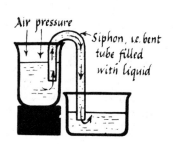

With a siphon you can move a liquid uphill without carrying it or using a pump. It works this way:

Imagine two tanks, an upper one full of water and a lower one empty. Now imagine a U-shaped pipe with one long and one short part. This is placed with the bend upward and with the short part in the water of the upper tank and the long one in the lower tank. If the pipe is filled with water and the ends are opened, the water will fall from the long part of the tube into the empty tank. This will begin to create a vacuum, a place where there is nothing. Now, the weight of air is about 15 pounds per square inch (1 kg/cm^2), and this presses down on the water in the upper tank. The pressure forces water into the short part of the tube to fill the vacuum that is forming. This water also falls into the empty tank. The process goes on until the water level is the same in both tanks or until air starts to get into the tube. Water can be lifted as much as 30 feet (10 m) this way.

SIREN

A siren is a noisemaking device, usually used on fire engines, ambulances, and other emergency vehicles to warn traffic to get out of the way. These are high-pitched sirens, but there are very powerful, low-pitched sirens for use on ships and lighthouses.

Many sirens today are electronic and can make many different sounds, but the first sirens were worked with compressed air. A disk with holes in it was turned quickly in front of a jet of air so that the air was cut off and let escape many times a second. The whirling of the disk at different speeds caused the rising and falling wail typical of such sirens.

SISAL

Sisal is a tropical plant, resembling a large cactus and having five-foot long, sword-like leaves. This plant produces a valuable fiber, called sisal hemp. Special machinery cuts and scrapes the leaves, removing the pulp and waste material. The remaining yellowish fiber is processed and used as twine and ROPE. It can also be made into matting, rugs, sacks, and brushes.

Sisal derives its name from Sisal, the former chief seaport of Yucatan, in Mexico. The plant is native to Central America. Since the 1930s, it has been cultivated in many parts of Africa, in Tanzania, and in Brazil.

SITTING BULL (1834?–1890)

Sitting Bull was a famous Sioux Indian chief. When white settlers and prospectors looking for gold invaded Indian territory, he led the Sioux on the warpath in the 1870s. The U.S. Army tried to force the INDIANS onto reservations (special lands set aside for just the Indians). Sitting Bull organized the Sioux, Cheyenne, and Arapaho Indians to fight back and directed many massacres of the whites. At the Battle of Little Big Horn in 1876, Sitting Bull's Sioux Indians killed General George Custer and several hundred U.S. Army troops. This was the Indians' last big victory against the whites.

Afterward, U.S. forces pushed the Indians back onto the reservations. Sitting Bull escaped with his band into Canada. In 1881, on the promise of pardon, he returned to North Dakota and surrendered. Later, Sitting Bull toured with Buffalo Bill's Wild West Show. During an Indian uprising on his reservation, he was shot and killed.

SKELETON

The skeleton is the strong structure that supports and shapes man and all other VERTEBRATES. Unlike the crusty outside skeleton of lobsters, spiders, and insects or the limy outside skeleton (SHELL) of clams, snails, and oysters, the bony vertebrate skeleton is formed inside the body. It helps to protect soft, delicate organs like the HEART and BRAIN and, by a wonderful system of joints and hinges attached to it, helps the MUSCLES to move.

There are about 200 bones in the human skeleton. The *skull*, including the jaw bone, is jointed onto the backbone or *spine*, made up of ringlike bones called *vertebrae*. The *ribs* are like a cage protecting the heart and LUNGS.

Arms are fastened to the *collarbones* in front and to the *shoulder blades* in back. Each upper arm (*humerus*) is hinged to the *radius* and *ulna* of the forearm, with its small, delicately jointed *finger bones* attached to 8 *wrist bones*.

The leg bones are fixed to the strong *pelvis*, that cradles the organs of the abdomen. Each leg bone consists of the thigh bone (*femur*), kneecap (*patella*), the shin bone (*tibia*), and *fibula*, plus the many small ankle, foot, and toe bones.

A baby's skeleton is made up of bone and *cartilage* or gristle.

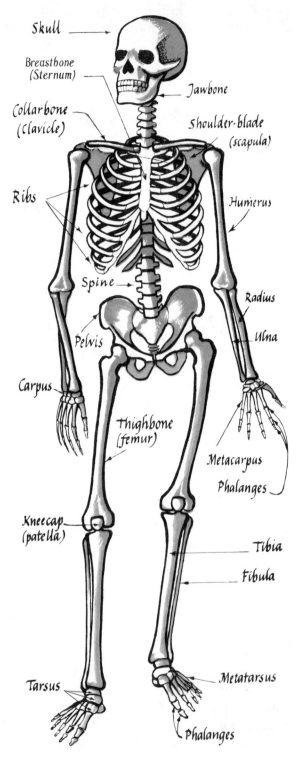

Skull

Breastbone (Sternum)

Jawbone

Collarbone (Clavicle)

Shoulder-blade (scapula)

Ribs

Humerus

Spine

Radius

Pelvis

Ulna

Carpus

Thighbone (femur)

Metacarpus

Phalanges

Kneecap (patella)

Tibia

Fibula

Metatarsus

Tarsus

Phalanges

Growing is the adding on of new cartilage as the old cartilage turns to bone. This process stops at about the age of 20 when a person has attained his full height. Bones are "padded" with cartilage at the joints to prevent them from rubbing together and to absorb the shock from a jump or fall.

Bones cannot move until the brain sends a message through the NERVES to the muscles that are attached to the bones by tendons. SEE ALSO: BONES.

SKIING

Men have used skis for thousands of years, finding them useful for travel, hunting, and waging war in snow-covered country.

Skis are made of hard wood, like ash, hickory, or spruce, or of fiberglass and aluminum. They are about 3 inches (7.6 cm) in width and usually about one foot (30.5 cm) longer than the height of the person who uses them. So that skis may move smoothly and easily they are waxed underneath and are curved slightly upwards at the tips. Ski bindings hold the skier's boots to the skis, and two strong ski poles with circular webbed rings at the bottom help the skier turn, climb, and keep balance.

Skiing became a popular winter sport after 1850. Today, people attend skiing classes and learn the various techniques of skiing. They must bend their knees and keep their hands forward so that they can go down a mountain, turn, and stop. Expert skiers compete in downhill racing and in the slalom (racing through poles on a downhill, winding course). Ski jumping and cross-country skiing are also competitive events that require great skill and strength.

SKIN

Skin is an outer body covering that is made up of tiny CELLS several layers thick. The top layer constantly dries and flakes off, usually unnoticeably, unless there is a case of dandruff or sunburn. The next layer contains NERVES and is thick and hard on the palms of our hands and the soles of our feet. Slightly deeper layers of skin contain blood vessels, sweat glands, hair roots, and little MUSCLES that cause "goose bumps" and make hair "stand on end."

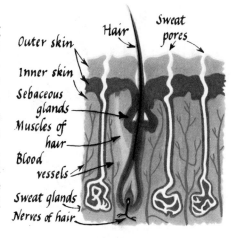

Hair
Sweat pores
Outer skin
Inner skin
Sebaceous glands
Muscles of hair
Blood vessels
Sweat glands
Nerves of hair

Aside from enabling us to feel pain, warmth, and cold, the skin prevents germs from entering the body. For this reason, we cover a cut on the skin until the skin has grown back. The skin keeps the body cool. More than 2 million tiny sweat glands continuously carry moisture and waste materials to the surface of the skin to evaporate.

SKUNK

All skunk species are American and all are much the same in habit. This black and white striped MAMMAL is known for its very bad odor, which comes from two scent glands located at the base of the tail. The skunk squirts out this foul smelling liquid as a way of protecting itself. Adult skunks are about the size of a large cat and are sometimes called "wood pussies."

Since skunks sometimes kill chickens, farmers do not like them. Skunks also dig up lawns in search of grubs. However, they are helpful by eating mice and many harmful INSECTS. Descented skunks are sometimes nice pets. Skunks are often hunted and trapped for their fur, which is occasionally sold as "Alaskan sable."

SKYSCRAPER

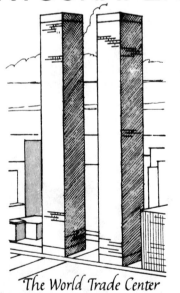

The World Trade Center

In the middle of the 19th century, land began to become very valuable in the middle of the American city. At the same time, business organizations began to become large, with many employees, and needed large buildings. And people who built office buildings to rent out to many small businesses wanted to have as much floor space as possible. Since it was expensive to buy a large amount of land in the central city area, the solution to these problems was to put many floors in one building.

There were two main difficulties, though. First, most people refused to walk higher than five floors to get to an office. Second, the outer walls of buildings in the mid-19th century were made of solid masonry, and the higher the building was, the thicker the masonry had to be. Such thick walls were expensive to build and lessened the amount of space for rent.

When an American, Elisha Graves Otis, demonstrated the first safe ELEVATOR in 1853, the first difficulty was solved. The second one was solved with the invention of the *skeleton frame*. The insides of the masonry buildings already used iron posts and beams, and by 1850 some building fronts were made of iron. It was simple, then, to make the whole building a riveted frame of wrought iron or steel, covered with masonry for weatherproofing, fire protection, and decoration. The first true skyscrapers were built in the 1880s in Chicago, and the first New York skyscraper was begun early in the 1890s.

For a long time, skyscrapers were built as tall boxes, as wide at the top as they were at the bottom. But this began to keep too much light and air out of the city streets. In 1916 the City of New York enacted a new law, requiring that skyscrapers become narrower as they rose. This forced architects to give them new and interesting forms. Many beautiful skyscrapers were built in New York and many other cities in the 1920s, using the tapering forms first dictated by the New York law. Today, most skyscrapers are boxlike again. Instead of occupying practically all of their land as they used to, they occupy only part of it. The law allows them to rise much further than they might otherwise do.

SLAVERY

Slavery is a social system in which certain persons are held as personal property by other persons. It was practiced among all the ancient peoples. Captives in battle and the people of conquered lands, such as the HEBREWS, were often sold into slavery. The Greeks and Romans used large numbers of slaves, many of whom were well treated and able to earn their freedom. During the 1st millennium A.D., there was a busy slave trade throughout Europe.

In 1503, the Portuguese took the first shipload of NEGROES from Africa to be sold as slaves in the WEST INDIES in Santo Domingo. The first slaves in the British American colonies arrived at Jamestown in 1620. During the 16th, 17th, and 18th centuries, the Spanish, Portuguese, and English, as well as some African blacks, engaged in a profitable slave trade of African Negroes, selling them for work on the plantations and in the mines of America.

During the 1800s, most European nations abolished slavery. In the U.S. in 1863, ABRAHAM LINCOLN issued his Emancipation Proclamation, which freed the slaves.

SLEEP

Sleep is a daily period of unconsciousness. This period of rest allows the bodies of most animals, including man, to build new CELLS to replace those that have been worn out and destroyed during the active awake period. It is a time for the body to store up energy. For some unknown reason, people also need sleep in order to dream. Scientists have learned that people become ill if they do not have dreams.

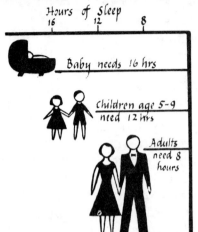

Hours of Sleep
16   12   8

Baby needs 16 hrs

Children age 5-9 need 12 hrs

Adults need 8 hours

During sleep, our body functions are decreased. The heart beats more slowly, breathing is slower and shallower, and muscles are more relaxed and looser. The brain is at rest, too. Preventing sleep leads to crankiness, forgetfulness, mental disorganization, and other strange behavior.

Babies need to sleep twice as long as they are awake (about 16 hours each day) because their bodies are growing so rapidly. Growing children need about 12 hours of sleep each day, and most adults need about 8 hours. Everybody occasionally experiences sleeplessness (*insomnia*), which can be caused by being overtired, upset, excited, or in pain. Being too hot or cold can also cause insomnia. Sometimes people sleep more than is necessary because they are bored or unhappy.

SMELL

Both man and animals have five senses—sight, hearing, touch, taste, and smell. Many animals have a much keener sense of smell than man has, though man's eyesight and sence of touch may be keener.

Every VERTEBRATE (an animal with a backbone) is able to smell because its nose has a sensitive lining with NERVES leading to the part of the brain recognizing smells.

Scents or PERFUMES in the gaseous state are drawn into the nose when we breathe. If we like the smell, we usually sniff to draw in more air; if we do not like the smell, we often hold our nose.

Our sense of smell easily becomes dulled, and it then becomes difficult to recapture a delicate scent or distinguish between a mixture of them. A dog, however, has a keen sense of smell and can follow his master's scent, even when surrounded by a great many other smells. SEE ALSO: PERFUME.

770

Captain John SMITH (1580?-1631)

Captain John Smith had a daring and adventurous early life, traveling, fighting the Turks in Hungary and Transylvania (now part of Rumania), and spending a period as a slave in Turkey. Around 1604, he returned to England and invested in the new Virginia Company. In December, 1606, Captain John Smith sailed with the first colonists to Virginia. He helped establish a colony at JAMESTOWN in 1607 and was named a member of the governing council.

His major service to the colony was his exploration of the surrounding territory. He also was able to get food for the starving colonists from the Indians. However, on one of his excursions, Smith was captured by some Indians and was supposedly saved by POCAHONTAS. According to legend, she held Captain John Smith in her arms and persuaded her father, Chief Powhatan, to let him go.

Captain John Smith governed Jamestown through the winter of 1608-1609, helping the colony through this "starving time." In October, 1609, he sailed back to England. Five years later, he led an expedition that explored the coast of what is now NEW ENGLAND. Returning to England with a valuable cargo of fish and furs, Smith encouraged the settlement of New England. Besides drawing maps of places in the New World, Smith wrote several books about it and about his adventures.

SMOKE

Smoke is the visible vapor or gases given off by a burning or smoldering substance. Smoke usually consists of hot gas with suspended particles of soot. Bituminous (soft) coal when it is burned produces heavy smoke. Wood produces little smoke if burned when dry and if the fire has an ample supply of air.

Smoke can interfere with sunlight, filtering out the most healthful rays. Smoke can leave deposits of grit, dust, and tar on buildings. Its oily deposits can hinder plant and animal life. Its tars and acids may cause problems in the respiratory (breathing) systems of human beings and animals. It is believed by many scientists that tobacco smoke causes cancer of the lungs.

Smoke from factories often combines with mositure in the air to form *smog*. Today, tough laws are being passed to prevent air POLLUTION. Where necessary, electricity, anthracite (hard) coal, and gas are used in place of fuels that make heavy smoke.

SNAILS and SLUGS

Snails and slugs are a kind of soft-bodied animal called a *mollusk*. Hundreds of different types of snails exist. Some live on land or in salt or fresh water. They all have one or two pairs of "horns," a tongue like a ribbon covered with as many as 4000 tiny teeth, and a single, usually coiled,

SHELL attached to the body. A snail can hide inside its shell to escape from danger.

Most land snails (and slugs) are active at night when they feed on leaves and shoots. Snails keep aquariums clean by eating the green algae that form on the glass. A few are flesh-eaters. Snails hibernate during the winter after sealing their shells with a hard slime from the foot glands.

They lay eggs, and most newly hatched young look like miniature adults. Some snail shells are the size of a pinhead, while those of the sea conches are more than a foot (30.5 cm) long.

Slugs look like snails without shells, though some species have traces of a shell. The largest slugs are not quite half the size of the largest snails. Like snails, they leave a silvery, slimy trail as they move along by means of a muscle or "foot" under their body. A "snail's pace" has been found to be from 23 inches to 55 yards (58-5010 cm) per hour for the common land snail.

The flesh of garden snails, whelks, and periwinkles is considered a delicious food in many countries.

SNAKES

Unlike most of their reptile relatives, snakes are legless. They are covered with dry scales. Those scales on the underside of their body help them to grip the ground as they wriggle along by movements of their ribs. Snakes can crawl about as fast as a child can run, and the black mamba of Africa can travel as fast as 15 miles per hour (24.2 km1hr) for short bursts. Snakes can climb, and they all are able to swim. They periodically shed their skins as they grow. Usually baby snakes hatch from leathery eggs; however, the garter snake carries her eggs within her until they are ready to be born.

Snakes are found in most parts of the world, except in the cold Polar regions, New Zealand, and Ireland; there are only a few in the Pacific islands. Some live in trees, in fresh water, and even in the sea. They prefer, however, the woods, forests, and deserts in warm climates. Those that live where winters are cold must hibernate in a sheltered spot.

Snakes feed upon other animals and their eggs. Their loosely hinged jaws make it possible for them to swallow animals much bigger than themselves. Usually their prey is swallowed alive; however, the PYTHONS and boas crush their victims and coat them with saliva before swallowing them. The tongue is simply a delicate organ of touch and smell.

The teeth are used for seizing and biting their food. Poisonous snakes, like the cobra, mamba, adder, VIPER, RATTLESNAKE, copperhead, and water moccasin, also have special teeth called fangs. Fangs have tiny grooves along which poison from a venom gland is squirted into a wound from a snake.

Many snakes, such as the grass snake and garter snake, are harmless. There are about 120 species of nonpoisonous snakes in the U.S. Some, like the king snake, eat poisonous snakes. Many snakes are helpful to man because they destroy rats, mice, and other pests.

Green Tree Boa

Grass Snake

Adder

Young Python eating mouse

SNOW

Snow is made up of tiny ice crystals joined together to form 6-sided or 6-pointed snowflakes. Snow is white because each

of the faces of the tiny crystals reflects all of the light to our eyes. The beauty of a lacy snowflake is best seen under a magnifying glass. Naturally, if snow crystals get warm, they melt and turn into a tiny water droplet.

In order for snow to fall, the water vapor in the air must freeze. Snow from the cold upper air may turn to rain at lower elevations near Earth. Thus, often the mountains receive snow, while the valleys have rain. Hail is frozen rain; sleet is partly melted snow.

In Antarctica and on very high mountains, snow remains all year round, while in the Arctic, it melts in summer at elevations below 600 feet (180 m). It never or rarely snows in some areas of the world; however, these areas may receive floods in springtime because of melting snow on mountains hundreds of miles away. SEE ALSO: WATER.

SOAP

Soap was invented two thousand years ago by the Gauls, who lived in what is now called France. The Gauls used soap to brighten the color of their hair. Shortly after hearing about it, the Romans began making soap, which they used for cleaning their clothes and bodies. Their soap was made from goat fat and beechwood ashes. A chemical called an *alkali* is found in wood ashes and is still mixed with some kind of fat to produce soap. During the Middle Ages, only the rich used soap; no one realized that cleanliness was important for good health.

The American colonists made their own soap once a month by boiling their cooking grease with water that had been poured over their wood ashes. The resulting thick mixture was called "soft" soap. "Hard" soap was cooked longer and had salt added to it. Today, colored dyes, perfumes, oils from fats derived from the almond, coconut, cottonseed, and olive, and sometimes sand and medicine are added to our modern soaps.

SOCCER

Soccer is an outdoor game played on a grassy field measuring 120 yards (109 m) by 75 yards (68 m). Two opposing teams of 11 players each try to drive an inflated ball past the opposing goalkeeper into his goal for a score. Also, each team tries to prevent the other from scoring. The ball is kicked (often dribbled with short kicks) or moved by other parts of the body such as the head and chest. Only the goalkeepers within the penalty areas (in front of each goal) are allowed to

catch or touch the ball with their hands. Players cannot hold, push, or trip an opponent.

Play begins with a kickoff in which a player kicks the ball to a teammate at the center of the field. Opposing players try to take the ball away and move toward their opponents' goal at the other end of the field. Play stops only when a goal is scored, when the ball goes out of bounds, or when the referee stops play for a rule violation, foul, or injury.

SOCRATES (470?–399 B.C.)

Socrates was a great Greek PHILOS-OPHER and teacher who lived in ATHENS.

As a young man, Socrates fought bravely in several battles during the Peloponnesian War between Athens and Sparta. Later, he spent his time wandering about Athens, talking to friends and teaching them.

Socrates liked to ask questions. Pretending to be ignorant, he encouraged people to find the answers themselves and to express what they thought life was all about. This method of teaching became known as the *Socratic method*.

To Socrates, virtue was knowledge. He believed people could be taught to be good and happy. Also, he felt that people who knew what was good and right would not willingly be bad and unjust. Socrates dressed very simply and thought money and possessions were unimportant.

Eventually, Socrates' opinions offended many Athenians, who accused him of misleading young people and neglecting the gods. During his trial, he made fun of his accusers, saying they should reward, not condemn, him. He was found guilty and ordered to drink a cup of hemlock, a fatal poison. His friends planned for his escape, but Socrates said that a man must obey the laws. He then bravely drank the hemlock.

Socrates never wrote a book about his ideas, but his pupil, PLATO, wrote much about his teachings and life.

SOIL

The action of wind, frost, rain, heat, cold, floods, and GLACIERS has broken rock on the Earth's surface into fine particles to form soil. Plant roots, animals, worms, and grubs also help in this disintegrating or breaking-down process.

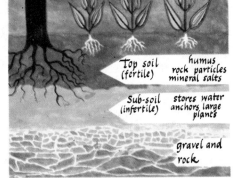

Soil, however, is more than just rock dust. It contains decayed plants and animals. Sunshine, air, and rain act upon MINERALS from the rocks to enrich the soil, supplying plants with such substances as phosphorus, sulfur, and iron.

In sandy soils, the particles are so big that rain quickly drains through. However, heavy sticky soils, such as clay, have their particles close together. Thus, sandy soil is poor and unable to hold minerals or moisture; clay is hard to dig and plow and gets water-logged, though it can eventually break down into useful soil.

Loam is the best soil; it contains a good mixture of minerals and decayed matter (*humus*) and is easy to cultivate. The particles in loam are not too small, big, heavy, or coarse in order for the farmer to grow crops in decent weather.

SOLAR SYSTEM

The SUN is a star with 9 PLANETS traveling around it in a counter-clockwise direction. Several planets have their own moons—JUPITER, for

Part of the Sun, on the same scale

example, has 14—and there are comets, meteors, and a ring of asteroids or small planets. These heavenly bodies all make up the sun's family called the solar system.

The paths or *orbits* of the planets are not exactly circular, but the planets are held in their positions by the sun's attraction. Like EARTH, the other planets have no light of their own but merely reflect that of the sun. VENUS, our nearest planetary neighbor, appears very bright, but NEPTUNE and PLUTO are too far away to be seen without a telescope.

Scientists used to think that the solar system consisted of bits of the sun that were hurled off into space and gradually became cool. This idea was proven to be unlikely, so it was suggested that a passing star pulled away many small fragments. A modern theory is that the sun was originally a double star until its giant companion exploded. As a result, a disk of gas began to orbit the sun and then condense into a few planets and smaller bodies.

Our solar system is only a speck in a great system of STARS called a GALAXY that turns like a gigantic wheel. The galaxy that our solar system is part of is called the Milky Way. It is only one of countless others.

SOLOMON (died 932? B.C.)

Solomon became the third King of Israel after his father, King DAVID, died. His mother was Bathsheba. During his reign, which began about 972 B.C., Israel was generally at peace with her neighbors and grew extremely prosperous.

He developed trade and commerce with Hiram, the Phoenician king of Tyre, and with Egypt. He constructed and fortified numerous cities that were used as arsenals and storehouses. To carry out his father's dream, Solomon erected a splendid temple at JERUSALEM, which was then a city of wealth and luxury.

Solomon also became famous for his wisdom. His wise sayings are reported in the Old Testament, particularly in the Book of Proverbs and Ecclesiastes. The Song of Solomon, a biblical love poem, has also been ascribed to him.

The HEBREWS paid heavy taxes to support Solomon's extravagance. When he died, rebellion occurred and the kingdom broke into two parts.

SONGS

The combination of words with music may be the oldest kind of music there is. Many old cultures have *work songs*, which do two things. First, they keep up the spirits of the workers. Second, they set a rhythm that helps people who are working together—pulling on a rope, for instance—to move at the same time. A sailor's CHANTEY is such a work song. Another old type of song is the BALLAD, sung in Europe and America. This tells a story, often a sad one. There are songs that make fun of people, songs to be sung at religious ceremonies, and songs of love. These are *folk songs*. They have been sung in this or that place as long as anyone remembers, and no one knows who made up the words or music.

Popular songs are different. They are modern, and their composers are known. Some of them are written for musical comedies or for special singers at first, but if the public likes them they are sung also by others. They often sound like folk songs.

Art songs are written by classical composers, who set poetry to music. They are often sung by one person with a piano accompaniment. There are other kinds of classical songs. An *aria*, for instance, is a song from an OPERA, sung at an important moment. Arias are often sung at concerts. The *madrigal* is a song sung by several people without accompaniment. Madrigals were intended to be sung in the home, and were very popular 300 years ago. Many classical composers have also written songs for large choruses. SEE ALSO: SINGING.

SOUND

Sound is produced when something is made to *vibrate* (move back and forth rapidly). These vibrations travel in WAVES until they reach our eardrums, which in turn also vibrate.

However, sound, unlike LIGHT, must travel through a *medium*. An electric bell enclosed in an air-free glass case will not make a sound even though the bell is seen ringing, for there is no medium of air through which the waves can travel. Wood, water, and metal are even better conductors of sound than air.

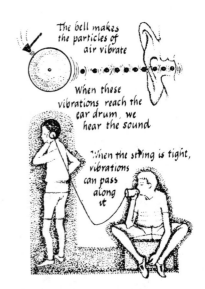

The bell makes the particles of air vibrate

When these vibrations reach the ear drum, we hear the sound

When the string is tight, vibrations can pass along it

Sound travels at about 760 miles per hour (1224 km/hr), while light travels at the rate of 186,300 miles per second (299,443 km/sec). This tremendous speed of light compared to that of sound explains why lightning arrives way ahead of the thunder.

Sound waves are *reflected* (bounced back) from solid objects. This effect is noticeable in an empty room or in a cave and is called an ECHO. SEE ALSO: EAR, ECHO.

John Philip SOUSA (1854–1932)

Many of the marches that Americans know, such as "The Stars and Stripes Forever" and "The Washington Post March," were written by John Philip Sousa, the March King.

Sousa was already a musician in a band when he was 11 years old. He joined the Marine Corps as an apprentice (student) in 1868, and by 1880 he was a leader of a Marine band. In 1892 he formed his own band, which was popular all over the world. During World War I he was in charge of training band musicians for the U.S. Navy. In all, he wrote 140 marches and several light operas.

SOUTH AMERICA

The continent of South America contains the Andes, the longest mountain range in the world. It stretches more than 4000 miles (6440 km) down the western side of the continent, from Panama in the north to Cape Horn in the south. This range has high plateaus, deep gorges, and numerous volcanoes, such as Chimborazo, (now thought to be extinct) and Cotopaxi.

East of the Andes is a vast plain that lies between the Guiana Highlands and the Brazilian Plateau. This plain is drained by the AMAZON and its tributaries, creating the largest river system in the world.

North of the city of RIO DE JANEIRO, South America has mainly a tropical climate, except for those regions in the mountains. Low areas have heavy rainfall and hot temperatures all year long. The climate is more moderate to the south, and the seasons are just the opposite of those in North America. July and August are winter months in South America. Patagonia, a bleak tableland in the extreme southern part, has cool, dry weather.

The tropical part of South America has dense rain forests that are unexplored. Here are abundant palm, bamboo, ebony, mahogany, and rubber trees. TAPIRS, anteaters, sloths, JAGUARS, and many kinds of colorful parrots live in the forests. Some of the rivers have large crocodiles and piranha fish, that can tear apart a big animal in minutes. Horses, cattle, and sheep have been introduced from Europe, but the LLAMA and the vicuña, both mountain animals, are native to South America.

Millions of cattle and sheep are raised

on vast grasslands, such as the Orinoco *llanos* in the north and on the *pampas* of ARGENTINA. Bananas, sugar, coffee, cotton, rice, and tobacco are grown in the tropical region.

The continent is rich in minerals. VENEZUELA has enormous oil fields; CHILE has copper, nitrate, and iron ore; BOLIVIA has tin and gold; Guyana and Surinam have large bauxite deposits. Lead, zinc, manganese, and silver are also mined.

Despite this great natural wealth, South America is still an underdeveloped continent. Many people live in remote areas or in slums, without jobs and enough food. The largest populations are near the coast, in such fine ports and cities as São Paulo, BUENOS AIRES, and Caracas.

In the 1500s, Portugal and Spain took control of South America, overpowering numerous tribes, such as the INCAS. It took almost 300 years for the Spanish and Portuguese colonies to gain their independence. Today, the people include many of European, Negro, and Indian ancestry, as well as mixtures of all of them. The Spanish language and customs are widespread, except in BRAZIL where Portuguese is spoken. SEE ALSO: INDIVIDUAL COUNTRIES OF SOUTH AMERICA.

SOUTH CAROLINA

South Carolina is a southern state on the Atlantic coast. It consists of two main regions—the Low Country and the Up Country. The Low Country covers about two thirds of the state and is part of the long Atlantic Coastal Plain. Marshes, inlets, and islands lie along the coast. To the west is the Up Country, consisting of the hilly Piedmont Plateau and Blue Ridge Mountains. Much of South Carolina is covered with forests, mostly pine. But there are also oak and gum in the Low Country and poplar, sycamore, and black walnut in the Up Country. Near the middle of the state is Columbia, the capital and largest city. About 2.8 million people live in the state.

The Spanish built a fort on Paris Island around 1566, but they soon abandoned it. The first permanent settlement was established by the English at Albemarle Point in 1670. Because of poor conditions there, the settlers moved up the Ashley River and founded Charles Towne, known today as Charleston. This became a trading center for furs, rice, indigo, and slaves. Negro slaves were used on South Carolina's cotton plantations until the CIVIL

WAR. The state was the first to secede (withdraw) from the U.S. In 1861, it fired on and forced the surrender of U.S. soldiers at Fort Sumter in Charleston harbor. The war ruined South Carolina.

The state has since recovered. Its main industry is textiles, but other important products are furniture, paper, lumber, and chemicals. Tobacco, cotton, and peaches are the principal crops. Tourists like the many sandy beaches.

SOUTH DAKOTA

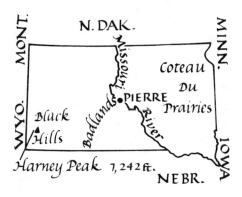

South Dakota, a state in the north-central United States, is cut by the great Missouri River, which flows north to south through the middle. East of the river the land is good for growing wheat, corn, rye, and oats. West of the river are the rolling grasslands of the Great Plains. Here graze millions of cattle and sheep.

About 1600, the Arikara Indians lived in the region. Later, they were forced out by the hostile Sioux Indians. In 1743, Frenchmen claimed the land where the town of Fort Pierre is today. (Pierre, the state capital, is right across the Missouri River from Fort Pierre). In 1763, the region was given to Spain, but France reclaimed it in 1800 and sold it as part of the Louisiana Purchase. LEWIS AND CLARK visited the region in 1804 and 1806. The first lasting settlement was built at Fort Pierre in 1817. It became an important fur trading center. When gold was found in the Black Hills, white men poured into the area and took land from the Sioux. The Indians fought back but were defeated by 1890. South Dakota is today the home of about 32,000 Indians (mostly Sioux), living on nine reservations.

Agriculture earns the most money for South Dakota. The processing of foods from the farms and ranches is the main industry. Tourists come for boating and swimming. Many go to see Mount Rushmore, in the Black Hills. Carved on its granite face are the heads of Washington, Jefferson, Lincoln, and Theodore Roosevelt. Nearby is another huge sculpture—that of the Sioux warrior, Crazy Horse. South Dakota has nearly 700,000 people.

SOUTH POLE
The South Pole, on the continent of Antarctica, is the southernmost point on the Earth's surface. In 1772, CAPTAIN JAMES COOK, a British explorer, sailed around Antarctica without sighting the mainland. Not until 1840 was this huge ice mass discovered to be a continent. Charles Wilkes, an American naval officer, completed in that year a 1500-mile (2415 km) voyage along the

coast. Afterward, other explorers pushed inland with dog sledges trying to get to the South Pole. In 1908, Shackleton, an Englishman, reached the glacier-covered, 11,000-foot (3410 m) high plateau and came withing 97 miles (156 km) of the South Pole.

At last the Pole was reached in December, 1911, when ROALD AMUNDSEN and his men arrived a month before ROBERT SCOTT. All five of Scott's party died from hunger and cold on the return journey.

This tragedy did not stop further exploration of the desolate continent. An Australian explorer, Sir Hubert Wilkins, was the first to fly over Antarctica, in 1928, and an American, Richard Byrd, flew over the Pole in 1929 and later established a land base

Wreck of 'Endurance'

Amundsen

Fuchs and Hillary

Byrd

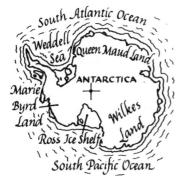

South Atlantic Ocean
Weddell Sea
Queen Maud Land
ANTARCTICA
Marie Byrd Land
Wilkes Land
Ross Ice Shelf
South Pacific Ocean

there. In 1958, two British explorers, Hillary and Fuchs, used snow-cats, weasel tractors, aircraft, and dog sleds to cross the continent via the Pole, becoming the first persons to make the 2158-mile (3474 km) trip from coast to coast.

Today, scientists from many nations go to this region to study glaciers, weather, and polar plants and animals.

SOYBEAN

This bean which has many uses is widely grown in Asia, especially in Japan and China. It has also been successfully cultivated in the United States, Canada, Brazil, and parts of Europe.

In each hairy pod, there are two or three yellowish-brown beans that are very nourishing. They can be eaten as a vegetable, and they can also be ground into a flour for making sausages, soup, candy, and sauces, and into meal for chickens and cattle. The meal is also used in manufacturing plastics and glues. Soybean oil is used in making MARGARINE, paint, varnish, synthetic rubber, and printer's ink.

SPACE TRAVEL

Man has always been curious about outer space, but it was only after World War II that two nations, the United States and the Soviet Union, could send objects far from the Earth. Germany had led the world in knowledge about ROCKETS during the war, and German scientists helped us in our work.

The first stage in exploring space was a series of *sounding rockets*, which went up about 100 miles (160 km) to investigate the Earth's outer atmosphere. By the late 1950s, it was possible to go further into space and launch SATELLITES. 1957–58 was declared International Geophysical Year, to be used for an international effort to examine the whole Earth. Satellites would be useful in this. The Soviet SPUTNIK I was the first satellite put in orbit. It was lifted by rockets in October, 1957. Sputnik II was the first to contain a living creature (a dog). Yuri Gagarin, a Russian, was the first man to go into outer space, in 1961. In 1969, Americans took the lead by being the first humans to walk on another heavenly body, the moon.

Unmanned vehicles have now landed on Venus and Mars, and have left the solar system entirely.

There are many problems in space travel. The vehicle leaves the Earth at great speed, and an ASTRONAUT has to lie down so as not be to injured on takeoff. He has to wear a special suit when he leaves the vehicle in outer space so that he has the right air pressure, body temperature, and oxygen. Beyond a certain point he and other objects in the space vehicle have no weight, because no heavenly body is pulling at them strongly, and he has to get used to that. The vehicle itself has to be kept on the right course at all times. It has to withstand very high temperatures.

Probably we shall never reach another star. Nothing can travel faster than light, and the light of the stars takes years to get to us.

SPAIN

Spain occupies most of the Iberian peninsula in southwest EUROPE. France is to the north, across the Pyrenees Mountains. Much of Spain is plateau crossed by mountain ranges and cut by deep valleys. Along its coast is a narrow, fertile plain. Rainfall is scarce. Summers are very hot, especially in the central region, where MADRID, the capital, stands. Winters are cold inland and mild along the Mediterranean coast.

Many Spaniards are farmers, growing wheat, olives, and citrus fruits. Others fish for cod, tuna, and sardines in the Atlantic or the Mediterranean.

In northern Spain, people mine enough iron ore for export. Cork trees are also cultivated, and their bark is exported.

Spain was ruled for many centuries by the Romans. The Visigoths overran the country in the A.D. 500s, and later the Moors from North Africa invaded and lived in Spain for about 700 years. The Moors were conquered by the Spainish kings, who also acquired an enormous overseas empire in

Central and South America and in parts of Africa and the East Indies. Wars and bad management led to the collapse of the empire. Since the 18th century, Spain has endured invasions, revolts, civil wars, and much poverty. Today, Spain's 37 million inhabitants live under a constitutional monarchy, with a parliament (the *Cortes*) and a king (Juan Carlos I). SEE ALSO: MADRID.

SPANISH-AMERICAN WAR

The Spanish-American War was fought between the United States and Spain in 1898. When a formal peace treaty was signed by both nations on December 10, 1898, Spain gave up control of CUBA, which became an independent territory under U.S. protection. Spain ceded to the U.S. the Spanish islands of Guam and PUERTO RICO. The PHILIPPINES were also surrendered to the U.S. for a payment of $20 million.

For many years, Cuba had been fighting for independence from Spain. Cuban rebels had many American sympathizers, who felt that Spain was too harsh in its treatment of the Cubans. The U.S. government was also upset by the heavy American economic losses because of guerrilla warfare.

The U.S. battleship *Maine* was sent to Cuba to protect U.S. citizens and property. While resting in Havana harbor, the ship was sunk by a mysterious explosion on February 15, 1898. Two hundred sixty sailors were killed. Newspapers in the U.S. printed headlines that blamed the Spanish for the disaster. "Remember the Maine" became the slogan for those Americans demanding Spanish withdrawal from Cuba. The U.S. Congress made a resolution enlisting volunteer troops and set terms for U.S. intervention. American ships blockaded Cuban ports. On April 24, 1898, Spain declared war on the U.S.

On May 1, American warships under Commodore George Dewey sailed into the harbor of Manila, in the Philippines, and thoroughly destroyed the Spanish fleet there. American warships blockaded another Spanish fleet in the harbor of Santiago, in Cuba. When the Spanish ships tried to escape on July 3, they were utterly defeated by the Americans.

Meanwhile, about 17,000 poorly equipped American soldiers landed in Cuba and undertook the capture of Santiago. There was heavy fighting at the fort of El Caney and at San Juan Hill, where THEODORE ROOSEVELT led a brave attack by an American volunteer regiment called the Rough Riders. After a week's fighting, Santiago surrendered on July 15.

An armistice (truce) was signed by the U.S. and Spain on August 12. Unaware of this, Dewey and Wesley Merritt commanded American sea and land forces during a successful capture of Manila on August 13. The U.S. emerged from the Spanish-American War as a world power.

SPARROW

The sparrow is a small kind of finch, having generally a dull coloring and a wheezy, weak song. It feeds and nests on or near the ground. The small, redcapped, brown-streaked chipping sparrow, perhaps the most familiar variety, builds a nest of horse hair or dog hair. The next best known American sparrow is probably the song sparrow, which dwells in neglected brushy fields and uses fine grasses and long hairs to line its nest built on the ground.

The native American sparrows, such as the white-throated and field sparrows, help the farmer by eating huge amounts of weed seeds and insects.

SPARTA

Sparta was an ancient city-state, situated in the Peloponnesus in southern GREECE. It had a strong defensive position on the plain of Laconia, beside the Eurotas River. Sparta, founded by the Dorian Greeks, developed a strong army for defense against invaders and unfriendly neighbors.

Spartan children were trained early to be tough, brave, and cruel. Their fathers lived in barracks and seldom went home. The comforts of life, art, and trade were discouraged, and rigorous military training was given to everyone. By the beginning of the 5th century B.C., Sparta had a wonderfully disciplined and efficient army and was master of the Peloponnesus states.

As the city-state of ATHENS in the north grew more powerful, it became certain that Sparta would fight her for supremacy. The great Peloponnesian War from 431 to 404 B.C. wrecked Athens, and Sparta became the strongest Greek city-state. But Spartan tyranny (cruel use of power) caused rebellions, and in 371 B.C. Epaminondas of Thebes defeated the Spartans at Leuctra, in central Greece. Sparta was never able to dominate the other city-states again.

SPEAR

The spear is a very old weapon. Early man probably used the sharpened end of a stick to stab the animals he was hunting. Later, he learned to make spear points out of flints and other stones that could be sharpened. Later, men learned to make points of bronze, iron, and steel.

There are two basic types of spear. One is the *javelin*, which is thrown. Ancient armies often threw javelins at the enemy, then charged with swords. The other type is the *lance*, used by the Macedonians in ancient times and by the knights of the Middle Ages. A fighter with the lance does not throw it. He charges, on foot or on horseback, thrusting it at the enemy. Some cavalry (horse) soldiers used lances until the early part of this century.

SPECTRUM

When white LIGHT passes through a solid, wedge-shaped piece of glass called a prism, the light is separated into a band of seven separate COLORS from red to violet. This colored band of light is known as a spectrum.

Drops of water can act like tiny prisms to produce a RAINBOW when rays of sunlight pass through them. The rays become bent or *refracted* and separate into the various colors. Crystals and objects of cut glass can also have the same effect on light.

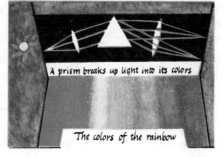

A prism breaks up light into its colors

The colors of the rainbow

SPEECH

Many animals can make noises to express their anger, fear, and pleasure, but they are unable to describe things and ideas. Because man's BRAIN is much more complex than that of an animal, he has ways of communicating with other people by using certain groups of sounds.

In order to speak, man must first make his breath pass through some throat muscles known as *vocal cords*. The resulting SOUND can be varied by using the tongue, lips, and teeth in ways learned during babyhood. Since speech is learned by imitating others, we tend to speak as do our parents, relatives, and close friends, using the same language and dialect and developing the same speech problems, if any, as they have.

SPHINX

A sphinx was an imaginary monster that usually had a human head and a lion's body. The Egyptians carved hundreds of sphinxes out of stone and placed them in rows leading to a TEMPLE.

The most remarkable of the Egyptian sphinxes is the Great Sphinx at Gizeh, near the Great PYRAMIDS. This colossal statue is 66 feet (20 m) high and 240 feet (74 m) long, with the face of a pharaoh. King Khafre is said to have built it about 2500 B.C. The Great Sphinx had a religious importance and may have been known as Horus, guardian god of the pyramids and the temples.

Ancient Greek legends mentioned a sphinx that had a woman's head, a bird's wings, and a lion's body. The frightening Sphinx of Thebes ate all travelers who could not solve her riddle, "What walks on four legs in the morning, two at noon, and three at night?" Oedipus gave the right answer, "Man," for man crawls on all fours as a baby, walks on two feet as a man, and uses a cane as an old man. The angry Sphinx then flung herself into the sea and perished.

SPICES

The people of the Middle Ages loved highly spiced food because most food was dull, especially in winter when there were no fresh fruits or vegetables and the meat was tough, salty, and often half spoiled. Spices masked any bad tastes that the food might otherwise have had. At that time, most spices came from the EAST INDIES (called the Spice Islands) in the western Pacific Ocean. Lives and fortunes were risked and great battles were fought in an effort to control the spice trade routes of the East Indies. Columbus was in search of a shorter, easier route to the East Indies when he discovered America in 1492.

Spices come from the different parts of plants. Black pepper comes from berries; ginger, from roots; cinnamon, from bark; cloves, from flower buds; nutmeg and mustard, from seeds; mace, from seedcases; and paprika and red pepper, from the fruit.

SPIDERS

Spiders are not insects. Spiders belong to a group called the *arachnids*. There are three main ways of distinguishing spiders from insects: (1) spiders have a 2-part body, whereas insects have a 3-part body; (2) spiders have 8 legs, while insects have 6; (3) instead of feelers (*antennae*) such as insects have, spiders have a pair of pincers.

Most spiders spin sticky webs for trapping insects. The silk comes from glands called *spinnerets*, whose position can be seen in the drawing. Depending on the species of spider, webs vary greatly in size from the 18-foot (5.6 m) wide ones, spun by spiders in the tropics, to webs the size of a small postage stamp. Spider silk is even stronger than steel wire of the same thickness. The finest, most beautiful web probably belongs to the common garden spider that spins a big cartwheel web. Relying on its speed to catch insects, the fierce wolf spider does not bother to spin a web. The crab spider does not spin one either, even though it is not swift; it simply lies in wait and then pounces on its victim. The striped zebra spider uses lengths of floating silk threads, called *gossamer*, to keep itself from falling off walls and trees. These threads are also used by the young spiders to swing quickly from one area to another.

Usually, the spider hides in a silk tube, pounces on his prey, and kills it with a poisonous bite when it becomes trapped in

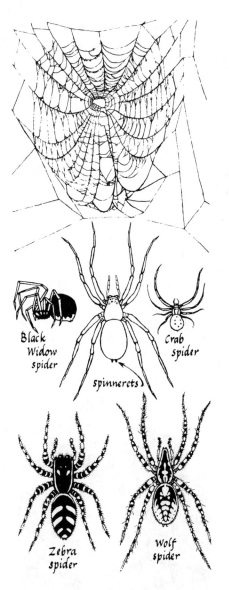

Black Widow spider

Crab spider

spinnerets

Zebra spider

Wolf spider

Tarantula

the web. A spider bite is usually not harmful to a person. The American black widow has a dangerous bite capable of causing a person's death, although such instances are quite rare. This species is easily recognized by the red "hour glass" on the underside of its black body. The bite of the scorpion and large hairy tarantula is painful but not as deadly as it was once thought to be.

The female spider lays her eggs in a silk sac or cocoon from which the young hatch in the spring. The babies, which look like miniature adults, must push their way out of the sac. As each grows, it sheds its skin several times.

The illustrations on pages 789 and 790 show a few of the thousands of kinds of spiders that exist in the world today.

SPINNING

Most natural cloth fibers are too short or too weak to be used alone. They must be twisted together with others to make threads or yarns. The twisting process is called spinning.

First, raw fibers are cleaned. If a mixture of different fibers is wanted, they are blended. Then they are *carded*. Cards are plates with tiny teeth that move through the masses of fiber, pulling them straight. In some cases the carded fiber is then combed so as to remove all short fibers and leave only long ones.

For many centuries, the spinning itself was done by hand. The fibers were wound on a long stick called a *distaff*, which the woman spinning held under her left arm. The spinner pulled some of the fibers from the distaff and tied them together around a short stick with a weight on one end. This was the *spindle*. Holding the fibers so that the spindle dangled from them, the spinner twirled the spindle in such a way that it spun around, giving a twist to the fibers as far up as her fingers. She wound the thread or yarn thus made around the spindle, putting the upper end of the twisted part through a notch that held it, then started the process again with a new length of untwisted fiber. The spinning wheel, known in Europe from the late Middle Ages, speeded the process by turning the spindle mechanically. It was run by a treadle moved by the spinner's foot.

Spinning Jenny

In the 18th century, the demand for threads and yarns became greater than the hand spinners could supply. James Hargreaves' spinning jenny of 1770 and Samuel Crompton's "mule" of 1779 sped up the process enormously.

SPONGES

This very simple SEA ANIMAL attaches itself to a rock or other support. A sponge is a group of separate living cells, that take in tiny plants, animals, and oxygen from the sea water. The water runs through hundreds of *pores* or tiny openings all over the surface of the sponge. A sponge skeleton may be a hard, beautiful shape, or it may be bendable, like the bath sponge. Some are glassy; others are of chalk. Some sponges grow in fresh water; however, most grow in warm, salt water.

SPRING

The SEASON called spring begins on March 21 in the Northern Hemisphere. The days then grow longer and hotter as the sun's rays hit the northern part of the Earth more directly.

The appearance of the ROBIN is said to be the first sign of spring, when birds return to the north after spending winter in the south. Hedgehogs, ground squirrels, and bears come out of hibernation. Insect eggs hatch; bees build hives; hares shed their winter coats. Lambs, calves, chickens, and the young of most animals and birds are born or hatched during springtime. Grass, trees, flowers, and farmers' crops begin to grow again. Spring festivals are sometimes held, celebrating the start of a "new" year.

SPRINGS

When rain water soaks through *porous* rock, such as chalk, it finally reaches an *impervious* layer through which it cannot pass. This non-porous layer may come to the surface further down a slope, where the water will gush out as a spring.

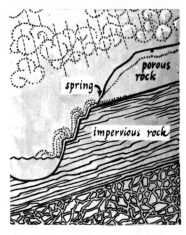

After journeying underground, water often is very cold and pure. But, if its underground journey is at great depths, especially in volcanic areas, it may reappear as a hot spring, like those in Hot Springs National Park in central Arkansas.

When large amounts of minerals are dissolved in the water, these mineral waters, either hot or cold, often become known for their healing powers and are also bottled for their good taste. Health resorts where such springs exist are called *spas*, such as Saratoga Springs, New York, and Warm Springs, Georgia. SEE ALSO: GEYSERS.

SPURS

A spur is used by a horseman to start his horse or urge him to go faster. It fits around the heel of his boot and has a long extension that jabs the horse's side. Early medieval spurs had spikes that injured the horse's hide. In the late Middle Ages, horsemen began to use *rowels*, spiked wheels that did less damage. Modern spurs have rowels with many short, blunt spikes.

Norman spur

In the Middle Ages, a knight wore gilt spurs that were sometimes decorated. To say that a person had won his spurs meant that he had been promoted from a squire to a knight.

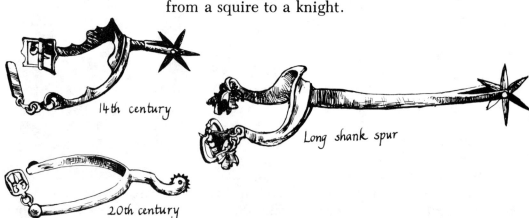

14th century

Long shank spur

20th century

SPUTNIK

In October, 1957, the Soviet Union launched the first artificial SATELLITE, which they called Sputnik. It weighed 184 pounds (84 kg) and circled the Earth every 96 minutes. The closest it got was 143 miles (231 km) and the furthest was 584 miles (942 km). After a few months of sending data, it returned to the Earth's atmosphere and burned up from friction with the air during its rapid fall. Other sputniks, some with live animals, went up shortly afterward.

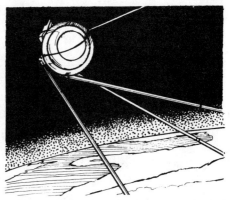

The United States tried to send up a satellite in 1957, but failed. There was great concern in the United States about the lead in space travel gained by the Russians. SEE ALSO:SPACE TRAVEL.

SQUIRRELS

Squirrels are RODENTS, found in all parts of the world except Australia. Squirrels live in trees and feed mainly on nuts. They will also eat grain, eggs, baby birds, and seeds, much to the distress of the farmer. Squirrels use their bushy tails to help keep their balance as they climb and jump in the trees. Also, making their tails into a kind of furry blanket, they often sleep with their tails over their backs.

In the fall, squirrels busily store away acorns and berries, sometimes forgetting where they hide them. In the winter, they take several long naps, but rarely hibernate completely. During the spring, they build nests of sticks, bark, and moss. Two or three young ones are born in the spring. Another litter of baby squirrels is sometimes born in August.

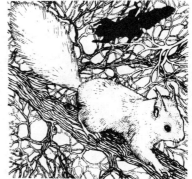

There are four kinds of squirrels in the United States. The most common species is the red squirrel. The fox squirrel is the largest, usually reddish or black in color. The gray squirrel is somewhat smaller and has a wider range than the fox squirrel. The flying squirrel has folds of skin connecting the front and back legs, making possible its long, gliding leaps between branches and trees.

SRI LANKA

Sri Lanka, formerly known as Ceylon, is an island in the Indian Ocean, lying 20 miles (32 km) off the southernmost tip of India. The coastal region is flat, but the central part is mountainous. The climate is hot and humid, with occasional cool ocean breezes. Sri Lanka's capital and largest city is Colombo.

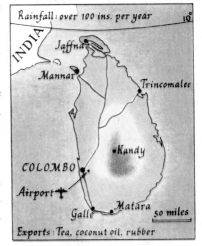

Much of the world's tea comes from the island, which also produces rubber, coconuts, cinnamon, and cacao. Sri Lanka has many minerals and metals, such as graphite, limestone, iron, and precious and semi-precious stones.

Most of the 14.5 million inhabitants are Sinhalese, whose ancestors came from India more than 2000 years ago. The rest are Tamils, who practice Hinduism. The Sinhalese, however, are followers of BUDDHA.

Sri Lanka came under Portuguese control in 1505, and later was ruled by the Dutch. In 1802, it became a British crown colony and in 1972 an independent republic.

STAGECOACH

Before there were many railroads, people often traveled by stagecoach. This was the forerunner of the modern bus. It traveled on a schedule, carrying anyone who could pay the fare, between stopping places called *stages*. These were usually inns, where the passengers could refresh themselves and where fresh horses could be harnessed to the coach.

Although many countries used stagecoaches, those of England and the United States are the most famous. English coaching began early in the 17th century, but the greatest period was that between 1800 and 1840, when beautifully painted coaches ran on the new, smooth roads of MACADAM. They averaged 10 miles an hour (16 km/hr), a fast speed for the day. They went out of business as the number of railroads increased.

Stagecoaches were popular along the east coast of the United States by 1800. They are best remembered, though, for their widespread use in the far West after the Civil War. Two main types were used, the Concord coach, which was often made in Massachusetts, and the mud wagon, a heavy, slow coach used on bad roads. Many in the Southwest were run by Wells Fargo and Company. There was a charge for carrying parcels and passengers.

STALACTITES and STALAGMITES

Limestone, which consists wholly or mainly of calcium carbonate, dissolves easily in rain water that flows or seeps through pores and cracks in the rock. In limestone CAVES, droplets of this water collect on the ceiling. Some of the water evaporates, leaving a limy substance that gradually grows into a hard "icicle." It hangs from the ceiling and is called a *stalactite*.

Some of this limy water can also drip onto the floor of the cave. Here evaporation again causes the buildup of hard material. This time, however, the column grows upward from the floor, creating what is known as a *stalagmite*.

Sometimes stalactites and stalagmites join together, forming strange and wonderful shapes, columns, or clusters. Long "curtains" of lime can also develop along the walls of caves. Among the famous American caves with these formations are Mammoth Cave in Kentucky, Luray Caverns in Virginia, and Carlsbad Caverns in New Mexico. SEE ALSO: CAVES, LIMESTONE.

STAMP COLLECTING

For centuries, all postage was paid by the people who received the mail, not by the ones who sent it. In 1840, though, Great Britain issued the first postage stamps, which were stuck to mail to prove that the senders had paid the postage. These first stamps showed a head of Queen Victoria. A black stamp cost one penny, and a blue one cost two pennies.

Other countries quickly took up the idea, which was a very useful one, and soon there were many kinds of stamps. By 1861, there were enough stamp collectors that catalogues of canceled (used) stamps were being issued, and in 1865 the hobby of stamp collecting received its special name, *philately*.

A modern collector can find many kinds of stamps, some very cheap, some extremely valuable. Each country has its own stamps, of course. There is a different stamp for each postal rate. Designs change from time to time. Commemorative stamps celebrate something that has just happened or something that happened in the past. Stamps show great men of a country, or its plants, animals, birds, or famous scenes. Some countries go to great trouble to print many kinds of stamps because they know collectors will buy them.

There is so much that could be bought, and some stamps are so expensive, that most collectors buy only special stamps— stamps from one part of the world, stamps from one period of time, for example. Some collectors want stamps that have certain perforations (rows of holes between stamps) or markings. Some want stamps badly printed, even, like the U.S. Air Mail stamp in which the plane is upside-down.

Every letter that comes to your house has a stamp, so some of the stamps you might collect are free. On the other hand, one stamp that is the only one left may sell for more than a quarter of a million dollars.

Sir Henry Morton STANLEY (1841–1904)

Sir Henry Morton Stanley was born in Wales and came to the U.S. as a cabin boy on a ship. He fought on both sides during the U.S. Civil War and afterward became a newspaper correspondent for the *New York Herald*. He won fame sending back news stories about the wars and political troubles in Turkey and Spain.

In 1869, the *Herald* asked Stanley to find DAVID LIVINGSTONE, the Scottish missionary and explorer who had been missing in Africa for two years. With a well-equipped caravan, Stanley forced his way through the jungles and discovered the explorer at Ujiji on Lake Tanganyika on November 10, 1871. Together they explored the north end of the lake. After failing to persuade Livingstone to leave Africa, Stanley returned to Europe in 1872.

The next year he went back to Africa to explore the continent further. He made a journey of about 1600 miles (2576 km) across Africa, learning much about the Congo region and tracing the course of the Congo River.

STARCH

Starch is the name of the food manufactured by all green plants in the process called *photosynthesis*. In order for photosynthesis to occur in plants, *chlorophyl* (the green coloring matter), carbon dioxide from the air, sunlight, and water must be present. Like all carbohydrates, starch is made up of three elements: carbon, hydrogen, and oxygen. Rice, corn, wheat, arrowroot, and potatoes are rich in starch. Starchy foods give us heat and energy, but they are not nutritious enough without meat and green vegetables.

Laundry starch is a dried form of the starch we eat. It is used for stiffening linen and other fabrics and for many industrial purposes.

STARLING

Starlings are blackish birds with feathers that shine like metal. They have long bills that are yellow in spring and summer. Starlings are common throughout the world.

Because starlings eat harmful insects and animal ticks, they are somewhat beneficial to farmers. However, they also do much damage to fruit and young wheat, as well as drive away smaller, more desirable birds. Starlings often steal the nesting sites of other birds, too. Their own nests are untidy and built almost anywhere. Starlings feed and perch in large flocks.

Some kinds are kept in cages as pets, such as the mynas and grackles of India. They have their own song but are also very good at mimicking (imitating) other bird songs and other sounds, such as car horns, bicycle bells, and even human speech.

STARS

On any clear night, a person can see about 2000 to 3000 stars with the naked eye. A small telescope would reveal about a half million more stars. Astronomers say, however, that there are probably as many stars in the universe as there are grains of sand on Earth.

Like our flaming gaseous SUN, each star is a heavenly body that radiates its own LIGHT. Because they are so far away from us, stars are only seen as tiny pinpoints of light, although many are far larger and hotter than our sun. Stars twinkle because their light is bent and scattered by the Earth's atmosphere. On the moon, where there is no air, they would be viewed as shining with a steady light.

Astronomers make their calculations in terms of *light-years*, rather than in miles or kilometers. The light from the sun reaches Earth, which is 93 million miles

A star cluster

A spiral galaxy

(150 million km) from the sun, in about 8 minutes. One *light-year*, then, is the distance light travels in one year, traveling at the rate of 186,300 miles per second (almost 300,000 km/sec). A body one light-year away is about 5.88 trillion miles (9.47 trillion km) away. Sirius, the Dog Star, the brightest of all, is 9 light-years away; the North Star, Polaris, is more than 400 light-years away.

On some dark, clear nights, the hazy band of brightness that is visible across the sky is the Milky Way, made up of millions of stars. This system of stars, rotating like a colossal pinwheel, is called a *galaxy*. It is one of many galaxies

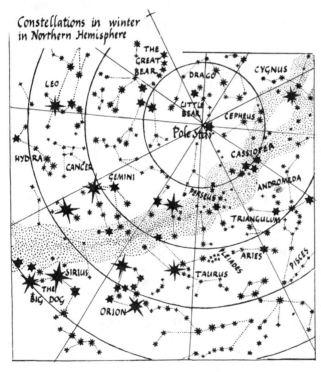

Constellations in winter in Northern Hemisphere

scattered throughout the endless universe. Andromeda is the name of another galaxy astronomers study.

Stars are different colors. The coolest are red. The hottest visible stars are blue-white. Some stars are actually two, or as many as six suns revolving about each other.

Stars appear in patterns or groups, called *constellations*, which the ancient peoples thought looked like pictures in the sky. The names they gave the constellations, such as Leo ("The Lion"), Taurus ("The Bull"), Canis Major ("The Big Dog"), and Cancer ("The Crab"), tell us what they saw. SEE ALSO: ASTRONOMY.

STAR-SPANGLED BANNER

In 1814, during the WAR OF 1812, the British attacked Fort McHenry, near Baltimore, firing rockets and shells at it. A Baltimore lawyer, Francis Scott Key, saw the attack from a British ship to which he had gone to obtain the release of a friend who had been taken prisoner. The fort held out against the British, and Key, back in Baltimore, wrote a poem, "The Defence of Fort McHenry," the next day. It was set to a popular 18th-century song as "The Star-Spangled Banner." This became the official United States anthem in 1931.

STATUE of LIBERTY

Shortly after the Civil War, the French historian Edouard de Laboulaye had the idea of a huge statue of *Liberty Enlightening* (giving wisdom to) *the World*, to be built in the United States. Both the French and the American peoples gave money for the project. The sculptor for the statue was Frédéric-Auguste Bartholdi, a Frenchman. It was made of sheets of copper supported by a steel frame. The right arm and torch of the statue were shown at the Centennial Exposition of 1876 in Philadelphia. The statue was built in 1886 on an island in New York Harbor that is now called Liberty Island. Its overall height, with the pedestal it stands on, is 302 feet (92 m).

Millions of people have seen the Statue of Liberty as they entered the United States at the port of New York. The statue stands for the freedom that the country offers to the people of the world.

STEAM ENGINE

Watt's steam engine

When steam is created by boiling water, it tries to expand. The force it uses in its effort to expand, and the fact that when it expands it takes up many more times the space it had when it was water, have been put to work in running machinery.

Although an ancient scientist had already invented a kind of TURBINE, steam was not really put to work until around 1700. Thomas Savery's engine of 1698 and Thomas Newcomen's engine of 1712 were not true steam engines, though. They were *atmospheric engines*, which used the weight of air pressing against a vacuum. Steam was let into a closed place, then was *condensed* by cooling it so that it turned to water. This created the vacuum.

Atmospheric engines were slow and wasted fuel, since the chambers that held the steam were cooled when the steam was. In 1765, a Scotsman, James Watt, invented a separate condenser that allowed the steam chamber to stay hot. He made many other useful improvements. Atmospheric engines were useful only for pumping. The Newcomen engine could give only an up-and-down motion. Watt's engines could turn a crank, and thus turn wheels.

A	Cylinder	D	Pump piston	G	Cold water
B	Boiler	E	Pump rod		tank
C	Piston	F	Fire	V	Valve

They had a *flywheel*, whose weight kept the engine moving smoothly even when the power was temporarily off. Most importantly, Watt used steam for power rather than air pressure.

An ordinary 19th-century steam engine worked this way. Steam under pressure entered one end of a CYLINDER, a chamber that looked like a circle when seen one way and a rectangle when seen another. Fitting snugly in this chamber was a *piston*, a sliding disk mounted on a rod called a *piston rod*. The expanding steam pushed the piston along the cylinder to the far end. The piston rod pulled or pushed on the end of a *connecting rod*, which turned a crank on a shaft outside the cylinder. The *crankshaft* could be used to turn wheels, pulleys, propellers, or other things. When the piston was all the way along the cylinder, the steam that pushed it was released to the open air or sucked into a condenser to be turned into hot water for the boiler. Then steam was let into the other end of the cylinder to push the piston back where it came from. This was a *double-acting engine*; each movement of the piston was a *power stroke*, turning the crankshaft halfway around.

As steam pressure grew higher thanks to the construction of better boilers, it became possible to use the expanding steam over again in one or more larger cylinders. It would go from a small high-pressure cylinder, where it had expanded a little way, and end in a large low-pressure cylinder where it expanded still further. An engine with two sizes of cylinder was called a *compound engine*, and one with three sizes was called a *triple-expansion engine*.

STEEL

Steel is a mixture of iron with other minerals. At least half of the mixture, or *alloy*, must be iron if it is to be called steel.

About one percent of the steel will be carbon. Wrought iron has very little carbon, while cast iron has a great deal. Many other ingredients go into the many different steels that are made. Carbon steels contain a small amount of manganese. They are used for construction and for making machinery. Low-alloy steels have up to 5 percent of several minerals besides iron, and are used for many special purposes where great strength is needed. High-alloy steels contain more than 5 percent of various minerals. Stainless steel, which resists rust, is a high-alloy steel made with chromium. It is used for tableware, kitchen utensils, parts of jet engines, and cutlery. SEE ALSO: IRON.

George STEPHENSON (1781–1848)

The 'Rocket'

George Stephenson, an English engineer, built some of the first steam locomotives to be used in England.

He was born in the mining village of Wylam, near Newcastle. Because his parents were too poor to send him to school, he worked at the coal mines and looked after the pumping engine. He learned how to repair steam engines during the day, and at night he learned how to read and write.

In 1814, Stephenson built a steam locomotive to haul coal

from the mines. He invented a miner's safety lamp at the same time SIR HUMPHRY DAVY did. Both men are given credit for this oil lamp, designed for safe use in mines that have inflammable gases like firedamp.

Stephenson became an engineer on the first English railroads, always urging the use of STEAM ENGINES rather than horsepower. In 1829, Stephenson's locomotive, the *Rocket*, won a famous competition on the Liverpool to Manchester Railroad. His locomotive safely hauled a passenger train along the railway, attaining a speed of 44 miles per hour (71 km/hr).

Robert Louis STEVENSON (1850–1894)

Robert Louis Stevenson was born in Edinburgh, Scotland, and studied to be an engineer. However, his poor health (he had tuberculosis all his life) turned him to the study of law. Though Stevenson became a lawyer in 1875, he changed to writing as a career. Soon he became a popular writer of essays, stories, novels, and verse (poetry).

Stevenson in Samoa

He traveled throughout Europe and the United States and lived in California for one year (1887). In 1889, after a long tour of the South Seas, Stevenson settled down in Samoa, where he built a house and became well-known among the natives. He died there, and, by his own request, was buried on Mt. Vaea near his island home.

Stevenson's famous books of adventure include *Treasure Island*, *Kidnapped*, and *The Black Arrow*. Two of his other popular works are *A Child's Garden of Verses* and *The Strange Case of Dr. Jekyll and Mr. Hyde*.

STOCKINGS

Stockings, or *hosiery*, seem to go back almost 2000 years. Before that time people lined their shoes with compressed animal hair or wrapped strips of cloth or leather around their legs.

Early stockings were made of materials that would not stretch, such as ordinary woven cloth. They were cut to the shape of the leg or foot, but they could not fit snugly. To do that, knitted stockings were needed, and were eventually invented. Even today, stockings are knitted.

10th century *16th century* *Early 16th century* *Late 16th century*

For many centuries, all stockings were knitted by hand. The number of stitches had to be changed in various places down the stocking so that it would fit. But in 1589, an English clergyman, William Lee, invented a machine for knitting stockings. Queen Elizabeth I refused to give Lee a patent for this machine, however, because it would put too many people out of work. Machine knitting began only in the 17th century.

Wool and cotton were the favorite stocking materials until this century. After 1920, when women gave up long dresses for much shorter ones, silk and RAYON became especially popular for women's hose. After World War II, nylon replaced silk almost entirely.

STOCKS

Today, people convicted of crime are often put in PRISON, where they may perhaps be reformed. In colonial America, they were often punished for a little while in some unpleasant way and then let go. Their wrists and legs were clamped between the two boards of the *stocks* and they sat for hours exposed to public ridicule. Or they stood in the *pillory*, with their necks and wrists held in the same way. They might be whipped at a *whipping post*, or ducked in a pond tied to a *ducking stool*. Prison was only for people who were dangerous.

Stocks also are the securities used by companies to represent money owed them. The stock MARKET or stock exchange is a place where these securities may be traded (bought and sold) in an organized way.

STONE

We find many stones or rocks in nature. They appear in many sizes and can be smooth or rough. Builders use many kinds of stone in construction projects.

GRANITE, a handsome gray stone with dark marks and shiny black flecks, is the hardest of all building stones. It is commonly used for foundations, lighthouses, piers, docks, and massive buildings, like colleges, banks, and town halls. New Hampshire is nicknamed the "Granite State," because of its large, valuable granite deposits.

Granite

an old method of quarrying granite

wedges being driven in to split the stone

planing stone

sawing stone

Stone is now cut and shaped by machines

Sandstone, made up of sand granules cemented together by silica, is also a good building stone. Sandstone is brown, yellowish, or white in color.

Softer than granite or sandstone, LIMESTONE is widely and easily used as a building material; however, it quickly darkens in smoky environments. The finest building stone of all is MARBLE, a kind of limestone. However, it weathers poorly in cool, wet climates so it is mainly used for the interiors of buildings. SEE ALSO: GRANITE, LIMESTONE, MARBLE.

STONE AGE

The Stone Age was a long period of time when man used weapons and tools made of stone. Scientists disagree about how long the Stone Age lasted, but they usually divide it into three main periods—the Old Stone Age (Paleolithic), the Middle Stone Age (Mesolithic), and the New Stone Age (Neolithic).

During the Old Stone Age, people hunted and gathered food. They developed a crude kind of hand axe, made by sharpening stones with other stones. They made stone knives, scrapers, and bone needles, with which they sewed clothes out of animal skins.

Scientists believe these ancient people dressed in thick skins and lived in caves as protection against the severe cold. Also, they discovered the use of fire during this period. Remarkable cave paintings, done by these people, have been found in Spain and France.

During the Middle Stone Age, people began to build houses and use stone saws, ivory tools, and bows and arrows.

During the New Stone Age, man learned how to grow corn and to herd animals. The PLOW and the wheel were invented, people lived in larger groups and sometimes in LAKE DWELLINGS. They discovered how to make cloth and pottery, as well as how to polish flint. Grass trails were used as roads. They buried the dead beneath mounds called *barrows*. Communities traded goods with one another in this period.

When man learned how to make bronze from copper and tin, the BRONZE AGE began. However, the way of life of the Stone Age did not immediately vanish. Some people continued in the Stone Age in one part of the world, while others used metals, made fine buildings, and learned how to read and write, as in ancient Egypt, China, Greece, and Rome. Even today, in remote parts of NEW GUINEA, people live as they did in the Stone Age.

STONEHENGE

We still know very little about Stonehenge, the mysterious open-air construction that stands on a plain in the part of England called Wiltshire. It seems to have been built and rebuilt several times between 1800 and 1400 B.C., but we do not know the purpose it served. The sun and moon rise and set so as to shine between some of its upright stones on important days, so it was probably a temple for some sort of sky worship.

The outer part of Stonehenge is a circular bank of earth about 340 feet (100 m) in diameter. Inside this are two circles of upright stones with

other stones on top crossing between them. The outer circle is about 100 feet (32 m) in diameter. These stones were brought from Wales, a long distance away. Inside the two circles are five constructions of two upright stones each with a third stone on top. They are set in a horseshoe, whose open end faces the direction that the sun rises on the first day of summer. A two-mile (3.2 km) avenue lined with banks of earth goes away from Stonehenge toward the rising sun.

The labor of building Stonehenge was enormous. Not only were some stones brought from far away, but some of the stones are 30 feet (10 m) long and weigh 50 tons (27,000 kg).

STORK

Storks are large, long-legged birds with long, slender necks and straight, sharply pointed beaks. The common European white stork, shown in the illustration, mates for life and builds a nest of sticks on a roof or chimney to which it returns with its mate each year. These nests are often very large. Since it is considered good luck to have storks nesting on the house, they are never driven away. After rearing their young, they migrate in the autumn to southern Africa. Storks are voiceless, but they chatter by loudly snapping their beaks together.

STORMS

Storms are severe disturbances in the atmosphere that produce bad weather. Windstorms, thunderstorms, snowstorms, sandstorms, CYCLONES, duststorms, and hurricanes are well-known examples. Storms are the result of the uneven heating of air. The sun causes some parts of the Earth to heat up faster than others, resulting in a great deal of warm air coming in contact with colder air.

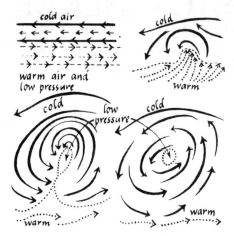

Cold air is heavy and dense and produces what is called a high air pressure system. The polar regions are in high pressure areas. On the other hand, warm air is light and tends to rise, cooling as it goes. It does not press as heavily upon the Earth's surface. The equator is in an area of low pressure with a belt of cooler, high pressure air on either side. Cool air from a high pressure area always tends to flow towards a warm, low pressure area, as if it were trying to fill a hollow.

Temporary disturbances of the Earth's magnetic field are called magnetic storms and are the result of radiation and streams of charged particles from the sun.

STRATFORD-ON-AVON

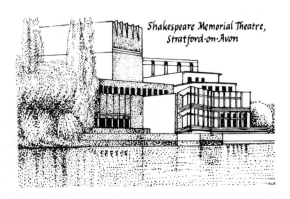

Shakespeare Memorial Theatre, Stratford-on-Avon

The market town of Stratford-on-Avon, in central England, is famous throughout the world as the birthplace of WILLIAM SHAKESPEARE.

Visitors come to the gabled house on Henley Street, where the poet and playwright was born in 1564. They can also visit the homes of Shakespeare's two daughters and of his mother. In the fine old Church of the Holy Trinity, his grave can be seen beside that of his wife, Anne Hathaway, whose cottage is in Shottery, very close to Stratford.

On the bank of the Upper Avon River stands the Shakespeare Memorial Theater, now called the Royal Shakespeare Theater. Each year festivals of poetry and drama are held there.

STRAWBERRY

The strawberry is a member of the rose family. The delicious red strawberry fruits contain tiny yellow seeds in small hollows which are all over the surface of the FRUIT. New plants, however, are not raised from seed but from the long, slender stems, called *runners*, that trail over the ground and root wherever they can.

Strawberry plants must be replaced every three years. Since the ripe fruit is so close to the soil, it can be ruined by heavy rain; therefore, straw is placed under the clusters of fruit—hence the name, *straw*berry.

SUBMARINE

Even in ancient times man was interested in the idea of going under the water. The first submarine actually to travel below the water was built by a Dutchman early in the 17th century. In 1776, during the American Revolution, a Connecticut man named David Bushnell built the *Turtle*, a submarine that tried without success to plant a mine under a British warship. The inventor Robert Fulton built the *Nautilus*, which worked fairly well. He could get no navy to buy it, however.

The Confederates used submarines in the Civil War, and during the late 19th century people in several nations suggested or built new types. The trouble with these early submarines was the lack of a good way of moving them. When the first really useful submarines were built, a little after 1900, the problem had been solved. The standard 20th century submarine had electric motors driven by batteries for undersea travel, and diesel or gasoline engines for use on the surface. The engines also ran generators that put electricity back in the batteries. They had water tanks that could be filled to submerge and emptied to rise. They had fins and rudders for moving in any direction, and a PERISCOPE for looking over the water while submerged. Their torpedoes, unlike 19th-century ones, were self-propelled and moved at high speeds.

Diagram of the 'Nautilus'

During World War I and II the submarine was very dangerous and sank many ships. But in World War I some submarines were also used to carry cargo. They were fairly safe from enemy warships and from storms while submerged.

The *Nautilus*, a U.S. submarine of 1955, was the first to be run by nuclear energy. Nuclear submarines are more expensive than ordinary diesel-electric ones, but the U.S., Russian, and other navies have built many because they can go long distances under water. SEE ALSO: PERISCOPE.

SUBURBS

The populated districts that surround a large city are called *suburbs*. Often a city will spread out to touch several smaller towns and villages around it, and they become its suburbs.

Suburbs were not very important until the mid- 19th century, when railroads allowed people to travel for many miles in a short time. Then, new little towns grew up around the railroad stations. The women and children could enjoy the suburbs all day. The men became *commuters*, going in to their offices by train every morning and coming back every evening.

As the suburbs became popular, more people wanted to live in them. Merchants wanted to have stores there. Landowners were tempted to build many little houses or apartments. Some suburbs became ugly places, while others passed laws to keep too much new building from taking place. Recently, the suburbs have realized that they now have some of the problems the original suburbanites fled the city to avoid. Many people are going back to the city, especially after their children are grown. They take apartments or buy and remodel houses in old city neighborhoods.

SUBWAYS

In many cities people travel by underground railroads called subways. The first subway was opened in London in 1863. The trains were pulled by steam locomotives, and the

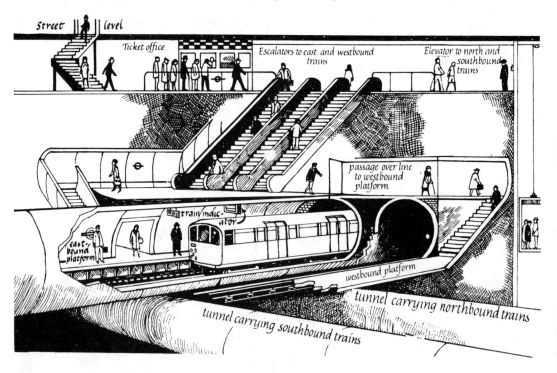

subway line was left open to the sky in many places to let the smoke escape. More subways were built in London, and in 1890 the first to use electric locomotives was opened there. The first subway on the continent of Europe was that of Budapest, Hungary, opened in 1896. The first American subway was that in Boston, opened in 1897.

Around 1900 subway construction became very popular, since it gave a way of moving around town rapidly without being delayed by street traffic. The famous Métro of Paris opened in 1900. The first part of the New York subway, now the world's largest, began operations in 1904.

A subway is often a very complicated affair, with many lines connecting so as to form a network under the city. Trains on different lines have to cross above or below each other. They have to go deep enough not to interfere with sewers, building foundations, and other things close to the surface of the earth. Sometimes they have to go under rivers. There have to be signals and switches, as on any railroad, and tracks where trains not in use can wait. The stations have to have stairs, escalators, or elevators to connect with the street. They have ticket agents and policemen. Often there are shops. Most subway stations are plain, but the people of Moscow and Leningrad in RUSSIA are very proud of their subway stations, which are richly decorated.

SUDAN

Sudan is the largest country in AFRICA, nearly four times bigger than Texas. Egypt is to the north; the Red Sea and Ethiopia to the east; Kenya, Uganda, and Zaïre to the south; and the Central African Republic, Chad, and Libya to the west. Sudan's capital is Khartoum.

The country is mostly desert in the north, except for the fertile valley of the NILE. The central region, especially around the Atbara, Blue Nile, and White Nile rivers, has good farmland for cotton, pastures, and gum forests. In southern Sudan there are dense tropical forests, with rich soil.

The 17 million Sudanese consist of Muslim Arabs, Negroes, and Nubians (of mixed Arab and Negro blood). They were ruled by Egypt until 1899, when England and Egypt decided to share control. The Sudanese gained their independence in 1956.

SUEZ CANAL

The Suez Canal links the Mediterranean Sea with the Gulf of Suez, an arm of the Red Sea. It is about 101 miles (163 km) long and has no locks because it runs through flat desert. Egypt lies along the west bank of the canal, and the Sinai Peninsula occupied by Israel is to the east.

The canal was built by an Egyptian company between 1859 and 1869.

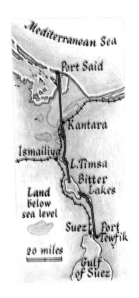

Ferdinand de Lesseps, a French engineer, directed the project from start to finish. In the 1880s, he led a French company that tried unsuccessfully to construct a PANAMA CANAL.

Parts of the Suez Canal are only 196 feet (61 m) wide. Ships must then wait to pass one another, staying in a special by-pass or in one of the lakes through which the canal flows. In one place, several large hollows are filled with water to create the Great and Little Bitter Lakes. Continual dredging is needed to keep the canal open.

Britain controlled the canal after it became the largest stockholder in the Suez Canal Company. In 1956, Egyptian President Nasser seized the canal. In the Arab-Israeli war of 1967, ships were sunk to block the channel, which was not cleared until 1975.

SUGAR

The major source of the sugar we use is sugar cane and sugar beet, two very different plants as the pictures illustrate. The sugar maple tree and the sugar palm of North America produce only small amounts of our sugar supply.

Sugar cane needs a hot climate in order to grow. India, Java, Cuba, Jamaica, the Philippines, Puerto Rico, and the United States in Texas, Louisiana, Florida, and Hawaii are places where sugar cane

Sugar cane

grows well in carefully controlled, irrigated fields. In less than a year, the canes grow 10 to 20 feet (3.1–6.2 m) tall. After the flowers fade, the canes are cut down and carted to the factory where the juice is squeezed out by rollers. Boiling the juice separates out the thick molasses syrup, and reboiling in huge pans causes brown sugar crystals to form at the bottom of the pans. This crude or unrefined sugar is then sent to refineries where it is boiled some more, and then

Boiling pans

treated to produce the white sugar needed for icing and granulated and cube sugar.

Sugar beets are large white roots with a high sugar content that grow in cool countries in good soil. They are the main source of sugar for Europeans. Germany, Austria, Russia, France, and the northern United States grow large quantities of sugar beets. In autumn, the leaves and tops are

Sugar beet

removed and used as cattle feed. At the factory, the roots are cut into chips and then crushed to remove the juice. The remaining pulp makes a rich food for domestic animals. Lime is added to the juice and the remaining processing is similar to that of sugar cane. Beet molasses is fed to livestock, for it is too difficult to purify for people to eat. The refined sugar from sugar beets is exactly the same as that from sugar cane.

Sugar was first brought to Europe in the 700s when the Moors brought it from

Harvesting sugar beets

the East to Spain. Later, Crusaders returned with "sugar loaves." Before the 1400s, sugar was so expensive that honey was really the only sweetener used by most people.

SUMERIA

Sumeria, or Sumer, was an ancient region in southern Mesopotamia, in the fertile valley of the Tigris and EUPHRATES Rivers. Later it became known as Babylonia and is today part of Iraq.

Sumerians developed a high civilization about 4000 B.C. They were good

Figures on the side of a box known as the Standard of Ur

farmers, builders, artists, and traders, and had a well-organized communal life and a complex nature religion. The first writing —CUNEIFORM—and the first use of metals came from the Sumerians. Kings ruled in the important Sumerian cities, such as UR, Erech, and Kish, and had temples called *ziggurats*—high towers with a series of terraces.

Sumeria was invaded about 2000 B.C. by tribesmen called Elamites. However, with the rise of Hammurabi, the country became part of the kingdom of BABYLON, and the Sumerians, as a nation, disappeared.

SUN The sun is a STAR more than a million times bigger than EARTH. Earth gets its light and heat from the sun, and it is one of the 9 planets in the sun's family, called the SOLAR SYSTEM. Although Earth is about 93 million miles (150 million km) from the sun, this distance is actually very small when compared to the vast distances between stars.

The sun is a mass of fiery gases that are intensely hot. The sun's internal temperature is believed to be about 57 million° F (about 14 million° C) and its surface temperature is almost 11,000° F (about 6000° C).

Leaping out for millions of miles from the main body of the sun are gigantic flames and tongues of fire, known as "prominences" or the sun's corona. Periodically, dark areas, called *sunspots*, appear on the sun's face. They are thought to be immense explosions, which seem to be the cause of electrical disturbances in our atmosphere.

earth

A solar prominence

SUNDEW

The sundew belongs to an unusual group of plants that trap and eat small insects. In the bogs and marshy places where they grow, the water-logged soil does not supply them with all the NITROGEN they need. Therefore, they are able to digest insects, which provide sufficient nitrogen for them to live.

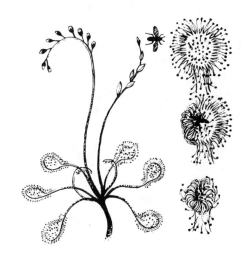

The leaves of the sundew are covered with hairs, each ending in a droplet of sticky fluid. These leaves attract and trap insects in the stickiness. The sticky hairs fold inwards and release a digestive fluid that dissolves the insect, which is then absorbed into the leaf. The hairs afterward uncurl. Any undigestable parts of the dead insect are blown away, and the leaf is ready for the next insect.

The Venus fly trap and the pitcher plant are other *insectivorous* plants—that is, plants that eat insects.

The SUPREME COURT

The Supreme Court is the highest court in the United States, established by the U.S. CONSTITUTION. It consists of eight associate justices (judges) and one chief justice. They are nominated by the President and approved by the Senate. They are also appointed for life and can only be removed from the Court by impeachment and conviction. However, many justices have resigned because of sickness or old age.

The Court has the authority to act in cases concerning the Constitution, laws, and treaties of the U.S. and in disputes between states or between citizens of different states. It decides maritime (navigation and commerce of seagoing vessels) questions and handles cases affecting ambassadors, consuls, and other public ministers.

In a case in 1803, Chief Justice John Marshall ruled that the Supreme Court has the power to declare a law unconstitutional. This power, called *judicial review*, was not expressly given by the Constitution, but it is now considered an "implied power" of the Court. Judicial review allows the Court to overrule some of the decisions made by the President, Congress, or state legislatures.

Much of the Court's business concerns *appeals* in cases affected by federal law. (An appeal is a request for a rehearing of a case by a higher court.)

SWALLOW

Swallows are swift flying birds with long pointed wings and usually with forked tails. Their short beaks can open very wide, allowing them to catch insects as they swoop and dive through the air. They have very short legs and walk awkwardly. They often perch on telephone wires.

The best known species is the barn swallow. It breeds all over the northern hemisphere in summer and migrates to the southern hemisphere for the remainder of the year. It seems to have given up its natural nesting sites, preferring to build its mud nest in rafters of barns or garages, especially those near large open fields with a pond nearby to draw insects.

The cliff swallow is the "swallow of Capistrano" that promptly returns each spring to its region. Formerly breeding in rocky places, this square-tailed swallow builds a gourd-shaped nest of mud pellets. It lives in barns with as many as a hundred pairs of other cliff swallows.

The tree swallow is the commonest, most widespread American swallow. It is greenish blue with white underparts. On the Atlantic coast and prairies, hundreds of these swallows gather in huge autumn migratory flocks and can be seen sitting lined up on telephone wires.

Because they are *insectivorous*, swallows are of great importance to the farmer. Like moles, hedgehogs, and shrews, swallows feed on harmful insects that destroy crops.

House Martin

Swallow

SWAMPS

A swamp is wet, spongy land with much rainfall, ground water, or tides. Thus, swampland is flooded periodically because of poor drainage. Swamps are common in low, flat areas of seacoasts, lake basins, and stream valleys, and also in the sloping highlands where

drainage is poor. Swamps are widespread in wet climates, but they are also common in arctic areas even though the precipitation is low.

Growth of plant life is usually dense in swamps. Cattails, grasses, willows, alders, buttonbushes, white spruces, mangroves, cottonwoods, bald cypresses, sycamores, cotton gums, and swamp maples are typical examples of vegetation.

The southeastern United States has large swampy areas, a famous one being the Okefenokee Swamp of Georgia.

SWANS

Swans are large water birds that are members of the DUCK family. They are bigger than geese. All swans, except a South American species, have necks that are long enough to reach the seeds and roots of water plants at the bottom of streams and shallow ponds. Sometimes they graze on grass and grain like geese do. They are great destroyers of fish eggs, and their aggressive behavior poses a threat to other waterfowl. Swans hiss like geese and use their powerful wings for attack or defense.

While the *pen* (female) sits on her six greenish eggs, the *cob* (male) fiercely protects their nest of reeds. The *cygnets*, or young swans, are gray for the first year. Afterward, the five North American species turn white, the South American species turn white with a black neck, and the Australian species turn black. Adult swans weigh up to 40 pounds (18 kg) and are one of the heaviest birds that fly. Swans may live for at least 50 years and they mate for life.

Most species of swans migrate. The whistling swan nests in northern Nrth America and winters as far south as North Carolina. The rare trumpeter swan breeds within the Arctic Circle and winters as far south as Texas.

SWEDEN

Sweden occupies the eastern part of the Scandinavian peninsula. It is separated from Norway on the west by the rugged Kjölen Mountains. Most of Sweden's east coast is on the BALTIC SEA and the Gulf of Bothnia, which is frozen in winter.

Half of the country is covered by forests, which supply timber for paper and matches. Sweden's rich iron ore is exported; it also has deposits of lead, copper, zinc, gold, and silver, though little coal. Its abundant waterpower provides electricity for homes and industries, which produce excellent steel products, glassware, and modern furniture.

Southern Sweden has many lakes and fertile land, on which wheat and potatoes are grown and cattle and pigs are raised. Here live most of the 8.3 million Swedes. Sweden's big cities, such as Göteborg, Malmö, and Stockholm, the capital, are built along the coasts.

The country is ruled by a king and a parliament, the *Riksdag*. Its government supports housing projects, hospitals, and schools that are open, free of charge, to everyone.

Jonathan SWIFT (1667–1745)

The English author Jonathan Swift wrote a famous book called *Gulliver's Travels*. It describes the fascinating adventures of Lemuel Gulliver during four voyages to different lands. He is first captured by the tiny people of Lilliput. Later, he comes to the land of giants, Brobdingnag, and then visits several other strange places. Finally, Gulliver reaches the land of the Houyhnhnms, a tribe of gentle horses endowed with reason, who rule the Yahoos, a stupid and cruel kind of people. Swift's story is a *satire* (writing that makes fun of people's petty ways, foolishness, greed, and so on) as well as a charming tale of adventure.

Jonathan Swift was a very clever man who felt he had not gotten the recognition and rewards he deserved. Although he became famous for his many satirical essays and political pamphlets, Swift failed to earn significant royal recognition for his efforts. Bitter and unhappy, he became first paralyzed and then insane.

SWIMMING

Swimming probably calls for the use of more muscles than does any other sport. Man has had to learn various swimming strokes in order to move easily through the water, for man is not a natural swimmer, like a duck, seal, or otter.

The fastest stroke is the crawl, developed by the Australians from the South Sea Islanders' method of swimming and later perfected by the

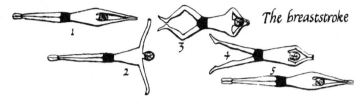

The breaststroke

Americans. There are four other strokes that are commonly used today—the backstroke, sidestroke, breaststroke, and butterfly. Beginners often do a dog paddle, similar to the way a dog swims, before they take swimming lessons at school, camp, or at the YMCA or YWCA.

Swimming races were held at the first modern Olympic Games in 1896. Also, swimming across the English Channel, about 21 miles (34 km) wide, has become popular since the first successful try in 1875.

SWITZERLAND

Switzerland is a small republic in central Europe, with 6.5 million inhabitants. It is divided into 22 districts, called *cantons*, and has four official languages—German, French, Italian, and Romansch (a form of Latin).

Much of the country is mountainous. Every year many foreigners visit the Swiss ALPS to ski and mountain climb. Others come to view the splendid scenery or to rest and relax at Swiss sanitariums (health resorts).

Through hard work and skill, the Swiss have built a modern, industrial nation. They make intricate machinery, instruments, watches, fabrics, and chemicals. Swiss craftsmen are famous for their music boxes and other carved wooden objects. Farmers raise cows, using their milk to make delicious Swiss cheese and chocolate. The cities of ZURICH, Basel, and GENEVA are great banking centers of the world.

Switzerland's capital is Bern, which is famous for its medieval buildings, arcades, fountains, and towers.

SWORD

When man learned to use metal, he was able to make a new weapon. This was the sword, whose long sharp edge and point allowed it to be used either for chopping or thrusting. The *hilt* of the sword was an extension of the blade, wrapped with rope or leather to give the hand a firm grip.

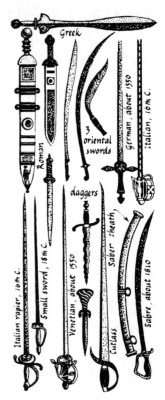

The invention of iron and steel helped to make a lighter sword and one that took a better edge. Ancient Roman soldiers used a *gladius* in their fighting, a sword with a blade only two feet (60 cm) long. The gladiators of the Roman arenas used these swords, too, as you can tell from their name. In the Middle Ages, on the other hand, the nobility fought with very long swords, meant mostly for chopping through armor. Such a sword was heavy, and was wielded with both hands. The hilt ended in a *pommel*, a rounded end that helped the swordsman to grasp it firmly. The best swords were made of thin layers of iron, hammered and rehammered and heated in such a way that they turned to steel. Toledo in Spain and Damascus in Syria were two cities famous for their good swords.

The invention of guns made armor useless, and in the 16th century swords became thrusting weapons. The swordsman thrust at his enemy with the light, straight *rapier*, holding a dagger in his left hand to turn aside the enemy's sword. The *foil* a modern fencer uses for thrusting is much lighter still. Cavalry used the *saber*, a curved sword with a sharp edge, in charges. Sailors used the *cutlass*, a shorter curved sword, in fighting from ship to ship.

Swords are not used in modern warfare, though officers sometimes carry them as part of their dress uniforms.

SWORDFISH

This striking, silvery blue fish is found chiefly off the coasts of North America and New Zealand, where it is greatly prized by fishermen. Swordfish range in size up to

12 feet (3.7 m), although larger specimens have been caught. Its sword-like beak is an extension of the upper jaw and makes up a third of the body length. The sword probably is used as a sharp, offensive weapon, as a "cutwater," and as an instrument to stun its catch. Swordfish will attack whales, sharks, and even boats. They travel at a speed of 50 knots (57.6 mph or 92.7 km/hr).

818

TAJ MAHAL

In 1631 the wife of Jahan, who was emperor of a great part of India, died. For her tomb, Jahan built one of the world's most beautiful buildings. A Turkish or Persian architect designed it. It took 22 years for the tomb and its surroundings to be finished, though 20,000 people worked on it at one time.

The tomb itself is faced with white marble with inlaid patterns of other colors of marble. With its great dome it is over 200 feet (60 m) high. It has four minarets, for Jahan was a Muslim. Jahan and his empress are buried in its basement.

The tomb, located in Agra, India, stands in grounds 1900 by 1335 feet (580 by 304 m) that contain a MOSQUE and other buildings as well as a beautiful garden with canals running through it.

TANKS

The first armored cars for military use were built around 1900, but when World War I started in 1914 they were already out of date. They could not drive over the trenches where the troops took shelter from the fire, and the barbed wire in front of the trenches tore their tires. But farm tractors with endless caterpillar treads of steel gave British designers the idea

Mark V British (1917-18)

for a new vehicle, heavily armed, heavily armored, and able to crush barbed-wire entanglements and bridge the gaps caused by trenches. The first tanks went into action late in 1916.

Early tanks were slow, no faster than a man could walk. They were often used to prepare the way for infantry attacks. Later, faster tanks appeared that acted independently. Lightly armed and armored fast tanks moved against enemy infantry, while heavier tanks protected friendly units, bombarded fortifications, or fought other tanks. New tank designs continued to appear, and tanks were important in World War II. Today some use guided missiles instead of cannons.

'General Grant' (U.S.A) World War II

TAPESTRY

A tapestry is a woven piece of decorative cloth, usually hung on a wall. To make one, the weaver stretches the threads that will go the length of the tapestry (the *warp*) between two beams. Then, following the artist's *cartoon* (full-sized design), he crosses the warp part way with colored thread that goes above one warp thread and below the next. The cartoon shows him what color of thread should go in each part of the tapestry. These cross-threads, which form the *weft* of the cloth, are pushed together side by side so that as the WEAVING goes on, the warp threads are covered and the whole tapestry appears as a pattern of different colors that usually make a picture. Most European tapestries use heavy woolen thread, but threads of linen, cotton, silk, and even gold and silver have been used in various parts of the world.

European tapestries in the Middle Ages were boldly colored and often had a flat design with a few figures against a pattern of flowers. Later, in the RENAISSANCE, weavers tried to imitate the illusions of real scenes that painters were creating. The tapestry weaver had to be very skillful to follow the artist's cartoons. In the 18th century, tapestry was used not only for the walls but for upholstery. Today, there is a new interest in tapestries. Many of them have gone back in spirit to the bold color and patterning of the Middle Ages.

Embroideries and similar cloths are sometimes called tapestries, but are not. In true tapestry the design is woven into the cloth, not applied to it.

820

TAPIOCA

Tapioca comes from the roots of the tropical cassava plant. The cassava grows in the tropics in western Africa, southeastern Asia, and Latin America, where it is also known as manioc.

There is a sweet and a bitter cassava, tapioca coming from the bitter kind that contains a poisonous juice. The roots are peeled, chopped, pounded, and boiled in water to remove the fibers and acid, which is used for flavoring and preserving. The rest of the root is dried into starchy flour, grains, flakes, or pellets. Tapioca serves as an important food for the natives and also provides us with tapioca for tapioca puddings and for a thickener.

TAPIR

Tapirs are heavily built, smaller relatives of the rhinoceros and horse. These hoofed mammals are found in tropical rain

forests, where they are fond of water and mud. These animals weigh up to 700 pounds (315 kg) and look somewhat like swine with their long, flexible snouts. These quiet, harmless vegetarians eat land and water plants and are often seen rolling in the mud to protect themselves from insects.

The Asian tapirs have a broad white band across the belly; the rest of the animal is black. This coloration camouflages them in their natural surroundings. American tapirs are all brown or black. The young of both types, however, are yellow with white stripes, until they are about six months old.

TAR

Tar is a thick, dark-colored, sticky liquid obtained from wood, such as pine, larch, and fir, and from COAL.

The strong-smelling coal tar is distilled from coal during the manufacturing of coal gas. Further distillation separates it into *naphthalene*, used in making dyes and as a moth repellent, *benzene*, a solvent also used in the making of chemicals and dyes, *creosote*, a wood preservative, and other substances. The final, almost solid, residue, called *pitch*, is used for surfacing roads, caulking the seams of boats and roofs, and in certain kinds of varnish. Various forms of tar are also widely used in making medicines, ointments, soap, explosives, perfumes, and insecticides. SEE ALSO: COAL.

TASMANIA

Tasmania is an island lying about 150 miles (242 km) south of AUSTRALIA. It is an Australian state with a population of about 400,000. Hobart is Tasmania's capital and chief port.

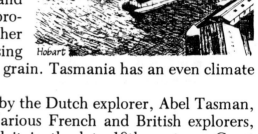
Hobart

Mountainous and partly forested, the island is rich in natural resources and hydroelectric power. Scattered mines produce copper, coal, tin, lead, and other minerals. Its farmlands are used for raising sheep and cattle, as well as for growing grain. Tasmania has an even climate with moderate rainfall.

The island was discovered in 1642 by the Dutch explorer, Abel Tasman, who named it Van Diemen's Land. Various French and British explorers, including Captain James Cook, visited it in the late 18th century. Great Britain took possession in 1803 and ran a penal colony there until 1853.

TASTE

There are four basic tastes —sweet, sour, bitter, and salty— or a mixture of these. The *taste buds* (tiny nerve cells) are located mostly on the TONGUE, but also in the mouth and throat. They work together with the sense of smell to produce the experience of taste. The important role of the nerves in the back of the nose is quickly realized when a head cold prevents them from functioning properly. Food, at such times, seems almost tasteless.

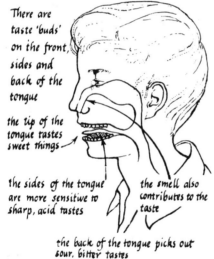

There are taste 'buds' on the front, sides and back of the tongue

the tip of the tongue tastes sweet things

the sides of the tongue are more sensitive to sharp, acid tastes

the smell also contributes to the taste

the back of the tongue picks out sour, bitter tastes

Children have a much keener sense of taste than adults and usually do not like spicy, strong flavors. As people age, their sense of taste and smell becomes lessened. Tests show that heavy smokers actually lose some of their ability to taste. SEE ALSO: TONGUE.

TAXES

Taxes are the money collected by the local, state, or federal government to pay for its services. Local and state governments levy (charge) taxes to pay for public roads, schools, water and sewage systems, and police and fire departments. Federal government's taxes support the armed forces, social security, welfare, Medicare, CONGRESS, and many federal courts and agencies.

The U.S. Federal Government and many state governments levy *income taxes* on a person's wages, salary, interest on savings, or dividends on stocks, and on a company's profits. An income tax is *graduated*—that is, the more money a person or a company makes, the higher the taxes on every dollar they earn.

Local and state governments levy *property taxes* on a person's or company's land, buildings, cars, and other valuable items. The U.S. CONSTITUTION does not permit the federal government to levy these taxes.

Many states have a *sales tax*. A person or company buying goods pays a tax, which is the same for everybody—rich or poor. Food and drug prescriptions, however, are usually not taxed. Sales taxes on special items are called *excise taxes*, and taxes on IMPORTS from other countries are referred to as *tariffs* or *customs duties*.

U.S. FEDERAL GOVERNMENT DOLLAR

Where it comes from

Where it goes

The Internal Revenue Service (IRS), an agency of the U.S. Department of the Treasury, collects all taxes imposed by federal law.

Peter Ilyich TCHAIKOVSKY (1840–1893)

This great Russian composer was a teacher of music at the Moscow Conservatory from 1865 to 1878. Then, a rich widow who greatly admired his early work, such as the ballet *Swan Lake*, gave him enough money to live on and devote himself to writing music.

Tchaikovsky's work includes six symphonies, several concertos, some beautiful songs and operas, and the ballet music of *Sleeping Beauty* and *The Nutcracker*. A very popular work is his *1812 Overture*, written in memory of the unsuccessful attack on Moscow by NAPOLEON. Tchaikovsky died of cholera shortly after the first performance of his Sixth Symphony, or *Symphonie Pathétique*.

823

TEA

Tea has been cultivated in the Far East (China and Japan) for at least 2000 years. It reached Europe in the early 1600s, but it remained too expensive for the common people to buy until about 1850. In Japan, the drinking of tea has become a special part of entertaining guests. The Japanese make the tea according to specific rules and then drink it in a special room. Today, coffee is drunk in Japan as much as tea is. Far more

coffee than tea is drunk in the United States, Europe, and Latin America. However, in England, tea is still very popular as a beverage.

Tea is made from young, dried tea leaves and buds, which grow on a small evergreen shrub. This shrub is kept bushy by constant pruning to a height of about 3 feet (.9 m). A tea bush, which is raised from seed, is ready for its first picking after three years. Many "tea gardens" grow on the hillsides of Asia and east Africa, where rain is plentiful and can easily drain away.

There are two kinds of tea: black and green. The difference is that the leaves of black tea are allowed to ferment, whereas those of green tea are crushed and heated without being allowed to fer-

ment. Because tea leaves easily absorb other flavors and odors, specially flavored teas can be made. Also, various kinds of tea leaves can be mixed to produce different "blends." For instance, jasmine tea is made by spreading jasmine petals over the tea leaves as they are being dried. Some people prefer to use tea leaves, while others prefer using tea bags.

TEAK

This valuable timber grows in huge teak forests in Asia. Teak trees grow to be 150 feet (46.5 m) tall. Their leaves produce a purple dye and are also used for thatching roofs.

The rich brown wood is very hard but is easy to work and polish. Because teak resists boring insects and withstands water for hundreds of years, it is

widely used in the tropics for building furniture, shop fronts, and park benches. However, its greatest use all over the world is in shipbuilding. Teakwood contains an essential oil which resists sea water. The oil also prevents the rusting of iron. Thus, unlike OAK, teakwood does not eat away or corrode the metal fittings and bolts used in boats and ships.

TECUMSEH (1768?–1813)

Tecumseh was a famous Shawnee Indian chief. He tried unsuccessfully to unite all the Indian tribes against the white settlers. In the early 1800s, the

U.S. government refused to agree to Tecumseh's plan to make the Ohio River the permanent boundary between the Indians and the whites. With his brother Tenskwatawa, called the "Prophet," Tecumseh said the United States could not buy land from any single tribe, for all Indian lands belonged to all the tribes in common. No individual tribe owned a particular area; thus it did not have the right to sell it to the white man.

Tecumseh's plan for an Indian confederacy came to an end after his brother was defeated at the Battle of Tippecanoe in Indiana. There, in 1811, U.S. troops under General William Henry Harrison destroyed the Prophet's town and killed many Indians.

In the WAR OF 1812, Tecumseh joined the British. He led the Indians against the U.S. and lost his life at the Battle of the Thames River in Ontario, Canada.

TEETH

People, like most MAMMALS, are born without teeth. At about the age of 6 months, an infant begins to get his 20 "milk" teeth, which begin to be replaced by permanent teeth at about the age of 6 years. Of the 32 permanent teeth, the last four, called the "wisdom" teeth, are the largest. They are located in the back of the jaw, and usually do not come in until early adulthood.

Since people eat both meat and plants, teeth for cutting, tearing, and grinding are needed. In each adult jaw, there are 4 *incisors* for biting, 2 *canines* for tearing and holding, 4 *bicuspids* or pre-molars for chewing but with a cutting edge too, and 6 *molars* for grinding up food.

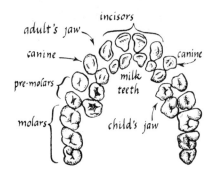

Each tooth has 3 parts: the *crown*, *neck*, and *root*. The crown is covered with hard enamel, called the *dentine*, which covers the major part of the tooth. Blood vessels and nerves within the dentine make up the dental pulp. The root of the tooth is the unseen part that is embedded in the jaw.

Since teeth play such an important role in preparing food for digestion, it is important to keep them clean and in good health. Toothaches result when bacteria change starchy foods, caught between the teeth, into acids that cause tooth decay. Proper brushing and regular dental check-ups help minimize problems with the teeth and gums.

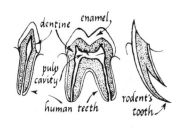

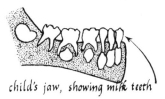

child's jaw, showing milk teeth

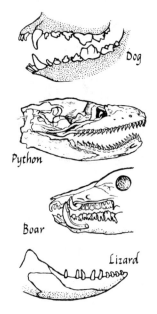

Birds do not have teeth, and the teeth of other animals are used for special purposes. The boar's tusks are enlarged teeth that are used as weapons. The elephant's tusks are also enlarged teeth. Carnivorous animals, such as members of the dog and cat families, have sharp teeth for killing and tearing. RODENTS have gnawing teeth that continuously grow, while grazing animals, such as cattle, deer, and horses, have front teeth for tearing grass and strong molars for chewing. The reptiles usually have backward slanting teeth so that their prey cannot escape while it is being swallowed whole.

TELEPHONE

The first practical telephone was patented in 1876 by ALEXANDER GRAHAM BELL. Thomas Edison helped improve the first models. By 1890, the telephone was popular in the United States and in many countries in Europe. In 1915, it was possible to make a phone call all the way across the United States. The first dial telephones were put in service in the early 1920s, and transatlantic telephone service, using radio waves, began in the mid-1920s.

A telephone works this way. One person talks into the *transmitter*. His voice vibrates (shakes) the air, and the air vibrates a thin plate called a *diaphragm* in the transmitter. The diaphragm moves another device which strengthens or weakens an electric current many times a second. This current is picked up by the telephone at the other end and vibrates another diaphragm in the *receiver* that the person listening holds to his ear. The receiver diaphragm vibrates just as the one in the transmitter does, so that the voice is reproduced.

TELESCOPE

Nobody knows who made the first telescopes. They were in existence around 1600, and Galileo, early in the 17th century, was already looking at the stars with telescopes he designed and made himself. Early telescopes were of the *refracting* type. In these, the light from an object passes through a large LENS called an *object glass*, which focuses it on a point. Somewhere either in front of or behind this point another lens, the *eyepiece*, causes the light to turn again into an image that the eye can see. Refracting telescopes have many good qualities and are the commonest sort still made. Binoculars are a type of small refracting telescope. But when such telescopes are large enough for astronomy they have great disadvantages. They are very long sometimes and hard to handle.

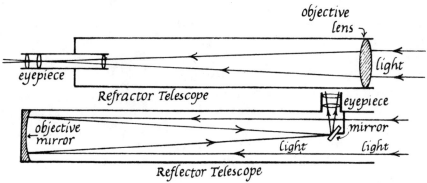

The *reflecting telescope* is much better for many astronomical uses. The light from the object is reflected from a curved mirror that magnifies the image as a lens would. Then the image passes to another mirror so placed that the eye can see it. The reflecting telescope can be much smaller than a refracting telescope of the same power. Still, some reflecting telescopes are big. There is one in Russia with a mirror about 20 feet (6.5 m) in diameter. It was cast of solid glass and took two years to cool properly after casting.

Astronomers use refracting telescopes for some purposes and reflecting ones for others. Today, though, they also use *radio telescopes*. It was discovered in the 1930s that stars give off radio signals, and astronomers are interested in studying them. One German radio telescope has a dish-shaped radio antenna, very sensitive to radio waves from outer space, that is 328 feet (100 m) across.

TELEVISION

Late in the 19th century, scientists already had ideas for television. But many of the parts had still to be invented, and only in the mid-1920s was a practical system worked out. The first regular television service began in Germany in 1935. Television service began in the United States in 1941, but did not reach many people

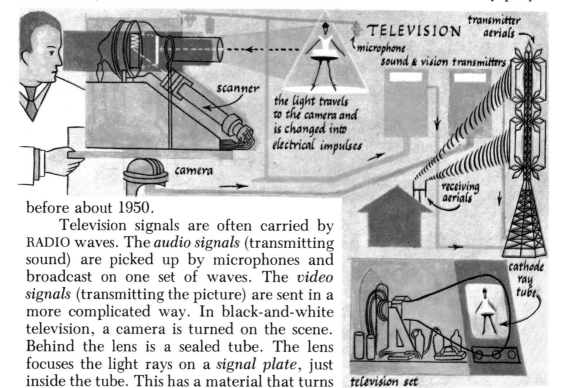

TELEVISION — transmitter aerials — microphone — sound & vision transmitters — scanner — the light travels to the camera and is changed into electrical impulses — camera — receiving aerials — cathode ray tube — television set

before about 1950.

Television signals are often carried by RADIO waves. The *audio signals* (transmitting sound) are picked up by microphones and broadcast on one set of waves. The *video signals* (transmitting the picture) are sent in a more complicated way. In black-and-white television, a camera is turned on the scene. Behind the lens is a sealed tube. The lens focuses the light rays on a *signal plate*, just inside the tube. This has a material that turns the areas of black and white into different strengths of electric charge. A *scanning beam* of electrons passes very rapidly back and forth over this plate, row after row, many times, picking up the electric charges and turning them into signals of different strengths. A television set in the home reverses the process, turning the signals back into dots of light of varying brightness. In the United States, the scanning beam crosses the signal plate 525 times, and in doing so creates 130,000 signals. It does this 30 times a second.

Color television is more complicated because the camera must break every sort of color on the scene down into three colors, red, green, and blue, each with its own signal. It must also send out a signal that black-and-white television sets can receive. A color television set receives the three separate color signals and combines them to reconstitute the scene.

Closed-circuit television passes signals along electric wires to just a few receiving sets rather than broadcasting them by radio waves. It is used by guards and others who have to be able to inspect places they cannot see directly.

In the last few years, *cable television* has become popular. In this, television signals from a broadcast arrive at the viewers' homes through an electric cable rather than in the form of radio waves. Sometimes the viewer is charged for the amount of time he spends watching the programs that come over the cable. Sometimes cable television is used to transmit programs from a radio antenna set up in a place where reception of programs is better than in the viewer's own neighborhood.

William TELL

William Tell is a legendary Swiss hero who stands for the fight for political and individual freedom. There is no evidence that Tell ever lived, but the story about his marksmanship (skill in shooting) is very popular in folklore.

Tell was supposedly a peasant in the Uri canton (district) of SWITZERLAND in the late 13th and early 14th centuries. At that time, the Swiss were ruled by the Austrians. One day, Tell went with his son to the town of Altdorf, where the Austrian governor, Gessler, had had his hat placed on a pole in the town square. Every passerby was ordered to bow to it, as a symbol of Austria's political power in Switzerland.

Tell, an expert archer, refused to bow before Gessler's hat. As a punishment, Tell was forced by Gessler to shoot an apple off his small son's head with a crossbow. Tell succeeded, but proudly said that he would have shot Gessler if his son was harmed. Tell was then arrested. As Tell was being taken to Gessler's castle dungeon on Lake Lucerne, a terrible storm arose and Tell escaped. Later, he killed Gessler and led the Swiss against their Austrian rulers.

TEMPLE

A temple is a place of religious worship. Christians usually prefer to call their place of worship a *church*. Jews call theirs a *synagogue*.

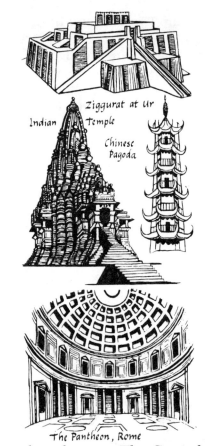

Ziggurat at Ur

Indian Temple

Chinese Pagoda

The Pantheon, Rome

In many parts of the world, temples have been large and splendid, much more so than any other kind of building. This was so with the Mayas and other Indians of Central America, the ancient Babylonians and Egyptians, the ancient Greeks, and many others. Even in India, China, and Japan, where there are magnificent palaces and other non-religious buildings, the temples have had the tallest towers. The *pagodas* of the Buddhist temples of China and Japan are the most famous buildings of the Far East.

For 2500 years, the Greek temple has been the most important influence in the architecture of Europe. Its rows of stately columns, carrying richly carved beams and eaves, have been imitated in different ways, especially in ancient Rome and in Europe during the RENAISSANCE. The same has been true in the United States since colonial times. The Capitol in Washington, D.C., owes much of its appearance to the temples of Greece in the form in which they were imitated by the Romans.

TENNESSEE

Tennessee lies in the east south-central United States. This state has three main regions: the Great Smoky Mountains and Cumberland Plateau in the east, highlands and the Nashville Basin in the middle, and broad plains and bottom lands along the Mississippi River in the west. Nashville is the state capital, and Memphis is the largest city and an important Mississippi port. Tennessee has about 4.3 million people.

The Chickasaw, Creek, and Cherokee Indians were living in the region when Hernando De Soto, a Spanish explorer, arrived in 1541. English fur traders crossed the Great Smokies and French explorers, Marquette and Joliet, came down the Mississippi in 1673. However, not until 1769 was the first permanent settlement made. Virginians then settled in the Watauga River valley of east Tennessee. Soon settlers arrived from North Carolina. The area was successively part of North Carolina, the separate "state"' of Franklin, a U.S. Territory, and a state of the U.S. in 1796. The Indians were forced westward in the 1830s, and Negro slaves were brought in to work in the cotton and wheat fields. In the Civil War, Tennessee went with the South, but many men fought on the Union side.

Today, massive dams on the Tennessee, Cumberland, and Clinch Rivers generate electric power for the state's many industries. Textiles, chemicals, metals, and forest products are manufactured. Tobacco, cotton, and soybeans are grown on Tennessee farms. Nashville, home of the Grand Ole Opry, is the nation's center for country music and is a major tourist attraction.

TENNIS

Tennis is a game played indoors or outdoors by two players (singles) or four players (doubles) on a grass, clay, or asphalt court. The court is 78 feet long by 36 feet wide (24 by 11 m), but only 27 feet (8 m) wide for singles. A net 3 feet (.9 m) high divides the court in half. The players use rackets to hit a ball back and forth over the net.

forehand volley

Backhand volley

The object is to hit the ball into the opponent's side of the court out of his reach or to make him return the ball out of bounds or into the net. A point is then won, and the points are scored in the progression 15, 30, 40, and game. The score of a player with no points is called "love." A tie score of 40 to 40 becomes "deuce," meaning a player must win two consecutive points to win the game. A set is won by the player first winning 6 games (by a 2-game margin).

Alfred, Lord TENNYSON (1809–1892)

Alfred, Lord Tennyson was a great English poet, born in Somersby, Lincolnshire, England. As a boy of eight, he was already writing poetry. Later, he attended Cambridge University but left upon the death of his father.

Tennyson was later overwhelmed by the sudden death of his very good friend Arthur Hallam. He spent much time afterward studying, thinking, and writing. In 1850, he published "In Memoriam," a poem in memory of Arthur Hallam. That same year, QUEEN VICTORIA appointed him poet laureate, royal poet, of England.

Some of Tennyson's short poems are "The Lady of Shalott," "The Charge of the Light Brigade," "Ulysses," and "Break, Break, Break." He wrote many long poems, including a group of 12 about King Arthur, entitled *Idylls of the King*.

TERMITES

Termites are small, soft-bodied INSECTS that live in organized colonies. They are sometimes called "white ants," though they are different from ANTS. Termites are widely found in the tropics, and some species live in the temperate regions of North and South America.

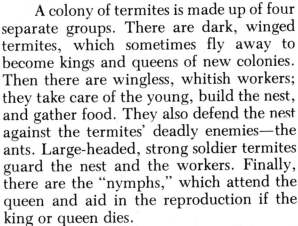

A colony of termites is made up of four separate groups. There are dark, winged termites, which sometimes fly away to become kings and queens of new colonies. Then there are wingless, whitish workers; they take care of the young, build the nest, and gather food. They also defend the nest against the termites' deadly enemies—the ants. Large-headed, strong soldier termites guard the nest and the workers. Finally, there are the "nymphs," which attend the queen and aid in the reproduction if the king or queen dies.

Termites eat mainly the cellulose in wood. They live either in the wood or in the soil, making nests with elaborate tunnels and passageways.

Because they eat paper and wood as their main diet, termites can do extreme damage to wooden buildings and wood products, such as books. To prevent the infestation of termites, buildings' foundations should be made of concrete, and no wood should be close to the soil. Specially treated wood should also be used.

One African species of termite builds its nest above ground, instead of underground as most termites do. Its nest is a very hard mound, varying from a few feet to 15 to 20 feet (4.7–6.2 m) in height. The illustration shows one of these nests.

TEXAS

Texas is the second largest state in the United States. It consists of wide coastal plains along the Gulf of Mexico, central lowlands, Great Plains, and mountain ranges. There is plenty of rain in the eastern part of Texas, near the Louisiana border. The climate is drier as you go west. Texas summers are hot. Winters are cold in the northern and western sections but mild on the Gulf of Mexico. Texas's largest city is Houston and its capital is Austin. The state has almost 13 million people.

The Caddo Indians inhabited the area when the first Europeans, the Spaniards, explored there in the early 1500s. The first Spanish settlement was Ysletta, near El Paso, in 1682. Many Spanish missions were founded to teach

Christianity and European trades to the Indians. The area was then part of Mexico, but Americans moved there in large numbers. In 1836, Texans battled unsuccessfully against their Mexican rulers at a fort called the ALAMO in San Antonio. At San Jacinto, Sam Houston's small army of Texans defeated the Mexicans under General Santa Anna, and Texas became an independent republic for nine years. The Republic of Texas joined the U.S. in 1845.

Today, the state leads all others in production of oil, natural gas, sulphur, and asphalt. It is a major agricultural center, raising cattle, sheep, and poultry and growing cotton, rice, sorghum, peanuts, and citrus fruits. Oil refining, chemicals, food processing, and machinery are its main industries. Commercial fishing is also important. Texas has abundant electric power for its homes and factories.

TEXTILES

CLOTH that has been woven is called a textile. The Egyptians were already WEAVING cotton and the Chinese were weaving silk 5000 years ago. The printing and dyeing of textiles with color also goes back thousands of years.

Until the late 18th century, SPINNING and weaving were done by hand, but after that time, complicated machinery was built to take over the hand work. The invention of this machinery was one of the most important parts of the Industrial Revolution, which changed our way of life.

The first commercial (rather than home) weaving in the United States began in Massachusetts in 1638. The first machine-operated cotton mill in the United States was built by Samuel Slater, an English immigrant, in 1793. This was also the year that Eli Whitney invented the cotton gin and made the mass production of cotton practical. SEE ALSO: CLOTH, COTTON, LINEN, RAYON, SILK, SPINNING, WEAVING, WOOL.

THAILAND

Thailand, which was once called Siam, is in southeast Asia. It borders Burma in the west and northwest, Laos in the northeast, Cambodia in the southeast, and Malaysia and the Gulf of Thailand in the south.

The climate is hot, damp, and tropical—suitable for growing rice and fruit. Cotton, tobacco, corn, pepper, and spices are also cultivated. Thailand has large teakwood forests, rubber plantations, and tin and tungsten mines.

The Thais are descendants of the Mongols of central Asia and are closely

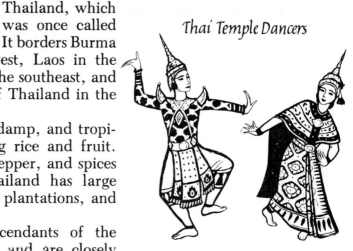

Thai Temple Dancers

related to the Burmese. Most of them worship BUDDHA. Every Thai man spends several months of his life in a Buddhist monastery. Children are taught by priests, who are often seen in the picturesque temples, called *wats*, throughout Thailand. The Thais have wonderful religious dances that Western people find particularly beautiful.

Thailand is the only southeast Asian country that has never been controlled by a European nation. Today, it is ruled by a military government.

THAMES

The Thames is the chief river of ENGLAND. It flows southeastward for about 210 miles (338 km) through good farmland, passing towns such as Oxford, until it reaches LONDON. Here the Thames widens into an estuary (inlet) that empties into the North Sea.

Twice a day, at high tide, the sea moves up the Thames, allowing ocean-going ships to go about 45 miles (72 km) upstream. In the "Pool" at London, large ships can be berthed at special docks, which are closed off from the river by water gates. When the tide goes out, the gates

hold water in the "Pool" at a high level.

There are about 25 miles (40 km) of wharves and docks along the Thames, many of which are no longer used because of the switch to container traffic. The universities of Oxford and Cambridge hold their famous crew race on the river each spring. SEE ALSO: LONDON.

THANKSGIVING

Thanksgiving is a national holiday in the United States, celebrated each year on the fourth Thursday in November. Families gather together that day and give thanks to God for the year's blessings, especially for the many good and plentiful things to eat. A big dinner is usually served, with a roast turkey, stuffing, cranberry sauce, and mince and pumpkin pies.

According to tradition, Thanksgiving is a harvest festival. It commemorates (honors) the first harvest reaped by the PILGRIMS in Plymouth Colony in Massachusetts in 1621. The Pilgrims had survived a miserable winter with much sickness and little food. In the spring, the Indians helped them to plant corn and other vegetables. William Bradford, governor of the small colony, proclaimed three days of "thanksgiving" in the fall. He invited the Indians to join the Pilgrims for a huge feast in celebration of the bounty of the season.

In 1863, President Abraham Lincoln officially proclaimed Thanksgiving as a national holiday. Canadians adopted Thanksgiving in 1879 and celebrate it now on the second Monday of October.

THEATERS

To put on a play you do not need a theater; you need only a place for the actors and a place for the audience. The ancient Greeks first had temporary wooden theaters, erected in market places, for special occasions. These had grandstands for the audience around a dancing and acting area called an *orchestra*. Behind them was a kind of wooden backdrop called a *skene*.

In the 4th century B.C., the Greeks built

their first stone theaters. These had many tiers of stone seats almost encircling the orchestra. Behind the orchestra was a stage, and behind the stage was the skene. This was now a *stage-house*, where actors could dress and wait for their turn to enter. The Greek theaters were dug into hillsides, but when the Romans started to build permanent theaters around 50 B.C., they built them on flat ground, supporting the seats with several rows of stately arches. The seats formed a semicircle of many tiers, facing a shallow stage and a tall, elaborately decorated stagehouse.

Elizabethan theater

Medieval actors had no theaters. They performed on temporary stages, on church steps, or in the courtyards of inns. But by 1600 permanent theaters were being built again. A few Italian theaters followed the Roman model. On the other hand, several theaters in the London of Shakespeare's time had many galleries in a square or an octagon looking onto a *thrust stage*, which came forward from the stage house into the midst of the audience.

Later in the 17th century, such simple plans were replaced by another one. The audience either bought seats in the orchestra, now the main floor of the auditorium, or in the enclosed *boxes* that surrounded the orchestra in a horseshoe pattern on several levels. The stage was beyond a huge archway called a *proscenium*. It was a deep stage with elaborate scenery that was intended to make the scene look as real as possible. Such theaters were still being built in the early 20th century.

After 1900, though, playwrights and scenery designers began to demand a new type of theater that would put the actors in the midst of the audience again with very little scenery. The proscenium was no longer used in this new theater, and architects also gave up the elaborate decoration that theaters had had since the 17th century.

THERMOMETER

Our common thermometer consists of a glass tube with a tube of MERCURY or alcohol at the lower end. As the air around the thermometer becomes warmer, the liquid also gets warmer, expands, and then rises up the tube; the reverse happens when the air temperature drops. A scale marked on or alongside the tube indicates the number of degrees reached by the liquid.

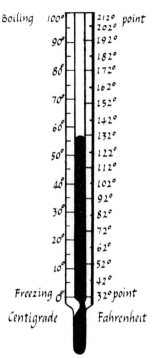

The two most commonly used scales are the *Fahrenheit* (marked F) and *Centigrade* or *Celsius* (marked C). The Fahrenheit scale has 180 marks or degrees, with 32° marking the freezing point of water and 212° marking the boiling point of water. On the Centigrade scale, 0° marks the level at which water freezes, and 100° marks the level at which it boils.

Doctors use a *clinical thermometer* with a short column of mercury for taking a patient's temperature. For ease in reading, the mercury does not drop when removed from the patient's mouth; however, it has to be shaken down before being used again. SEE ALSO: MERCURY.

THESEUS

In Greek mythology, Theseus was the son of King Aegeus of Athens. He offered to go as one of the group of seven boys and seven girls whom the Athenians were forced to send to CRETE to be eaten by the MINOTAUR.

This monster, half bull and half man, was housed in a large labyrinth (maze). Ariadne, daughter of the king of Crete, fell in love with Theseus and gave him a ball of string which he was to fasten at the labyrinth's entrance and unwind as he went on. Theseus killed the Minotaur with his bare hands and retraced his steps following the string.

Theseus sailed home. Nearing Athens he forgot to hoist the white sail of success as he had promised his father. The usual black sail was seen. King Aegeus thought Theseus was dead and in grief threw himself into the sea, thereafter called the AEGEAN.

The THIRTEEN COLONIES

The Thirteen Colonies is the term used for the British settlements in North America that joined together during the AMERICAN REVOLUTION. They adopted the Declaration of Independence in 1776 and became the thirteen original states of the United States of America (U.S.A.).

They were:

Massachusetts,
Connecticut,
Rhode Island,
New Hampshire,
New York,
New Jersey,
Pennsylvania,
Delaware,
Maryland,
Virginia,
North Carolina,
South Carolina,
Georgia.

Virginia had the earliest lasting British settlement, JAMESTOWN, in the New World (1607).

THOR

In the Norse mythology of SCANDINAVIA, Thor was the god of thunder and the protector of warriors and the peasants. He was the son of ODIN and lived in a palace called Thrudwanger.

The dwarfs made Thor a magical, red-hot hammer that always returned to him when he threw it. As Thor drove his chariot through the heavens, he hurled his hammer, creating great thunderbolts of lightning. Armed with his hammer, iron gloves, and belt of strength, he constantly fought wicked monsters and giants.

Being a god of the people, Thor was also connected with marriage, the hearth, and agriculture. Thursday (Thor's Day) is named for him.

Henry David THOREAU (1817–1862)

Henry David Thoreau, an American writer, was born in Concord, Massachusetts, and spent most of his life there. Unable to earn a living by writing, he worked as a teacher, pencilmaker, and surveyor. He also became associated with a group of New England thinkers that stressed the spiritual life over the habits and concerns of everyday life. RALPH WALDO EMERSON, another American writer, was a good friend of his and a member of the group.

In 1845, Thoreau built a small cabin beside Walden Pond, near Concord. He lived there for more than two years, away from worldly cares. He grew his own food, watched the changes in nature, and kept a journal of his simple life in the woods. Later, in 1854, an account of his life at Walden Pond was published as *Walden, or Life in the Woods*. Today, this book is considered a classic in American literature, representing one man's struggle to live honestly and freely.

Thoreau's other writings include some poems and essays, including the famous one called "Civil Disobedience."

TIBER

The Tiber is the second longest river in Italy, about 250 miles (403 km) long. It rises in the Apennines Mountains and flows south through Tuscany and Latium. The Tiber passes through ROME, where it is about 100 yards (91 m) wide. In Rome 14 bridges span the river, including the beautiful Bridge of Saint Angelo and the Fabricius Bridge, built in 64 B.C. and possibly the oldest bridge in the world. The Tiber empties into the Tyrrhenian Sea, part of the Mediterranean.

Unlike the Mississippi, the Rhine, and the Thames Rivers, the Tiber is not an important commercial waterway for ships and barges, for it is only navigable by small boats.

TIBET

The little-known country of Tibet is separated from India on the south by the HIMALAYAS and from China on the north by the Kunlun Mountains. It is the world's highest plateau, where the climate, altitude, and desolate countryside make life very difficult.

The 2 million people of Tibet lead primitive lives as nomads, farmers, shepherds, or monks. Sheep, cattle, and yaks (oxen) are raised, and barley, rice, and some vegetables are cultivated. Thousands of monks live in huge Buddhist monasteries situated high in the

Tibetan mountains. It used to be the custom for families to send a son to a monastery to be taught by a *lama* (Buddhist priest) and thus to become a monk.

The Dalai Lamas (priest-kings) were the supreme rulers of Tibet for more than 300 years. They lived in a high palace just outside Lhasa, Tibet's capital, also known as the Forbidden City because foreigners were not allowed to enter it. However, in 1959, the Chinese Communists seized complete control of Tibet, and the Dalai Lama fled to India.

TIDES

Twice a day, the ocean waters rise and fall. The sun and moon are the cause of tides because their gravitational pull causes the water to pile up where the pull is the strongest. Because the Earth is turning on its axis once every 24 hours, your spot on the Earth will be in line with the moon or opposite it twice every day. At those times the tide is high. Six hours after high tide your spot on the Earth will have low tide because the Earth has turned away from the pull of the moon.

Since the moon is closer to the Earth than the sun, it has a greater influence on the tides. When both the moon and the sun are pulling from the same direction or from opposite sides of the Earth (that is, at new or full moon), the extra pull from the sun causes the tides to be higher and lower than usual. Such tides are called *spring tides*. When the sun and moon are pulling at right angles to each other, the gravitational pull is lessened, and the tides rise and fall less than usual. Such tides are called *neap tides*. SEE ALSO: GRAVITY.

TIGER

The tiger is the second largest member of the cat family, although occasionally a Bengal tiger may be bigger than a LION.

Tigers are found wild in parts of Asia, mostly in jungles, but some live in Siberia and have paler, softer, longer fur. Their deep yellow coat with black stripes camouflages them in tall jungle grass. Tigers generally hunt at night, killing deer, antelopes, wild pigs, monkeys, and young cattle. Sometimes they become man-eaters when they are old or when food is scarce.

Tiger cubs stay with their mother for about two years. They begin killing small animals for themselves when about seven or eight months old.

Tigers adjust well to captivity and are popular attractions in zoos and circuses all over the world.

TILES

A tile is a hard, thin piece of building material. Some tiles are made of plastic now, but for centuries they were always made of baked clay. In many places tiles are used to cover roofs, for instance in Spain, Italy, England, China, and Japan.

Flat tiles are also used to pave floors and cover walls. Bathrooms often have floors of tiny tiles, glazed in various colors to make a MOSAIC. Some porches and rooms have floors of big red tiles. Fireplaces sometimes have blue-and-white Delft tiles, first made in the Netherlands. In Spain, Portugal, and Latin America blue-and-white tiles and tiles of many colors are often used on walls. They are easy to clean, help keep rooms cool, and look very handsome. In Mexico, some churches have domes covered with colored tiles laid to make brilliant patterns.

TIMBER

Timber may be softwood or hardwood. As a rule, the PINE family is softwood. This type of wood does not resist dampness or hard wear, but it is easily worked and plentiful. Paper and rayon are made from softwood pulp.

White planks of wood from spruce and silver fir and yellow planks from Scotch pine are used in houses and for furniture that is veneered (covered with fine wood).

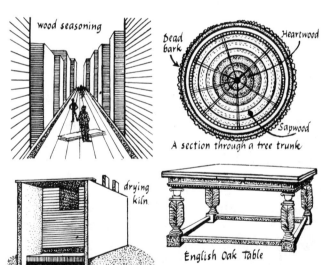

Hardwood, such as OAK, TEAK, and mahogany can be used indoors or out. Oak and teak are very strong and are not affected by water. WALNUT, MAPLE, rosewood, SYCAMORE, and beech are beautiful woods for furniture but are not strong enough for heavy work.

ELM is a hard, strong timber that does not split; ebony is hard and dark. Ash is tough, while WILLOW is springy. Most fruitwoods are dense and much valued by woodcarvers and makers of special pieces of furniture.

TIME

Generally speaking, a *day* is the important basic unit of time. Weeks, months, and years are all multiples of a day; hours, minutes, and seconds are all fractional parts of a day.

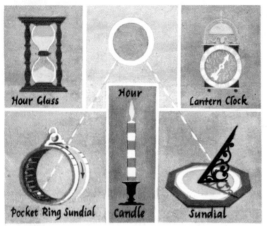

Hour Glass

Hour

Lantern Clock

Pocket Ring Sundial

Candle

Sundial

A *solar day* is the time it takes the Earth to make one complete turn on its axis. During that time, each place on Earth has daytime and nighttime. Actually, the Earth takes a little less than 24 hours to spin once on its axis. The length of the solar day varies a little because the Earth is on a tilt and also because its orbit (path) about the sun is not a perfect circle. Twenty-four hours is the average (*mean*) length of a solar day. Time measured in this way is called *Mean Time.*

At any given moment, the clocks around the world show a different time. This difference is due to the fact that the sun shines overhead in different places at different times. When it is 12:00 noon in Chicago, it is already 6:00 p.m. in London and only 10:00 a.m. in San Francisco. Since it would be very awkward to be changing one's wristwatch every few minutes one traveled east or west to keep accurate time, the world has been divided into 24 time zones. The time throughout any one zone is considered to be the same. This *standard time* is called *Greenwich Mean Time* (G.M.T.). Places east of Greenwich, England, are ahead in time; places west of Greenwich are slow in time. In other words, if you travel east, you must set your watch ahead one hour everytime you cross a time zone; if you travel west, you must set your watch back one hour per time zone. In the summer, many areas of the United States have *daylight savings time*. Clocks are moved ahead an hour in order to give people more hours of sunlight after work. SEE ALSO: DAY AND NIGHT.

TIN

Man has used tin for at least 5000 years. It was sought after by ancient traders, because, mixed with copper, it was used to make BRONZE for tools and weapons.

Tin is a soft metal that does not rust. Therefore, it is often used to coat iron. The United States has almost no tin, yet it uses more than half of that produced by the rest of the world. Half of the tin imported goes into making "tin cans," which are actually iron cans thinly coated with tin. Squeeze tubes for shampoo, toothpaste, and shaving cream are pure tin. Pewter is an ALLOY of tin and lead. Tin foil has now been replaced by aluminum foil, which is a cheaper material for wrapping candy, foods, and other things.

Tin ore comes from Bolivia, Malaysia, Indonesia, Mexico, Thailand, and Nigeria.

TOADS

Toads are AMPHIBIANS and have the same life cycle. They spend their early life in water breathing with gills and their adult life on land breathing with lungs.

Sometimes it is difficult to tell frogs and toads apart. Compared to frogs, toads generally have drier, warty skins, are heavier, slower moving, and are more frequently seen on land than in the water. In spring, toads come out of HIBERNATION, and the females lay strings of eggs, called toad spawn, in the nearest pond. The tadpoles that hatch out are smaller and darker than those of a frog.

The idea that handling a toad causes warts is strictly superstition. Like frogs, they are quite harmless to people. Toads live on insects, woodlice, slugs, and snails. SEE ALSO: FROGS.

TOBACCO

The first Europeans arriving in America found Indians chewing tobacco leaves and inhaling tobacco smoke through hollow canes. This habit was brought to Europe by a Spanish doctor and popularized by SIR WALTER RALEIGH in England. Originally, smoking was thought to be good for all diseases; now, research has proven it is bad for health, especially for the LUNGS.

Tobacco grows 2 to 6 feet (0.6–18.6 m) tall. The large leaves are dried in various ways. Strong pipe tobaccos come from rich, dark soil, while light colored cigarette tobaccos come from sandier soil.

Virginia is believed to be the home of tobacco. Today, the plant is cultivated in the southern United States, as well as in Central and South America, the West Indies, Turkey, India, and the U.S.S.R.

TOKYO

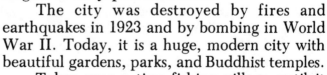

Tokyo, the capital of JAPAN, has about 11.5 million people and is situated around the Bay of Tokyo, on Honshu, the largest of the Japanese Islands.

The city was destroyed by fires and earthquakes in 1923 and by bombing in World War II. Today, it is a huge, modern city with beautiful gardens, parks, and Buddhist temples.

Tokyo was a tiny fishing village until it became the residence of feudal lords in 1457 and of *shoguns* (army leaders) in the 1600s. Its name was changed from Yedo to Tokyo in 1868, when the Japanese emperor made it his capital. SEE ALSO: JAPAN.

TOMATO

The tomato is a red or yellow, juicy, acid fruit, high in vitamins A and C. The tomato is a native of the Peru-Ecuador-Bolivia area of South America. Cultivated tomatoes were being grown in Mexico before 1500.

The first European forms, called "love apples," were yellow and ornamental. They were believed to be poisonous, probably because, like the potato and tobacco, they were related to the deadly nightshade (a poisonous plant).

About 200 years ago, tomatoes were part of the European diet. There is no record of any grown in the United States until Thomas Jefferson grew them in 1781. Until almost 1900, many people believed them to be poisonous. Today, tomatoes are a major crop in America, where they are grown in every state except Alaska.

Tomatoes are eaten fresh or canned. They are also made into juice, soup, sauces, and ketchup.

TOMB of the UNKNOWNS

The Tomb of the Unknowns is a white marble memorial in the Arlington National Cemetery in Virginia, just across the Potomac River from Washington, D.C.

On November 11, 1921, an unknown soldier who had been killed in France was buried here in a solemn and impressive ceremony. He represented all the unidentified American soldiers killed during WORLD WAR I. On November 11, 1932, his tomb was dedicated as the Tomb of the Unknown Soldier and became a national shrine. On the tomb was written, "Here Rests in Honored Glory an American Soldier Known but to God."

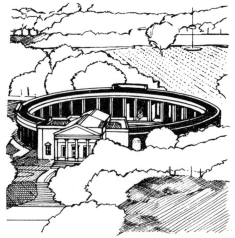

On Memorial Day, May 30, 1958, two more unknown soldiers—one killed in WORLD WAR II and the other in the KOREAN WAR—were buried in the tomb, which was then renamed the Tomb of the Unknowns. Honor to America's war dead is paid each year on Veterans Day (November 11), which is a national holiday.

TONGUE

The tongue is a movable muscle attached to the floor of the mouth in most VERTEBRATES. In man, it is important not only in chewing and swallowing but also in producing the sounds of SPEECH. The upper surface is covered with tiny cones called *papillae* that produce the roughness of the tongue. TASTE buds are among the papillae and the saliva glands that produce the fluid to moisten the mouth, especially during eating. The tongue also senses changes within the mouth and is an aid in locating pieces of food lodged between the teeth.

Usually pinkish red, the tongue can become discolored, swollen, ulcerated (broken or cut), asymmetrical (lopsided), and painful with a burning sensation during various illnesses. SEE ALSO: SPEECH, TASTE.

TOOLS

Man's imagination has caused him to make many kinds of tools. He began with pieces of wood and stone, picked up for hammering, chopping, and puncturing. As he learned to use metals—first bronze, then iron, then steel—he was able more and more to create exactly

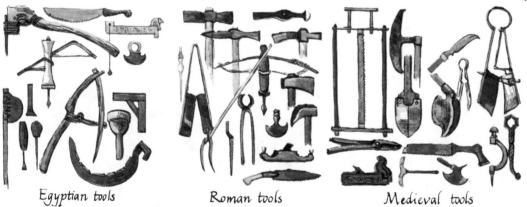

Egyptian tools   Roman tools   Medieval tools

the right tools he needed for the kind of work he wanted to do. He invented tools that helped in making other tools, and tools that could measure the accuracy of his work. In addition to knives, saws, shears, drills, hammers, and so on, ancient man invented tools such as the lathe and the potter's wheel, which spun the material to be shaped so that it ended up perfectly round.

Early tools were operated by hand or foot, or in some cases by animal power. When something had to be accurately made, the craftsman worked with hand tools, inspecting his work carefully as he went along. During the RENAISSANCE, though, water power came into

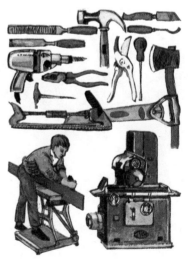

use to run saws, grinding wheels, and other tools that did rough work.

The INDUSTRIAL REVOLUTION could not have taken place without highly accurate tools able to work quickly. A steam engine cylinder and its piston had to be true circles, for instance, so that the steam did not leak. Inventors around 1800 created highly accurate, powerful *machine tools*, run by water power or by steam, that were able to produce many parts of exactly the right size. Later, such tools were often run by electric motors. Over the years they have needed less and less control by human beings. Today a tape, much like a recording tape, controls many of them as they go through the procedure of shaping materials.

TORONTO

Toronto, the capital of ONTARIO, is the second largest city in Canada. It is situated on the north-west shore of Lake Ontario. Long before the arrival of white settlers, the Indians gathered there, calling it "toronto," meaning "the place of meeting." Today, Toronto is a large port and an industrial and financial center. It has the largest cattle market in Canada and many meat-packing plants.

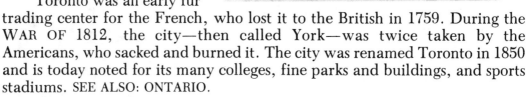

Toronto was an early fur trading center for the French, who lost it to the British in 1759. During the WAR OF 1812, the city—then called York—was twice taken by the Americans, who sacked and burned it. The city was renamed Toronto in 1850 and is today noted for its many colleges, fine parks and buildings, and sports stadiums. SEE ALSO: ONTARIO.

TOUCH

Of the five senses, touch is the least sensitive in man. Unless the sensation is quite strong, there is little body response to touch. Touch is, however, a very important sense. It not only supplies the body with information about what is happening outside of itself but it also warns the body of any possible danger. A hot or sharp stimulus received by the nerves in the skin causes the body part to withdraw quickly even before the brain has time to report what the danger is.

Nerve endings in the SKIN send signals to the BRAIN. Signals from the right side of the body are received in specific areas on the left side of the brain; the opposite is true for those signals received from the left side of the body.

The tip of the tongue is the part of the body most sensitive to touch; the skin over the backbone is the least sensitive to touch. However, the sense of touch can be made keener with use. Many skilled workers develop a very highly specialized sense of touch. The blind have an extremely keen sense of touch. They read the fine, raised BRAILLE letters and make delicate articles in a way impossible for those who have sight.

TOWER of LONDON

The Tower of London is an old stone castle, situated on the north bank of the Thames River in LONDON, England. The oldest part of the castle, known as the White Tower, was built by WILLIAM THE CONQUEROR about 900 years ago. All thirteen towers of the castle are enclosed by a massive wall and a moat, now dry.

During the Middle Ages, the Tower of London was a royal palace. Later, it was used as a prison by the kings and queens of England. SIR THOMAS MORE and two wives of King Henry VIII were executed in the Tower. Elizabeth I (as a princess) and SIR WALTER RALEIGH were prisoners there.

In the White Tower, there is a splendid exhibit of armor and weapons, and in the Wakefield Tower are the CROWN JEWELS of the British royal family. The Tower of London still houses a small garrison of soldiers, the most admired of which are the Yeomen Warders, commonly called "Beefeaters," in their elegant red and black uniforms. In recent times, captured spies and some notable traitors have been imprisoned in the castle.

TOYS

Children have always played with toys. They seem to have an instinct for doing so. With toys they can play many games. Toys help them imitate the activities of grownups. Toys even help them to learn things.

A ball is a very simple and extremely old kind of toy. So are dice, jackstraws, marbles, and other very simple things used in games. Puzzles, which test how much you know or how clever you are, are a kind of toy.

Many toys are imitative. They look more or less like real things and help children pretend that they are keeping house, fighting wars, running railroads, and so on. DOLLS and PUPPETS imitate the looks and even the actions of human beings. Some dolls can even speak a few words. Masks allow children to pretend to be people they are not. Toy soldiers and fighting equipment can be used in mock battles around toy forts. All kinds of cars, trucks, buses, and so on are imitated too as toys.

Model railroads are a favorite, even with grownups. Some adults build hundreds of feet of track in real-looking landscapes, with real-looking buildings, and send real-looking and real-sounding trains running through them. These are run by electricity and are modern, but the old-fashioned wind-up toys, invented a hundred or more years ago, are still being sold. Many of them come from Japan.

Some toys are educational. They are supposed to help the child to use his mind, to tell him things, or to test how much he knows.

TRACK and FIELD

Track and field refers to a group of sports performed either on an oval track (for running and hurdling events) or on a large field enclosed by the track or in some similar area (for jumping and throwing events). These events are held either indoors or outdoors in competitions called *meets* between individuals or teams.

The running events include dashes or sprints of 100, 200, and 400 meters (or corresponding U.S. distances of 100, 220, and 440 yards). There are also running races of 800 meters (880 yards), 1500 meters (one mile), 5 kilometers (3 miles), 10 kilometers (6 miles), and the marathon (26 miles 385 yards). Hurdling events are races in which runners jump over a series of barriers called hurdles. There are hurdling races of 110 meters (120 yards), 200 meters (220 yards), and 400 meters (440 yards). Teams often compete in relay races of 400, 800, and 1500 meters. The field events include the broad jump, high jump, pole vault, shot put, javelin throw, discus throw, and hammer throw. The OLYMPIC GAMES have all these events, as well as the running hop-step-and-jump and the *decathlon* (a contest comprising 10 different track and field events).

TRANSPORTATION

Transportation means the carrying of goods and persons over land, over water, or through the air. Transportation of any kind probably began with the carrying of things by women and men, usually on their backs. Donkeys, camels, oxen, and horses were then used to carry or haul things. Also, the use of animals made transportation much faster.

After the invention of the wheel, man built simple two-wheeled carts that were pulled by a horse, ox, or other animal. The ancient Egyptians and

Greeks developed the crude cart into a beautiful chariot. At the end of the 12th century, four-wheeled carriages were built, pulled by many horses. However, these carriages were only used by the rich. In the late 18th century, public stagecoaches began to operate in France and England. In the United States, the strong CONESTOGA WAGON became an important means of transportation for families traveling across the mountains, the Great Plains, and westward.

The invention of the STEAM·ENGINE and the RAILROADS in the 1800s enabled large numbers of persons and many goods to be carried quickly over long distances. After World War I, AUTOMOBILES, buses, and trucks powered by gasoline engines werc developed, and they soon exceeded the railroads in importance.

Transportation over water started with small canoe-like BOATS. Then small wooden sailing vessels, large square-rigged galleons, and speedy schooners and clippers were successively built, until steel-hulled steamships in the late 19th century replaced the wooden sailing vessels. Today, nuclear powered ships are being built in greater numbers.

Transportation through the air developed in the 20th century. The AIRPLANE has become an important means of transportation, moving goods and persons comfortably and quickly to virtually any place in the world. Manned space travel became a reality in the 1960s. U.S. astronauts have even transported themselves and goods to the Moon. Scientists are today finding new ways to improve the transportation of persons and goods around the world and into space.

TREES

Trees are the largest members of the plant kingdom. They differ from bushes and shrubs in that they usually have a single stem or trunk.

There are two main kinds of trees—*deciduous* and *evergreen*. Deciduous trees shed their leaves for part of the year, whereas EVERGREENS start growing new leaves before the old ones fall. The oak, maple, elm, beech, birch, and ash are deciduous, whereas the pine, fir, redwood, and holly are evergreens. Trees bearing cones are called CONIFERS and are usually evergreens.

The age of a tree can be determined by the number of annual growth rings in a cross section of the trunk. The oak and olive trees are some of the kinds that live to be hundreds of years old. The bristlecone pine and the giant SEQUOIA live more than 5000 years.

Among the largest trees in the world are the giant sequoia of California, the Australian eucalyptus, and the Douglas fir of Washington. These trees have attained heights of more than 300 feet (93 m).

Until 1900, enormous numbers of trees in America were cut down and never replaced. Conservation of timberland has been a major concern for the last 50 years. In many countries, such as Greece, the lack of *reforestation* has caused the topsoil to wash away in heavy rainfall, so that the land has become barren.

With modern advances in technology, timber is no longer the principal material used for ships, houses, furniture, and fuel, as it was in ancient and medieval times. SEE ALSO: INDIVIDUAL KINDS OF TREES.

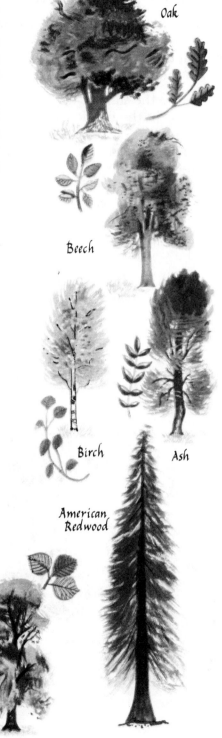

Oak

Beech

Birch

Ash

American Redwood

Silver Fir

Scots Pine

Elm

TROPICS

The tropics extend in an imaginary, broad belt around the Earth from the Tropic of Cancer (23.5°N of the equator) to the Tropic of Capricorn (23.5°S of the equator). These two points mark the most northerly and most southerly points at which the sun can be overhead at noon.

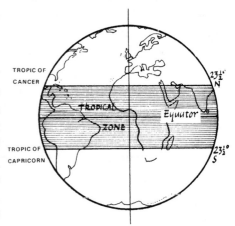

Since the sun's rays are almost directly overhead in the tropics, this area is always very hot, and there is very little difference between the seasons. Here there are great differences in rainfall. The dense JUNGLES on the equator have heavy rainfall throughout the year. Elsewhere in the tropics, rain falls only in summer, except in the DESERTS, where it almost never falls and the vegetation is very sparse.

Central Africa, southern Arabia and India, the East and West Indies, northern Australia, Mexico, Brazil, and Peru are the regions of the world having a tropical climate. SEE ALSO: EQUATOR, JUNGLE.

TROUBADOUR

Like the minstrels, the troubadours were singers and poets. They lived in southern France and northern Spain and Italy, and composed their poems in Provençal, the language often used in those regions. The MINSTRELS were traveling entertainers from the lower class of society, but the troubadours were usually noblemen. Even kings, for instance, Richard the Lionhearted of England, might be troubadours. Their poems were usually poems of praise for women. Troubadours usually composed their own music but not always.

The great period of the troubadours was from a little before 1100 to a little after 1300. Most of them disagreed with the official teachings of the Catholic Church, and many of them were killed because of this. A similar kind of poet and musician, the *trouvère*, was active in northern France around the same time.

TROUT

Trout are freshwater fish that belong to the salmon family. They have a great variation in color, ranging from nearly black to light olive. All species 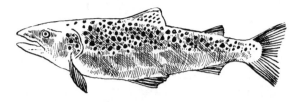 of trout have black or red spots. The average weight of a trout is one pound (.45 kg), but some have been caught that weighed more than 20 pounds (9 kg).

Trout are found in swift-flowing streams and in cool, deep ponds. They often hide beneath submerged objects and in riffles (rapids). They are native to the Northern Hemisphere but have been brought to other areas. Between fall and spring, trout spawn (reproduce) and bury their eggs in nests of gravel under the water.

Fishermen enjoy catching trout, luring them with special fly bait. "Tickling" is another way to get them. A person carefully and quietly feels beneath the bank for this fish. The movement of his fingers on the trout's body seems to hypnotize it into a quiet state, so that it can be quickly grabbed and thrown onto the bank.

TROY

Troy was an ancient city in ASIA MINOR. Here the Greeks and Trojans, the inhabitants of Troy, fought the Trojan War, which was said to have lasted for ten years (1194–1184 B.C.).

According to the *Iliad*, a poetic story probably written by HOMER, the Trojan War began when Paris, the son of King Priam of Troy, ran away with HELEN, the beautiful wife of King Menelaus of Sparta, a Greek city-state. Menelaus called on all the Greek kings and princes to help him bring Helen back.

ACHILLES, ODYSSEUS, and Agamemnon sailed with their armies across the Aegean Sea and laid siege to Troy. In the tenth year of the war, the Greeks gained entry to the city because of Odysseus' clever thinking. They hid some of their warriors in a huge, hollow, wooden horse and left it outside the gates of Troy. The Trojans believed it was a gift from the gods and dragged it inside the walls. At night, the warriors opened Troy's gates to the Greek armies, which then destroyed the city.

Archeologists have discovered that nine successive cities were built on the site of Troy, dating back to about 3000 B.C. Homer's Troy was the seventh city. SEE ALSO: ACHILLES, HELEN, ODYSSEUS.

TRUCKS
Wagons to haul freight have been used for thousands of years, of course. But when we speak of a truck we usually mean a freight vehicle moved by a motor. The first truck was built in Germany in 1896, and by 1910 trucks were fairly common. For many years they had gasoline ENGINES just as most cars do, but most trucks today are powered by diesel engines.

There are trucks for all sizes and weights of cargo. A *panel truck* is a small delivery truck with a fully enclosed body. A *pickup truck* is a small truck with a low-sided open body. A *stake-bodied* truck carries its load on a flat, open platform, but stakes can be raised around this to hold the load together. A *dump truck* has high, heavy, open sides. It carries coal and other heavy, loose material, and its body can be tilted to dump the material. An *articulated truck* consists of two or more parts, a *tractor* that does the pulling and a *trailer* that carries the load. Most trailers are *semitrailers*, in which the front part rests on a platform behind the tractor cab while the rear is supported by wheels belonging to the trailer itself. When a semitrailer (or *semi*) is coupled to a tractor, the combination is called a *tractor-trailer*.

Harry S. TRUMAN (1884–1972)

Harry S. Truman, the 33rd President of the United States, served as an officer in the U.S. Army during World War I. Later he ran a haberdashery (men's clothing store), but the business failed. He then turned to politics, holding several public offices in Missouri and attending Kansas City Law School. Having a reputation of honesty and efficiency, Truman was elected to the U.S. Senate in 1934 and reelected in 1940. He became well-known through the reports of his Senate committee which uncovered waste and inefficiency in war production during World War II.

In 1944, Truman was elected U.S. Vice President along with President FRANKLIN ROOSEVELT. On the death of Roosevelt, he assumed the presidency and made the controversial decision to drop two ATOMIC BOMBS on Japan. After the war ended, Truman opposed Communist aggression in Greece and Turkey in 1947. The Truman Doctrine was established, giving economic and military aid to nations threatened by "armed minorities or by outside pressure." Truman supported the Marshall Plan, suggested by his Secretary of State George C. Marshall. It gave money and materials to rebuild European countries bombed in the war.

Truman was reelected President in 1948, though the polls predicted his defeat. When Communist North Korea invaded South Korea in 1950, he quickly got U.N. approval to send in American forces. Later in the KOREAN WAR, he removed General DOUGLAS MACARTHUR from command for not obeying orders. Truman was hurt by the discovery of corrupt officials and charges of Communist spies in his government. He refused to run for reelection in 1952.

TRUMPET

The trumpet is a brass instrument. The motion of the player's lips creates a vibrating column of air inside the trumpet tube, and this causes the sound. The *natural trumpet* is the trumpet in its simplest form, that of a long tube that flares outward at the end. It can play only a few notes in one key. Such trumpets can

be changed in key by the use of *crooks*, pieces of curved tubing added to the trumpet that change the length of the air column. Modern trumpets are usually *valve trumpets*. Valves called *pistons* open extra lengths of tubing so that the length of the air column can be changed in a moment.

Sojourner TRUTH (1797–1883)

Isbella Baumfree was born to an African slave couple in Ulster County, New York. After she raised a family of five children, she asked her master to set her free. When he refused, she ran away and changed her name to Sojourner Truth. Sojourner Truth visited many cities in the northern United States, making public speeches against SLAVERY. She defied a law that banned blacks from riding on street cars in Washington, D.C., and she tested other laws that limited the rights of minority people.

Harriet TUBMAN (1820?–1913)

Harriet Tubman was born a slave on a plantation in Maryland. In 1849, she escaped from the plantation and fled to the north. Wishing to free other Negroes from SLAVERY, Harriet joined the Underground Railroad—a secret network by which slaves could escape to the northern states. During the 1850s, she became one of the most successful "conductors," leading more than 300 slaves to freedom. Sometimes she had to force the timid or the tired ahead by threatening them with a loaded gun. Because of her great courage, strength, and reliance on God, she came to be known as the "Negro Moses."

In the Civil War, Harriet Tubman worked as a nurse, laundress, and spy in the Union Army in South Carolina. After the war, she settled in Auburn, New York, where a bronze tablet on the courthouse wall rests in her honor.

TULIP

Tulip comes from the Turkish word meaning "a Turk's cap" or "turban," which the flower resembles. This member of the lily family blooms in late spring.

Early in the 1500s, the first tulip bulbs were brought to Vienna, Austria, from Turkey. Soon they reached Holland where the climate and soil were especially suited to them. By 1634, tulips became so popular in Holland that people paid as much as $5200 for a single bulb. Fortunes were made and lost during this sudden craze, called *tulipomania*. Although financially disastrous for many people, this craze, stopped by government intervention, helped to establish Holland as the tulip capital of the world. The states of Washington and Michigan are also noted for their tulip raising. SEE ALSO: BULB.

TUNNELS

Tunnels are useful in a number of ways. They save travel time in hilly country, especially for trains and other vehicles that cannot climb steep slopes. They allow water to flow by gravity alone. And they allow vehicles, water, sewage, and other things to go under rivers where bridges are impractical. Some tunnels are very short, just long enough to go through a hill. Others go for miles. The longest tunnel is 105 miles (168 km) long; it brings water to New York City.

Tunnels are difficult to make. Sometimes they must penetrate hard

Men working behind a tunnel shield

Railroad tunnels

rock, and sometimes they go through loose soil, water, or sand that threaten to fill the tunnel. Unless the tunnel is driven through firm rock, it is necessary to build a *lining* that will keep the earth around the tunnel firmly in place and that will keep water out. Tunnelers often use a *shield*. This is a strong drum of steel that can be opened at the far end to allow the soil to be dug away bit by bit. When enough soil is removed, the shield is pushed forward as far as it will go. Workmen build up the lining as the shield advances. Another device for tunneling is a *mole*, a machine that grinds away at rock by turning. It leaves a round opening big enough for a circular lining. Where water and loose sand threaten to fill the tunnel, air under pressure is used to resist them. There are many different ways of tunneling for different types of ground, each intended to be as quick, cheap, and safe as possible in a special case.

TURBINE

In the 18th and 19th centuries most engines were *reciprocating*. That is, steam or the explosions of some fuel like oil caused pistons to move back and forth. Rods to the pistons connected with cranks which turned the back-and-forth motion into the *rotary* (turning-around) motion needed to drive most machinery. Much power was wasted in starting and stopping the pistons many times a minute.

A turbine, on the other hand, is a rotary engine. In an *impulse turbine*,

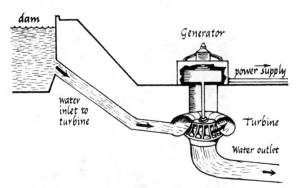

the force of a moving fluid such as steam, water, or burning gas strikes the blades of a *rotor* (turning part) as it passes through them. This causes the rotor to turn. A windmill is an impulse turbine of a special kind. In a *reaction turbine*, the fluid comes out of the rotor. Because of a law of physics, the force with which the fluid emerges creates an equal and opposite force that drives the rotor around.

Reciprocating engines are still practical for many purposes, but engineers use turbines wherever possible.

TURKEY

Turkey lies partly in Europe but mostly in Asia, occupying all of what used to be called ASIA MINOR and stretching eastward to Russia and Iran. European Turkey, bordering on Greece and Bulgaria, is separated from Asiatic Turkey, sometimes called Anatolia, by the Turkish Straits (narrow passages of water). These straits connect the Black and the Aegean seas; they consist of the Dardanelles, near which stand the ruins of TROY, the Sea of Marmara, and the Bosporus, by which stands ISTANBUL, Turkey's largest city and chief port.

Central Turkey is mainly a high plateau, with salt lakes, hot springs, mountains, and active volcanoes. Earthquakes sometimes occur in this region. The climate is hot and dry in summer and cold in winter.

The 42.2 million Turks, who are mostly MUSLIMS, are farmers, miners, and factory workers. They grow tobacco, cotton, grains, figs, olives, and poppies. Angora goats and cats, both of which are known for their long, soft hair, are raised in the region around Ankara, the capital. Chrome, copper, coal, and lignite are mined; and silk, textiles, and machinery are manufactured.

From about 1300 to 1918, Turkey was the center of the Ottoman Empire, ruled by the Sultans. In World War I, Turkey joined Germany, and its defeat caused the loss of much land. In 1923, it became a republic, with Kemal Ataturk as its first president. SEE ALSO: ASIA MINOR, ISTANBUL.

TURKEYS

Turkeys are large game and domesticated birds. They are related to the grouse, the pheasant, and the peacock. The American turkey was named after a similar bird from the country of Turkey, with which it was confused.

Turkeys are native to North America. The Spanish conquerors of the 16th century brought the Mexican turkey back to Europe. The Pilgrims in New England ate the wild eastern turkey at the first Thanksgiving feast.

Turkeys like to live in woodlands and are usually friendly, except at breeding time. Wild turkeys are quite rare today, but domesticated turkeys are raised in large numbers on turkey farms. Baby turkeys can be easily killed by dampness, coldness, or overcrowding.

TURPENTINE

This oily substance containing RESIN is made from the sap of CONIFERS, especially the pine. It is collected in barrels as it slowly oozes out of cuts made in the bark of these trees. The sap is then heated in a copper vessel, where the turpentine evaporates and the vapor, when cooled, liquefies into a clear liquid called oil of turpentine. A very pure form is called "spirits of turpentine."

Tar, pitch, and other useful substances come from the rest of the sap. Some of it hardens into a clear, yellowish solid called "rosin."

Turpentine is widely used in the manufacture of paints and varnishes. It is often used as a paint remover and thinner. It is also valuable in making some antiseptics, liniments, and plastics.

TURTLES and TORTOISES

Turtles are the only REPTILES with a shell. The shell acts as a protection for them. Each turtle is able to withdraw completely its head, legs, and tail inside its shell.

Some turtles live on land, and some live either in salt or fresh water. Land turtles are often called *tortoises* and pond turtles are often called *terrapins*. Some species only grow a few inches long, while others grow as long as

7 feet (2.2 m) and weigh as much as 1000 pounds (450 kg). None has teeth but instead turtles have a sharp-edged, horny substance in their jaws for cutting the plants they eat.

Females lay their eggs in a hole on land. The round, white, leathery eggs are then covered with earth or sand and kept warm by the sun. There is no attempt at further care. Baby turtles have to struggle hard to break through the tough shell. Soon after hatching, they head at once for water or woods.

Tortoises are the longest-lived VERTEBRATES and may live to be well over 100 years old. The giant tortoises of the Galápagos Islands, off the northwest coast of South America, are the slowest moving turtles. Even when they are hungry and encouraged with food, they cannot walk any faster than 5 yards a minute (4.6 m/min) or 0.17 miles an hour (0.27 km/hr). Over long distances their speed is greatly reduced.

Mark TWAIN (1835–1910)

Mark Twain, whose real name was Samuel Langhorne Clemens, grew up in Hannibal, Missouri, on the Mississippi River. He worked as a printer, steamboat pilot, silver miner, and reporter. When he began to write, he adopted the pen name of "Mark Twain," a phrase meaning "two fathoms deep" that was shouted by pilots on the Mississippi River.

Twain went to California in 1864 and soon won fame with a humorous short story called "The Celebrated Jumping Frog of Calaveras County." He traveled around the world and gave humorous lectures in the late 1860s. Twain was married in 1870 and settled down in Hartford, Connecticut. Here he wrote some of his best books: *Tom Sawyer, Huckleberry Finn, The Prince and the Pauper, A Tramp Abroad, Life on the Mississippi,* and *A Connecticut Yankee in King Arthur's Court.*

In 1893, he found himself in debt after an unwise investment in a publishing firm. Perhaps this and the deaths of his wife and two of his daughters made him a bitter man, for much of his later writing was deeply pessimistic.

TYPHOON

Tropical CYCLONES form on the western side of great oceans. They are called hurricanes in the western Atlantic and typhoons in the China Seas and near the coast of Japan.

These violent storms have winds of tremendous force that swirl counter-

clockwise in the Northern Hemisphere and clockwise in the Southern Hemisphere at speeds up to 250 miles per hour (403 km/hr). Houses, cattle, and automobiles can be swept into the air, but the greatest damage is apt to come from tidal waves that strike the shore with great speed and from the torrential rainfall which may amount to as much as 50 inches (127 cm).

The disastrous typhoon that struck Japan in 1934 lifted ships from the sea and hurled them over seawalls and into the streets beyond.

UNCLE SAM

Uncle Sam is a nickname for the government of the United States. The term Uncle Sam originated with Samuel Wilson, a businessman in Troy, New York. During the WAR OF 1812, Wilson stamped "U.S." on the barrels of meat that he supplied to the U.S. army. One story says that the initials U.S. were meant by Wilson to indicate government property. But another story says that U.S. stood for "Uncle Sam," which was what Wilson was called by his friends and townspeople.

Before too long, the name Uncle Sam came to represent the United States. American cartoonists, especially Thomas Nast, created a white-haired gentleman, dressed in swallow-tailed coat, vest, high hat, and striped pants. This figure, known as Uncle Sam, became very familiar during the two World Wars. In 1961, Congress recognized Wilson as the namesake of Uncle Sam, the national symbol.

UNITED NATIONS

The United Nations is an international peace organization founded in 1945 by 51 nations. According to its charter, the U.N. seeks to promote peace and security, to create friendly relations among nations, to encourage respect for the rights of others, and to develop a system of international law.

The United Nations not only tries to settle quarrels that might lead to war among nations, but also, through numerous agencies, seeks to improve the quality of life around the world. It is concerned about the health, education, trade, communications, and energy in underdeveloped nations, as well as in industrial nations.

The headquarters of the U.N. are in New York City, where the Security Council and the General Assembly meet to discuss world problems and to make recommendations on how to solve any problem. Two other important bodies of the U.N. are the Secretariat, the administrative branch headed by a Secretary-General, and the International Court of Justice at THE HAGUE in Holland, where disputes among nations are settled by discussion and law.

UR

Ur was an ancient city in SUMERIA, in southern Mesopotamia. The Bible identifies "Ur of the Chaldees" as the birthplace of ABRAHAM.

A Ziggurat or Temple

Little was known about Ur until Sir Leonard Woolley, an English archeologist, excavated the site between 1922 and 1934.

About 4500 years ago, Ur was a very prosperous city, with skilled craftsmen, traders, and scholars. A priestly king ruled the people from his vast temple (ziggurat) which dominated the city. Later, Ur fell to the Elamites, tribesmen from Persia, and then became part of the kingdom of BABYLON. Through the centuries, Ur was destroyed and rebuilt by various kings, including NEBUCHADNEZZAR. About 500 B.C. Ur lost its importance, perhaps because of the change in the course of the Euphrates River, which had been the reason for the city's wealth. SEE ALSO: SUMERIA.

URANIUM

This hard, silvery, radioactive element is the heaviest metal. It was discovered in 1789 and named after the planet Uranus, discovered a few years earlier. Uranium is never found in a pure state in nature, but as a COMPOUND. For centuries, uranium compounds had been used in Europe by glassmakers; the American Indians used a bright yellow uranium compound for making war paint. By the mid-1900s, scientists were hunting the world over looking for uranium to supply NUCLEAR ENERGY.

The smallest piece of an element that can exist is called an ATOM. More than 2 billion billion uranium atoms would fit on the period at the end of this sentence, yet these atoms are the largest found in nature. Scientists have discovered there are three types of uranium atoms—U-234, U-235, and U-238—differing in the number of neutrons in the nucleus. U-238 is the most common; U-234 is the most rare. Atomic power has been produced by splitting the U-235 atom, and also by producing the element plutonium from U-238 and then splitting plutonium. When Uranium atoms are split, enormous energy is released and a chain reaction causes more uranium atoms to split. The result is an atomic explosion or, when controlled, heat for generating electricity.

Because it gradually loses energy, uranium is called *radioactive*. Eventually, it changes to lead. SEE ALSO: ATOMIC BOMB, NUCLEAR ENERGY.

URANUS

Uranus is a large PLANET, about 31,000 miles (49,910 km) in diameter. The distance of Uranus from the sun is about 19 times that of the Earth, and the density of the planet is less than one quarter that of the Earth. It takes slightly more than 84 years for Uranus to complete one trip around the sun. However, like Neptune, which is often called its twin, Uranus has a short day, completing a rotation of its axis every 10 hours and 48 minutes.

Uranus, which has five known satellites or moons and a dark set of rings, was discovered by William Herschel in 1781. Herschel, an English astronomer, probed the sky with his powerful telescope, believing at first that Uranus was a comet. SEE ALSO: PLANETS, SOLAR SYSTEM.

URUGUAY

Uruguay is one of the smallest countries in SOUTH AMERICA. Slightly larger than Missouri, it borders the Atlantic on the east, the great *estuary* of the Plate River on the south, and the Uruguay River, which separates it from Argentina, on the west. To the north lies Brazil.

Half of Uruguay's 3 million people live in or near the capital city of Montevideo. Most Uruguayans have a Spanish or Italian background and are mostly Roman Catholic. Many work for the government, which owns the power, telephone, railroad, oil refining, and other industries. Others work on Uruguay's great ranches,

where sheep, cattle, and horses are raised for their wool, meat, and hides.

The first settlers were the Spanish, who founded a colony at Soriano in 1624. Portugal competed with Spain for control of the country; later Brazil and Argentina fought over Uruguay, which finally won its independence in 1828.

U.S.A.

The United States of America is the fourth largest country in the world, following the U.S.S.R., Canada, and China. It consists of 50 states, the District of Columbia—in which stands WASHINGTON,

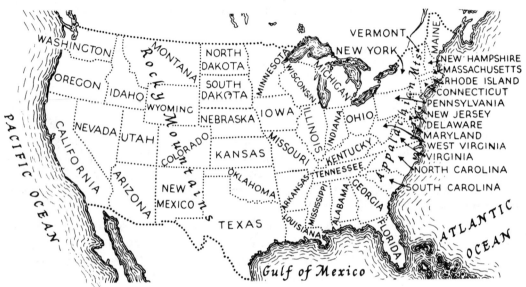

the capital—and several outlying dependencies, such as Guam in the Pacific Ocean, PUERTO RICO, and the Virgin Islands. There are about 220 million people in the U.S.A.

In the western United States are the great ranges of the ROCKY MOUNTAINS. Vast plains cover the central area, and the Appalachian Mountains run along the eastern part. Mount McKinley in Alaska, rising 20,320 feet (6299 m), is the highest mountain in the country and in North America. The islands of Hawaii have many volcanoes that are still active.

Hawaii

Alaska

The United States is drained by the Mississippi River and its tributaries in the central region, by the Colorado and Rio Grande rivers in the southwest, by the Columbia and Snake rivers in the northwest, by the St. Lawrence and Great Lakes system in the northeast, and by the Yukon River in central Alaska.

The United States has developed its great natural resources of oil, copper, coal, iron ore, natural gas, and other minerals. It has vast timberland and rich farmland, on which large crops of corn, wheat, cotton, and tobacco are grown. Cattle, sheep, pigs, poultry, fruits, and vegetables are also raised in great amounts. American factories manufacture every kind of product, from automobiles to xylophones.

The U.S.A., popularly called AMERICA, was first settled by the British, French, Dutch, and Spanish, all of whom brought slaves from Africa (see NEGROES). Then came the Germans, Scandinavians, Irish, Poles, Russians, Asians, and many others. Today, English is their common language, and "life, liberty, and the pursuit of happiness" is their common belief. SEE ALSO: AMERICA, INDIVIDUAL STATES OF THE U.S.A..

U.S.S.R. The Union of Soviet Socialist Republics is the official name of RUSSIA. The name tells us a great deal about the country since the RUSSIAN REVOLUTION. When the Bolsheviks seized control of the Russian government in 1917, they announced that thereafter the country would be ruled as a *socialist* state. A Supreme Soviet (Council) of the U.S.S.R. was set up to make laws, with representatives from every Russian republic (state). However, behind this "constitutional" government was the strong Communist party—the real ruling power. Today, the Supreme Soviet is completely controlled by the Communists.

The U.S.S.R. is a federation of 15 republics. The largest republic is the Russian Socialist Federated Soviet Republic, which includes territory in Europe and Asia and occupies almost 80 percent of the whole country. The other republics are Ukraine, Byelorussia (White Russia), Moldavia, Estonia, Latvia, and Lithuania—all in Europe—Azerbaijan, Georgia, Armenia, Turkomen, Uzbek, Tadzhik, Kazakh, and Kirghiz—all in Asia.

the Kremlin

Slightly more than half of the 260 million people of the U.S.S.R. are Russian. There are about 160 ethnic groups, including Ukranians, Uzbeks, Tartars, Kalmuks, and Letts—many of which have regional names and speak their own native language.

The U.S.S.R. is now one of the leading nations of the world, both in industry and in agriculture. In formerly isolated areas, huge cooperative farms and hydroelectric dams, factories, apartments, railroads, and airports have been built. SEE ALSO: RUSSIA.

UTAH

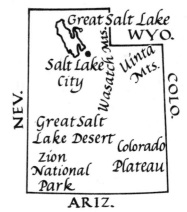

Utah lies in the western United States. This state is divided into two almost equal parts by the Wasatch Mountains. To the west is the Great Basin region, which includes the Great Salt Lake and the surrounding desert. To the east are the high Uinta Mountains near the Wyoming border. Southward lies the rugged Colorado Plateau, cut by the deep canyons of the Green and Colorado Rivers. Here the scenery is magnificent, with colorful rock formations carved by the rivers and the weather.

Spanish missionaries came to the area in 1776 and found several large Indian groups—the Ute, Paiute, and Shoshone. Canadian and American fur trappers hunted beaver and other animals there in the early 1800s. The MORMONS came in 1847, seeking a peaceful spot where they would be left alone. When their leader, BRIGHAM YOUNG, saw the green valley of the Great Salt Lake, he said, "This is the place." He founded Salt Lake City, the present-day capital of Utah. Later, the area was named a U.S. Territory. Congress named it Utah, a form of the Indian name Ute. It became a state in 1896.

Since the time of the early Mormon settlers, farming has been carried on there by irrigation. But, manufacturing and mining are the main source of income. Utah mines much copper and uranium. Tourists come to boat, fish, and ski, as well as to visit the many scenic national parks. About 1.25 million people live in Utah today.

VALLEYS

Valleys are lowlands between uplands, hills, or mountains. Usually valleys are formed by the erosion of streams and RIVERS, but they can also be formed by GLACIERS.

The shape of a river valley depends upon the rate of erosion of the river bed and the geological age of the river. A "young" valley has steep sides, with a narrow flood plain. A river will cut out a V-shaped valley. An "old" valley is usually U-shaped, formed by a slow-moving, meandering (winding) river. However, if a river has to erode hard rock, a V-shaped valley may be "older" than a U-shaped one formed by a river wearing away soft rock.

Many valleys are sheltered from the wind and have good, rich soil for growing crops. Also, many have a natural water route for transportation—the river. For these reasons, valleys have usually been the centers of early civilizations, such as those in the Tigris-Euphrates and Nile valleys. The early pioneers in America often settled in fertile valleys.

VALVE

A valve is a mechanism for lessening the flow of a liquid or gas, or for stopping it altogether. There are several types of valve. The simplest is the *butterfly valve*, a plate that pivots in a pipe so that one side goes up while the other goes down. In the *gate valve*, a plate slides up to leave the opening clear. A *poppet valve* has a plug that rises and falls on a spindle to open and close an opening.

A *globe valve* is like the ordinary household FAUCET. It has a plug that screws up and down, and gets its name because it bulges around the place where the plug is. In a *needle valve*, a thin, sharp plug slides in or out of a very narrow opening; this is used for sprays. A *plug valve*, or *cock*, has a cylindrical plug with a hole drilled across it. When it is turned off, the hole is sideways to the opening and

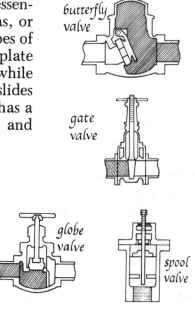

butterfly valve

gate valve

globe valve

spool valve

allows no liquid through; when it is turned on, the hole is lined up with the pipe on either side. In a *spool valve*, a sliding piston covers or leaves free openings into the valve chamber so that fluids can move between different openings at different times. SEE ALSO: FAUCET.

VANCOUVER

Vancouver in BRITISH COLUMBIA is the third largest city in Canada. It is also Canada's

most important Pacific coast port, having a fine natural harbor. This deepwater port, with many docks and grain-elevator facilities, handles freighters, a fishing fleet, and ferries to Vancouver Island and is linked to mainland Canada and the U.S. by four major railroads. Other industries include wood processing, shipbuilding, and metal fabricating.

Stanley Park, one of Vancouver's many parks, has a zoo, aquarium, arboretum, and famous gardens. An international airport serves the city, which has two universities and many attractive residential suburbs. SEE ALSO: BRITISH COLUMBIA.

VANDALS

The Vandals were a warlike people who lived in the valley of the Oder River in northern Germany during the time of the Roman Empire. They were unaffected by Roman civilization for many centuries. In A.D. 406, the Vandals moved westward across the Rhine River and invaded Gaul (now called France).

Refused permission by the Franks (another barbaric tribe) to settle in Gaul, the Vandals moved

southward into Spain. Here they fought the Romans and the Visigoths, a Germanic people that had settled in Spain. Pressed by the Visigoths, the

Vandals crossed to Africa in A.D. 429 and seized control of the Roman provinces along the Mediterranean. In A.D. 439, they took CARTHAGE and built a powerful kingdom. Their fleet soon ruled the Mediterranean.

The Vandals conquered Sicily, Sardinia, and Corsica. In A.D. 455, Gaiseric, their greatest king, invaded Italy and his troops sacked ROME, destroying priceless art treasures. The Vandals' power declined after Gaiseric's death in A.D. 477. Later, the Eastern Roman Emperor Justinian sent troops under General Belisarius, who captured Carthage in A.D. 533. The Vandals then fell apart as a nation.

The Vandals left no artistic monuments of their reign. However, our word "vandal" comes from their cruelty and senseless destruction.

VASCO da GAMA (1469?–1524)

Vasco da Gama, a Portuguese explorer, was the first to reach India from Europe by sailing around the continent of Africa.

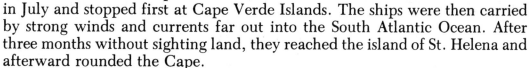

During da Gama's youth, Portuguese sailors traveled down the west coast of Africa, trying to discover a sea route to the riches of India and Asia. In 1488, Bartolomeu Dias reached the southernmost tip of Africa—later called the Cape of Good Hope—and sailed around it.

In 1497, King Manuel I of Portugal placed four ships under the command of Vasco da Gama. The expedition left Lisbon in July and stopped first at Cape Verde Islands. The ships were then carried by strong winds and currents far out into the South Atlantic Ocean. After three months without sighting land, they reached the island of St. Helena and afterward rounded the Cape.

Exhausted and sick with scurvy, da Gama's men wished to turn back, but da Gama persuaded them to continue up the east coast of Africa to Malindi, in Kenya. With help from a native chief, the expedition sailed across the Indian Ocean to Calicut, a port in southern India. Here, on May 20, 1498, almost eleven months after leaving Lisbon, da Gama exchanged gifts with the Indian rulers and then sailed home. He was rewarded with land, money, and titles. In 1502, da Gama made another voyage to India and later died there on his third visit.

Da Gama's discovery of a sea route to India brought great wealth to Portugal through trade and colonization. COLUMBUS did the same for Spain when he opened up the riches of America in 1492.

VENEZUELA

Venezuela is a country in SOUTH AMERICA bordering the Caribbean Sea and the Atlantic on the north, Guyana on the east, Brazil on the south, and Colombia on the west. Its population is 12.7 million, and its capital and largest city is Caracas with about 2.5 million people.

Venezuela has tropical rain forests, swamps, grasslands, and snow-capped mountains. One of the world's great rivers, the Orinoco, more than 1600 miles (2576 km) long, flows through the central part of the country. In the upper course of the river are flat, grassy plains called *llanos*, where enormous herds of cattle and horses are raised.

Coffee, cocoa, rice, sugar, and fruits are grown, but it is the large oil field around and beneath Lake Maracaibo that is the main source of Venezuela's wealth. Other minerals include iron ore, salt, copper, gold, coal, and diamonds.

Modern apartments, Caracas

Most Venezuelans are *mestizos* (people of mixed Spanish and Indian blood). The rest are native Indians, Negroes, or whites.

COLUMBUS discovered Venezuela in 1498. In the 1500s, the Spanish conquered the native Arawak and Carib Indians and colonized the country. In 1819, SIMÓN BOLÍVAR, the national hero, freed Venezuela from Spanish rule. In his honor the nation's coins are known as "bolivars."

VENICE

Venice is a magnificent Italian city that stands at the northern end of the ADRIATIC SEA. It is built on about 120 islands. Among the islands are scores of canals, which are crossed by hundreds of bridges. People often travel about the city by motorboat or gondola, a long, narrow, flat-bottomed boat with a high, decorative stem and stern.

From the 11th to the 15th century, Venice was a great seafaring and trading center. Ruled by the Doge (chief magistrate), the city acquired enormous wealth from jewels, silks, perfumes, and spices that were brought overland from the East. Also, Venetian merchants traded throughout the Mediterranean and in Flanders (now western Belgium and northern France), England, and the Baltic.

The power of Venice declined after the Turks seized Constantinople (ISTANBUL) in 1453 and cut off trade routes to the eastern Mediterranean. The discovery of America and of the Cape route to Asia shifted commercial power to Spain, Portugal, and other nations in western Europe.

VENUS

Venus is one of the 9 PLANETS in the SOLAR SYSTEM. As the second closest planet to the sun, Venus travels between the orbits of Mercury and Earth.

It is slightly smaller than Earth, but its year, consisting of 225 days, is much shorter. Venus turns so slowly on its axis that one day (243 Earth days long) is longer than its year!

Like the moon, Venus reflects the light of the sun and goes through similar *phases*— sometimes appearing crescent-shaped and sometimes disc-shaped.

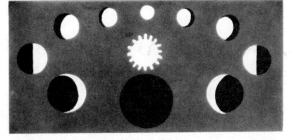

Being closer to the sun, it is much hotter than Earth. It is surrounded by a thick cloud of gases, containing mainly unbreathable carbon dioxide that trap this heat and cause the surface temperature to rise to 887°F (475°C).

According to data from a 1972 Soviet spacecraft landing on Venus, faint sunlight manages to pass through the planet's dense atmosphere onto the surface, which is composed of granite-like rock. SEE ALSO: PLANETS, SOLAR SYSTEM.

VERMONT

Vermont is a lovely New England state, noted for its peaceful villages with white steepled churches, clear mountain lakes and streams, and thickly forested mountain ranges. Through the middle of the state run the Green Mountains. Lake Champlain and the fertile Champlain Valley lie in the northwest. Along Vermont's border with New Hampshire in the east flows the long Connecticut River. Vermont's natural beauty brings visitors all year round, especially in the fall when the leaves change color. Skiing, hiking, and fishing are popular activities in Vermont.

In 1609, Samuel de Champlain explored the lake that bears his name, and later the French built forts in the Champlain Valley. The British built Fort Dummer, near present-day Brattleboro, in 1724. With the help of the Iroquois Indians, the British pushed the French out of the area. At the start of the American Revolution, ETHAN ALLEN and his "Green Mountain Boys" captured Fort Ticonderoga from the British. In 1777, Vermont declared itself an independent republic, but joined the United States in 1791.

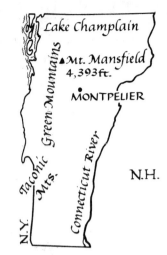

Vermont is famous for its maple sugar and syrup, fine marble, and Cheddar cheese. Much asbestos and granite also come from the state. Its leading manufactured goods are machine tools, computer components, and wood products. Dairying is the principal kind of agriculture in the state. Montpelier is Vermont's capital. About a million people live in the state.

Jules VERNE (1828–1905)

Some of the earliest science fiction is still some of the best. Jules Verne's *Twenty Thousand Leagues Under the Sea*, *Around the World in Eighty Days*, and *The Mysterious Island* are still being read and enjoyed, though they were written a century ago. Verne, who lived in France, studied to be a lawyer but

became interested in the theater and in literature. His stories were very popular from the start, for he combined careful scientific study with a talent for creating interesting situations for his characters.

872

VERTEBRATES

All animals, including man, that have a backbone are called vertebrates. The illustration shows the 5 groups of animals, from the simplest to the most complex, that have backbones: the FISH, AMPHIBIANS, REPTILES, BIRDS, and MAMMALS.

Every vertebrate except sharks and rays has a bone skeleton. The backbone is the main part of this framework. It is made up of many separate bones called *vertebrae*. The vertebrae can be likened to beads strung on a cord, called the spinal cord in animals. The spinal cord is the main nerve from the brain down the backbone.

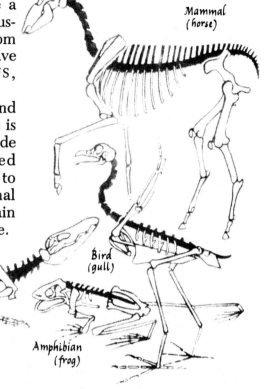

Mammal (horse)

Bird (gull)

Reptile (crocodile)

Fish (perch)

Amphibian (frog)

VESUVIUS

Vesuvius is an active VOLCANO on the eastern shore of the Bay of Naples in southern Italy. The height of the main cone changes with each eruption; the present height is 4190 feet (1299 m). The sides of the volcano are scarred by lava flow, but its lower slopes are covered with vineyards, orchards, and villages.

The earliest recorded eruption occurred in A.D. 79, when it buried the prosperous Roman cities of POMPEII, Herculaneum, and Stabiae. These cities were destroyed by millions of tons of volcanic cinders and ash and lay buried for many centuries.

Since then, Vesuvius has erupted more than fifty times, sometimes violently as in A.D. 512 and 1631. Its most recent eruption was in 1944. Despite the danger, about 2 million people live in the area.

VICE PRESIDENT

The Vice President of the United States is the official next in rank to the President. He is elected at the same time as the President and must have the same qualifications—be at least 35 years old, a native-born citizen, and a resident of the U.S. for 14 years before running for office. The Vice President succeeds to the PRESIDENCY on the resignation, removal, death, or disability of the President. Though the U.S. CONSTITUTION is unclear about whether the Vice President becomes President, this has been the custom ever since Vice President John Tyler in 1841 succeeded President William Harrison, the first President to die in office.

The only specific duty of the Vice President is to preside over the SENATE during sessions of Congress. He has no vote there, except in case of a tie during a vote on a bill or some other measure. He then has the deciding vote. In this century, the Vice President has gotten increased duties such as adviser on defense and foreign affairs and roving ambassador for the U.S.

Queen VICTORIA (1819–1901)

In 1837, Victoria became Queen of Great Britain and Ireland. During her long reign, Britain was the strongest nation in the world. It is often called the "Victorian Age."

Victoria was born in London and, before she was a year old, her father died. She was brought up strictly by her mother and became queen at the age of 18. Victoria soon took an interest in government, agreeing and disagreeing with the policies of her ministers. The prime ministers during her reign included Melbourne, Peel, Palmerston, Gladstone, and Disraeli.

In 1840, Victoria married her German cousin, Prince Albert of Saxe-Coburg-Gotha, who became her adviser in affairs of state. Their marriage was very happy, and most of their nine children married into other royal families in Europe. When the Prince died of typhoid fever in 1861, Victoria was stricken with grief. For three years she did not appear in public, and for the rest of her life, she wore black mourning clothes.

In 1876, Victoria took the title Empress of India, and Britain's empire stretched around the world. The INDUSTRIAL REVOLUTION had brought great power and wealth to her country.

VICTORIA FALLS

In 1855, DAVID LIVINGSTONE, a Scottish missionary and explorer, discovered some spectacular waterfalls on the upper ZAMBEZI River and named them for QUEEN VICTORIA. Situated on the border between Zambia and Zimbabwe (Rhodesia), Victoria Falls are divided by islets into four waterfalls, each about a mile (1.6 km) long and 355 feet (110 m) high. The thick mist and the thunderous roar produced by the falling water can be heard 25 miles (40 km)

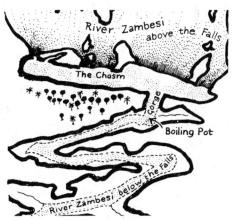

away, thus giving the falls their native name, "the smoke that thunders." The waters flow into a huge chasm just below the falls and then through a narrow gorge named "the Boiling Pot." Afterward the waters rush down a deep zigzag channel for 40 miles (64 km). A railroad bridge spans the gorge, and a modern hydroelectric plant stands nearby.

VIENNA

Vienna, the capital and largest city of AUSTRIA, lies on a plain beside the DANUBE River. Around the city are forested hills, the most famous of which is the Wiener Wald (Vienna Woods).

the Opera House

Vienna was controlled successively by the Celts, Romans, Huns, Avars, and Franks. Soldiers during the CRUSADES stopped there, and in 1296, it became the residence of the Hapsburg emperors of the Holy Roman Empire. The Turks besieged Vienna in 1529 and 1683 but never captured it. From 1867 to 1918, it was the capital of the Austro-Hungarian Empire, and from 1938 to 1945 it was a part of Germany. Since the 13th century, Vienna has been the chief artistic and cultural center of eastern Europe.

Old Vienna (the inner city) was encircled by high walls, which were torn down in 1858 and replaced by the famous boulevard, the Ringstrasse. Vienna's great buildings include St. Stephen's Cathedral (built in 1433), the Imperial Palace, the Gothic city hall, the stately Houses of Parliament, and the Imperial opera house. Vienna also has a distinguished university, founded in 1364, and many parks and art museums. SEE ALSO: AUSTRIA.

VIETNAM

Vietnam is a long, thin country that lies along the eastern coat of the Southeast Asian peninsula. The jungle-covered hills of the mountainous Annamese Cordillera stretch from the north into the south. To the east of the mountains are fertile coastal lowlands. In north Vietnam is the DELTA of the Red River, on which lies Hanoi, Vietnam's capital. The Mekong River forms a large delta in south Vietnam. Vietnam has about 48 million people, most of whom are Buddhists.

The principal food of the country is rice, which grows abundantly in the delta regions. There are rubber, tea, and coffee plantations in the south. Vietnam has large amounts of coal in the north, as well as some iron ore, tin, and phosphate. Its industries produce steel, textiles, glass, paper, and machinery.

The region was settled by the Viets, a people from central China. For more than 900 years, China controlled it, until in A.D. 938 independence was established. In 1859, the French captured the city of Ho Chi Minh (known as Saigon until 1976). France then gained control over most of the region, making it an Indochinese colony. Japan occupied Vietnam during World War II. Afterward, Communist guerrillas under Ho Chi Minh fought the French from 1946 to 1954. The French were defeated at Dien Bien Phu, and the Communists took over the northern half of Vietnam. The UNITED STATES was involved in the VIETNAM WAR. After the war ended, the Communists seized the southern half of the country and reunited Vietnam.

VIETNAM WAR

After 1954, the Communists in northern VIETNAM tried to take over the southern provinces of the country. Vietnam was at that time split into two separate nations—North and South Vietnam. The Communist North Vietnamese supported the Vietcong (Communist guerrilla forces in South Vietnam), who were working to overthrow the government of South Vietnam. The United States, under Presidents EISENHOWER and KENNEDY, gave advice and economic assistance to South Vietnam. However, the country's civil war grew worse.

In 1964, two U.S. destroyers in the Gulf of Tonkin were fired upon by North Vietnamese torpedo boats. The U.S. Congress then passed the Gulf of Tonkin Resolution that gave President Lyndon Johnson power to repel any armed attacked. In 1965, bombing raids were started over North Vietnam, and U.S. soldiers were committed to the war in Vietnam. By 1967, there were 474,000 American men fighting in Vietnam.

As the war got worse and American casualties increased, large protests against the Vietnam War erupted in many cities in the U.S. While bloody and heavy battles went on, peace talks were begun between the U.S. and North Vietnam in 1968. The next year, new peace talks included the Vietcong and South Vietnam.

By April, 1969, American troops in Vietnam reached a high of 543,400, and American battle deaths were more than in the Korean War. Large demonstrations against the war continued in the U.S., and secret police negotiations were carried on by President Richard Nixon's advisor, Henry Kissinger. Fierce attacks were made by both sides, using bombs, artillery, machine guns, and grenades.

Finally, in early 1973, President Nixon stopped all U.S. offensive military operations and began withdrawing American soldiers. A peace pact was signed in Paris by the U.S., the Vietcong, and North and South Vietnam. U.S. troops were all out of Vietnam at the end of March, 1973. Later, fighting continued between the South Vietnamese and the Communists, who gained total control of Vietnam in 1975.

VIKINGS

The Vikings, also called Norsemen, were early inhabitants of Scandinavia. They were great seafaring warriors who raided and terrorized the settlements along the coasts of Europe from the 8th to the 11th century A.D. This was the Viking Age.

The Vikings lived in tribes in small villages along the coasts of present-day Norway, Sweden, and Denmark. They wrote using a 16-letter alphabet, called the *runic* alphabet. They were highly skilled craftsmen in wood and iron, producing superb tools, weapons, armor, and ships. The Vikings were very loyal to their tribal chief and proud of their military courage.

About A.D. 700, the Vikings grew too large in number for their rocky and barren land to support. This and their adventurous spirit drove the Vikings southward. In their swift, seaworthy warships, the "long ships," they made attacks on coastal towns in present-day England, Germany, France, and Holland.

In A.D. 878, ALFRED THE GREAT pushed the Vikings out of England. King Charles III of France was unable to drive Rollo, a great Viking chieftain, out of northern France. Thus, the king gave Rollo certain lands, on the condition that Rollo become the king's subject. In A.D. 911, Rollo married the king's daughter and later converted to CHRISTIANITY. Later, the Danish king Canute ruled a Viking kingdom that included Norway, Denmark, and England. Other Vikings sailed west and made settlements in Iceland and

Greenland. The two most famous Viking seafarers are probably Eric the Red, who discovered Greenland, and his son LEIF ERICSON, who explored the coast of North America. The Vikings also roamed south to the Mediterranean Sea, establishing footholds in Italy and Sicily for a while. Vikings from Sweden traveled eastward along the waterways into what is now Russia.

The Viking Age ended when Christianity became the chief religion of Scandinavia. The Vikings were Christianized by 1100 and developed into farmers and peaceful settlers.

VINEGAR

Vinegar is a sour liquid consisting chiefly of acetic acid and water. It is produced by the fermentation of wine, cider, beer, or ale. Most of the best vinegar is made from cider. Vinegar is used in cooking for flavoring, preserving, and softening tough foods. It is also used as a mild disinfectant.

As a natural by-product of wine, vinegar has been known to man for about 5000 years. The name *vinegar* comes from the French *vin aigre*, meaning "sour wine." Wine vinegar is common in most European countries. Malt vinegar, made from sour beer, is used in England, and cider vinegar is preferred in much of the United States.

VIOLIN

The violin is the best-known member of a family of instruments that first appeared in the early 16th century. It plays the highest notes of any instrument in the family. The other members are the *viola*, which is a little lower in pitch; the CELLO, lower still; and the *double bass*, which plays very deep notes.

The violin is usually played with a long, straight

bow. The stretched hairs of the bow, which are rubbed with a piney substance called *rosin* to make them less smooth, scrape on the four catgut strings of the violin and cause them to vibrate. The violinist sometimes plays with the wooden back of the bow, or plucks the strings with his fingers.

A violin has 84 parts, which are carefully glued together and varnished. Some persons feel that the very best violins were made in the 17th century in the Italian city of Cremona. The Stradivari family there was especially famous. But excellent violins are still being made for those who can afford them.

VIPER

The viper is a very poisonous snake. When it bites, its poison is injected through one of its sharp, hollow teeth, known as *fangs*. These fangs fold back into the roof of the mouth when not needed. If one of the fangs becomes broken or old, a new one soon grows to replace the old.

Viper comes from the contraction of the Latin word *vi(vi)pera*, meaning "bearing young alive." (Our English word *viviparous* means just that.) People in the ancient world believed all vipers produced living young rather than eggs. A few vipers do lay eggs, like most other REPTILES.

Among the true vipers of Europe, Asia, and Africa are the adder and gaboon viper. The pit vipers of America and Asia, which have a deep pit on each side of their heads, include the dangerous water moccasin, copperhead, and RATTLESNAKE.

VIRGIL (70–19 B.C.)

Virgil was a famous Roman poet. He wrote the long poem called the *Aeneid*, that described the adventures of Aeneas, the legendary "father" of the Roman people. After the fall of TROY, Aeneas, a Trojan prince, escaped and wandered to CARTHAGE. Here Dido, the founder and queen of Carthage, fell in love with Aeneas and killed herself when he left her to sail northward. After landing in Italy, Aeneas fought and slew Turnus, the king, and established the beginnings of the Roman Empire.

As a young man, Virgil lived on his father's farm, where he studied and wrote poetry. In 41 B.C., he lost his land and went to Rome, where he became the favorite poet of Augustus Caesar. In addition to the *Aeneid*, Virgil wrote about country life and work on the farm in some poems called the *Bucolics* and the *Georgics*.

VIRGINIA

Virginia is considered the most northerly of the southern states of the United States. Its Atlantic Coastal Plain, known as the Tidewater area, is generally flat and partly swampy. Four great tidal rivers—the Potomac, Rappahannock, York, and James—flow southeastward across this area to the Chesapeake Bay. The state's central region, the Piedmont Plateau, rises in the west to the Blue Ridge

Mountains. The beautiful, fertile, historic Shenandoah Valley lies between the Blue Ridge and the Appalachian Mountains. Many forests cover the land.

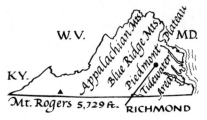

The Algonkin, Siouan, and Iroquoian Indians were living in the area when English settlers founded JAMESTOWN in 1607. It soon became a British colony. Tobacco was grown and exported abroad, and Negro slaves were used on the plantations. British restrictions led to the AMERICAN REVOLUTION. After George Washington's victory at Yorktown, Virginians like WASHINGTON, JEFFERSON, MADISON, and MONROE provided the first federal leadership of the nation. Virginia seceded (withdrew) from the U.S. in 1861, at the start of the CIVIL WAR. It was the scene of many battles, until General ROBERT E. LEE surrendered at Appomattox in 1865.

Today, Virginia manufactures many goods, such as chemicals, cigarettes, foods, and furniture. It produces eggs, hams, poultry, apples, peaches, and peanuts. Coal, stone, and lime are mined. Tourists enjoy the lovely countryside, beaches, and numerous historic sites, such as Colonial Williamsburg. Virginia's capital is Richmond. There are nearly 5.25 million people in the state.

VIRUS

In 1935, Dr. Wendell M. Stanley, an American scientist, demonstrated that a virus can be both a living and a non-living thing. When a virus is within living CELLS, it acts like a living organism; when it is outside the cells, it can be dried indefinitely to form harmless, non-living crystals.

These tiny bits of matter are so small that they pass through filters that trap the smallest bacteria. They cannot be seen with ordinary microscopes but are visible with the aid of the electron microscope.

When this parasitic agent infects a living cells, the normal activities of the host cell cease and its energies are diverted into reproducing new viruses. Finally, the host cell disintegrates to release the many new infective particles. Those viruses infecting man are generally spherical and those infecting plants are generally rod-shaped. Others look like coils, tadpoles, and 20-sided polygons.

Polio, viral pneumonia, measles, mumps, cold sores, chicken pox, and the common cold are some of the known viral diseases of man. Several types of cancers, parrot fever, rabies, and distemper are viral diseases of animals. Tobacco mosaic is one of the plant diseases caused by a virus.

VITAMINS

Vitamin comes from the Latin word, *vita*, meaning "life." Around 1911, when people knew about airplanes and automobiles, people just began to learn about vitamins. About that time Casimir Funk, a Polish-born American scientist, separated pure vitamin

Vitamin A			For general health
Vitamin B			This is really a group of vitamins, all important for health.
Vitamin C			For protection against colds. Helps wounds to heal. For general health.
Vitamin D			Essential for the healthy growth of bones and teeth.
Vitamin E			Probably helps growth of babies before birth

B₁ (thiamine) from rice husks. He originated the term *vitamine* (now vitamin) and claimed the existence of four such materials for normal health and for the prevention of disease.

During the 1800s, the English knew that their sailors would not become sick and die of scurvy if they drank lime or lemon juice. At that time, no one understood that it was the vitamin C in these citrus juices that kept these men free from the disease.

Scientists have discovered today that there are about 15 vitamins, the most important being listed on the chart above.

Although vitamin pills can supply us with what our bodies need, it is better to rely mostly on a well balanced diet of body-building proteins, energy-giving fats and carbohydrates, and "protective" foods such as fruits and vegetables. These various foods may also contain some essential undiscovered vitamins. SEE ALSO: FOODS.

VOICE

Sounds are produced by vibrations or waves in the air. When we speak, air passes through our *larynx* ("voice box"). Inside this "box" are fibrous bands called *vocal cords* that move back and forth or vibrate when air is forced from the LUNGS out of the body. When the vocal cords are tightened, high sounds are produced; when they are relaxed, low sounds are made. More air produces a loud SOUND; less air, a soft sound.

In addition to the vocal cords vibrating to make sound, the lips, tongue, and teeth also assist in producing the sound of the voice. SEE ALSO: SOUND.

VOLCANO

The word *volcano* comes from Vulcan, the Roman god of fire whose home was supposedly Mount Etna in Sicily.

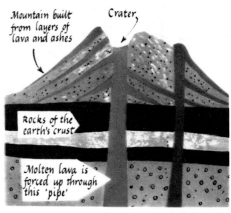

Mountain built from layers of lava and ashes

Crater

Rocks of the earth's crust

Molten lava is forced up through this 'pipe'

A volcano is an opening in the Earth's crust through which hot, molten rock (called LAVA) and ash erupt out under tremendous pressure. A cone that grows higher and higher is formed by the outpouring of lava. Eventually, a mountain forms with a vent or chimney inside and a CRATER or mouth at the top.

Many years may pass without any volcanic activity. Then, suddenly, a violent eruption may occur. Streams of burning lava will flow out and scorch the sides of the mountain, and red hot ash will shoot up like a column of smoke.

Around the world there are distinct belts of volcanoes, which are found usually near the sea along the edges of continents. The Pacific Ocean is surrounded by volcanoes. They are also located in Iceland, in the Mediterranean, and even in Antarctica. VESUVIUS, KRAKATOA, Etna, and Mauna Loa are some of the world's most famous volcanoes. SEE ALSO: MOUNTAINS.

VOLLEYBALL

Volleyball is an outdoor or indoor game played on a court, 60 feet (18.6 m) long by 30 feet (9.3 m) wide. The court is divided in half by a net, the top of which is 8 feet (2.5 m) from the ground. The game is played between two opposing teams of six players each (three forwards and three backs).

An inflated, rubber ball is served from behind the back lines of the court. Using an open hand or fist, the server has only one try to hit the ball over the net into the opponents' court. The ball must be returned before it touches the ground and must be kept within the boundaries of the court. The players use any part of their bodies to hit the ball. A team's players are allowed to hit the ball no more than three times before returning it over the net. A player may not hit the ball twice in a row.

Points are won only by the serving team. If the serving team fails to return the ball, the other team gets a chance to serve and thus to score points. When a team regains service, its players rotate clockwise so that a new player becomes server. A team wins with 15 points, and it must have a two-point advantage if the score is tied at 14.

VOTE

When boys and girls at school want to choose their class president, they hold an election. Two, three, or four members of the class are "proposed" or nominated as candidates for president. Then everyone votes for that one candidate he or she thinks will do the best job. The candidate receiving the most votes wins and becomes president.

Voting can be done openly by having everyone raise his hand or secretly by having everyone write or indicate his choice (vote) on a slip of paper called a BALLOT. By using a ballot, no one is supposed to know the vote of anyone else. Since the vote is secret, the final outcome is supposedly more truthful. SEE ALSO: BALLOT.

VULTURE

A vulture is a large bird of prey that feeds on *carrion* (the flesh of dead animals). It has an ugly, bald head and neck, and its feet are big with claws suitable for holding a carcass. In some vultures, the hooked beak is very powerful and heavy. However, the American vulture has a weak beak and weak feet. Because of its lack of

strength, it seldom attacks a live animal, as the European and Asian vultures do.

Vultures have keen sight and may stay aloft for hours, skillfully soaring on their long, broad wings. They live in many kinds of terrain, roosting and nesting together on high mountain cliffs and trees. The female vulture lays one or two eggs, which take 7 or 8 weeks to hatch. Vultures are valuable scavengers that eat up rotting flesh, garbage, and other waste.

WALES

Wales is a principality of GREAT BRITAIN, occupying a broad peninsula to the west of ENGLAND. Though this region has been connected with England for more than 400 years, the Welsh people, however, have kept their language, literature, and way of life. Wales has about 3 million people.

It is a land of rocky sea cliffs, *heather*-covered hills, and lush, green valleys. The Cambrian Mountains, which run from north to south, contain

the highest peak in Wales and England—Mt. Snowdon (3560 feet or 1104 meters).

South Wales is the industrial area, with coal mines, tinplate works, oil refineries, and one of the biggest steel factories in Europe. Also situated here are the busy seaports of Swansea, Newport, and Cardiff, the capital. Central Wales has few people, most of whom raise sheep for a living. North Wales has beautiful scenery that is enjoyed by tourists and climbers.

About 200 B.C., the Celts were the dominant people in Wales. Welsh princes and chieftains fought almost constantly with the English kings. In 1282, the last Welsh prince, Llewellyn, was defeated by King Edward I of England. King Edward gave his son the title PRINCE OF WALES.

WALNUT

The walnut belongs to a family of deciduous trees characterized by large, compound leaves. These trees live mainly in the north temperate regions of the world.

Walnut trees are commercially important for their edible nuts and for their hardwood TIMBER. The nut of the walnut is one of the most valuable food nuts of the U.S.

The dark-colored wood of the English or the black walnut is hard, durable, and well-grained. It is used for furniture, gunstocks, musical instruments, and interior paneling.

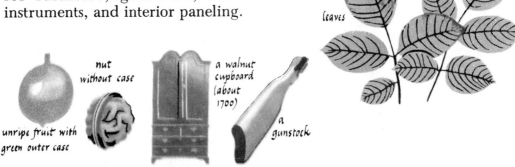

tree in winter

leaves

nut without case

unripe fruit with green outer case

a walnut cupboard (about 1700)

a gunstock

WALRUS

Walrus comes from a Dutch word meaning "whale horse." This member of the seal family is a large MAMMAL adapted to living almost entirely in the sea. The walrus has bristly whiskers, elongated upper teeth called tusks, and a thick, tough skin. The hind limbs are webbed and twisted under like fins to make them fine swimmers. On land, they are able to hobble about more easily than other SEALS. Adult males weigh about a ton (907 kg) and are about 10 to 12 feet (3.1–3.7 m) in length.

Herds of walruses live among the ice floes along the edge of the Arctic Ocean. They eat mainly shellfish which they pry off the rocks with their long tusks. Like seals, they have a sharp bark and a gusty bellow. Although normally gentle and unaggressive, walruses will fiercely defend their young. As a group, they will also assist a wounded member of the herd. SEE ALSO: SEALS.

WAR

War is an armed conflict between nations or organized groups of people. Since prehistoric times, wars have occurred between tribes, groups within a country (civil war), and independent nations (international war).

The reasons people give for going to war are often complicated, but usually beneath them is the real reason—power. For instance, Sparta fought for power over Athens; the many wars among England, France, and Spain were often over control of trade and colonies. Sometimes, civil wars and revolutions began because a government had grown too powerful and harsh. People wanted more freedom and more control over their lives, as was the case in the American, French, and Russian revolutions.

At the start of the CRUSADES, men went to war with high religious ideals, but they often prolonged it for selfish reasons —to gain glory, wealth, and power.

During the Middle Ages, the upper classes regarded war as a hobby. Also, men like Alexander, Napoleon, and Hitler have made war because it brought glory and power through new territory and domination of other peoples.

Victory in war has generally gone to that side with the better weapons. Flint-tipped spears were replaced by bronze swords, which gave way to iron weapons. Then came the disciplined Roman armies and the power of the cavalry. Later, armored knights on horseback were no match for the *longbow*. Castles were made useless by the use of gunpowder. Muskets were replaced by rifles, rifles by machine guns, and machine guns by artillery, rockets, and missiles. Today, power is in the hands of those with atomic, hydrogen, plutonium, and nitrogen bombs, whose destructive force could kill everyone on Earth.

Nations have made *treaties* to keep peace, but these agreements have often been broken. In 1945, the United Nations was formed to try to promote better understanding among nations so that there will be no wars.

WAR of 1812

In the early 1800s, the United States decided to remain neutral (not to take sides) in the war between France and Britain. NAPOLEON agreed not to interfere with American trade to Britain. However, the British said that neutral ships must first stop at British ports and pay duties (taxes). This offended the U.S., which also disliked the British for stopping U.S. merchant ships on the high seas and impressing (forcing) American seamen into service on British warships.

At the same time, American frontiersmen in the West wanted more free land. They felt that the British were preventing American expansion and were encouraging armed Indian raids from Canada. These frontiersmen were supported in Congress by Henry Clay, John Calhoun, and other "war hawks." Finally, a declaration of war was signed by President JAMES MADISON.

At first, American plans to invade Canada failed. However, on the sea, the frigate U.S.S. *Constitution*, known as OLD IRONSIDES, captured the British frigates *Guerrière* and *Java*. The U.S.S. *United States* also seized the British ship *Macedonia*. In September, 1813, the American fleet under Oliver Hazard Perry defeated and captured the whole British fleet on Lake Erie.

Then American soldiers led by General William Henry Harrison moved into Ontario, Canada, against the British, who had recently burned Detroit. On October 5, 1813, Harrison defeated British and Indian forces at the Battle of the Thames River, in which Tecumseh, the great Shawnee Indian chief, was killed.

The British fleet blockaded U.S. ports. In August, 1814, a British landing force took Washington, D.C., burning the White House and the Capitol. The British fleet was halted at Fort McHenry, in Baltimore, where Francis Scott Key was inspired by the American defensive efforts to compose the STAR-SPANGLED BANNER.

In the summer of 1814, a British army advanced from Canada into New York State and seriously threatened the Hudson River valley. However, the U.S. *Saratoga*, commanded by Captain Thomas MacDonough, defeated the larger British ship *Confiance* during a furious naval battle on Lake Champlain. Afterward, the British army retreated into Canada.

Weary of warfare, both sides signed a peace treaty (the Treaty of Ghent) on December 24, 1814. Before news of the treaty reached the U.S., about 5000 American backwoodsmen under General ANDREW JACKSON decisively defeated more than 8000 British troops at the Battle of New Orleans. The battle occurred on January 8, 1815.

WARSAW

Warsaw, the capital and largest city of POLAND, stands on the left bank of the Vistula River. For more than 700 years, the city suffered invasion by foreigners—Swedes, Prussians, Russians, and the French. During World War II, the Germans almost completely destroyed Warsaw, once considered one of the loveliest cities in Europe. Today it has numerous modern buildings, wide streets, parks, and beautiful gardens. SEE ALSO: POLAND.

Modern Warsaw

Booker T. WASHINGTON (1856–1915)

Booker Taliaferro Washington was born a slave on a plantation in Franklin County, Virginia. He moved with his family to West Virginia, where he worked in salt furnaces and coal mines. He studied and went to school when he could. In 1875, he graduated from Hampton Institute, where he worked as a janitor to earn his room and board. After teaching for a while in a Negro school in West Virginia, Washington was appointed an instructor at Hampton in 1879.

In 1881, he was asked to start a school for NEGROES in Tuskegee, Alabama. He accepted and founded the famous Tuskegee Institute, of which he was the president and guiding spirit for the next 34 years. Tuskegee Institute emphasized industrial, vocational, and agricultural education. Washington believed that this kind of schooling would enable Negroes to gain self-respect and economic independence.

Booker T. Washington made many speeches in the U.S. and Europe about his work and philosophy. He believed that Negroes could not gain social equality before they had attained economic equality. He wrote *Up from Slavery*, *The Future of the American Negro*, and *My Larger Education*.

George WASHINGTON (1732–1799)

George Washington, the first president of the United States, was the son of a well-to-do tobacco planter in Virginia. His father died when he was 11, and his older half brother, Lawrence, then took care of him. He received little formal schooling but studied surveying and learned to ride, hunt, and shoot well. As a young man, Washington served as a lieutenant colonel in the British forces during the FRENCH AND INDIAN WAR.

When the American colonists fought against the rule of King GEORGE III and the AMERICAN REVOLUTION broke out, Washington became commander of the colonial army. Through his courage and steady leadership, and with help from the French, the British were defeated. Then, after he helped draft the CONSTITUTION, Washington was chosen President in 1789.

In the hard job of governing a new country, Washington's wise, sensitive, and strong character won him much respect. In 1793, Washington was unanimously reelected and continued to give the United States a strong central government. Later, weary with political life, he refused to run for a third term and retired to his home, MOUNT VERNON, where he died two years later. He belonged to the Federalist party. SEE ALSO: AMERICAN REVOLUTION.

WASHINGTON

The state of Washington lies in the northwestern corner of the United States. It is divided by the high Cascade Mountains into two main regions. To the west are fertile lowlands around Puget Sound, an arm of the Pacific Ocean. Here are also the Olympic Mountains and the Coast Ranges.

East of the Cascades are thickly forested mountains and the Columbia Plateau. Irrigation with water from the Columbia, Snake, and Walla Walla Rivers has made much of eastern Washington a rich farming region. The state's largest city is Seattle and its capital is Olympia. Washington has more than 3.6 million people.

Many different Indian tribes once lived in the region. They included the Quinault, Makah, Chinook, Klickitat, Sahaptian, and Nez Percé. The Spanish sailed along the coast in the 1770s. An American, Robert Gray, discovered the Columbia River in 1792. Later, LEWIS AND CLARK came by land and fur traders set up various posts. The first permanent settlement was Tumwater, near Puget Sound. This was the end of the OREGON TRAIL, which brought new settlers to the area. The Indians were defeated and moved to reservations. For a while the area was part of Oregon, but it broke away and became a state in 1889.

Washington now has many industries, producing such goods as airplanes, lumber, paper, chemicals, and foods. Wheat, apples, and dairy items come from the state. There is a large fishing industry, with salmon the main catch. Many vacationers come for hunting, boating, and fishing.

WASHINGTON, D.C.

Washington is the capital of the U.S.A., situated on the Potomac River in the District of Columbia. It contains the Capitol (the seat of the CONGRESS) and the White House (the home of the U.S. PRESIDENT). Other fine buildings are the Library of Congress, the National Gallery of Art, and the Smithsonian Institution. The Jefferson Memorial, Washington Monument, and Lincoln Memorial stand in honor of three great U.S. presidents.

The city was designed by Pierre L'Enfant, a French architect and friend of GEORGE WASHINGTON, after whom the city was named. During the War of 1812, the British burned the White House and other government buildings. Washington was rebuilt, and after the Civil War it developed into a large, beautiful city with parks, museums, universities, and a lovely, historic suburb called Georgetown. Today, more than 3 million people live in and around Washington.

WASPS

These stinging insects are close relatives of the BEES and ANTS. They can be distinguished from their relatives by their slender waists. Like ants and bees, wasps have 4 stages to their life cycle: egg, larva, pupa, and adult.

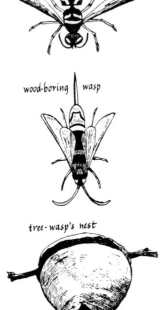

common wasp

wood-boring wasp

tree-wasp's nest

There are thousands of kinds of wasps. Some are social, like bees and ants, and live in large colonies in nests; others live alone.

In autumn when workers and males die, the social queen wasp finds a sheltered spot in which to hibernate until spring when she begins a new colony. The paper nest she builds is made of chewed up wood. It is located in a bank where she lays her eggs. The workers that hatch and mature finish building the nest. Only one queen and a few males live in a colony.

Wasps are attracted to sweet, ripe fruit, but young, wormlike grubs have to be fed animal food, such as captured flies.

The non-social, solitary queen wasp stings a caterpillar or spider, pushes the paralyzed insect into a hole, lays an egg on it, closes the hole, and flies away. Thus, the young hatches with its own food supply. When fully developed, the adult wasp eats its way out of the sealed paper nest and flies away.

WATER

Water covers about 75 per cent of the Earth's surface and is essential for life. Water is a compound, created when 2 ATOMS of HYDROGEN chemically join with one of OXYGEN— written in chemical shorthand as H_2O. It can exist in 3 states: solid, liquid, and gaseous. As a solid, it is called ice. Ice is hard and dry. As a liquid, it is wet and can be poured. As a vapor, it is dry, invisible, and cannot be felt. Water freezes at 32°F (0°C) and boils at 212°F (100°C). When pure, it is colorless, odorless, and tasteless.

All living organisms are at least 50 per cent water; the human body is 70 per cent water and can go much longer without food than without water.

Water is used for drinking, cleaning, cooking, growing plants, dissolving many substances, and fighting fires. Man uses water to produce electric power and depends on water transportation to carry goods. Man builds recreation areas along rivers, lakes, and oceans.

WATERLOO

Waterloo is a village in central Belgium. At the Battle of Waterloo, NAPOLEON Bonaparte, the French Emperor, was decisively defeated on June 18, 1815.

In February, 1815, Napoleon escaped from exile on the island of Elba and returned to France. With a large French army, he defeated a Prussian (German) army on June 16, 1815. Assuming that the Prussians were retreating, Napoleon's soldiers marched northward and met a British army led by the DUKE OF WELLINGTON.

Meanwhile, the Prussians had recovered and marched to Waterloo to help the British. Late in the day, when Wellington's soldiers were starting to weaken, the Prussian army arrived and attacked. Napoleon was beaten and fled from the battle, during which the French lost about 40,000 men. On June 22, 1815, Napoleon surrendered formally to the British.

WATER PLANTS

There are a great variety of water plants, ranging from the handsome yellow iris to the fast-multiplying duckweed, whose tiny leaves can cover the

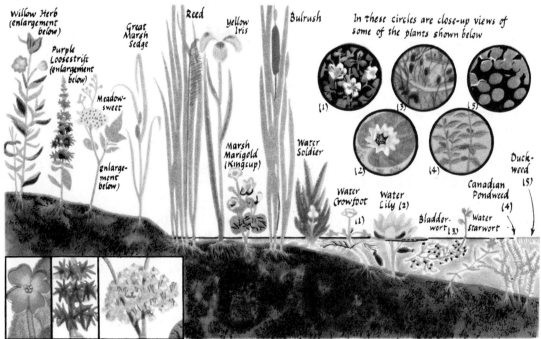

surface of a pond in one night. Duckweeds are among the fastest growing water plants.

Some water plants, like the watercress, LOTUS, and other water lilies, have roots; their leaves and flowers grow above the surface of the water. Other water plants float on the water's surface, where they obtain their nourishment. They include the water hyacinths, the bladderworts, and the duckweeds, which are the smallest flowering plants.

Water plants which grow entirely underwater include the curled pondweed, the water violet, and the Canadian waterweed. Some of these can cause trouble in reservoirs and lakes. These underwater plants do not drown because they obtain their oxygen from the air that is dissolved in the water.

Many water plants grow in marshy areas and on the banks of streams. Among those that need a waterlogged environment are cattails and other various reeds and rushes, kingcups, marsh mallow, rice, and peppermint-scented water mint with its lilac flowers. Weeping willows, alders, and bald cypresses are trees that like a watery location. SEE ALSO: LOTUS.

WATER POLO

Water polo is a swimming game that began in England in the 1870s. There are seven players on each of two competing teams. The object of the game is to maneuver— by hand, head, or feet—a rubber ball into net-enclosed goals at opposite ends of a swimming pool. The ball is passed and thrown with only one hand, and it must be carried on the surface of the water. Players may hold, pull back, and dunk any opponent who is holding the ball. The game consists of 7-minute quarters (5-minute quarters in international play) and is conducted by one or two referees. Since 1900, water polo has been part of the OLYMPIC GAMES.

WATER SUPPLY
We often take our water supply for granted. It is very cheap, is almost never interrupted by breakdowns in the supply system, and is free of the germs that might give us disease. We use so much water in different ways that a modern *waterworks* counts on supplying 100 gallons of water or more per day for every person.

In many primitive communities, even in some large cities, water was once sold from door to door by peddlers who brought it in tanks carried on the backs of animals or in carts. Other communities depended on wells, as people in the country still do. But some ancient civilizations already had piped water supplies and complete plumbing systems. The AQUEDUCTS of the ancient Romans brought water from distant streams to their cities. There it was distributed to public fountains, bath houses, and other places.

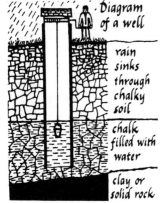

Diagram of a well

rain sinks through chalky soil

chalk filled with water

clay or solid rock

During the Middle Ages, the ancient aqueducts went out of use, but in the 16th century some cities began to have waterworks again. Watermills in a river ran pumps in some cases, though water sometimes flowed by gravity from springs in high places. Wooden and iron pipes were laid to carry the water to different parts of the cities. River water was often polluted, though, and could cause disease. Early in the 19th century, some waterworks began to filter water through sand to remove pollutants. Around 1900, some waterworks began to put chlorine and other chemicals in water to kill germs.

In a typical modern waterworks, the water arrives by aqueduct and pours into a *reservoir*, a huge basin where it stays until the mud it carries has fallen to the reservoir bottom. Then the water is *aerated*, sprayed or allowed to fall so that it is mixed with air. This removes bad tastes and smells as well as some minerals. After this, *coagulants* cause other impurities to drop to the bottom of *settling basins* where the water is once again stored. *Softeners* remove minerals that make the water hard to wash with. Then the water is *filtered* through sand, crushed rock, or special sieves to remove tiny plants that grow in water. Finally, the water is *disinfected*, and is ready to send through the *mains* to the users. SEE ALSO: AQUEDUCT.

James WATT (1736–1819)

James Watt was born in a small fishing village in Scotland. As a boy, he liked to make models and later, at the age of 19, went to London to be an instrument maker. The hard, poor life in London caused him to return home, where he became an instrument repairer for the University of Glasgow.

In 1764, Watt was asked to repair a model of Thomas Newcomen's STEAM ENGINE, which was used to pump water out of mines. He greatly improved Newcomen's clumsy engine and later devised a new type of engine that worked faster and did more varied work. He also constructed a rotary engine.

In 1775, Watt went into business with Matthew Boulton, whose money helped Watt in manufacturing his steam engines. His engines were used in many European and American factories, and Watt became very wealthy. He continually sought to improve his machines, developing a double-acting engine, a centrifugal governor, and a pressure gauge. The "watt," a unit of electrical power, was named after James Watt.

WAVES

When a stone is thrown into a still body of water, it pushes particles of water out of the way. Ripples travel outwards from the point where the stone enters the water. The water itself does not change position as ripples or waves move across the surface of the water. Only the up-and-down movement of the water is passed on. If a slip of paper is placed on the water as the waves go by, it moves up and down, not with the wave across the water.

SOUND is simply *longitudinal* waves of the air. When a horn is honked, the air around it is disturbed. You hear the horn when the waves of sound, traveling at 760 miles per hour (1224 km/hr), reach your ear. Sound waves can pass through steel and other solids, but they can not go through a vacuum (a space without matter and air).

A beam of LIGHT consists of a series of very tiny waves, which vary in length. Red light, for instance, has a longer wavelength than a blue light—that is, the distance between two crests of a wave of red light is longer than that between two crests of a wave of blue light. Radio waves have even longer wavelengths than those of ordinary, visible light waves. As a result, radio waves are invisible to the human eye.

The wind causes waves on the surface of the ocean. These waves move in the same direction as the wind. The shallow water near the shore causes the top of the ocean waves to travel faster than the lower part, eventually causing the waves to "break." SEE ALSO: LIGHT, SOUND.

WEAVING

The making of CLOTH by interlacing threads or yarns is called weaving. It is done on a frame called a LOOM. Some threads run the length of the loom; these are called the *warp*. Others cross the loom, carried by a device called a *shuttle*; these threads are called the *weft*. As the shuttle carries the weft back and forth, the cloth is woven.

Hand loom

Power loom

In a *plain weave*, every warp or weft thread goes above one thread that it crosses, below the next, above the next after that, and so on. This is the simplest kind of weave. In a *twill weave*, some threads pass over two or more of the crossing threads in such a way that an easily seen diagonal pattern is set up. In a *satin weave*, some threads cross several others, but in a way that does not create a pattern.

There are much fancier weaves than these, used for making velvet, lace, and other decorative cloth.

All weaving was a slow process, done entirely by hand, until the 18th century. The flying shuttle (Joseph Kay, 1735) and the power loom (Edmund Cartwright, 1785) turned the loom into a modern piece of industrial machinery.

Noah WEBSTER (1758–1843)

Noah Webster was a famous American educator and writer. He made the first American DICTIONARY, which was the forerunner of *Webster's New International Dictionary*.

Born in West Hartford, Connecticut, Webster graduated from Yale College and later studied law. While teaching in Goshen, New York, he became dissatisfied with the British textbooks used in the schools. He believed that spelling, grammar, and usage should be based on the living, spoken language in America. In 1783, he published *The American Spelling Book* and later wrote a grammar and a reader, all of which helped standardize American English.

After Webster's marriage in 1789, he practiced law in Hartford. Four years later, he moved to New York, where he founded and edited two newspapers. In 1803, however, Webster sold out and moved to New Haven. There he devoted himself to compiling an American dictionary.

In 1806, his first dictionary was published, but he soon began work on another. He traveled to France and England, gathering materials on language unavailable to him in the U.S. In 1828, his *American Dictionary of the English Language* came out in two volumes, containing about 70,000 entries and about 35,000 definitions that had not appeared in any earlier dictionary. Webster's dictionary helped to establish common American spellings, pronunciations, definitions, and usage.

WEEDS

Weeds are plants that compete with valuable crops for water and minerals in the soil and for sunlight. Actually, any plant that grows where it is not wanted is considered to be a weed. Weed seeds may be spread by wind, water, birds, animals, and man.

A garden or farm that is full of weeds will produce poor crops, because weeds usually grow faster and reseed more quickly than those plants that are cultivated. Much money and time today is being spent on research to discover new and better ways and means of weed control.

Some weed killers are "selective"—that is, they are made up of chemicals that kill only the harmful plants. Many weed killers contain special substances that cause the weeds to grow and develop so quickly that they exhaust themselves and soon die. The chief methods for controlling weeds are still mainly hoeing and plowing. In gardens, mulching—the covering of the ground with straw or leaves—is a common way to control weeds, as well as to enrich the soil.

The one important function weeds perform is helping to keep soil from washing away after a heavy rainfall.

WEEK

A week is a period of seven days, commonly the cycle beginning with Sunday, the first day of the week, and ending with Saturday, the last day. However, like a MONTH, it is not a precise division of a year, and we are not sure how or why it arose.

The ancient civilizations of China, Persia, Babylon, and Egypt used a week as a division of time. The Egyptians used to have a 10-day week, and the early Romans had an 8-day market week. The 7-day week probably came from Mesopotamia, and by Roman times the week was connected with the sun, moon, and five of the bodies recognized today as planets. The days became known as Sun-day, Moon-day, and then the days of Mars, Mercury, Jupiter, Venus, and Saturn. In the English language, some of the Roman names have changed to corresponding Norse names. Mars became Tyr, or Tiu (Tuesday); Mercury became Woden (Wednesday); Jupiter, Thor (Thursday); and Venus became Freya (Friday). Sunday, Monday, and Saturday have not changed.

The Hebrew week is based on the observance of the Sabbath, which comes every seventh day, because the world was created in six days, and on the seventh, the Lord rested from his labors. The Christian week and the Muslim week were probably derived from the Hebrew week, though the holy days are different (Hebrew, Saturday, seventh day; Christian, Sunday, first day; Muslim, Friday, sixth day).

WEIGHTS and MEASURES

No one knows exactly when man began to recognize the need for measuring different things. Man needed to measure the height of flood waters, the amounts of grain grown, the lengths of cloth woven, or the weight of precious metals. Man needed measurements when he built temples, houses, and statues. Measurement began when man compared distances to parts of his body. The *cubit*, mentioned in the Bible, was the distance from the tip of the elbow to the tip of the middle finger, and one cubit was equal to 7 *palms*.

The ancient Greeks originated the "foot" as a standard measure of short distances. The Roman Empire later used it as the chief measure of small distances. The inch was considered to be the width of one's thumb. Even in Roman times, 12 inches equaled a foot, although these two lengths were not identical to ours.

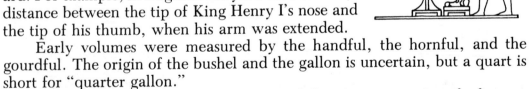

An Egyptian balance in use over 3,500 years ago

Since body measurements vary so much, measurements were usually very inaccurate. As governments recognized the problem, they would often use their king or ruler's body measurements as the standard. For example, in England the yard used to be the distance between the tip of King Henry I's nose and the tip of his thumb, when his arm was extended.

Early volumes were measured by the handful, the hornful, and the gourdful. The origin of the bushel and the gallon is uncertain, but a quart is short for "quarter gallon."

Early weighing of precious metals and drugs was in grains of wheat or barley which man noticed had a uniform size. The use of the *grain* as the name of a unit of weight for these things still exists. The seed of the carob, a Mediterranean evergreen, was once used as a unit of weight, and the name *carat*, used as a measurement of diamonds today, traces its origin back to carob seeds.

Gradually, as trade and commerce increased in importance, people recognized the need for accurate measurement. In 1854, the United States and

Great Britain established the standard yard. It was the distance between two fine lines crossing two gold plugs set in a bar of platinum, which was kept at a constant temperature and pressure in the Exchequer Office in London. The legal standards today, fixing our units of length, weight, and capacity, are carefully preserved at the National Bureau of Standards in Washington, D.C.

About 150 years ago, the government of France decided to discard its old measurements and invent a completely new system. It chose the *meter* as the basic unit of measure. This is one ten-millionth of the distance between the equator and the North Pole. This whole new system of weights and measures is called the metric system, and it is now used widely in Europe, South America, and by scientists all over the world. The United States is gradually trying to convert to the metric system to simplify measurement.

Today, modern measurements are so accurate that scientists are able to measure in millionths of inches, centimeters, and grams.

The Duke of WELLINGTON (1769–1852)

Arthur Wellesley, the first Duke of Wellington, was one of England's greatest soldiers.

He was born in Dublin, Ireland, and went to school in England and France, where he attended a military academy. At 18, he became a British army officer and later served in India. From 1809 to 1813, Wellesley commanded the British army in Spain, where he crushed the French armies of NAPOLEON. He was rewarded with the title of Duke of Wellington.

After Napoleon returned from Elba and raised another large French army, Wellington took command of the allied armies in Belgium. At the Battle of WATERLOO, he defeated Napoleon and afterward was the most famous man in Europe.

In 1828, Wellington became prime minister of Great Britain. When he allowed passage of the Catholic Emancipation Bill, admitting Roman Catholics to public office and Parliament, he lost the support of his party, and his ministry fell in 1830.

Herbert George WELLS (1866–1946)

H. G. Wells was an English shopkeeper's son. When he was nearly 30, he decided to give up teaching and make his living as a writer. He became one of the early writers of science fiction. *The Time Machine* (1895), *The Invisible Man* (1897), and *The War of the Worlds* (1898) are still famous. Later he became interested in what was happening in the real world of science and politics, and tried to make people aware of the danger to which civilization was exposed. He died a few months after the first atomic bomb was exploded.

WEST INDIES

The West Indies are a large group of islands between North and South America. They stretch from Florida to the coast of Venezuela and form a barrier between the Atlantic Ocean and the Caribbean Sea. The West Indies were named by COLUMBUS, who thought he had reached India by sailing west. For many years, the islands were colonies of Britain, France, Holland, or Spain. Most of them are now independent or semi-independent.

Most of the islands are rocky and mountainous, with plains along the coasts. There are numerous lagoons, mangrove swamps, and coral reefs. The climate is tropical, and hurricanes occur sometimes in the summer.

On the islands' lowlands are grown sugarcane (the principal crop), cotton, tobacco, bananas, coffee, and cacao. Some oil and natural gas have been found in CUBA and Barbados, bauxite in Hispaniola and JAMAICA, and asphalt in Trinidad. Manufacturing industries include rum distilling, fruit canning, cotton ginning, and cigar making.

The first inhabitants of the islands, the Carib and Arawak Indians, died of diseases brought by the Europeans. In the 18th century, many NEGROES were brought from Africa to be slaves on the plantations. Today, most of the 30 million West Indians are black or of mixed ancestry.

WESTMINSTER ABBEY

The London church known as Westminster Abbey is one of the most interesting places in England. There has been a church on this site for at least 1200 years. In the present church there are parts of an earlier church finished in 1065 by Edward the Confessor, but most of what we see today was built between 1245 and the end of the 15th century. The original architect for this church was French, and the style is that of French Gothic in the 13th century. Henry VII added a large chapel to the Abbey, begun around 1503. It has lacy fan vaults, which spread in all directions above the floor of the chapel. The two towers at the entrance to the Abbey were built early in the 18th century, although they are also Gothic.

The church is 531 feet (162 m) long and is 105 feet (33 m) high inside. Its Gothic architecture is beautiful in itself, and it also has many fine tombs, some of them brightly painted, that are a pleasure to see. With two exceptions, all of the reigning kings and queens of England were crowned here, and many are buried here in highly decorated tombs. So are many other famous English persons. The Poet's Corner has the tombs of literary figures such as Chaucer, Tennyson, and Browning. Famous scientists such as Darwin, Livingstone, and

King Henry VII's chapel

Newton are in another part of the church. Many English statesmen are buried here too. England's Unknown Warrior of World War I has a special place of honor at the center of the church.

WEST VIRGINIA

West Virginia is a rugged state in the east-central United States. Its eastern part is in the Appalachian Mountains. Most of West Virginia, however, consists of highland, called the Allegheny Plateau, that slopes toward the Ohio River on the western border.

There are large deposits of coal, oil, natural gas, and salt in the plateau region. Coal and salt are used in West Virginia's factories to make a wide variety of chemicals. The state also manufactures much steel and glass. Coal is burned in West Virginia's power plants that supply electricity to many cities and factories outside the state. Charleston, on the Kanawha River, is the capital. There are about 1 million people in West Virginia.

Not many Indians lived in the area when frontiersmen from Virginia, Maryland, and Pennsylvania arrived in the 1700s. DANIEL BOONE and GEORGE WASHINGTON both explored the region, which was then linked to Virginia. Differences between the frontier territory (now West Virginia) and Tidewater Virginia led to much fighting and bloodshed. In 1863, the region broke away from Virginia and became a separate state.

Visitors to West Virginia enjoy trout fishing and turkey, deer, and bear hunting. There are many historic sites, like Harpers Ferry. Here John Brown and his men in 1859 seized the arsenal as part of their plan to end slavery in the U.S. West Virginia has mineral water resorts at White Sulphur and Berkeley Springs.

900

WHALES

A whale is not a fish. It is a MAMMAL that has a body that can live entirely in the sea. In order to move forward, the whale moves its great tail up and down while a fish moves its tail fin from side to side.

Like all mammals, whales cannot breathe underwater. Since they have LUNGS, they must come to the surface occasionally to breathe out carbon dioxide through a nostril or blowhole on the head. When they expel this used air, they do so with such force that the warm breath liquefying in cold air looks like a jet of water.

Whalebone (or baleen) whales, like the giant blue whales, are often 100 feet (31 m) long. They strain great mouthfuls of water through a sieve of

The Blue Whale is greater in bulk than...

....2,500 people

...36 elephants

...the largest dinosaur

whalebone inside the mouth where millions of microscopic sea creatures are trapped. Toothed whales, like the sperm whales and killer whales, feed on larger creatures, such as the squid and their own relatives, the porpoises. Although most whales are timid, they can be dangerous if attacked. They show great affection towards their young and the other members of their herd or "school."

A thick layer of fat or blubber, a source of whale oil, lies under a whale's skin to provide warmth in the cold, icy seas. Although whales inhabit all the oceans of the world, they live mostly in the Antarctic Ocean, where they are hunted for their oil and whalebone. The body and bones are made into fertilizer, and *ambergris*, a valuable substance found in the intestines, is used in making PERFUME.

Since so many whales have been killed, most countries have agreed to limit the number killed each year in order to prevent their extinction.

901

WHEAT

Originally a wild grass, wheat was probably first grown in ancient Egypt. It is closely related to corn, oats, rye, rice, and barley. Wheat and rice are the two most widely eaten grains in the world.

Winter wheat is sown by farmers in autumn. It begins to grow, and then rests under a blanket of snow until spring. *Spring wheat* is sown in February or March and is harvested in late summer. Wheat grain or seed is ground into flour. The best quality bread comes from wheat flour, which is used more than any other flour in the United States.

Flour wheat requires "stiff" soil because the kernels are heavy. Since it takes a great deal of nourishment out of the earth, wheat cannot be grown on poor soil or in cool, wet climates.

The United States, Canada, Australia, and Argentina are leading growers and exporters of wheat.

WHITE HOUSE

The White House is the home of the President of the United States. It was designed in 1792 by a Philadelphia architect, James Hoban, but has been remodeled, rebuilt, and added to many times. The temple-like north porch and the rounded south porch were added in the 1820s. Many presidents have refurnished and redecorated the interior, and two office wings have been added. In the 1950s, the whole interior was taken out and rebuilt, since it was in dangerous condition.

The building was called the White House almost from the start, since it was built of limestone and everything around it was of red brick. In 1814, the British, who captured Washington in the War of 1812, burned the outside, and the smoke-blackened stone has been painted white ever since. President Theodore Roosevelt was the first president to call the building the White House formally. Before that it was formally called the President's Palace or the Executive Mansion.

Eli WHITNEY (1765-1825)

As a boy, Eli Whitney showed great interest in machines and business. In his father's farm workshop in Westboro, Massachusetts, he tinkered with the lathe and other tools. He also repaired violins. During the American Revolution, he made badly needed nails, as well as ladies' hatpins.

After graduating from Yale College, he took a job as a tutor on a southern plantation. There the COTTON planters encouraged him to use his talents to invent a machine that would rapidly separate cotton fibers from seeds. In 1793, he designed the cotton gin, which in one hour did a full day's work of several slaves. Whitney then formed a partnership to manufacture gins in New Haven, Connecticut. However, others had copied his invention, and thus Whitney earned little money from the business.

In 1798, Whitney built a factory in New Haven to make firearms for the U.S. Army. He devised machines, like drill presses, to make parts for rifles and used workers to put the parts together on assembly lines. His rifles were the first to have standardized, interchangeable parts. Whitney introduced the American system of mass production.

Frances E. WILLARD (1839–1898)

Born in Churchville, New York, Miss Willard attended Northwestern Female College. She taught in public schools for a few years, then went to France for further studies. She became president of Northwestern Female College in 1871.

In 1874, Miss Willard was chosen to be the new president of the Women's Christian Temperance Union (WCTU). She helped to establish the Prohibition Party in 1884, and became president of the World Women's Temperance Union in 1891. Miss Willard and CARRY NATION exerted a powerful influence upon American politics.

WILLIAM the CONQUEROR (1027?–1087)

William I, known as William the Conqueror, was born in Normandy, a region in northwest France. His father, duke of Normandy, died when William was eight. Later, young William, as duke, fought against the lawless Norman lords, whom he defeated and ruled over.

When his cousin, the King of England, died in 1066, William claimed that he had been promised the throne of England. However, Harold, duke of Wessex, was crowned king. William immediately landed a Norman army on England's shore and defeated Harold at the BATTLE OF HASTINGS. On Christmas Day, William was crowned the new king. He then built castles, gave land to his Norman followers, and crushed several rebellions.

He introduced the FEUDAL SYSTEM into England. To the Church and to those who obeyed him, William was just and merciful. In 1086, he gave orders to survey all land and property in England, the results of which became a document called the Domesday Book. SEE ALSO: BATTLE OF HASTINGS.

WILLOW

This tree family has about 300 members which grow in the cold and temperate climates of both hemispheres of the world. The willow tree thrives in damp places and on riverbanks where its complex root system is useful in binding sandy soil together.

The black willow, the tallest North American species, grows to be 120 feet (37.2 m) tall, whereas small shrub species, such as those found in the Arctic, are only a few inches tall. Weeping willows are often found gracing parks and gardens as ornamental trees. The pussy willow of eastern North America with its silvery gray silky catkins is one of the favorite signs of spring.

Male and female catkins grow on separate trees.

The slender young branches, called *osiers*, are woven into baskets and wicker work. The wood is prized in the manufacture of charcoal, and the springy wood of the white willow is used in making cricket bats. Medicines are made from willow bark, and paper pulp is made from the wood.

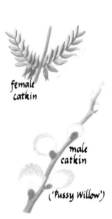

female catkin

male catkin

('Pussy Willow')

Woodrow WILSON (1856–1924)

Woodrow Wilson, the 28th President of the United States, studied and taught history, law, and economics. His reputation as an excellent teacher, scholar, and writer grew steadily. In 1902, Wilson was named president of Princeton University in New Jersey. He introduced a number of educational reforms and became well-known as a fighter for democracy against the snobbery of privilege. In 1910, Wilson was elected governor of New Jersey and made several important changes in the laws. He won national attention, and in 1912 he was elected U.S. President as a Democrat.

He reformed some of the economic policy of the United States. A Federal Reserve System was set up to improve the banking system, and a federal income tax was established. He persuaded Congress to pass laws to help small farmers and to regulate big business.

In foreign affairs, Wilson protected American interests in revolutionary Mexico. He worked to make good relations with all Latin American countries.

Wilson was reelected President in 1916, largely because he had kept the U.S. out of WORLD WAR I. However, his policy of neutrality became too difficult to maintain, especially after Germany's unrestricted submarine

warfare on American shipping. He asked Congress to declare war in 1917.

Two years later, Wilson went to Paris to help negotiate the peace. The Allies agreed to many of his proposals, including the establishment of the League of Nations. The League would settle disputes between nations without war. However, the U.S. Senate rejected the peace treaty and the League of Nations. To win public support, Wilson made a cross-country speaking tour, but was stricken with paralysis. He retired from public life at the end of his term.

WINDMILLS

Windmills were first built in the Near East 1000 or more years ago, and the idea for them was probably brought to western Europe by Crusaders late in the 12th century.

The earliest European mills were *post mills*. The whole mechanism of the mill and its enclosing structure stood balanced on a central post. When the wind changed, everything had to be turned. Early in the 14th century, the French invented the *tower mill*, which made things much

easier. The machinery was housed in a solid tower, and only a cap that held the sails and their supporting shaft had to be turned. In the 18th century, a *fantail* was added. This was a little set of sails at right angles to the main one. When the wind changed, the fantail began to spin, turing gears that turned the mill cap in the proper direction. In the middle of the 19th century, the American *wind pump*, an open metal tower with a ringlike sail, was invented to supply water for farms. Many of these still stand in the country.

Medieval Post-mill

Scientists hope that new, scientifically designed windmills will be able to generate the large amounts of electricity we need so that we can save oil and coal. Many new types of windmill, unlike the old ones in appearance, are being tried out.

WINDS

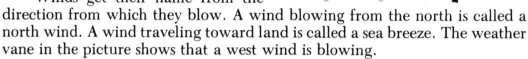

Anemometer

Weather Vane

When various areas on Earth heat up unevenly, AIR is heated and its MOLECULES move farther apart and rise. As a result, cooler air flows in to take its place. In other words, air flows from a region of high pressure to a region of low pressure. Wind, then, is moving air.

Winds get their name from the direction from which they blow. A wind blowing from the north is called a north wind. A wind traveling toward land is called a sea breeze. The weather vane in the picture shows that a west wind is blowing.

Weather is influenced by wind. Warm weather often comes from a south wind; cold, from a north wind. Weather predictions are based on wind direction.

The weatherman has instruments to tell him the speed and direction of the wind. One instrument he uses is called an *anemometer*. The number of revolutions per minute the whirling cups make is converted to wind strengths on the Beaufort Wind Scale. Force 4 on the scale, for example, is a moderate breeze of 13 to 18 miles per hour (21–29 km/hr); force 8, a gale of 39 to 46 miles per hour (63–74 km/hr); and force 12, a hurricane of speeds above 75 miles per hour (121 km/hr).

The most destructive winds are the TYPHOONS of the tropical western Pacific area and the hurricanes of the tropics in the West Indies area, including the Caribbean Sea and the Gulf of Mexico. SEE ALSO: AIR, BAROMETER, CYCLONES AND ANTICYCLONES, TYPHOON.

WINDSOR CASTLE

There has been a royal residence at Windsor, a town near London, since the 9th century A.D. The castle we see today dates from later times, though. The big Round Tower in the middle of the castle was built partly in the 12th century, though it was enlarged early in the 19th century. The chapel is a beautiful work of late English Gothic, built around 1500. Many English kings and queens who are not buried at WESTMINSTER ABBEY are buried here. The rest of the castle is built around two large courtyards. It has been added to or remodeled many times. Much of the work was done in the 17th century and the 1820s.

George III and Queen Victoria both lived at Windsor for many years. In World War I the royal family, whose name had been a German one, began to call itself the House of Windsor. When Edward VIII resigned as king in 1936 to marry a woman not approved of by the king's councillors, he took the title of Duke of Windsor.

WINE

When grape juice undergoes FERMENTATION, wine is produced. Freshly picked grapes are put in a container and the juice is squeezed out, then drawn off, and allowed to stand. In a very few wine producing areas of the world, wine makers still insist that the ancient methods, which include having workers trample the grapes in a large stone vat, are necessary for maintaining the traditional excellence of their wines. However, most modern wine making industries use machines to press out the grape juice.

Grape juice is made up of sugar, water, and small amounts of acid. In the vats, microscopic plants called YEASTS grow on the grape skins and break down the grape sugar into alcohol and carbon dioxide. "Sweet" wines are those which have not had all the grape sugar fermented away; "dry" wines are those that have. The sparkling or "fizzy" wines, like cold duck or champagne, are those that continue to ferment after being bottled. Other wines are "aged" in wooden casks—sometimes for several years—before they are bottled.

The color of grape wine varies from greenish yellow to dark red. Red wine gets its color from having the grape skins present during fermentation; "white" wines are those in which the skins were removed during fermentation. Red wines are usually served with beef; white, with chicken or fish.

Grapes need a temperate climate, plenty of rain, and well drained hillsides. The type of soil and the amount of sunlight and rain all affect the taste from year to year in a particular region. Wine fanciers therefore want to know the year in which a wine was made and how long it was allowed to age.

France and Italy are the world's leading wine producers. Other important producers are Spain, Portugal, Yugoslavia, Germany, Australia, and the United States. California produces most of the wine in America and has set by law the highest standards for quality and labeling of any state or country in the world.

Wine is also produced from elderberries and CURRANTS, as well as rhubarb, parsnips, tomatoes, and dandelions. SEE ALSO: FERMENTATION.

WINNIPEG

Parliament building

Winnipeg, the capital of MANITOBA, is the largest city in the prairie region of Canada. Lying in the middle of vast wheat fields, the city has huge grain elevators and flour mills, as well as stockyards, meatpacking plants, and other industries. Winnipeg is one of the world's largest exporters of grain. Cheap hydroelectric power for industry is supplied from plants on the Winnipeg River, about 60 miles (97 km) east of the city.

Here, in 1738, a Frenchman named Vérendrye built Fort Rouge, and later other trading posts were set up along the Red River, which flows through Winnipeg. In 1821, the Hudson's Bay Company set up a trading post there.

WIRE

Wire is a piece of thin, flexible metal, usually circular when viewed on end. It can only be made of *ductile* metals—that is, only those which can be drawn out into threads without breaking. Ductile metals include gold, silver, platinum, tungsten, copper, iron, aluminum, and various ALLOYS. Platinum wire can be made as fine as a hair; gold can be made into a thread fine enough for embroidery.

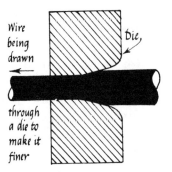

Wire being drawn through a die to make it finer

Die

Wire is made by drawing a narrow tube of the metal through a series of bell-shaped holes of decreasing size. The holes are called *dies*. The metal surrounding each die is particularly hard and has to be oiled constantly as the wire passes through.

Wire is very useful and is widely used in making ropes, cables, springs, electrical conductors, strings for musical instruments, and precious jewelry.

WISCONSIN

Lake Superior
Superior Upland
MICH.
Timms Hill
1,952 ft.
Green Bay
MINN.
Lake Winnebago
Lake Michigan
MADISON
IOWA
ILL.

Wisconsin, in the north central United States, has huge, rolling plains, lovely, clear lakes, and large forests. This state is known as "America's Dairyland," because it produces more milk and cheese than any other state. It is also a leading producer of butter, corn, hay, alfalfa, and cranberries. Large numbers of cattle, hogs, and turkeys are raised in the state.

Manufacturing, however, earns the most money for Wisconsin. Machinery, paper, and food are important products. The state is the nation's largest supplier of beer, with many breweries situated in the Milwaukee area.

A French explorer, Jean Nicolet, reached the south end of Green Bay in 1634 and became the first European to visit the region. The Indians called the area *Wees-Konsan*, meaning "our homeland." The Winnebago, Menominee, Sauk, and Fox Indians traded furs with the Frenchmen who came from Canada. France claimed the whole area but lost it to Britain in 1763. The U.S. took control after the American Revolution, but many British fur traders remained until the War of 1812. When lead was discovered about 1830, miners poured in and took Indian lands. After the Indians were beaten in the Black Hawk War of 1832, the area became a separate U.S. Territory. Many German, Scandinavian, Irish, and English farmers settled there. In 1848, the territory became a state.

Wisconsin's capital is Madison, situated in a rich, agricultural region. The state has more than 4.6 million people.

WITCHES

For thousands of years, people have believed in magic and evil spirits and have felt that certain individuals have extraordinary powers. Women called witches were supposed to be able to cast spells, to cause pain, to talk with the Devil, and even to kill a person. Male witches were called *warlocks*, or wizards.

In the Middle Ages, witches were said to fly about on broomsticks and to meet at night in groups called *covens*. They could supposedly tell the future by studying the insides of animals.

Witches - from a 15th century drawing

In the Bible, Saul went to the Witch of Endor to learn what would happen to him in battle. The Bible clearly condemns witchcraft in Exodus 22:18 and Galatians 5:20. In 1431, JOAN OF ARC was burned as a witch. In 1692, twenty women in Salem, Massachusetts, were accused of being witches and killed.

It was thought that witches had one place on their bodies that could not feel pain, the Devil's spot. Some people believed that a witch would float if she were tied up and thrown into a pond, so this test was used to convict women as witches.

WOLF

Wolves, like hyenas, jackals, and foxes, belong to the dog family. However, unlike the faithful domestic dog, the wolf remains a wild animal.

Wolves have powerful teeth and bushy tails. The North American wolf or timber wolf is gray. Wolves have become extinct in Great Britain and are

fast disappearing in many parts of the United States. However, they are still abundant in the wilder parts of Europe, Russia, and Asia.

Wolves live in forests, prairies, and on mountains. Their dens may be a hole dug in the ground, a hollow tree, a cave, or a thicket. The breeding season for wolves is in the spring, with 3 to 12 pups in a litter. The pups remain with their parents at least until the following winter.

Usually the wolf hunts alone and feeds on small birds and animals; in winter, he becomes bolder and hunts in packs. These packs may attack sheep, poultry, reindeer, bison, and other large animals.

The long, low, mournful howl of a wolf is perhaps one of the most eerie sounds in nature.

WOOD CARVING

Many carvers and sculptors like to work in wood. It is much easier to find than good stone and can be carved very delicately without breaking. Its grain and its warm color make it pleasant to look at. It must be protected from the weather, however.

Many primitive cultures have done excellent wood carving. The totem poles of the Indians of the Pacific Northwest are famous. So are the elaborate carvings of the New Zealand Maoris, the central Africans, and the natives of the South Pacific. Much of the sculpture of China, Japan, and medieval Europe was carved from wood. It was often covered with a thin plaster-like substance called gesso that was painted.

Japanese wooden mask

English wood carving

Carved head, Congo

Highly carved wooden furniture, often unpainted, was popular in Europe from the 15th through the 19th centuries. In Europe, the Germans and the Swiss have been the best carvers.

WOODPECKER

Woodpeckers are found in wooded areas of every country, except Australia. Their rat-ta-tat-tat pecking at a tree, roof, or telephone pole is a familiar sound. Sometimes they peck for insects and insect eggs in the bark; sometimes they are pecking themselves a hole in which to nest; and sometimes they peck to signal their mates.

Woodpeckers have sharp pointed, short stubby tails that are used to brace themselves against the tree they are pecking. The long, sticky tongue with sharp points at the end is specially designed for extracting food lodged in the wood. Flickers eat enormous quantities of ants and are unusual in that they are often seen on the ground.

Since most woodpeckers eat insects that are harmful to trees, they are a valuable help in our parks and forests. The yellow-bellied sapsucker, however, is not a welcomed species because it drinks the sap from trees.

Red-headed Woodpecker

Flicker

Downy Woodpecker

Yellow-bellied Sapsucker

Hairy Woodpecker

WOODWIND

Certain musical instruments are called woodwinds, because they are made of wood (or were made of wood at one time) and because they are played with the breath. The player blows into such instruments in special ways. This starts a column of air vibrating inside the instrument. The vibration creates a sound that is high or low in pitch depending on whether the column of air is short or long. By opening and closing holes in the instrument, the player can change the length of the column and play different notes.

The FLUTE is the simplest type of woodwind. The player blows across a hole at one end. It has a rich, rather high-pitched sound. The *piccolo* is much like the flute but smaller, and has a much shriller sound. The *fife* is another high-pitched instrument, much used in military bands at one time. These instruments used to be made of wood but are

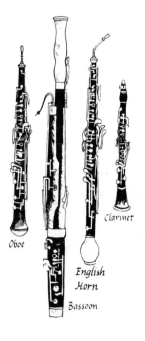

Oboe

English Horn

Bassoon

Clarinet

Bandsman playing fife

Flute

Piccolo

now made of metal. The *recorder* is an old-fashioned form of flute. It is blown from the end, not the side, and is made of wood.

The *clarinet*, *oboe*, *English horn*, and *bassoon* are *reed instruments*. The vibration of a reed (shaped length of cane) from the blowing of the player gives them their special sounds. These instruments are made of wood. The *saxophone*, a brass instrument that also has a reed in its mouthpiece, is sometimes considered to be a woodwind.

Wool-bearing animals

vicuna

llama

sheep

WOOL

Wool was probably the first fiber man wove into cloth. WEAVING woolen cloth began in prehistoric times. Wool comes from the whole coat or fleece of SHEEP. Similar soft hair from other animals, such as the vicuña, llama, goat, and camel, is sometimes called wool.

There are many types of wool. Some is long; some is short. Merino wool from a

Spanish sheep is regarded as the world's finest. Sheep of the same type do not produce the same grade of wool. Quality depends on diet, age, health, and even weather and climate. Lamb's wool is the fine wool that comes from the first shearing; "pulled wool" comes from slaughtered animals.

Today, most of the cleaning, sorting or "carding," SPINNING, weaving, and dyeing is done in factories called woolen mills.

Felt is unwoven woolen cloth in which the fibers are merely steamed and pressed together. The tangled wool is held together by the tiny overlapping scales on each fiber.

Wool is widely used in the making of clothing, rugs, and blankets. Newer fabrics are often interwoven with synthetic fibers, such as nylon, to make a hard-wearing product.

Australia is the leading wool producer. New Zealand and Argentina are also wool producers. Since the United States uses more wool than it can produce, it must import wool from other countries. SEE ALSO: SHEEP.

William WORDSWORTH (1770–1850)

William Wordsworth, the great English poet, spent much time as a boy wandering about the hills and woods of England. Left an orphan at 13, he lived with an uncle and attended various English schools, including Cambridge University. As a young man, Wordsworth traveled abroad and became deeply involved in the French Revolution. Later, he settled with his wife, his sister, and his three children in the Lake District of northern England. Since Wordsworth had received several legacies (gifts of property by will), he was able to devote himself to poetry for much of his life.

In 1798, he and his friend, Samuel Coleridge, published *Lyrical Ballads*. In 1805, Wordsworth finished his long autobiographical poem, *The Prelude*, which was not published until after his death. Wordsworth's poetry was influenced by his great love of nature. His work shows the poetic beauty of the commonplace, as in "Margaret," "Lucy," and "Daffodils."

WORLD WAR I

World War I lasted from 1914 to 1918 and was fought between the Central Powers and the Allies. The Central Powers consisted of Austria-Hungary, Germany, the Ottoman Empire (Turkey), and Bulgaria. The Allies were Great Britain, France, and Russia, joined by Italy, Japan, the United States, and various smaller nations.

In the early 1900s, European nations were building up their armies and navies, developing military alliances, and making certain they were ready for any possible enemy. Many countries lacked strong leadership and were suspicious of each other. Europe was a bomb about to explode.

On June 28, 1914, Archduke Ferdinand, heir to the throne of Austria-Hungary, was assassinated by a Serbian who wanted to free Serbia (now part of Yugoslavia) from Austro-Hungarian rule. Austria declared war on Serbia, and Russia mobilized (readied its troops) to aid Serbia. Austria was supported by Germany, which declared war on Russia on August 1, 1914. Two days later, Germany declared war on France, an ally of Russia, and moved its armies westward. Great Britain then came into the war to help France.

German troops moved to cut off supplies from Britain, but the Belgians delayed them by opening their DIKES on the North Sea and flooding the battlefield. Finally, the French stopped the German drive toward Paris. Now the war became deadlocked with opposing armies holding themselves in trenches extending from Switzerland to the English Channel. The war settled down to many unsuccessful attempts to break through enemy positions. Movement was nearly impossible because of machine guns, artillery, and nerve gas. The British introduced the tank, which at first bogged down in the mud and had mechanical problems. Later, tanks helped greatly to end the bloody trench warfare.

In 1916, the Germans made desperate attempts to break through the western front at Verdun, in northeast France. They failed, with both sides suffering enormous losses and becoming exhausted.

A German U-boat (submarine) had sunk the British passenger ship *Lusitania* in 1915, killing more than 125 Americans on board. This catastrophe and the increasing attacks by U-boats against all ships angered neutral countries like the United States. After many merchant ships were sunk by German torpedoes, U.S. President WOODROW WILSON signed a declaration of war on April 6, 1917. American troops were sent to Europe. The Allies felt that they had almost an unlimited supply of men and materials and that victory would eventually be theirs.

Meanwhile, the RUSSIAN REVOLUTION had occurred, and many Russian soldiers had left the battlefield because of lack of food, clothing, weapons, and ammunition. When the Bolsheviks under NIKOLAI LENIN took control of Russia, they began to make peace with Germany. Russia was now out of the war.

Allied forces in the BALKANS defeated the Bulgarians. British troops conquered PALESTINE and Mesopotamia in the Near East, and Arab rebels seized ARABIA. The Ottoman Empire, realizing it was defeated, concluded an armistice (truce) on October 30, 1918. Austria-Hungary surrendered on November 4 after its armies were disastrously beaten by the Italians at Vittorio Veneto, in northeast Italy.

Allied armies under the French leader Marshal Foch halted terrific German attacks in northern France and pushed the Germans back, crumbling their defenses. Many German soldiers mutinied because of lack of food and supplies. Discontent led to revolution in Germany. Kaiser (emperor) Wilhelm II was forced to give up the German throne,

and finally Germany signed an armistice on November 11, 1918.

By the Treaty of Versailles, signed on June 28, 1919, Germany was completely disarmed, forced to pay $33 billion, and lost much territory and its overseas colonies.

WORLD WAR II

World War II was fought from 1939 to 1945. Germany, Italy, and Japan (the Axis Powers) were opposed by Great Britain, France, Russia, China, and the United States (the main Allies).

After WORLD WAR I, Germany grew angry because of the harsh treatment it had received from the victorious nations. It could not repay what the Treaty of Versailles ordered. The German people suffered from lack of food, jobs, and money. These miserable circumstances helped ADOLF HITLER, head of the Nazi Party, to become Chancellor of Germany in 1933. He wrongly blamed much of Germany's troubles on the Jews, whom he set out to kill. Hitler promised to make Germany the strongest nation in the world and began to build a huge military force.

The League of Nations, an international organization that was set up to keep the peace after World War I, failed to stop Japan's attack on China in 1931. Seeing the powerlessness of the League, Hitler in 1936 moved German troops into former German lands along the Rhine River. Then Benito Mussolini, premier of Italy, sent Italian troops to conquer Ethiopia. Hitler took over Austria in 1938. The following year, he seized Czechoslovakia and invaded Poland. Immediately, Britain and France declared war on Germany. The German army attacked and occupied Denmark and Norway.

In May, 1940, German troops invaded Holland and Belgium and then moved into France. British forces in Europe were forced to the port of Dunkirk on the English Channel where they withdrew back to Britain. On June 14, 1940, Paris was captured by the Germans, and soon all of France was occupied by them. The powerful German *Luftwaffe* (air force) tried to defeat

Britain by bombing ports, factories, bridges, and airfields. London was later heavily bombed. But the British air force managed to check the Germans.

Although Hitler had earlier signed a peace agreement with Russia (the Soviet Union), he decided to invade and seize Russia in June, 1941. He had underestimated Russian strength, for the Germans suffered severe losses, ran out of supplies, and were forced to retreat after two years of fighting. Some of the bloodiest battles occurred in Stalingrad (now Volgograd).

In 1940 and 1941, Japan seized parts of southeast Asia. It felt that the U.S. naval base at Pearl Harbor, in Hawaii, was a threat to Japanese interests. On December 7, 1941, hundreds of Japanese planes made a surprise attack on the base, bombing and destroying much of the U.S. fleet. The following day U.S. President FRANKLIN D. ROOSEVELT signed a declaration of war against Japan. Soon Germany and Italy declared war on the U.S. in support of Japan.

Japan conquered most of Southeast Asia, the Dutch East Indies, and the Philippine Islands. However, at the Battle of the Coral Sea, on May 7 and 8, 1942, American warships prevented the Japanese from taking Australia.

Gen. MacArthur

In Europe, the Allies started heavy bombing of German industrial cities. In North Africa, Allied soldiers under British General BERNARD MONTGOMERY and American General George Patton forced the German Afrika Korps to retreat in 1943. British and Americans then invaded Sicily and Italy, where Mussolini had been dismissed as premier. Soon the Italian government joined the Allies and declared war on Germany in October, 1943.

In the Pacific, U.S. troops under General DOUGLAS MACARTHUR drove the Japanese from New Guinea. After much Japanese resistance, U.S. forces

Gen. Eisenhower

also conquered the island of Guadalcanal. Gradually, Japan lost control of Burma, Malaya, the East Indies, Thailand, and Indochina, as well as many small Pacific islands. In 1944, most of the Japanese naval fleet was destroyed at the second Battle of the Philippine Sea. U.S. planes based on Pacific islands began heavy bombing of TOKYO and other Japanese cities. But Japan would not surrender. U.S. President HARRY TRUMAN ordered the ATOMIC BOMB to be used. On August 6, 1945, the atomic bomb was dropped on Hiroshima, and three days later on another Japanese city, Nagasaki. Japan formally surrendered on September 2, 1945.

Meanwhile, U.S. General DWIGHT D. EISENHOWER was placed in command of an Allied invasion of Europe. On D-day (June 6, 1944), Allied forces invaded Normandy and began to push the Germans out of France, Belgium, and Holland. Despite a great German counterattack, the Battle of the Bulge, the Germans were forced to retreat in early 1945. On March 7, 1945, the Allies—whose main field commanders were Montgomery and U.S. General Omar Bradley—crossed the Rhine River and proceeded to overrun Germany. Knowing the end was near, Hitler committed suicide in his underground headquarters in Berlin, and Germany surrendered on May 7, 1945.

After the war, Germany was demilitarized and later split into two countries. Berlin was divided into four sectors—one each for Russia, France, Britain, and the U.S. Japan was demilitarized and occupied by American troops until 1952. The UNITED NATIONS was set up in 1945.

WORMS

Worms are soft bodied, crawling creatures. True worms have no legs, feet, or backbone. They are usually made up of a number of segments or rings that have tiny hairs to help them crawl along. Other worms are not segmented, such as roundworms and flat worms.

Earthworms that are segmented play an important role in improving soil. They aerate it as they crawl underground, and they take leaves below the surface. As they move their way forward, they take in organic matter from the earth. Some of it is digested and some passes through their systems as worm casts. Worms are also good fish bait.

There are worms, such as the fisherman's lugworms, that live in the sea. Doctors once used leeches, another type of worm, for sucking blood from their patients. The hookworm, pin worm, and tapeworm are harmful parasitic worms that live inside animals.

WREN

The wren is a tiny, plump, brownish bird with a short, sharply cocked tail, and tiny black bars on its feathers. Wrens are found throughout the world, especially in the tropics of the western hemisphere.

In the United States, the most common wren is the house wren or Jenny wren, found in tall brush that provides cover for them. They are especially common in the North and East. Males build many false nests. They often build nests in boxes and crevices in or about houses. They perform a valuable service to man by eating garden insect pests. Bewick's wren, native to the American South and West, is similar in appearance to the house wren, but its song is less bubbly and sounds more wiry.

All wrens defend their nests fearlessly. They are very curious and are much attracted to squeaking and shushing noises.

WRESTLING

Wrestling is a sport in which two unarmed opponents struggle hand to hand with one another. Each tries to secure a *fall*—that is, to pin his opponent's shoulders to the floor or mat for a full second. Wrestling is a test of strength, quickness, and endurance. A wrestler also knows a variety of body grips or holds, which he uses on his opponent to throw him to the ground.

There are two basic styles of wrestling: freestyle and Greco-Roman. In freestyle, a wrestler is allowed to apply holds on his opponent's legs. He can also use his legs to trip and throw his opponent and apply holds. The freestyle is common in the U. S. Greco-Roman wrestling, which is popular in Europe, is similar to freestyle except that a wrestler cannot apply holds to his opponent's legs. Also, he cannot use his own legs to hold or trip his opponent.

Wrestlers compete in different weight classes, and a referee conducts the matches. Wrestlers win points for falls, for applying various holds, and for aggressiveness.

WRIGHT BROTHERS

Orville Wright (1871–1948) and Wilbur Wright (1867–1912) first designed and built printing machinery. Later, they designed, manufactured, sold, and repaired bicycles. From the study of the flight of birds and from wind-tunnel experiments, the two brothers taught themselves *aerodynamics* (the study of the motion of air and its effects on objects). They became very interested in problems of flying.

In their bicycle factory in Dayton, Ohio, the Wright brothers built *gliders* (unpowered aircraft). At Kitty Hawk and Kill Devil Hills, in North Carolina, they tested their gliders, learning how to control and maneuver them while in flight. In the winter of 1903, the brothers designed and built an efficient propeller driven by a lightweight gasoline engine. This was mounted on a biplane, named *Flyer I* (now called the *Kitty Hawk*). On December 17, 1903, at Kill Devil Hills, Orville Wright made history's first controlled and sustained flight in this powered AIRPLANE. Four flights were made that day;

the first lasted 12 seconds; and the last, made by Wilbur, covered a distance of 852 feet (264 m) in 59 seconds.

The Wright brothers continued to build new and improved airplanes. They established a company and made public flights of their new machines in Europe and the U.S. Their airplanes could turn, bank, circle, do figure eights, carry passengers, and stay airborne for more than an hour. In 1908, Wilbur stayed in the air for a record 2 hours and 20 minutes.

Wilbur died of typhoid, but Orville continued to make important contributions to aviation. At Kitty Hawk, the U.S. government erected the Wright Brothers National Monument in honor of their accomplishments and the first flight. SEE ALSO: AIRPLANE.

WRITING

Without a way of recording words, a civilization like ours would be impossible. People would forget—or pretend to forget—the laws they were to obey and the agreements they had made. News would be spread by word of mouth, and everyone would tell it differently. Authors would not make up long stories and have every word they used preserved. And no one would be able to record what was happening, and so our society would be forgotten; we would have no history.

Today, we have films, tapes, and records to preserve our words. But a hundred years ago people had only writing with which to do so, and printing (which is a form of writing, really). Writing is still the best way of recording many facts.

Primitive man drew pictures to put his ideas on record. We use these *pictographs* ourselves, for instance on highway signs. An arrow curves around to the right as the road does. A railroad crossing sign is two lines crossing.

Egyptian Hieroglyphs

Sumerian cuneiform writing

Mayan numerals (S. American)

Red Indian script

Polynesian script

But drawing pictures is clumsy and slow, and there are many ideas that cannot be represented exactly by pictures of things. The Chinese and some other cultures have reduced their old pictures to a system of signs called *ideographs*, which can be easily made. These represent not only things but also ideas. Thus a Chinese ideograph can mean "road" but also "the course of events the world follows naturally." Such a system forces people to memorize thousands of ideographs.

Our system is *alphabetic*. Our words do not look at all like the things they describe, but they are spelled so as to give us an idea of how they sound. We have to memorize the idea that goes with the sound. Thus, if we see the word "snath," we know from its appearance how to say it but have to be told that it is the handle of a scythe. No one knows how old the first form of our ALPHABET is, or where it was invented. It is probably about 2800 years old. It was invented by some of the Semites, the population group that includes the original Jews. From them it went to the Greeks, who changed its form, and from them to the Romans, who changed its form again. It is basically the Roman alphabet that we use, though the exact form of the letters has changed from time to time. The Greeks are still using their ancient alphabet, and the Russians use another form of the Greek alphabet called the Cyrillic.

John WYCLIFFE (1324?–1384)

John Wycliffe was a famous English churchman who publicly attacked the abuses of the Church, especially the greed and wealth of the clergy and the Pope. Also, he preached many sermons on the right of any person to form his own opinions on the basis of what the BIBLE said. Thus, he is often called the first Protestant and a forerunner of the REFORMATION.

He made the first complete English translation of the Vulgate, the Latin version of the Bible. Wycliffe was condemned as a heretic, and his followers, known as "poor priests" or Lollards, were severely persecuted. However, his ideas were revived during the English Reformation of the 16th century.

WYOMING

Wyoming is a large state in the western United States. The Rocky Mountains stretch from the northwest corner to the middle of the southern boundary with Colorado. In eastern Wyoming is the rolling high country of the Great Plains, cut by many rivers and covered with grasses, sagebrush, and cactus. Here and in the basins of the mountain section graze many cattle, sheep, and horses. Wyoming also grows hay, wheat, and sugarbeets, often on irrigated

farmlands. Cheyenne, situated in the state's southeast corner, is the capital and largest city. Wyoming has about 410,000 people.

The Crow, Sioux, and Cheyenne Indians inhabited various parts of what is now Wyoming. In 1807, an American fur trapper named John Colter explored the Yellowstone territory and brought back fantastic stories of its steaming geysers and great canyons. Trappers and fur traders made their way there. Fort William, later named Fort Laramie, was established in 1834—the first permanent settlement. As pioneers went west by way of the Oregon and California Trails, they sometimes settled in the region. Indians fought settlers and soldiers but were finally crushed about 1880. Meanwhile, people kept coming, seeking gold and coal. The railroad brought homesteaders, and cattlemen and later sheepmen battled over the precious grasslands. In 1890, Wyoming territory became a state.

Its largest industry today is mining, particularly of oil, natural gas, coal, iron ore, and uranium. Agriculture is second. Many tourists come to hunt, fish, ski, or to visit the beautiful national parks.

X-RAYS

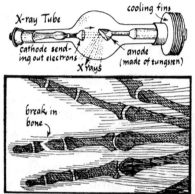

In 1895, a German scientist named Wilhelm Roentgen discovered a form of radiation, something like LIGHT. However, unlike light, the rays were invisible to the eye, and they were powerful enough to pass through solid objects. He named them X-rays. X-rays are produced when a fast stream of electrons is shot against a tungsten "target." The rays then radiate from this rare metal.

X-rays are important to medical science. The shadow pictures that they take are used by doctors to detect where bones are broken, where accidentally swallowed objects are located, and the condition of the teeth below the gums. They are also used to determine the progress of certain diseases inside the body. X-rays can also be used in treating some diseases, such as certain types of cancer.

In industry, flaws in metals and in the quality of many products are detected by X-rays. Even old paintings can be checked with X-rays to see if they are genuine.

XYLOPHONE

Two percussion musical instruments are the xylophone and the marimba.

The *xylophone* (whose name means "wood sound" in Greek) has rows of wooden bars of different lengths that are struck with padded hammers. The longer a bar is, the deeper a sound it makes. The xylophone is found in various

forms in central Africa and southeast Asia. It was in use in Europe by the early 16th century, but became popular only about 150 years ago.

The *marimba* is a xylophone with a gourd or metal tube under each piece of wood. These strengthen the sounds by echoing them.

YEAR

A year is the length of time taken by the Earth to orbit the sun. This journey takes exactly 365 days, 5 hours, 48 minutes, and 45.5 seconds, which is slightly less than 365.25 days. Because we can not have one-fourth of a day that stands alone, we say there are 365 days in a year. However, every four years we add up the extra one-fourth-days and make that year have 366 days, giving the month of February one more day. That fourth year is called *leap year*.

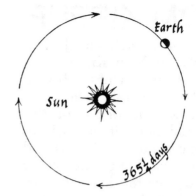

An old Roman year used to begin in March, not January, so that September, October, November, and December were respectively the seventh, eighth, ninth, and tenth months, as their Latin names mean. In 45 B.C. Caesar set up the Julian calendar with a year like ours, and in 1582 Pope Gregory VIII made the year's length more exact with his Gregorian calendar.

YEAST

Yeasts are tiny fungi that cause FERMENTATION, a process in which sugar is broken down into carbon dioxide gas and alcohol. With the help of yeast, grapes are made into WINE, barley becomes beer, and dough "rises" to become BREAD.

A single yeast plant is too small to see without a microscope: 2800 yeast cells would form a line an inch (2.54 cm) long. Warmth and dampness will cause yeast to grow and multiply either by budding or dividing into living cells called *spores*.

A yeast cake is made up of millions of dry yeast plants in a state of rest. SEE ALSO: FERMENTATION.

YOKOHAMA

Yokohama is the port city of TOKYO, situated on the western shore of Tokyo Bay. It was destroyed in 1923 by earthquakes and fires and again in 1945 by Allied bombs. From the ruins arose an enlarged city with wide streets, parks, modern buildings, and fine universities. It has steel, automobile, and chemical plants, as well as oil refineries and shipyards. Since Yokohama was first opened to foreign trade in 1859, it has become a major exporting center for Japan's manufactured goods. The city has more than 2 million inhabitants.

YOM KIPPUR

The most solemn Jewish holiday is Yom Kippur, the Day of Atonement celebrated in the early fall. The Bible describes the origin of this holy day in Leviticus 16:1-19. People confess their sins and ask the pardon of each other and of God for the harm they have done. In some congrega-

Blowing a ram's horn (shofar) to announce the beginning of Yom Kippur

tions, they spend hours praying and meditating. They neither eat nor drink. In ancient times, the leader of the congregation drove a goat away from the community. This *scapegoat* was supposed to carry away all the sins of the congregation. We still call a person blamed for the sins of others a "scapegoat."

YORK

York is a famous historical city in north central ENGLAND. Visitors come to see the old Cathedral of St. Peter, commonly known as York Minster, the notable guildhall, and The Shambles, a medieval street of butchers' shops. Among the other historic features are York Castle, which is on the site of a castle built by WILLIAM THE CONQUEROR, and the ruins of Fountains Abbey, a monastery built in the 12th century.

York was an ancient Roman stronghold called Eboracum. In A.D. 120 Emperor Hadrian built earthen walls around it to keep out the Picts and CELTS. York became an important education center in the time of CHARLEMAGNE.

Today, the city has many light industries that produce such items as chocolate, cocoa, furniture, glass, and scientific instruments.

York – the Shambles

Brigham YOUNG (1801–1877)

Brigham Young, born in Whitingham, Vermont, joined in 1832 the newly organized Church of Jesus Christ of Latter-Day Saints, or MORMONS. Three years later, he became a member of the Council of Twelve, the ruling body of the Mormons. Through his preaching and missionary work in the U.S. and

England, Young converted many to Mormonism. At the death of Joseph Smith, founder of the Mormon Church, in 1844, Young kept the Mormons together and became their undisputed leader.

Because of continuing persecution of the Mormons by outsiders, Young organized a great westward migration. In 1846 and 1847, he led about 5000 Mormons to what is now UTAH. There he founded the settlement of Salt Lake City. Under his strong leadership, the Mormons became self-sufficient and prosperous, establishing farms, industries, and a peaceful, cooperative society. They also built a great temple and university. In 1850, Young was made governor of the new territory of Utah. SEE ALSO: MORMONS.

YUCCA

The yucca is a member of the lily family. About 30 species are native to the American Southwest and Central America. The yucca is the state flower of New Mexico.

All yuccas have a dense cluster of sword-like leaves that grow from the ground on short woody trunks. Depending on the species, the stems range from 2 to 50 feet (0.6–15.5 m) high. The flowers form a cluster shaped like a pyramid and depend on moths for their pollination.

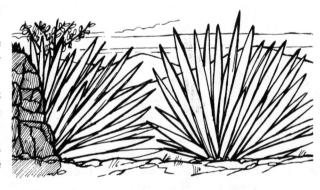

The coarse fibers of the stem and leaves of many species are used in manufacturing rope. Many species have grass-like leaves which are used for stuffing cushions. The roots of some provide a substance used as a substitute for soap in some countries.

YUGOSLAVIA

Yugoslavia is a rugged, mountainous country that lies on the eastern shore of the ADRIATIC SEA. It is about the size of Wyoming, with a population of about 22 million. BELGRADE is the capital.

The Yugoslav people include several important groups—the Serbs, Croats, Slovenes, Macedonians, and Montenegrins. There are also Bosnian Muslims, Albanians, Hungarians, and Turks. Most of them differ from each other in religion and language.

925

The country is rich in minerals, such as coal, iron, copper, oil, bauxite, and antimony. Its dense forests provide good lumber. Most of its industry is owned by the state, which also controls many big, modern farms. The chief crops are cereal grains, tobacco, and fruits.

Yugoslavia became a nation in 1918 when King Peter I of Serbia united the Serbs, Croats, and Slovenes. During World War II, the Germans occupied the country, but they were driven out by Yugoslav partisans. Marshal Tito then seized control, declaring Yugoslavia a Communist people's republic. SEE ALSO: BELGRADE.

YUKON

The Yukon is a wild, rugged territory in northwestern CANADA. The land is mostly mountainous, with more than 20 peaks higher than 10,000 feet (3100 m). Mount Logan, the highest peak in Canada, is in the southwest, near the Alaska border; it rises 19,850 feet (6154 m). The Yukon River, about 2000 miles (3220 km) long, and its tributaries drain much of the territory. In the south is Whitehorse, the territorial capital and largest town. The Yukon has only about 22,000 inhabitants.

Most people work in the mines, which produce silver, copper, gold, lead, zinc, and coal. There is little farming; only the hardier grains and vegetables can be grown in such a severe climate. Numerous sportsmen come each year to fish for the Arctic grayling, lake trout, and northern pike and to hunt for bear, moose, caribou, and mountain sheep and goats. Tourists enjoy the natural beauty of the spectacular scenery.

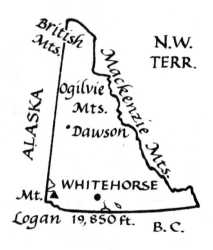

When gold was discovered on the Klondike River in 1896, more than 30,000 prospectors flocked to the region. The Yukon GOLD RUSH ended about 1910, when most of the gold had been taken from the streams.

ZAÏRE

Zaïre is a large country in equatorial AFRICA, with a narrow coastline on the Atlantic. It has rain forests, grasslands, and mountains as well as rich deposits of diamonds, copper, gold, and cobalt. Most of Zaïre's 26.5 million people belong to 200 tribal groups that speak Bantu languages. Kinshasa, the capital, lies on the Congo (or Zaïre) River, which flows through eastern Zaïre.

In the 1880s, SIR HENRY STANLEY explored the region on behalf of the King of Belgium, who later made it a colony, called the Belgian Congo. In 1960, it gained independence and eleven years later was renamed Zaïre.

ZAMBEZI

The Zambezi is one of Africa's longest rivers. It flows for about 1600 miles (2576 km), chiefly through Zambia, Zimbabwe, and Mozambique, and empties into the Indian Ocean. The Zambezi is navigable in three separate sections, but its main course is broken by many *rapids* and the great VICTORIA FALLS. The Kariba Dam, one of the largest in the world, stands on the river's border between Zambia and Zimbabwe.

DAVID LIVINGSTONE discovered the Zambezi in 1851.

ZAMBIA

Zambia is a landlocked country in south central AFRICA. The terrain (land) is mostly high plateau covered with forest and grass, suitable for farming and grazing. Zambia is rich in copper, cobalt, lead, and zinc. Most of Zambia's 5.3 million people belong to Bantu-speaking tribes and still make their living as farmers. Lusaka, the capital, is a large, modern city with an international airport.

ZEBRA

The zebra is related to the horse. However, unlike the donkey and the horse, it is always striped and very difficult to train. Zebras are usually bad-tempered.

They are found wild only in Africa. Depending on the species, small herds roam grassy plains, inaccessible mountain ranges, or hill forests.

Regardless of species, they all have a black and white striping. This camouflages them from lions and other meat-eating animals.

Before laws protected them they were hunted for their meat. Their valuable hides are used for leather and are made into rugs and other ornamental articles.

ZEPPELIN

In 1900, the German Count von Zeppelin demonstrated a new type of BALLOON. It was a *dirigible*, with motors and a rudder so that it could go where it pleased. It was cigar-shaped, with a light, rigid frame. Zeppelins were used as bombers during World War I. They dropped the first bombs on London.

After the war, several nations tried to use them as passenger aircraft. The Germans had the most success. The *Graf Zeppelin*, built in 1928, crossed the Atlantic Ocean 144 times and made a famous round-the-world trip. The zeppelins were dangerous, though, because they were inflated with hydrogen, which easily caught fire. In 1937, the large new zeppelin *Hindenburg* burst into flame while landing at New Jersey. Zeppelin construction ended shortly afterward. SEE ALSO: BALLOONS.

ZEUS

In Greek mythology, Zeus was the supreme god. He was the son of the Titan Cronus, who ruled Mt. Olympus before him. Cronus was said to have swallowed his sons to prevent them from replacing him as chief of the gods. But Rhea, wife of Cronus, saved Zeus by substituting a stone for him. Later, when Zeus became Chief, he forced Cronus to vomit his other sons out. Then Zeus and his brothers divided up the universe. Poseidon received the sea, Hades the underworld, and Zeus heaven and Earth. Zeus married Hera but had many love affairs with other goddesses and mortal women.

Zeus represented power, law, and order. His sacred bird was the eagle, and his mighty weapon was the thunderbolt. The Romans named him JUPITER.

ZINC

Zinc is an element that is never found in the pure state in nature. Pure zinc is a shiny, bluish-white METAL. It is one of the most widely used metals and is often found together with silver and lead. The United States produces about one-third on the world's supply.

Zinc is used mainly to give a protective coating to iron and steel. *Galvanized* iron is iron coated with zinc to prevent rusting. The plates in a dry cell BATTERY are made of zinc. Zinc oxide is used as a white pigment in paints, dental fillings, and ointments.

Zinc is mixed with copper to form brass and with copper and tin to make bronze. (See ALLOYS.) Zinc has been known since prehistoric times.

ZOO

A zoo, short for zoological garden, is a place in which wild animals are kept for exhibition. People enjoy zoos because of the many different kinds of animals, and experts in ZOOLOGY learn much about animals by studying them in zoos.

Most zoos have mammals, birds, reptiles, and amphibians, like frogs and tortoises. However, there are some small zoos that display only the animals that they know and care for especially well. The United States has more than 150 zoos, among which are the Bronx Zoo in New York City, the San Diego Zoo, and the Philadelphia Zoo, which is the nation's oldest—founded in 1874.

Most animals in a zoo are bought from professional animal dealers, who obtain tigers from India, zebras and elephants from Africa, parrots and boa constrictors from Latin America, and so on. Some animals cost many thousands of dollars. However, many are born in zoos, which are constantly trying to find ways to breed animals that are scarce or nearly extinct.

ZOOLOGY

Zoology is the study of ANIMALS. Since there are about a million different kinds of known animals, a zoologist usually specializes in the animals or problems that interest him most. He discovers, for example, where animals live, how their bodies function physically and chemically, what their diseases are, why they behave as they do, and how new and better animals can be developed.

Aristotle, who lived in ancient Greece, was the first great zoologist. He classified animals into two groups: those with red blood and those without red blood. Other famous zoologists are Lamarck, who divided animals into VERTEBRATES and invertebrates, Linnaeus, who named animals in Latin by their genus and species, and DARWIN, who theorized that animals evolved.

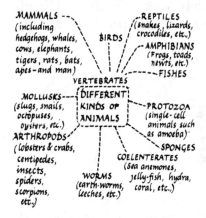

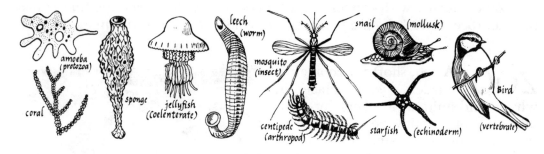

ZUIDER ZEE

Windmill were used to pump the sea water from the land into a canal, and from the canal into the sea.

Zuider Zee, meaning "southern sea" in Dutch, was the name given to the shallow sea formed in the 13th century when north central HOLLAND was flooded by the North Sea.

Since 1920, much of the region has been drained and reclaimed from the sea. Today, farms are producing crops on hundreds of acres of this low, fertile farmland, known as *polder* land. In 1945, the Germans flooded parts of the polders, but these lands were quickly drained in the same year.

The pumping out of this sea water has also left a lake, called the Yselmeer or Ijsselmeer. At the lake's southern end lies the city of Amsterdam. SEE ALSO: HOLLAND.

ZULU

The Zulus are a tribal people who live along the coast of southeast AFRICA. Tall and well-built, they live in compounds called *kraals* and grow some corn and raise cattle. Many Zulus today work in the African cities and mines and have become skilled laborers.

In 1838, the Zulu chief Dingaan ambushed and killed 500 Boers (Dutch) who had settled in Zululand. Later, he and his followers were killed by the Boers. In 1879, the Zulu chief Cetewayo fought against the British but was eventually defeated. Zululand was then made part of British Natal, which is today a province in the Republic of South Africa. There have been no major Zulu wars since 1907.

ZURICH

Zurich, the financial and commercial center of SWITZERLAND, is situated on both banks of the Limmat River where it flows from Lake Zurich. Its industrial products include machinery, textiles, locomotives, paper, and chemicals. The city is also a printing and publishing center and has a large tourist trade.

Zurich has old, narrow streets, and broad, modern boulevards, which are lined with lovely shops comparable to those of Paris. It has a famous cathedral known as the Grossmünster, built about 1100, and the largest Swiss university, founded in 1832. It was one of the key cities of the Swiss REFORMATION led by Ulrich Zwingli. Zurich has about 440,000 people, most of whom speak Swiss German. SEE ALSO: SWITZERLAND.

INDEX

A

ABACUS, 1
arithmetic, 49
numbers, 591

ABBEY, 1-2
monastery, 540-541
Westminster
Abbey, 899-900

ABORIGINES, 2
Australia, 67-69

ABRAHAM, 2
Hebrews, 385
Mecca, 522
Ur, 862

ACCORDION, 3
musical
instruments, 558

ACHILLES, 3
Hector, 385
Homer, 399
Troy, 853-854

ACROBATS, 4

ACROPOLIS, 4-5
Athens, 63
Greece, 364
Pericles, 634

ACTORS and
ACTING, 5

ADAMS, John, 6
American Revolu-
tion, 27-29
Declaration of
Independence,
245-246

ADAMS, John
Quincy, 6
Jackson, Andrew,
431
Monroe Doctrine,
543
War of 1812, 886-
887

ADAMS, Samuel, 6
American Revolu-
tion, 27-29
Boston Tea Party,
118

ADRIATIC SEA, 7,
map of, 7
Venice, 870-871
Yugoslavia,
925-926

ADVERTISING, 7

AEGEAN SEA, 8

AENEAS
Virgil, 879

AFRICA, 8-12, maps
of, 8, 10, 11, 12
Arabs, 42-44
Carthage, 160
desert, 249-250
Egypt, 273-274
elephants, 277
Ethiopia, 285
Ghana, 349
giraffe, 351
hippopotamus, 395
jungle, 447
Lake Victoria, 462
Livingstone,
David, 490
Negroes, 565-566
Nigeria, 578
Nile River, 579
oasis, 593
pygmies, 684
Rhodes, Cecil, 706-
707
Stanley, Sir Henry
Morgan, 796-
797
Sudan, 809
Suez Canal, 810
tropics, 852
Victoria Falls, 875
Zaïre, 927

Zambezi River,
927
Zulu, 931

AGRICULTURE, 12-
13
cereals, 172
farming, 298-300
Industrial
Revolution, 416
industry, 416-417
plow, 656-657

AIR, 13
barometer, 89-90
carbon, 156-157
lungs, 500-501
nitrogen, 580
oxygen, 611
respiration, 703-
704

AIRPLANE, 14-17
airport, 18
gliders, 354
helicopter, 386-387
jet engines, 441-
442
parachute, 618-619
radar, 690
Wright Brothers,
919-920

AIRPORT, 18
airplane, 14-17

ALABAMA, 18, map
of, 18
Civil War, The,
190-192

ALAMO, 19
Crockett, Davy,
226
Texas, 832-833

ALASKA, 19-20, map
of, 19
Eskimos, 285
London, Jack, 495

ALBANIA, 20

ALBERTA, 20, map
of, 20
Canada, 148-150

ALCOTT, Louisa
May, 21

ALEXANDER the
GREAT, 21-22
Aristotle, 48
Asia Minor, 59
Persia, 635-636

ALFRED the
GREAT, 22
England, 283-284
Saxons, 738-739

ALLEN, Ethan, 22-23
American Revolu-
tion, 27-29

ALLIGATORS, 23
crocodile, 226
reptiles, 702-703

ALLOYS, 23
brass, 122
bronze, 129
chromium, 186
copper, 217-218
gold, 356-357
lead, 470
magnesium, 506
mercury, 526
metals, 526
nickel, 577
steel, 801
zinc, 929

ALMANAC, 24
dictionary, 252-253
encyclopedia, 281

ALPHABET, 24
braille, 121
cuneiform, 232
deaf, the, 244
hieroglyphics, 394
writing, 920-921

M

N

NAMES, 560

NAPOLEON BONA-
PARTE, 561
France, 327-328
Louisiana Pur-
chase, 498-499
Malta, 510
Moscow, 548-549
Nelson, Horatio,
566
Waterloo, Battle
of, 891

NATION, Carry, 562

NATIONAL PARK,
562

NAVIGATION, 563
buoys, 135
compass, 208-209
latitude and longi-
tude, 468-469
lighthouses and
lightships, 482
maps, 512-513
radar, 690

NAVY, 563-564

NAZARETH, 564
Jesus, 440-441

NEBRASKA, 564,
map of, 564

NEBUCHADNEZ-
ZAR, 565
Babylon, 73-74
Jerusalem, 439-440
Seven Wonders of
the World, The,
750-751

NEBULA, 565
galaxy, 336

NEGROES, 565-566
Africa, 8-12
Carver, George
Washington, 161

King, Martin
Luther, 452
Marshall,
Thurgood, 518
Mays, Willie, 522
Nigeria, 578
Owens, Jesse, 610
races, 688-689
slavery, 769
Truth, Sojourner,
856
Tubman, Harriet,
856
Washington,
Booker T., 887-
888

NELSON, Horatio,
566

NEON SIGNS, 567

NEPTUNE, 567
planets, 651-652
solar system, 776-
777

NERVES, 568
brain, 121-122
cells, 168
heart, 383-384
muscles, 556
skeleton, 766-767
skin, 767-768
smell, 770
taste, 822
touch, 846-847

NETHERLANDS, see
HOLLAND

NEVADA, 568-569,
map of, 568
Death Valley, 244

NEW BRUNSWICK,
569, map of, 569
Canada, 148-150

NEWCOMEN,
Thomas
industrial revolu-
tion, 416
steam engine, 800-
801
Watt, James, 893-
894

NEW ENGLAND,
569-570, map of,
569
Connecticut, 212
Maine, 508-509
Massachusetts, 519
New Hampshire,
571
Rhode Island, 706
Vermont, 871-872

NEWFOUNDLAND,
570, map of, 570
Cabot, John, 143
Canada, 148-150
fishing, 312-314

NEW GUINEA, 571

NEW HAMPSHIRE,
571, map of, 571
New England, 569-
570
Thirteen Colonies,
The, 838

NEW JERSEY, 572,
map of, 572
Thirteen Colonies,
The, 838

NEW MEXICO, 572-
573, map of, 572

NEWSPAPERS, 573
paper, 617-618
printing, 673-674

NEW TESTAMENT
Bible, 103-104

NEWTON, Sir Isaac,
574
atronomy, 61-62
color, 204-205
gravity, 362
light, 480

NEWTS, 574
amphibians, 31

NEW YORK, 575,
map of, 575
Hudson River, 406
New York City,
575-576
Thirteen Colonies,
The, 838

NEW YORK CITY,
575-576
Hudson River, 406
New York, 575

NEW ZEALAND,
576, map of, 576

NIAGARA FALLS,
576-577, map of,
577

NICARAGUA
Central America,
170-171

NICKEL, 577
steel, 801

NIGERIA, 578, map
of, 578
Africa, 8-12

NIGHTINGALE, 578

NIGHTINGALE,
Florence, 578-
579
nursing, 592

NILE River, 579,
map of, 579
Africa, 8-12
delta, 248
Egypt, 273-274

NITROGEN, 580
air, 13
fertilizer, 305
gas, 338
light bulb, 481

NOAH, 580
ark, 50

NOBEL PRIZE, 580

NOBILE, Umberto
Amundsen, Roald,
31-32

NORMANS, 580-581
castle, 162-163
feudal system, 305-
306
Robin Hood, 715
William the
Conqueror, 903